financial SEASONS

DEVOTIONAL

Daily Inspiration About
Money & Emotions

Lisa Y. Jones

ISBN: 0960010103
ISBN-13: 978-0-9600101-0-3

Dedication

For Jonathan

Never in a million years would I have believed you would not be with us today. The joy you brought to so many is still deep in the hearts of all you touched. And while we believe your time on earth was way too short, we know that ultimately, God is in control. You accomplished more in sixteen years than many people accomplish in a much longer life time.

You taught us that most successes in life are "earned…not given."

I am thankful for you. I miss you. I love you.

See you in heaven.

The Spirit of the Sovereign Lord is on me, because the Lord has anointed me to proclaim good news to the poor. He has sent me to bind up the brokenhearted, to proclaim freedom for the captives and release from darkness for the prisoners, to proclaim the year of the Lord's favor and the day of vengeance of our God, to comfort all who mourn, and provide for those who grieve in Zion— to bestow on them a crown of beauty instead of ashes, the oil of joy instead of mourning, and a garment of praise instead of a spirit of despair. They will be called oaks of righteousness, a planting of the Lord for the display of his splendor.

Isaiah 61:1 – 3 NIV

Free Gift For You

Thank you for purchasing Financial Seasons. I wish I had this devotional when my husband Keith and I were getting out of debt. I pray it provides you with hope and encouragement.

But you may also need some tangible tools to help with your journey to financial freedom. To help you, I want to offer you a free budget bundle. Use the tools in this bundle to either start or accelerate your debt reduction plan.

You can find your free bundle at www.lisayjones.com/budgetbundle. While you're on the site, please also check out our other resourses. Keith and I want to give you everything you need to live a life free of debt.

We're praying for you!

Contents

Acknowledgements

To My Lord and Savior Jesus Christ

Thank You. Thank You for the courage to complete this divine assignment. You knew it was never my desire to put my financial life on paper for the world to read and critique. But You called me to do so. I have learned so much from this season and I am thankful for the privilege to be a part of your Master Plan in a small way. I pray for more courage to embrace the next season and its unknown challenges and opportunities.

I pray for wisdom and tenacity. I ask for compassion and grace. I pray for humility and discernment. I am prayerfully requesting the embodiment of the Fruit of the Spirit and the covering of the Full Armor of God.

I am a willing vessel, ready to be used by You. I am so thankful You chose me.

To Keith

Wow. I could never have imagined this would become my life when you slid in next to me during Sunday service all those years ago. It has been a wild ride. I could not have known how much beauty you would add to my life by being a part of it. Thank you.

I love your transparency and your heart for "chasing after Jesus." I love the way you challenge me to be better, to be more, to fully embody the woman God has called me to be, to let my flowers bloom. I love your patience and your desire to serve. I love your heart for our children, family and friends.

I thank you for supporting me in this. For giving me space to write. For grocery shopping with a detailed list and making zoodles, since they require no cooking. For proofing and questioning. For pushing me when I wanted to quit before I even got started. For holding me accountable and calling me on my crap.

I thank you for praying with me, and **for** me. I thank you for placing value on our three-strand cord.

I love you and am thankful God has not only given us a marriage steeped in Him, but also a ministry we get to do together. I can't wait to see how he uses us next! Thank you for being my best friend.

To Our Kids

Thank you for the hundred times you asked me *"Mrs. Lisa, are you done with the book yet?"* I know it was your way of encouraging me to finish and I thank you for caring about what I care about.

Thank you for choosing to embrace me as your stepmom. You are both incredible and Daddy and I are so proud of you.

I am so thankful God fulfilled my desire to be a mom by allowing me to marry you guys. Continue to showcase God's will for your lives by making good choices and remembering that He loves you and desires only what is best for you. We do, too.

To Our Life Group

Who could have known a random sign-up for Wednesday night Life Group would have led to an amazing extension to our family? We have laughed together, cried together, worshipped together and played together. You have challenged us and loved us and cared for us in ways we could never have imagined. We could not have done this journey without you.

You were there with us in the beginning when God gave me this assignment and you stayed on your post of encouragement 'til the very end. Thank you for your love and support. We are so blessed to call you family.

To the Team

There is no way I could have done this without you!

Vicki Julian (www.vickijulian.com). Thank you for your patience and practicality as we went through so many rounds of edits. I thank you for your keen eye and insight. I thank you for reading every single word and stretching me to go back and ask God for more. I look forward to what God has in store for us in the future!

Maria Morris (www.mariaportrait.com). You. Are. Beauty. Everything you touch just oozes beauty. From the professional headshots to the cover design for the book to the creation of the website, your handiwork is all over this project! I am so thankful you helped me open my mind to all the possibilities. Thank you for helping me implement what seemed incredibly overwhelming in the beginning. You are amazing.

Carolyn Sheltraw (www.csheltraw.com). There is nothing like being one degree of separation from one of the most competent designers I have ever worked with. Your interior design work is stunning! Thank you so much for being open to this project. You picked up the ball, put your mark on it and have helped us create an amazing and beautiful final product. Thank you. I look forward to many more endeavors together.

To **Jessica Lynn** (www.jessicalynndesign.com). One conversation for less than thirty minutes solidified a sisterhood which was steeped in the blood of Christ thousands of years ago. Thank you for your passion and energy. Your knowledge and ability were just what we needed to prepare our online image for the volume it would receive with the launch of this book. You are the real deal and a gem to all who know you. Excited to have you on our team.

Launch Team. You know who you are!!!!!!! Your words of encouragement, prayers and willingness to be first on the ground with this book mean more than you will ever know. Thank you for all of your support. Best seller, here we come!

To the Masses

There are so many others who have encouraged me on this journey. I thank you from the bottom of my heart. I pray God's blessing on you. I thank Him for allowing our paths to intersect. I so appreciate your words of encouragement, reassurance, hugs, prayers and overall well wishes. You have added so much value to my life and I am blessed to know you. Thank you for being you.

Introduction

When my husband Keith and I got married, we brought to our union $191,000 in unsecured debt. There was every kind of debt imaginable: Student loans, IRS repayments, car loans, credit cards, personal loans, 401k loans, loans to friends, and more. We were paying a huge amount of money each month in interest charges. I could barely breathe. I remember thinking, "Lord, how on earth are we going to get through this?"

At the same time, we found ourselves on a long and drawn out medical journey. The cost would eventually total an additional $110,000. We chose to pay cash for our medical expenses to keep from incurring any more debt. Many months it was a juggling act.

We wanted to be debt-free, but it seemed so overwhelming. We honestly did not know where to begin. We decided to invest in financial coaching. I say "invest" because the monthly payment amount could easily have gone to debt. I cringed when we set it up because there was so little money actually going to debt. I questioned whether it was the right decision.

Our current process obviously was not the solution. We did not yet know what we needed to know to lead a life free of debt. We were practicing insanity. We were doing the same things we always did but were expecting different results. A change was definitely needed. We saw the value in having fresh eyes on our situation and believed a financial coach could guide us through our storm to freedom. Financial Freedom.

Our coach worked with Crown Financial Ministries, a Christian finance organization. He taught us the importance of budgeting and using the envelope system to divide out our income. We began to track our debt and pay attention to our spending habits. We began to manage our money instead of our money managing us.

Crown introduced us to the understanding that God truly did care about our financial lives. The ministry caused us to rethink what it meant to be generous towards the Kingdom of God. We were hungry to learn all we could.

A year or so into our journey, we were introduced to "The Dave Ramsey Show." We read *The Total Money Makeover* and discovered a faster game plan for debt reduction. When we combined the game plan with our financial coaching, we began to understand how we could increase the intensity of our journey to financial freedom.

We did not have enough money to purchase the Financial Peace University (FPU) class materials so we borrowed the CDs from the library. Our eyes were opened even more, and our debt-reduction process got "gazelle intense." The amount of debt we repaid each month increased and we began to get traction on our situation. We also met people along the way who encouraged us, and others we were able to encourage.

Crown Financial Ministries and Dave Ramsey taught us two very important lessons about money. First, we learned we are not the owners of anything in our possession. God is. We are simply managers (stewards) who have been called to take care of things on His behalf.

When we have no debt, our money is free to be used to glorify God and His Kingdom. When we have no debt, we can give and support ministry in ways we cannot fathom when payments consume our income. When we have no debt, we can support God's Kingdom more completely because our money is working for us, not against us through interest payments and fees. When we have no debt, we not only receive our own personal reward, but God is glorified because His work is completed by His stewards.

The second lesson we learned was God's Word was filled with His thoughts about money. In fact, Crown Financial Ministries discovered 2,350 scriptures in the Bible where money is the subject. This devotional calls on those scriptures to help provide a sense of hope for you on your financial journey. It is my prayer it will help sustain you along your path. It is not an easy journey for most. And depending on your financial circumstances, it may not be quick. But debt reduction is more than just an idea. It can be a reality for you. Rest assured the Lord is with you.

These are my stories. Most are circumstances I experienced myself. A few are the experiences of friends, FPU class members and coaching clients we have walked with on their own journey to financial freedom. They are lessons I have learned as we reached a place of financial peace.

How to Use This Devotional

The reflection questions at the end of each day are designed to help you look inward at your own thoughts and perceptions about money. Please ponder them and be honest – not with me, but with yourself. They may make you uncomfortable but keep going.

Each day is meant to take about 15-30 minutes of time to complete. I encourage you to read each devotion early in the morning, prior to getting deep into your day. It will allow your subconscious mind to digest the reflection questions throughout the day. Ultimately, find a time when you can be still and allow the day's story to be used by the Lord to minister to you in whatever way He chooses.

The devotional is broken up into seasons. Each season is a phase of my life. As with all seasons, each of these is different. Some are longer than others. Each is filled with highs and lows. Some include other people, while others are just about me.

All scripture references are listed in the back of the devotional. They are New International Version (NIV) unless otherwise indicated. Please refer to them each day for a deeper experience.

Romans 12:12 says to "be joyful in hope, patient in affliction, faithful in prayer." Your situation may not look great today, but better days are ahead of you.

Keith always says achieving financial peace is a marathon and not a sprint. I pray as you work your way out of debt and into a place of financial peace, you find comfort, wisdom, hope, and encouragement from this devotional. These are the gems I received as I lived out the words found in this book. I thank the Lord for being with me the entire way. May He be with you also.

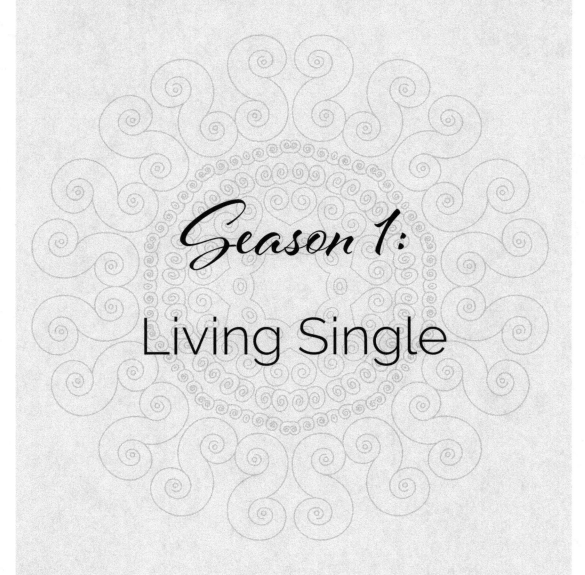

Season 1:

Living Single

Day 1
What About Mine?

My mother became a widow at 26 when my dad died. I was four, and my brother was six months old. She was a teacher in rural South Carolina and attended graduate school at night to increase her income. I do not remember a time when she did not work two jobs. She did the best she could with what was available. We were never hungry and never experienced homelessness, but we did not have a lot of extra.

I might have been ten or twelve years old when my mom sat us down one day and explained that she could no longer buy for both of us without it being a necessity. Until then, we both got something whenever the other experienced a need. If I needed new shoes, my brother might also get a toy truck. If he needed new clothes, I might get new barrettes during the same shopping trip.

She explained that money was tight, and she would have to focus on providing our needs. Wants could wait for Christmas or birthdays. She asked if we understood and we both shook our heads to acknowledge the statement. I did not understand. But I would soon find out just what she meant.

My brother needed shoes. The three of us piled into the car and drove to the local clothing store. My mom, brother and the sales person took way too long to pick out a pair of shoes my brother liked, and which my mom could afford.

I was bored, so I began to wander around the store. I slowly fingered the pretty dresses and sweaters. I casually looked at the price tags to see if they were within asking range. If they cost too much, I knew not to ask. If they were on sale or cost less, my mom might consider them as the add-on purchase. I made my way to the pretty lace slips and eyed them longingly. Surely this could be the add-on.

I looked over and saw my mom, brother and the sales person heading to the counter. If I just stayed where I was, I knew my mother would see me and ask if I wanted the slip. I circled the display a few times to make sure she knew I found what I wanted. She never glanced my way.

My mom paid for the purchase, handed the bag to my brother and called for me to join her at the door. It was time to leave. I hung my head and slowly walked out of the store. She was quiet until we got in the car. Once we were all settled, she turned and told me how disappointed she was in me.

Surely, as the oldest I would have understood her need to take care of the essentials for our little family. Surely, I would have been more supportive and set a good example of what it meant to only buy what we needed. But I did not. Instead I pouted over an unpurchased slip.

There was nothing to say. She was right. The sting of her words caused hot tears to form in my eyes. I never wanted to disappoint her, but I surely did that day. It was a day I would never forget.

Your Turn…Your Perspective: Who have you disappointed by not fulfilling your part of a financial arrangement? Who has disappointed you? What changes did you make because of both?

Prayer: Lord, I cannot begin to imagine how much I have disappointed You. Thank You for loving me anyway. I pray to be more mindful of Your provision and ask for the prompting of the Holy Spirit when I tend towards selfishness.

Day 2
Not Quite Enough

DEUTERONOMY 8:16

My mom taught my brother and me to work hard and not settle for average. It was never a real discussion but was more like an unspoken law of the house. We grew vegetables in the summer with the rest of our family to provide food for the rest of the year. We were active in the community and held leadership positions in school.

We knew we would go to college. We knew we would have a career and not a job. We knew we would move beyond our meager economic beginnings. It was baked into our DNA from the very start of life.

Despite the healthy foundation to work hard and be my best, I always struggled with having enough. I constantly felt as if "enough" was an illusion. It always seemed to remain just outside my grasp. A feeling of anxiety about the future was always firmly planted in the bottom of my stomach. I felt as if my life was built on a foundation of sand. At any moment the winds of life would turn, and my safe little haven would topple.

This feeling carried me through college. It carried me into my first job and one-bedroom apartment after college. I remember writing out what I thought was a budget on a steno pad in my living room each pay period. I was constantly fearful of not being able to make ends meet.

After Keith and I started following Dave Ramsey, I realized what I was experiencing was a result of not having margin. There was no real understanding of how to put distance between my life and the "winds" responsible for toppling so many safe havens. I did not understand what it was to have an emergency fund. I never thought to pay cash for large purchases, and never saved more than a few hundred dollars.

As we worked our way through our debt snowball, the anxiety of not having enough was strong. But, the more debt we paid off, the more I worked my way through it. Even if I did not yet have "enough," I finally knew with certainty the day would come when I would. The years of diligently managing debt re-payment began to build in me the muscles of fiscal confidence. I became confident in my ability to save. I became confident in my ability to spend wisely. I became confident in my ability to negotiate. I became confident in my ability to say "no" and not associate it with a feeling of lack. It was a powerful process.

I noticed my new attitude manifesting itself in several areas of my life. Emergencies no longer created a knot in the bottom of my stomach. I became more patient with others as it related to money. I no longer freaked out at missing a sale but knew paying full price with cash in hand was better than a sale on credit any day. I stopped looking for short cuts, even as I constantly searched for a good deal. It was subtle, but effective. I was learning how to create the mindset where "enough" was the norm.

My circumstances and early life experiences may not have been the best start financially, but they served as stepping stones to a more secure financial future. I became a much more financially secure woman because I learned what it meant to truly have enough.

Your Turn…Your Perspective: What experience has caused you to question if you have enough? How did you get through it?

Prayer: Lord, thank You for enough. Thank You for contentment. I pray to always be mindful of when I'm losing sight of both. Please help me to stay focused on Your provision and not my own.

Day 3
Work and Study, Not Work-Study

PROVERBS 6:9-11

I was clueless when I filled out my Free Application for Federal Student Aid (FAFSA) form the spring before my freshman year of college. I only knew I needed lots of scholarships and grants to graduate and get a degree. I knew enough to limit the number of student loans, but not much else.

When I got to the Work-Study portion of the FAFSA form, I chose not to check the box. "Federal Work-Study provides part-time jobs for undergraduate and graduate students with financial need, allowing them to earn money to help pay education expenses." [1] The result was a financial aid package very different from most of my friends. They were assigned jobs the moment they came to school our freshman year. I did not have a job, but it did not take long to realize I needed one.

I asked around on campus and found a job as a file clerk in the graphics department. I filed artwork and did miscellaneous jobs around the office. I learned a lot about the operational side of the university and began to meet some influential staff members. These relationships served me well through the years, and several of them became references when it came time to start a career after graduation.

My friends worked 10 hours a week for minimum wage. I worked 15 hours a week for $1 more. I did not understand the difference in pay, and the number of hours available. I asked my boss and was told Work-Study hours were regulated by the government. Students receiving Work-Study could only work a set number of hours and could only make a set amount of money.

I also learned I got more money towards my tuition and books because I did not have Work-Study. It turned out Work-Study wages were subtracted from the total financial aid package, creating the need for loans for most students. I was amazed at my good fortune! My relationship with Jesus was in its infant stages back then, and I did not know to give Him the credit. However, I did recognize my initial naiveté about the financial aid process was a blessing.

I eventually changed campus jobs and was able to raise my hourly rate another $3. My new office also allowed me to accumulate hours to be paid later. In the weeks when I worked more than 20 hours, I banked the time and was paid on it at the end of the semester. I also worked through breaks. Instead of leaving campus the first week of December after fall semester, I worked until just a few days before Christmas. By doing this, I was able to significantly reduce the outside money needed for my education.

We rarely know how the small decisions we make today will impact our lives in the future. Not checking the box for Work Study changed my life. Most of my friends relied on Work-Study. The result was tens of thousands of dollars in student loans for them, and less than $5000 for me. My future was made bright because I chose to work and study instead of having Work-Study.

Your Turn…Your Perspective: Think of a time when you received an unexpected blessing. What long term impact did you experience?

Prayer: Lord, thank You for guiding my steps even before I fully knew who You were. Thank You for providing even when I did not know I had a need. I pray to look for Your hand in every part of my life and to be mindful of how You continue to bless me. I praise Your Holy name.

Day 4
Earthly Benefactor

I went to college at Clemson University in Clemson, South Carolina and received a BS degree in Computer Engineering. I was involved in lots of activities on campus, including student government. One of the things I enjoyed most about being a part of student government was the opportunity to work side-by-side with school administrators, and the university president.

I went to Clemson on lots of small scholarships, one large tuition-only scholarship, and a few student loans. I was also a part of the Cooperative Education Program, which meant I worked every other semester as an engineer. The good part about the Co-op program was I graduated with work experience. The bad part was it took me longer to graduate. By my last year at Clemson, I depleted all my small scholarships and did not quite have enough to finish paying for my education. I did not know where the money was going to come from. Loans were not an option because I did not want to increase the balance on my existing student loan, and I had no real savings to rely on.

I decided to network. I called and made an appointment to see the president of the university. He knew who I was because we worked closely together during the previous two years to implement new policy for the university. Additionally, he was the benefactor of one of the scholarships I originally received. I simply asked him if he could grant an extension on the scholarship. He was disappointed to not be able to help and told me he would let me know if something changed. I thanked him for his time and went home. I was not sure what I was going to do, but I knew I was too close to graduation to not finish.

The next afternoon, there was a message to call the president's office. When I did, I learned he received a check in the afternoon mail the day before. He met a businessman at a luncheon a few weeks prior who was impressed with him. The businessman sent the check to the university with a note for the president. He instructed him to not simply put the check into the university's general fund, but instead, to use the money in a way which would bring about the greatest impact. The president of Clemson University told me the greatest impact from the donation would be me finishing the year and earning my degree. He gave the donation to me. And the most beautiful part was that the check was for the exact amount I asked him for less than 24 hours earlier. Glory to God!

I thanked him for his generosity and asked if it would be possible for me to send a thank you note to the businessman who sent the check. The president gave me his address and we began to correspond. I learned he was a Christian and wanted to serve the Kingdom in any way he could. We then began to talk once a month, and he became my mentor. I valued our time and we continued our monthly connection for several years.

My earthly benefactor was a key part of my transformation from student to successful adult. He impacted my life, my career, and my walk with Christ in ways I could not have expected. The gifts of his mentorship and generosity were reminders of the Lord's Master Plan at work in my life. I was so thankful to be the recipient.

Your Turn...Your Perspective: How have you seen God at work in your life? How do you respond when His answer is yes? No? Not yet?

Prayer: Lord, I pray for favor. I do not always understand Your plan, but I choose to trust You anyway. I pray I never lose sight of all You have already provided for me. Thank You for loving me enough to share Your bounty.

Day 5
Gift Return

I do not know when I was first introduced to the biblical principle of tithing. I grew up in a Baptist church, so it was probably one of my earliest memories. I began to tithe when I got my first job the summer after my sophomore year in high school. I felt very grown up when I dropped my check in the basket every other Sunday after being paid the previous Friday.

I continued my tithing during my freshman year in college when I began working. I attended a local church, which was popular with many of the students on campus and chose to tithe locally most Sundays. If I happened to be home visiting family on a weekend after payday, I tithed to my home church. I never gave much thought to the act of tithing; I just knew I needed to do it.

One year I was visiting my family during Thanksgiving. I gave my tithe to the church near the university the Sunday before. However, when the time came for the offering, I felt compelled to give again. I admit hesitating because I did not have much money. I knew I needed to buy gas to get back to school and would not have much money left until I got paid again. Yet, I still felt the desire to give.

I thought through what purchases I needed to make in the next week. I knew there was food in my pantry, and my mother would send me back to school with groceries and clean clothes. I would not need to drive my car once I got back to campus. I reasoned I could make it with no money if I did not have an emergency. Operating with no money concerned me a little, but I chose not to focus on it. After lots of pondering, I put aside my gas money and gave the rest of what I had as an offering.

The rest of the church service passed without fanfare. Near the end of service, a church elder stood and asked all the college students in the congregation to stand. Typically, the church gave a monetary gift to the college students for Christmas, but this year they decided to do so early!

I received a check for three times the amount I gave as an offering. I was stunned. It was as if God wanted to see if I trusted Him before giving me His gift. He wanted to see if I would be willing to let go of the little I had in my possession and trust Him with the rest.

As I drove back to school later, I could not help but wonder what would have happened if I withheld my small gift? What would I have missed out on receiving? How would not seeing God's hand in my life have impacted my life?

I was so thankful for the choice I made to trust God with my small gift. The gifts I received in return (both the money and the lesson) were so much more than I could have ever expected. The truth was clear – you truly cannot beat God giving.

Your Turn…Your Perspective: Think of a time when trusting God did not seem to make sense. What happened? What was the end result? Any regrets?

Prayer: Lord, thank You for Your gifts. You ask me to give, but only because You want me to be like You. I am made in Your image and want to be like You as much as possible. Thank You for teaching me Your ways. I pray to not lose sight of the joy which comes from giving.

Day 6
Postal Gifts

JAMES 2:15-16

One of the things I loved about my time as an undergraduate student at Clemson University was the post office. I kept the same box number the entire time I was a student and loved going to check the mail. There were usually some bills (I used credit cards in those days), pizza coupons, mail order catalogs and every now and then…letters. It was the letters and cards I most looked forward to finding.

There were no internet or cell phones back then. To communicate with someone, you needed to be intentional. And the communication almost always came with a cost. It was either a long-distance call or the cost of a postage stamp. Either way, you knew the person reaching out wanted to communicate. This knowledge was what made receiving cards and letters so exciting for me.

One day, when I checked my box, I noticed a very plain envelope with no return address. The stamp cancellation told me it was mailed somewhere near Greenville, SC (about an hour away). I did not know anyone who lived in the Greenville area and had no idea who sent the envelope. With a little caution and a lot of curiosity, I slowly opened the envelope. Inside were a $100 bill and a note.

I do not remember the exact words written, but I do remember being greatly impacted by them. In summary, the note told me I was admired and to not give up. It told me I was making a difference and God had a plan for my life. I remember standing there just staring at it, slowly shaking my head in amazement.

My college life was so ordinary to me. I did not see myself making an impact on anything, and I certainly did not know how God would use me. The note caused me to become more aware of my actions and how they affected others. For the first time, I began to think I could make a difference for my fellow man.

Of course, I found a use for the $100. It took care of any number of needs (i.e. groceries, gas, and a trip to my favorite Chinese restaurant). I was thankful for the gift. It was so much more than just money, however. I knew it was ultimately an offering from the Lord.

I never found out who sent the note, but I will never forget the influence it had on me. I became more aware of my actions and how they may be perceived by others. I became intentional with how I lived and how I spent my time. I knew in the back of my mind someone, other than family, wanted to make an investment in me and it was my responsibility to ensure a good return.

Even though I was never able to thank the person for the gift, I hoped to live my life in a way which said, "thank you." I hoped to make my life significant. I hoped to live for the Lord. I hoped to make a difference to others. A small note and a $100 bill changed my life. I was forever changed by the generosity of an unknown friend.

Your Turn…Your Perspective: Have you ever gifted someone anonymously? Have you been the recipient of an anonymous gift? How would receiving an anonymous gift today change your perspective on your community?

Prayer: Lord, thank You for the support of others. Thank You for their investment in me and my family. I pray I continue to live in a way which creates a positive return on their investment and Yours.

Car Savvy

PROVERBS 12:20

I got my first car while I was in college. I felt very grown up and was determined to take care of it. I got the oil changed regularly and rotated the tires according to the odometer's reading. Every 3000 miles for an oil change, every 6000 for a tire rotation. It lasted through college and into my first few years as a working adult.

When I graduated and moved to my new city, I found a local car maintenance chain and thought I was set. They put the little sticker in the driver's side window, so I would know when it was time to get the oil changed. I did not see why I needed to actually check the oil if I was going to use my little sticker as a guide.

One day, just a few miles from my mother's home, my car just stopped. It made a horrible sound and would not start. This was years before cell phones, so I simply waited for the next person to come along to take me to my mother's house. We towed the car to a local garage and found out the motor was locked tight. My last oil change was incomplete. Either no oil was added back after the initial change, or the oil plug was not replaced properly, and it all leaked out. In any case, I needed a new engine.

I could not afford to buy a new car. I could not afford to buy a new engine. I was barely making ends meet. There was only a few hundred dollars in my savings account. I never stopped to think about what would happen if I experienced an emergency. There I sat with no plan.

My stepdad found a guy, who knew a guy, who was able to find me a used engine. We found a mechanic in my city to do the repair and towed the car to the shop. My stepdad was gracious enough to allow me to use his truck until my car repair was completed. I arranged to pay the mechanic monthly until the $750 debt was repaid. Once the debt was repaid, I could get my car. It was a humbling experience.

I learned to check my oil. I learned to check my transmission fluid. I learned to look for stains on the concrete and investigate strange noises I heard while driving. I began to feel much more confident in my skills as an informed car driver. I did not want to ever again find myself without a reliable vehicle.

There were also other lessons to be learned from the experience. It was frightening to not be prepared for an emergency, but my education about financial preparation was far from over. Back then, I associated financial preparation with the amount of available credit on a credit card. Credit cards created the false margin I used for emergencies. The balances went up, I paid them off, and the balances would come back down. The process was simply repeated for the next emergency. I lived this way for the first 25 years of my adult life.

It took Financial Peace University, and an understanding of the cost of paying interest, for me to realize the false margin associated with credit cards. I remember the first time Keith and I realized the balance in our savings account was over $1000. It felt like such an accomplishment! It was the beginning of a new way of managing emergencies and our financial lives in general. We were determined to no longer view credit as an option for emergencies. It was the first of many decisions which led to a life of financial freedom.

Your Turn…Your Perspective: What lessons do you have about financial margin? How did you learn them?

Prayer: Lord, I thank You for a game plan. I thank You for new knowledge and new wisdom. I pray I embrace Your way of managing money and the lessons which Your Word provides. I pray for wise counsel in every area of my financial life.

Day 8
Early Budgeting

PROVERBS 15:25; JOHN 14:2

When I graduated from college, I moved to Charleston, SC to start work as a Systems Engineer. Since it was an entry level position, I did not make a lot of money. I chose to rent a one-bedroom apartment to keep my expenses as low as possible. After rent, utilities, credit card payments, student loans and my car payment, there was not a lot of money left over.

I managed to make ends meet each month, but it was a tight fit. I wrote out my version of a budget each month on a steno pad and thought I was managing my money responsibly. I did not think of the debt I carried. Everyone carried debt, right? I never accumulated more than a few hundred dollars in my savings account before "something" caused me to use it. I had no plan for my money.

I stayed in the apartment for three years. Over time, my income increased, and I felt a little more comfortable with my financial situation. I eventually paid off my car, but always maintained credit card balances. I still did not know the meaning of debt-free living.

A few months before it was time to renew my lease, a series of mishaps took place in my apartment complex. My apartment was vandalized; the nice neighbors moved out and not-so-nice neighbors moved in. I also discovered mold in my apartment. It was time to leave.

Instead of thinking through my next steps, I decided to buy a house. I knew nothing of the home buying process. I just knew I needed to leave my current address, and buying a house seemed like a good idea. I went back to my steno pad to see if I could squeeze in a mortgage payment.

I found a banker who arranged my financing and then borrowed the down payment from my 401(k). Instead of signing a new lease, I bought my first townhouse. Because I gave no thought to the purchase, I was not prepared for the increased utility payments. I was not prepared for the need to plan for repairs. I was not prepared for homeownership.

Slowly the credit card balances got higher and higher. Before long, all my cards reached their limits and I realized I was in over my head. I took out another 401(k) loan to "consolidate" my loans. But my money management skills were no better than before, so it was not long before the balances returned. It was a vicious cycle which continued until I sold the house to move to Virginia five years later.

Unfortunately, I still did not learn my lesson about revolving debt and repeated my mistakes. I bought another house I could not afford and did the same thing all over again. Looking back, I see clearly all my mistakes. So much worry, so much anxiety and all because I was unwise with my money. I never asked God for guidance. I never asked Him for education. I thought I knew it all, and it cost me more than I would ever know.

Your Turn…Your Perspective: Describe your budgeting process. Describe a purchase you regret making. How has it impacted your life and your financial well-being?

Prayer: Lord, thank You for delivering me from my former self. I thank You for loving me enough to lead me to a place of Christ-centered financial wellness. I do not want to go back. I pray for the courage to stay on Your plan for my life.

Day 9
Interest on the Loan

PROVERBS 12:24

My brother has always been an amazing athlete. Built like Shaquille O'Neal, he was one of the top ranked basketball players graduating from high school. His passion for the game fueled his discipline and earned him quite the reputation. The year he graduated, his team ended the season with an overall record of 30-1. Almost 30 years later, no other team has come close to what my brother and his teammates achieved his senior year.

During his final year, all the top colleges in South Carolina followed him. He was also on the radar for several other powerhouses in the NCAA. Everyone was waiting to see which team he chose to further his athletic career.

But he was on a different type of mission. He knew two things: a career in the NBA was a long shot, and he wanted to be an engineer. Because of those two pieces of information, he decided to sign his college letter of intent during the early signing period (November) instead of waiting for the regular signing period (April).

Once an athlete signed a letter of intent with a university, all recruiting efforts by other schools were off limits. The recruiting period could be incredibly stressful for an athlete. School recruiting trips, constant calls from scouting coaches, and special workout sessions were all common. During his senior year, my brother was taking Advanced Placement (AP) calculus and physics, along with his honors classes. He did not want the distractions associated with waiting until the spring to sign his letter of intent.

Everyone was surprised by his choice of schools. Instead of signing with a large basketball powerhouse, he signed with a lesser ranked school with an adequate basketball program. The important part for my brother was their stellar engineering program. Basketball would indeed pay for his engineering degree.

Fast forward a year and it is the start of his freshman year in college. It was his first time on the big stage of the NCAA Division 1 basketball world. He was so excited. Memories of his final high school season and all the accolades flooded his mind. It was time to do it again.

The problem was his new team was not his old team. He struggled to find his place on the team and found it difficult to settle into a rhythm. Instead of racing out the season's gate with lots of wins, my brother's team was 3-7 for their first ten games and finished the season 10-18 overall. He was so disappointed.

We spoke often, and I constantly talked him out of transferring. He was a winner and was really having a hard time not being on a winning team. I encouraged him by reminding him how he came to his decision to attend this school. It was not the basketball program which drew him in; it was the engineering program. I told him the losses he was experiencing were simply the interest on the loan. Instead of taking out loans for his education, he needed to simply endure the string of losses and focus on the bigger win.

The basketball team never had a winning season. But my brother was a winner. Four years later, he graduated with a degree in electrical engineering from one of the top schools in the country. He kept his eye on the goal and paid his interest on the loan. He chose to endure the frustration of a losing team to win in the end.

Your Turn...Your Perspective: What "interest on the loan" experiences have you had in your life?

Prayer: Lord, thank You for opportunities for a better future. Thank You for helping me stay on the narrow path even when it is lonely and uninviting. Please help me to keep my eyes on You and Your plan.

Day 10
No Plan

PSALM 119:24

I was 25 when I bought my first house. So much about the purchase was just wrong. I was completely clueless about how to go about purchasing a home. I attended no seminar. I read no book. I sought no counsel. I just knew I wanted out of my one-bedroom apartment. I wanted to own a home. The entire thought process was reactionary.

It was as if I woke up one morning and said, "Today I will buy a house." And while it did not quite happen so quickly, my actions showed just how ill-prepared I was for home ownership. Since I could afford the payment, I thought all would be well.

Shortly after I moved in, I began to receive the "you just bought a house" mail. I succumbed to the free offers in exchange for an hour-long presentation. Within a year, I bought a new vacuum cleaner, a whole house water filtration system, a new HVAC system, and brand-new windows. All were financed. All were purchased without thinking through the impact on my budget.

My skin was softer from my newly treated water. My carpets were clean enough for my baby nephew to happily crawl around. My electric bill went down because my new windows kept air from leaking in. And I used my new programmable thermostat and high SEER rating to slowly recoup the cost of the HVAC system without knowing I put a property lien on my house to do so. So much for reading the fine print of the contract.

Unfortunately, none of the improvements were able to improve the hole in my checking account. I was broke. There was no margin. There was no room for anything to go wrong. I prayed nothing did go wrong because there was also no emergency fund. Only Visa, Discover and American Express. They were ready to come to the rescue. They were each already growing balances to offset the need for continued repairs.

When the toilet leaked and damaged the downstairs bathroom, the insurance deductible was financed. When the exterior faucet malfunctioned, and the water bill was over $100, I paid for it with a credit card. I was obviously in over my head, and the sad part was I did not even know it. I thought how I lived was normal. I never thought about completing the repairs in phases. I just financed it all.

Looking back, I see God's hand of protection. He prevented me from feeling the fullness of my poor choices. Nothing else can explain how I managed to escape the poor financial choices I made with my first home without bankrupting myself.

It took me decades to even recognize how poor my choices were, and many other bad decisions littered my past before I did realize. When I finally learned how to make better choices, God was right there waiting to applaud my efforts and encourage me to keep going. I was thankful He never gave up on me. He will not give up on you either.

Your Turn…Your Perspective: What poor financial choices have caused you to hang your head? What did the experiences teach you?

Prayer: Lord, thank You for protecting me from myself. Thank You for never giving up on me. I pray for the courage to stay on this journey and to begin to think before taking financial action. Thank You for Your patience with me as I figure this out.

Day 11
Car Fever

ROMANS 7:8

After working for a few years and receiving several raises, I was finally beginning to breathe financially. There was a little more financial margin in my life, and I no longer felt afraid of every purchase. The year after I purchased my home, I got a very large tax refund. I knew enough about finances to know I would benefit from having more income monthly instead of a large year end refund.

Increasing my take-home pay gave me even more financial margin. But I still did not know what to do with it. Should I save it? Spend it? On what? The questions went unanswered. I still primarily reacted to money instead of being proactive. I knew nothing of saving to pay cash for future purchases. In the end, I decided to use my extra monthly income to buy a new car.

I always wanted a convertible and felt I deserved to buy whatever I could afford. "Afford" at the time meant whatever payment I could manage in my budget. I did not have money for a down payment and did not know anything about negotiating. I just knew I wanted a silver convertible Camaro, and I should get one. I believed it was my "right" to have a nice vehicle.

Since I did not have enough in savings, I arranged for a no-money-down loan from my credit union. Armed with my financing, I headed to the local Chevrolet dealership. I explained to the sales person what I wanted and proceeded to pay full price for the car of my dreams. I thought I was getting a bargain because they were able to "fit" the car into my loan amount. It never occurred to me to work the price down below the amount I was eligible to finance.

I also only looked at new cars. The thought of buying a used vehicle literally never crossed my mind. I even took it a step further and bought a car which needed to be shipped in from another state. Color, after all, was very important. Paying a transport fee in my mind was a small price to get a silver convertible Camaro with a black rag top. I was so happy to have my new car.

The payment for my dream car was two-thirds of the amount I spent on a monthly mortgage payment. My insurance and property taxes doubled. I was a 26-year old with a sports car, and the insane expenses to prove it. The cushion of newly found money in my paycheck was quickly absorbed with new car expenses. I convinced myself I also needed a car cover, touch-up paint, and monthly car detailing.

Within a few months, the financial pinch was back, and I was again afraid to breathe when it was time to make financial decisions. The extra income in my bank account was nowhere to be found. Paycheck to paycheck once again became the norm.

How did I end up back here? was the question I asked myself. My trusty notepad, which held my monthly budget, provided no answer. I once again put myself in a financial bind. I once again made a poor financial decision. It was a vicious cycle I would repeat for many years to come.

Your Turn…Your Perspective: What cycle of poor decision making have you been in? What did it take for you to finally break the cycle? How do you keep from going back?

Prayer: Lord, thank You for helping me to find my way out of the crazy cycle of good and bad financial decisions. I pray I do not forget the cost of the lessons I have learned. I do not want to repeat them.

Day 12
Convertible Joy

JOB 34:19; JOHN 10:10

The object of my car affection was a 1995 convertible Camaro with a 5-speed transmission. It came complete with a muscle car engine which literally rumbled when I started it. Friends and family found it odd for a girl to want to drive a muscle car, but I did not care. It was everything I always wanted. And the amount of power I felt when I shifted from 2nd to 3rd gear was sheer joy.

Even though I thoroughly enjoyed driving my new car, I struggled with whether I actually deserved it. It took years for me to feel worthy of the car. My mind was constantly struggling with the purchase. *Who did I think I was, driving a sports car? Did I really have to buy a new car? There was still life left in my college car. Do I know how many kids I could feed with the money I spent on a car payment?*

It was a constant stream of negative thoughts and emotion. I was not worthy. I wasted my money. I was a disappointment to God. I was not a good steward. The fight in my head was real, and I daily felt as if I would lose the war. Did I deserve it? I could not convince myself I did.

The guilt associated with my car stayed with me the entire time I owned it. I never felt worthy of the purchase. I was not sure where the strong negative emotion came from, but it was my constant companion, never leaving my side.

And while the purchase of the convertible was the first time I experienced the feelings of unworthiness, it was not the last. I questioned every purchase of substance. I was often embarrassed to wear certain clothing items or pieces of jewelry for fear of being judged by others. It was an endless "head" game.

Years later, as I learned to understand God's Word and His promises, the weight associated with unworthiness began to subside. It also helped when I began to understand the value of budgeting and living within my means. What it meant to "afford" something shifted from being able to make the payment to actually paying for it outright.

Eventually, I learned the value of taking my time and waiting before making bigger purchases. I learned to shop around and get additional bids. I learned to prayerfully consider each purchase and to seek God's guidance. It took years for me to not hear the voice of condemnation in my head after a purchase.

My convertible was long gone, but the memory of what I learned from the purchase was still very clear in my mind. And while I was not sure if I would ever own one again, I knew whatever vehicle I owned would be free of guilt and condemnation. I was finally free to enjoy what God blessed me with, and I was finally able to embrace His gifts.

Your Turn…Your Perspective: Name a time you felt unworthy. How did you get past it? What purchase have you made which you knew you deserved? How did it make you feel?

Prayer: Lord, thank You for freedom from condemnation. Thank You for Your Son, Jesus Christ, who died so I could live a life of abundance, and not one of fear. Thank You for helping me find my way to Christ-centered financial wellness.

Day 13
I Had a Feeling

PSALM 32:8; 1 KINGS 19:11-12

I lost $80,000 once. I was moving from South Carolina to Virginia and needed to sell my home. I was discussing my move with a friend and she mentioned her dad would be happy to help. The realtor I used to purchase the home did a great job and it was my plan to use her again. But I liked my friend, and allowing her dad to represent me, sounded like a great way to help him out and gain favor in the eyes of my friend.

Mixing friendship and business did not turn out well for me, however. I did not interview my friend's father the way I would a realtor I did not know. And I never called my former realtor to give her the opportunity to compete for the sale. By not doing my due diligence upfront, I did not know my friend's father was not actually licensed to sell real estate.

A random number was chosen for my home's purchase price instead of comparable sales being considered to set the price. By the time I found these things out, we were under contract and I was a week away from moving.

I was devastated, angry, and confused. I did not understand how my friend could put me in this situation. She knew her father was not licensed but recommended him to me anyway. At first, all my negative emotions were directed at my friend and her father. How could they take advantage of my kindness? Why would they intentionally deceive me? What happened to honesty and integrity in business and friendship? The questions and anger built up like a pressure cooker. I fought back angry tears every time I thought of the deception and betrayal.

It took years to get past the loss of the money and all the negative emotion associated with the transaction. Finally, I realized my anger was directed at the wrong people; I should have been angry at myself. How could I have been so foolish? Why did I not listen to the sinking feeling welling up inside before I hired my friend's father? My desire to impress a friend resulted in a horrible loss, both financial and emotional.

I did not use due diligence in the largest business transaction of my life – the sale of my home. I took from myself the opportunity to create a firm foundation for my move to a new city. It was not my friend's fault. It was not her father's fault. It was finally clear to me. It was all my fault and I was the one to blame. My lack of follow-through cost me an entirely different future. It would take years to undo the financial mess I created.

After closing costs, there was barely enough money left to put a down payment on my new home. There was certainly none left to invest. I knew the Holy Spirit was prompting me to go with my former realtor, but I rationalized the benefits of helping my friend's father. I learned a costly lesson at the expense of friendship and financial solvency.

Over time, I was able to forgive myself. While the decision to use my friend's father was not a good choice, the lessons learned were etched in my heart, and would stay with me for a lifetime.

Your Turn...Your Perspective: Have you ever experience the "sinking" feeling indicating you made the wrong choice? What did you do about it? How could you have handled the situation differently?

Prayer: Lord, thank You for the Holy Spirit Who lives inside me and serves as my guide. Help me to listen to Your still, small voice and to use discernment when making decisions. I pray I stay in tune to You enough to hear You.

Day 14
Walking on Water

PSALM 33:18; MATTHEW 14:29-30

I clearly heard it. It was 2A.M. and I clearly heard the Lord tell me I would qualify to become a Sales Director with Mary Kay Cosmetics in just one month. The company requirements allowed someone to take up to four months to qualify, but I did not need four. I only needed one. I was awestruck. I did not think sleep would come again as I asked many questions. How will I do this? Where will I find the people?

This was a milestone I tried to reach for over three years. I came close several times, but still failed. I amassed war stories of how difficult it was, and how much I learned about myself in the process. My pride was hurt, and my ego and self-confidence were badly beaten as I tried and failed six times.

The qualification required at least 30 team members and $16,000 in production in no more than four months. My team consisted of 12 people and we never reached more than $4500 in production in a month. Growing from 12 to 30 with $16,000 in production for one month was laughable given my previous track record. I was way out of my league and knew it. The only way I could meet the requisite was with the help of the Holy Spirit. There were only 31 days to get it done.

I went to work. I booked, coached my clients and team members, sold a ton of product, and added team member after team member. I worked like a mad woman and never lost sight of the goal. Momentum was building and soon my team caught the vision also. We were a well-oiled machine and our goal was coming into view.

On day 28, our team reached 32 with just under $13,000 in production. We were almost there. I looked at my list of prospects over and over to see where I could find the other $3000. I was running out of time and knew I needed to get fresh momentum if we were going to make it.

I made phone call after phone call. Nothing. I held additional appointments with minimal sales. Promises for orders disappeared and the addition of new team members slowed to a crawl. I was so close but did not see how I could finish.

On day 30, I gave up. Day 31 came and went. And while we experienced a wild ride, we did not finish our goal. We ended up being short by less than $2000. I sat quietly thinking about it all and wondered where I went wrong. It was then the still small voice of the Holy Spirit showed me the error of my ways. I never prayed for God's help. I did in the beginning, but not in the end when I needed Him most. I took His challenge, but when things got complicated, I took my eyes off Him and looked to my own ability.

Wow! What a revelation. How many times had I taken my eye off the Lord? What else was lost because I did not trust him? I asked for forgiveness and another chance. He was gracious and granted it. This time I prayed. I finished qualifications in two months with over 50 team members, and $22,000 in production. Praise the Lord!

Your Turn…Your Perspective: When was the last time you had to trust God to get you through something? What was the end result? What experience did He use to teach you the life lesson?

Prayer: Lord, thank You for second chances. Thank You for showing me where I fall short, but also showing me grace. I pray I keep my eyes on You and not on my circumstances. Help me to trust You.

Day 15
To Tell the Truth

PROVERBS 12:19

Becoming a Sales Director with Mary Kay Cosmetics was one of the most incredible accomplishments of my professional life. There were strict guidelines associated with attaining the position, and only 2% of the sales force ever reached it. It was the pinnacle of my career and I was excited about this new season of professional opportunity.

Because it was a new leadership position, the company provided a week of training for all new Sales Directors. My training was scheduled for December, and the annual Leadership Conference for all Sales Directors was scheduled for January. Thanksgiving and Christmas were also on the horizon and spending time with family for the holidays was important. I could not fathom not going home for a visit. It all added up to a need for lots of vacation time.

The amount of time needed off from my full-time day job was not the issue – the vacation hours were available. I rarely took vacation and simply held on to my hours for future use. The problem was my boss was a micro-manager and did not want anyone to take vacations. In his mind, vacation hours were reserved for emergency use only. He was known to create special projects for people specifically to keep them from leaving on time. If your vacation was scheduled to begin on Monday, he would wait until Friday afternoon to assign an "urgent" matter.

I really wanted (and needed) to attend the Mary Kay events if my business was going to grow. I also wanted to spend time with my family during the holidays. I moved to the DC Metro area without many contacts and was anxious to head home for a reprieve. I did not know what to do. I kept praying about it, but no answer came.

I decided to step out on faith. I booked my flight to Dallas for both Mary Kay events and made my hotel reservations. I was committed to going, but just did not know what to do about my day job. My mind was a whirlwind of thought. I could simply ask for the time I needed and suffer the wrath of my boss. Or I could get creative by suddenly becoming sick for a week. The flu typically lasted a week, right? I could just call in each day in my best nasally voice and no one would be the wiser.

I literally felt like there was a little angel and a little devil whispering in each ear. The little angel told me to be honest and deal with the consequences. The little devil told me it was only a white lie, and no one would know. For days, the volley in my head went back and forth between the two. I did not want to lie, but I also did not want to deal with the wrath of my boss. My time was running out.

One morning as I was sorting through the day's email at my day job, the HR manager asked to see me in his office. When I arrived, I was surprised to find my boss already there. They called me in to fire me. My immediate thought was "Praise the Lord! I don't have to lie!" I was giddy with excitement. I knew it was a strange response, but I felt so much relief at not having to lie to get the vacation time I needed. It was the first day of the rest of my life, and I was excited. Time was on my side.

Your Turn…Your Perspective: When was the last time you battled to do the right thing? What happened? How did it change you?

Prayer: Lord, thank You for the Holy Spirit who helps me with moral issues. Please help me to always be sensitive to His promptings. I pray to not compromise my integrity because it seems easier in the moment.

Day 16
The Prayer of Jabez

PSALM 145:18; 1 CHRONICLES 4:10; ISAIAH 55:11

The day I lost my job started out as any other. I struggled to fit in with my new company. I was hired to create a quality improvement department for a tech company but was met with constant resistance from leadership. After six months of trying to make it work, we reached an impasse.

A Mary Kay client requested I deliver some "thank you" gifts the same day. My original plan was to deliver the gifts after work, but since my day was suddenly free, I decided to drop them by early. My client told me to "ask about Jabez." I thought it was a strange question but was intrigued and chose to be obedient.

When I arrived, I presented the gifts and then asked about Jabez. One of the team members immediately jumped up and handed me a copy of Bruce Wilkinson's powerhouse little book, *The Prayer of Jabez*. I sat in the car for a few minutes and read the first chapter.

Wow! Who knew such a small book could pack such a punch? The book chronicled a seemingly insignificant prayer, prayed by a seemingly insignificant man named Jabez. The prayer was found deep in the book of 1 Chronicles in the Old Testament and was surrounded by obscure genealogy. But what seemed insignificant to many was more profound than anything I had come across in a long time.

In less than 30 days, I became a Sales Director with Mary Kay Cosmetics, lost my job, and was given a copy of *The Prayer of Jabez*. It seemed to be too much of a coincidence to ignore. Was my new "territory" my new business opportunity? It was my prayer for years to transition into Mary Kay full-time. It was sooner than I expected, but I could not deny the opportunity. I saw the book as confirmation to start my new season of entrepreneurship.

I read *The Prayer of Jabez* over and over in the first few months. When I woke up from my fog and realized no more salaried checks were coming in, I panicked. Jabez helped me breathe through the initial anxiety and get my business in high gear. I needed to replace "momentum" with true activity quickly.

Fear of failure became my motivator. I needed to make this work. I was flying by the seat of my pants and I knew it. I needed traction quickly or I would not survive. Jabez and his little prayer were my inspiration to keep going and not let the unknown slow me down.

I truly believed I was exactly where the Lord wanted me. I knew there was no chance of succeeding on my own. I needed the Lord on my side. My prayer life deepened immensely, and I stayed in the Word. I found scriptures about work, success, faith, and trust in God. I read them all daily. When I fell short on a goal, I dug a little deeper in the Word. I was determined to find my way, and I knew Jesus was my guide.

I truly believed the experience set me up for the debt-reduction journey Keith and I began when we got married. I knew exactly what to do. I got on my knees, found scriptures of support and encouragement, and got to work. *The Prayer of Jabez* provided the foundation I needed for success yet again.

Your Turn…Your Perspective: What territory has the Lord enlarged for you? What did the experience teach you?

Prayer: Lord, thank You for the promise You give us in Isaiah 55:11. I know Your Word will not return to You void. It will accomplish what You have set forth for me. Thank You for the reminders of You being with me always. Keep me focused on You, Lord. Keep me on my knees.

20 • Lisa Y. Jones

Day 17
Striking Out on My Own

MATTHEW 25:16; ROMANS 8:28

I never stopped to ask God if He wanted me to pursue a career with Mary Kay full-time. I did not fall to my knees the day I was fired, or the day after to lay my dilemma before Him. I did not see it as a dilemma at all. My logical mind was firmly in control and did not recognize the need for guidance from the Holy Spirit. I prayed in the past for the opportunity to run my business full-time. My prayer was answered.

At least, I thought it was the answer to my prayer. On the same day I was fired, I decided not to look for a new engineering position, but instead, chose to pursue Mary Kay full-time. I made a life altering decision without any prayer whatsoever. I did not call a mentor to ask their opinion. I sought no guidance at all. It was a dangerous move.

I was not a new Christian but was new to including God in my decision making. I did not yet understand His desire to be a part of all aspects of my life. I saw myself as competent and capable, without need for outside assistance unless it was "important." I was short-sighted and did not even know it.

I sought His guidance when I accepted the position which moved me to Virginia, but there were so many other crucial decisions I made without seeking His input. It was years before I even realized the impact of not putting this life-altering decision before the Lord.

Hindsight is always 20/20 and this case was no different. I jumped into the deep end of the pool head first without a life vest. Not only was I learning how to run my new business, but now I depended on it for income. It was not a great combination. I was too blinded by pride and the potential for success to see the danger signs. I thought all I needed to do was book, sell, coach, and recruit for my business to succeed.

I spent years trying to keep my poor choice from overtaking me. I went for long periods of time with little or no health insurance. I was constantly in a reactionary state of mind about money, and very rarely had the luxury of a plan of action. Despite my haphazard approach to business, I managed to maintain my position as a Sales Director for a full decade.

The blessing in all of it was my relationship with Jesus Christ. If I gained nothing else from my decade of hasty career decisions, I did gain a deeper faith. A Christian psychologist once told me the Lord tests us in the area of our heart's desire. It was definitely true with me; my business kept me on my knees.

My decision to not find a new engineering position was probably a mistake, but the decade of living out the mistake was amazing. The woman of faith I became, born of the trials of the season, could not have existed otherwise. If given the chance, I am not sure I would do it all the same, but the deeper relationship with Jesus Christ made it worth the trials endured.

God took my unvetted decisions and created an incredible woman of faith. I would use that faith daily in a different season, when Keith and I worked hard and long to get out of our debt. God worked it out for my good.

Your Turn…Your Perspective: What poor choice have you had to live with? How has it grown you spiritually?

Prayer: Lord, thank You for being with me, even when I take the wrong path. Thank You for working out all things for good.

Day 18
"I Got Work to Do"

PSALM 41:2

When I lost my job and made the decision to pursue a career with Mary Kay Cosmetics full-time, I did not realize how difficult it would be to manage my time. My business was over three years old and I typically worked about 10-15 hours each week. I worked 40-50 hours each week on my "day job," and therefore, spent very little time at home.

When I was home, I was exhausted. It was not uncommon for me to pass out on the sofa watching mindless television until I could get myself together enough to actually go to bed. My home was a place for me to rest, not a place of work.

It did not take long for me to realize I needed to rethink how I viewed my home. I could not watch mindless television all day if I was going to make a living and support myself. My home could no longer be a place of rest; it needed to become a place of work, also.

My office in the basement was ready and waiting for me to use, but I did not have office hours. I did not have a set schedule. I did not think about how to spend my day in order to be intentional in growing my business. If I did not make a change soon, I would be out looking for another job.

I thought about my situation and knew I needed to retrain my brain. My mind saw my home as a place to relax, and I needed it to see my home as my office.

I decided the first thing I needed to do was get dressed. Until this time, I stayed in lounging pajamas all day unless there were appointments scheduled. And often, I found myself forcing appointments to other days because I did not want to get up and get dressed. If this was to be a full-time job for me, I needed to at least dress the part.

I also began to set an alarm. Until then, I slept until I woke up. It was not uncommon for me to still be lounging around at noon each day. If I was going to make this job full-time, I needed to get up and get out of the house. I needed to create more order to my day.

The last thing I did was the most significant. Singer Vanessa Williams released a single the year before and I purchased it and put it on repeat. From the moment I finished my devotion, until I walked out of the door each day, I played "I Got Work to Do." It was the reminder I needed to shift my mindset, from viewing my house as a place of rest, to a place of work.

Over time, I was able to set a routine for my new career. I learned what days were best to work from home during the day, and which days needed to be the days I held appointments away from home. I learned which areas of the house needed to be reserved for work, and which were places of rest and relaxation. Shifting my focus to working from home was a crucial step in being able to grow my business in those early years. I was thankful it was a lesson I learned early.

Your Turn…Your Perspective: How have you had to adjust your work environment (now or in the past) to accommodate change? What did you learn from the experience?

Prayer: Lord, so much of this journey is about mindset. I pray to keep You at the forefront of my mind. Please help me stay positive in my thinking and actions. I praise Your holy name.

Day 19
Dressed for Success

PROVERBS 15:19

As a brand-new Sales Director with Mary Kay Cosmetics, I needed to not only shift how I managed my income (going from a salaried position to 100% commission), but I also needed to shift how I managed my time.

Northern Virginia was one of the most congested areas of the country and traffic was always a factor. Before I understood the importance of organizing my day around my appointments, I often found myself racing around the city haphazardly. I started many days without much structure and attempted to adjust midstream. I inevitably got caught on the wrong side of town at the wrong time. It was costing me time and money, neither of which could I afford to lose.

If I did not get it together quickly, I would have to find a salaried job. I realized my wardrobe was a big part of my problem. If I did not have appointments scheduled for the day, I did not give much thought to what I wore. I would throw on a pair of jeans and a top to run errands and end up missing a networking opportunity because I was not dressed professionally.

Sometimes I would not get dressed at all if I did not have plans to leave the house. Then I would scramble to throw together an outfit and race out the door if a telephone conversation turned into a more immediate opportunity.

After months of expending energy on random activity, I stumbled on the solution. Get up, get dressed to work, and do it every day. I needed more structure in my routine; I needed more structure in my wardrobe. If I wanted my new career to pay me like a business, I needed to treat it like one. I had to dress for the career I wanted.

Jeans pretty much disappeared from my wardrobe. Every day became a day for a suit, or at least a professional skirt and top. Rarely did I wear slacks.

I got dressed right after I finished devotion and was ready for whatever opportunities became available. My sales increased, and my gas budget dropped. I no longer needed to run back home to change clothes to make a last-minute appointment.

I also learned to work in sections of the city. Instead of scheduling appointments all over the city for any part of the day, I began to book appointments according to the address. All appointments held in Washington, DC were made for Tuesday mornings. Appointments on the western side of the county were scheduled for Fridays after Bible study.

It was difficult in the beginning to find my way, but I was determined not to give up. A year into my full-time status, my system was down to a science. My income began to climb, and for the first time in a long time, I felt like I would make it. I was thankful to rise to the challenge once again.

Your Turn…Your Perspective: What changes have you had to make recently to get more out of your day? What was the catalyst for the change?

Prayer: Lord, thank You for the lessons which stretch me. Thank You for loving me enough to not allow me to simply settle for status quo. Please help me stay focused on the main thing and not be sidetracked by impulse.

Day 20
Debt Cancellation
HEBREWS 2:8

A few months after I lost my job and began to work my Mary Kay business full-time, I was surprised to get a letter from the South Carolina Student Loan Corporation (SCSLC). I was fortunate to not have a large amount of student loan debt after college because I earned a significant number of small scholarships which collectively paid for most of my undergraduate degree. My internship also paid for tuition.

After college, I set up my monthly payment to SCSLC and promptly forgot about it. The payment came out automatically each month. I knew I was paying interest but had not yet learned I could have a life without payments and interest. I just knew it was a debt which needed to be paid. I did not want to go down the path of not paying my loans because I knew it would only create more trouble.

When the letter arrived, I was curious because I knew all my payments were made on time. I did not understand why they would contact me. After reading the letter twice, I called the toll-free number. I was still confused by what I was reading. The words "debt" and "cancellation" were not ones I was used to seeing together in one sentence.

The customer service representative on the phone chuckled a little when I explained why I was calling. She explained the SCSLC was a non-profit agency and they underestimated the amount of money they would collect the year before. They could not keep the excess and their policy was to give it to those clients who historically made their payments on-time. I was stunned. The letter was authentic. My debt had been cancelled. All my student loans were forgiven.

All I could do was praise the Lord! I thanked the customer service representative, hung up the phone and did a happy dance in my kitchen. What a blessing! SCSLC may have seen me as a good business investment, but I knew the debt was cancelled because the Lord wanted it to be cancelled.

The timing of the letter was not lost. The previous few months were very stressful. I lost my job, my income was cut to a fraction of the previous amount, and I started a new, commission-only business – all as a single woman. I took a huge risk in making the business full-time, and not looking for another engineering position. It was "sink or swim" time and I wanted desperately to stay afloat. Having an entire chunk of debt forgiven made my monthly expenses much more manageable.

I thanked the Lord. I saw the debt cancellation as permission to pursue my dream and build my business. It made the decision to pursue Mary Kay full-time, and not look for a salaried position, a lot easier. The debt cancellation made me feel as if my stepping out on faith was simply following the path He laid out for me.

The season of full-time entrepreneurship was one of huge spiritual growth for me. I grew in ways I could never have experienced in a salaried position. I had to rely on Him, and not my own abilities. I was so thankful He trusted me enough to give me the opportunity.

Your Turn…Your Perspective: Think of a time when you received an unexpected gift. What was your first reaction? When was the last time you had to trust God for provision? How did you do?

Prayer: Lord, thank You for making a way out of no way. Thank You for provision. I pray to not lose sight of just how much You love and care for me. I know You have my best interest at heart and it is wonderful to see You work things out on our behalf.

Day 21
Mink

PROVERBS 13:7

A few months into being full-time with Mary Kay, I found myself at my first ever Leadership Conference. It was an annual event for the top 2% of all Mary Kay Consultants. It was held in January, which was the first full month of my new commission-only life. All of the payouts associated with my former job were gone.

It was amazing to see so many successful women in one place. They were dripping with diamonds, fur coats, and all the outer signs of success. I was wearing my own diamond ring, which I won the year before, but it paled in comparison to the four and five carat diamonds worn by others.

I felt so out of place. My clothes did not feel up to par, my hair seemed too simple, and my makeup was not quite polished enough. I felt like the country bumpkin attending the finest pageant in town. After being a Sales Director for all of three months, I already felt the weight of maintaining success.

After the sessions ended one night, I was making my way through the exhibits when a friend came running up to me. She grabbed me by the arm and literally pulled me to a booth a few feet ahead. There, in front of my eyes, was a display of fur coats. Every style, color and size imaginable was on display. These were not just any fur coats; they were from the most famous furrier in the country. I knew nothing about fur coats, except I always wanted one. My eyes were wide with excitement.

When the salesman chose a floor length, mink coat for me to try on, I could not believe the woman who stared back at me. Gone was the country bumpkin and before me was an elegant, classy woman who obviously knew how to be successful. The transformation was amazing. The salesman immediately worked his magic and created a layaway plan for me to have my coat. It was all so simple – a down payment of $100 and a year to pay off my coat. I hesitated only for a moment before signing my name and writing the check.

It took less than 24 hours for buyer's remorse to set in. What on earth did I do? I recently lost my job, was trying to make a commission-only career work, and just committed to paying for a mink coat for the next year! Foolish, foolish, foolish! It was the only word to describe my actions. It was a huge mistake.

I wanted so much to fit in and feel as if I were truly a part of this elite group of businesswomen. The mink was supposed to help me belong. But how could I belong when I could not afford the purchase? I was setting myself up for failure right from the beginning. I gave no thought to the financial burden I created for myself.

I struggled to make payments on the mink for an entire year. I reached the same crossroad many times where I wrestled with pouring good money after bad. I did not want to lose all I invested, but there were so many other uses for the money I spent on coat payments. It was a horrible feeling.

Finally, the day came when I made the final payment and the coat appeared at my door. Wearing it lacked the excitement I remembered, and I knew it was because I finally understood the real cost. I knew I would never get the full enjoyment out of it simply because of all I lost by purchasing it. It served as a constant reminder of how costly it was to attempt to buy status. The truth was, it was not for sale.

Your Turn…Your Perspective: In what ways have you attempted to purchase status? How was your life impacted?

Prayer: Lord, thank You for the hard lessons. Please help me to exercise wisdom in purchases and not be fooled by outward appearances. I pray to not be impulsive when making large purchases.

Day 22
Confidence in the Making

LUKE 12:27-28

It was quite an adjustment to go from a significant salaried income to being self-employed with a 100% commission income. There was a lot to learn. My thought process on everything changed. The way I shopped and spent in all categories needed to adjust to make ends meet as I made the transition. I knew this from the beginning and was on high alert. I could not afford to create debt when my income was still so uncertain.

One of the first areas I addressed was my wardrobe. As a test engineering manager for a laser technology company, I wore pants to work most days. I ran a test lab and the equipment I tested day in and day out was quite bulky. In the Mary Kay arena, I usually held appointments in the evenings and on Saturdays. My typical wardrobe was a skirt and my Mary Kay beauty coat. There was not much in my wardrobe which did not fall into one of these two categories.

When I made the decision to pursue Mary Kay full-time, I realized I did not have the clothes to support my new career. I also did not have much money to use on a new wardrobe. I finally decided to work with what was currently in my closet. It was a very uncomfortable feeling. Not only was I unsure of what I was doing in my new career, I also felt self-conscious of my wardrobe.

My self-confidence took a huge blow when I lost my job. I knew I needed to adjust my self-talk to not sabotage my efforts at success in my new career. Instead of incurring debt to relieve my feelings of inadequacy, I chose to see my situation as an educational opportunity. I watched other Sales Directors in the area and made notes on their clothing choices. I became a student of the women around me. I needed to learn how to dress like the professional career woman I wanted to become. With my new-found knowledge, I slowly transformed my wardrobe.

I learned to shop differently and discovered new ways of using my existing clothing to create variety. I learned how to accessorize the same suit with different scarves and jewelry. I mixed and matched pieces to extend the range of my small wardrobe. The transformation took well over a year, but the result was a much more confident woman who felt capable of becoming successful as an entrepreneur.

One day I caught a glimpse of myself in the mirror as I was about to leave for an appointment. I was a different woman than the one who lost her job and her confidence so many months prior. I had a fresh haircut and my makeup was impeccable. My suit was tailored and looked professional. My pumps added flair, and my jewelry was elegant and tasteful. I realized I looked the part of the career woman I always wanted to become and did not spend a significant amount of money to do so. It was a great feeling.

I learned it was more important to have confidence than a wardrobe. By focusing on the activity and not my appearance, I made the transition to full-time Sales Director without breaking the bank.

Your Turn...Your Perspective: What unfulfilled dreams do you have? What would it take to be able to achieve it?

Prayer: Lord, I pray to trust You for what I need and to not depend on my own abilities. Help me to look for ways to stay relevant and on budget. I ask for guidance in how to makeover my financial life during this season of change.

Day 23
Faith Zone

GENESIS 22:14

Even after a few years as a Sales Director with Mary Kay Cosmetics, I still struggled with what it meant to be a 100% commission sales person. Not only did I manage the income I needed to live on, but I also managed the resources needed to run the business. I separated my household expenses into daily and monthly expenses.

Daily expenses were things like gas and groceries I could purchase from my sales. Monthly expenses were things like the mortgage and utilities which were allocated from my monthly commissions check and bonuses. This system worked great unless my sales were low, and/or the monthly commission check and bonuses were lower than my monthly expenses. In those instances, I needed to adjust and find a new way to get by.

This particular day was in the middle of a rather slow sales month. The number of new appointments were down and my reorders from existing clients were also low. I was beginning to feel overwhelmed. There was only one selling appointment on my calendar for the day. It was about 30 minutes away and I was down to the last quarter tank of gas in my car. I also scheduled a haircut for later in the afternoon. I would have to cancel my haircut if the appointment was not productive. I would also have to work hard to keep the dollar signs out of my eyes as I worked through the appointment. It was important to keep my client's needs at the forefront of my mind. My need for a sale could not supersede my client's needs or budget.

As I got dressed, I knew I was in what I called a "faith zone." There was no way I could accomplish what I needed on my own. I needed divine intervention to have a successful day. I paused and asked a simple prayer: "Lord, please let this appointment go well. I need to sell at least $75 in products, and I need her to pay me with a local check or cash. I know You *can* provide for me. I pray You will."

A sale of at least $75 would give me enough profit to get my haircut and put gas in my car. But an out of town check or credit card meant no funds would be available for the next few days. I would have to cancel my hair cut and find another way to pay for gas.

It was a beautiful appointment. She lived in an area of town I did not frequent often, and her home was surrounded by trees. It was springtime and the birds gave great entertainment outside her kitchen window. She was beautiful in the makeup options we chose, and she loved her new look.

As the appointment came to an end and we discussed her needs, I again prayed to not focus on myself. I knew if I focused on my client and not myself, I would somehow get what I needed in the end. The sale was $85. She wrote a check and it was drawn on the bank right next door to where I got my hair cut! The Lord provided and made it convenient, too! What a blessing.

I learned a lot from my cry out to the Lord. I learned to trust Him even when I could not see Him at work. I learned to praise Him through my circumstances. And I learned to care for my clients regardless of my own needs. I held on to those lessons and they continued to serve me well through my career.

Your Turn...Your Perspective: Think of a time when you had needs the Lord met. How did it feel to watch Him at work in your life? How did the experience impact you?

Prayer: Lord, thank You for Your constant faithfulness. Thank You for always providing what I need. I pray to stay focused on You and Your plan even when I can only see a few steps ahead of me.

Day 24
Family Time

MATTHEW 6:20

I was a full-time Sales Director with Mary Kay Cosmetics for 10 years. From my first introduction to the business plan, I was in awe of being able to set my own hours and map out my business the way I wanted. Unlike a business owner with a storefront, I enjoyed the flexibility of working when, where and how I wanted. I knew it was a blessing, and I was thankful to have it.

A year after I started growing my business full-time, I got a call from my mom. She wanted me to know my stepdad would be undergoing surgery in a few weeks. She recently suffered a mishap herself and was not able to drive so she asked if I would come home to assist. Of course, I told her I would.

For the next few weeks, I tidied things up in Virginia. I held extra appointments to create cash flow, and rescheduled appointments already on my calendar to accommodate everyone before I left town. My plan was to only be gone a week, so I booked additional appointments for the week of my scheduled return to have work waiting for me when I got back.

We drove my stepdad to the hospital on Monday morning and settled in for the routine procedure. My brothers called to check in, and the ones close enough to visit came by later in the day. What should have been a routine 2-3-hour surgery took over 10 hours. It was not good.

Each day, my mom and I got up, ate breakfast, and drove an hour to the hospital. We stayed all day and returned home emotionally and physically exhausted. We did this every day for almost a week. My stepdad passed away five days after the surgery.

It was obvious I would not be returning home any time soon. Instead of calling a supervisor to explain the need to be with my family, I simply cancelled the appointments on my calendar and continued the grieving process. I managed my existing clients from my cell phone and computer by filling orders and shipping them instead of delivering them in person. I continued to reach out to clients for follow-up.

I was incredibly thankful to be in the position of anchor that my family needed during our grief. Because I was there to give support, my brothers were able to make the necessary arrangement with their families and employers to get home when they could. They did not need to worry about the day-to-day decisions.

So much of my time as a single, commissioned-only salesperson was spent scraping by just to make a living. There were times when I was not sure I would make it. But the month I was able to take to be with my family during a great loss was more special than any other experience associated with my career with Mary Kay. The cars and diamond rings did not compare to the joy I experienced, knowing my time was my own and I could schedule it as I needed to. It was a priceless opportunity.

Your Turn…Your Perspective: When have you had a need for flexibility during an important life event? How did you manage it? What did you learn through the experience?

Prayer: Lord, thank You for a season of flexibility. Thank You for family. I pray to be reminded often of the importance of having margin to be available for the important things.

Day 25
Do You Trust Me?

EZEKIEL 28:4

June was the last month of the Mary Kay Cosmetics fiscal year. It was the stretch month where year-long goals came into focus for the last possible push to reach the finish line. I managed to eke out a living as a Sales Director with Mary Kay Cosmetics for a few years and was finally in the middle of one of the best months of my career.

It was the end of the month, and I was fast and furiously bringing all the loose ends to a tight close. No stone was left unturned. No phone call left unanswered. No order unfilled. It was not uncommon for me to be up until the early hours of the morning wrapping up the day, only to get a few hours of sleep and do it all again. My motto was "I can sleep in July!"

During this time, a client placed an order for her usual items. She was also in sales and understood the demands of year-end and month-end goals. As I sat with her chatting over small things while she wrote the check for her purchase, she shared her desire to start a business selling Mary Kay.

We got her business started later the same day. As I sat with her at her kitchen table and laid out her inventory options, I asked her again if she was sure. She seemed so defiantly against the idea of starting a business a few months prior that it just seemed hard to believe she was now ready to jump in with both feet.

Hours later, I processed her order and finally went to bed. When I awoke a few hours later, I found her email telling me she was experiencing a change of heart. The problem was her order was already processed and could not be cancelled. Several thousand dollars' worth of inventory was headed her way.

After communicating with the company, we found a solution. She was to simply refuse the order when it was delivered, and after it was returned to the company, a refund would be issued. It might take a few days to undo the transaction, but she would no longer be a consultant.

The problem was I earned almost $1000 in commissions on the order. I would be initially paid for it in July but would then need to return the commission when the company refunded her order. I struggled with whether I should keep the $1000 in savings until it was time to repay it, or should I use it in my monthly budget?

I decided to put the money in savings and wait until it was time to repay it. Immediately, I felt a prompting from the Holy Spirit. He reminded me of the call to keep my resources working and to not be afraid. I was to trust God to provide what I needed. With a huge financial leap of faith, I put the $1000 in use when it was deposited a few weeks later. I chose to trust God to show up in a big way when the refund was deducted. And He did.

The refund was deducted from my November 2012 commissions. It was my highest month ever. Even with the deduction, my commissions were almost double what they were for June. God asked me to trust Him and He blessed me mightily because I did.

Your Turn…Your Perspective: When was the last time you had to trust God for something big? What was the end result? How did your faith mature because of the experience?

Prayer: Lord, thank You for the prompting of the Holy Spirit. Thank You for Your provision. I pray I always have the courage to trust Your plan, even when I don't understand it.

Day 26
Friendship Gift

PROVERBS 3:3; 18:24

At the peak of my Mary Kay career, I led a team of almost 100 women. We retailed over $300,000 in products in our best year, and our modest years were all over $200,000.

My personal client base averaged over 200 clients in any given year. My own sales ranged from $20,000 - $40,000 each year for almost 20 years. It felt good to be a part of a transformation which helped many women see themselves as beautiful for the first time.

Most of my clients were people I did not know prior, but I did have a few friends as clients. Serving them was a blessing, and I enjoyed being able to add another dimension to our relationship. One year, a friend made a routine order. This was before online credit card processing, so my friend was to mail me a check.

I shipped the order to my friend and expected to receive payment in a few days. After a week, I called hoping the check was not lost in the mail. She explained they were having a small emergency and she would mail payment the next week. I assured her it would not be a problem.

Another week passed. Then another. Still no check. I was beginning to get concerned. It was uncomfortable having to call my friend for payment and I was not sure how to proceed. Should I wait another week before calling? What should I say to put her at ease? I was stumped.

I decided to wait another week. My call went to voice mail. I was pretty certain she was avoiding me, and my heart ached. We had been friends for years, and I did not want this type of misunderstanding. I was running a business and could not simply give away so much product. I decided to wait it out.

Years passed. I thought of my friend often but did not know what to do. It was beyond awkward to have a conversation about payment now, and I was not sure she would even take my call. I did not know what was going on in her life, but I knew it must be a difficult time for her and her family when I did not hear from her for so long. More than anything, I missed our friendship.

I prayed. I asked the Lord what to do. I had long since written off the lost product, but I did not want to write off our friendship. Years of non-communication could be overcome if we were both willing to meet in the middle, but I was not sure the relationship was salvageable.

During my prayer time one day, my friend again crossed my mind. The familiar pain of loss and confusion touched my heart, and I finally knew what I needed to do. I picked up the phone and dialed her number. Her voice mail clicked on. I told her I missed her, and the cost of the product was not worth our friendship. I asked her to please call. I wanted to get past the uncomfortable first few moments and move on.

She called. We both cried. She thanked me for the gift, and I thanked her for her friendship. We never spoke of it again, and I was very thankful to have my friend back in my life. Thankful to not be ruled by profit.

Your Turn…Your Perspective: Has money ever come between you and a friend or family member? What lessons have you learned from mixing business and friends/family?

Prayer: Lord, thank You for teaching me people matter. Thank You for the reminder to protect the relationships closest to us. Thank You for the ultimate Friend, Your Son, Jesus Christ.

Day 27
Raining Hope

PSALM 73:24; 2 CORINTHIANS 4:8-10

As much as I loved my time as a Sales Director with Mary Kay Cosmetics, it was far from easy for me. It was hard to watch my colleagues make and meet their goals with relative ease, while every goal I set seemed to be met with challenge after challenge.

I think I loved this period of my life, however, because I met God there. He always seemed to be with me and I felt His presence often. Many times, I felt like I was at a place in my life where my career served as a pruning tool for Him. He had my attention and used my business to grow me spiritually almost daily. I never experienced God before then with such intimacy.

One night I was feeling especially frustrated. The best thing about my business was helping other women reach their goals. The worst thing about my business was trying to instill in them the desire to reach their goals. It was tough to watch them set goals and not follow through.

On this particular evening, my frustration stemmed from having just spent hours preparing for a training session where only a handful of consultants attended. It was disheartening to see the lack of enthusiasm in their eyes and to hear the excuses of why they did not work on a goal yet again.

It was raining hard when I returned home, and I felt weary. Instead of going inside, I took my shoes and jacket off and sat on my front step, just within shelter from the raindrops. I watched and listened to God replenishing water to the earth and hoped He would replenish me, too. I questioned whether I was doing the right thing. Could I actually make a living helping other people reach their goals? Would it ever get easier?

I asked those questions and many more during the time on my front porch. I just sat, and waited, and hoped God would hear me and answer me. It was not too much longer before I recalled a scripture. I knew it was the answer I sought:

2 Corinthians 4:8-10 stated "We are hard pressed on every side, but not crushed; perplexed, but not in despair; persecuted, but not abandoned; struck down, but not destroyed. We always carry around in our body the death of Jesus, so that the life of Jesus may also be revealed in our body."

I got my Bible and brought it back to the rain. I read the words over and over to make sure I did not miss anything. I did feel pressed on every side, but God said I would not be crushed. I was perplexed, but God said not to feel despair. I did feel financially persecuted, but God said He would not abandon me. I did feel struck down by want, but God said I would not be destroyed. He showed me my efforts were to make me better. My efforts were to complete the assignment Jesus had given me. Don't give up. Keep going.

My hope was restored on a rainy Tuesday night. My passion renewed. I did not work for others; I worked for Jesus. I just needed to be reminded.

Your Turn…Your Perspective: Think of a time when you felt financially frustrated. How did you get through it? How did God use the experience to grow you?

Prayer: Lord, thank You for the still small voice You use to speak to me. Thank You for showing me Your love through Your Son, Jesus Christ. Please help me to be reminded of my assignment to You – to represent You in all I do.

Day 28
Cranberry Glass

LUKE 12:25-26; PROVERBS 13:12

When I bought my first home, a lot of the previous owner's style was still intact. I did not know much about decorating, so I did not change much. When I moved in, I found a single wine glass in the back of a cabinet. I instantly liked it because it was my favorite color – burgundy. Years later, while on vacation, I discovered this was not just a burgundy wine glass; it was hand-blown and rare. The name given was cranberry glass. It felt good to know I owned something unique. I did not know if it was expensive, and it did not matter. I chose to enjoy it, knowing someone took great care to make it.

Fast forward several years, and I was living in a different home. I was in Northern Virginia with a career as a Sales Director with Mary Kay Cosmetics. I was surviving, but I was not thriving. Poor money management, and expenses too high for my income, left me in a financial crunch. I was beginning to lose hope. I was not sure I could make it work.

I chose not to share my burden with anyone, which only made the hopelessness deeper. I could not figure out why my efforts at building my business were not leading to greater results. I tried to not compare my business flaws to the successes of my colleagues. It was easy to want to compare and ask, "Why not me, Lord?" It took all my effort to keep my eyes focused on my own business and not be envious of the success I saw around me. I failed miserably and added it to the long list of perceived disappointments I experienced in my career.

I was thinking about my current state of affairs while doing dishes one day. I allowed my mind to wander too much and dropped my beloved wine glass. It shattered on the counter. Although I did not get cut by the broken glass, my heart shattered right along with the glass.

I began to cry. I felt so hopeless. I cried for the broken wine glass and what I believed to be a broken life. I just stood there and cried. I felt overwhelmed by my choices, and pride limited my options on what to do next. I thought I made the right choice in pursuing Mary Kay full-time. I thought it was an answer to prayer. At that moment, standing at my sink, however, I was not so sure.

Slowly, my sniffles turned to sentences and I began to pray out loud. The more I prayed, the less I cried. I prayed for God's peace and provision. I prayed for fresh energy and creativity in my business. I prayed for a breath of hope to fill my heart again.

Finally, the tears subsided, and my reality settled into my thoughts. I realized a pity party would not serve me well at all. I was faced with two viable choices. I could give up hope and accept defeat, or I could choose to trust the Lord knowing He would continue to make His way plain to me.

I must decide if I would believe the lie which stated I was a failure or trust the truth of God's plan still unfolding before me. With new resolve, I swept up the pieces of the wine glass and threw them in the trash. I chose to not focus on what was "broken" about my life, but instead focused on the One who would always be there to put the pieces back together.

Your Turn...Your Perspective: What is the dream in your heart? Have you ever lost sight of it? How do you keep it in focus as you work to fulfill it?

Prayer: Lord, thank You for loving my brokenness. Thank You for Your plan. I pray I not lose hope but continue to hold on to the dream in my heart.

Day 29
The Lamp Post

MATTHEW 6:1

I was house poor. There was no question about it.

Month after month, I worked feverishly to increase my sales and team building efforts of my business. In the meantime, the list of repairs around my house grew. I kept a list of what needed to be done but keeping the lights on along with food and gas were a much bigger priority than a toilet seal. As much as I wanted to manage the repairs, without more income, there was no real plan to execute any of it. Since nothing was an emergency, I justified putting the list off another month.

A couple in my neighborhood befriended me shortly after they moved in. They were vibrant, fun, and full of laughter. We often shared meals and enjoyed watching the neighborhood change as the trees and the kids grew. The longer we were neighbors, the closer we became as friends. I welcomed building community with them.

One year for my birthday, they rang my doorbell. I opened it to find my friends grinning before me with a huge, birthday wrapped box. I loved gifts just as much as the next person, but we were not at the gift exchange stage of our friendship. I panicked. I am sad to say my first thought was *"Oh, no! Now I will have to buy gifts for their birthdays."*

My response was an indicator of my financial state of mind. Friends came to bless me on my birthday, and all I could think about was how little money I would have to spend on their birthdays.

I invited them in and we settled in the living room. "Open it! Open it!" came from "Mrs. Friend" while "Mr. Friend" hung back to capture the moment. I opened the huge box and several emotions mixed with the tears which began to fill my eyes. My friends bought me a lamp for my lamp post in the front yard.

I was thankful, grateful, and embarrassed. The lamp was in disrepair and was an eyesore to our quaint little neighborhood. I added it to my fix-it list several months earlier, but it was an incredibly low priority. I could not justify replacing a lamp when I could barely pay for the power to run it.

There was no money to repair the lamp post. I saw it every time I entered my home, and every time I left. Obviously, my neighbors saw it too. I was embarrassed at not being able to do anything about it. I was embarrassed to be discovered.

I sheepishly thanked my friends. I did not share how much I appreciated them not simply reporting me to the HOA (Home Owner Association). No report was really necessary since the disrepair was open for all to see. Instead of condemning me, my friends gave me the gifts of graciousness and kindness. Instead of looking down on my financial state, they supported me beyond the requirements of being neighborly. They chose to be my friends, instead of just being neighbors. I was grateful.

Your Turn…Your Perspective: When was the last time you experienced the kindness of someone who covered you with grace? When have you covered another with grace? When have you not? How has each experience impacted your current financial situation?

Prayer: Lord, thank You for the good friends in my own life. I pray for humility and the removal of pride. Please help me be a good neighbor to those around me in whatever way I can. Help me be like the best Neighbor…Jesus Christ.

Friday Morning Bible Study

HEBREWS 2:6; 1 THESSALONIANS 5:17

Have you ever bargained with God? I did. I wanted so desperately to be a full-time Sales Director with Mary Kay Cosmetics, I reasoned it was a bargain which would be good for both of us. "Lord, if You allow me to do this, I will attend a daytime Bible study."

In my mind, a daytime Bible study would allow me to go deeper in my study of the Word. In my mind, I did not have time to do an intense study in the evenings if I were working a straight nine-to-five job. I wanted to know the Bible more and I wanted to be a full-time Sales Director. I knew I would be better at both if I did them together.

God accepted my bargain. He did His part by allowing me to become a full-time Sales Director. I did my part by joining my church's Friday morning Bible study.

It was intense. Every Friday I met with women from my church to study God's Word. The studies were full of concepts I never previously experienced – inductive Bible study, scripture memorization and diagraming, and daily homework assignments and reading. I was challenged every week. And I loved it. I soaked it up like a sponge. It was one of the most rewarding experiences of my life.

The women in the group became one collective mother to me. They comforted me when I hit a wall in my business, and in my relationship with Christ. They challenged my beliefs and kept me open to the Christian views my very immature spiritual mind was experiencing. They loved me through the tough times and applauded my successes. They were some of my biggest cheerleaders.

One of the hardest things I ever did was leave the group when my financial picture forced me to go back to a regular job. I experienced separation anxiety for weeks because I missed them so much.

What I did not know at the time was just how much I learned. I did not know the impact or the power of my bargain with God. It was if He said, "Ok, you want a morning Bible study, I'll give you one. And one more thing…you're gonna need it!"

It was the scriptures and Bible study tools I learned during Friday morning Bible study which later sustained me on our journey to debt-freedom. I knew how to find what I needed in my well-worn Bible because I studied those scriptures for years. I understood what it was to "pray without ceasing" because I learned how to do it years earlier. It sustained me through the new season of debt reduction. I was less afraid to face the fiscally irresponsible woman I was because I was equipped. I was spiritually trained to endure the tests.

The Lord took my request to bargain, and He made me better through it. I had no idea what I signed up for in the beginning, but I quickly found out. It was a blessing to have such an impactful season in my life – one which impacted another tough season years later.

Your Turn…Your Perspective: Name an experience where you were challenged for a season. How did it impact you? When was the last time you bargained with God? What were the results?

Prayer: Lord, I pray to be strengthened by Your Word. Please help me to stay focused on You and not on my circumstances as I work through this current financial season. I pray for the endurance to run this race and get to the finish line. I want to serve You well with my finances.

Day 31
The Flower Factor

I loved fresh flowers. I knew a woman once who loved fresh flowers so much she arranged to have fresh flowers delivered to her office every day. I thought her approach was a bit extreme, but I did not see why I could not get fresh flowers each week. So, I did.

Every weekend I bought myself a new bouquet of flowers from the local market or grocery store. I enjoyed seeing what was in season and experiencing God's beauty in a different way. Over time I amassed quite the collection of vases to hold my flowers – short, round vases for daisies and tall, square vases for tulips. I experimented with using them all. It brought me a lot of joy and was a high point of my week.

As my business continued to fail, I worked to cut back on my spending. I did not have a real budget back then, or an idea of how much I spent on anything. Budgeting for groceries never crossed my mind because I simply bought what I wanted. I did, however, change how I shopped for clothes by simply spending less on clothing. I also did not budget for car repairs or eating out. I still did not understand what it meant to set a specific amount before spending any money.

The only thing I could think to cut was flowers. It was time for my weekly dose of fresh flowers to go. I did not know how much I actually spent on them, but estimated I was spending anywhere from $750 to $1000 a year on fresh flowers. I could not believe it. I knew it was a conservative estimate, which meant I most likely spent over $1000 a year.

Author David Bach invented the concept of "The Latte Factor" and I realized, although I made my coffee at home, I was not immune. Mine was a flower factor. The Latte Factor was "a metaphor for how we dribble away what should be our fortunes on small things without ever really giving it much thought."[2] I realized I could potentially stay in business if I cut my flower factor. No more flowers.

As friends came to visit, they would inevitably ask, "Where are your flowers?" I then explained my "flower factor" and they would immediately express amazement at the amount. Some felt a little sorry for my loss and would occasionally buy me a bouquet. When we got married, Keith would use his spending money to bring home a bouquet every now and then. He knew what a sacrifice it was for me to not have fresh flowers in our home on a regular basis.

I did not know if I would ever get back to weekly bouquets (the opportunity cost was too great), but I did look forward to the time when I could enjoy them more frequently. In the meantime, I continued to savor the times I did have fresh flowers in our home. The sacrifice was more than worth it to me. I was thankful I saw the tradeoff for what it was – a faster journey to financial freedom.

Your Turn...Your Perspective: What kind of "factor" do you have? How much does it cost you a year to maintain? What could you do with those funds if you chose to divert them to a different place in your budget?

Prayer: Lord, thank You for helping me keep my priorities in order. Thank You for the love I have for Your creation. I am forever grateful for the joy it brings to admire what You have created, including discipline.

Day 32
Absolutely Nothing

PROVERBS 14:23

Pride was my nemesis. It controlled so much of my life, and I was clueless about what to do about it. It was so ingrained in who I was that I did not even recognize it as an issue. It was particularly prevalent in my Mary Kay career.

I struggled with the difference between pridefulness and self-confidence. Goal setting was difficult because I could not always separate what I wanted from what I felt God calling me to obtain. I was constantly at war over how big a goal to set for myself. If I knew with certainty that a specific goal was from the Lord, I worked at it with my whole heart and sought His guidance during the process. If I just "thought" about a goal and received no confirmation the goal was what God wanted for me, I found it difficult to stay the course and was easily swayed.

One of the ways this struggle manifested was in how I defined myself. I was not a woman, or a Christian, or a friend, or a daughter or a sister. I was first and foremost a Sales Director with Mary Kay Cosmetics. Every other description was secondary.

When my business began its downward spiral, my definition made it difficult to increase my income by working outside of Mary Kay; I could not rationalize doing anything else. I felt a sense of betrayal to the idea of being independent by earning a pay check to add to my commissions. I even burned the idea into my head at every Mary Kay event.

When I introduced myself, I always included the sentence, "Outside of Mary Kay, I do ABSOLUTELY NOTHING!" I wanted others to know I was successful as a single, commission-only, sales person. It was the ultimate declaration of independence.

I felt like a fraud when I was no longer able to support myself solely with my business income. How could I continue to say I did "ABSOLUTELY NOTHING" outside of Mary Kay when I needed temp assignments to bridge my income and expenses? How could I encourage others to grow their businesses enough to quit their jobs when I was looking for one myself?

The questions were without answers. My income kept falling, and I kept digging in my heels in attempts to slow the descent. I refused to get another job. I refused to admit my business could no longer support me. I refused to believe the days of "ABSOLUTELY NOTHING" were over.

My pridefulness cost me greatly. My pridefulness cost me my home. My pridefulness created massive amounts of debt. My pridefulness was nearly the end of me financially. But it also drove me to my knees.

Pridefulness forced me to see the sin in my life and ask God for help. It caused me to look at work and goals in a different way. God used it to draw me closer to Him. It created a testimony and a ministry of financial transparency. Acknowledging the sin of pridefulness gave me a greater respect for all work. It helped me no longer devalue anyone based on their occupation.

Your Turn…Your Perspective: What sin takes first position in your life? How has it affected you financially? What changes has it caused you to make in Your relationship with God?

Prayer: Lord, thank You for the discipline of correction. I pray for deliverance from the sin which has me bound. I ask for Your guidance as I choose to live for You in all areas of my life.

Day 33
Let's Split It

PROVERBS 11:15

One day I was talking with a friend and we ended up on the subject of good food. I enjoyed trying new restaurants, and the one she mentioned was one I had never visited. A few weeks later, when she invited me to join her and her sister for dinner, I jumped at the chance. I was looking forward to good food and good fellowship since I did not spend much time with her.

As we got closer to the night of the dinner, I decided to go online and check out the menu. It was a slow sales week and I did not have much cash. I wanted to make sure I had enough money to enjoy the evening and still be able to pay all the bills coming due over the next week.

A peek at the menu revealed prices which made me cringe. I literally felt my heart constrict with panic as I looked at it. I could not afford this restaurant. It was way out of my league, but pride prevented me from calling and canceling. I did not want my friend to know just how strapped I was for cash. I was embarrassed about my financial situation and not ready to own how little margin was in my life. I carefully counted and calculated exactly how much I could spend.

Entrees were out of the question. So was dessert. I would definitely be drinking water with lemon, not because it was chic, but because it was free. I realized a large appetizer and a salad was all I could afford.

The night of the big dinner arrived. I put on a nice dress and met my friends. We were seated at a table with a beautiful place setting which enabled us to watch the sunset over the river. It was incredible. The wine menu came. I said, "No thank you" while my friend ordered a glass of her favorite. It was then time for appetizers. Since I took time to carefully scan the menu beforehand, I knew exactly what I would order, only what I could afford.

My friends ordered heavily and enjoyed the fullness of the menu. They offered to share new items with me, but I declined because I did not want to then be on the hook for a portion of the cost. I was content to eat the plentiful bread basket, my appetizer, and my salad.

I thought I would get away with my ruse until the bill came. My friend suggested we simply split it three ways. I panicked. I could not afford to split it three ways! Their portions would easily add another $20 to my bill. But I said nothing. Pride snatched my voice and forced my silence.

I was so angry driving home. "How dare she?!" I cried to the Lord with another rant about selfishness. It went on for several days. Finally, during my quiet time one morning, the Lord showed me my mistake. I did not speak up. I was not truthful about my financial situation. They did not know my menu choices were based on the amount of money I could spend because I did not tell them. There was no one to blame for overspending but myself.

Once again, pride made a fool of me. I asked the Lord for forgiveness and vowed to never put myself in the situation again. It was an expensive lesson, but I'm thankful I learned it.

Your Turn…Your Perspective: When was the last time pride cost you money? What did you do about it?

Prayer: Lord, please help me to not live a life laced with pride. It is such a big weakness for me. I pray for the courage to be transparent. Please help me to not hide.

Day 34
Business Acumen

LUKE 12:15

Running a business as a single person in one of the most expensive areas of the country was not for the faint of heart. I learned everything I could about the marketing and customer service portions of my business. I studied team building and personality types. I spent hours each month listening to training material to learn everything I could about growing my business. But something was missing.

I did not have a great understanding of how to manage the business side of business. There were foundational elements about running a business full-time I did not understand. Taxes and bookkeeping were skills where I lacked competence. I certainly knew nothing about using my business income to both manage my business and manage my household.

I struggled every year to pay my taxes. I opted to pay a penalty at the end of the year instead of budgeting for quarterly taxes. There were financially challenging seasons when I went without health insurance because I did not budget for the premiums. I often needed to sell May Kay products just to have money to buy groceries because I did not allocate my profit and commissions appropriately. I understood how to run a business; I just did not understand how to live off my business earnings. I did not understand how to allocate for both personal and business expenses from my sales and commissions.

I could have simplified my life by selling my home but decided against it. I was afraid people would think I could not afford my house. I could have gotten a roommate to help with expenses, but I did not want to give up my privacy. Instead, I continued to fall into the downward spiral of being house-poor. There were many times I did not have enough money to make necessary repairs – the garbage disposal was broken for months.

Finally, I decided to refinance. I found a mortgage broker and arrived at his office ready to hear how he was going to rescue me from my financial mess with the equity from my home. After he reviewed the documents, he asked the most horrifying question I ever heard. He said, "Lisa, why don't you sell this house?!"

I just looked at him and began to cry. I felt like a failure. Pride did not want to release me, and I was almost too afraid to let go. I was an independent woman making my own way. Selling my home felt like the ultimate betrayal of my ability to take care of myself and be successful. Homeownership was synonymous with success in my book. How could I be successful if I did not own a home?

I did not want to believe my home was just an address. I bought into the lie that it was a part of my identity. Pride, yet again, firmly held me in its grasp. It felt like quicksand pulling me under. The mortgage broker before me offered a line to pull me to safety. If I did not take it, it would not be long before I was lost for good.

I sat quietly in his office and began to see the gift God was granting me. The equity in my home was a lifeline out of the dark tunnel of debt. I would be foolish not to take it and the market was on my side. Three weeks later I received a ratified contract. I was thankful for the opportunity to start again.

Your Turn...Your Perspective: Have you ever been blinded by pride? What "things" have you held onto too long? What would it mean to you to "start over?"

Prayer: Lord, please help me let go of my stuff and my pride. I do not want to be more concerned with what people would think of me than in following Your path. Please help me resist the lure of pride.

Day 35
A Tenth

I heard it said, when you learn to truly embrace tithing, the amount given will not matter. A decision to tithe on $200 would evoke the same emotion as the decision to tithe on $200,000. When you get to the place when the amount leaving your checking account is not as important as making sure the check is written, you know you have embraced tithing.

By this definition, my tithing commitment still needed some work. I found it much easier to tithe when I worked in a salaried position than when I was self-employed. The safety of a "guaranteed" income appearing every two weeks like clockwork created a false sense of security for me. When I became self-employed and no longer knew the amount of each pay check, I began to worry about not having enough. In my mind, I needed to "hold on" to my income, just in case.

Over time, I realized this was directly associated with faithlessness. I said I trusted the Lord, but I learned I could not fully trust if I could not showcase obedience by tithing. In the lean financial seasons where I did not tithe, I chose to focus on my circumstances instead of completely trusting in God. I began to understand tithing was like developing a muscle. It always hurt more in the beginning than at the end.

It was a complete leap of faith to tithe, and I knew the growth and development of my spiritual life depended on me getting it right. I found myself in one such "low faith" season when my business was flat lining and my tithing was non-existent. I chose not to "blame" my lack of tithing on the downward turn of my business, but I did recognize how much harder growing my business became. When I made less money, I tended not to tithe, which in turn led to less money. It was a vicious cycle I was desperate to get out from under.

My business continued in its downward spiral to a point where it became clear I needed to sell my house to stay afloat financially. I already held on to it too long. I could barely pay the mortgage and did not have enough money to do much more. I was trapped in an address.

I consulted with a mortgage broker and he confirmed what I already knew. It was time to sell. While a money pit to me, my home value was significantly more than it was when I purchased it. I could reset my financial life and start over. I was thankful for a way out.

Six weeks later, I sold my house and received a check for $130,000. The very first thing I did was tithe. I did not tell anyone. I failed in this area so many times, I certainly did not want to boast when I got it right. I wanted it to be different this time. I wanted to be consistent in my obedience. I wanted to trust the Lord more than I trusted my own abilities to make money.

My prayer was to make the turn towards tithing for good. I was so thankful for a "do over" on life, and I did not take the opportunity for granted. My tithe was an act of obedience and a wake-up call. There was not another house to sell to fix my mess. I had to get it right this time.

Your Turn…Your Perspective: What area of your life needs to be turned over to the Lord? What was your "do over" moment?

Prayer: Lord, thank You for being the God of second chances. Thank You for loving me even when I do not trust You. I pray for the courage to trust You completely in every area of my life. Please keep me mindful of the areas of life I'm tempted to keep away from You. I trust You, Jesus.

Day 36
Karen

PROVERBS 13:10

I had a surrogate mother when I lived in Northern Virginia. Her name was Karen and she was a real estate agent. We met through a networking organization and shared breakfast with a group of business owners every Tuesday morning for almost ten years. Her heart was as big as the ocean and she was always willing to help anyone in need. She was known for popcorn and chocolate chip cookies and always kept a meal ready for anyone who dropped by.

The day I decided to sell my home, the first call I made was to Karen. I told her I decided to sell, and I needed her professional help. She told me to come on over. When I arrived at her home, I was greeted with a hug and lunch. She told me she knew it was an emotional decision and she wanted to be sure I made it on a full stomach. Hot tea and chocolate chip cookies were added to comfort me.

I felt like such a failure. I purchased the home four years earlier and never really settled in. Now I was selling. Keeping it was an option, but it did not seem like a viable one. I knew selling was the right thing to do. My heart was broken over my poor choices and ultimately, my pride was wounded. I was not just making a business decision, I was on display for all to see how poorly I managed my money. Or at least it felt like it.

As I described what I felt and what I knew I needed to do, she gently patted my hand and told me everything would be okay. Then she wrote me a check, so I would have some extra cash until the house sold. When I left her home a few hours later, I felt more hopeful than I had in years. I saw the sale of my home as the blessing I knew it was.

Within the week, Karen's husband completed the necessary repairs to the home. We staged it and put it on the market. I was fortunate to sell during the height of the housing boom and I received competing offers after only one open house weekend. By the end of the next week, we received a ratified contract and set a closing date.

Karen knew I was emotionally attached to my home. I never felt rushed. Unlike my previous experience with selling a home, she made sure I understood every part of the process. It felt wonderful to know I was in such capable hands, even though I felt like a failure as a business woman. And I certainly did not feel as if I was a good steward of God's resources.

I knew I was fortunate to have the opportunity to start over. The Lord sent Karen to make sure I was able to do so. The entire process was seamless, and I was thankful to have such a competent realtor who took care of everything. I felt cared for at a time when I was at my lowest. I was thankful to have Karen with me every step of the way.

There was no doubt. She was a Godsend.

Your Turn...Your Perspective: Who is the "Karen" in your life? And are you a "Karen" to someone else? Have you ever had the opportunity to fill a need in someone's life? What did it feel like?

Prayer: Lord, thank You for knowing what I need even when I do not. I thank You for timeless friendships. I pray for guidance in how to be a good friend. I want to offer what is needed without judgement. Thank You for the reminder to love others where they are.

Day 37
An Opportunity to Hide

PSALM 34:13; LUKE 8:17

The weekend I put my townhouse on the market, I took the time to house hunt. I needed to find a place to live, and my realtor did not want me at home anyway. Armed with a few listings, I headed out to find my new home.

I was not happy to need to house hunt. It would have been so much easier to have a magic wand wave away all my financial issues, so I could stay in my home. I did not want to move, and more importantly, I did not want anyone to know I needed to move. I was more concerned with what people thought of me selling my home than I was with the financial relief it would bring.

This was my mindset when I met Jason and Heather. They were getting married and planned on renting out Jason's townhouse. I was there to interview with them and submit an application to become their renter.

I do not remember how the conversation turned to my current living situation and the sale of my own home. Before I knew it, Jason was offering to buy my house and allow me to rent it back from them. I stared at them in disbelief. Were they serious? This was too good to be true! I would not have to move, and more importantly, no one would have to know I could no longer afford my home.

They were planning on purchasing other rental properties in the future, so why not buy mine? It came with a built-in renter, they knew I would take care of it, and they could grow their rental portfolio without much effort. They were very serious and asked if I would entertain an offer. I immediately accepted and skipped/ran back to my car.

I saw it as an incredible blessing to meet them the same weekend my house went on the market. Selling and closing would be a piece of cake, and I could quickly put this phase behind me and move on. I was thankful God had not made me go through the embarrassment of having to move.

The next day, I got a call from Jason. He did not qualify for the loan necessary to buy my house. I was heartbroken. It all seemed like the perfect arrangement. It looked like I would, indeed, have to move.

The next morning during my devotion, I asked God for understanding. Why were Jason and Heather not being allowed to purchase my home? I sat for a long moment before I saw a glimpse of myself, filled with excitement at the opportunity to hide. I could not sell to Jason and Heather because to do so would allow my pride the opportunity to remain hidden.

To stay in my home meant not dealing with the truth about how much I valued the opinions of others. To stay in my home meant keeping my financial situation a secret. To stay in my home meant I would not have to come face to face with my pride.

I hung my head in shame and asked God for forgiveness. Pride was proving yet again to be my downfall. I prayed for the courage to let go and to fully trust God's plan for my life. I prayed for His peace to get me through the process.

Your Turn…Your Perspective: What sin binds you? How is God using it to draw you closer to Him?

Prayer: Lord, thank You for loving me enough to show me the error of my ways. I pray I am always open to Your correction. Help me stay moldable to Your will.

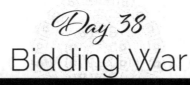

Day 38
Bidding War

PSALM 37:11; ISAIAH 61:3

My house went on the market priced at almost twice what I paid for it just four years earlier. The market was hot, and my real estate agent did not expect it to sit for more than a weekend without multiple offers.

Her estimate was great news for me because I was broke. The idea of being able to wipe away all my debt and financial mistakes with the profit from the sale of my home was music to my desperate ears. I was ready to start over and was more than thankful the Lord gave me the opportunity to do so.

I did not think about the other side of the transaction, however. Even though I was expecting a bidding war on the sale of my home, I did not stop to think about being on the other side of the same war. There was a shortage of available housing. Demand pushed prices through the roof on rentals, also.

I would have to get out into the frenzy and fight with all the people who were looking for a place to rent. For several weekends straight, I searched for a new place to live. The listed rental prices would be reasonable, and when I showed up to view the property, it was only to be told the price was increased by several hundred dollars.

I was in the middle of a bidding war for rental property. I could not believe it. People were actually paying hundreds of dollars more than market value per month to RENT a house. It was insane. Multiple times I removed my name from consideration because the rate increased literally overnight.

I was running out of time. I was scheduled to close in less than 30 days and still did not have a place to live. I vowed to never again live in an apartment, but the reality of my situation meant I needed to go back on my vow if I did not find something soon.

Even though I was about to be debt-free, I still had expenses and a business on life support. I was nervous about stretching my rental budget too far because, as much as I hated to admit it, I did not know if I could turn my business around. Things would need to be drastically different to make it work.

With two weeks left before closing, I made the hard decision to stop looking at rental houses and turned my search to apartments in the area. I already felt like a failure because my past financial choices were forcing the sale of my home. I felt even more like one when I signed the lease on the two-bedroom unit a few miles away from the house I was about to sell. I was out of viable options. Apartment living once again.

I could not have known all the spiritual growth I was about to experience. My life changed in ways I never previously imagined. I was right where God wanted me, and He was not shy about letting me know it. It took years to appreciate the experience to its full extent. It was not the first time I received beauty from ashes. And it would not be the last.

Your Turn…Your Perspective: When was the last time God moved you into His plan? How long were you there? What did you learn?

Prayer: Lord, thank You for loving me enough to have a plan for my life. I do not always like or agree with Your plan, but I am thankful I have learned to trust it. You never cease to amaze me. Please keep me open to You always.

Day 39
Number 401

Failure. It was the first word I thought of the day I signed an 18-month lease on a two-bedroom apartment. I swore I would never again live in an apartment, yet there I was. My poor financial choices were once again on display for all to see. I dreaded the move and struggled to keep the tears at bay until I got back to the car.

What a mess. It was hard to be excited about being debt-free. It seemed like such a high price to pay for what appeared to be a loss of my life as I knew it.

I found a unit on the top floor of a four-story building with a balcony and enough space for my essentials. The other items were either sold or moved to a girlfriend's basement. I did not plan on renting any longer than necessary. I thought a year and a half should be enough time to get my life and my business back on track. I prayed my business would turn around quickly and I would be back on a positive track financially.

I filed my change of address with the post office and proceeded to make all the address changes. Several people asked why I moved, and I found myself uncomfortably trying to explain why I chose to sell my house. I did not want people to know I needed to sell to stay solvent. It seemed pride moved in with me. As much as I hated selling my house, I hated the prideful embarrassment which accompanied the move even more.

The biggest frustration with my new address was the apartment number. It was not a big deal to live on the 4th floor. It was a big deal to live in an apartment. I found myself writing "Number 401" instead of "Apartment 401." In my pride filled mind, I hoped people would see "Number 401" and think condo, and not apartment. It was a façade I created, and I was determined to maintain it. It lasted for years.

It turned out my plan of staying in the apartment for a maximum of eighteen months was a joke. It seemed the Lord had a sense of humor when it came to removing pride from my life. If I refused to let go of my pride, He refused to let me move. I ended up living in "Number 401" for over seven years. I was absolutely miserable. Many of the lowest moments of my life took place in "Number 401." The pride was rooted deeply and needed a strong root extractor. Fortunately for me, Jesus was up to the task.

Slowly, after many nights on my knees, I chose to embrace my situation and turn my living situation over to the Lord. Pride's hold on me seemed to lessen as I asked the Lord for His help. While I never viewed my apartment as a home I would have voluntarily chosen, I did finally begin to see it as the location where the Lord and I came to know each other best.

I could no longer deny the heart change I experienced in "Number 401." I reached a level of spiritual growth I had never experienced before. The Lord took me to the lowest point in my life and I made an altar there. Pastor Jack Hayford said an altar, "represents the occasion and place where we have had a personal encounter with God."[3] "Number 401" was certainly an altar, and I was thankful for the personal encounter.

Your Turn…Your Perspective: What situations has the Lord used to get your attention? How did you respond?

Prayer: Lord, thank You for the painful lessons designed to grow me. Thank You for "not yet." I pray to always be open to the growth You have in store for me, even when it comes in the valley.

You'd Better Ask Somebody

PROVERBS 11:14; MATTHEW 25:18

Selling my home at the height of the real estate boom and receiving a profit of over $130,000 allowed me to become debt-free. I just knew my money issues were over. I was so excited. And thankful. But there was one thing I was not. I was not wise.

I did not surround myself with good counsel. I did not have investment knowledge. I did not understand financial jargon. I did not yet know the advice Keith and I often now share with our financial coaching clients: "Never invest in any financial product you do not understand." Instead of choosing to educate myself, I relied on the opinion of a financial advisor without completely understanding what was offered. Rather than asking for options, I took one recommendation and got no second opinion.

I put my financial decisions in the hands of someone else and ended up with a plan which did not fit my circumstances. And since my underlying attitudes about money did not change, four years after being completely debt-free, the $130,000 I made from the sale of my home was gone.

It was not frivolous spending. It just was not wise spending. There were no lavish purchases or trips. I did, however, make many poor business decisions. I took financial risks I would have passed on otherwise. I propped up my failing business much longer than I should have. Shortly after, I was in debt again.

Filmmaker Billy Wilder said, "Hindsight is always 20/20." In hindsight, I could clearly see how important it was to not only ask questions, but to continue to ask questions until I fully understood the information being presented.

I knew I did not fully understand what I was purchasing but did not want to showcase my ignorance. By choosing to remain ignorant, I purchased investments which did not fit my needs and set up my ultimate return to debt. The experience taught me just how costly it was to be ignorant.

The Lord entrusted me with the responsibility to care for some of His possessions, but I failed. I was worse than the servant who dug a hole and buried his master's possessions in the ground. The experience taught me to be an avid researcher and to prepare for all financial appointments with a list of questions. I learned to take responsibility and not decide until I had a full understanding.

I used to be angry at the financial advisor who poorly advised me, but I have since realized it was my own fault for not surrounding myself with a MULTITUDE of counsel. Good counsel. Second opinions are not just for medical procedures; second opinions are for anything you do not understand. I learned the need to have the heart of an eager student. One who was not only willing to learn but was also adamant about understanding. Even though my poor choices cost me money, I finally learned the benefit of not choosing to remain ignorant.

Your Turn...Your Perspective: How much control do you really have over your finances? Do you have a multitude of counsel you trust? How comfortable are you to walk away from a purchase until you can make an informed decision?

Prayer: Lord, please help me to continue to seek good counsel. I pray for discernment as we make decisions about the financial future of my family. I thank You for guiding me through this journey to financial peace.

Day 41
I Know the Plans

Shortly after I moved into my new apartment, I went home to South Carolina to visit my family. I stopped to have lunch with a friend on the way back and ended up wandering around a Christian bookstore while waiting for her to arrive.

A stone carving of Jeremiah 29:11 caught my eye. It was one of my favorite scriptures and I just stood there staring at it. After lunch, I went back and bought it. When I arrived home, I placed it on the balcony of my new apartment, which looked out onto the courtyard.

I awoke every morning, made a pot of tea and sat on the balcony to do Bible study. If it was too cold to be on the balcony, I would sit in an oversized chair and look out at the balcony and the stone carving. This is where I was one day when I had the revelation which changed my life.

I was not happy with the current state of my life. I felt like a financial failure. My career and business seemed to have stalled. After owning two homes, I found myself living in an apartment again at age 39. And I was single with no marriage prospects. There was so much I did not like about my current situation. I did not feel excited about where my life was going.

I wrote those statements in my journal and asked the Lord, "Why?" Why was I not successful? Why was I not married? Why did I have to sell my home? Why was my business failing? I just sat there staring out the sliding glass door, looking onto the balcony. I was waiting for Him to answer.

And then I saw it. Suddenly, the stone carving held fresh meaning and the words seemed to jump off the surface. I saw the word "I" emphasized in a way I had never seen before. I knew the Lord was telling me it was **His** plan for my life which was important, not mine. It was **His** plan I was to follow, not mine. It was **His** plan which would bring about my chosen future, not mine.

I sat there and cried at the realization. I needed to trust His plan for my life if I wanted to experience spiritual fulfillment. If I meant it when I committed my life to Him, I must let Him lead. And I would need to be okay with the path He chose, even if it was not the one I would have chosen for myself.

As I sat in my chair, overlooking the balcony, staring at the scripture, I resolved to follow Him completely. I knew my future was in His hands. He was in charge. It was His plan.

There were so many examples of His faithfulness to me. I knew the future would be more of the same if I simply allowed Him to have free reign in my life. I must let go and let His plan unfold. I realized the words of the prophet Jeremiah were not only engraved on a piece of stone, but also on the tablet of my heart. It became a constant reminder of His plan and His love for me.

Your Turn...Your Perspective: What ways have you seen God's plan for your life unfold? How did you respond when His plan did not match your plan?

Prayer: Lord, thank You for loving me. Thank You for having a plan for my life. Thank You for not allowing my faulty vision to create a detour in Your master plan. I praise Your name for what is yet to come.

Day 42
Money Market Account

PROVERBS 1:32-33

I decided to put about $20,000 of my $130,000 profit in a money market account. It was a random number I literally chose because it sounded good. I gave no thought to what purpose it was to serve. I simply stuck it in an online account and breathed a sigh of relief at having a little money set aside.

A few months passed, and a new business opportunity presented itself. Several of my business associates were participating, and I decided it would be foolish to pass up on what seemed like a good thing. The only problem was I did not have enough money to pay for it. My business associates were using credit cards, but I was debt-free. No credit cards for me. Instead, I wrote a check from my money market account.

A few more months passed, and it was a slow sales month. My commissions were low, and so were my sales. My income for the month was much lower than I expected. Instead of adjusting to live off the commissions I received, and increasing my sales to compensate for the shortage, I wrote a check from my money market account. Groceries, gas, and a haircut were needed, and the money market account was there to pay for it all.

A few more months passed, and I wanted to take a trip with a friend. It was not a big trip, but more like a long weekend. The problem was my sales were on a slow decline. Month after month saw a slightly smaller commission check deposited in my checking account and I did not feel comfortable paying for the trip out of my monthly commissions. You guessed it. I wrote a check from my money market account.

Within the year, the entire $20,000 was gone. I committed the cardinal sin of wealth building. I used my money market account as an extension of my checking account. I did not go to Vegas and gamble. I did not buy a new wardrobe or an expensive piece of jewelry. I simply nickeled and dimed it all away.

I was horrified to once again have no safety net. There was no back-up; no emergency fund. I went from debt-free and flush with cash to living less than pay check to pay check in less than a year. I could only blame myself. I felt like a failure in the worst way. Foolish. Foolish. Foolish.

What on earth would I do now? was the question I asked myself. It was not like there was another house I could sell. I hung my head in shame. I was right back where I was a few years ago. No savings and no plan.

I was so proud of becoming debt-free, but I failed to change the habits which sent me into debt in the first place. I did not create a plan, nor did I think about how my current purchases would affect my future savings. I did not use a budget. I did not think about my money.

I have since come to learn and understand many things. I learned the importance of financial boundaries. I learned what it meant to have margin. I learned to create and use a budget. And most importantly, I learned the finiteness of my checking account, regardless of the tempting opportunities around me.

Your Turn…Your Perspective: How do you approach saving? What is your long-term strategy for money management? What is the most significant lesson on saving you have learned?

Prayer: Lord, thank You for being the God of second and third chances. I pray for Your guidance as I work to gain a full understanding of Your will and Your plan for my life. Please help me learn the hard, financial lessons today to be a better steward of what You have given.

Day 43
Temp

COLOSSIANS 3:22; 2 CORINTHIANS 12:6-8

I read a statement somewhere which completely described an era of my life: "The hardest thing for an entrepreneur to do is to get a job." I was fighting hard to keep my business afloat but was failing miserably. I simply was not making enough income to pay all my bills. I sold my home and moved into an apartment to streamline my life. It worked for a year or so, but since I did not know to change my spending habits, I soon realized something more drastic needed to be done.

A colleague began supplementing her commission-only income by temping and recommended I look into it. I held out for as long as I could before calling to set up the placement assessment. After a day of tests, I was ready to get started. Over the next few months, I found myself with a constant stream of temp assignments.

One day I got a call about a long-term temp opportunity. Until then, my assignments were a day or two in length, never more than a week. This assignment would be months, and I would need to work 20 hours each week. The pay rate was also more than I made at any other placement. I knew I was prideful, but a fool I was not. I took the assignment.

On my first day, I showed up at the appointed hour to meet my new supervisor. Her name was Nancy and she was an HR manager. She was also blind. It turned out their company was preparing for a large wave of retirements which would take place over the next few years. All the records associated with this set of employees were still in paper form. Because Nancy could not read the documents, they all needed to be digitized for her to process them. My job was to make that happen.

We disliked each other from the very beginning. We had only two things in common. Neither of us wanted me to be there, and we both suffered from an extreme amount of pride.

It was hard. I hated giving up the precious daytime hours I previously used to build my business. I felt trapped by my financial circumstances. I hated having a schedule where I was told where to be and for how long. I felt out of place and caged in.

Nancy hated having to depend on someone else. She created a system which worked for her and felt intruded upon to have to share the inner workings of the system with me. She was nervous about being needy and prided herself on her independence. For me to be assigned to her was an insult to her professional abilities, and she was angry because she knew she needed me. She had no idea how much I needed her too.

It was a long nine months, but we got through it. While I would not say we became friends, we did grow to respect each other, and we learned to appreciate what the other offered. After a bumpy start, we finally settled into a rhythm.

When my tenure was up, I think we were both sad I was leaving. I remember calling her a few months after I left because I missed her quirky sense of humor. She told me she was glad to hear from me and I believed her. God used Nancy to humble me. It worked.

Your Turn…Your Perspective: What is the thorn in your flesh? How has God used it for His glory recently?

Prayer: Lord, thank You for giving me opportunities to lessen my pride. I pray to not be held hostage by pride any longer. Please show me the way out.

Day 44

Working through the Pain

JOB 1:9-10

Single. Self-employed. Commission only. Not the best combination when you live in one of the most expensive parts of the country. While it was exhilarating to set my own hours and have unlimited flexibility in my schedule, I missed the little things most employees took for granted, like sick days.

It did not take long for me to learn the importance of staying healthy. There were no sick days to use when I was not feeling well. If I did not work, I did not get paid. I was fortunate in the first few years to stay relatively healthy. Besides the occasional headache, I did not have many health concerns at all. This all began to change a few years into being self-employed.

I struggled to keep good health insurance since the beginning of my career as a full-time Sales Director with Mary Kay. As a result, I did not always schedule the basic annual exams every woman needed. In one season, I got caught in the world of fine print and went almost two years without an annual exam. It was during this time when the monthly pain began to increase. I knew something was wrong but was afraid to schedule an appointment since I was uninsured.

I could not afford anything more serious than a paper cut, and this was definitely not a paper cut. What on earth was I going to do? The question stayed with me for a lot longer than it should have. It stayed with me for years. Yes, years.

The thought of a medical procedure created so much fear, I lost all rational thought. I did not stop to think about how my actions were endangering my life. I only thought about how much I could not afford to be seen by a doctor. I never once thought about seeking assistance through public outreach organizations; I did no research to find alternative ways to receive the care I needed. I honestly did not think there were any options I could afford.

Each month I worked through pain. Each month I put on my mental gear to get me through the ten days of torment. I adjusted my schedule as much as I could to give myself time to rest. I scheduled a morning appointment, returned home to nap, and went out again for an afternoon appointment. It was exhausting.

I became a master at managing my time. During the times of the month when the pain was greatest, I only scheduled appointments within a small radius of my home. I found parks and parking garages where I could nap quietly when the weather permitted. I did not linger at a client's home or run errands. I worked, and I napped. It was all I could manage most days. I eventually got adequate health insurance and surgery followed soon after. Fortunately, it was not life threatening and I was thankful to be free of pain.

Looking back, I realized just how out of order my priorities were. Without health, nothing else should have mattered. I was in financial survival mode, not basic survival mode. I neglected my health in order to make a living. It was only the grace of God which got me through it.

Your Turn…Your Perspective: How has your health (or the health of those in your household) impacted your journey of Christ-centered financial wellness?

Prayer: Lord, thank You for the hedge of protection You place around me. Please protect me from foolish choices, instead of allowing me to experience their full impact. Thank You for grace.

Streams in the Desert

PSALM 128:5; ISAIAH 43:18-19

It was a day I would never forget –the Friday after Valentine's Day in the Washington, DC Metro area. Snow was on the ground from the night before, and I was checking the weather to see if my last standing appointment would hold. Since it was a seminar held at a local university, it would only be cancelled if the school cancelled classes. The ticker rolling at the bottom of the "Good Morning America" broadcast showed my appointment would indeed go on as scheduled. The university was open for business.

I did not watch morning television often. I do not know why I left the television on after finding the weather information. But there I found myself watching the show as the TV host introduced the next segment.

Robin Roberts was one of my favorite TV personalities. She always seemed warm and friendly. I watched her struggle on national television as she battled cancer. Twice. So, when she shared a little devotional her grandmother introduced her to years earlier, my interest perked up. She talked about how much she gleaned from the little book, and how much it blessed and impacted her life.

I was so moved by her story, I immediately went to the book store and picked up the devotional. The title was *Streams in The Desert* by L. B. Cowman. The name came from Isaiah 43:18-19:

> *"Behold, I am about to do something new; even now it is coming. Do you not see it?*
> *Indeed, I will make a way in the wilderness and streams in the desert."*

There was no way I would have ever known how my life was about to change as a result of the TV segment and subsequent book purchase. The words written in the devotional spoke to me in a profound way. I went on to use it as my primary devotional for years and Isaiah 43:18-19 became my life verse.

After I purchased the devotional and spent a little time with it, I went to my appointment. After it was over, and through another set of seemingly random events, I was offered the position as the Director of the Women's Business Center of Northern Virginia. The offer was unexpected but came at a crucial time. My business could no longer support me financially, and I needed a more stable income. I also needed the benefits.

I could not deny the relief of finally having health insurance, sick leave and a 403(b) retirement account. I needed all those things during this financially lean season of my life. And, they were all offered after I read a scripture telling me to embrace the newness I was about to experience.

I was standing face to face with my future. My choice was a pivotal one. Would I allow pride to keep me saddled with debt, fear, and worry about my future, or would I take the offer extended to me and begin to heal so many broken areas of my life? I chose the path to healing.

Your Turn…Your Perspective: When was the last time you were at a crossroads in your life? How did God reveal Himself to you during this time?

Prayer: Lord, thank You for the timing of Your Word. Thank You for loving me enough to get my attention. Thank You for presenting options for my future, just as You have for so many others. I choose to trust You and accept the newness You offer.

In the Nick of Time

1 CHRONICLES 29:17A; MATTHEW 11:30

The pain was severe, but I did not go to a doctor. I was in yet another season of my life where I did not have health insurance. I was more afraid to seek care than I was to be without coverage. But the longer I held off, the worse the pain became. I knew I would need to go to a doctor soon. This was not the first time I waited too long to go to the doctor. You would think I would have learned my lesson. Sadly, fear of the medical bill was more the focus than getting the medical assistance I needed.

Fortunately, I was the new Director of the Women's Business Center of Northern Virginia. Pride almost prevented me from accepting the position. But as prideful as I was, I recognized the beauty of God's hand on my life. I could tell He was at work behind the scenes. As much as I did not want to, I knew I needed to sign on the dotted line…quickly.

I needed the money from my new job since I was unable to turn my business around. More importantly, I needed the benefits. I needed health insurance desperately, and having sick days would not hurt either. I gulped down my pride and accepted the position.

My new agency was very good to its employees. It was March 27th, and if I got my paperwork filled out before the last business day of the month, my health insurance would take effect on April 1st. I was already scheduled to see my doctor on April 2nd so the timing was perfect. I knew it was no coincidence.

I went to the doctor and was told I needed surgery. I was stunned for so many reasons. I was embarrassed at not taking better care of myself. I was incredibly thankful for the brand-new medical coverage I would get to test out. It was humbling to know the diagnosis was not life threatening. Yet.

I sat in my car for a long time after I left the doctor's office. Things could have gone so badly. I gambled on my health and almost lost. My desire to be self-employed, and the pride which kept me from managing my financial life better could have cost my life. I felt foolish and very small.

I was relieved to have avoided a medical disaster. The timing of the activation of fully-loaded health insurance was not lost on me. I thanked my Heavenly Father for stepping in at just the right time.

When would I learn to trust the Lord? When would I trust Him to take care of my every need? My pride was so thick, I wondered just how long it would take to break through it. But a breakthrough is what I needed. God was giving me yet another chance. I prayed I learned this time.

Your Turn…Your Perspective: Describe a time when pride caused you to take unnecessary risks. How did the experience change you? How did it impact how you make decisions now?

Prayer: Lord, thank You for caring about my every need. I pray for the courage to reach out for assistance when I need it. I pray to finally and completely give it to you and leave it for you to carry.

Hurricane Dean

JOB 30:25

Life took a toll on me for quite some time before I finally acknowledged my harsh reality. My Mary Kay business could no longer support me. And if I were honest, I would admit it had not supported me fully in a long time. There was nothing left of my savings. I could no longer afford to be self-employed.

Even though getting a job brought the relief of income, it did not help my self-esteem. I could not shake the feeling of loss. A friend recommended I take a vacation to take my mind off my situation. My cash reserves were gone, and I was beginning to accumulate debt again, but the idea of some time away seemed like a reprieve. I looked around online and found a cheap, week-long trip to the Dominican Republic.

I chose an all-inclusive resort and did not venture too far away. I wanted to stay safe and frugal. I did not buy any souvenirs and did only one excursion. I spent most of my days sleeping and reading, reflecting and journaling. I needed the rest physically, but I also needed some emotional and spiritual healing.

At the end of the week, I boarded the transport for the two-hour drive back to the airport. All the tourists were monitoring the weather closely because Hurricane Dean was headed towards the island. Flights were still scheduled for departure and I prayed I would not get stranded. I did not have much cash left and knew my checking account was also low.

I used all my excess money to take the trip, and there was just enough money for my monthly expenses in my checking account. Staying longer in the Dominican Republic was not in my budget. The closer we got to the airport, the more I realized my trip was a mistake. I did not plan for an emergency and should not have taken a trip so far away from home with so little money. But hindsight is always 20/20. It was too late for regret.

Sure enough, all flights were cancelled. I was two hours away from the resort, by myself, with no money and nowhere to go. I did not speak the language and was not sure who I could trust. I looked and acted like a tourist, which meant I was a prime candidate for someone to take advantage of me. "Lord, Jesus. Please keep me safe," was my prayer.

A taxi driver, who spoke great English, approached me. "My friend has a clean hotel not far from here. May I take you there?" I reluctantly said yes and prayed this man was sent by God. The driver waited while I checked in. The hotel would not take my debit card, so he took me to a bank machine a few blocks away. Cash in hand, I finally checked in and settled into my room for the storm. I prayed God would continue to keep me safe. He did, and my flight departed the next day. I thankfully made it home safely.

What started as a great and necessary respite nearly ended in disaster because I traveled with no money. I could not believe how foolish I had been. God protected me (including sending a taxi angel) and kept me safe through it all. I was incredibly thankful and humbled beyond words.

Your Turn…Your Perspective: Name a time when you cried out to God for protection. How did you experience His protection and His presence? What did the experience teach you?

Prayer: Lord, thank You for Your constant protection. Thank You for being with me and covering me. I pray for You to help me to make sound financial decisions. Please help me to take care of all aspects of my financial, spiritual and emotional needs. I pray for Your hand to always be upon me.

Day 48
Unexpected Sanctuary

PSALM 37:16

The financial slide continued. I could not seem to get my business to turn. I taught others how to grow their business, but what I taught others was not working for me. I was at a loss for why it was so difficult to make the shift back into positive business momentum. I tried everything I could think of. I hired a business coach. I sought out additional mentors. I expanded my sales circle. I shrunk my sales circle.

But no change in my business came. Each month the slide continued, and soon I was relying on debt again to bridge the gap between my commission-only income, and the expenses I created.

Not only did I feel the financial restriction returning, but I never shed the spiritual restriction which moved with me. I felt trapped by my circumstances and did not understand why God did not rush to my aid. While I was not bitter or angry, I certainly was not clinging to Him. I was having a spiritual temper tantrum and my Father was allowing me to tire myself out.

I was not foolish enough to turn my back on Him, however. I continued to pray and search His Word. My journal was heavy with words describing my frustration at my situation. Why was my business failing? Why did I have to sell my home? How long would I be condemned to this apartment? Why am I here, Lord? When can I go, Lord? The questions streamed with tears most days. I was exhausted with hopelessness. It was clear there was a lot still to learn from my current situation.

Two years came and went in a blur. Before I knew it, four years had passed. My business was still on life support and I finally realized I needed to find a job.

Every morning I sought the Lord in my tiny living room. Over time, I stopped asking "why." I resigned myself to the apartment, and finally began to make the best of it. So many amazing revelations came during this financially low season of my life. I was broken, and He was slowly putting me back together again. The pridefulness which shaped my life in the past held less of a grip on me. I cared less about what people thought of me, and more about how I could serve Him.

During one such morning, I looked out onto the courtyard from my balcony. I heard the sweetness of early morning nature and breathed in the scent of spring. It was my second favorite time of the year (fall was my first), and I was enjoying the gift of it. The Holy Spirit took advantage of my complete attention and reminded me of my location. The feeling of peace and wholeness I was currently experiencing was taking place in the apartment I hated so much a few years earlier.

My current state of mind would not exist if I had not moved. He needed to slow me down and remove all distractions to get my attention. The place He used was no longer a prison of my mind, but a sanctuary where I was able to fully meet Him. I was thankful in ways I never thought I would be. I accepted the blessing and gave thanks for my sanctuary.

Your Turn...Your Perspective: Describe an experience God used to create a sanctuary in your life. How long did it last? What did you learn from it?

Prayer: Lord, thank You for loving me enough to move me out of my comfort zone. I have experienced both pain and joy there. I am thankful for Your devotion to me and pray I never forget just how far You will go to keep me close to You.

Day 49
A Good Time

PROVERBS 1:10

My nephew Jonathan came to visit one summer, and I was determined he was going to have a good time. He and I were both excited for him to come to Northern Virginia for a visit with Aunt Lisa. He was six years old and I wanted to expose him to as much of the Washington, D.C. area as possible. There was only one problem. I was broke. My business was failing and took all my reserves. I was barely making ends meet each month and could not figure out how to stop my checking account from hemorrhaging.

Instead of paying for one cool thing for us to do and exposing my nephew to "free D.C.," I succumbed to the "I deserve it" mantra playing in my head. I convinced myself my six-year-old nephew would not enjoy himself unless I was able to "splurge" on all the niceties associated with D.C. I did the unthinkable. I got a loan.

I actually borrowed money to take my nephew to a play, a major league baseball game, an amusement park, three movies, and dinner out almost every night. He got souvenirs from the play, the baseball game, and the amusement park; popcorn and a drink at each movie; and random toys during trips to the super-store for groceries. There was no budget and no thought to how much was spent. He thoroughly enjoyed himself. But when he left at the end of the week, I was still broke.

The only difference in my financial situation was the new monthly payment added to my list of expenses to remind me of just how foolish it was to take out a loan. To make matters worse, when asked what part of the visit he enjoyed most, he gave the typical six-year-old kid answer. He most enjoyed having silver dollar, chocolate chip pancakes for dinner. Total cost for his favorite part of the week, $2.99. Total cost of the lesson learned for Aunt Lisa, priceless.

I fell for the trap. I fell for the lie told to so many parents, and aunts, and uncles: You must spend money for your kids to have a good time. I allowed the enemy to convince me I was not creative enough to entertain my nephew for a week. The same nephew who loved outdoors and would have been happy for a day in the park. The same nephew who enjoyed our time baking cookies. This was also the same nephew who would have loved the FREE Air and Space Museum. He would have had a blast walking the National Mall or simply driving around the city, stopping when something caught our eye.

I failed miserably. And, I learned a valuable lesson. Fortunately, by the time I married Keith and subsequently our kids, I was ready. We thoroughly enjoyed ourselves every time they visited. Keith and I were pros at creating free memories. We explored Kansas with a picnic basket, and experienced theater in the park with stadium chairs and a giant bag of homemade popcorn. We invited friends over for dinner and shared our famous red velvet cupcakes with anyone who stopped by. We played games and watched movies and made homemade ice cream. Every visit was packed with laughter and, "do you remember when we…?" moments.

I was thankful I learned the lesson early. It would have been very difficult to learn it while trying to get out of debt. I was thankful Keith did not need to learn it himself but was happy to learn from my painful experience. We set a budget each time the kids visited and stayed well within the limits. I no longer needed to believe a lie. There was enough truth to remind me of how little money was needed to make memories.

Your Turn…Your Perspective: What lies have you chosen to believe as truth? How much did it cost?

Prayer: Lord, thank You for the hard lessons. Thank You for second chances. Thank You for loving me even when I disappoint you. I pray to learn from my mistakes and find triumph in the trials.

It's Not Where You Start, It's Where You Finish

PROVERBS 11:28

Keith and I met in 2009 at church. We each told our own version of the story, but the unified version was the Lord knew we were ready for the other. What stood out most to me about our romance was we were both at our lowest point financially when we met.

Keith lost his job in St. Louis the year before moving to Virginia. It was difficult to find suitable employment afterwards, so he moved to accept an internship. The program started with a small salary but offered the opportunity to develop a long-term career.

The cost of living in the DC Metro area was much higher than St. Louis and his debt was huge. Fortunately, a friend offered him a room in his basement for a year to get him on his feet. He ate as cheaply as he could and managed to live on about 30% of his take home pay.

I was struggling to keep my business afloat. I held on to it for three years longer than I should have. The result was a depletion of all my savings and a re-entry into the world of debt. My self-esteem was severely wounded, and I was gun-shy about trying to do more than just survive. My dreams of entrepreneurship were dim, with the flame flickering out.

We were perfect for each other. Two people at their lowest, hanging on to the promises of God with not much else to offer anyone. I often told Keith I knew with certainty I would have overlooked him as a potential suitor if I met him when I was on a financial high. I would not have seen him for the man he was becoming. All I would have noticed was what he was not, and what he did not have.

Because we were both at the bottom of our financial mountains, we could relate to the journey of the other. We provided support to one another and were able to begin to dream of a future together. He made it clear he would not be able to spend a lot of money on our dates. I understood, and we split the cost of most of our excursions. Fortunately, free entertainment was plentiful in Washington, DC.

Our first Easter was spent with a picnic and a trip to the National Arboretum. The annual Cherry Blossom Festival offered a beautiful canopy for jazz and a lazy afternoon reading to each other under the trees. Sunday afternoons were spent watching sports in my apartment instead of at a restaurant with friends. Fourth of July was a road trip on Skyline Drive (with a picnic of course). We saw each outing as an adventure. We were able to discover the city around us and grow in our relationship as a couple. We dreamed of our future and made plans of a life together.

After we got married and joined our financial messes into one big mess, we were able to make more headway with debt reduction. Instead of two sets of utility bills and rent payments, there was only one. We simply moved the extra money into our debt snowball and kept going. The future looked brighter every day. We were thankful we allowed the Lord to guide us and did not get side tracked by how unsightly our financial situations were when we met. We were two rock bottom people headed up...together.

Your Turn...Your Perspective: When was the last time you looked past someone because of their circumstances? How did the situation make you feel?

Prayer: Lord, please help me to not discount others because of their financial situation. I pray for compassion and kindness to be primary virtues in my life.

Day 51
Authentic Self

PROVERBS 19:22

The church Keith and I attended had three service times. I switched to the 11am service for a new ministry opportunity. He sat next to me one Sunday and we worshipped together. I began to see him around the church serving in different capacities and we began to talk more. Our first telephone conversation lasted more than an hour. During the first week, we logged over 20 hours on the phone.

We talked about a variety of subjects – music, the Bible, movies, family, goals, and everything in between. I thought we knew a good bit about each other by the time we got around to our first date. However, I did not know his financial story. Over dinner he told me about the foreclosures and failed business ventures, losing his job, and his divorce. He chose to share all the "bad stuff" up front so I could be well informed as I decided if I still wanted to pursue a relationship.

He made it clear he would not be able to buy me trinkets or take me to dinner at expensive restaurants. He told me he barely made enough money to take care of his basic needs. He accumulated a very large amount of debt which would eventually need to be repaid. He told me about his desire to move back to the Midwest as soon as possible to be closer to his children.

I had never met a man who chose to be so painfully honest with me. It was a lot to take in. I knew it must be true because it did not make sense for him to exaggerate the amount of negative information he shared. After a lot of prayer and conversations with a few girlfriends, I began to appreciate his honesty and was impressed by his desire to be transparent.

There were days, however, when I needed to remind myself of our early conversations. Those were the days when I was disappointed because our date night consisted of me making dinner and him bringing a video from the library to watch. I especially chose to remind myself of those early conversations when I was annoyed when he did not bring me flowers.

I removed my expectations of what I thought a date with him should resemble. Fortunately, I did this early in our relationship, and as a result, I was able to settle into our way of dating. My girlfriends sometimes questioned our date night choices, and many of them told me I deserved someone who could offer me more.

But I chose to see Keith for the authentic person he was and did not attempt to make him into something he was not. Because of my choice in mindset, I was more appreciative of the times when he did bring flowers or arranged little surprises as a part of our date night. Our dating relationship was genuine, and we grew to love each other without pretense. It created an incredible foundation for our marriage and the journey of financial stewardship which began long before we said, "I do."

I was thankful I did not allow the world's expectation of dating to taint the special relationship we were able to build because we chose to be true to ourselves.

Your Turn...Your Perspective: Have you ever discounted someone because of their financial situation? How do you showcase your authentic self to others? Do you ever feel tempted to present a different version of who you are when meeting others for the first time?

Prayer: Lord, I pray to not be judgmental. Help me to see each person in my life through Your eyes. I pray to not create false expectations based on the world's standards.

The Sting of Expectation

PROVERBS 27:9; PSALM 107:9

I hated how I felt. The sting of sadness crept into my mind at least once a month the entire first year of our relationship. I was incredibly embarrassed by the disappointment I felt at not receiving flowers. I absolutely loved fresh flowers and had treated myself to them on a weekly basis for years. I recently stopped buying them when I realized just how much it was costing me. However, I was completely unprepared for the level of disappointment I felt at not receiving flowers from my new beau.

I prayed for release from the obvious entitlement I was feeling. I had never met a man so transparent before. He told me of his financial woes. He told me he would not be able to give, give, give. He shared his desire to lead a better life, spiritually, emotionally and financially. He talked about what he wanted the future to look like. He laid it all out for me in the first few weeks of our relationships. Now that we were in the midst of it, I was struggling to do my part; I felt so selfish. "Please, Lord, shift my focus away from receiving. Help me to focus on giving instead." It became my daily prayer.

A few weeks passed, and Keith came over for dinner. When I opened the door to greet him, there he stood…with flowers! I cannot describe the emotion I felt standing there watching him grin back at me. It was a beautiful gesture and I was just as excited about him bringing them as I was at the flowers themselves. I recognized the sacrifice he made to give me the lovely bouquet, and it caused me to appreciate the gift even more.

As I sat in my favorite chair after Keith left for the evening, I could not help but think back to a different time of expectation. I was new to the area and looking for a church to join, but I kept comparing the ones I visited to my former church. I kept a mental checklist of things I wanted in my new church, and none completely met the list. I refused to see each church for what it offered, but instead focused on what each was lacking. My expectations kept me from benefitting from what God planned for me.

Fortunately, one day the Lord showed me the error of my ways. He showed me the importance of not comparing, but instead taught me to see each experience for what it offered me. By changing my perspective, I was able to enjoy the experience of finding a new church home and ended up choosing a community which spiritually fed me well.

As I thought about the experience of choosing a church home, I realized the same opportunity existed with Keith. I did not want my expectations of wanting to be wooed with flowers and gifts on a regular basis to cause me to miss the incredible opportunity to get to know a wonderful man with a heart for God.

Psalm 107:9 says: "For he satisfies the thirsty and fills the hungry with good things." The Lord chose to fill my need for the gift of flowers through Keith and taught me to limit my expectations in the process. I was thankful for both the gift and the lesson. It would serve me well in the years to come as we worked our way out of a massive amount of debt.

Your Turn…Your Perspective: When was the last time you transferred your expectations to someone? What was the outcome? What did you learn?

Prayer: Lord, I pray to learn to limit my expectations and to watch for Your presence in my life. I pray for constant wisdom in this area.

Day 53
Mine, Mine, Mine

DEUTERONOMY 10:14

During our second year of dating, Keith suggested we participate in a Crown Financial Ministries Bible study on money offered at our church. I was apprehensive for many reasons. It was 10 weeks long and it was on Sunday afternoon for 2 hours. There was a fee to participate. And most importantly, I was afraid to look at my financial picture with my "boyfriend" watching.

I was filled with negative emotions about money and was not ready to unpack them. I did not know this at the time, but I did know I was not excited about digging into the skeletons in my financial closet. I avoided the discussion for about two weeks.

Finally, my future husband put his foot down. He told me he believed we could have a future together. He was ready to tackle his financial situation and was hoping I would be ready also. He wanted us to be proactive about our money. For us to move forward, we needed to go through this class together. Reluctantly I agreed to attend.

One of the first assignments for the class was to sign a declaration acknowledging God as the actual **Owner** of all our possessions. I remember how difficult it was for me to sign the declaration. I fretted over relinquishing control of my "things." It was quite an ordeal, and frankly, I did not want to do it.

It took a while, but I finally realized the purpose of the exercise: to acknowledge God's place of authority in my life. If I truly meant it when I said, "I trust You, Jesus," I needed to freely give everything to Him. Besides, it really belonged to Him anyway.

Slowly over the course of several days, I listed everything I owned in the booklet. As I listed each item, I literally felt a weight being lifted. It was amazing to recognize how much lighter my countenance was when I acknowledged God's place as **Owner** of all **I** possessed. I started with the big items, but also included smaller items which created an emotional response (like my 600-thread-count sheets and mink coat).

Over time, I began to see my possessions differently. I became less attached to things. I still took good care of them, but I did not freak out when my friends' kids jumped on my sofa. I did not stop everything to try to keep a scratch from "ruining" the dining room table. A chip on a china plate or a broken crystal glass did not send me into a tailspin. I relaxed more and began to enjoy sharing my possessions with those around me. I knew my need to control every aspect of my possessions was not completely resolved, but I was thankful for the realization of God's ownership.

Gospel artists BeBe and CeCe Winans released a song entitled "Things." It was a great illustration to me of what can happen when possessions become the center of someone's life. The exercise of relinquishing all my "things" to the Lord helped me to begin to put safeguards in my life to prevent possessions from taking God's place at the center of my life. I was thankful to learn the lesson.

Your Turn...Your Perspective: What is your attitude towards your possessions? What emotions do you experience when you feel someone has mishandled your things?

Prayer: Lord, please help me embrace You as Owner of everything. Thank You for allowing me the privilege of taking care of your possessions for You and sharing them with others. Help me to not be selfish. Help me to be consistent in my sharing of the gifts You have given.

Day 54
Federal Safety

PROVERBS 29:14

When Keith and I met, I was still trying to rebuild my Mary Kay business. It was now a side business while I worked full-time managing the Women's Business Center of Northern Virginia. However, my income was not keeping pace with the rise in the cost of living. Even as a side business, the downward slide continued. It no longer supplemented my income. It was barely providing enough income to cover my business expenses.

When I took the position as Director of WBC, I intended to be there no more than two years. The goal was to rebuild my Mary Kay business to a point where it could support me financially again. The goal was still unmet. And since my income from Mary Kay was continuing to decline, my financial outlook was similar to what it was before I sold my house. If I could not rebuild my Mary Kay business to a consistent income level soon, I would have to look for another job.

The problem was, I did not know what I wanted to do. My engineering technical skills were old and outdated. It was a full decade since I worked in the field, and I honestly was not sure I even wanted to go back to engineering. But what could I do? What marketable skills did I actually have? Even with degrees in computer engineering and information management, I felt like a poor job candidate. I possessed a great set of sales skills, but I was not sure I wanted to sell anything other than Mary Kay. In fact, I was not sure I knew how to sell anything other than Mary Kay.

"Lord, what on earth am I going to do to support myself?" was the question I constantly asked.

I was looking around job placement sites one day when Keith called. When he asked what I was doing, I shared my job concerns. He was quiet for a minute before saying, "Lisa, did you forget you have twelve years of service with the federal government? Why are you not looking to go back?"

I honestly never thought of going back. In my mind, I could not go back. I forgot about the incredible benefit of working for the federal government and the flexibility I possessed as a former federal employee. I did not have to go back to the same agency; I just needed to go back to the federal government. My tenure would be restored as if I never left.

My retirement timeline would also restart. My pension would be restored and begin to grow again. I would have a 401k with a 5% match in addition to my pension. My vacation time would accrue at the same rate it did when I left ten years earlier. I could not believe I forgot all the benefits associated with being a federal employee. Fortunately for me, Keith was there to remind me.

I began my search, and a few months later I was hired by the US Department of State. I was reinstated with full benefits. My income doubled and would literally triple in the next three years. I could breathe again as I began to dig myself out of the financial hole I dug for myself. I began to put distance between me and my financial mess. I was thankful for yet another financial reset. Praise God for federal service.

Your Turn...Your Perspective: How has God provided for you lately? When was the time when His constant provision made the biggest impact on your life?

Prayer: Lord, thank You for caring for my every need. All You ask is for me to ask! Please help me to always remember how well You provide for me.

Day 55
Grocery Money

PSALM 15:1-2

Dating on a budget was real. Keith and I wanted to spend as much time together as possible, but our limited income made it a challenge. We were both broke. Neither of us could afford to try and impress the other. We both took it as a challenge to find as many free activities as possible to occupy our time. Fortunately, we lived in one of the most culturally rich cities in the country.

Instead of expensive entertainment, we borrowed lots of movies from the library, went for walks and picnics in the many parks in the area, and enjoyed the free museums. We scoured public service announcements and found as many other free activities as we could. I also cooked for us. A lot.

Keith visited a few times during the week, and we saw each other at least once or twice on the weekends. We enjoyed our time together and spent as much time as we could getting to know each other. But as much as I enjoyed the new romance, feeding two people was beginning to take its toll on my grocery budget.

I was too embarrassed to tell Keith just how pinched my budget was. While he chose to be completely transparent about his financial situation, I had not yet been completely transparent with myself, let alone him. I honestly did not allow myself to see just how bad my money situation was, so I continued to juggle and move things around.

I looked for opportunities to stretch a meal as far as I could. I changed what I ate when Keith was not joining me for dinner to create room in my budget to feed us both when he did. I allowed myself no extravagance in my meals for one. I never needed a lot of meat, so meatless Mondays also became meatless Tuesdays. I saved dishes with meat for the times when Keith joined me for dinner. This went on for about six weeks. Then one day it all changed.

It was a Wednesday when Keith came over for the evening. After greeting me, he handed me a $20 bill and told me he knew he was impacting my budget by joining me for so many meals each week. He told me again how much he enjoyed spending time with me and felt it was important to pull his own weight by contributing to the grocery budget each week from then on.

I was speechless. And thankful. And embarrassed. Why did I not believe in him (or us) enough to tell him I needed assistance with groceries? I did not have to wait long for the answer. It was pride. Pride pinched me into a corner. Pride caused me to believe Keith did not care. Pride caused me to wonder how long I could sustain the relationship.

I thanked Keith for his offer and shared my pride-laced confession. I desperately needed help with groceries and looked forward to sharing many more meals with him. It was the start of newfound transparency which became foundational to our relationship, and later, to our marriage. What a blessing it was to us both as we learned how to navigate what it meant to achieve financial freedom.

Your Turn…Your Perspective: Name a time when pride caused you to do something you later regretted. What emotion did it stir in you? What did you do about it?

Prayer: Lord, I pray for deliverance from whatever sin has me bound. I pray to embrace transparency as the light it is. Please help me to look to You for grace and trust. I pray for the courage to break free.

Day 56
Christmas Ornaments

PSALM 39:6

When I moved into my 1000 square foot apartment after selling my 2100 square foot townhouse, I obviously needed to downsize. I believed apartment living would be short term and did not want to give away the items which did not fit in my new home. I was fortunate to have a girlfriend who had recently built a home, complete with a very empty basement. She offered to store my extra furniture and boxes until I was ready for them. What I thought would be a year or two turned into seven years.

When Keith and I started dating, my tenure in the apartment was five years. During that time, I never put up a Christmas tree. I reasoned the next year would be the year I would have a home large enough to put up a tree. Next year never came.

Our first Christmas as a couple was special for both of us. It was literally decades since I spent the holidays with someone special. We were excited to start new traditions. Keith was a little disappointed when he found out I did not put up a tree. I explained the space issue and proceeded to purchase a tiny tabletop tree with tiny ornaments to match. His expression showcased just how far from the mark this gesture landed. Fortunately, all the other aspects of our first Christmas together left us with great memories.

As we approached our second Christmas together, I announced my plans to put up a tree. I explained we would need to pay a visit to my girlfriend's house to pick up the ornaments. Since I had not seen (nor used) any of the items currently being stored, I decided to use the trip to purge. The three of us went through all the boxes, and I decided what I still wanted to keep and what needed to be donated. It felt good to let go of the past.

After dinner, we loaded up Keith's truck with all the boxes which needed to be donated and put the Christmas ornaments and decorations in the cab of the truck to keep them separate. The next day, Keith dropped everything off at the local donation center.

When I say he dropped off everything, I mean EVERYTHING! He donated all the ornaments and Christmas decorations. When I realized what happened, I was devastated. I owned an angel ornament collection, crystal ornaments, table decorations, and a beautiful tree topper. They were all donated.

Keith apologized profusely. I could see the disappointment on his face. It matched my own. He did not know how I would react and was bracing himself for a negative response. What was supposed to be a magical time was suddenly overshadowed by a huge mistake.

I literally felt the crossroad I was standing in. I had a choice to make. I could rant and rave about stuff I literally had not seen in seven years, or I could see the situation as the genuine mistake it was and move on. I hugged him. I thanked him for the apology and told him I looked forward to collecting new ornaments with him for our future home. I did not want to be defined by stuff any longer. It was the beginning of a deeper purge the Lord would take me through as we cleared all our debt. I was thankful I chose to start over.

Your Turn…Your Perspective: What sentimental item or items have you lost recently? How did you respond? What did the experience teach you?

Prayer: Lord, I pray for the strength to let go of the past and embrace the future You have for me. Thank You for guiding me on this journey of new memories made without debt.

Day 57
Preparing for Rain

PROVERBS 28:19; REVELATION 3:8

In the movie "Facing the Giants," a man went by the school to deliver a message from God to the struggling football coach. He told him God was at work in his life and he was not to give up. If he wanted to see the blessings in store for him, he needed to prepare for rain. He was referencing the world of farming and how a farmer must make his fields ready to receive the benefit of the rain when it came.

I experienced something similar when the Lord told me to move to Kansas. Keith also experienced it when God told him to move to Kansas. When I got my message, I was not excited. We were not yet married. We were not even engaged, but I knew my message to move was clear. I struggled with the decision. Even though I knew I heard God's instruction, I was concerned about what others would think of my decision to move before Keith and I were married.

I said I would never move for a man, and here I was, following my "boyfriend" halfway across the country without any commitment to a future together. I did not want to face what I knew would be a juicy rumor. But ultimately, I knew it was not a move to follow Keith. It was a move to be obedient to God's instruction. As much as I wanted to not have others talk about me and my decision, I could not concern myself with anyone other than the Lord. He gave me my marching orders, and if I wanted to be in His Will, I needed to get going.

I started looking for a job immediately. I started assessing my living arrangements and began to put a plan in place to get me and my household halfway across the country. It was overwhelming. There was no extra money in what I called a budget, and I did not want to add to my already bulging debt. I needed to get creative if I were to get myself and all my belongings to the Midwest.

I knew I did not have enough money to hire a moving company. I would have to do it myself. Keith would pitch in for labor, but financially I was on my own. I shared this information with a friend one day and she told me about Craig's List and all the people who often gave boxes away for free. Free was what I needed. I began to check Craig's List daily for boxes and collected as many as I could find. Storage in my small, two-bedroom apartment was at a premium. I also did not know when I was moving. It could be weeks, or months, or (heaven forbid) years. I had to trust. The Lord told me to get ready to move so I chose to assume I would be moving relatively quickly.

I found a small business owner who received glass bottles and jars, delivered each week. His boxes were sturdy and large. He agreed to give me all of them and called me whenever he received new shipments. I wanted to be ready when the time came. I was preparing for rain.

I collected boxes for months. I applied for every position possible. I ignored the naysayers and chose to trust God's plan. When the time did come to move, the Lord showcased His faithfulness in grand style. I was so thankful I chose to not waiver. I was thankful I chose to prepare for rain.

Your Turn...Your Perspective: Think of a time when you needed to do something which went against what others believed was the right thing to do. How did you approach it? Has God ever spoken to you?

Prayer: Lord, please help me to hear You and not be afraid to embrace what You tell me. Help me to have the courage to share what you tell me with others. I am thankful for Your love and Your plan. Help me to embrace both and not be swayed by the ways of the world.

Day 58
Relocation Package

PSALM 25:12

Keith and I were not surprised when we each individually got our call to move to Kansas from the Lord. Since we were still single, we made major decisions as singles. We discussed our individual situations with the other, but the decision was made by just one of us.

Keith decided to take a transfer from the Washington, DC office, where he worked, to Kansas City, KS. Moving to St. Louis where the kids lived was not offered and did not appear likely to become an offer, so he accepted the transfer to Kansas. Four hours of travel to spend time with the kids was a lot less than fourteen.

While I supported his move to Kansas, and believed it was the right thing for him, I made it very clear I would not move with him as his girlfriend. If he wanted me to move, he needed to "put a ring on it." He agreed with my decision, and we decided to settle into a long-distance relationship for the time being.

A few weeks later, I awoke for a 2A.M. encounter with God. It was not uncommon for Him to awake me in the early hours of the morning to chat about something. I was not sure where the conversation would take us but was anxious to hear what He had to say so I could go back to bed.

Back to bed proved to be quite difficult when I realized He wanted me to move to Kansas before Keith and I were engaged. WHAT?! You can't be serious! What will people think? This was contrary to the promise I made to myself. I would never move for a man!

The questions and exclamations kept pouring out of me. I could not journal my disbelief fast enough. "Lord, You can't be serious?" The biggest question hung in the air like a heavy fog and encompassed the prospect of marriage. What if he doesn't propose? What if I move to Kansas and our relationship does not survive? What on earth would happen then?

Quietly, the Lord reminded me of the small tidbit of information I missed. Keith was not asking me to move to Kansas. He was. He would continue to provide for me and take care of me. He was and always would be my first priority. I must trust Him. So, I did.

I told Keith about the charge from the Lord for me to move and began to search in earnest for a new job. Keith supported my decision and encouraged me to not be afraid. We moved him to Kansas in June, and my job offer came in July. AND IT CAME WITH A FULL RELOCATION PACKAGE!

Not only did God provide a job, but He also arranged for me to be relocated without one dime coming out of my pocket. My new employer packed me, loaded me, shipped me, and unloaded me. My sole responsibilities were to drive myself to Kansas, submit my receipts for reimbursement, and unpack my household goods. It was incredible. And it never would have happened if I did not trust Him. I was more thankful than ever, especially since I had no money and no idea how I would have moved myself otherwise.

Your Turn…Your Perspective: Name a time when you had to go against what you believed in order to follow God. What was the end result? How has your life changed as a result?

Prayer: Lord, thank You for loving me enough to make a way out of no way. I pray I always stay in tune to Your voice. Please help me to be obedient, even when I do not understand Your plan.

The Red Sea Parted

ISAIAH 45:3; EXODUS 14:21

When I moved from Northern Virginia to Kansas, I experienced what I call a Red Sea Moment. If I were one of the Children of Israel, I was sure I would have felt the same way when the Red Sea parted, and we walked across on dry ground. They trusted God to deliver them from the hands of Pharaoh's army, and I needed to get myself and my household goods moved to Kansas with absolutely no money to spend on moving expenses.

In preparation for my move to Kansas, I decided to sign a month-to-month lease on my apartment in Virginia. It increased my rent by almost $500 each month. The cost of breaking a lease was more than I could have afforded, and I knew in my heart I would be moving soon. I did not know when, but I trusted God's Word. He told me to move to Kansas; I needed to do all I could to be ready.

The very first month of being on a month-to month lease, I got a job offer. It meant I only owed one month of inflated rent. In addition, my job offer came with a full relocation package. Relocation packages were extremely rare as all businesses (the federal government included) trimmed their overhead by limiting surplus expenses. Since my new position was mandated by Congress, moving expenses were authorized.

Within three days of accepting the position, I received a call from my move coordinator who happened to be a Christian. I honestly do not remember how we ended up discovering we were both Christ-followers. When I told her the story of God telling me to move, she began to pray for a smooth transition. I was relocating during the busiest season of the year and was given only three weeks to do it. She did not know if she could get me a packing team, find a truck to pick up my household goods and deliver them before my start date. Her prayer was for me to not experience any delays because of the heavy logistics.

Her prayers were answered almost immediately. A packing crew was arranged to arrive two weeks before my start date. The labor crew arrived the same day to build the crates needed for fragile furniture. All I could think about was how difficult it would have been for me to get my furniture to Kansas without it breaking. I did not even know I needed crates for fragile furniture. I certainly did not have the money to pay for them.

The movers arrived on schedule and were able to load my belongings directly onto the trailer which would transport them to Kansas. The driver was available the next day to begin the trip west, and my checkout at the apartment was scheduled for the day I left for Kansas. I arrived in Kansas on Friday, and my household goods arrived on Monday, which was a day early. Nothing was lost, and nothing was broken.

During our post-move call, my move coordinator shared her amazement. She had never seen a move go so smoothly. We both praised God for His blessing. It was obvious to us and all who watched my journey unfold. My Red Sea did part and dry ground was created to get me to Kansas safely. Incredible!

Your Turn...Your Perspective: How have You seen God at work in your life? In what areas of your life do you need to trust Him more?

Prayer: Lord, thank You for Your faithfulness. You continue to show Your plan is better than any plan I can come up with on my own. I thank You for loving me enough to give me the opportunity to serve You in a new way.

Pay Cut to Privilege
DEUTERONOMY 7:13

I looked for a new position in Kansas for about 4 months before I found one. Changing agencies within the federal government was not always easy, so I took the position even though it meant a $10,000 per year pay cut and did not have promotion potential.

My first thought was to not accept the position and wait for a higher paying one., but I had no idea how long it would take to receive another offer. God told me to move, and a position was offered. I needed to take it and start the next phase of my life. I could not focus solely on the money.

Since the cost of living in Kansas was lower than it was in Northern Virginia, I knew I would still be able to manage my finances on the smaller budget. I also knew I was following God's plan for my life by moving to Kansas. I chose to believe the change in salary would be less of an issue than it presented on paper. But I was still not sure what kind of future I would have with no promotion potential.

I chose to take one day at a time and trust God's plan for my life. I worked well in my new position, kept a positive attitude, and made myself a valuable member of my new team. It was hard sometimes to stay motivated, but I knew I needed to make the best of it. I learned a great deal and knew I would learn even more if I stayed engaged in my work.

The Lord moved me to Kansas without any additional expenses, helped me learn to live on a tighter budget, and allowed Keith and me to start a life together as husband and wife. Surely, He could help me find a more fulfilling job and ultimately begin to build a career.

I chose to trust Him and be patient. I studied techniques on resume building and learned how to fine tune my search parameters to widen my options. I began to look for virtual positions in addition to those based in Kansas City. I knew I would stay with the federal government but was not opposed to switching agencies again. Most importantly, I chose to maintain my good attitude.

I found a new position in the same agency about 18 months after moving to Kansas. New challenges and opportunities were available in the new position, and so was more income. Five years after moving to Kansas, I increased my income by almost $30,000. I saw it as a gift from the Lord for choosing to follow Him and His plan for my life. I would never know what delays would have been put in motion if I held out for a position with more money instead of trusting the position He provided.

It felt like I took two steps back initially, but the Lord blessed me with four steps forward. In the end, His master plan for my life unfolded because I chose to be obedient. I decided to trust the Lord and not my own abilities.

Your Turn...Your Perspective: Think of a time when a step back seemed like the right idea. What did you do? How did you know if you made the right decision?

Prayer: Thank You, Lord, for the blessing of financial abundance. I thank You for showing me a sample of the goodness available to us when we choose to trust You. I pray I am constantly reminded of the love You show us and not lose sight of Your perfect plan.

Day 61
Separate Spaces

PROVERBS 13:8; MATTHEW 5:13-16

When Keith moved to Kansas City, he moved into a one-bedroom apartment. When I moved to Kansas City, I moved into a three-bedroom duplex. Everyone thought we were crazy. Why did we not just move in together? It was a great way to save money and we were planning on getting married later, right? Surely God would understand our situation. We completely disagreed.

We decided 2 ½ years earlier to follow the Bible's plan for dating, which meant an abstinent relationship. It also meant living together prior to getting married was out of the question. We were not willing to risk the purity of our relationship to save money on rent. When we decided to embark on an abstinent relationship, it was because we both wanted to honor the Lord (and each other) with our commitment. Saving money had nothing to do with it.

All our finances were kept separate until after we got married. We talked about money often and kept each other up to date on any extra spending which was necessary, but we were intentional in not co-mingling our money. It was a lot more expensive: Two sets of utilities; two rent payments; two different rental insurance policies. It all added up. But none of it was as important as honoring God with our relationship. We knew the Lord would continue to honor our commitment if we honored Him with our living arrangements.

Keith's one-bedroom apartment was about 20 minutes away from where I lived. It was something he could easily afford on his existing income. My three-bedroom duplex was situated 30 minutes away from where I worked, and 30 minutes away from where Keith worked. When we did get married and he moved in, we would both have a 30-minute commute. It was also large enough for Keith and the kids to join me after we got married.

It was a little sad for me to have so many people question why we did not move in together. Many of them were Christians, and all of them knew we chose an abstinent relationship. The world's way of managing money and managing relationships seemed to be seeping into the thinking of our friends. But we chose to continue to do things God's way.

Ultimately, we knew we must honor the Lord in our relationship and living arrangements, and hoped we were setting a good example for our kids. It was a reminder, however, of the value system of the world we lived in. A system where it was commonplace to go against what the Lord asked of us.

Financially, we could have started paying down our debt snowball a lot sooner if we chose to move in together and consolidate our finances before we were married, but the cost was simply too great. We could either follow the world's way of living or follow the Lord's. We chose to follow the Lord. We knew by doing so, we were setting our marriage up from the beginning to spiritually thrive.

We knew God was our provider and would redeem the money "lost" following His plan for us.

Your Turn…Your Perspective: When was the last time you needed to defend a decision you knew aligned with the Lord's will for your life? When was the last time you gave into the temptation to follow those around you? How did each decision impact you?

Prayer: Lord, thank You for helping me stand firm in my decisions to honor You with my finances. I pray I can be salt and light to those around me.

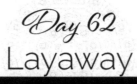

Day 62
Layaway

Many people questioned my move to Kansas. Keith and I had been dating for over two years, with no proposal in sight. They asked if I was sure it was a good idea to move and continue a relationship with someone for so long without a commitment.

Frankly, I asked the Lord the same question. We were both 43 years old and I was not sure how much longer I was willing to simply date. Not only did I have a desire to be married, but it was much easier to abstain without a boyfriend than with one. It was getting harder and harder to resist a physical relationship and neither Keith nor I wanted to risk breaking the covenant we made with the Lord.

We discussed marriage several times while we lived in Northern Virginia. We discussed it even more as we both began the transition to Kansas. When Keith asked if I would attend pre-engagement counseling with him, I was not sure where it would lead. It seemed a little odd to start counseling before we were engaged, but our counselor (a clinical psychologist and a licensed minister) thought it was a great idea.

We began counseling the week after I moved to Kansas. It was not easy. Many weeks we touched difficult subjects, and always left with homework (not to mention the occasional hurt feelings). The more sessions we completed, the more I began to think we were getting closer to making an engagement official. The emotional baggage we were uncovering did not send either of us running for the fences, so we must be getting close.

Keith proposed on my birthday. We spent the entire day together, exploring our new city and discovering gems of God's beauty. The evening ended with a lovely dinner at a nice restaurant. Keith enlisted the assistance of our waiter to set up his surprise. He made a pedestal out of the little box and perched my Crème Brule on top. When I noticed it, Keith got down on one knee and asked if I would marry him. The restaurant erupted in applause as I said yes, and the celebration began. It was an incredible experience.

As the fanfare died down and we were able to enjoy the moment, Keith quietly told me it took a while for him to propose because he was still paying for my engagement ring. It was on layaway for almost a year, and he did not want to propose without it. He told me he knew it was frustrating for me, but he was not able to pay for it any faster. The move to Kansas was tough for him financially and there was simply not a lot of money.

I was stunned. I knew his financial picture was bleak, but I did not think about how it impacted our future. I thought about all the times I questioned his love for me. I thought about how many times I asked the Lord if I was foolish to wait for him. All along, he was saving money and making payments on a ring.

The look in his eyes said it all. They showed resolve. They showed his love. They told me we would get through everything waiting ahead of us. I asked the Lord for a man who followed Him, and He gave me Keith. I was thankful I did not allow the world's definition of what a dating relationship should look like influence my decision to wait.

Your Turn…Your Perspective: When has going against the crowd proven to be a good decision? What about a time when you did not resist the temptation to follow the crowd? What did you learn from each decision?

Prayer: Lord, please help me to not be moved by the world's way of thinking. I want to live for You in every way. Please give me the courage to make the tough decisions to not follow the crowd.

Day 63
"I Do" on Sunday

2 THESSALONIANS 3:8

A few years before we were married, I visited Keith in his hometown of St. Louis, Missouri. He was on a temporary work assignment and I flew in for a weekend visit. Since we were in an abstinent relationship, we intentionally chose to not spend time in his apartment. Instead, we chose to spend the day in public.

Keith gave a lot of thought to how we would pass the time because we did not have much money. He looked for ways to show me his city in a way I would appreciate, and not spend a lot at the same time.

We drove around for a few hours as he shared the different places he lived growing up, his high school and college campuses, and where he worked. After lunch, he took me to The Jewel Box in Forest Park because it was an arboretum and he knew I loved flowers. During the tour, we also discovered that the newly renovated Jewel Box was a special events venue. It was beautiful.

It was early afternoon and there were no other visitors. Our guide shared all the history of the building and the grounds with us. We decided then and there to have our wedding ceremony at The Jewel Box if we chose to get married. Three years later it was time to make arrangements.

The Jewel Box turned out to be a very popular place for weddings. Many couples chose their date as much as 18 months in advance to insure the location was available on their special day. When we began planning our wedding, we discovered Sundays were discounted. We could also save an extra 50% discount if we booked a date less than a year away. While scouting locations for our reception, we found a venue which offered a 30% discount if we got married on Sunday. The DJ and the limousine company also offered discounts for bookings on Sundays.

The decision was made. We were getting married on Sunday. We knew some of our guests would not be able to make the ceremony because of our choice. Even though it was disappointing, we needed to be frugal and spend wisely. We were 43 years old, with lots of debt. Having an extravagant ceremony on a prime-time Saturday afternoon was simply not in the budget.

The value of the savings was literally thousands of dollars. We knew we made the right decision for us and our newly combined checking account. The decision to choose an unpopular day for our wedding was probably the first good financial decision either of us had made in a long time.

It was a beautiful Sunday wedding day. The guests who were able to join us shared in creating memories which were magical and unforgettable. We were not stressed about the cost of the day because we knew we were good stewards. We chose wisely. Everything from the lack of wedding favors to the choice of hors d'oeuvres was viewed through the lens of creating a lovely experience for our guests without going over our budget. We appreciated all our guests sacrificing their time to join us. There were no regrets about the decision to be untraditional.

Your Turn...Your Perspective: When was the last time you made the decision to be untraditional? How did it feel? Did you feel the need to justify your actions?

Prayer: Lord, I want to make good financial decisions, even when it is not the popular choice. Help me to not be moved by tradition, but to do what is right in Your eyes and for my budget. Help me to always be a good steward.

Day 64
Can We Have Both?

LUKE 12:24

When Keith and I were planning our wedding, we decided to create a budget and stick to it. My brother always told me I had champagne taste on a beer budget, and our wedding was proof I could make a beer budget work.

One of the big-ticket items was the reception menu. The hotel we chose gave several options and worked with us to narrow down our choices. We decided to have a plated meal instead of a buffet since it was more cost effective. They offered a great selection of entrees in our price range, and we were able to choose from a long list of side dishes. We narrowed our selection to three entrees and six side dishes. The final decisions were determined at our tasting. Neither of us ever experienced a tasting before, and we enjoyed the opportunity of choosing our meal.

The hardest decision was to either have all chicken, or both chicken and salmon. Chicken fit our budget best, but we really wanted to offer our guests both types of protein. Not only was it an elegant choice (Keith did not care about presentation, but I did), it also meant everyone would have a better chance of enjoying the meal. But it must work financially.

Our reception coordinator told us we could wait until one week before the wedding to make the decision. We knew it would all be based on the number of people who RSVP'd. As we worked through all the other details of the wedding, we realized we needed to get the menus printed long before we made the decision of what entrée to serve. The cost of waiting until the week before the wedding to have them printed was much higher than we wanted to budget.

We decided to print two sets of menus: one with chicken, and one with chicken and salmon. By printing two sets, we were able to save on the overall printing costs and still wait until the last possible moment to make the final decision on the meal. I know we would not have made the decision to print two sets of menus if we were not committed to our budget.

We chose to have small paper menus on the table, since they were cheaper than having posters printed. Printing two sets costs much less than paying expedited shipping if we waited longer to make the final menu decision.

We chose chicken and salmon. The plate was beautiful (for me!), our guests enjoyed the variety, and the budget survived the last-minute change. The choice to spend a few dollars on a second menu ahead of time proved to be a big part of the cost savings needed to serve our guests the meal we both desired to serve.

Your Turn...Your Perspective: Think of a time when you needed to delay a financial decision because you needed more information. What did you do? How did you resolve the issue? Did you rush or wait to review the information?

Prayer: Lord, please help me make smart decisions with my money, even when it is for "wants" instead of "needs." I pray for contentment as I balance my desire to change my financial situation with the desire to enjoy "things." I pray for discipline and discernment in all financial decisions.

Day 65
Chicken Nuggets

PROVERBS 23:6

The average cost for a wedding in 2012 was around $25,000. Keith and I set a budget of $8000 for our wedding and our honeymoon combined. Our reasoning was simple. We were broke. We were drowning in debt, had recently relocated to a new city, still maintained two separate households, and could not afford to spend what most people spent on a wedding.

We opted for a very simple décor, invited 70 of our closest friends and family, and were determined to not go over our budget. We designed our paper items ourselves and used an online print service to decrease the cost of printing. We served cupcakes instead of buying a wedding cake and did not serve alcohol at all.

The limited number of flowers used for the ceremony were purchased from a wholesale floral company. We bought river rocks from a dollar store to create our centerpieces.

Food was one of our big stressors for the reception. There were so many choices. We finally opted for a sit-down dinner instead of a buffet, and really struggled over the menu. We wanted a simple and elegant meal but needed to stay within the budget. It was not easy. We went back and forth on the menu items and did not make the decision until the very last possible moment.

We also limited the number of children invited to our wedding. We previously attended "no kids please" weddings, and understood the request was just as much about keeping costs low as it was about having a more adult-friendly party. But there were many kids who were special to us and we wanted them to be a part of our special day. Ten of the 70 people to attend our wedding were kids, and we wanted to make sure they enjoyed themselves, too.

We did two things to help the younger invitees feel a part of our special day. We created a coloring and craft table to give them something to do while the adults enjoyed dinner and dancing, and we served them chicken nuggets and French fries. Both were a big hit with kids and parents alike.

We were unaware of an unexpected advantage of the chicken nuggets, however. Not only did the kids and their parents enjoy the kid-friendly meal, but the cost was half of an adult plate. Because we focused on the kids enjoying themselves and not just our own desire to have a celebration for adults, we received the blessing of a lower food bill for the reception.

We struggled so much with the budget and found it to be a blessing to have a line item come in lower than we estimated. It also helped us enjoy the planning process just a little more knowing our kids would enjoy themselves. It was a reminder to stay focused on others and not just ourselves, even on our wedding day.

Your Turn...Your Perspective: When have you had an opportunity to be a blessing to a special child in your life? How did it impact you financially?

Prayer: Lord, please help me to be mindful of others, even during my difficult financial times. Help me to look for ways to serve others. Show me when I am inward focused and help me turn back to You for direction. Thank You for always being there to show me the way.

Day 66
Hand It Over

HAGGAI 2:4

I remember the conversation as if it happened yesterday. It was easily 10 years before I got married and a girlfriend and I were having dinner and discussing life. We were both single at the time with absolutely no prospects for marriage. We were both engineers and possessed the logical brains to prove it. We both wanted desperately to be married.

As we dissected our situations, I shared with her a thought which was niggling the back of my brain. I wanted to turn over my checkbook to my husband the moment I got married. I did not want the responsibility of managing my money any longer than necessary. I was happy to hand it over and let him (whoever he turned out to be) deal with all the financial decisions. I was ready for someone else to take care of my financial needs.

Fast forward a decade. Keith and I are planning our wedding. We discussed what it would mean to merge our lives in every way. I held on to the thought of giving my husband full financial control over my life and was ready to do so. I was sure he would agree.

We were having dinner one night while going over the latest round of things we needed to do before the wedding. Our merger of stuff was the topic. Keith looked at me brightly and said a topic during his prayer time was who should manage our family finances. He was sure the Lord wanted me to do it. What?!

I just stared at him for a long moment. He did not understand why I looked so deflated. I asked him if he was sure he wanted me to handle our finances. He said he was sure it was what God wanted for our family.

I prayed for a husband who prayed, and I got one. I was simply not prepared for what it meant to have a husband who prayed. I was certainly not prepared for the answers to his prayers to contradict my desires. I was about to come face-to-face with one of the biggest fears of my life. I made a horrible mess with my finances, and Keith was now entrusting our combined financial mess to me.

Why was the Lord doing this? I thought it was a good thing to want to submit my money wholeheartedly to my husband. Instead of getting an "attagirl," I was being punished.

It was not a pleasant conversation. Keith did not fully understand the impact of his declaration, and it took me a while to help him comprehend it. I hoped my explanation would cause him to feel sorry for his soon-to-be wife and come to her rescue. He did not. He simply held my hand, looked me in the eyes, and told me God would get us through it.

It took me several years to understand why the task was assigned to me and not my husband. God knew I needed to confront my fear to overcome it. I learned so much about myself and my attitudes about money because I was forced to confront them. It truly was a blessing in disguise. Yet again, God knew what was best.

Your Turn…Your Perspective: What financial fears have you experienced? How did you get through them? What did you learn about yourself in the process?

Prayer: Lord, thank You for always providing for me, even when I don't like the direction. I pray to serve You in every way. Please help me not fear money or anything else. Give me the courage to get through my financial situation.

Season 2:

Joining Debt

Day 67
Yours or Mine

1 CHRONICLES 29:16; MARK 10:8

Long before Keith and I got married, we knew we would have one set of bank accounts. We took the "and the two shall become one" literally. I spent years watching married couples, taking note of the things which seemed to create a healthy marriage. One habit which stood out to me was joint accounts. Keith did not have joint accounts in his first marriage but was open to doing something different in hopes of achieving a different result.

It was not a stretch for either of us to add the name of the other to the accounts. The biggest issue was choosing which bank to use. He was a long-time member of a credit union, and I was a long-time member of a national bank. Both institutions offered lots of perks, but we knew we could only choose one.

My bank's branch was just a few miles from where we lived. There were no branches in our immediate area for the credit union Keith wanted. We would have to drive almost 40 miles to do any business inside a branch. The decision was a no-brainer to me. We should use my bank.

But this did not sit well with Keith. He was incredibly attached to the credit union and did not want to change. I honestly did not see why it was such a big issue. It was not like we were moving millions of dollars. In fact, there was very little money to move. What was the big deal?

I decided to take it to the Lord during my prayer time one morning. The discussion stretched on for more than a week and we still did not have a decision. I remember writing feverishly in my journal asking God for clarity on the issue. Why was this such a big deal to him? I sat and waited for a very long time. Finally, I heard an answer. It was not what I wanted to hear.

"Why do you have to have your way?" was the response which came back. There it was. I wanted to make the decision. I wanted it to be my bank, not because my bank was better, but just because I wanted my way. If Keith was so passionate about using his bank, and there was no real emotional attachment to my bank, would it really hurt me to move to his bank?

I sat at a crossroad early in our marriage, faced with the choice to compromise or dig my heels in and insist on being right. Was this how I wanted to start our financial lives together? Was the negative emotion worth it? What was the ultimate goal? The choice to me became clear. Credit Union, here we come.

When I shared the thought with Keith, his response was filled with emotion. He was incredibly loyal, and in a way, the credit union was like family to him. It was a trait I came to respect more and more over time. It was a key to the character of the man I married. I was thankful I did not miss an opportunity to experience it fully by allowing pride to win.

Your Turn…Your Perspective: When was the last time you fought to have your way? Why was it so important? What did the experience teach you?

Prayer: Lord, thank You for the truth. Thank You for being able to hear You when my pride is getting puffed up. I pray I am always mindful of the end goal and work to keep Your will ahead of my personal agenda.

A Need to Give

PROVERBS 3:10

So much merging to do. We merged two homes into one, including dishes, pots and pans, linens and furniture. We merged two schools of thought on chores and housekeeping. We merged two sets of finances, two sets of bank accounts, and two stacks of debt.

We also merged our thought process on giving. Merging the concept of giving proved to be more difficult than either of us expected. Keith was a natural giver and I was not. He would give you the shirt off his back and deal with the cold. I would keep my shirt and help you to find your own. Keith wanted to give to anyone who asked of us, and I wanted to put all extra money towards our debt snowball. It was not easy or fun finding a common ground.

I hated not being on one accord about giving. On one hand I felt cheap, selfish and insensitive. On the other hand, I felt protective of our income, motivated to get out of debt as soon as possible, and passionate about meeting our own goals before helping others meet theirs.

I literally felt like I was between a rock and a hard place. It was difficult for me to reconcile someone else's needs with ours. I also did not want my new husband to be disappointed in me. I truly did not know what to do. It was not something I ever thought we would experience as a newly married couple.

We prayed a lot and worked to find a solution. It took several months to find one we agreed on. We finally decided to allocate a small amount of our budget each month to give outside of tithing. This did not include the charitable giving already in the budget. Whatever was not used by the end of the month would be left to accumulate with the amount budgeted for the next month. It was one of the few envelopes we did not move into the debt snowball envelope at the end of the month.

The giving envelope was allowed to grow because we only gave what was in it. If there was no money in the envelope, we did not give any extra. If there was money in the envelope, we were able to give to whatever cause was requesting a donation.

This process worked well and helped to cut down on the number of disagreements about giving. It was easier for me to be okay with extra giving since it was in the budget. It was easier for Keith to limit what we gave to the amount only available in the extra giving envelope.

We were thankful we were finally in one accord about something as important as giving. We each wanted the other to feel their opinion was valued and heard. It was a huge learning experience for us as a newly married couple. Being able to find common ground on giving made us believe we could find our way through anything…if we kept prayer in the midst.

Your Turn…Your Perspective: Have you ever felt it necessary to defend your monetary beliefs? Who was the other person? Were you able to discuss your feelings and feel heard? What was the result?

Prayer: Lord, please help me reconcile helping others with helping myself. I want to serve You and serving You means serving others. I pray for discernment when others have requests of me. Please help me to not incur debt, but to give appropriately. I pray for wisdom and peace in my finances.

600 Thread Count

PSALM 35:27

While we both owned a lot of stuff, I brought most of the household linens to our marriage. I was called a "linen snob" in the past, and honestly, it was a title I did not mind. I liked high thread count sheets and richly absorbent towels. I enjoyed the daily pampering they gave me and did not see the need to justify the cost.

Getting married and merging everything meant also merging linens. The towels were not such a big deal because there were enough of "my" towels to justify us not using the towels Keith brought to our union. But sheets were a different story. All my sheets were at least 600 thread count and fit my queen-size bed perfectly.

Keith brought a king-sized bed to our union, complete with sheets of a lot less thread count. I felt like the heroine from the childhood story *The Princess and The Pea.* I absolutely hated those sheets. Of course, my new husband looked at me blankly when I tried to explain how these sheets were unacceptable and we needed to buy new ones. He actually entertained the idea briefly until he saw how much they cost.

The price tag created an emphatic, "NO!" Keith refused to allow us to buy new sheets. There were bills coming out of our ears, and the cost of the sheets could easily have paid at least two or three minimum payments. No new sheets.

I brought it up at least once a month. "Look, Honey, sheets are on sale!" or "Honey, check out this pattern. They match the lamps you brought to our marriage," and "Honey, can we please buy new sheets this month?"

The answer was always the same – no new sheets. As small as it seemed, it was a big deal to me. I wanted nice sheets. I was used to having nice sheets. Our kids were sleeping on wonderful sheets since they slept on queen-sized beds with MY 600-thread count sheets. I was struggling.

Finally, after months of me whining (it was not pretty), Keith came to me with a great idea. Since I was the one who wanted "luxury" sheets, I could be the one to pay for them. I could buy as many sets of sheets as I wanted, as long as I paid for them out of my monthly fun money. No house money could be used.

Deal! I was so excited I could hardly stand it. I went out the same week to get prices to set my savings goal. It took me three months, but I finally got my sheets. Sleep improved immediately! Keith still did not get it, but I was one happy woman.

The entire experience was a great communication lesson for both of us. My needs were met, and the budget was intact. It was win, win, win for me, Keith and our marriage. We used the approach many times during financial discussions and avoided a lot of frustration over purchases. We learned to not discount the needs of the other person and how to listen with an open ear, heart, and mind. It was a valuable lesson for our marriage.

Your Turn…Your Perspective: When was the last time you had to justify a purchase? How did you manage it? What did you learn from the experience?

Prayer: Lord, I pray for patience and endurance as I run this race. I pray to respect my budget and properly manage wants and needs. I pray for the discipline to save for my wants and keep my focus on debt reduction first. Thank You for keeping me motivated to live my financial life Your way.

Day 70
Wise Counsel

PROVERBS 19:20

Before Keith even got settled into his one-bedroom apartment, he began looking for a church home. He visited two different churches on Sundays (8am and 11am services), and a different one on Wednesdays. Co-workers, the radio, and driving through neighborhoods were his sources for leads. He called me after each visit and shared if he found one which made the cut for a second visit. He did this over and over those first few months.

I got a call from him one Wednesday night as I was packing to move to Kansas City. He was so excited. A church on his list warranted a second visit and he chose this time to go to Bible study. He was very intrigued by the topic of the evening. The study fascinated him, and he made a point to thank the instructor after the class ended. Through conversation, he learned the Bible study instructor was a licensed minister and a clinical psychologist.

Keith mentioned our courtship and asked if the minister/psychologist would be open to pre-engagement counseling. The minister thought it was a great idea to start counseling before the engagement and agreed to meet with us. I arrived in Kansas City on Friday, and our first counseling session was held on Tuesday.

We went to counseling every Tuesday from August until December. We learned so much about ourselves and began the difficult task of understanding each other. When the kids visited, they went with us and waited in the lobby area. They liked "Mr. Alex" and always enjoyed seeing him. After about a month of visits, we asked Alex if he would officiate our wedding when the time came.

A few months after the wedding, Keith thought it would be a great idea to get a "tune up." Outside of discussions for the wedding, our communication with Alex was limited after we finished our official pre-marital counseling. We were settling in to married life and wanted to see if we were on the right track. Our tune up went so well, we decided to take the kids with us the next time.

The four of us showed up for our session, not having any idea how it would drastically change our lives. We knew the statistics on blended families were not good, and we were determined to not be a casualty. We decided to make room in the budget each year for our family to have counseling sessions.

The kids thought nothing of it. "Mr. Alex" was a part of our family from the very beginning; meeting with him was a natural part of coming to Kansas. As they got older and were faced with teenage issues, Alex recommended separate sessions. We expanded the budget to accommodate.

We learned so much. From difficult parenting situations and family dynamics to family bonding exercises – all were a regular part of our visits. We even discovered one child liked movies, while the other preferred games.

Being a blended family was certainly not easy. But Keith and I had a not-so-secret weapon named Alex. We thanked him often for the impact he made on our family, one referral at a time.

Your Turn…Your Perspective: Where do you turn for wise counsel? What area could you use counsel on right now?

Prayer: Lord, thank You for wise counsel. I pray I continue to be open to receiving it from those with the expertise I do not have. I pray for guidance in choosing well those who support my life and my desire to live out Christ-centered financial wellness.

Day 71
STEM

HAGGAI 1:14A

Keith and I spent a good bit of time preparing for our summers with the kids. Five weeks was not a lot of time and there was a lot we wanted to teach them. The first year we were married, they were 8 and 10, and there was no money whatsoever. We took turns tele-working because we could not afford camp or day care.

They were stuck in the house all day every work day. We took advantage of our library's extensive DVD collection and tried to entertain them in between conference calls as best we could. It was not ideal for any of us, but we made it work.

The next summer, I knew more of what to expect. I found as many free camps as possible, and they were able to get out a little more. We decided to put a little money in the budget for a few other camps and were able to round out the summer.

The kids enjoyed themselves, and we felt much better about them being able to get out and enjoy the summer instead of being cooped up in the house. It was also a learning experience for me. There was no frame of reference the first summer we were together as a family. The second year was much easier to manage since I better understood what it took to manage our new little family.

The third year, Keith and I really used the power of budgeting. We began to put camp in the budget as soon as the school year started. It gave us a much larger budget to work with, and as a result, we were able to send the kids to a wider variety of camps.

STEM (Science, Technology, Engineering & Math) camps became our focus. Since I was an engineer, I understood the power of a STEM career. We wanted the kids to understand this power also. We used the camps as an opportunity to expose them to some of the options they might have available to them if they chose a STEM career.

We knew many young adults who spent many years and a ton of money on an education, only to find out it was not what they wanted. We wanted our kids to have viable career options. We wanted to expose them to as much educational opportunity as we could.

While we understood their career choices would ultimately be their decision, we made certain STEM camps were a part of the lineup almost every summer. If we could open their eyes to the career possibilities associated with STEM careers, we hoped to limit the confusion they would face when it came time to choose a college and a career.

Prayer was our constant companion for our kids. We prayed for them daily, and their career choice was a big part of our prayer strategy. It was too soon to know how it would all turn out, but exposure to the options certainly would not hurt their chances of choosing a good career.

Your Turn…Your Perspective: How has your career choice impacted your financial life? If you could change anything, what would it be?

Prayer: Lord, thank You for options and good choices. I thank You for the opportunity to positively impact my life and the lives of those around me through my work. I pray for guidance for any upcoming career changes. Help me to always keep Your plan for my life as my primary focus.

Put It in the Budget
PROVERBS 21:5

When we first started doing a budget, we used the same numbers in each category each month. The food budget was always the same. The budget for gas for the vehicles never changed. And so on. Then we would spend several hours each month trying to adjust the budget on the fly to match what we really needed.

We spent more on groceries in the months when the kids were with us, but we did not actually budget any extra money for food for those months. Even though I no longer worked at home and needed more money in the gas envelope, we did not make the adjustment. The result was several months where we ran out of gas money as we neared the end of the month.

This way of budgeting made me crazy. I was constantly concerned about having enough money for basic expenses as the end of the month drew near. I was fearful of using our debt snowball allocation for debt payments because I knew chances were high we would need to redirect it to a basic expense later in the month. We budgeted this way for several months into our marriage. There were so many minimum payments to manage, and by not budgeting properly, we inadvertently added another layer of stress to our money management. We did not see the error of our budget process until we completed Financial Peace University and began to go through it again as coordinators. It was an incredible paradigm shift.

By approaching each month as its own entity, we were able to account for the times when we needed more money in certain areas and less in others. We made the adjustment to the food and gas envelopes to accommodate the kids being with us for the entire month of July. Instead of using our debt snowball money to pay for summer camp in the spring, we began to put a small amount aside each month. This allowed us to pay for camp for the kids and still have a debt snowball payment in the spring months.

We always budgeted for basic household items like utilities, cell phones and car repairs. It just seemed lost on us to include things like extra money for the food envelope in December to accommodate holiday cooking. Once we got the hang of it, we felt so much more control over our money. For us, it was freeing to know we would be able to invite friends over for Thanksgiving and Christmas dinner, and still make a sizeable debt snowball payment in November and December. We no longer felt we were being held hostage by our financial situation. We still chose to put most of our extra income towards debt, but the guilt was gone. I no longer stressed about spending a little extra on ingredients for a nice meal to share with friends a few times a year.

It was a blessing to know life was not being put completely on hold while we walked our journey of debt reduction. It was also a blessing to know our sacrifices would create an incredible financially-free future for our family.

Your Turn...Your Perspective: In what ways can you be more diligent in your financial journey? How has God taught you His ways recently?

Prayer: Lord, thank You for wisdom. Thank You for the lessons learned in the trenches, for teaching me to pray diligently. Please help me to be open to new ideas about managing the resources You have provided. I am thankful to grow in my knowledge of You.

Day 73
Family Ministry

PROVERBS 28:12A

In the first year of our marriage, Keith and I were more focused on surviving than thriving. The debt seemed to be taking over. Collection notices were everywhere. I was overwhelmed by it all. We could not see our way out and did not know how long it would take to get through it.

Setbacks occurred often, and there were many months where no progress was made on repaying the debt. We were struggling to keep our financial footing.

During this time, we went to dinner with an older couple. At some point during the conversation, they asked us what our family ministry would be. We stared back at them blankly and told them we did not have one. They recommended praying and asking God to make our ministry clear to us.

We began to pray about our family ministry each day during our prayer time. We were not sure what it would look like, and we certainly did not feel we knew enough about anything to call it a ministry.

One day, Keith and I were talking about the cost of an item and its impact on our budget. I was feeling frustrated at missing yet another opportunity to do something and feel normal. I told Keith I did not think we could afford it.

He stopped what he was doing, turned to me with fierceness and said defiantly, "Don't ever say we cannot afford something again. We CHOOSE to put our money elsewhere!" There was such conviction in his voice; it was clear my words hit a nerve. As I processed the conversation, the Holy Spirit said to me, "Financial stewardship is your family ministry."

It all made sense. Even though our debt was huge, we were determined to work our way through it. We made the commitment to live our financial life as directed by God's Word. There were many others who were in similar situations. If we chose to share what we learned on our own journey, we would be able to help others do the same.

We began to listen for opportunities to share our story with others and taught what we learned. Shortly after, we began teaching Financial Peace University at our church. There were almost thirty people in our first class. It was clear our ministry was needed.

We chose to be very transparent with our class members. We shared our struggles and temptations. We shared our plan and how well we executed it. We shared our successes and failures. We wanted to help as many people as possible avoid the mistakes we made.

What began as a marriage built on debt turned into a ministry built on a solid foundation of faith, courage and perseverance. We stayed open to how God chose to use our ministry to grow the Kingdom and celebrated each success someone else achieved. It was amazing to see how God used our pain to bring so much joy to others. We were thankful we chose to be open to His plan for our marriage.

Your Turn…Your Perspective: How has God used a place of pain in your life to bring joy to someone else? What did you learn during the process?

Prayer: Lord, I pray to stay open for opportunities to be used by You to assist others. Help me to never discount the power of my own story. Show me who can benefit from me sharing my story.

Day 74
Check, Please

PROVERBS 17:18; TITUS 2:7

Keith and I were about a year into eliminating our debt when we discovered Dave Ramsey's Financial Peace University. We immediately began implementing the principles outlined in the program. We also began reading everything we could find on God's ways of handling money. It made so much sense to us. With the incredibly large amount of debt we needed to pay off, we knew we would need God's help to get rid of it. To receive His help, we also knew we needed to do things His way. We always told our kids we would not reward disobedience, and we believed God operated the same way. If we wanted Him to bless us financially, we needed to follow His financial plan.

A few weeks into our new-found way of managing our money, I got a call from a very close friend asking me to co-sign for a loan. The request was a first and I knew how hard it was for them to ask. I also knew their financial picture was bleak. The Bible talked about co-signers being foolish because they did not follow the lender's lead. If the lender did not see the borrower as a good risk, the potential co-signer should not either.

I was torn. I really wanted to help, but I knew I could not. I also could not get past the timing of the request. It was within weeks of our commitment to follow the financial plan outlined in the Bible. I saw the request as a test from the Lord. He seemed to be saying, "Do you trust Me? Are you serious about managing your money the way I asked you to manage it? Are you willing to be unpopular to follow Me?" I knew I must say no to my friend.

It was a sad day for me. On the surface, it should not have been a big deal. But it was. I knew I was at a crossroads. By saying no to the request, I was choosing to not only be obedient, but to be unpopular. My friend did not take my response well. I was criticized for my choice to not participate in their folly, just as I knew I would be. Even through the pain of the ridicule, I stood by my decision. I knew it was the right thing to do.

For a long while, I owned the negative energy my friend gave when I delivered the bad news. Keith comforted me, but made it clear I needed to work through this on my own. We chose to draw a line in the sand and knew we would not be popular with most. I prayed the relationship with my friend was not damaged by my decision. Ultimately, I did what I needed to do for our family's financial health and well-being.

It took about two years for the relationship with my friend to mend. I continued to pray, and we never spoke of the event again. I continued to provide support in every way I could and was eventually able to encourage my friend to attend Financial Peace University. Even though they chose not to, I knew my job was to continue to model God's way. The rest would be up to them.

Your Turn...Your Perspective: Have you ever been on either side of a co-sign situation? If so, what was the result? How did the relationship fare through the experience?

Prayer: Lord, You never said following You would be easy. Thank You for providing a path which is simple to understand, even if it is not popular. I pray for continued strength to do what is right although it may be difficult for others to comprehend. I pray others see You in our actions and choose to follow Your ways also.

I Think I Can. I Think I Can

TITUS 1:7; 2 TIMOTHY 2:15

Keith and I started teaching Financial Peace University about a year and a half after we first took the class. Even though we were not yet out of debt, the class drastically changed our lives and the way we handled our finances. We were excited to lead other families through the process which helped us make such great progress on getting out of debt.

The class created financial structure in our lives and we easily embraced most of it. The one exception was using cash envelopes. We were using an online budgeting tool to manage our money, which included an electronic envelope for each category. In my mind, having electronic envelopes for our budget items meant we really did not need to use cash envelopes. Yes, our grocery budget was quite large, but we were not using credit cards. I really did not see where we needed to make a change.

A few weeks into teaching our first class, I knew my thought process was being challenged. I could not get cash for groceries out of my mind. I did not want to switch to cash, but knew God was calling me to do so. I was not sure why it was such a challenge. I journaled about it, prayed about it, talked with Keith about it, and ultimately knew what I needed to do. It was time to create a cash envelope for groceries.

The first time I went to the bank machine to pull out cash for groceries, I felt sick to my stomach. I just knew I was going to get in line at our favorite discount warehouse and not have enough money. I imagined people glaring at me for holding up the line to count out cash, especially when it was so much "easier" to swipe my debit card. But I was committed.

I got to the warehouse armed with cash, a grocery list and a calculator, and got to work. I began my normal shopping process and realized I might not have enough money. I was used to buying two of everything, but I quickly discovered a shift in perspective was needed. I went back around the store, put half of my items back, and recalculated the cost.

During check out, my palms were sweating. I nervously fingered the $20 bills in my possession and miscounted when I paid the attendant. But I got through it and there was money left over! The reason I was not able to trim our food budget in the past was because I was buying in bulk. I would never have realized it without switching to cash. I began to think differently about grocery shopping and was able to cut our food budget by 20% the first month.

More than anything, I felt authentic. Dave Ramsey talked about using envelopes, and as coordinators, we encouraged our class members to follow his lead. Now we could speak about it from our own personal experience. I recalled a leadership principle I learned during my time as a Sales Director with Mary Kay: "You cannot teach what you do not know; you cannot lead where you do not go." I now felt truly ready to teach and lead.

Your Turn...Your Perspective: What parts of your budget do you have difficulty controlling? Do you use cash? Why or why not?

Prayer: Lord, I hear You convicting me to make changes in my management of money. Thank You for the desire to be authentic. Thank You for Your patience with me as I work through my fears of money.

Day 76
Too Much to Rent

1 TIMOTHY 6:6-8; PHILIPPIANS 4:19

We were renting. When I moved to Kansas from Northern Virginia, there was no way to know what was in store for me. Keith and I were not yet married. I did not know anyone in the city other than him. Everything about my job was new and I did not know what my future held. I purchased a home in the first few months of moving to Northern Virginia a decade earlier, and while it was not the worse decision I ever made, it certainly was not the best. This time I decided to rent for a year before I purchased a home.

My life changed quickly. We got engaged, planned a wedding, got married, combined households and finances. I was ready to buy, but financially we could not afford to do so. We decided to wait another year and then leave our rented duplex behind. Shortly after, however, we discovered Financial Peace University and realized it would not be wise to purchase a home before we were debt-free. Since our debt numbers were huge, I knew it would be years before my desires of being a home owner again were realized.

I did not like renting. It felt like money was being tossed down the drain. I hated dealing with the management company. The appliances and fixtures were cheap. I felt insulted when the maintenance guy came to replace the kitchen faucet and it came with a plastic water sprayer. It was obvious they did not expect us to take care of the property, so they invested as little into it as possible. The carpet was cheap, the insulation was only what was required to pass the building code, and all these things reminded me I lived in a rental.

One day, I was especially frustrated with how long it was taking to get rid of our debt and I shouted out, "Lord! We make too much money to be renting!" There was silence. No feeling of comfort from the Holy Spirit; no scripture popped into my mind to reassure me. I just stood there, waiting for the Lord to acknowledge my cry.

And then it hit me. I was having a temper tantrum. Why would I expect the Lord to run to me and coddle me when I was behaving like a two-year-old not getting her way? A wave of sadness washed over me, and I hung my head in shame. I was completely out of line. Poor decisions placed Keith and me in this situation, and I wanted the Lord to bless our mess.

Dave Ramsey often said, "renting buys patience." He talked about wanting home ownership to be a blessing and not a curse. Buying a home before being debt-free and not having a fully funded emergency fund would be a huge risk. It would set us up for misfortune. Ultimately, I knew renting until we were debt-free was the right thing to do. My flesh was not excited to admit this. I wanted what I wanted, and I wanted it now.

It took me a long time to embrace renting as an investment in our future. I learned my issue was not really with renting, but with contentment. I could not see the blessing of where we were because I was so focused on where I wanted to be. Years would pass before I made real progress in this area. The seed of discontentment was deeply rooted. Only with constant prayer and a deep desire to not limit my family's prosperity did I begin to shift my perspective. What I wanted most was to not lose sight of the lessons learned. I knew they would serve us well as we continued our journey to financial freedom.

Your Turn...Your Perspective: What causes you discontentment? In what ways are you more focused on the future than on the present? How can you readjust your attitude towards contentment today?

Prayer: Lord, thank You for loving me enough to not give me what I wanted when I was not ready to handle it. Thank You for supplying all my needs and showing me grace.

Day 77
Wait Well While I'm Waiting

PSALM 112:1; DEUTERONOMY 1:2-3

During my transition time from Northern Virginia to Kansas, I learned a great lesson in patience. Keith and I were not yet married, but the Lord gave me instructions to move to Kansas. He gave Keith the same instructions a few months prior. I was afraid people would think I was moving because of my boyfriend.

The opinions of others were center stage in my life and I struggled immensely with the fear of criticism. Anytime someone asked about the upcoming move, I shifted in my seat and felt the heat rise to my face. I felt the need to explain my upcoming move even before the question was asked.

Four months after I started my job search, I attended a single's event at my church. The youth pastor spoke on the topic "I Wait Well." A very engaging speaker, he captured my attention immediately. He demonstrated how we were to "wait" (as in serve) while we waited (as in patience) on God to fulfill His promises. The statement resonated with me because it perfectly described my current season.

The problem was my attitude sucked. I may be waiting, but I was not waiting well. The phrase became my new mantra. "I Wait Well While I'm Waiting." I prayed and meditated on it daily to stay focused on God's plan. Very shortly thereafter, a position became available with a full relocation package. Not only did the Lord fulfill His promise of a position, but He ensured I would have no trouble getting there.

Fast forward a year or so, and Keith and I were knee deep in debt, fighting hard to get out. It felt daunting and sometimes overwhelming. Our life felt chaotic and all my dreams of what our married life would become seemed to be on hold. My attitude was again suffering as I struggled with yet another season of waiting.

During my prayer time one morning, the Lord reminded me of my old mantra. Again, I was called to wait well while I waited. The five months of looking for a new position seemed like a cake walk compared to what we were currently going through. It would take years to pay our debt, and roadblocks were a monthly occurrence.

A bad attitude was not a great accessory for this trip. I certainly needed to wait well. Our future was on the line and I did not want to stay in debt any longer than necessary. I chose misery in the past and did not want a repeat performance. I needed to shift my perspective while in the valley experience.

Deuteronomy 1:2-3 tells us the children of Israel took 40 years to make an 11-day journey. Over and over, they made the same mistakes. They constantly whined and complained and were continuously ungrateful for what they had. I did not want to repeat their mistakes. I did not want our journey to be prolonged because of my attitude.

I decided to wait well while I waited. Only the Lord knew how long our journey would take, but I knew my attitude must remain positive. With each experience, the choice was mine to make. I determined how each experience impacted me and every choice was my choice. I knew my attitude would dictate our length of stay in this season.

Your Turn…Your Perspective: What "wait well" experiences have you had? How was your attitude during the process? What did the experience teach you?

Prayer: Lord, thank You for the desire to be better. Thank You for the reminders of what my life can be, both good and bad. I pray You help me to keep my blinders on and stay focused on You and Your plan for my life.

Day 78
Pink and Blue

PROVERBS 16:6; EPHESIANS 5:21

Keith and I were working hard at paying off our debt. We were both committed to becoming debt-free as quickly as possible. We also supported each other when one of us experienced some form of financial weakness which threatened to derail our progress. But even with a high level of commitment to the goal and the desire to work together, there were still moments when a heated discussion caused us to feel frustration.

There were more heated moments early on than we cared to admit. Looking back, we could tell it was not only the sheer amount of debt we were working through with a smaller income, but also the two of us learning how to become one. Healthy communication took more effort than we realized. Fortunately for us, we were committed to finding a way, and neither of us would accept anything less.

I do not remember how we discovered the book *Love and Respect* by Emerson Eggrichs, but we were incredibly thankful we did. After reading his book, and later going through a companion Bible study, we discovered the root of our frustration. Keith was a boy and I was a girl! The reason we were attracted to each other was the same reason we struggled to figure out why the other did not understand our perspective.

As Emerson put it, Keith was speaking and hearing with a blue megaphone and hearing aids, and I was speaking and hearing with a pink megaphone and hearing aids. He did not automatically understand me, and I did not automatically understand him. Some translation would be required if we were to make this communication thing work.

The theory of our dilemma was based on Ephesians 5:33. Men were called to love their wives when it was the most unnatural thing for them to do, and women were called to respect their husbands when it, too, was the most unnatural thing for them to do. It seemed so simple, but it was far from it.

We each needed to be aware of the other's inability to naturally understand what we were communicating. We also needed to be patient as the other person attempted to decipher what was said. Once we learned how to decipher each other, we no longer stayed as long on what Emerson called the "Crazy Cycle." It did not mean we did not get on the "Crazy Cycle," it just meant we did not stay on as long.

What a gift this realization became. While we were both committed to our marriage, spending five plus years getting out of debt could have been a miserable experience if we did not learn how to communicate and love each other according to Ephesians 5. It was essential to work together to accomplish our financial goals.

We shared our new-found knowledge with as many people as we could, especially couples. We were not shy in sharing our struggles, and how Emerson's concepts helped us find our way. Just as we felt a huge responsibility to educate as many as we could about God's way of managing money, we felt an incredible responsibility to help couples understand the importance of learning how to have an Ephesians 5 marriage.

Your Turn…Your Perspective: *If you're married:* **How is your communication with your spouse? What ways can you work to better understand each other?** *If you're single:* **How are your communication skills with those around you? What can you do to limit confusion?**

Prayer: Lord, thank You for Your Word, which gives me everything we need. Thank You for the desire to seek out the tools I need to grow in You and in every area of my life. Please help me not hide behind my sin but be transparent. Help me seek out the assistance of others when I need it.

Day 79
Just One

PSALM 30:6

Since Keith and I both worked for the Federal Government, we shared all aspects of Human Resources. Our agencies shared the same insurance options, the same retirement plans, the same pay and promotion schedule. It was all identical. The only difference in our employment was how our agencies received money from Congress. Keith's agency received money on a yearly basis. My agency received money every other year.

So, in 2013, when the President and Congress could not agree on a budget and shut down the Federal Government for two weeks, our household was definitely affected. But only partially. Keith's agency was affected; mine was not.

Instead of losing both of our incomes, we only lost one. It was truly was a blessing and God's hand was on full display in our financial life. We certainly saw the averted disaster for what it was. Our journey of becoming debt snowball free was only a year old. Progress was slow, with at least 15 debt payments going out each month.

There was no way we could manage financially if we lost both of our incomes. We were literally living paycheck to paycheck. There was no margin in our lives, and every dime which came in was sent back out. Or so we thought.

The immediate blessing (besides still having one income for the household) came when we discovered we could cover all our minimum payments with just one income. We never stopped to calculate it before, but there it was. All our extra debt payments and savings were covered out of the second income. If we tightened down our food budget, cut savings for future purchases and repairs, and discontinued all giving (not tithing), we could live on one income. Just one.

Wow! What a blessing it was to discover margin. Even though we were far from being out of the financial woods, it was a beautiful reprieve to know we could continue to tread water on just one income.

It was also a wake-up call. We could certainly not afford to lose both of our incomes. And while we could manage on just one, we could not make any forward progress. There was only room for minimum payments on everything. There was no room for anything extra. One emergency would surely take us out.

The reality of our situation sobered us and simultaneously gave us great relief. We were thankful God chose to allow us to keep one of our incomes during the government shutdown, but we also clearly saw just how close to the edge we were living. We could choose to continue to live a status quo life with lots of debt, or we could press in and do the hard work of cleaning up our financial life. We chose the latter. We were thankful it was a choice we were able to make before no choices were available.

Your Turn…Your Perspective: Name a time when you know you were spared the full force of a bad situation. How did it impact you? What did you change as a result?

Prayer: Lord, thank You for giving me glimpses of what my life could look like. Thank You for protecting and providing for me. I pray to stay open to all You show me. Help me not take my circumstance for granted. As difficult as it can be at times, I know it could be worse.

Breaking Ground in the Wrong Location

1 CORINTHIANS 14:40

Shortly after we got married, we decided to build a home instead of buying and renovating an existing one. We started researching locations and builders, and began to think about what the home would look like. We were paying off our debt slowly but were not yet using the method taught by Dave Ramsey. Our goal was to pay off everything except our student loans. We did not want to wait until we were completely debt-free to build, and we told ourselves it would take too long to get completely out of debt. We unknowingly were flirting with disaster and were excited about it.

About a year later, we were making progress on the non-student loan debt. It looked as if we would be able to start our building project the next year. Around the same time, we discovered Dave Ramsey and began to implement the strategies he taught. Through our education, we realized we needed to pay off all debt and save at least three months of expenses before we started our building project. I was not happy.

I felt defeated and incredibly disappointed. I certainly did not want to wait until we were done paying off student loans to get started on building our home. We were already two years into paying off our debt with at least another year before we could start our fully-funded emergency fund. To wait until after it was funded to save for a down payment meant we needed to rent at least another three years. I wanted out of our rental duplex as quickly as possible, and three more years did not sit well with me.

I wondered what Keith was thinking. I did not want to ask for fear he was thinking the same thing. If I talked to him about it, it would seal our fate to wait until after our emergency fund was saved to begin saving for a down payment. When I finally asked, his thoughts were the same as mine. As much as I hated it, we agreed to delay our home building until we finished paying off all our debt.

Fast forward three years, and we were making significant progress on paying off our debt. There was more debt paid off than we still owed. I started to feel more hopeful about when we would be able to build our home.

While we were paying off debt, we continued to look at potential lots for our future home. We found several lots which suited our needs. One day, Keith reminded me our original lot choice was no longer a contender. What he said next was incredibly profound. He reminded me of when we were ready to jump the gun on building three years earlier. If we had, we would have broken ground in the wrong location.

Keith's revelation stayed with me for days. 1 Corinthians 14:40 clearly stated the importance of being decent and in order. It was a reminder to not be in such a hurry, and to be mindful of how costly it could be to take shortcuts. Patience was a fruit of the Spirit for a reason.

Your Turn…Your Perspective: When was the last time you had to make a tough decision about a large purchase? Have you ever delayed a purchase and then decided against it altogether? How did you feel after making your decision?

> *Prayer: Lord, thank You for obedience. I know following a Godly plan will not lead me astray. Please help me continue to be mindful of this as I make every decision. Help me remember the income I earn belongs to You and I am simply a steward acting on Your behalf.*

Day 81
Feed Me, Feed Me

2 CORINTHIANS 8:12

Birthday celebrations were always important to me. As a child growing up in rural South Carolina, my family always placed a big emphasis on birthdays. Part of the celebration was having your favorite meal. Typically, the celebration would take place on the Sunday before or after your birthday, and you were given the opportunity to create your menu and invite whomever you wanted to join the family. It brought me great joy to celebrate my birthday with my family in this way.

When Keith and I got married and began celebrating birthdays with the kids, I realized I missed the tradition of celebrating with food. It was not uncommon for me to ask Keith what he wanted for his birthday, but it was a tradition not yet implemented with the kids.

The next year, I was intentional in making food a part of their birthday celebrations. Several weeks before each of their birthdays, I told them we would have a grand meal as a part of their special day. I asked them to think about their favorite foods and give me a list of what they wanted as a part of their birthday meals.

The menus they chose were elaborate. It was not only necessary to invite friends over to celebrate, but we needed help to eat all the food I prepared! Our son's menu included turkey burgers and fries, salmon, broccoli, lemonade and red velvet cupcakes. Our daughter's menu included salmon, asparagus, shrimp and grits, fried green tomatoes and red velvet cupcakes.

They were both excited to be allowed to choose such a grand meal, and I was excited to be able to accommodate their requests. Keith got a kick out of it also because he loved all the foods they loved. He knew birthday celebrations were a time when we got to veer off our very limited menu and include dessert.

It was important for them to know how important their special day was to us. We always served birthday meals on fine china, added sparkling cider for a special birthday toast, and made sure candles were lit. Many of our friends thought we went overboard and were in awe of our celebrations. Once we explained the significance, they joined in and were just as excited as we were. Everyone enjoyed it.

I realized how important it was for our kids to be able to create their own birthday menu. I also realized how inexpensive it was to add another level of celebration to their birthdays. The meals were elaborate, but they really did not cost any more money. I simply reallocated the grocery money to accommodate their choices, and we ate the leftovers for future meals.

Not only did these special menus become a great way to celebrate our kids, we were able to stay true to our desire to not overspend on special occasions. We created some great memories and continued a family tradition of birthdays with food. I always heard of people talking about how much they enjoyed bringing their childhood traditions into their new family, and birthday dinners gave me a way to do the same thing with my new family. It was truly a blessing for me, my new husband, and my new kids.

Your Turn...Your Perspective: What special memories do you have of childhood celebrations? How have you incorporated them into your adult life?

Prayer: Lord, thank You for old traditions which become new again. Help me rethink how to enjoy special occasions without overspending. I pray for the contentment which comes from working with the resources available to me.

Day 82
Third Check

PSALM 119:36

Keith and I got paid every other week. We followed the zero-based budget format which meant every single penny was assigned to a line item. We completed the process a month at a time and made sure it was in place prior to spending any money for the new month. We funded for monthly expenses and added to our sinking funds for purchases like future car repairs, summer camp for the kids and property taxes.

Because of how the calendar fell, twice a year we received a third pay check in a month. Before making the decision to live a life of Christ-centered financial wellness, we saw our third checks as a super-sized allowance. The third check was the time to splurge and make large purchases. We treated our third checks the same way many people treat a tax refund. Lots of toys and fun. Little to show for it when the month ended.

After we got serious about digging our way out of debt, we slowly began to see the third check as an opportunity to make a huge dent in our debt. We learned how to project our income and expenses, and then used the third check to set up the next month for a win. We also planned for a few non-debt snowball expenses like funding our Christmas gift purchase envelope for the kids and setting up our medical envelope with a large influx of cash. Very little (if any) went to allowance-type purchases.

It was all very adult-like. We were serious about our money and making mature decisions. It felt good. It felt good to see the progress made on our debt elimination plan. It felt good to be able to project huge chunks of cash leaving our checking account with a purpose. It felt good to know we were shortening the amount of time left to make payments to creditors. It all just felt good.

The shift into fiscal maturity was happening and we were responding well. We were becoming good stewards of what God gave us to manage. And because we were more intentional with our third check, we began to have more and more large chunks of money show up. Random medical reimbursements, unexpected bonuses from work, class action lawsuit settlements were coming every few months.

Instead of having two "third checks," we once experienced a season with six in one year. On an average of every other month, a large sum of money showed up. We did the same thing with each one. We sat down, devised a strategy and paid off a huge chunk of debt.

For as long as I could remember, it was my desire to feel financially savvy. I wanted to feel as if God could trust me with more because I was managing well what He already gave. And slowly, with each third check, I began to settle into the feeling. It felt so good to know I was becoming financially trustworthy. It was a feeling I never wanted to forget, and I knew I never would. This time, I finally found my financial rhythm.

Your Turn…Your Perspective: Name a time when you felt financially weak. When have you felt financially strong? How do you know when your financial strength is wavering?

Prayer: Lord, thank You for the opportunity to finally get it right. Thank You for not giving up on me. Thank You for the growth of spiritual and financial muscles. I want to feel strong and capable. I pray to stick to Your plan, so that one day, I will be.

Day 83
Plugging Money Holes

PROVERBS 1:25

Keith firmly believed a car dealer service center was superior and was adamant about getting all our maintenance performed at dealerships. Since we both drove older vehicles, it was not uncommon to have a laundry list of repairs presented to us every time we went in for routine maintenance. It created a great deal of anxiety for me. I knew Keith would want to get everything repaired and I fretted over not having the money to do so.

There was very little extra money in our early budgets because of all the minimum payments going out. We did not have a lot of financial room for unplanned repairs. I prayed every time we needed an oil change. "Please, Lord. Please let there be no immediate maintenance issues this time."

We were intentional in making sure we did not get oil changes on both vehicles in the same month. Only $100 was budgeted monthly for maintenance during our early budgets and there was no way we could get the oil changed in both vehicles and stay within budget.

One day, Keith took his truck in for an oil change. When he came home, he told me some additional repairs were needed and the total bill was $283. I was stunned. I just looked at him. I asked him where the money to pay for the extra repairs would come from. He did not have an answer. In his mind, since he did not use a credit card, everything was okay. He gave no thought to our budget process. The concept of saying no to the added repairs, and scheduling them for another day, never crossed his mind.

I was so angry. Hot tears sprang into my eyes. I wondered if we would ever get out of debt. Even though we received a "great income" by most people's standards, we saw very little of it. It came in and it went out in the form of debt payments, medical bills and car repairs.

What made matters worse was the amount of the overage. It was only a difference of $183, but we were held hostage because of it. There was no financial margin in our lives. I was angrier at the state of our financial affairs than I was at Keith not following the financial plan.

It took me a few hours to work through my anger. I asked Keith to sit with me, so we could rearrange the budget to make up for the amount he overspent. I knew he was remorseful. In his mind, it was his responsibility to keep our vehicles safe and well maintained. I knew his overspending was not malicious, but I really needed him to see the importance of staying on budget.

We agreed to both give up our personal "fun" money, in addition to our date money, to make up the difference. It was not an easy month. I had to make the decision to not be bitter, and to embrace the realization of us being in this together. It was an important lesson which taught us the value of working together. It also taught us the importance of not making purchases without consulting each other *and* the budget.

Your Turn...Your Perspective: In what ways have you neglected to follow your budget? How did you adjust to include the added expense? What did you learn about yourself from the experience?

Prayer: Lord, I pray to give and receive grace to my loved ones. Help me to see them through Your eyes. I pray to not hold grudges, but to be kind and considerate. I pray for peace as I am faced with difficult financial decisions. I pray to make good money choices.

Medical Meltdown
LUKE 12:29-30; JEREMIAH 33:6

In the first few years of our debt-reduction process, Keith and I were also still trying to find solutions to his mystery health issues. We found a local naturopath who seemed knowledgeable and we began the process of implementing a new food and medication regimen. We did not yet have a medical fund; we simply reallocated money from as many envelopes as we could to pay for the visits.

Allocations were very random, and as a result, I always felt nervous before a doctor's appointment. On one such visit, the total cost of the appointment was over $600. I literally felt weak in the knees and began to have a panic attack right in the office. Keith held on to me while I attempted to regain my composure. We paid the bill and he got me to the car.

I was in tears before we got completely out of the building. We did not use a credit card. The money to cover the expense was in the bank. Why was my response so overwhelming? Why did I emotionally (and physically) crumble? What was the root of the anxiety? There were so many unanswered questions. I was embarrassed to have responded with such fear.

As I paid the bill, all I could think about was how much money was being diverted from debt payments. At the rate we were going, we would never get out of debt. I saw every extra payment as a dagger in our already hemorrhaging budget. I felt so much despair at our circumstances. I never felt as hopeless as I did standing in the doctor's office handing over more money.

We both sat in the car feeling defeated and stunned. I felt defeated at my response to the amount of the medical visit, and he was stunned by my meltdown. We sat quietly for several moments before we held hands and prayed. We prayed for understanding and peace. We prayed for courage to continue the very long journey before us. We prayed for health and healing.

Over the next few months, we began to create a medical fund. By choosing to move money from payments toward the debt snowball ahead of time, it did not feel as if we were taking money away from debt reduction to pay medical bills. It was amazing how much peace of mind I began to have because money was allocated for medical expenses.

Our attitudes also changed. We began to see the true extent of our financial resources. We really were making progress. And the medical bills were only a setback, not a complete derailment. If we truly trusted God's plan, we would continue to walk in the promise of it until it was fulfilled.

It was a powerful lesson which took time to embody completely. We were determined to see it through to the end, no matter how long it took.

Your Turn…Your Perspective: Think about the emotions you have about your financial situation. Do you feel hopeful or overwhelmed? How much of what you feel has to do with your spiritual walk?

Prayer: Lord, thank You for hope. Thank You for helping me to trust You completely, even when I cannot see Your plan unfold. I pray You continue to show me the way to financial freedom.

Day 85
Living in Lack
NEHEMIAH 9:21; JOHN 10:10

About a year into our marriage, Keith and I experienced a breakthrough. It was building for a few months as we continued to tread water financially. There were 19 debt payments leaving our checking account each month. At the same time, we were learning how to be married and merge our money. Added to the mix was the mountain of medical expenses surrounding our mysterious illnesses. We were barely surviving financially.

Each change in the budget sent me into a tailspin. Keith's responses were not as extreme as mine, but he was also affected. Medical meltdowns, cringes at car repairs, and financial fiascos from the food bill all created a heavy air in our home. We felt defeated and dazed by our situation. We were losing the war being waged on our finances. We could do nothing but pray and continue to take it one day at a time.

We discovered Financial Peace University around this time, and it became our life line. We began to form a concrete strategy for debt reduction and felt major victories with each small win. One day, we were down to 17 debt payments and our debt snowball was turning over. A few months later, a few more debts were gone and the spring in our financial step created confidence in our ability to make it through.

We were hungry for more information on how to live well financially. We began reading more and discussing what we learned with each other over dinner every night. Gone were the fictional characters who consumed our time and mental energy. We replaced them with books on wealth, success, and God's plan of abundance.

We began to recognize the patterns of behavior which led to so many poor financial choices. Slowly, over time, our choices began to change. We were less reactive and more proactive financially. With each passing month, we made slow progress – one financial foot in front of the other.

One day we were having dinner and discussing the latest financial issue to which I responded poorly. The money was available to cover the emergency, but I allowed the situation to temporarily remove the sense of plenty we were experiencing. Keith stopped mid-sentence and stated with authority, "I am tired of living in lack! I will not continue to be poor!"

There it was. So subtle, but so true. The core of our issues, the root of our problems was the spirit of lack which clung to us like an ill-fitting coat. It was there in the back of our minds at every turn, ready to remind us of our financial deficiencies. It was ingrained in each of us since childhood. We brought it into our marriage and it multiplied and spread like a bad germ. It was the ultimate form of financial baggage.

Keith's statement was a blessing in disguise. It hung in the air and we both breathed it in. It was the statement needed for us to turn financially and head in a different direction once and for all.

We drew a line in the sand right then and there. No more living in lack. We decided to no longer have a poor state of mind. Our future was upon us, and we embraced it abundantly.

Your Turn…Your Perspective: What financial baggage do you carry? What is your "living in lack" story? What can you do today to no longer live in lack?

Prayer: Lord, thank You for provision. I have no reason to feel poor because You promised abundance. I stand on Your word and boldly claim Your promise as my own. Please show me the areas of my life where I still cling to the spirit of lack. Give me the courage to completely trust Your provision for my life.

Teach My People

PROVERBS 12:15; JOHN 10:10B

Teaching FPU was more than just a way to serve our community. To Keith and me, it provided a lifeline which kept us tied to our goal of becoming debt-free and leading a life of Christ-centered financial wellness.

We saw teaching FPU as a way for us to stay "gazelle intense" and help others at the same time. It made our journey more meaningful by frequently sharing our stories with our class members. In many instances, they were more hopeful because we just experienced a situation they were currently going through. We took the opportunity to walk "the baby steps" with our FPU classes.

We decided early on to be very transparent with our class members. We shared our successes and failures; details about our spending, income, major purchase decisions and more. It was as if we moved ourselves into a glass house for all to see how we lived. It was our desire to take away all excuses about why FPU would not work for them. We wanted our class members to see their situation was not too big to overcome. We could do it, and they could do it too.

We were cheerleaders and accountability partners. We prayed with couples on the brink of divorce and pleaded for them to not give up on their marriages. We implored them to trust God and each other just a little while longer. We knew money problems were the symptom of a bigger issue, and recommended counseling and books for them to read. We gave them examples of how we communicated about tough subjects in hopes they would see the value in openly discussing their frustration with their spouse.

We also gave tough love to those who needed it. We refused to allow singles to settle for their current situations just because their income may be lower than a married couple. We reminded them of just how valuable they were to God's kingdom and all they could do with their income when they were debt-free.

Our classroom was a "no excuse" zone. Everyone was expected to do their homework. We made ourselves available before class and afterwards to help clear any confusion still unresolved. We were patient with those who did not quite "get it" and applauded those who were moving full steam ahead with their budgets.

It was also a safe haven. The deepest fears shared were prayed over. Our prayer journals were full of the needs of our class members; no concern was overlooked. Hope was a three-course meal served every week with chips, salsa and trail mix.

It was our desire to make sure our FPU class members left with more than just a financial strategy for life. We wanted our students to know the hope of abundant living in Christ. He made it available to each and every one of us. All we needed to do was own it for ourselves. The Lord gave us a game plan for abundance and tasked us with the awesome responsibility to make sure as many people embraced it as possible. Game on!

Your Turn...Your Perspective: Who do you know who needs encouragement in their finances? Who encourages you? What is your level of transparency towards both?

Prayer: Lord, I pray to stay sensitive to the needs of those around me. Keep me mindful of my journey and not forget the pain and victories of it. I pray to not shrink away from any opportunity to help someone learn what I am learning. In Jesus' name.

Week Three

The first time Keith and I taught Financial Peace University, we were so excited. We were following the plan ourselves and saw a drastic improvement in the speed of our debt reduction. We were gaining significant momentum and felt great about the progress we were making.

The first two weeks were great. There were 25 people in our class and the diversity was incredible. Married couples and singles, people with young kids, no kids, adult kids and grandkids were all represented in our class. We stayed late each week and scheduled individual coaching sessions to help as many as we could. We were on a spiritual and emotional high, humbled to see how the Lord was using us.

It all went according to plan until the third week of class. Keith and I had a horrible argument. We were not immune to disagreements, but nothing like the week three argument. It was awful and lasted for days. We could not seem to get past it. It started on a Wednesday, and by Friday, it was no better. I made an appointment to see our family counselor since we could not seem to find our way though it on our own.

Week four of our FPU class was strained. It was hard to be a team when we were at such odds with each other. We did not know what hit us. Our marriage foundation was shaken, and we still did not have our footing. Keith added his own counseling sessions to the calendar and we both tried to reason our way to a solution to our struggles.

During our life group after week four, we asked for prayer. We also asked for prayer for our FPU class. We were in the section of the class which dealt with budgeting and many were struggling to get through it. As our life group covered us in prayer, one of the members reminded us of the importance of all ministry leaders being covered in prayer.

Suddenly, I realized the source of our issues. We were under spiritual attack. We were at the heart of teaching people how to budget, get out of debt, and manage their money God's way. Wow! If the enemy could keep Keith and me from being a team, he could limit our effectiveness in our ministry. It almost worked.

We immediately began to pray and ask for a covering for our marriage and our ministry. We repeated the request each time we started a new class. Weeks three and four were still sometimes stressful, but they never reached the level of attack we experienced during the first session. In the years since, we became much more aware of the possibility of spiritual warfare and worked to limit its effect on our ministry.

We could have stopped teaching or limited how we interacted with our class, but instead chose to move into our ministry full throttle. We saw the attack as proof we were on the right path. The enemy never bothered those who did not make a difference. We were confident in making a difference for the people in our FPU class and were proud to be on God's team. We knew He was protecting us, and nothing could keep us from doing our part.

Your Turn…Your Perspective: How have you worked to grow God's kingdom? What difficulties have you experienced in the process?

Prayer: Lord, use me to grow Your kingdom. I want to be a part of someone else's financial growth and development. Show me how to impact someone through my financial and spiritual growth. I pray to not be afraid to serve You this way.

The Jones' Family Cornerstones

PROVERBS 13:22A

During the first years of our marriage, Keith and I worked hard to create an emotionally healthy environment for our kids. Since they were not with us most of the year, adjusting to the expectations of our way of parenting was sometimes difficult. They were eight and ten when we got married. It was quite an adjustment for all of us to merge our lives together.

We sought the advice of our family counselor, and using his suggestions as a guide, Keith, the kids and I created the Jones Family Cornerstones. It was important that the kids be involved in the creation of the cornerstones since their lives would be affected by them also.

The Jones Family Cornerstones:
1. Respect
2. Follow Directions First Time Asked
3. Chores and Self Care
4. School and Education
5. If You Don't Know…Ask

We typed them up and made them law by putting them on the refrigerator. All discussions with the kids and their behavior were framed in the Cornerstones. The Cornerstones helped us to not argue with them about our expectations. They already knew.

If an issue arose, a simple question was asked, "What number is that?" The kids immediately knew what the response needed to be. We were able to have conversations with them about their choices and consequences in a way which gave them ownership of the situation at hand.

The application of the Cornerstones was universal. They applied to every situation including issues in school ranging from completing assignments on time to talking in class. "What number is that?" Sibling frustration, or no compassion for others. "What number is that?" Chores or homework incomplete. "What number is that?" Tone of voice too strong or body language unbecoming. "What number is that?"

It was a lot of work to restructure their behavior to match the Jones Family Cornerstones, but we were committed to the process. Each year got a little easier and we learned to adjust our parenting style to account for our kids' personalities. Failure was not an option and we were determined to hardwire the Cornerstones in our kids.

Andy Andrews once said our role as parents was not to raise great kids, but to raise great adults[4]. Keith and I believed the Cornerstones, and a healthy understanding of how to manage money was God's way to help us on our path to raise two good adults. It was our desire to leave them more than money as an inheritance.

Your Turn…Your Perspective: What guiding principles do you have for your life? Who has benefitted from your use of them?

Prayer: Lord, help me to be a good role model to those around me. Give me the courage to go against the ways of the world. I pray for guidance on how to leave a Godly inheritance to my loved ones.

Day 89
Ooh-Rah

PROVERBS 21:20

Keith is a Marine. Notice I said, "is." Even though he was no longer active duty, he still is and always would be a Marine. When his platoon announced plans to have a reunion in Florida, he announced to them he would not be attending. The guys did not understand. Many of them knew of our goal to become debt-free but did not get how this impacted their military reunion. Keith explained his commitment to being debt-free before taking any trips.

They could not imagine the reunion without him. Several of his closest friends decided to chip in and pay for his airline ticket. Another friend offered to share his hotel room. All Keith would need was spending money for the week. He was so excited when they presented him with their offer.

Since the date for the reunion was almost a year away, Keith decided he would save his "blow money" to use for the trip. We each received $40 a month for clothing and $40 to spend any way we decided ("blow money"). Keith did not distinguish between the two categories of money, but instead counted his as $80 for the month.

He saw the reunion as a challenge to save for something important. It meant a lot to him for his friends to make an investment in him, and he wanted to do his part. He had not seen many of his platoon members in years and looked forward to reconnecting. He calculated how much he wanted to take with him and set about budgeting his expenses to make sure there was enough money for the trip.

He faced several financial crossroads during the year. Simple "Ooh, I want one!" purchases were later returned in favor of saving for his upcoming trip. He resisted the urge to buy more workout gear. Book buying from Amazon was limited. He was very thoughtful with every purchase. He kept his goal at the forefront of his mind and viewed every purchase through the lens of how it would impact his trip.

I encouraged him along the way and often asked how his goal was progressing. He would proudly share the new amount saved and we would both celebrate his success. As the trip approached, he reassessed how much money was saved. He began to scrutinize his purchases even further and purchased fewer and fewer items. He put all unnecessary purchases on the back burner as he worked to hit the goal of funding his portion of his trip.

It was wonderful watching him work on such an important goal. And it felt good to know Keith was just as committed as I was to us being debt-free. I was thankful to know we were in one accord. Becoming debt-free would be so much sweeter because we worked together to achieve it.

Your Turn…Your Perspective: What things do you need to delay to meet your goal? What goal do you have which is worth delaying small, daily pleasures to achieve? What areas in your life still need to be tweaked to fit your long-term goals?

Prayer: Lord, please help me be more intentional with saving for what I want. I pray for the willpower to say "no" to impulse purchases. I want to see being debt-free as a priority. I pray to align myself to Your Will and stay on the path You have set before me.

Day 90
Sacrificial Giving

LUKE 12:30

A friend of ours lost her job. She was single and was relatively new to the city. None of her family lived in the area. Several months passed and she was still without employment. We saw her every week at church and Bible study, and always tried to encourage her.

One day, during my morning devotion, I felt the Holy Spirit prompting me to give her money for groceries. We were in the early stages of paying our debt snowball and did not have a lot of room in our budget. While I felt sad about her predicament, I did not immediately understand this new prompting to assist her.

Our last Bible study was on sacrificial giving. I understood the concept and thought understanding was good enough. I saw the irony in the situation as I slowly embraced the lesson I was in the midst of learning. When I realized the gift of grocery money was to come from our own grocery budget, I was not excited. I did not get all warm and fuzzy inside. Instead, I felt apprehension and fear.

I told Keith about my time with the Holy Spirit. I shared the idea of giving some of our grocery money to our friend. I thought we should give her $40. I knew it was not much, but I rationalized since she was single she would not need a lot of groceries and $40 would go far. I knew it was a "comfortable" sacrifice, but it was a sacrifice nonetheless.

Keith huffed at my suggestion and said it was not a sacrifice at all. Since we worshipped together, he learned what I learned about sacrificial giving – only *he* embraced it fully. When he said we would give her $100, my heart sank. How on earth would I make our grocery budget meet our needs with a $100 reduction?

Did Keith not realize how difficult it was to buy groceries on our existing budget? Obviously, he did not! There was no way we could take a $100 budget cut and have enough groceries for the month. On and on I went in the split second after his response. There must be another way.

Then it hit me. My thoughts were contrary to the very idea of sacrificial giving. I was incapable of meeting our needs, but God could. And He did. We did not miss the $100 reduction and our friend truly benefited from the gift. And most importantly, God got the glory all the way around.

It was an incredible lesson for me and it pushed my faith to new levels. I learned to trust the Lord in a way I did not even know I needed. I always knew He was there, but this experience taught me to really see Him for what He could do.

It was easy for me to trust when I knew the stakes were not high. It took a much greater faith to trust Him when groceries were on the line. It was like jumping off a ledge when the ground is only a few inches away compared to taking a plunge from 12 feet in the air. Ultimately, I chose to trust He would catch me. I was thankful I chose to be obedient.

Your Turn...Your Perspective: Have you ever given sacrificially? If so, how did the decision to sacrificially give impact you? If not, have you ever had the opportunity to give sacrificially? Is it something you can consider now?

Prayer: Lord, thank You for gently prodding me to trust You always. Thank You for loving me enough to teach me the importance of sacrificial giving. Thank You for allowing me to see the beauty of Your Will being done.

Jones' Family Barbecue
1 KINGS 17:16

Mealtime was a favorite time in our house. Except for the occasional TV trays in the living room to watch a movie, all our meals were eaten at the table. It gave us the opportunity to bond and catch up. It was the perfect setup for us since I loved to cook, and my family loved to eat. A match made in heaven.

As was the case with most families with kids, our food budget expanded as the kids got older. One year, it practically doubled during their summer visit. Our overall budget took a big hit and I knew I needed to rethink the menus for the next year in order to not completely eliminate paying on our debt snowball for the summer months.

Keith's one comment on our family dining was it must taste good. Since we only ate chicken and fish, I needed to get creative. Our evenings were almost always full, which meant I chose meals which did not require a great deal of prep.

I tried my hand at pulled barbeque chicken in the crockpot. It was a new dish for us and I was not sure how it would turn out. I was prepared to freeze individual portions and eat it all myself if it did not turn out well. No chance of that happening! It tasted amazing and took very little time to prepare. I was able to get four days of dinner for four people from just three pounds of organic chicken. It was as if the chicken multiplied.

I added an inexpensive homemade organic coleslaw (cabbage is the cheapest vegetable on the planet) and a salad for our son (we always kept romaine lettuce in the house). Our daughter, Keith, and I preferred eating our barbeque served over tortilla chips instead of a bun. Since we bought the tortilla chips from the local wholesale warehouse, they were always in the house and in great supply.

When guests came to visit, they ate what we ate. Since the recipe made so much, very rarely did having guests impact the rest of the meal planning for the week. I enjoyed watching the kids educate our guests on the best way to enjoy our crockpot barbeque chicken. No one knew its place on the menu was to keep the grocery budget from bulging. And it did not matter. They were full; they were happy; they were satisfied. It was all I needed.

The result was about $30 for dinner for four, for four days. I learned to rotate a two-week menu through the summer, and our new favorite meal of pulled barbeque chicken and coleslaw was on the menu for three of the five weeks. The kids loved to see the crockpot come out because they knew pulled barbeque chicken was on the menu. Our daughter and I mastered the coleslaw recipe, which also created a great bonding opportunity.

It felt good to give my family food they enjoyed, and it helped us come in under budget for the summer. Our time around the table was incredibly valuable to us. Even though they rarely said so, we knew the kids enjoyed it as well. A new family favorite was born out of a desire to eat good food and still keep our debt snowball turning over. What a blessing!

Your Turn...Your Perspective: What ways have you stretched areas of your monthly budget? How have you gotten your family involved in your financial goals?

Prayer: Lord, I pray for creativity and the resolve to stay on budget. I pray to never justify ambivalence. Help me to be content.

PROVERBS 11:1

When I moved to Kansas from Northern Virginia, I left behind a lot of favorites. My favorite Thai restaurant still held a top spot in my heart. It was second only to my favorite neighborhood American grill and the pumpkin cheesecake which graced its menu every fall just in time for my birthday. The autumn leaves were not nearly as vibrant in Kansas as in Virginia, and I missed the little hole in the wall with the best fried fish I ever tasted.

At the top of the list of things I missed, however, was my eye doctor. I never met anyone like him. He was incredibly thorough and attentive, right down to the little tube of breath spray he used before coming in for the up close and personal part of the exam. He diagnosed my dry eyes years before they became an issue and was always sure to explain any changes in my vision. He was cool.

When I moved to Kansas, I found it difficult to find a suitable replacement. Our vision insurance was excellent and offered lots of providers for me to choose from, but none offered the care and service of my optometrist in Virginia. Finally, after three years of searching, I found an acceptable eye doctor.

My dry eyes were getting worse, and a new procedure was recently available. My new eye doctor felt I would be a perfect candidate. The problem was it was not covered by insurance and was over $900 per eye. With all our other medical expenses, I struggled justifying the amount.

A few months later, I decided to check out the home page for the procedure. My new doctor boasted about being the only doctor in the area performing the procedure, but the website said otherwise. As I researched the other two doctor offices that were authorized to perform the procedure, I discovered their fee for the procedure was 30% less than what my eye doctor quoted! What? Was my new doctor price-gauging?

Hoping it was an isolated incident, I found the website for the frames I purchased from him. Sure enough, the Manufacturer's Suggested Retail Price (MSRP) for my frames was literally $200 less than the amount I paid.

I was angry for days. I thought of calling and confronting him, but knew it was a moot point. I thought of reporting him to the Better Business Bureau (BBB), but the reality was his practices were not illegal, just immoral. I was left with one course of action. It was time to resume my search for another eye doctor.

I learned a lot from the experience. I learned it was our responsibility to make sure our money worked for us, and not those around us. It was our responsibility to ask the questions and vet the vendors before simply handing over our hard-earned money. I was too trusting and paid the ultimate price of overpayment because of it. A second opinion is always needed when large sums of money are involved.

Dave Ramsey's Financial Peace University included a lesson called "Buyer Beware." The premise of the lesson was to teach class members how to put separation between sales people and the class members' money. The experience with the eye doctor really hit home. I was the buyer and it was my job to beware.

Your Turn…Your Perspective: What instances of "buyer beware" have you experienced? What lessons did you learn?

Prayer: Lord, thank You for insight. Please help me not be foolish and gullible with the resources You have given me. Give me patience to vet my purchases and shop wisely before making final decisions. I pray for true financial wisdom.

Day 93
The "House"

PSALM 16:7

Keith and I used a budget every day of our marriage. The first year was tough going. There was a ton of debt and not much disposable income. We wanted very much to honor the Lord with our finances. Because of the size of our debt, the numbers for non-essential items got smaller over time to increase the amount of money going to debt reduction.

I do not remember when it happened, but at some point, the budget became known as the "House." The "House" paid for one pedicure a month for me, but I used my personal money if I wanted a second one. The "House" paid for the occasional dinner out with Keith's Bible study group, but he contributed to the office fundraiser from his own money.

The "House" was a very real part of our debt-reduction process, and we spoke about it as if it were a real person in our home. Our kids would sometimes ask if the "House" would contribute to an event. They knew the decisions were ultimately made by us but understood the process of budgeting for everything.

Once the budget was set for the month, no changes were made without extensive discussion. They learned to inform us of what they needed sooner instead of later. If they wanted Keith to chaperone a field trip or attend an event at school, they told us the day the flyer was sent home, not two days before the event. Since we lived four hours away, trips during the week needed more coordination. This concept took a while for them to learn, although it did get easier as they got older.

The kids both experienced the disappointment of us not attending a special event because they informed us too late. We also were not without our own disappointment. We wanted to attend every event we could but needed to draw the line with the expenses associated with last minute trips.

There was no point having a budget if we ignored it every time a new opportunity to spend money presented itself. Our kids knew we were working to get rid of debt but did not understand how much it impacted them. Saying, "No," to them was one of the most difficult parts of our journey, but we decided it was more important for them to learn the lessons associated with financial responsibility than to simply ask and receive what was requested every time. We wanted to teach them the importance of timely communication and financial planning. By making the "House" a part of day-to-day discussions, we were also able to teach them the importance of setting a budget and sticking to it.

The key for us was to be consistent and remind our kids how much we loved them and wanted to be a part of their lives. While it was hard for us to say no, we knew it was necessary. We chose to be governed by the "House," which meant our kids were too. Our hope was for them to one day have their own budget, with their own version of the "House" as part of it.

Your Turn…Your Perspective: How do you handle tough discussions with the young people in your life? What unique ways do you use to teach fiscal responsibility?

Prayer: Lord, please help me to see my budget as an essential part of my journey of Christ-centered financial wellness. I pray for discipline and consistency. Please help me to resist impulse spending, even when it is a "good" purchase.

Day 94
Trade Off

PROVERBS 3:28

I always loved a good massage. It was one of the guilty pleasures I enjoyed most; I especially loved when someone else paid for it. Our Flexible Spending Account (FSA) viewed massages as eligible submissions, so I usually scheduled one or two when FSA money was available.

Even though it was something I knew I greatly benefitted from, I struggled putting it in the budget. While it probably needed to be a monthly expense, I still viewed it as a luxury item. Keith disagreed every time I requested his assistance with a backrub. My tight shoulders and rock-hard neck muscles were the indicators of my need for more time on the table.

When we moved to Kansas City, I left behind two really good massage therapists. It took me years to find them, and I knew I would miss their expertise. Three years after our move, I still did not have a suitable replacement. Then I received a gift certificate for my birthday. I was excited to be able to get a massage but hoped I would not be disappointed in the therapist.

In addition to not being sure if the massage therapist was skilled, the salon was quite a distance from our house. Another drawback. I was not sure if this would be a good experience but tried to keep an open mind.

I was pleasantly surprised with the skills of this massage therapist. She used heat (which I loved) and was able to get rid of several of the knots living in my shoulders. Her hands were strong, the environment was serene, and the music was soothing music. I was thoroughly impressed.

After the appointment, I took time to ask her a few questions about her business. I learned she had been a massage therapist for almost ten years but just recently opened her own salon. She mentioned the struggles she encountered with marketing and business development. I could tell she could use some help by the images used on her flyers and business cards. I told her of my experiences with my own small businesses, and of my time managing a small business resource center. I expressed to her my desire to help in any way I could.

She was shocked at the offer. Her body language and facial expressions indicated she was used to figuring things out on her own. Someone offering her assistance was foreign to her and the relief on her face was visible. She asked me how much I charged for my time. I explained I did not want payment, but simply wanted to help her. She shook her head in disbelief. Her next statement caused me to also shake my head in disbelief. She asked if she could pay me in massages. She wanted to barter? Wow! Talk about win-win.

We were both excited about the possibilities. I was a firm believer in small businesses supporting each other whenever possible. Even though I no longer assisted small businesses for a living, I relished the opportunity to assist whenever I could. Add really good massages to the mix and it was a match made in heaven.

I was thankful not to miss this chance by letting distance and unfamiliarity keep me away. Stepping out of my comfort zone created a great new adventure for me and my new friend. So thankful!

Your Turn…Your Perspective: Describe a time when you were able to bless someone with the gift of time. When were you last blessed by someone else sharing their time?

Prayer: Lord, I pray for the courage to step out of my comfort zone. I pray not to lose sight of the importance of being available to others. I thank You for the many people who have supported me on my journey and pray for those who are still in need.

Day 95
Liquid or Solid

PROVERBS 30:25

We spent a lot of time driving. We were four hours away from the kids and traveled back and forth to St. Louis often. We also did a good bit of sightseeing when the kids were with us. The result was a lot of time in the car.

Our routine was down to a science. I drove out from the house; Keith drove back. Each child had his/her preferred spot. Snacks were always with us, and if the trip was long enough, a picnic was also included. We were never without food or bottled water because planning ahead kept us from spending money on restaurants and random food purchases.

The one exception to our planning was the occasional fountain drink from our favorite convenience store. There were locations throughout the Midwest, and Keith and I often treated the family to a fountain drink when we stopped for gas. We each got to choose what we wanted.

Keith and I included the cost of drinks in our budget for the trip. It seemed like such a small thing to budget, but we still chose to include it. We knew the danger of forgetting the small items. If we were not careful, and did not think through every purchase, we could blow our budget with small, random purchases.

I noticed a trend with our son during these outings. He would ask for a frozen drink instead of the regular fountain drink. Each time I said, "no." On the surface, it was a small request. The price difference was less than $1, but we wanted our kids to understand the sacrifice necessary in sticking to the budget.

We knew how much drinks cost and saw the purchase as a treat. If we gave in to the request for frozen drinks, we set the stage for our kids to believe the budget was flexible and could be changed for any reason. We needed them to learn the value of thinking though each purchase, and how small purchases today would impact the ability to purchase tomorrow.

One day I decided to try a different approach. As we pulled into the gas station, and all piled out to get our fountain drinks, I told our son he could purchase a frozen drink if he paid the difference. His eyes perked up and he asked how much it would cost. I walked him through how to determine the total based on what size drink he wanted. He thought about it for a few minutes, and then decided to increase the size of his drink and make it frozen.

He was so excited about his purchase, and I was excited to be on both the giving and receiving end of a valuable lesson. While it was important for them to understand budgeting, it was also important for them to have a say in what they wanted.

Our son received ownership and a sense of purpose, but I had forgotten the value of both. I was thankful for the reminder.

Your Turn…Your Perspective: What was the biggest lesson you have learned from a small purchase? How different is your thought process around a large purchase versus a small one?

Prayer: Lord, please help me balance the need for frugality with the opportunity to experience Your gifts. I pray for discernment as I work towards Christ-centered financial wellness. Thank You for grace when I get it wrong.

Day 96
Can We Talk?

PROVERBS 15:22

Budgeting became a way of life for Keith and me pretty quickly. We understood our situation was not ideal and would not get better if we did not make major adjustments. We saw the value of having a financial coach early on, and our coach required us to maintain an active and up-to-date budget.

It took several months to figure it out, but we did. Once we got our system down, it only took us a short amount of time each month to fine tune our expenses and get our budget set for the next month. Creating the budget was the easy part. Maintaining it was a different story.

Several times each month, we needed to go back and adjust. The constant changes to our diet because of our health care needs, meant the food budget was a moving target. Medical expenses also adjusted midstream most months, and we had to adjust right along with them.

Car repairs were another area requiring constant monitoring. We worked hard to make sure both cars were not scheduled for maintenance in the same month. But since both vehicles were over 200,000 miles, it was not always possible.

Communication was key through it all. Many times, I found myself on the phone with Keith. "Organic chicken is on sale this week. Are you okay with me moving some extra money into the food budget so we can stock up? The mechanic said it will only cost $200 more if we do it now because they already have the car open. If we do it next month, the labor will be more. We can move the money from the kid's camp fund to cover the difference."

On and on the conversations went. We talked about moving money at least two or three times a week in the beginning. It was all very reactionary. Over time, however, the conversations lessened. The car repairs went down once we purchased newer vehicles and we finally found a rhythm with the food budget. Medical expenses were still a moving target, but because we were paying off debt and our income was increasing, there was more money to put towards them.

We talked about every purchase. We even discussed our personal purchases. It was all a part of casual daily conversation.

No arguing, limited frustration, always ending in agreement became our modus operandi. It was beautiful. With all the other frustrations we managed, it felt good to not argue about money. In our financial coaching business, we coached many couples who wondered how we did it. We chose to be very transparent with them, and shared our beginning struggles and how we managed to evolve through it all.

We wanted others to experience the financial peace and harmony we experienced in our home. We thanked the Lord often for the growth and maturity we enjoyed and worked to help as many others as we could.

Your Turn…Your Perspective: If you are married, how is your communication with your spouse about money? If you are single, who do you use as a sounding board about financial matters?

Prayer: Lord, I pray for transparency with my finances. Please help me to not hide. I thank You for the desire to be better in this area of my life. I praise Your holy name.

Day 97
Leftovers

PSALM 136:25

I grew up on leftovers. Keith did not really care if we ate leftovers or not. He could eat the same thing every day for a week and not grow tired. When we first got married, I did not do meal planning. Most days we ate yesterday's dinner for lunch, but there was no rhyme or reason to the process.

As we tightened our budget and began to divert all extra money to our debt snowball, I realized we were throwing away food every week. From the old perspective, it was not a lot – half a serving of pasta sauce, a few stalks of steamed broccoli, one or two chicken wings. But, it was still money being thrown away. If we were serious about making our budget as efficient as possible, we needed to plug every money hole.

We hemorrhaged grocery money through the lack of food planning. Meal planning required forethought and I was not thinking ahead at all when it came to the kitchen. It was not uncommon for me to need to run to the store midweek because I changed my mind about what to cook. I reasoned we were okay since we were not eating out. I did not think about the wasted food, wasted money in extra ingredients (buying more chicken because I did not thaw what was in the freezer ahead of time), and wasted energy. There was a lot of debt left to pay off and I needed to make some big changes in how I approached groceries and meals.

Big changes always started with small changes, and in the season of debt reduction, our small changes started in the kitchen. The first change I made was to decrease the amount of food I cooked. I liked leftovers but did not like to eat them more than two days in a row. Fewer leftovers meant less chance of food being thrown away. I still believed in making larger amounts of staple foods (pasta sauce, chili, soup, etc.) but froze half right away. I also put those foods back in the meal rotation sooner to keep them from being in the freezer too long.

We began having a leftover meal on either Friday or Saturday. All leftovers were pulled out of the refrigerator and heated up. Most weeks I needed to add something else to make sure everyone got enough to eat. I learned to not make a big deal of our mismatched meals, and neither did my family. There was more than enough food for everyone to get full. We all enjoyed the meal and the conversation.

It was a valuable learning experience. During the early years of our marriage, I spent so much time trying to make dinnertime a special event that I forgot it was more about the company kept during the meal. My family did not care if what we ate "matched." They only cared if it tasted good.

Our mismatched meals became our family's solution for too many leftovers. Coupled with better planning (both for meals and grocery shopping), we were able to cut the food budget significantly.

It felt good to tighten the budget and still know my family ate well. The sacrifice did not feel like a sacrifice at all. So much of our life centered on the kitchen and the food we prepared. This was true before our budget adjustment and continued to be true afterwards. Just the way we liked it.

Your Turn…Your Perspective: What activities anchor your family? How do you work those activities around budget restrictions?

Prayer: Lord, thank You for the small pleasures of life. I pray to enjoy each one, even when they need to be adjusted to keep the budget tight during this season of financial growth. I pray the lessons I learn while I'm in this place of life keep me focused on the joy of pleasing You.

Day 98
Furlough

PSALM 33:19; 2 TIMOTHY 1:7

The Federal Government did not have a history of laying off employees. The age range of employees was wide enough to use attrition to manage the need to cut the workforce. When someone in an office retired, or left for any other reason, the position was simply not filled, and the work was absorbed by other employees and no one lost employment.

Occasionally however, it became necessary to balance the budget of an agency by cutting back on the number of hours each employee worked. It was called a furlough.

During the second year of paying on our debt snowball, Keith's agency announced the need to institute a furlough for all employees. Over the course of a two-month period, each employee would lose four days of pay. They would all be required to reduce the number of hours worked by eight each pay period. We received a 30-day notice to prepare for the reduction in income.

It was a small amount of money, and it was embarrassing to think what a significant impact it made on our budget. Our progress on debt reduction was just getting started. The majority of the original nineteen debt line items were still in our budget. Losing a few hundred dollars a month seemed like we were losing thousands of dollars.

I tried not to panic, but I could feel my anxiety increasing each time Keith came home with new information. The closer we got to the start of the furlough, the more anxious I became. I wanted to trust God to get us through, and there was ample evidence of His provision for us. It just seemed so big at the time, though. I was not sure I could give it completely over to Him.

Fortunately, we were working with a financial coach at the time, and we shared our news during the next monthly call. He became the voice of reason for us. He reminded us of the $1000 emergency fund we saved months earlier. He reassured us of our ability to plan for the upcoming financial event, just as we planned for anything else.

He helped us go back through our budget and tighten our categories even further. We looked at our spending for the previous few months to determine which areas could go unfunded for the two-month period. We decreased payment to the debt snowball to zero and padded our checking account with cash. We prepared to hunker down and ride out what felt like a financial hurricane. We prayed. We prayed for God's provision. We prayed for peace and the removal of fear. We prayed for our faith to increase.

We got through it. We got through the furlough without missing any payments, and without incurring any new debt. We weathered a huge financial storm. God once again provided for all our needs. I did not give in to the spirit of fear which hovered nearby the entire time. I trusted God and His plan, and He remained faithful through it all. It was an incredible reminder in letting go and allowing Him to control it all.

Your Turn…Your Perspective: Describe a financially turbulent time in your life. What did you learn from it?

Prayer: Lord, thank You for the many opportunities You have given me to exercise my faith in You. Please help me learn the lessons in order to not repeat them. I pray to never forget all the times You got me through the tough times.

Day 99
Denied

1 JOHN 4:16; ISAIAH 55:8; EPHESIANS 3:20

One day Keith and I found out an expected settlement was denied. I spent months checking the mailbox for a big check. I imagined the amount and what we would be able to do with it. Sometimes I imagined it would be enough to pay off all our remaining debt. Other times it would be enough to get rid of all debt, fully fund an emergency fund, and buy a plot of land for the home we would one day build. I even imagined what it would feel like to sit with Keith as we opened the envelope. Would it be summer or fall? How would it feel to pay the tithe on the sum? Would I cry out with joy or just be silently and humbly thankful? I imagined so many different scenarios of what it would feel like to receive this check.

It was such a letdown to find out it was not coming, and I was beyond disappointed. It took me several days to process it all. It seemed impossible to wrap my mind around the reality of the answer being "No." I resisted the prompt to ask the Lord, "Why?" I knew He was not required to answer me. Ultimately it was His decision how we got out of debt. If He saw fit to not send us a windfall check, it must not be in our best interest.

I was sad for several days. I was so ready to be out of debt. I saw this check as a springboard to the finish line. As I reflected on it, I realized my reaction to not getting the check was the exact reason it did not come. The check could not be our savior. Jesus was our Savior. He would never allow us to replace Him with anything else. Once I realized this, I asked the Lord for forgiveness. I did not want debt reduction to displace Him as my Savior. I also apologized to Keith. I often said I did not want to be the reason we missed a blessing, and yet I did exactly what I did not want to do.

God used this situation to remind me His ways are not our ways, and His thoughts are not our thoughts. I thought God would wipe out our remaining debt in one big sweep using this settlement. The reality was I did not know how He would do it.

I realized this was the beauty of serving a Sovereign and All-Powerful God. This was the beauty of trusting a God who sat high and looked low. This was the beauty of a having faith and knowing God's plan was bigger and better than all we could ask or imagine. I was hoping the settlement check would be the miracle I knew God could provide. But how could it be a miracle if I was able to predict what it looked like?

God was so much bigger than my small mindedness. There was no way to predict how His plan would unfold. It was our responsibility to stay focused on our journey and not get sidetracked by our desire to finish our plan. We were to continue to do the work and have faith in God's ability to deliver us from our situation. While it was difficult to not be disappointed when the circumstances did not unfold the way we thought they would, it was important to not allow our disappointment to cause us to become immobile. We kept moving towards our goal. We knew God would honor the commitment and rejoice with us on the day we were finally debt-free.

Your Turn...Your Perspective: When was the last time you felt disappointed with God's timing? How did you recover? How will you manage disappointment when it shows up again?

Prayer: Lord, thank You for reminding me Your plan is bigger than all I can imagine. Thank You for helping me to hold on to hope. Thank You for being all I need. I trust You, Jesus.

Day 100
Shirts

PROVERBS 3:27; DEUTERONOMY 29:5

Keith was on a small clothing budget long before we got married. He owned a good number of suits, shirts and ties from years of purchases, but they were beginning to look dated.

When we got married, I coaxed him into letting go of some frayed items, but we were not able to replace them right away. Because we were more interested in being debt-free than in being fashionable, we set our clothing budget at just $40 per month for each of us.

His new office in Kansas City was not a suit and tie office. The dress code was much more relaxed. People wore everything from jeans and a polo shirt to a shirt and tie. Slowly, he gravitated to the business casual theme of his coworkers.

I admit I was not excited when Keith began to make the shift to casual attire. I approached work with professional dress and found my productivity tended to be higher on days when I dressed the part. It was ultimately his decision, however, and I supported him in his choice.

After a year or so, Keith announced he was going back to a shirt and tie. He, too, seemed to notice a correlation between dress and productivity, and wanted to elevate his work ethic and efficiency to the next level. He was not fazed by his small wardrobe. He was committed to professional dress.

One day while at work, a colleague dropped by to see Keith. They occasionally hung out together, and we even joined him and wife on a marriage retreat earlier in the year. We all got along well, and Keith was happy to take the break to chat with his friend.

The guy seemed a little nervous at first, and Keith did his best to put him at ease. It turned out his friend came with a gift but did not want it to offend him. He told Keith he owned several dress shirts he wanted to donate but preferred to give them to someone who needed and appreciated them. Keith put his friend at ease. He was the fourth of eight children and was used to "hand me downs." He told his friend he was happy to receive them and thanked him for the offer.

The next day, Keith came home with over thirty new, or almost new, dress shirts. The tags were still on many of them, and they were all designer labels and fit well. It was a humbling experience for Keith. With the switch back to professional dress, this new addition allowed him to rotate several weeks' worth of shirts before wearing the same one again.

Keith appreciated his friend's gift and saw the shirts as confirmation of his decision to step up his level of professionalism. He could have justified the need to increase his clothing budget but, instead, was the recipient of incredible generosity.

He believed the Lord honored his decision with the gift of the shirts. He felt certain he would have missed the gift if he continued to approach work with a casual attitude toward dress. The Lord provided, and Keith saw the value of staying true to his own values. He was blessed by both.

Your Turn…Your Perspective: How does your work ethic honor the Lord? Improvements?

Prayer: Lord, thank You for my work. I pray to not take it for granted. I pray to approach my work with a positive attitude and view it as an opportunity to serve You.

Day 101
Liquid Gold

ACTS 20:35B

Keith was diagnosed with heavy metal poisoning a few years after we got married. A large portion of our monthly budget was allocated to pay cash for medical expenses. Even though it was a huge chunk of cash not going to the debt snowball, it was a blessing to be able to cash-flow all the expenses and not incur any new debt.

Part of the healing process was eating lots of green vegetables. As a result, we ate salads for lunch almost every day. Each week I poached several pounds of organic chicken breasts to use as protein for our lunches. The result was quarts and quarts of seasoned, organic chicken broth. It was like liquid gold. Only once did I pour it down the drain. I learned my lesson quickly and stocked up on quart-sized containers and got busy storing chicken broth.

Keith teased me about how much chicken broth we kept. When I sent him to get something out of the deep freezer, he would come back and say, "Bag number 72 said hello!" There was more chicken broth in the freezer than anything else and I could not use it fast enough. At times it was comical to attempt to manage it all.

I finally decided to give it away. We began to look for opportunities to give away our chicken broth as a way to bless others (and make room for more in our freezer). Quarts and quarts were given to those who were sick, those who were low on funds, and those who knew what to do with it! And of course, we used it ourselves.

Our neighbor was battling cancer…chicken broth for him. A friend had a rare brain disease… chicken broth for him. A friend from church was struggling to make ends meet…chicken broth for her. Life group members loved to cook as much as I did…chicken broth for them. Friends came to visit for dinner…chicken broth for the ride home. We left it on the porch in a cooler for a friend to pick up when she was getting over a cold. We carried freezer bags of it to church and dispensed it from the trunk of our car in the parking lot. It felt good to give. Since we chose not to do any extra giving outside of our tithe during our debt snowball, chicken broth was our way to help our community.

As long as we needed chicken for salads, we would have chicken broth, and it was important to make sure it always had a home. Our friends laughed at our determination to constantly find a new way to give away chicken broth. I did not care.

I knew it was not a lot, but it was my prayer to make a difference for someone with our chicken broth. After we completed paying our debt snowball, we would again be able to give to the charities which were important to us. In the meantime, it was chicken broth for whoever needed it.

Your Turn…Your Perspective: What is your attitude towards giving? What have you shared recently? What are you waiting on until you have more to share?

Prayer: Lord, I pray to always have a heart to share. I pray to be generous to those around me. I pray to give when I can and look for opportunities to serve when I cannot. I pray to keep an open spirit towards Your people.

Day 102
It's Time for Tuna

LUKE 9:24-25

We were in a season of our life which required lots of cash going out for medical bills in addition to our debt snowball. As a result, our food budget once again found itself on the chopping block. So many of my struggles around the budget were related to food. It was hard to wrap my mind around how much money we spent on food. We only ate out a few times a year, but I still constantly tried to find ways to reduce our costs. It was time to review the food budget again.

This particular budget review came with a new game plan. It was time for tuna. Organic chicken breasts were the primary protein in our diet, and we spent almost $25 every week just on chicken. I knew I could recover a significant amount of money each month if I cut back on the amount of poultry we ate. The problem was I was not a big fan of tuna. Keith did not mind it so much, but it was certainly not my favorite.

The bigger question I asked myself was whether getting out of debt and managing the increased cost of our food and medical bills, was worth the sacrifice of eating tuna. Others may not have seen it as a big deal, but to me it was huge. So many niceties from our budget were already gone. Changing to tuna was just another example of how extreme we needed to be to get through this season of debt and emergencies.

When would it end?

I was at a crossroads. I could continue leave the grocery budget as it was, or I could find a way to make tuna more palatable. I chose to work my kitchen magic to find a way to make tuna more than a mundane meal. I learned I could actually enjoy tuna if I ate it the day after making it. The key was small batches.

When we ate chicken for lunch, I poached several pounds every Sunday evening. This process did not work with tuna. I struggled to eat it for lunch after Monday. To make this new meal work, I needed to make less of it more often to enjoy it. It created a little more work but was worth it to be able to cut the cost of our lunch.

I did my research and found our favorite discount warehouse carried a brand of tuna which was environmentally friendly and low cost. It meant I could reduce the cost of our lunch from roughly $5 per day to around $2. Over the course of a year, it was a significant savings. And it all went to debt reduction.

I knew I would not have to eat tuna for lunch forever. But for this season of our journey, I did see it as a necessary sacrifice. The change was one of those small, incremental ones which did not make much of a difference on its own. But each incremental savings chipped away at our debt and got us closer to the next financial season of our lives.

Making the change to tuna was like a dripping faucet which would eventually overflow and flood a house. By itself, it did not have much impact, but added to all the other small, incremental changes we made, we knew the effect was significant.

Your Turn…Your Perspective: Think of your last major sacrifice. What did you give up? For what? How did the outcome impact you?

Prayer: Lord, please help me to keep my eyes focused on You. Help me to see the value in small sacrifices for a greater gain. Thank You for the plan You gave. It never changes. Yesterday, Today, Tomorrow – You are always the same.

Day 103
The Spirit of Lack

1 CHRONICLES 29:11; 2 TIMOTHY 1:7

Keith and I coined a term we used when working with our clients and Financial Peace University class members. While not all our clients and class members fell into this category, the majority of them did. We experienced this phenomenon for most of our lives and were newly free from it ourselves. We called it the Spirit of Lack.

We based the term on 2 Timothy 1:7 (AMP): "For God did not give us a spirit of…fear, but [He has given us a spirit] of power and of love and of…a calm, well-balanced mind and self-control."

The spirit of lack operated in much the same way as the spirit of fear. It stole your future by causing you to question your ability to break old habits and patterns. It caused you to think your life would never be any different than it was in the past. The spirit of lack created fear around money and "poor" thoughts. Poor was a state of mind, and a person with the spirit of lack lived with a mindset of being poor.

We were quite familiar with the spirit of lack and lived with it for what seemed like forever. Our minds were filled with experiences where the spirit of lack ruled our lives. We made financial decisions with a defeatist mindset instead of from a place of strength and power.

The day we broke the spirit of lack was one neither of us would ever forget. It was a doctor's appointment. We budgeted $200 for the appointment, but in the end, it was over $600. I panicked right at the checkout counter. My knees went weak, and I literally could not breathe. Keith did his best to comfort me as we paid the bill and slowly made our way to the car where I burst into tears.

Keith did not understand what was happening. The money to pay the bill was in our checking account; no debt was used. We did not even have to transfer money from our emergency fund. What was my issue? I did not want to spend debt snowball money on medical expenses. I did not want to delay debt reduction yet again.

We sat quietly for a long while. Finally, Keith looked at me and said, "Never again. Never again will we be afraid of money. Never again will we make decisions from a place of financial fear. God has not given us the spirit of fear, even when it comes to money."

In the parking lot of a doctor's office, with well over $150,000 in debt still to be repaid and over $100,000 in medical bills yet to be uncovered, we broke the spirit of lack. Everything about how we viewed money and financial decisions changed. We began to approach each financial decision knowing God was with us, and we would make it through, even if the situation seemed impossible.

We prayed before making big money changes and slowly matured financially to a place of financial freedom. We let go of the spirit of lack long before we were debt-free. It was as if it was a requirement for us to move to the next financial level. We were thankful to be on the other side.

Your Turn…Your Perspective: What was your most profound "spirit of lack" moment? What changes did you make afterwards?

Prayer: Lord, thank You for the many promises You clearly gave me in Your Word. Thank You for guiding me through difficult financial times. Please help me to never lose sight of all Your plan.

Day 104
We Are "The" Joneses

1 CORINTHIANS 12:8

Keith loved to tell people we were the Joneses and keeping up with us would not be a good thing. It would always get a laugh out of the group. We were deep in debt and were years away from becoming free of the bondage we created for ourselves. "The Joneses" in our case were not the ones others wanted to follow. We encouraged them to not follow in our footprints.

Then one day we decided we did want everyone to be like us. We wanted to be debt-free and live a financial life which was pleasing to God and we wanted the same for everyone around us. We embraced the phrase "keeping up with the Joneses" and shared it with as many people as we could.

It was a thought at the very heart of who we were and the legacy we were creating for our family. We understood what value would come for our families, friends and church members when they became debt- free. We just needed them to see it too. But it was counterintuitive to what was currently the American way.

To be like our kind of Joneses, someone would have to be okay with being different. They would need to be thick skinned and go against what was considered normal. We knew it would not be easy for many but prayed others would take up our challenge to be different.

We decided to teach Financial Peace University to be on the front line. We worked with each family one-on-one to help them learn the basic principles played out each week in the videos. We encouraged them, and even after the class ended, checked in every few months to help them navigate their new way of life. We encouraged them to continue to be different and not stop until they crossed the finish line into a life free of debt.

It felt good to give people a different perspective on what it meant to be "the Joneses." It made some uncomfortable since we were so clear to give Jesus credit for our journey, but we did not want to tarnish our witness by holding back. We also worked to give hope to those who did not think they could do it. We told our story as often as we could and were quick to share both the wins and the losses of our journey.

Keith even often used our story as material for his Toastmaster's speeches. We attempted to encourage our coworkers. We shared with members from our church, our friends and family, and our neighbors. If the opportunity presented itself in the grocery store, we shared there also. Anytime we could get someone to stop and think differently about debt, we did. It became our mission.

We did not want people to think it was easy for us. We wanted them to see the sacrifice and the victories of our journey. It was our hope they would see the possibilities of their own debt-freedom if we shared enough of our story. The fear of others thinking we were weird did not deter us. We were on a mission to share our story with as many as we could. And we would not stop until everyone we knew were just like us – debt-free!

Your Turn...Your Perspective: How has your spiritual journey inspired others? When was the last time you gave a testimony about something in your life?

Prayer: Lord, help me to be bold and proclaim the good news of the Gospel. I pray You give me opportunities to share my story and not be afraid. Use me to bring hope to Your people.

Day 105
Road Trip

ROMANS 11:36

When Keith and I moved to Kansas, we knew there would be lots of travel in our future for the next few years. We wanted to spend as much time with the kids as possible. The first year after getting married and starting our new family, the trips created anxiety for me. We attempted to budget for them, but always seemed to go over the limit. Then we would spend the next few weeks scrambling to rearrange other budgeted items to "find" the money we needed to make up for the extra we spent during our road trips.

When we started taking Financial Peace University, we realized our problem was we did not budget enough for the trips! It seemed so simple. Adjust the budget each month to have the money we needed to make the trips work. A small change made the world of difference, and my anxiety over money for time with the kids got smaller and smaller.

We increased the amount budgeted, but still did not want to go overboard and spend a large amount of money on activities and entertainment. We realized we needed to get more creative in how we spent our time with the kids. I spent hours searching Groupon and other online discount sites, looking for inexpensive activities for us to enjoy together as a family. We also traveled with games to make our time in the hotel as much fun as possible.

Our kids were just like other children and outgrew their clothes almost overnight. We budgeted for clothing for church and shopped at consignment shops when possible. It was not uncommon to need to replace shoes and dress clothes every few months, even though they were not worn often. Anything the kids grew out of was donated to a local shelter. We often took them with us when we donated items to help reiterate the importance of sharing and giving back.

We packed meals to cut down on the amount spent on eating out. Since we stayed in hotels (typically paid for with points) which provided small kitchens, I cooked full meals for our weekends away. It was a lot of work, but the money saved was a huge tradeoff. It meant paying on our debt snowball did not take a major hit every time we spent the weekend in St. Louis.

Over time we stayed in St. Louis less and less. Instead we began to drive back to Kansas on the Friday-Sunday weekends. We could no longer justify the cost of a weekend of hotel expenses when there were no hotel points to cover the cost. We lost a good bit of time in the car on those trips because of the distance, but knew it was necessary to keep our expenses low.

It took us a while to find a rhythm. We were committed to finding a solution which did not derail our budget and still give us healthy time with the kids. It was one more way we worked to create tradition for our new family.

Your Turn...Your Perspective: What are your budget busters? How do you respond when you have to make changes to your budget mid-month?

Prayer: Lord, thank You for the desire to keep my budget in line and to live a life free from debt. Help me to make the seemingly hard choices today to have a better tomorrow. Help me to ask for guidance when I need it, and to not be afraid to step out of my financial comfort zone.

Day 106
Business Partners

PROVERBS 6:5

Keith and I decided to build instead of buying a home. The problem was we discovered Financial Peace University before we got started. FPU taught us to wait on our building project until we were out of debt with a fully funded emergency fund. I was not excited.

I was looking forward to undertaking a building project and getting out of a rental. Waiting until we were debt-free meant our project might take years before it got started. I wanted to build now, not later. As frustrating as it was to be delayed indefinitely, I knew it was the right decision. Our debt was huge.

To keep myself busy during the wait, I built our home in my mind and on our vision board. I researched how to design a net-zero energy home. I determined which appliances consumed the least amount of energy, and which style of roof offered the best savings on energy costs. I learned why Volatile Organic Compounds (VOCs) were bad, and how window placement could lower the amount of heat used in the winter.

I found vendors for bamboo floors and porcelain tile while ruling out cabinet makers who were not Forest Stewardship Council (FSC) certified. We interviewed builders and architects and looked at plots of land. I wanted to make as many decisions as possible before it was time to start our building project.

During the first few years of research, we were almost certain we had chosen our general contractor and architect. They were always helpful when we asked questions, we sent them many referrals to help build their business and they specialized in the type of home we wanted to build. Their business was growing steadily, and we felt confident it would be a good experience. But since we were nowhere near ready to begin building, all we could do was watch them work on other projects.

Over time, however, I began to sense some shady business practices. One partner was always level headed and thoughtful. The other seemed to fly by the seat of his pants. Time and time again, the referrals we sent their way reported to us a sense of apprehension in doing business with them. Further discussions also revealed their company was heavily leveraged, and one partner carried an extreme amount of personal debt. One red flag after another appeared over the course of a year. We began to see a pattern of poor business practices, which caused us to reevaluate their company as a potential builder.

Perhaps the delay in our plan to wait was to keep us from choosing the wrong building firm. Could it be our lengthy debt snowball was such to keep us from entering into agreement with shady business partners? I thought of the money, time and negative energy we would have spent if our project started earlier. Building a home was complex enough without adding lack of trust to the list of variables impacting the process.

We chose to be obedient and were blessed in an unexpected way because of it. We decided to keep looking for a suitable builder and vowed to pray our way through the process. No more important decision making without consulting the Lord. He showed us grace during this experience and we did not want it to be in vain.

Your Turn…Your Perspective: What disaster has time saved you from? What lessons did you learn from the experience?

Prayer: Lord, thank You for protecting me from myself and my impulsive tendencies. Please help me to slow down and consult You before executing any decision. I pray for discernment in all money matters.

Day 107
Give. Save. Spend

MATTHEW 25:14

The farther into paying off our debt snowball we got, the more we wanted to learn how to use God's resources wisely. We were hungry for knowledge and gleaned as much as we could. We also wanted to teach our kids everything we learned. Even though we started late, we knew there was still time to get a solid foundation of God's ways of handling money planted in our kids.

We used Dave Ramsey's Financial Peace, Jr™ program as the starting point in the educational process for our kids. The concepts were very applicable to our family, and we made use of them long after we stopped using the visual aids included in the original kit.

The "Give, Save," and "Spend" envelopes were where we put most of our educational focus. Every Saturday was "pay day" in our house, and after they each received their "commissions," we helped them divide it all out into envelopes. Any money in the "Give" envelope was given to the church the next day. They knew we tithed, and we explained the concept to them to apply to their own "income."

The Save and Spend envelopes were harder for us all to implement. Our kids saw our way of living as extreme and did not understand why we spent so little money on activities, eating out and vacations. Neither Keith nor I went shopping without a specific purpose, and all spending was done on a budget.

The kids knew we were paying off debt, but the concept was not tangible to them. They did not see many purchases outside of necessities and found this difficult to comprehend. Since we did not spend much money, it was hard for them to embrace the idea of spending money when they were with us. We encouraged them to take their spending envelopes with them whenever we traveled, but they rarely spent it.

I always felt like we missed the opportunity to make a greater impact in this area. I could have lamented about not having enough time to teach the lessons we wanted them to learn. Instead I chose to focus on what we could teach with the time we were given with our kids. Perspective was a wonderful gift.

Keith and I reinforced the message of healthy spending whenever the opportunity presented itself. A trip to the game room was paid for with "Spend" money. The sweater in the department store was not purchased because our daughter did not want to spend so much on a sweater she liked but did not love. Every decision was discussed, and they were encouraged to actively think through each decision to spend their money. We were always nearby by to provide guidance.

I continued to silently pray for the opportunity to make a bigger impact in their lives financially. Sixty days a year did not allow a lot of time for complex money lessons, but we did the best we could. I knew ultimately it was in the Lord's hands; our job was simply to teach what we learned and provide insight. I chose to leave the rest at His feet and try not to pick it up again every time a missed opportunity passed. If I meant it when I said, "I trust You, Jesus," I must let Him fix it. It was a tough lesson, one which took years to learn.

Your Turn…Your Perspective: What money lessons do you remember from your childhood? Which impacted you the most? How old were you when you realized the value of what you were taught?

Prayer: Lord, so much of what I want takes time and effort to come to pass. I pray for patience as I continue to work the plan You have laid out for me. Please help me to leave all my cares with You. I trust You, Jesus.

Day 108
Coupon Queen

PROVERBS 11:16

One of the things I loved about teaching Financial Peace University was the sharing. The class members were all so different. Each came to class with a unique set of circumstances, life experiences and limiting beliefs. Some were just fed up with not having more to show for their money. Our classes included singles, empty nesters, retirees, blended families, and everyone in between.

During one semester, we discovered a coupon queen in our midst. She knew couponing inside and out. She and a few of her friends studied the system of couponing and had it down to a science. She knew which stores offered double coupon days and which stores offered price matching. She knew which websites offered coupons for organic foods and which were the best for paper products and toiletries. She knew it all.

Most of the rest of us (myself included) did not do much with coupons. I did not even know you could get coupons for organic foods, except the ones right beside the product in the store. We all knew couponing was a great way to stretch the food budget but did not know how to maximize our efforts.

It all seemed so overwhelming. We all agreed it was easier to find another way to cut the food budget than deal with couponing, but our couponing expert was happy to come to our rescue. The week after the last class ended, most of our group reconvened for a crash course in couponing, including the guys.

Our coupon queen taught us how to read the local circulars to discover the best deals. She told us which stores did coupon matching, double coupons and when. She showed us websites and blogs to follow, and even walked us through the sign-up process. She showed us how to buy organic with coupons. We all left with a better understanding of how to incorporate couponing into our budget and overall financial strategy.

She took the time to create handouts for us and sent us home with our own copies of circulars to get started. Her generosity and time were so appreciated. I was especially thankful because I knew she was an incredibly busy woman. She owned two businesses and was married with two kids. They were in the middle of renovating a home, in addition to implementing all they just learned in FPU.

I could tell from her presentation how much effort she put into the preparation. It warmed my heart to see her passion for helping her classmates. It was obvious she saw the value in couponing and wanted to make sure others did also. I realized then the community we were creating. A room full of random people who were now forever connected because of a 9-week commitment. It lasted a lot longer for those who chose to remain in our little family.

When Keith and I decided to teach FPU, we did not know the impact the class would have on us. We did not expect to receive so much love and support from our class members. It was truly a blessing to be a part of the lives of these amazing people, and to have them be a part of ours.

Your Turn...Your Perspective: What random associations have changed your life? How have you added to theirs?

Prayer: Lord, I pray for my own community of like-minded people. I pray to keep an open mind to new ways to stretch my income and make the most of the resources You have given. I thank You for guiding me to the financial finish line.

Day 109
Cheap Organics

We decided to switch to organic foods. The decision was made after Keith was diagnosed with heavy metal poisoning. An organic diet would help limit the number of toxins being added to his body as we worked to get rid of the ones already present. Organic food was not cheap. Once the decision was made, we increased our grocery budget by 50% to have enough money to purchase the food he needed.

Vegetables were a major source of toxins since most commercial farmers used a variety of pesticides on their crops. The Environmental Working Group list, "The Dirty Dozen," helped me to see which vegetables were grown with chemicals and therefore needed to be organic. This was compared to "The Clean Fifteen" list of vegetables which were grown with minimal chemicals and did not need to be organic. Sweet potatoes and avocadoes did not need to be organic, but apples and white potatoes did.

Meats were another area which needed to be adjusted. We ate mostly chicken and fish, so all chicken became organic. I found the stores with the lowest regular price on organic chicken. I also learned to stock up on clearance organic chicken by shopping at stores which froze fresh chicken right before it expired. It was typically discounted by 10-15%. The discount made the marked down prices as affordable as fresh organic at the lowest price. We did not eat much canned foods, but organic canned tomatoes were purchased by the case. We did the same with beans for chili and pumpkin for fall cooking.

Organic tortilla chips, salsa, eggs, spices, non-dairy milk substitutes, etc. were all priced out to determine where they needed to be purchased. Certain items were more economical when purchased in bulk. I learned to put aside a little of our grocery budget to pay for bulk items and began to spread out bulk purchases so there was still enough room in the budget to buy the other items needed.

People did not understand why we chose to eat organic when we cut our budget so drastically in other areas. It was not easy in the beginning; I was very systematic in how I went about choosing our organic foods. It did not change the anxiety I felt about spending such a large portion of our monthly budget on food, however. It took months to fully embrace the reality of this new way of shopping and I continued to look for organic bargains where I could. More importantly, I made sure I stayed within our new, expanded budget.

Ultimately, I realized Keith's health was more important than getting out of debt a few months faster. If he was not healthy enough to enjoy our financial freedom, what was the point in working to become debt-free? We did not view having a larger food budget as a sacrifice. It was a necessity to maintain a healthy quality of life for Keith. It was a tradeoff worth making.

Your Turn...Your Perspective: What are the non-negotiable items in your budget? Are they justified? What are you willing to give up to keep them?

Prayer: Lord, I want my new life more than my old one. I want a different financial life. Please help me make the tough changes to get through this season of my life. Show me who can help me. Show me what to change. I thank You for a community of people who share information. Thank You for helping me keep my priorities in order.

Day 110
The Shelter

ECCLESIASTES 4:14

One year during Christmas break, we chose a homeless shelter as our service project. The kids were with us for the second half of Christmas break, and I found a shelter which needed assistance taking down all the Christmas decorations. We arranged to be there for the entire day and set off on a new adventure.

The kids always reserved judgement about our adventures until after they found out what we were doing. Sometimes they got excited about it, and sometimes they did not. Nevertheless, we knew they would learn something from the experience. As was the case for all of us, it was always a better experience when we approached adventures with a good attitude.

This shelter was different than any shelter we visited previously. Not only was it a shelter with actual residents (many shelters were day shelters), this shelter was home to families and children. Our host gave us a tour of the facility before we began work and shared a little about their mission. They provided emergency shelters and recovery programs for men, women, and families along with after-school and summer programs for kids.

Our kids were quiet during the tour and did not say much as we gathered our supplies and mapped out our strategy to remove several hundred ornaments and strings of lights. After about an hour working and singing Christmas carols, our daughter quietly asked if the children we saw lived there. I told her they did. She asked why, and I explained how some families were having a hard time with the economy. One or both parents either lost their job, or the family just did not have enough money to take care of their household expenses.

Our daughter asked the question, but I knew our son was also listening. I fell silent and allowed this new information to settle into their minds. I was careful not to push. I wanted them to grasp the seriousness of the situation the residents faced.

I wanted to remind them of the two separate Christmas celebrations they experienced while the residents of the shelter did not have one celebration of their own. I wanted to call attention to all the food our son and daughter enjoyed, the gifts exchanged, and the warm beds with internet and television. I chose instead to silently work beside them and only answer the questions asked.

We continued to work for the next several hours and finished removing all the decorations. I watched our kids as we put the supplies away and said goodbye to the new friends. They were very somber as we drove home, and it was a quiet evening. Neither of them ever mentioned the shelter again, but I prayed it left an indelible mark on their minds of what it meant to be blessed.

We learned through the years to lead our children to the place where they could begin to make decisions for themselves. We desperately wanted them to serve others and have a heart to serve God. We knew the more we exposed them to the need, the less they would be able to ignore it. Only time would tell what they chose to do with it. In the meantime, we would keep sharing and praying, and wait for the Lord to do the rest.

Your Turn…Your Perspective: How would your service be different if you were in a different place financially? What can you do to bridge the gap while you work on your goal?

Prayer: Lord, thank You for the blessings I take for granted. I pray to be mindful of all You have continued to provide for me. Please help me to not lose sight of those who are less fortunate then I and treat them with compassion.

Untimely Check-Ups

PROVERBS 1:29

Both Keith and I struggled with an area of the budget. Mine was the grocery budget, his was the car repair envelope. Where I struggled to stay within the limits of our budgeted amount for food, he struggled with scheduling routine car maintenance according to the budget, and not the odometer. In his mind, if it was time to get the oil changed, you got the oil changed. What was the issue?

By this time, we were up to $125 per month for car repairs. We tried to keep our vehicles on alternate schedules so they both did not need routine maintenance at the same time. The problem was Keith did not always check the car repair envelope before scheduling repairs.

It was a constant struggle for us. He wanted to get the cars serviced when the odometer reached a milestone, and I wanted to keep the car repairs on budget. Keith wanted to pull the excess from debt reduction at the time of the car repair, and I wanted to wait another month. Time and time again, we reached an impasse. Frustration, anger and disappointment became a constant part of the car repair process.

I did not know why Keith did not understand my concerns. He did not know why I did not understand his. Neither of us was malicious in our desires. We actually both wanted the same thing – safe vehicles with repairs paid for in cash. Why was it so difficult for us to find common ground? It was foundational to our marriage.

I decided to approach it a different way. I began to pray (what a concept!). I prayed for direction in how to help him see my viewpoint. I prayed for the Lord to help us communicate better. I prayed to not be frustrated and to be more understanding of his viewpoint. I prayed for more money for the car repair envelope.

I prayed for months and slowly began to see a shift. Over time, we argued less about the car repair envelope. He began to talk about upcoming appointments weeks before scheduling them. We also began to review the budget before either of us took a car in for servicing so we both knew exactly how much money was available. The entire situation began to have less stress around it.

We did not make drastic changes. It was small shifts which created the change. I wanted to see his side of things more than I wanted to be right. I believed he wanted the same thing. We wanted to find a way to communicate on car repairs because we knew it would only make our communication stronger in other areas. I wanted to show more compassion and so did he.

We both significantly shifted our attitudes, and I knew it was because of prayer. While my prayer started out as a selfish prayer (Lord, please change Keith's viewpoint!), the Holy Spirit knew what we really needed. We finally found our way to a place of mutual agreement and open communication.

We did not compromise, but instead figured out how to both be heard and how to both feel secure in our journey. It did not happen overnight, but instead was a slow, steady progress. Learning how to communicate about small things made it much easier to communicate when bigger issues came at us full throttle. We were strengthening a key attribute of our marriage, and I knew it would pay dividends in the years to come.

Your Turn…Your Perspective: How well do you communicate in a crisis? How can you improve?

Prayer: Lord, please help me to remain open to communication about my finances. I pray to never lose sight of the need for community, even in money.

Day 112
Scholarship Drafts

The summer after our daughter turned 13, we added a new activity for her to work on during our 6 weeks together. She needed to begin applying for scholarships. When we approached her with the task, she looked at us with the teenage "my parents are weird" stare. We explained our madness, reminding her of the agreement to get as many scholarships as possible to assist with her college education.

While she understood her commitment, she did not understand why she needed to apply now. In her mind, she only needed one scholarship. And of course, it would cover all her expenses for the entire time. She certainly did not think she would apply for a scholarship and not get it. She did not know what it meant to compete in a larger arena than her current peers.

Competition for scholarships was incredibly intense. Most students were easily discouraged and gave up after applying for only a few. Many believed no scholarships were available at all, but we knew otherwise. I funded most of my undergraduate degree with lots of small scholarships. The smallest ones did not carryover past a single semester. As they ran out, I replaced them with student loans.

Our strategy built on what I did to get through college. We taught our children how to apply for scholarships early and often to gain familiarity with the process. While most donors targeted high school juniors and seniors, we found many scholarships open to kids as young as 13. We worked with both of our kids and their essay writing skills early on to expose them as soon as possible. The goal was for them to not be intimidated.

Our 11-year-old got into the action earlier than expected. He did not want to be left out. While he was not able to submit his applications, nothing prevented him from practicing. We printed out each application and he went through the process of filling it out and completing his essay as if he were submitting it. We were able to help him understand the concept of writing essays long before he began to do so in school.

Our kids were amazed how quickly they reached 300 words. They were not used to condensing their thoughts and struggled at first to stay under the word count. We coached them through the process and explained the importance of following directions. It was an incredible exercise.

We learned through the years the importance of layering the lessons we wanted our children to learn. This was no different. Essay writing and applying for scholarships took a great deal of discipline. If we could teach our kids the discipline necessary to follow through on applying for lots of scholarships, they stood a much better chance of getting into a great school the family could all afford. Debt was not an option, so scholarships would be maximized to ensure money was available for both kids.

Hebrews 12:11 stayed in our focus. "No discipline seems pleasant at the time, but painful. Later, however, it produces a harvest of righteousness and peace for those who have been trained by it." The training for our kids began long before it was needed. We prayed the payoff would be big.

Your Turn…Your Perspective: What innovative ways did your parents use to build discipline? How did those innovations shape your work ethic today?

Prayer: Lord, discipline can be so ordinary sometimes. I pray to stay excited about my financial journey and to be mindful of opportunities to grow. I thank You for the desire to serve You in this area of my life.

Day 113
Game Night, Movie Night

Game night, movie night was the foundation of our blended family since we did not have any money for entertainment when we first got married. In the beginning, we watched movies and played games because it was cheap entertainment.

Somewhere along the way, however, we learned one of our kids preferred to play games and the other preferred to watch movies. Once we figured it out, we became intentional in alternating. What could have been a point of contention for the entire family became a great opportunity. Each child was able to experience family time in the way he or she enjoyed it. And because they were enjoying themselves, we all ended up enjoying ourselves.

Whenever they came to visit, and regardless of how long they were with us, we scheduled game night, movie night. It was not about a specific day of the week. It was the next time we were home together. During the summer months especially, we might have several days without either. But the next time we were all together as a family, we either watched a movie or played a game.

We had our favorites. Sorry, Uno, and The Game of Life were all at the top of the game list. Facing the Giants, Elf, Transformers & Mission Impossible were all at the top of the movie list. The kids did not argue over what to watch or what to play. We simply put our requests in the queue and eventually we would get to all of them.

We held Star Trek and Star Wars marathons. Games of Uno literally went until the wee hours of the morning. There were many "remember the time when…" moments centered on game night, movie night. A deck of Uno cards stayed in the glove compartment of the car in case a spontaneous game needed to break out in a hotel room.

Occasionally, we took our game night, movie night outdoors. Putt-Putt and the arcade made an appearance a few times a year as did one or two action movies at the theater. We were careful to not go overboard on the amount we spent on entertainment to keep our budget tight. We all looked forward to the times when we were able to get out and enjoy some time outside of the house.

It was amazing how much the kids enjoyed our simple life of entertainment. Most of our movies came from the library which meant there was no cost to us at all. The games were usually given as a part of Christmas. Any movies seen at the theater were matinees. Putt-Putt was paid for with a Groupon. The arcade came with a $20 spending limit. They were encouraged to use their own money if they wanted to stay longer.

What started out as a simple way to keep both kids engaged in our family became a tradition which only got stronger with the passing of time. It felt good to create memories with them where little to no money was associated with our time together.

Your Turn…Your Perspective: What inexpensive activities have made the most lasting memories for you? How does your current financial situation impact your entertainment choices today?

Prayer: Lord, I pray to allow creativity free reign in my financial life. Help me to see beyond the immediate need to spend money and find those hidden gems of life which are tucked away, waiting to be discovered.

Day 114
Which Path?

PROVERBS 10:5

One year we bought our son the game called Life. It was one of my favorite games growing up, and I thought the kids would enjoy it also. It took a while to find the classic version which used money and not credit cards, but after some searching online, I found it. It was wrapped and placed under the tree for Christmas. After a few times of playing, everyone got the hang of it, and we enjoyed lots of laughs and long nights trying to become millionaires on paper.

Over time, it became clear our son seemed to have an aversion to attending college. Every time we played Life, he announced to all of us his decision not to go to college. He made it very clear it was his decision to make. He was so adamant about it, Keith and I wondered if this was a conversation we would have in a few years in real life.

Our kids were in middle school during this time, and the discussion of how to prepare for college was a common topic in their classrooms. We discussed it any time the kids were with us, and we purposely planned summer activities around camps which showcased what careers were possible with a college education. They both knew they were expected to go to college. But during the game of Life, our son refused to go.

We did not make a big deal out of it. It was a game and we wanted him to have the opportunity to see how it played out. Each time we played, our son chose not to go to college. And each time we played, our son came in last. The rest of us all went to college, and while we experienced some bumps and bruises along our journey of Life, we always finished the game with more money than our son.

We kept encouraging him. We told him it was not about how much money he made, but more about the quality of life he was able to lead. What did he want to do when he grew up? We knew there was plenty of time for him to decide, but we hoped the game of Life would help him understand the importance of choosing a career which would support the lifestyle he ultimately wanted to lead.

Finally, his desire to win made him begin to think he may need to reassess his decision. The next time we played, he still again announced he would not go to college. But when he was given the opportunity to make a career change, he opted to get a college degree to see where it led him. This time, he still did not win, but he no longer came in last. Having a college degree made a difference after all.

We continued to encourage him. Slowly, he decided to go to college more and more. And finally, after several attempts, he won! We all cheered. He chose college and ended up being a doctor with well over a $1 million-dollar net worth at the end of the game. Talk about a turnaround. He was so excited.

We were not sure if this meant he would have the desire to actually go to college when he got older or not, but we were thankful for the life lesson. The final decision was still years away. We would continue to encourage him in the meantime.

Your Turn...Your Perspective: How did your career decisions impact your current financial situation? If you could go back and change one career decision, what would it be?

Prayer: Lord, thank You for life lessons. I pray for the opportunity to learn them while the cost is low. I pray to stay alert to new opportunities to change my financial life and to not be afraid to stretch myself.

Blended Family Peace of Mind
PROVERBS 16:3

Keith and I were married for about two years when we got around to getting our wills executed. I was nervous about not having wills, especially since we were a blended family. But we were having a hard time determining if we needed a will or a revocable living trust. We were also not very far along in paying our debt snowball and did not have a lot of money to spend on a will. When we began taking Financial Peace University, we realized having a will was more important than paying extra on debt. So, we diverted our debt snowball money to a will fund, and began looking for an attorney to assist us.

I began doing research on the best approach to estate planning and was really confused at what I found. Our first attempt was to use a generic, online version, but quickly realized it was not the best option for our family. It would have been fine if we were the typical American family with 2.5 kids, a dog and a white picket fence, but it was not set up to handle the nuances of a blended family. Our unique family situation required a more specialized approach than an online fill-in-the-blank program could offer. We decided to pay the extra money to have someone sit with us and help us map out our estate plan.

We interviewed three attorneys before making a final decision. The first two chose a cookie cutter approach to creating a will and did not understand our family's unique needs. Both also attempted to steer us towards a revocable living trust. I was not convinced it was the best solution for our family. Neither attorney was able to clearly explain why a revocable trust fit our situation best and I was uncomfortable using a tool I did not understand. We decided to keep looking.

The attorney we finally chose was one who sat with us for over an hour and listened to the details of our life. Afterwards, he mapped out a strategy. He took time to explain the differences between a will and a revocable living trust. He drew diagrams to show how our assets would be managed based on which of us passed away first. He asked questions about our kids and what made them special. He pointed out areas we still needed to address, including a document giving me limited power of attorney for guardianship of the kids. We were able to include this document in their school records. It allowed me to pick them up if it became necessary. It also gave me access to their grades and schedules.

Our attorney was not the cheapest, nor the most expensive. We chose him because we felt satisfied in his ability to understand what we needed. He was then able to translate our wishes into documents which accurately reflected our wishes. We were thankful we chose to keep looking. We were also thankful we did not choose an estate product which we did not understand.

After we signed all the documents, I felt as if a weight were lifted. I felt safe and protected. Our last wishes were now documented, and we were in a place of strength to manage what could be a difficult time in the future. We received good counsel which created a peace of mind.

Your Turn…Your Perspective: Do you have a will? Do your parents, friends, siblings, co-workers and neighbors have wills? If not, please protect yourself and your family by doing so as soon as possible. And encourage others to do the same.

Prayer: Lord, help me to not be afraid to face financial scenarios I do not currently understand. Please help me to look for wise counsel and to not sign documents I do not understand. I pray for the courage to keep looking when necessary. Help me to protect those I love from my past financial mistakes.

The Giving Tree

HEBREWS 11:4

The holidays were always bittersweet for our family. Most blended families experienced the happiest and saddest times of the year during Thanksgiving and Christmas. Our parenting plan was the same as many blended families – if the kids were with us for Thanksgiving, they were with their mother for Christmas and vice versa. The blessing for us was the opportunity to split the Christmas season. It may not be Christmas day every year, but at least we got to spend time with them during their holiday break.

It took a few years to settle into our schedule, and Keith and I worked hard to establish some traditions for our new family. One of these was the giving tree. Each year we made sure the kids were given an opportunity to choose a gift to give to a child their age. It was important to us for them to learn the importance of giving. We were all born knowing how to receive, but the idea of giving must be taught.

They were 9 and 11 when we started the giving tree tradition and they did not fully understand how blessed they were. Not all children received everything they wanted for Christmas. We explained how our gifts would help these kids experience a slightly better Christmas than they would without our gifts. We encouraged our kids to choose gifts they wanted to receive themselves. They were given a budget for the gift, and we used the opportunity to teach about managing costs for gift giving.

The first few years were slow going. They viewed the exercise as more of a chore and did not enjoy shopping for someone else. Gift cards were not an option, so our kids were expected to actually think about what to purchase and make sure it fit within the budget. If they were with us for Thanksgiving, we shopped for the gifts and turned them in to the agency in early December. If the kids were with us for Christmas, we made special arrangements with an agency to drop the gifts off closer to Christmas. This gave us the time we needed to take the kids shopping for the Angel Tree gifts, and still get them delivered before Christmas.

It required a good bit of leg work on our part to find an agency willing to accommodate our parenting plan timeline, but we were committed to participating each year to give back a portion of what we received. We expanded our budget each year in either November or December to have enough money for the kids to shop for their gifts. Lowering payments to the debt snowball for the month proved to be a small sacrifice compared to the opportunity to help our kids better understand how important it is to give.

By the third year, the kids were more excited and looked forward to the shopping trip. They got creative with their gift selection and came up with some really cool gifts to give to kids in need. As they warmed to the idea of shopping for someone else, they tried to imagine how the child would like the gift and attempted to gauge their reaction.

It became one of our favorite family traditions, and Keith and I were thankful for the opportunity to teach our kids it is more blessed to give than to receive.

Your Turn...Your Perspective: How do you teach giving? What family traditions do you have which showcase what it means to live for Christ?

Prayer: Lord, thank You for Your generosity. I pray I am mindful of the need to be generous to others. Please show me how to love those around me.

Teacher! Teacher!

PSALM 3:8

When Keith and I began teaching FPU, we could not have known what was in store for us. We simply knew our family ministry was to be financial stewardship, and teaching FPU was a great way to stay engaged. The first session consisted of almost 30 people. To date we have helped approximately 420 people to learn God's principles of finance.

What we were not expecting was the impact teaching FPU would have on us. Not only were we able to help others begin their journey of Christ-centered financial wellness, but we were also able to keep our skills sharp. Five years was a long time to work on a goal. Teaching FPU helped us do more than just pass the time as we worked to fight our own way out of debt.

Just as each class brought its own unique challenges, each class helped strengthen our resolve, and honed our skills needed to live a life free from debt. Even though we viewed each video many times, it was not uncommon to hear a phrase or comment and see it from a fresh perspective. It was almost as if we were Bill Murray's character from the movie *Ground Hog Day*.

We lived each lesson with our class members, knowing what they were about to experience. It gave another opportunity to make adjustments in our own process. We became masters of the budget because we spent so much time teaching it to others. We knew exactly what our life, health and other insurance policies needed to consist of because we viewed so many policies belonging to our class members.

Countless couples came to our kitchen table with feelings of fear, betrayal and hopelessness only to leave hours later with the glimmer of a smile, a better understanding of their personal finance situation, and more hope than they thought was possible. We were the accountability partner for the singles who came through our class and offered the tough love necessary to help them see the changes necessary for a future free from debt. It was exhausting. It was exhilarating. It was incredibly rewarding.

While I never doubted we would eventually become debt-free, I knew our journey through debt was made richer because we chose to include so many others. Our transparency may have given them hope, but it helped us be accountable. A mentor once said to me, "You cannot teach what you do not know. You cannot lead where you do not go."

Keith and I needed to teach FPU. We needed to hear the lessons weekly to create new paths of knowledge and understanding in our brain. We needed to have the information hardwired to ensure we did not go back. We needed to be the difference for others to see it was possible to become and stay debt-free.

Teaching FPU was our way of impacting our community one family at a time, one budget at a time – including our own.

Your Turn…Your Perspective: What/Who motivates you to stay on your financial plan? How has being accountable impacted your financial goals? If you do not have accountability, why not?

Prayer: Lord, thank You for Your Word being so clear on what You desire for me financially. I thank You for the tools You have provided for me to use to become debt-free. I pray to stay on the path set before me until I reach the goal of being financially free.

Day 118
Symphony with Friends

PROVERBS 13:20

Keith and I went to St. Louis for a parent-teacher conference. Since both kids were in middle school, we were able to coordinate to see all the teachers during the same visit. Band was the one subject where they shared the same teacher. They both enjoyed being in band and their teacher was always a joy to visit. During our visit with her, we learned she was a member of the St. Louis symphony orchestra.

As we talked more about orchestra and her love of all things musical, she shared that the orchestra would be performing later the same evening. She then asked if our daughter could attend. Our daughter was a flutist and was quite good. Her band teacher knew the performance would contain several flute solos and thought our daughter would enjoy the experience. Since the band teacher was in the orchestra, she told us she would arrange to have tickets waiting for us at the will call window.

As we planned the trip weeks earlier, we chose to reserve a room, just in case the opportunity to spend more time with the kids presented itself. It was still early enough in the day to cancel the room and simply head back to Kansas City after the conferences. If we did, we would save a night's hotel cost but miss an excellent opportunity to spend time with our daughter.

We saw the cost of a hotel room for the night as a worthwhile investment. It would allow us to hang out with our daughter and her best friend. We picked them up and arranged to return them both after the concert and a late-night meal. The girls were excited to go to their first symphony; we were excited to have time with them for the evening.

The venue was beautiful. Our free tickets were in a great section, and the orchestra was amazing. The girls were on the edge of their seats with excitement. While Keith was not a big orchestra fan, even he knew the importance of the evening which we all thoroughly enjoyed. The girls continued to talk about the music and how cool it was to experience it firsthand all through dinner. It felt good to watch them experience culture. And it felt even better to create a memory with our daughter.

The extra night in St. Louis was worth the added cost to the trip simply because of the beautiful time we were able to share. Our daughter may or may not remember it, but we would. We were thankful to have the resources to use. Our debt payoff date may be delayed, but it was worth it.

Managing our debt-reduction process, in terms of our activities with the kids, was extremely important to us. We did not go overboard on spending for activities, but we wanted to be as available as possible to take advantage of those unexpected moments of quality time with each of them. We were thankful for the opportunity.

Your Turn…Your Perspective: Think of a time when you chose to spend instead of saving. Why was it important for you to do so? Was the end result worth it?

Prayer: Lord, I pray for perspective. Please help me to be mindful of when to take a short detour and when to push through to the end. I pray for wisdom. Help me to view each potential detour through the lens of living a life free of debt. I do not want to lose sight of my goal. I do not want to stay in debt any longer than necessary. I pray for discipline.

Day 119
Health Makes Money

MARK 5:25-26

Medical expenses were a regular part of our monthly budget. We did not do multi-vitamins, but instead tested our blood twice a year to determine what vitamin and mineral deficiencies existed. We also kept monthly appointments with our chiropractor. We did not use traditional "western" medical care, but instead used a naturopath, an osteopath, and eventually an environmental healthcare specialist (eight hours away from our home) as our primary care physicians. It was not cheap.

Many of our friends questioned our decision to spend so much money on medical care when we said debt reduction was so important. Sometimes I questioned it also. But one day a simple thought changed my mindset completely. Without good health, the benefit of being free from debt lost its luster.

Debt-freedom without good health meant having little energy to enjoy our lives. Debt-freedom without good health meant spending more money long-term on life-threatening illness. Debt-freedom without good health meant a lower quality of life. Debt-freedom without good health also meant a potentially shorter lifespan.

We saw good health as a part of our lives and did not want to wait for years to experience it fully. There were chronic illnesses on both sides of our family tree. Poor dietary choices and lack of exercise were a part of the issue, but it was also steeped in our culture. We came from families where you went to the doctor only when something was wrong, not to see what to prevent. We wanted to break the mold of what was expected and be proactive about our health and wellness.

But it did not happen overnight. I kept telling myself the delay in reaching our goal to become debt-free was worth the newfound health and wellness we would receive in the end. So instead of delaying the specialists, organic foods, semi-annual blood tests and expensive care, we put all of it into the budget.

In the beginning, I saw the reallocation of funds as necessary to find a solution to our mystery illnesses. Over time, however, I began to understand the value of our new approach to healthcare. It was just as much preventative as it was finding a solution. I came to appreciate being proactive about healthcare.

To off-set our medical expenses, we found the least expensive locations to purchase everything. We began to use Community Supported Agriculture (CSA) to supply vegetables a large portion of the year. We ordered our dietary supplements online and in bulk to save money. We used frequent shopper programs at the office of our local naturopath. All were our efforts to stretch our medical dollars as far as possible.

I was still frustrated at the pace of things occasionally. I wanted us to be healed AND debt-free. Both were more than possible for the God I served. "When, Lord?" was the question I asked most often.

Over time I accepted the delay, accepted the slow healing process, and accepted the realization of God's ultimate control of our lives. If I meant it when I said my life belonged to Him, I needed to settle down, not be anxious, and watch Him work miracles out of our lives and our health.

Your Turn…Your Perspective: What about your current situation makes you anxious? How do you reconcile it with God's plan for your life?

Prayer: Lord, please heal my heart. Heal my desire to have more today than You think I can handle. Help keep me content in my circumstances and not get ahead of Your plan. I am thankful for Your love. I know it is big enough to cover all my frustration and anxiety.

Day 120
High-End Health Insurance

PROVERBS 24:5

As federal employees, Keith and I were fortunate to have access to one of the largest networks of health insurance options available in the United States. This was important since we were not only making healthcare decisions for our own care, but also for our kids. It was very important to choose a company and plan which fit our needs and was easy for our kids' mother to manage in a different state. We wanted to make sure wellness programs were available in addition to co-pays being low.

We did not realize how important these decisions would be until we both began to have "mystery" illnesses. Traditional treatment options were available under our insurance plan, but we were not getting the assistance we needed from those medical professionals. Each appointment yielded more questions than answers. We decided to take a different approach, hoping to find more answers and more relief.

We began to seek care from non-traditional medical arenas. We started with a Naturopath, switched to an Osteopath, and eventually ended up with a specialist in environmental medicine. We knew we would incur more expenses since they were out of network, but at least our health insurance reimbursed out of network expenses. We diverted a portion of paying our debt snowball to medical to continue our search for solutions.

Because our family deductible on our health insurance plan was only $700, it did not take long each year to reach the point where the insurance plan covered 80% of the expenses for in-network providers. Our insurance did not cover as much for out-of-network providers, but we were thankful for the reimbursements we received. We worked with each physician's office to make sure the appropriate medical codes were used, and then we submitted the expenses to our insurance as quickly and concisely as possible. When we received a reimbursement, we simply applied those funds to the next round of medical care.

We made sure to use in-network diagnostic companies for blood tests and other care whenever possible. Doing so reduced the cost of those expenses tremendously. One such visit was $45 instead of $600, simply because we requested to use the in-network diagnostic company. We spent countless hours on the phone with our insurance company to make sure we knew exactly what we needed to do to get the best results. If claims were returned, we followed through to find out why, and resubmitted them to make sure we were refunded as many expenses as possible. It was a daunting task, but we were committed to following each claim through until it closed to minimize our costs.

It was not easy going through so many medical tests and procedures. Slowly, we began to see progress, both in our health and in our ability to process medical claims effectively. We also learned a lot about the medical claim process, and were able to decrease the amount of time between our out-of-pocket expense and the reimbursement being received. It was a blessing to receive care and limit the added strain of the costs. Time and again, our high-end health insurance proved to be money well spent. Our medical expenses were still high, but we knew they were lower than they would be if we chose a lesser plan.

Your Turn...Your Perspective: How often do you research the healthcare plans available to you? How do you take advantage of your company's health insurance Open Enrollment to adjust your coverage?

Prayer: Lord, show me ways to get creative to stretch my money. Please help me to not be afraid to embrace change. I pray for guidance in the areas I do not understand. Show me how to be a better steward of the resources You have provided.

Day 121
I'm Good for It

As Keith and I were paying off our debt snowball, we eventually got to the unpaid personal loans from his days as a real estate investor. Getting to the point in the snowball where we could repay these loans was very important to him. These people were his friends and he felt he let them down in a big way.

He had not spoken with them in years and was unsure of how the reunions would go. His anxiety level was high as he contemplated how to best start the conversation. He wanted to repay them, but also hoped he could rekindle the friendships. His own journey took him out of St. Louis, into Virginia, and on to Kansas. He was curious about their journeys and wanted to share details of his own.

When the time came to make the calls, pleasantries did not seem appropriate. Instead, Keith chose to get right to the point. "I'm calling to make arrangements to pay back what you loaned me…with interest." The conversations were flat and business like, with few reminders of the friendships he wanted to salvage. In the end, all the debts were repaid, and only one friendship survived.

Keith and his friend were able to get past the financial issues which initially caused the rift, and Keith was thankful to have reconnected. As the two talked more, it became clear Keith's friend was in financial trouble. The first clue was his overall enthusiasm for the repayment; he spoke of the call from Keith coming "just in time." Through the next few phone calls, more and more of the story began to unfold. Keith's friend was heavily in debt, his business was not doing well, and he was not sure how to fix it.

Keith felt compelled to help. He arranged to meet with his friend and proceeded to lay out Financial Peace University and how it worked. He told his friend our story. He shared our struggles and our desire to educate as many people as possible on the FPU system. The surprise came when Keith's friend revealed he was already familiar with FPU, having taken the class years prior. We knew of others who were exposed to FPU but did not fully embrace its principles.

A few weeks later, Keith's friend called and asked if he could borrow some money. There was an awkward silence as Keith sat with the question hanging in the air. The Bible was clear on the dangers of loaning money, and both men experienced firsthand what it felt like. The irony of the question saddened Keith immensely. When he declined, his friend promised to repay. It took almost seven years for Keith to repay his debts to friends, and we did not want to go through it again, even from the other side of the loan. We knew we would not loan the money, but knowing this did not remove the sadness Keith felt.

Unfortunately, Keith did not hear from his friend again. Even though he was disappointed at not being able to restore the relationship, he knew he did the right thing. He chose to refocus his energy on helping those who desired to make a change, and not lose hope over the people who were not there yet. Our prayer was to reach as many as we could in the meantime.

Your Turn…Your Perspective: How do you handle money requests to or from friends or family? What is your response when friends disappoint?

Prayer: Lord, I pray for the courage to embrace Your plan for my finances and not waiver. Please help me to seek out assistance when I feel overwhelmed. I pray for wise counsel as I continue this journey of Christ-centered financial wellness.

Yours, Mine and Ours

ECCLESIASTES 4:9

One of the things I admired most about Keith was his transparency. He shared all the highs and lows of his life in the very beginning of our relationship. He told people he wanted me to fall in love with all of him, not just the good parts. As the relationship progressed, I also began to share more of who I was and what made my life unique.

Inevitably we got around to discussing our finances. Since we were both in debt, I knew it would take a while for us to work through it. We each continued to manage our money separately until we got married. Once we did, we combined all our bank accounts and got to the matter of our debts. We listed all of what we owed and added it up. The number was staggering – $191,000. I struggled to wrap my mind around how long it would take to get through it; the thought made my head spin.

We finished paying off all my debt and all of Keith's non-student loan debt in the first two years. But because the student loans were so big, over half of our debt was still unpaid. I was frustrated to see so much money leave our checking account each month while our debt shrank by what seemed like a small amount. I began to feel like we were held hostage by student loans. We could not build a home. We could not take a vacation. We could not do anything extra because of student loans.

Bitterness began to set in and I began to blame Keith. "His" student loans were keeping us from building our home. "His" student loans were the reason we could not take a vacation. "His" student loans were why we did not eat out or go to a sporting event or concert. It was all because of "his" student loans.

My attitude lasted for weeks and Keith did not know why I was so sullen. I did not share what I was feeling. I just let it fester and get worse. One day, during my prayer time, I realized I was in a dangerous place in our marriage. I was not sharing my feelings with Keith and I was holding a grudge. I knew I was wrong on both accounts.

I prayed and asked the Lord to reveal to me what I needed to do. Even as I said the prayer, I knew the answer. I did not need God to tell me the right thing to do was to confess to Keith what I was feeling and repent to God. Neither was something I wanted. It would be so easy to hold onto the grudge, but I knew my relationship with Keith and with the Lord, would suffer if I did nothing.

A few nights later, I sat down with Keith and shared what I was feeling. I asked for his forgiveness and apologized for blaming him for our situation. The reality was I married his debt when I married him. And he made the amount known from the very beginning; it was never a secret. We prayed together, and I recommitted myself to paying our debt snowball. Over time, I was able to see the value in the process. Keith and I learned a lot about ourselves, each other, and financial stewardship as we worked through "our" student loan repayment.

Your Turn...Your Perspective: What "ownership" issues have you had about money? How have you worked through them?

Prayer: Lord, I pray to stay focused on You and not on my circumstances. Please help me to not allow excuses to hinder my progress. Help me to keep moving, regardless of the pace of the progress.

Day 123
Gifts from the Heart

2 CORINTHIANS 9:12

As Keith and I got farther into our debt-reduction journey, we began to look more closely at our budget to see what areas could be cut even further. We decided gift giving to family members needed a drastic reduction. Keith came from a large family and they did not have a tradition of extended family gifting. My family, however, always gave gifts to the extended family. Our Christmas list included six nieces and nephews, my mom, two brothers and a sister-in-law. In the years we did not travel to South Carolina for Thanksgiving, the cost of postage was also an expense.

In addition to the gifts themselves, I needed to manage my own thoughts and feelings about giving. Gift giving was important to me. I never liked giving gift cards. I wanted to give a gift I thought each person would enjoy. My mother liked to change her bedding a few times a year, so one year she got a bedding ensemble. Another time, all my nephews and my brothers got baseball related items. My older nieces wanted to be nurses, so they got stethoscopes. Each year the cost of postage alone was close to $100.

I needed to rethink the holidays. Not only was I spending way too much on the gifts, but the postage was ridiculous. I decided to purchase several gifts online and shipped them directly to South Carolina. It was a start and saved on postage, but more cutting needed to be done. There must be another way.

The next year I decided to get creative and make Christmas gifts for my family. This was not an easy decision because I am not very creative. Making anything except food from scratch caused me great anxiety. It was one thing to have a lovely handmade creation presented to you at Christmastime, but quite another to receive a gift from an adult which rivaled the best kindergarten creation.

I decided on scripture name art. I created a print for each family member using key words from scriptures to spell out their name. Each piece contained three to eight scriptures which were meant to encourage my family member during their current season of life. My mom was always one to worry, so her passages were about God taking care of things. My brother was in a difficult season of loss, so his were about the peace and the comfort of the Holy Spirit. The scriptures for the kids spoke prosperity and favor over their lives.

I printed each piece in the person's favorite color. Instead of frames, I used paper document holders to mail the art. I was still able to wrap each gift and write a special note explaining the meaning of the scriptures. Everything fit neatly inside of one Priority flat-rate envelope. I bought the frames in bulk and shipped them directly to my mother's address for free!

It was the first year I handmade all the gifts for my family. It felt good to not just put thought into the gift itself, but also to make it with my own hands. I knew the sacrifice to not spend several hundred dollars on Christmas for my family was necessary to see a bigger increase in paying our debt snowball. I saw it as a short-term sacrifice which would yield a long-term gain. It made the Christmas season a little more special and gave me even more incentive to be debt-free. And my family loved the gifts.

Your Turn...Your Perspective: What are your gift giving habits for Christmas and through the year? What ways have you been creative in giving? If you chose to make gifts by hand, what would you give?

Prayer: Lord, thank You for the resolve to make the tough decisions necessary to get my debt paid as soon as possible. I pray You continue to show me ways to showcase Your love to others without spending money.

Rallying Cry
PROVERBS 20:18; HEBREWS 12:11

Keith and I read a great deal. We averaged about 2-3 books a month and focused mostly on non-fiction. A lot of the books we read were financial and/or spiritual in nature. It was not uncommon for us to both read the same book at the same time, and then discuss what we learned.

One book which made a powerful impact on our lives and our marriage was *Three Big Questions for a Frantic Family* by Patrick Lencioni. The focus of the book was teaching the reader how to create a strategic plan for their family. The idea was to have a goal statement and a "rallying cry" so all members of the family were on the same page. The "standard objectives" represented the family's overall direction for the long term. The "rallying cry" represented the family's focus on one specific area for a set period of time. By choosing a rallying cry, the family could be sure all decisions made during a specific timeframe were designed to support the stated short-term goal.

As we read the book, we realized this would be something great for our family. And it was right on time. I was struggling with all the money we were spending on medical bills. With both of us having "mystery" illnesses, it felt as if we were throwing away money on medical guesses. I wondered if we would ever get any closer to a viable treatment plan for either of us.

Our doctor told us about a clinic in Dallas, TX which specialized in mystery illnesses and recommended we both make appointments. It was not cheap. We realized we would need to redirect our debt snowball money to health expenses for about three months to pay for the initial consultation for both of us.

Before reading *Three Big Questions for a Frantic Family*, I would not have been so easily convinced to pause paying on our debt snowball for three months. It would have been difficult for me to redirect so much money away from repaying debt. The process of choosing an objective helped me remove the emotion from the decision and view it in terms of what made sense for our family at the time. I was still disappointed, but at least the thought of reallocating money away from the debt snowball did not cause me to go into a tailspin. I was able to logically process the decision with Keith and together we came to an agreement. He did not have to convince me it was a good idea.

Choosing to focus on health for a three-month period to get a better idea of what our long-term medical plan needed to be made sense to us. We hoped it would allow us to finally have a solution to our health issues. Then we would be able to fully focus on completing repayment of our debt snowball and finally achieve financial peace.

Having a plan with a definitive start and end helped me not be overwhelmed by the amount of money we needed to allocate to health care and away from our debt snowball. Recognizing we could get back to reducing our debt in three months also provided a sense of calm I was not used to experiencing. I was thankful for our "rallying cry."

Your Turn...Your Perspective: What challenges do you have in completing your next financial step? When was the last time you felt torn between two financial decisions which were both important?

Prayer: Lord, thank You for the desire to learn and be educated. I pray for a calm spirit as I grow in my knowledge of managing money Your way. I pray You help me not be anxious, but to constantly look to You for discernment and peace. I thank You, Jesus, for always being with me.

Day 125
Lights On; Lights Off
PROVERBS 17:26

Like most parents, Keith and I spent a great deal of time teaching our kids to not be wasteful. There were constant reminders to not stand with the refrigerator door open, turn off the water, and eat the food they put on their plates. The biggest offense, however, was leaving the lights on. Their bedroom lights were on; the bathroom lights were on. There was a trail of light behind them wherever they went.

We expected an increase in our electric bill when they were with us for more than a few days, but the spike always seemed higher than we anticipated. Finally, we decided to put our money where our mouths were. It was time for our kids to take ownership of their portion of the family budget.

During a family meeting at the beginning of summer one year, we informed the kids of a change to their work assignments. The change was to deduct the cost of electricity from their commission every time the lights were left on. We explained we could either pay them a commission or pay the electric company, but we would not pay both. If they wanted to receive their commissions, they needed to turn the lights off.

We started charging a quarter every time the lights were left on. At the end of the first week, they each owed over a dollar. Obviously, the pain point was not high enough. The next week, the fee was increased to fifty cents every time the lights were left on. The issue still remained.

As we entered week three, Keith informed the kids of the new fee – one dollar every time the lights were left on. Since they received ten dollars a week, it would not take many infractions to consume their entire commission. If it took the loss of a week's wages to make the point, we were willing to do it.

An amazing thing happened. There were no lights left on the third week. As a matter of fact, lights being left on was no longer even a discussion in our house. The kids automatically turned the lights off when leaving each room. They even began to help each other out, prompting the other to go back and turn the lights off.

Keith and I thought it was amazing. The kids learned the value of money and were helping to save electricity all at the same time. It reminded me of the "costs" associated with our own hard-to-learn lessons. Keith and I were living proof of the importance of learning financial lessons sooner versus later. It would always cost more to delay embracing the truth.

Just as we wanted to teach our kids how to not take resources for granted, God wanted us to learn the same lesson. And just like our kids, Keith and I were on the path to greater understanding. It was a beautiful lesson for all of us.

Your Turn…Your Perspective: What life lessons did you learn from your parents the hard way? How have those lessons impacted you as an adult? What financial lessons have been the toughest to learn in this season of your life?

Prayer: Lord, thank You for the life lessons You teach me. I thank You for Your patience as I learn the ones which are harder to grasp. I pray for an open heart. I want to embrace Your plan for me. I know being a good steward of the resources You have made available to me is one of them. Help me to always be open to You.

Day 126
Caught or Taught

JAMES 2:14

When Keith and I decided to embrace the principles of Financial Peace taught by Dave Ramsey, we were intentional in living them out, so our kids could see them at work in our lives. We knew we needed to be consistent so our message about being good managers of God's money was clear and not watered down.

We listened to "The Dave Ramsey Show" when the kids were with us in the car. We discussed our budget with them. We paid them a commission for completing their chores and having a good attitude instead of giving them an allowance. We loved their curiosity when we paid cash for groceries and openly discussed how much money was available for specific purchases. When it was time to shop for clothing and shoes, we always discussed the purchase with them prior to going to the store. We gave them the opportunity to add their own money to the total if they felt they really wanted something which cost more than was allocated.

We wanted our kids to dream with us about what we could do as a family when we were debt-free. We often discussed our goals of building a home and took them with us to look at potential neighborhoods and model homes. We sometimes spent Saturday afternoons window shopping, learning about soft-closed drawers and dovetailing.

It was a family giggle the day our daughter became fascinated with the character of design elements and discovered corbels. She spent weeks talking about the cabinet pulls she loved so much. We took pictures to make sure we remembered when the time came to plan and design our spaces.

Our children asked how much progress we made on our debt snowball. We talked openly about how much we paid off and how much was still unpaid. We explained what it meant to pay interest and the importance of us getting out of debt as soon as possible to limit the amount paid.

They knew our desire for them to live debt-free lives and to live within their means when the time came for them to strike out on their own. They understood our plan to assist with their college education, but only if they did not use student loans and chose a school which fit the entire family's budget. As early as ten and twelve years old, we talked with them about getting good grades, having good behavior and the impact both would have on their future.

We were intentional with our kids. Our message of living a life of Christ-centered financial wellness needed to be consistent if they were to embrace it.

We knew it would be years before we saw the fruit of our labor, but continued to pray our kids would "get it." It was our desire to teach them what we did not learn as kids. We wanted them to understand God owned it all and we were just the managers. We saw it as our responsibility to give them as much of a solid financial foundation as we could. The rest we left up to the Lord.

Your Turn...Your Perspective: How have you been intentional in modeling God's plan for managing money to the kids in your life? What habits of yours are they "catching?"

Prayer: Lord, help me to be intentional with my finances. I want to experience the abundance You have for me. I do not want to settle for what the world believes is the right way. I want to live for You.

Day 127
There Is No Place Like Home

ROMANS 8:28; MATTHEW 7:14

After we got married, I wanted to make sure our kids knew their third set of extended relatives. Keith knew how important family was to me and supported the idea of our kids getting to know my side of the family. The GPS showed Kansas as 16 hours by car from my home state of South Carolina. Because I grew up in rural South Carolina, purchasing plane tickets also meant renting a car and driving for at least an hour to get to my home town. As a result, we chose to drive when visiting my family. It also meant we did not go often, but we did try to visit annually.

One year, we experienced a significant number of emergencies. Lots of medical expenses and car repairs significantly reduced the amount we were able to pay towards our debt. A trip to South Carolina would have added another $1000 to the total amount diverted from debt for the year. And of course, we did not know what other "surprises" might be in store before the year ended.

I kept analyzing our budget numbers. Progress on our debt reduction was lower than it had been in years. We needed to get some traction quickly. We obviously could not do anything about the medical expenses and emergency car repairs. We would have to cut other areas of the budget if we were going to be able to gain some ground on our debt-reduction process.

The more I thought about it, the more I did not want to take another financial hit. I told Keith I did not think we should go to South Carolina for our annual visit. His response to me was, "Are you sure?" He knew how much of a sacrifice it was for me to not visit my family. He knew it was a tough decision and wanted to be sure I weighed all the costs (both financial and emotional).

The financial costs were the easiest because they were tangible. The cost of the trip to visit family would create a financial dent in the budget I did not want. Not going would allow us to use the $1000 for debt reduction.

It took a while longer to work (and pray) through the emotional costs. I really wanted to see my family. In the end, however, the financial future of my nuclear family outweighed the sense of loss associated with delaying the visit to my extended family. Both were important parts of my life; both impacted who I was as a person. But ultimately, we made the commitment to become debt-free as soon as possible. For our goal to be accomplished, we needed to make tough choices. We would have to deny self and do the wise thing.

Dave Ramsey was often quoted as saying, "Adults devise a plan and follow it. Children do what feels good." Our financial season of constant emergencies made it hard to be an adult. It was hard to say, "No," to the longing to spend time with my family. It was hard to call my family and tell them we would not be visiting. In the end, I knew we made the right decision. The day would come when vacations and family visits would happen more frequently. And when it did, I could celebrate with no guilt. I would have excitement, not anxiety. The delay in gratification would be worth it.

Your Turn...Your Perspective: Describe a time when you made the decision to deny yourself. What did it feel like? What was the reaction of those closest to you? How did you respond to their reaction?

Prayer: Lord, thank You for the Holy Spirit Who lives inside me. I am thankful He serves as my conscience and helps me to make the tough choices. I thank You for perspective and a sense of peace when making difficult decisions. I thank You for discernment. I pray to stay on the path and remember the gate is narrow for a reason. I must trust in You always.

Day 128
Good Debt

PHILIPPIANS 2:3

When we first started working to reduce our debt, I was always sure to highlight the fact that most of it was student loans. It was as if we got a pass on being foolish with money because we carried student loan balances and not payday loans. There was a sense of pride associated with having "good" debt. In my mind, ours was justified as "middle class," not commonplace.

After attending FPU, I realized student loans were no different than credit cards or any other loan. Just as the Lord did not make a distinction between types of sin, He also did not make a distinction between types of debt.

The more I studied God's Word with a focus on money, the more I began to understand there was no such thing as "good" debt. It all needed to be paid off as quickly as possible. Debt was keeping us from using our resources to serve the Kingdom and taking our hard-earned money in interest payments.

The experience also exposed just how much pride was associated with the student loans. Pride was my primary sin. It was the one I struggled with the most. Choosing to see student loans as better than the other debt was yet another way pride held me hostage. When I chose to no longer see them differently, the shackles of pride began to break.

It was harder to stay motivated when we reached the student loans. We were able to pay off the other loans much faster since they were smaller. The student loans were huge, and each took months to reach zero. We worked hard to stay encouraged. We kept the goal of being debt-free clearly in front of us to keep from losing hope. It felt daunting at times, but we were committed to seeing it through.

There was no celebration when we finally got to the student loans in our debt snowball. We marked off the last non-student loan debt as paid in full, and moved on to the next without fanfare. I saw the lack of acknowledgement as a victory over pride. It was a reminder of how far we still needed to go to become debt-free. I did not want to slow down our progress to celebrate when there was still so much work left to do.

When I looked back on how I used to view our debt, it seemed foolish to have boasted about having student loans. If there was any debt, we were limited in what we could do for the Kingdom. It was time to get rid of all of it, including student loans.

I was thankful to remove one more layer of pridefulness. As I learned how to view all debt as equal, I removed the pride associated with our student loans being better than the debt of others. There was no more "good" debt, and soon there would be no more debt at all.

Your Turn...Your Perspective: In what ways have you sought the approval of others? Have you ever attempted to justify poor choices? If so, what value were you looking for?

> *Prayer: Lord, thank You for showing me Your plan for my finances. Thank You for helping me see Yours as the only opinion which matters. I pray You continue to provide insight into Your plan for my life. Help me stay focused on You and not on what others may think of my desire to serve You.*

Day 129
Intense Moments of Fellowship

PROVERBS 4:24; EPHESIANS 5:33

A minister at a church Keith and I attended coined the phrase "intense moments of fellowship" to describe the heated discussions couples sometimes have. We thought it was a great description because these discussions were not full-fledged arguments but sometimes contained a lot of passion. This passion could get out of hand if both parties were not careful.

Dave Ramsey tried to prepare FPU couples for these intense moments of fellowship by explaining the different personality traits people tended to exhibit. By Dave's definition, people were either "Nerds" or "Free Spirits." "Spenders" or "Savers." Each family was a combination of each. In our house, I was the "Nerd" and Keith was the "Free Spirit." We both were "Spenders" at times, "Savers" at other times. Let the fun begin.

We were a typical married couple following Dave's plan, and most of our intense moments of fellowship were when we did the budget for the next month. I did not want to spend any money on anything other than debt reduction, and Keith reminded me we did have fun money.

Almost every month-end (and sometimes in between) we held this conversation in one form or another. They never escalated to arguments, but we both used our voice. It was important to keep communication open. To keep us mindful, we began each discussion with prayer. Inviting the Holy Spirit in to join us for the discussion was a great way to get through it without hurting each other with our words.

Each line item was discussed (sometimes only for a few seconds), and a decision was made. The first few took forever, but the more we worked together, however, the simpler it got. After a few months, our initial discussion lasted on a few minutes and the number of emergency meetings began to decrease.

I no longer fretted at the increase in food budget when the kids showed up. I finally understood it cost more to feed a family of four (really?), and we simply needed a bigger food budget. In the beginning, I did not make the adjustment and scrambled to find grocery money the last week of the month. All expenses were factored in before determining the amount set aside for debt reduction.

Through this adaptive budget process, we learned to create "sinking funds" for things like annual insurance premiums and property taxes to not deplete the debt-reduction envelopes in the months they were due. And we chose to use online budgeting software to assist us instead of using a spreadsheet. It made it easier to run reports at the end of the year to see exactly where our money was spent.

After a few years of intense moments of fellowship, we found they did not last as long. Our budget meetings became simple discussions with very little anxiety. We were able to agree on what we needed and what should be delayed. Changes to the budget were not met with panic, but with a sense of purpose. Time was on our side, and it felt good to see the growth in our relationship and our debt-free journey.

Your Turn…Your Perspective: <u>If you're married,</u> what is your communication like with your spouse? What improvements can be made? <u>If you're single,</u> how does your style of communication affect your relationships? What improvements can be made?

Prayer: Lord, thank You for the muscle of discipline. I pray to not get discouraged when the changes I am implementing are not always exact. I pray for patience with myself and others. I ask for clarity and understanding of the budget process. I thank You for grace.

Day 130
Family Radio

PROVERBS 14:5

When the kids were with us in the summer, we made sure to not make exceptions to how we normally lived. There were chores to complete. We did grocery shopping on the weekends. We all went to church on Sundays. They went with us when we ran errands. We lived our life with them in the summers the same way we would if they lived with us full-time.

So many blended families fell into a trap of trying to entertain their kids instead of exposing them to the normalcy of life. We made sure to not make the same mistake. It was important for them to know our way of life was just as normal as their life in St. Louis. They were not on vacation. They simply lived in two locations.

For Keith, living life the way he always did meant listening to "The Dave Ramsey Show" on the way to work. Our routine was typically for him to take the kids to camp on his way to work, and I picked them up from camp on the way home. While they were driving to camp in the mornings, the three of them listened to Dave.

As the kids grew older, they began to understand what the show was about. They asked Keith questions about the people who called in and their financial situations. They were curious about how people got into debt, how much debt we still needed to pay off, and when were we going to Nashville to do our debt-free scream.

Keith answered all their questions and explained every scenario. They even took turns guessing how Dave would answer the questions. The beauty of a podcast was the opportunity to pause and rewind a segment to listen to it again. The debt-free screams were a favorite for all three.

When the four of us gathered in the evening for dinner, the question Keith and I asked each other several times a week was shared by all of us. "Did you listen to Dave today?" was now the dinnertime topic for all of us, and not just Keith and me. It was exciting to share with our kids our desires to be debt-free and be good stewards of the resources the Lord gave us.

The phrase "more is caught than taught" was a primary thought in our house. Just as we wanted to teach our kids how to live for the Lord, we wanted to teach them how to logically approach money and money management. I wanted them to "get it" so badly. I wanted them to understand the mistakes we made and not repeat them. I wanted them to not be ruled by materialism, but by the desire to give and share with others.

We chose to expose our kids to good money habits early and often. We prayed for them to align their lives to the way God taught us to manage our money, and set the best example possible. Listening to the "The Dave Ramsey Show" and discussing the segments with them was a key component we used. It was our prayer to use this small opportunity in time to potentially make a big impact. Only time would show how successful we were.

Your Turn...Your Perspective: Who is watching your financial management practices? What are they learning from you? Who are you watching? What are you learning from others?

Prayer: Lord, I want to be a good example for those around me. Please help me to be the light others use as inspiration to manage their money well. Even when I get it wrong, I pray the experience can be used as a testimony for someone else. I praise You and thank You for guiding me through the process of living a life free of debt.

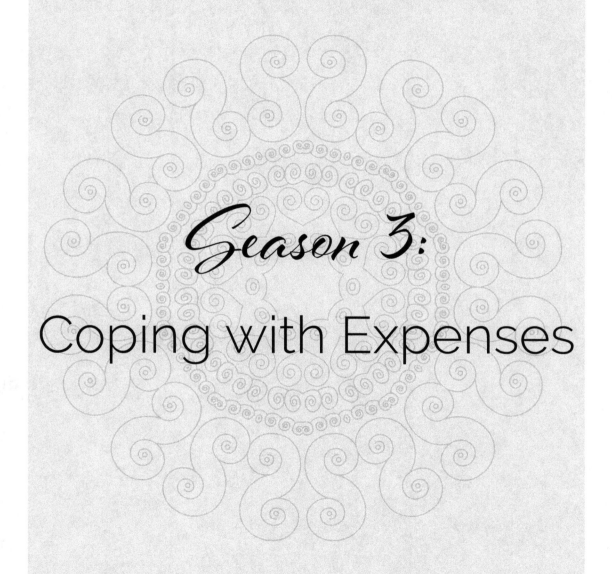

Season 3:

Coping with Expenses

Day 131
New for Me, Please

PSALM 73:25

When Keith and I started our journey to financial freedom, we knew the chances of us finishing without having to replace one or both of our cars were slim. Both vehicles were over ten years old with 200,000 miles or more showing on the odometer. Our kids lived four hours away which required us to be on the road quite a bit. Instead of putting all our extra money towards debt, we opted to save a small amount of money each month to purchase a decent, road worthy car when the time came.

My car died first so I was in the driver's seat during the test drive. I was excited to test out a "new" vehicle, but part of me was really struggling. The car was 10 years old, with 125,000 miles on the odometer. It was dingy and a little worn on the inside. It smelled dusty. Years of wear and tear showed on the dashboard and console. On the positive side, the seats were in good condition and comfortable, and it drove well. But still, it was struggling with the appearance.

I heard Dave Ramsey's voice in my head. He often talked about the price point of the vehicle being the deciding issue. We were not buying our car for looks, but instead were buying for function and reliability.

I realized this car purchase would be the first time I ever owned a used car. My college car was a new car. My mother bought it for me the summer after my sophomore year. She made the car payments and paid the insurance premiums until I graduated. I took over the payments the very next month. My first "adult" car was a brand-new convertible. I could afford the payments and thought I "deserved" a nicer car. I knew nothing of paying cash for a car back then and thought I was being responsible by choosing a car with payments I could afford.

I was a successful Mary Kay consultant and sales director, and the next four cars I owned were free cars. I would drive the car for two years and then get another one. The company paid the lease payments on my behalf and I paid 20% of the car insurance.

It was quite an adjustment to actually choose to purchase a used car. I was at a crossroads. Either I embraced owning a used car, or we would never be out of debt. I would have to decide if I could get past the used interior of my "new" car. I also needed to wrap my mind around the idea of never driving new cars again.

A few months after purchasing our vehicle, I began to settle into my latest mode of transportation. I realized I made a big step in living a life of financial freedom. New cars were a thing of the past. In the book, *The Millionaire Next Door*, Dr. Thomas Stanley's research showed the average millionaire paid cash for a car which was at least two years old.

Since I believed millionaire status was in our future, I saw our car as the first of many used car purchases. Once I shifted my perspective, I began to enjoy the car. I was thankful I was no longer defined by what I drove. It was a freeing feeling.

Your Turn...Your Perspective: How do you approach buying cars? What material possessions do you feel define who you are? How do you manage how others feel about what you own?

Prayer: Lord, thank You for helping me not be defined by what I own, especially since You own it all. I am thankful I am learning to not put my focus on things but instead, be mindful of all You provide. Please continue to refine my character and beliefs to align with You.

Show Them the Way

PROVERBS 22:6

We looked at several different websites to locate a suitable replacement for my car. We found one which met most of our requirements in St. Louis, MO. The timing was great because we were already scheduled to be there to spend Thanksgiving with Keith's family.

Instead of going to a mall or shopping center on Black Friday, we went car shopping. We knew how much money was available for the purchase and were determined to not go over the allocated amount. We went to the bank, withdrew the cash, and headed to the car lot.

On the way, we shared the upcoming potential purchase with our two kids and our nephew. Our son and nephew were 11 and our daughter was 13. We told them we were going to look at a car and asked if they knew why. Our 13-year-old daughter correctly figured we were looking to buy a vehicle because the other one was no longer working.

We explained what a negotiation was and instructed them to listen to the conversation between us and the car salesman, and then make a note of any questions which crossed their minds. We made it clear they were not to interrupt or add comments to the discussion. They were thrilled at the prospect of listening in on an adult conversation.

We were excited to share the experience with the kids. They listened in as we discussed the vehicle with the salesperson, and they watched as our information was collected for the test drive. They piled into the back of the vehicle and tested out the components they would have access to if we decided to purchase the vehicle. They listened as Keith and I talked about the pros and cons of buying it. When we returned to the car lot, they listened as we negotiated the price. They watched as we counted out $100 bills, and they watched as we signed the contract and got the details on the title transfer.

After the transaction was completed, we answered their questions. Our daughter was concerned about the vehicle not being as "pretty" as she thought it would be. I told her I shared the same concern. We both agreed getting the car detailed would help with the "pretty." Our son was in awe of the cash. We told him we saved a small amount each month, so we could buy a car when the need arose. Having cash made it easier to stay within our budget. Our nephew enjoyed watching the negotiation; it fascinated him to know we chose the final price of the car.

It was a great experience for everyone. The kids learned a lot, and Keith and I felt proud of the knowledge we gave them. We showed them the power of paying cash. We helped them have a better understanding of what it meant to negotiate. We were glad we chose to share the experience with the kids. Black Friday shopping took on a completely different meaning.

Your Turn...Your Perspective: What opportunities have you had to influence the kids in your life on the principles of money? How can you be more intentional with showcasing God's thoughts on handling money with the kids in your life?

Prayer: Lord, I pray to not be so focused on the crisis that I miss the lessons You want to teach me. I am thankful for the journey, even when I do not always understand Your plan. I pray You continue to teach me ways to be a better steward. Help me to pass on what I learn whenever possible.

Day 133
Fools Rush In

PROVERBS 1:30-31

Before we left to test drive my would-be replacement vehicle, we set some ground rules for ourselves. We were just looking. And while we were prepared to purchase a car, we did not have to do so right then. We told ourselves to not finalize the purchase without having it inspected by a mechanic since we were buying a used car. All we learned through listening to "The Dave Ramsey Show," teaching FPU and reading about how millionaires lived told us our decision to get a car inspected prior to purchasing it was a good idea.

We called the dealership to find out what the process was for getting a car inspected. We wanted to be armed with information before going to the car lot. It was Black Friday and the dealerships gave most of their staff the day off. Only oil changes and tire rotations were available. No full-service technicians were available to check out the vehicle.

Keith and I decided to check out the car anyway. We chose to take it for a test drive even though we knew we could not get it inspected by a certified mechanic. We told ourselves once we did the test drive, we could then make the decision to stay in St. Louis an extra day to get it inspected if we chose to follow up with a purchase. If the car dealer did not allow an inspection, we would not purchase the vehicle.

We followed our plan…almost. We test drove it. We liked it. We bought it. Without an inspection. We allowed ourselves to believe any repairs would not cost much since the car ran well. We "kicked the tires," and even though we knew little about cars, we convinced ourselves the vehicle was a great deal.

After returning home, we took our new "steal of a deal" to a local certified mechanic only to discover several thousand dollars' worth of repairs were needed to make the vehicle roadworthy. I was horrified. We drove the car over 200 miles when it could easily have stranded us on the side of road at any point during our trip home. In addition, our debt snowball and emergency fund would take a huge hit because many of the repairs needed to take place right away to make the vehicle safe to drive – all because we did not get an inspection beforehand.

I was sick with frustration. Our haste ended up costing a significant amount of money over the next few months. Dave Ramsey always talked about waiting 24 hours before making any major purchases. If had chosen to follow his advice, we either would have spent less on the car or not purchased it at all.

We learned two expensive lessons. Never buy a used car without getting it inspected, and never, ever, ever make a major purchase without prayerfully considering all aspects of the purchase first. We immediately began to share our new knowledge with others so they could learn from our mistakes and not endure the frustration we experienced. The sting of our mistake was a constant reminder to do better the next time.

Your Turn…Your Perspective: What hasty purchases have you made? What lessons did you learn? Do you have a system to keep from making hasty decisions in the future?

Prayer: Lord, thank You for the lessons of money management. They are sometimes painful but always necessary. You send the Holy Spirit to help me with discernment, but I must pay attention. Please help me to consult You and not make quick decisions. Thank You for the reminder to not be hasty.

Day 134
Bird in the Hand

PROVERBS 30:9; 1 CORINTHIANS 10:13

Our poor choice in the replacement car meant extensive repairs were needed immediately. What started out as a proactive, we-refuse-to-create-new-debt, let's-be-wise-with-our-money experience ended up as a huge fiscal disaster.

We drove our new purchase back to Kansas and took it to the local dealership the next day. I was heartbroken. Thousands and thousands of dollars would be needed to get our brand-new purchase road-worthy. My head was swimming with the reality of it all. How could we have been so foolish? What happened to our resolve? What on earth were we thinking when we made this decision? Ugh! It was beyond frustrating and we could blame only ourselves.

More money. More money. More money.

Our cash was low and so was our morale. Our next decisions were incredibly important. We needed to prove to ourselves that we could be wise and make good choices. Our debt was still almost $100,000, and the medical bills were pouring in. We could not afford to get this next decision wrong.

Dave Ramsey taught his listeners to sell their vehicles by private sale whenever possible. The amount of cash received for private sales over wholesale could be significant. The difference was time. Selling a car by private sale could take months unless a buyer was already lined up. We did not have a buyer for my car and did not have the time to wait to find one. Private sale was not the best choice for us.

We decided to sell the car wholesale. Having the cash available to assist with the repairs on our new purchase was more important than having a few hundred dollars extra several months later. We took the car to the local car mega center and sold it for $700. Again, I was heartbroken. I hoped for more but understood the business of wholesale. The more they gave us, the less profit would be available for them.

We took the $700 and the December debt snowball money, and reallocated it all to car repairs. We paid for the first round of repairs, our property taxes, and license plates. We then settled in to save for the next round of repairs. It would take another two months to get the car completely roadworthy, but it was all done with no debt.

We probably would have made an additional $300 if we used the private sale option, but it would have simply delayed the repairs needed to make the car roadworthy. We chose to see the experience for the lesson it was.

No crying over spilled milk for us. We chose the "bird in the hand" instead of waiting for the "one in the bush." We made it through a major emergency without creating any new debt. One down, many more to go.

Your Turn…Your Perspective: Describe your most recent "bird in the hand" financial decisions. What was the end result? What did you learn about yourself and your ability to make sound financial decisions?

Prayer: Lord, I pray for guidance through the tough decision times. I pray to not allow anxiety to overtake me when I am faced with difficulties. I pray to remember the way out is always provided by You. Help me always turn to You.

Day 135

The Cost of Premium

PROVERBS 30:15A

The goal for the entire decade I was a Sales Director with Mary Kay Cosmetics was to drive a pink Cadillac. It was an icon in the company since the first one was ordered by Mary Kay Ash herself in 1968. Any time I mentioned my affiliation with Mary Kay Cosmetics to a passerby, I got the question, "Do you drive a pink Cadillac?" My answer was always the same, "No, but I do drive a Mary Kay car."

Because it was such a big goal, it was hard to let go of it. Long after I ended the team building portion of my business, I still wanted a Cadillac.

Keith and I discussed it one day early in paying off our debt snowball. We just finished paying for repairs for my car and knew another vehicle for me would be on our radar sooner versus later. We also knew it needed to be larger than my current car to accommodate our growing kids.

Keith wanted me to have a Volvo SUV. He liked the safety rating associated with the vehicle and knew it would be large enough for our tall family.

I wanted a Cadillac. It was still in my mind after all the years of being at the center of my goals. We were at odds. But one day while we were running errands, Keith suggested we go by a Volvo dealership to take a look around. He felt I might change my mind if I drove one.

It was not the test drive which changed my mind. It was the sales person telling us about the features of the Volvo. I knew all about the safety ratings. I knew it was a solid vehicle which was known to last several hundred thousand miles. I knew it was roomy and comfortable. But what I did not know was it took regular gasoline instead of premium. I was stunned. Regular gas? A Volvo? Wow!

My mind began to calculate just how much money we would save by not buying premium gasoline. We planned on keeping whatever vehicle we purchased for as long as possible, and I imagined at least three to four years. The more I thought, the more the savings compounded.

I never thought about the maintenance associated with a vehicle in terms of its overall value. I just always purchased what I wanted without regard to anything other than "I want it." The idea of considering the cost of maintenance in the decision was a foreign concept. But it made so much sense. If we were called to be good stewards of the resources God gave us, why should the cost of gas not be included?

We bought a Volvo. And I loved it. The status of driving a Cadillac was no longer important. I wanted to get the most out of every dollar we spent, and spending our hard-earned money on premium gas, while we were working our way out of debt, made no sense at all. Maybe a Cadillac would be in my future after we finished paying off our debt snowball, but for the time being, it was a Volvo and regular gasoline.

Your Turn…Your Perspective: What item have you always wanted to own? How does it align with your overall financial goals?

Prayer: Lord, thank You for paradigm shifts and new ways of viewing the resources You have given me to manage. Thank You for teaching me to always have an open mind. I pray to not just learn the financial lessons You are placing before me, but to implement them in my life.

Delay, Not Denial

PROVERBS 10:2

The day I realized we were already over $50,000 in medical expenses was not a good day. I do not remember why I felt compelled to add up all the numbers, but I did. I simply stared at the total for the longest time and could not believe it was so much. Then I did a foolish thing and added up how much debt was left to pay off. The number was $62,500.

My heart was sad. Even though the numbers were not the same, the truth was clear in my mind. We could have been debt-free if not for medical expenses.

I wanted to be angry at someone. I could be angry at the Marine Corps for sending Keith to the Gulf War, but what was the point? I could be angry at all the medical experts we saw over the years who were clueless about a diagnosis. But being angry did not change the facts; it did not solve our issues at all.

It took me days to get past my new knowledge. I kept mulling the numbers over in my mind. I was numb as I thought of all the money we spent to understand our illnesses. All the blood tests. All the medications. All the food changes. All the travel. All the medical specialists. All totaling over $50,000 in four years.

So much cash out, but not to debt reduction. And we were not done which meant more money would go to medical needs before we reached the end of our journey to financial freedom. When would it end? How much would we spend before we were healed?

I knew I needed to shift my focus. Instead of focusing on the amount spent on medical care, I chose to remind myself the Lord used these circumstances to grow my faith in Him. I would have to decide if I would allow my new knowledge to create bitterness or blessings. It was all up to me.

I consciously decided to choose blessings. If we had become debt-free years earlier, we would have missed an opportunity to grow our mental toughness about money. If we had become debt-free years earlier, we would have missed the opportunity to learn key financial skills while the cost was lower.

Our experiences gave us so many examples to share with our coaching clients, and others around us, who wanted guidance on how to become debt-free. And most important, the trials we experienced caused us to have a much deeper relationship with Jesus Christ.

Slowly, the numbness subsided, and the bitterness which began to creep in, no longer claimed a foothold. I decided to continue to trust the Lord's plan and focus on the faint light of financial freedom ahead in the distance. Instead of lamenting over the $50,000 we spent on medical expenses, I chose to concentrate on the $62,500 left to repay.

We would be debt-free one day, and when we were, we would shout with joy for all the Lord taught us on our journey. Until then, we would be diligent and trust His plan.

Your Turn…Your Perspective: How have you been impacted by a huge disappointment? How did you rebound from it?

Prayer: Lord, thank You for the tiny light at the end of the tunnel. Please help me to focus on it and not my current mile marker. I trust You, Jesus.

Day 137
Emotions and Money

PROVERBS 18:11; 2 CORINTHIANS 12:7

The first few years of our marriage were filled with reactions to our financial situation. We did not have a solid financial plan. We found it difficult to stay ahead of all the magnets pulling at our money. It was a constant fight with life to make progress on our debt reduction. Many months we made no progress at all. I struggled to not go into a tailspin every time something new came up. We were determined to keep going.

As we continued to work through our debt and make small amounts of progress, I began to relax a little emotionally. My prayer to not respond to every small issue with negative emotion was slowly answered by the Lord. It certainly was not a prayer which was answered quickly. I knew I was not yet done with the lesson of trusting God to provide our every need. I was still a work in progress.

One day, during my quiet time, there was a moment of clarity. I realized my emotional responses to our financial situation were rooted in my desire to be in control. I was trying to fix it myself instead of laying it at the feet of Christ. I knew how to lay before the Lord and place the really big issues on the altar. But I was struggling with letting go of the day-to-day issues which seemed to constantly eat away at my joy.

I began to understand how I was stunting my own financial growth. If I wanted to experience the truly abundant life the Lord carved out for us, I needed to trust Him completely with every area, including our finances. The poor mindset I carried with me since childhood would only be removed when I saw my life as already being abundant.

It took years and many Bible studies, but I slowly began to shift my mindset. We still experienced constant money issues, but my response was different. I was more aware of each situation as it happened instead of reacting to it after the fact. I chose to believe what God gave was enough. He would get us through.

Once I became aware of how much my emotions impacted our journey, I clearly saw progress as progress. Small progress was still progress. The little steps were just as important as the big hurdles in the race to become debt-free.

As we passed through year two, year three and entered year four of our journey, we paid off more debt than what remained. We also spent a significant amount of money on medical bills and I was able to take it all in stride. New emergencies were discussions and not emotional outbursts. I no longer cried out, "Oh, Lord!" every time we hit a financial snag.

I realized this was probably an area I would never fully conquer. I saw it as a thorn in my flesh. It meant I would constantly be in prayer for deliverance from the negative emotions associated with money. My progress showed me I could do it. But the little seed of anxiety I always felt in the back recesses of my heart, told me there was still more of my will left to surrender. I was thankful the Lord was always there to help me through.

Your Turn…Your Perspective: What is your thorn in the flesh? How has it affected you spiritually? What can you do to lessen the impact it has on you?

Prayer: Lord, thank You for the reminder of Your presence in my life. Thank You for always being there to catch me when I experience a moment of weakness. I pray to never lose sight of You and Your will for my life.

Day 138
The Switch

PROVERBS 16:11

The more Keith and I taught Financial Peace University, the more engrained in the culture we became. We knew it was hard to teach a concept you do not fully embrace yourself. Every time we went through the class, we learned something new.

The third time we taught FPU, the highlight was car maintenance. We were getting our cars serviced at two different dealerships. Keith insisted on us establishing service for our vehicles when we moved to Kansas City. He was a firm believer in well maintained vehicles, and in his mind, the best service came from a dealership.

During FPU, Dave Ramsey reviewed a series of myths people embraced about why they spent their money the way they did. Sure enough, one of the myths was the service received at car dealerships was better than smaller, independent service centers. It was time to find another way to maintain our vehicles.

We replaced my vehicle a few weeks earlier and the new dealership provided horrible service. FPU solidified the timing by pointing out just how much more we were paying for the horrible service we were receiving. The new dilemma was which service center? We were not sure how to go about finding one. Shady mechanics from the past made us cautious, and we did not want to experience poor service again.

Sometimes, the Lord answers prayers when you have not even prayed them.

Shortly after we realized our need for a new service center, I was reading the latest AAA® magazine. There before me was a review of their certified service center program. They identified all the highly qualified service centers in our area. All we needed to do was pick one. They even offered a free 45-point inspection to make sure the vehicles were roadworthy and a 10% discount on all labor! I shared my find with Keith, and he shared in my excitement. Yet again, the Lord stepped in to assist us. We were so thankful.

We did a little research and settled on a quirky little shop a few miles from home. It was on the way to work for both of us, offered free loaners (my new dealership charged for loaners), and gave incredible service. The staff and management were friendly and knowledgeable, and became almost like extended family.

We often came home with fresh salsa from the kitchen of the front desk manager, fresh flowers if our appointments were on Fridays, and invitations to cookouts at the garage on the weekends.

They loved our cash-only policy and worked with us to prioritize repairs. They were such a blessing to us. And we loved supporting a small business in our area, especially one which understood customer service.

We did not miss our dealerships, and we certainly did not miss the extra money we spent on oil changes and tire rotations. Our new service center took excellent care of our car needs, and we knew they would be in our lives for years to come. Yet again, the principles of FPU saved us money and changed our paradigm. All we needed to do was embrace it.

Your Turn…Your Perspective: What paradigm shifts have you made about money recently? What habits are you holding on to which may be costing you money? Why have you not let them go?

Prayer: Lord, thank You for caring for even my small needs. Thank You for leading me on the path to better financial decisions in every area of my life. Please help me remain open to change. Help me to trust You with the big choices and the small ones.

Day 139
Standing in the Gap

PROVERBS 16:16

We loved our life group for lots of reasons. It was simply a random group of couples who all wanted to serve the Lord and love their spouses the way the Bible outlined. We were able to be vulnerable with each other. We prayed with and for each other often. We enjoyed our time together so much on Wednesday nights, we often carried the conversations over to Sunday mornings after service.

I found myself with one of the couples from our group one such Sunday morning. The three of us stood together laughing and enjoying each other's company. I honestly do not remember what we were talking about, but it was funny. As we settled down and began to say our goodbyes, I asked if there was anything specific I needed to be praying about for them. They reminded me of a few standing prayer requests and I did not expect their next question.

They asked me how they could pray for Keith and me. Why the question shocked me, I was not sure. All I know was it caused a flood of tears to fill my eyes. I was completely caught off guard by the level of emotion their question brought to the surface. They immediately embraced and comforted me. They asked what was wrong. It took me a moment to figure it out myself.

We learned a few weeks earlier about a new doctor in Dallas, TX. We decided to pause payments to our debt snowball to save money for what was expected to be at least a $5000 visit. It created huge anxiety. Previous tests and appointments resulted in no real answers. I was hesitant to spend so much money with no guarantee of results.

My friends hugged me. They reminded me God was in control. They recapped the tenacity with which Keith and I were attacking our debt. They reminded me the appointment was a referral from our doctor, and she would not be sending us if she did not believe we would find value in it.

I was so thankful for their friendship. I was thankful Keith and I chose to be transparent with our life group to keep from going through life alone. I was thankful our church placed emphasis on small communities of people to keep from getting lost in the fray of activity on Sundays. I was just thankful for everything.

When Keith and I joined our group, we did not know what blessings were in store for us. We simply wanted to learn more about God's word. We also wanted to build our relationship as a couple with other couples who wanted the same thing. We did not know we would receive such grace and encouragement from people we literally did not know a few years prior

I dried my tears, hugged my friends again, and felt new hope. I knew Keith and I were doing the right thing by going to the new doctor. I knew our time of debt-free living would come when the Lord was ready for us to experience it. I knew I was learning the valuable lesson of trusting Him, regardless of how the situation looked. I prayed it would stay with me forever.

Your Turn…Your Perspective: With whom are you most transparent? Why this person? In what areas of your life do you need to trust God more?

Prayer: Lord, please show me my community. Help me be transparent and not hide. I want to be blessed and be a blessing to others. Help me to trust You with every situation.

Day 140
Timely Testing

PROVERBS 11:4

When Keith and I planned the first visit to our new doctor, we knew it would be expensive. The center was out of network and out of town. We knew some testing would be required for both of us in addition to our initial patient visits. We did not know what else to expect but we did know the entire visit would be paid for in cash and our cash was limited. We decided to not do any optional testing to keep our costs down.

We planned to stay for two days. We found a hotel a little farther away to keep our costs low. It was complete with a kitchen and served both breakfast and dinner. I packed a travel lunch for us to keep our expenses low.

After the first day and our initial diagnosis, we realized we could maximize our visit if we altered our schedule and stayed an additional two days. Hotel costs doubled; food costs doubled. I heard cash register noises in my head. The office staff was very accommodating when I came back every day to get an update on the cost. I was determined to stay on top of the expenses.

On the third day, we found out there were two additional tests needed. Technically, they were optional tests and not cheap. Our original plan of not including anything optional was in question. If we took them during the first visit, the results could be factored into the at-home recovery process. If we waited, we would save money, but would delay a large portion of our treatment plan until the test was performed.

Keith and I huddled in a corner with a calculator. How would we make it all work? The value of the trip was already evident, and we knew we were on the right path. For the first time in years, our medical team understood us and were prepared to treat us. We just needed to pay for it.

Our monthly debt snowball money was used to pay for the first two days of the visit. If we were going to add the other tests, something else would have to go. We kept several sinking funds in our budget to save for larger purchases we knew were in our future. There was one for camp for the kids in the summer and another for car repairs. A third was for property taxes due in nine months.

We finally decided to empty the kids' camp fund because camp was not a necessity. We knew it was the logical choice. Neither car repairs nor property taxes were luxury items. As much as we wanted to send the kids to camp, paying cash for medical care was the pressing need.

The test results came back, and our treatment plan was set. The cost for the visit topped $4000. It was another medical expense paid for in cash to add to the ever growing total. We were still thankful. Sound judgement prevailed, and we came out of the trip with what we intended – no new debt. Payments to our debt snowball may have been paused, but we stayed true to our new desire to live a cash life.

It would have been so easy to set up a payment plan. It was all so convenient. We were determined, however, not to incur debt. We paid for our expenses as we incurred them. The line was drawn in the sand and it would not be crossed.

Your Turn…Your Perspective: When was the last time you decided to forgo the future for an immediate need? How did it impact you?

Prayer: Lord, I pray for resolve. I pray for the courage to think of Plan B and Plan C. Please help me to look ahead at all my expenses and to make decisions based on all available resources. I pray to not erase the line drawn in the sand of my financial life.

Day 141
Medical 401k

When we switched to an environmental health specialist in Dallas, TX, it was as if we entered a world of misfits. The diagnoses were weird health issues which were previously undiagnosed by western medicine. Our own journey was four years old. Our medical expenses were over $65,000 when we reached the point where our osteopath recommended we transfer. Many of the people we met came with similar stories.

One such couple literally spent the last of their retirement on the trip. They were from the northeast, and his diagnosis was sewer gas exposure. He was the onsite maintenance man for a large apartment complex when his health began deteriorating. In addition to eventually losing his job because he was no longer able to maintain the level of work required, they lost their home since they lived in the complex rent free.

They were seeking proof to support a worker's compensation claim. The company who owned the apartment complex disagreed and argued the health issues were simply the result of early onset Alzheimer's. The couple went to Dallas hoping to receive test results to prove their case. They were literally homeless, without health insurance, and down to their last few hundred dollars.

Hearing their story was sobering. We were so fortunate to be able to pay cash for all our medical expenses. Doing so drastically slowed our debt repayment, but we were not adding any new debt. We were also blessed to have both of our incomes (and health insurance) still intact. The blessings continued when we included the significant amounts of vacation and sick leave available to cover our salaries.

The couple's story was a reminder of the importance of having an emergency fund. They were not the first people we knew who resorted to using their 401k plans to fund emergencies. It was a horrible spiral of lost revenue and heavy tax implications at the worse possible financial time. I knew firsthand how hard it was to dig out of the financial hole created by taking money out of a 401k. It took me years to recover when I resorted to using my 401k because of poor money choices.

All we could do for them was pray. We prayed with them in the waiting room as they shared their story, and we shared our tears. We continued to pray for them in the months to come. Unfortunately, we did not think to get their contact information to stay in touch so there was no way of knowing how it all worked out. We simply asked the Lord to be with them. We prayed they would find resolution and healing.

I was often frustrated by the time it took to get out of debt. I was also frustrated by the time it took to get well. Meeting the couple in Dallas helped me be thankful and grateful for our circumstances. While our journey of healing and freedom from debt was far from over, we were blessed with so much more than most. For the first time in a long time, I chose not to complain. Instead, I rested in all the Lord provided. It was a sobering reminder of God's grace.

Your Turn…Your Perspective: Do you have 3-6 months of expenses saved for an emergency? (Please, please, please get it saved if you do not. If you do, please ensure it is in a savings account and not in an investment account. It should never be at risk to be lost. It is insurance and not an investment.)

Prayer: Lord, thank You for Your grace. Please help me to not take it for granted. I want to always be mindful of all You have provided. Help me to choose to see even the difficult circumstances as an opportunity to lean on You. I trust You, Jesus.

Day 142
Flexible Spending Account

ROMANS 13:7; 8:28

Since we were both federal employees, we were each able to participate in a Flexible Spending Account (FSA). "It is a special account you put [pre-tax] money into that you use to pay for certain out-of-pocket health care costs."[5]

The FSA doubled the amount of pre-tax money we could apply towards medical expenses. Our program also allowed us the opportunity to use the full amount at the beginning of the year. Our medical expenses were a huge part of our monthly budget, and it was a wonderful relief to use the FSA for costly tests and appointments during the first part of the year.

We needed to find as many ways to reduce our taxes (and our medical expenses) as possible. The FSA was one of the best options available for us. Each year we registered for the largest amount possible and each year we used it all, usually before the end of April.

We saw it as a blessing to be able to pay for our medical expenses using tax deferred dollars. It truly stretched our money and allowed it to work as hard as possible for us. It required a little work on our part to make sure all the paperwork was completed correctly, but it was a worthwhile investment of our time to receive the benefit of tax-free money to pay for our costly medical expenses.

Instead of choosing to be frustrated at the amount we spent on medical care, we chose to focus on the tax-exempt status of the expenses we could claim through our FSA. It made a huge difference in our attitudes to focus on what we could control instead of what we could not. Each year we repeated the process.

We could easily have chosen to be the victims of our circumstance. We could have allowed the sheer volume of medical expenses to prevent us from becoming debt-free. We made the decision early on to confront each financial obstacle as we encountered it, and managing our healthcare costs was no different. Our FSA was simply the weapon we used to beat down the obstacle called medical expenses.

A former business coach changed my perspective on paying taxes years ago. His thought was to focus on the amount of income, not the tax bracket. Instead of being frustrated at the <u>amount</u> of taxes paid, focus on the blessing of a good income which created the taxes.

By shifting our perspective, we were able to see God's grace in our ability to work and earn an income, despite our medical conditions and the expenses associated with it. His grace was called into action with the robust FSA available to us. It created flexibility in the financial management of our medical conditions and created a much-needed tax deduction at the same time.

We chose to follow Romans 8:28 and find the good in the midst of what, at times, was a very frustrating and costly situation. Our time of freedom from debt would come. In the meantime, we kept going.

Your Turn…Your Perspective: How do you manage your tax shelters? Have you pursued all the shelters available to you? (If not, please sit with a tax professional as soon as possible, preferably not from a franchise. If yes, please review your shelters every few years to be sure they are still valid.)

Prayer: Lord, I pray for the ability to find the good in even the difficult and costly situations in my life. Please help me to stay focused on the journey and not the obstacles. I can do this. You told me I could, and I trust You.

Day 143
Jesus in the Kitchen

PROVERBS 20:13; PHILIPPIANS 4:19

I faced many challenges in the past, but I always managed them head-on. Losing my job and jumping into entrepreneurship full-time was nothing compared to implementing the 4-day meal rotation. Two cross-country moves as a single person was a piece of cake. Buying and selling two homes by myself was like breathing. Being hired to start entire departments from scratch only increased my heart rate a little. Traveling by myself in foreign countries without knowing the language was something I did often.

Nothing ever got the best of me. Even working on our debt snowball, over such an extended period, did not affect me as much as implementing the new meal plan. This new discipline did what nothing (or no one) was able to do in 47 years. I was completely out of my element with no idea how to make it through.

Finally, I cried out to the Lord. I needed help. I needed wisdom. I needed Him to rescue me. I knew the plan was an essential part of our healing process. But how could I implement it, continue working nine-hour days, write this devotional, teach Financial Peace University, build our financial coaching business, continue to serve at our church, and find a moment for myself and Keith? I simply could not do it alone.

After many tears and cries, the Lord answered my prayers. He told me to hire the help I needed. What? We were trying to get out of debt and the Lord wanted me to divert debt-reduction money to hire help for the kitchen? It made absolutely no sense to me and I waited for another answer. Any other answer. But none came. It was as if He said, "You asked. This this is my answer. Take it or leave it." There it was. I took it.

My next prayer was: "Who, Lord? Who should help us with this task?" And sure enough, the answer came. I called to explain what I needed, and was greeted with a heartfelt, "Of course, I'll help you!" The relief I felt was palpable. I was so thankful. We met in the middle on price (I wanted to pay more, she wanted to accept less), and found a rhythm which fit both of our hectic schedules. It was an incredible blessing.

In addition to my new assistant, the Lord sent a wonderful friend to help in the kitchen for the rest of the weekly cooking. Keith became the full-time grocery shopper in addition to dish washer. In time, I was able to create a new system to manage all the grocery shopping, planning and preparations needed for Keith and me to successfully implement the plan. Slowly, it all began to come into focus.

I never felt so needy in my life. But the Lord provided for every need. All I needed to do was let go. Let go of pride. Let go of cash allotted for the debt snowball. Let go of control. Once I let go, He stepped in and took care of everything.

I did not know how long we would need to follow the four-day meal rotation. I prayed it would not be for the rest of our lives. But regardless of the time, I knew God would take care of it all.

Your Turn…Your Perspective: Name a time when you were completely overwhelmed. Did you turn to God? Why or why not? How did you get through it? What did you learn from it?

Prayer: Help me let go, Lord. I want so much to trust You. But I'm scared. Will You promise to be there always? Please help me get through this. Show me the way.

Four-Day Meal Rotation

PROVERBS 16:26

Once we settled into our new meal plan, it was not quite so overwhelming. Meal planning and grocery shopping still required more time than in the past, but I no longer felt paralyzed by the process. I also felt hopeful because both Keith and I were beginning to feel the effects of a simpler diet.

I learned what could be prepared and frozen a few weeks in advance, and what meals were best eaten fresh. I power cooked (cooking in large quantities and then freezing portions) when it made sense and prioritized everything else.

The food we ate was mostly organic. There were several items which cost significantly more than our previous meal plan. Almonds, almond oil and almond flour were combined with peaches for a very simple (but pricey) peach cobbler. Avocado oil, sunflower oil, walnut oil, and seaweed oil all became a part of our new plan. Walnuts were added and removed. Sesame oil came and stayed, but sesame seeds were no longer options. Shrimp reappeared, and tuna made an exit. Goat cheese (my favorite!) was back in, but not brie. Ground turkey left, but organic ground beef became a mainstay.

It was a lot to manage, but I was making it work. It felt like juggling. Every meal hung precariously in balance with every other meal. I knew our health depended on me finding my way through the maze of ingredients. I prayed the effort paid off, literally and figuratively.

I was also concerned about making sure we liked our new menu. I felt overwhelmed every time Keith asked for a new item. He missed his old favorites and wanted to try to incorporate as many of them in our new plan as possible. But with every ingredient came a potential conflict. It was simply not possible to give him all the foods he enjoyed and stick to the plan. Finally, I drew the line. No more changes.

Through it all, I kept a close eye on the grocery budget. I was afraid it could not handle the strain. With all the money going out for supplements and doctor's visits, I certainly did not want to increase our grocery budget.

Even though our ingredients were more expensive (quinoa flour was $15/pound), there were fewer ingredients and less variety. I bought as many items in bulk as I could, including ordering online when it made economic sense. Our freezer was always filled with the results of my days of power cooking.

I slowly began to exhale and focus more on getting healthy, and less on being able to afford to get healthy. It was a huge paradigm shift for me. I did not know how long we would need to follow the new plan, but I needed to be prepared for the long term.

Once again, I was reminded of how important it was to be healthy, even if we were not yet debt-free. The slow and steady progress we made not only gave us hope, but also gave us peace of mind. We would get through this challenge, just as we got through every other one. The Lord gave us everything we needed. All we had to do was continue to trust Him.

Your Turn…Your Perspective: In what ways can you see God at work in your life right now? What level of gratitude best describes your attitude as God continues His work in you?

Prayer: Lord, thank You for my challenges. As hard as it is to see them as blessings, I know You are using them to grow me. I pray for a good attitude as I continue to work my way through my own circumstances. Please help me choose to be grateful through it all.

Day 145
Due Diligence

PROVERBS 4:25; JAMES 1:2-4

Medical bills were everywhere. We surpassed the $65,000 mark when we hit year four of our journey to freedom from debt. The only thing bearable about the number was cash. We cash flowed all of it. Every medical expense was paid without incurring any debt.

Paying cash slowed down the debt reduction but did not add to it. In my mind, I saw the blessing of having the money to manage our complicated and expensive healthcare needs. In my heart, I worked to not be frustrated by the constant trial of new diagnoses and costly care. Our Flexible Spendable Account was a godsend. We depleted it each year by April. We were also blessed to have an incredibly low annual deductible.

Since most of our medical care was out of network, we learned everything we could about the process. We learned to call our insurance company and find out the proper codes to use before our appointments. We learned which blood tests could be processed through an in-network provider, and which ones could not. We learned to read each Explanation of Benefit (EOB) carefully to ensure it was processed completely.

In many instances, the insurance company sent the EOB as a request for additional information, which meant the claim was still open. We often submitted claims two or three times to insure all the information was received and the claim process finalized. No request for information was ignored.

It was a lot of effort. It was a lot of time on the phone and online researching what the insurance company needed to finish the claim. But we were not deterred. We wanted to ensure we received the largest reimbursement possible. No claim was left unprocessed, no receipt unfiled.

When reimbursements came in, they were allocated to either new medical expenses or debt reduction. We reused the money repeatedly. Medical expenses were in the monthly budget and we planned bloodwork, travel to out of state doctors, supplements and office visits as money was available. We did not schedule or purchase anything we could not pay for in full.

Through it all, I worked to keep a positive attitude. It was frustrating at times to see the amount spent on medical care, but we were committed to finding a solution to our health issues. We were fortunate to have excellent health insurance, still be working, and not incur debt. Such was not the case for many.

We also believed the Lord would use all we experienced. Maybe it was the new list of people (other patients of our doctor) we added to our prayer list. Maybe it was speaking life into the staff as they cared for us and others so diligently. Maybe it was so we could say, "I understand," and mean it when someone else spoke of mysterious, bank account draining illnesses. Maybe it was just to keep us humble.

We did not know the reason for this portion of our journey, but we chose to trust Him through it and count it all joy. The journey was long, but we remained hopeful. It was frustrating at times, but we remained humble. We chose to stay the course and knew we were victorious because of it.

Your Turn…Your Perspective: What difficulties has the Lord used to stretch your faith? How have you responded to them?

Prayer: Lord, thank You for trials. I do not always understand them and would certainly not ask for them. But I trust You, Jesus, and trust the words of James 1:2-4. I know Your perfect work [patience] will make me perfect and complete, lacking nothing.

Day 146
Transparency

EPHESIANS 4:25A

As we taught more and more FPU classes, we began to develop our process. We sent weekly emails to encourage the class, and added the class members to our prayer list. We created a prayer box where class members could add anonymous prayer requests and arrived early to answer questions from those who were too shy to ask them out loud in class.

We sat with the families who needed a little extra assistance getting their budgets together and acted as accountability partners to any who needed one. We called each class member at some point between week three and week five to make sure they were still following along. We believed the personal touches we added helped our class members embrace the changes they would need to make progress in the class.

The single most important thing we did with each class, however, was share our financial situation with them. It was not something we ever discussed beforehand. Over time we simply realized our class embraced the concepts more completely when they saw real application. FPU was a paradigm shift for most people. Many thought it was impossible to live without debt. Others thought those who lived without debt never faced difficulties managing crises in life. We wanted our class members to know the truth, so we shared the intimate details of our financial life.

We told them our beginning debt totals. We told them how much was left to pay before we would be debt-free. We told them our income. We shared the details of financial decisions which needed to be made during the time they were taking the class. We detailed our thought process when we needed to adjust the budget mid-month. We walked through our uncomfortable disagreements about money and how we worked through them. We allowed them to sit in a box seat and watch our financial life unfold on the big stage.

We did not hide. We laughed with them and cried with them as we talked about our financial successes and failures.

Our desire was for them to be encouraged by our circumstances. We wanted them to stay hopeful in their own situations by having the opportunity to see how we worked through ours. We wanted to make the class material more real and less like theory by openly showing how we applied it to our own lives. We wanted our class to walk through our circumstances with us and feel more empowered about their own.

We often saw class members in the months following the end of a class term. They were always excited to share their success stories. It felt good to know we helped others to achieve their financial goals as we worked to achieve our own. We knew it was not a requirement for us to share so much of our lives with our classes, but doing so allowed us to provide practical application in a very meaningful way. At least we hoped so.

Your Turn...Your Perspective: In what ways do you show transparency in your life? How have others impacted you with their transparency?

> *Prayer: Lord, help me to be transparent and not hide. I want to face my financial issues head-on and not be embarrassed by the changes needed to bring me to a place of Christ-centered financial wellness. I pray to face my fears head-on and leave it all in Your hands. I trust You, Jesus, to get me through.*

Day 147
The Right Thing

PROVERBS 23:23; LUKE 8:17; MARK 12:17

When Keith and I found ourselves in need of a replacement for his 15-year-old truck, we were in a little bit of a tough spot. It was a crazy season of car repairs and we were feeling the financial blows. After all we spent getting my car roadworthy, there was only about $1500 available to purchase a vehicle for him.

Debt was not an option. We began to pray for the Lord to direct us to the best value for our money. Our backs were against the proverbial wall and prayer was the only way out. Surely God would provide what we needed. It was what He did best. We did not know what His provision would look like, but we trusted it.

A few days later, we got a call from our mechanic. He confirmed the death of the F-150 and asked what we wanted to do with it. We told him we would be selling it for parts and we asked him if he knew a good used car lot to purchase a cheap car. Imagine our surprise when our mechanic told us he could help. He owned an SUV he was willing to sell. It was not pretty, but it would get us from point A to point B. If our mechanic thought the vehicle was safe to drive, we were good to go. The Lord came through. Just as we knew He would.

When we arrived to pick up the 1994 4Runner (with well over 250,000 miles) and complete the paperwork, we noticed the purchase price was missing from the title. We asked our mechanic if he wanted to fill in the amount prior to signing it. He said it did not matter what amount we used.

It was, however, important to us because the purchase price determined the amount of sales tax we would pay the county. We needed to decide whether to lower the amount on the title to save money on the sales tax, or pay the sales tax on the actual amount paid. That was an epic moral dilemma.

God gave us a car we could afford, from a seller we trusted. Did we trust Him to provide the funds for the sales tax or would we take matters into our own hands to create our own "savings?" Was our faith for sale for a few hundred dollars? I prayed quickly for guidance in how to proceed.

I looked at Keith and he looked at me. I held my breath, waiting for him to lead us in the decision. He looked me in the eyes and said, "Write $1500 as the purchase price." I was ecstatic! In the past, I would have been tempted to write in a lower amount to "save" money, but those days were long gone. I saw every financial crossroad as a test of our faith in the Lord and His process, and I refused to fail for few hundred dollars.

We often told our kids, "What happens in the dark, will one day come to the light," paraphrasing Luke 8:17. This situation was no different. We wanted the Lord to bless our efforts to get out of debt, and we often prayed for Him to miraculously decrease our debt in whatever way He chose. How could we ask this of Him when we were unwilling to be truthful? How could we ask this of Him when we circumvented the process?

"Render unto Caesar what is Caesar's" were words from Jesus' own lips. They were a reminder of the importance to do the right thing, not because we wanted to be rewarded, but because it is what is asked of us.

Your Turn…Your Perspective: How have you been tempted to "stretch" the truth? What justification did you give yourself?

Prayer: Lord, thank You for the reminder to do the right thing. Thank You for the character-building moments You give me. I pray to stay in tune to You and the promptings of the Holy Spirit. Keep me mindful of all who see You through my actions.

Day 148
Goodbye, Old Friend

LAMENTATIONS 4:1A

When our mechanic told us the repairs needed on Keith's beloved F-150 would cost more than the truck was worth, our hearts sunk. We just finished paying a small fortune buying a car for me and getting it roadworthy. There was only $1500 left for the purchase of another vehicle. We knew finding another for him would prove difficult.

We sat with the thought for a few days before deciding to buy another vehicle. Our mechanic was in possession of a 20-year-old SUV which was still in working condition. He agreed to sell it to us for $1500, knowing it was all we could afford at the time. It needed a few minor repairs, along with registration.

We decided to sell Keith's F-150 to the local wholesaler. We took the cash we received from the sale and added to what was in savings. We had sold my car to the local wholesaler a few months earlier and were familiar with the process.

It was a wholesale transaction so we knew we were not getting as much as we would from a private sale, but we needed the money to help with the registration of our new purchase. The entire transaction took less than an hour.

The sales agent asked if there was anything we wanted to take out of the vehicle. We removed everything before driving to the dealership, but Keith requested time for one last check. He stayed longer than expected, and I was surprised by the level of emotion I saw on his face when he finally returned.

Even before I asked what was wrong, I knew. He had driven the truck for 15 years. It was like an old friend. It was an end of an era, but also the beginning of one. We both knew getting out of debt was more important than the vehicles we drove. We decided previously not to spend much money on vehicles until after we became debt-free.

For Keith, saying goodbye to his F-150 meant saying goodbye to driving a truck for the next few years. And the car we purchased for him was far from comfortable. He traded down instead of up.

My heart hurt for him. I knew his pride was taking a beating. I also knew he chose the path we were on. We both did. The loss of the F-150 was just another sacrifice along the journey to become debt-free. We did not know when we would be able to purchase another truck for Keith, but we both knew the delay in gratification was worth the reward of freedom from debt.

Keith would be a truck guy again. His time of comfort and leisure would eventually return, as soon as we were done with our goal. It would make the next truck purchase so much sweeter and we both looked forward to it.

Your Turn…Your Perspective: What have you recently gone without in order to meet a financial goal? Was it worth it? Why or why not?

Prayer: Lord, I know the tough choices I face as a part of my own financial journey. Thank You for humility. Please give me the courage to not succumb to pride. Help me not put my wants ahead of the plan You have for me.

Day 149
Treads

PROVERBS 20:15

When Keith and I replaced his beloved Ford F-150 with a $1500 Toyota 4Runner, we opted not to replace the tires right away. The first reason for waiting was cash flow. We were only able to save about $2000 before needing to replace his vehicle. After paying for the 4Runner, taxes, title, and tags, we were quite low on cash. We needed to rebuild the emergency fund and get back on track with debt-reduction as soon as possible.

The second reason we chose to wait to replace his tires was because there was still a little life left in them. It was not a lot of life, but it was enough to get him back and forth to work for a few months. We decided this would give us enough time to save for the tires, and still make some debt-reduction payments. And quite honestly, we also wanted to make sure our $1500 vehicle was going to be with us long enough to invest in tires.

Several months later, we began to look for tires. Because the truck was almost 20 years old, the tires were not easy to find. They were also expensive. The cheapest set we found cost almost $600. We were faced with a dilemma: Do we put $600 tires on a $1500 vehicle, or do we risk our safety and ride the tires a little longer until we could buy another vehicle? We wanted to keep the truck as long as we could before replacing it. The longer we kept it, the more money we would be able to save for the next vehicle. It was not an easy decision.

We prayed for a few weeks and finally decided to buy the tires. We found a coupon which gave us a slight discount, and then negotiated the inclusion of free tire rotation and balancing for the life of the vehicle. We did not know how much use we would get out of the extra benefits but wanted to save money wherever we could.

Just a few weeks later, the 4Runner blew a head gasket and was dead in the water. Our worst scenario had come to life. Almost $600 was gone on tires for a vehicle we could no longer drive. It was heartbreaking, with the worst possible timing. It seemed like such an incredible waste of money. I had to make a conscious decision to keep a positive outlook about it all.

I chose to join Keith in seeing the entire ordeal as a simple business decision. I could allow it to take me into an emotional tailspin (as other emergencies did in the past) or I could choose to embrace the truth. We saved for tires and we bought tires. We could not control the timing of anything else.

I spent so much time reacting to emergencies, I was not sure I knew how to do anything else. It was obviously frustrating to lose so much money on the purchase of the tires, but what did we gain? Where was the good in the situation? The simple answer is we learned to work through difficult circumstances, regardless of the outcome, and we learned to trust God and His plan. Through all of it, we paid cash. No new debt for any of it. It was a powerful lesson.

Your Turn…Your Perspective: When has an adversity derailed you? How did you recover? What did you learn?

Prayer: Lord, thank You for opportunities to grow my faith. Help me to be mindful of the role of adversity. I pray to always trust You and not blame You when difficulties show up in life. Thank You, Jesus.

Day 150
Car Conundrum

PROVERBS 29:3A

After we purchased a $1500 replacement car for Keith and completed the repairs on the vehicle we purchased for me, we truly needed a moment to breathe. It was a tough few months in the car department, and our emergency fund took hit after hit. In the end, we were thankful to have a good-sized debt snowball payment because it was repurposed to help cover the cost of our car woes.

It was months before we could again pay anything other than minimum payments on our debts. We weathered the expensive financial storm without breaking, and as a bonus, the experience taught us just how resilient we could be when faced with a financial crisis. Our line in the sand had not been erased. No new debt was introduced. Praise the Lord.

Unfortunately, the reality was we weren't finished with this particular storm. We simply put a bandage on our car issues. Keith's $1500 vehicle would not last long and we knew it. It was just a matter of time before we needed to search for a vehicle again.

We needed to decide just how much to save for his next vehicle and how to do it. Should we take a month or two and pile up cash until the $1500 vehicle died? Or, did we take our chances by saving only a small amount each month, and see how far it took us? All money saved would come from payments to our debt snowball which meant a delay in paying off debt. We did not have many options.

We prayed and asked the Lord for guidance. "Which way, Lord? What would You have us do?"

After several days, we decided to put $300 aside each month for the next car purchase. We also decided to stop saving after we reached $3000. With our $1000 emergency fund, we felt it was enough to purchase a slightly better vehicle for Keith, and still not delay payments to our debt snowball too much. Armed with our new plan, we slowly began to rebuild momentum and were once again making headway on our debt snowball.

Fast forward ten months. Our $3000 was saved. We redirected the monthly $300 allotment back to the debt snowball. Just a few weeks later the $1500 car died. I was amazed at how calm we both were, especially me. I did not feel anxious when Keith called to tell me the car died. I did not feel fear at what might happen next. We had a plan and enough cash to put it into action.

There was very little emotion surrounding the need to buy another vehicle, and none of it was negative. We viewed it more as an inconvenience than anything else. We quietly went about the rest of our week and planned to start looking for another vehicle over the weekend.

I was amazed at the difference in my demeanor from previous car issues. I felt so thankful to have moved past the panic associated with "emergencies." We knew the day was coming and appropriately planned for it. It was not really an emergency after all.

Your Turn…Your Perspective: What emergency has caused you to have a negative emotional response? How did you work through it?

Prayer: Lord, thank You for growth and faith. Thank You for helping me embrace change and prepare for it. Please keep me mindful of this moment when I am faced with other challenging circumstances.

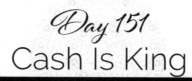
Cash Is King

When Keith and I started following Dave Ramsey and the principles of Financial Peace University, our unsecured debt level was over $191,000. In addition, both of our cars were over 10 years old with almost 200,000 miles of wear. We knew chances were slim we would make it through our debt snowball journey without having to replace one or both of our vehicles. Since we made frequent trips to St. Louis to pick up our kids, we needed at least one road-worthy car to handle the 400-mile trip we regularly made.

Our starter emergency fund of $1000 was in place, but we felt it would be beneficial to have a separate car fund. We also did not want to decrease paying on our debts any more than necessary. We were in a quandary.

After praying for several weeks, we decided to put $300 a month in a car savings fund. Every month the account was able to grow. There were several times when major car repairs were funded from the car savings envelope because the emergency fund was not enough to cover the cost of the repairs. Each time the emergency passed, we resumed saving $300 a month.

When the first car died, about $4000 was in the account. We added our emergency fund and debt snowball money to the car fund and paid cash to replace it. I did not want to continue saving for a car fund because I was ready to increase payment on our debt snowball, but we knew Keith's car was already showing signs of the need for costly repairs. We decided to continue putting away money for car replacement. Three months later, the second car died.

After making my car roadworthy and getting it registered, there was only $1500 saved to replace Keith's vehicle. It was not good. We did not know how to buy a $1500 car, but we were committed to not adding to our debt. The Lord truly answered our prayer when our mechanic called and told us he found a $1500 car for us. His shop maintained it also and he was familiar with its history. It was not the best-looking vehicle, but it would get Keith to and from work without major issues.

Keith's replacement car was a 1995 model with over 250,000 miles on it. It was rusty on the outside and barebones on the inside. But it was what we could afford and was deemed safe by our mechanic. It was all we could ask for.

We did not know how long Keith's "new" car would last, so we continued saving for another one. Our prayer was to save at least $3000 to get him into a slightly better vehicle. We would not buy before the car died, but simply keep saving.

We realized through the process just how committed we were to becoming debt-free. We knew we would have ended up with two new car payments beginning within months of each other if our resolve were not so strong. We were so thankful we made the hard choice to split our focus and put a small portion of our debt snowball payment amount aside to use for replacement vehicles. It saved us more than we would ever know.

Your Turn...Your Perspective: What process do you use to determine how and when to save for large purchases? What limitations do you place on yourself to prevent overspending?

Prayer: Lord, thank You for favor and wisdom. Please help me stay focused on the plan You have for me. It sometimes seems hard to manage, but I know my diligent hands will help me reap the reward if I do not lose sight of the goal.

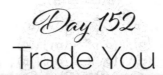

Day 152
Trade You

PROVERBS 29:7; 1 PETER 5:7

The day Keith's $1500 Toyota 4Runner died was a Tuesday. We were to teach an FPU class at the church and Keith was on his way to meet me when I got the call. He was stranded on the side of the road and AAA had to send a tow truck to get him. We taught the class, shared our story to give an example of how to work through an emergency, and headed home.

The next day, our mechanic called with the news of a blown head gasket. There was no need putting a new engine in a car worth less than $1500. But there was another cost which needed to be considered. We literally just put $600 tires on the vehicle a few weeks earlier.

It was hard to not feel defeated at the loss of so much money. I did not want to dwell on the loss, but $600 was a lot of money when we were still in the midst of so much debt. "Lord, help me to not be defined by this" was the prayer I prayed. I wanted to respond well and not worry. I wanted to prove just how much I had grown spiritually to both God and Keith.

I breathed deeply and prayed for God to calm my spirit. "Show me Your plan, Lord."

A friend of ours also owned an older model 4Runner. She was young, single, and did not yet understand the nuances of maintaining a vehicle. Keith looked at her vehicle a few months earlier and recommended she start saving for tires. Even though months passed since we last saw her, I reached out hoping we could sell her our tires.

If we could get $400 for the tires, I knew I would feel better. Losing $200 was a lot better than losing $600, but we needed to make a decision soon. Several days later, our friend was ruled out as an option and our mechanic wanted to know what we wanted to do with the 4Runner; we needed to arrange to have it towed somewhere. He would only be able to store it for a few more days. We were running out of options.

The next day, we called our mechanic to ask his advice. Keith and I exhausted all our options and wanted to get his opinion. We told him we were holding out on getting the vehicle towed because we did not want to lose the tires. Sending brand new tires to the scrap yard was not our idea of a good investment. We asked him if he knew anyone who would be in the market for tires.

He thought a moment and blew us away with what he said next. They were a full-service repair shop and offered an apprentice program for their technicians. Someone may start out as an oil change guy but could graduate to more responsibility over time. There was a new technician who wanted to certify on rebuilding engines. Our 4Runner would be the perfect practice vehicle.

He offered us $400 for the 4Runner. Praise the Lord! It was the exact number we prayed to receive to recoup most of the money from the tires. What a blessing! Yet again, God showed us He cared for all our needs. Wow!

Your Turn…Your Perspective: How has God shown His care for you recently? What did you learn from the experience?

Prayer: Lord, thank You for caring for my every need. Thank You for showing Yourself even in the difficult times. I pray I am always reminded of just how much You love me. I know You are with me always.

Day 153
Good Customer Service

PROVERBS 21:8

We loved our new mechanic. Over and over they showcased what a good decision it was for us to switch from the dealer service centers we used to use. They took great care of our vehicles and helped us out in a pinch many times.

Another incentive was the desire for better service. We really did not like the level of service we received from the dealership for the our newly purchased SUV. They were the only dealer in town for our make and model, and they acted like it. The air of superiority experienced during prior service visits did not leave us with a warm and fuzzy feeling. We felt like we were being sold.

Our new mechanic was a little shop with a big heart. It felt good to know we were supporting a small business in the heart of our community. They always went above and beyond and we were thankful to have found them.

One night, Keith was on his way home when the $1500 car we purchased for him died on the highway. He called AAA and they sent a tow truck to pick up the vehicle. We paid for the mid-level membership, which gave us a 50-mile tow radius. When the driver arrived, he asked where Keith would like the take the car. No need to take it to our house. Keith told the driver the name of our local mechanic.

We knew the garage was already closed. The car would have to sit outside of the garage, which was not ideal. There were security cameras outside to deter theft, but ambitious car thieves might still attempt to remove parts accessible from underneath the car. It was a chance we would have to take.

Imagine our joy and surprise when the tow truck driver told Keith he had a garage door opener for our mechanic. As it turned out, our mechanic was quite the networker. He and the tow truck driver worked together so much, they established a system for after-hour deliveries. He would put our car inside our mechanic's garage instead of just dropping it off in the parking lot.

What a blessing! We were so thankful. We knew we would not have gotten this type of care with the dealership maintenance department. It was yet another example of the level of customer service we received from our new mechanic. It also reminded us of the importance to take the time to choose business relationships carefully.

We trusted the integrity of our mechanic and came to appreciate his way of doing business. But protecting our vehicle after hours went above and beyond. We certainly felt cared for with our new mechanic.

Our journey of Christ-centered financial wellness was filled with examples of how to be good stewards. Choosing quality business relationships not only saved us money, but also gave us peace of mind. Our new mechanic was proof of God's desire to help us save money and have peace of mind.

Your Turn...Your Perspective: What business relationships in your life have taught you the most about money management? What was the lesson? How did it impact you?

Prayer: Lord, I pray to always be mindful of the small blessings which come even in difficult circumstances. Please help me get past this crisis. I want to make good choices for today and long term. I pray to be proactive and not reactive when I choose business relationships.

Day 154
The God Car

PROVERBS 13:21; GENESIS 12:2

Car drama. Car drama. Car drama.

It had been going on for months. From the repairs leading up to replacing my car, and subsequent cash out to get it roadworthy, to Keith's truck dying and then his replacement vehicle dying, we were up to our eyeballs in car drama. This did not even include all the medical drama we experienced during this same time. One issue after another was there waiting for our attention.

The only solace we found in all of it was cash. We managed to get through all of it with cash. No debt was used for any of our money drama. We were armed with $3000 to get another vehicle for Keith. We were better prepared to do our due diligence and make a sound purchase. The weekend car shopping trip would commence in just a few days.

The Wednesday after Keith's car 4Runner died, we went to our life group meeting just as we did most Wednesdays. After going through our Bible study, our group took time to go through prayer requests and praise reports. Since I recorded the requests for historical purposes, Keith and I typically went last. When it was our turn, we shared what happened with the group, thanked the Lord for our tow service, and asked the group to pray for us as we headed out over the weekend to look for a car for Keith.

The group knew we were working hard to get rid of debt, and knew all of the emergencies we had been through in the previous months. We knew they would support us in prayer as we searched for a reliable vehicle in our price range. All we expected was prayer. Imagine our surprise when one of them offered not only to pray for us, but to give us a car!

Our friends were given a car by one of their mothers a few months earlier. She had upgraded her vehicle and passed her slightly used car on to our friends. Since both of their cars were older, but still in good condition, they decided to gift their oldest vehicle to continue the string of blessings.

They first chose a young man to receive the car several months prior, but he had not followed through on the few items needed to transfer the title. So, when Keith and I mentioned we would be shopping for a car, they decided to gift the car to us instead. We could not believe it! Our entire life group erupted in praise and excitement; we were all thankful for the opportunity to be a part of this cycle of blessings. We all then went outside to check out the car – our new replacement vehicle.

The Lord told Abraham he would be blessed to be a blessing. Our friends took those words to heart when they chose to give us their car. We knew we too were blessed to be a blessing, and we wanted to kick our blessing into high gear by working fervently to get out of debt as quickly as possible. In the meantime, Keith's "God" car was an incredible testimony of faith. We shared it often with all who would listen.

Your Turn…Your Perspective: When have you been blessed to be a blessing? When did someone last bless you? How did each experience impact your life?

Prayer: Lord, thank You for blessings. I pray for a circle of friends to support me on this journey. Please help me to showcase Your love by blessing Your people whenever possible.

Day 155
Google Fiber

PHILIPPIANS 3:7; JOHN 17:16

Keith and I struggled with internet and cable prices since we started repaying our debt snowball. Prices were driven by packages and contracts, and the best rates were those where services were bundled together. The cost of internet itself was almost as expensive as the packages.

We continued to keep very basic cable service and an internet plan with moderate speed. The problem was "moderate" kept getting slower and slower. It was so frustrating. We knew the rate of speed was kept slower as a way to force us into a more expensive package. We finally decided to just deal with the speed. We did not want to decrease payments to our debt snowball to increase the speed (and cost) of internet.

When Google Fiber (Google's internet and cable service) came along, we were very excited to make the switch. Kansas City, MO was the first city to receive the service, and it was extended to the entire metro area after only a year on the market. The service provided incredibly fast internet and cable television services at competitive prices. More importantly for us, we were able to get the services independent of each other.

Being able to purchase the services independently meant we could drop our cable plan and purchase an internet-only plan. We were able to drop our overall cost, increase our internet speed, and were no longer locked into a 2-year cable contract. We opted to watch the few television shows we followed by streaming them on-demand. We were no longer paying for services we did not need! And, we finally had internet speed which was more than "moderate."

Not everyone understood our decision to cut cable. Many could not understand how we could give up the convenience of having television at our fingertips. The cut in cable did not seem to be worth the effort to them. In their minds, it was only a savings of a few hundred dollars a year. What difference could it possibly make in the long run?

We decided to manage our own household without regard to what people thought about it. We often heard this mentioned on "The Dave Ramsey Show." We chose to "live like no one else, so later [we] could live (and give) like no one else." We chose to stand firm on our decision to switch to Google Fiber for internet and not have a cable plan at all.

We decided to continue with the internet-only plan, at least until we were debt-free. If we opted to reconnect cable television afterwards, we would make the decision knowing it was a luxury and not a necessity.

The best part was making our own decision. We were not at anyone's mercy; not a cable company or our friends. We weighed all the factors and made the best decision for our family. It felt good to know we were in control, and not simply doing what society thought was best.

Your Turn…Your Perspective: What are you willing to give up to reach your goals? How well do you manage sacrifice?

Prayer: Lord, thank You for the discipline to go against what is popular. You said in Your Word I am in this world, but not of this world. Please help me to keep this mindset as I continue the plan You have set before me.

Day 156
Three Strand Cord

PROVERBS 6:2; ECCLESIASTES 4:12; JOHN 10:10B

A few years into paying on our debt snowball, a song by Christian artists Casting Crowns was released and really captured the essence of how we felt about our journey to debt-freedom. "Broken Together" was about a couple struggling in their marriage. They finally got to a point where they realized neither of them was perfect, and they must accept each other's brokenness to survive as a couple. While our marriage was not in danger of failing, there were many old scripts playing in our heads about money.

Our childhood, our early adult years, foolish business decisions, and simple ignorance all played into who we were the day we got married and became united as a couple. We each brought our own share of financial baggage, and the weight of it all was daunting. We worked to support the other as best we could but were each responsible for the personal healing we needed. If a flight attendant were instructing us in marriage, we would have been told to put our own mask on first before assisting the other.

It was not easy. Keith grew up poor in the inner city of St. Louis. He spent his formative years in the Marine Corps. He knew how to survive but did not know how to thrive. I grew up on a farm in South Carolina. I was taught a strong work ethic and making a difference was in my DNA, but I knew little about money.

Keith experienced foreclosures and I lost over $200,000 because of a series of poor financial decisions. He brought student loans into our marriage. I brought credit cards and personal loans. We both owed the IRS. He wanted to give all our money away, and I was afraid to give at all. A lot of financial weariness joined us at the altar.

It could have been enough to break us, but we were already broken.

The first few years were filled with confusion and a strong desire not to blame the other. Our financial coach helped us learn the basics and taught us how to build a strong financial foundation for our marriage. The budget became our friend and helped teach us how to communicate. I began to let go of the fear of not having enough, and Keith learned his home was his first ministry.

With fingers interlocked with the Holy Spirit, we held on tight, determined to get to "better together." We may have put our own mask on first, but we refused to leave without the other. We were determined to not only be debt-free, but to be free of the old money habits which bound us our entire adult lives.

Instead of drifting apart, we found our relationship strengthening. One by one, the old scripts we lived with the first 43 years of our lives were replaced with stronger, healthier, Bible-centered scripts. These new scripts taught us how to dream, how to be free in our thinking, how to balance generosity and wealth, and how to be at peace with what we had while working towards the next Godly goal.

In John 10:10b, Jesus says, "I have come that they may have life, and have it more abundantly." We were no longer bound in debt, but free to live in abundance – a journey we happily accepted.

Your Turn…Your Perspective: What old scripts have kept you from being free? What impact has living with old scripts made on your financial well-being?

Prayer: Lord, I pray for continued awareness of old scripts. Help me to spot them quickly and bind them with Your Word. I pray for the courage to learn new scripts, based on truth and fact. Help me resist the world's way of managing money and follow Your will for my life.

Day 157
Tax Time

PROVERBS 21:6

In the first few years of our marriage, we dreaded tax time. We owed the IRS over $6,000 the first year we filed jointly, and over $8,000 the second year. Each time we set up a payment plan. We did not have the cash to pay our taxes outright. Each time we incurred interest and fees until the amount was paid off. It was brutal and sent me into an emotional tailspin. We were hemorrhaging money and could not figure out how to stop the bleeding. The interest and fees alone were adding close to $1,000 a year to our debt.

We knew the IRS moved to the top of the list of debts. Their ability to literally take money from your bank account at a moment's notice meant we needed to get them out of our lives as quickly as possible. We also knew we must to do a better job of determining our withholdings each pay period to not owe again the third year. It was time to get serious and smart about our tax bill.

The number of deductions available to us was low, and our tax bracket was high. Not the best combination in the world of tax planning. We tithed and gave to a few charities which helped a little. We maxed out the non-cash donations category. We each took advantage of our Flexible Spending Account contribution which allowed pre-tax money to be used for out of pocket medical expenses. My Mary Kay business also helped tremendously in terms of providing small business tax deductions. No other deductions were available.

We decreased our tax withholdings even further and made the adjustments in our budget. We cut every category in our budget as much as we could and then decreased the amount allocated to the debt snowball. The new amount for our net income was significantly lower each pay period, but it was the only way to prevent a third year of owing on our taxes.

The next step was to dig in and work to get rid of the gigantic tax bill. The debt snowball money went to the IRS. Interest, penalties and fees accrued daily, so we sent multiple payments each month. Any "extra" money we found during the month went straight to the IRS. It took well over a year to get rid of it all. We were thankful when it was gone. It was a huge relief to no longer owe the IRS.

In the years after we paid off our "mega-debt" to the IRS, we became much more proactive at tax time. Our taxes were completed by the middle of February. We always owed Federal, but typically got a refund from both states (I worked in Missouri, we lived in Kansas). The refunds were always applied to what we owed Federal, and the difference was budgeted and paid long before April 15 arrived.

Our decisions meant no more racing to beat the Notice of Payment announcing more interest, penalties and fees. No more random IRS envelopes in the mailbox. No more fear.

The peace of mind associated with not having a huge payment to the IRS was beautiful. It was a reminder of how far we had come, and exactly where we were going. We were realizing financial freedom even before being debt-free, simply from not owing the IRS.

Your Turn…Your Perspective: How do you handle tax time? Do you dread it or embrace it? Why?

Prayer: Lord, please help me confront my debt head on. Give me the strength to look forward to the future and not be fearful. I know You are with me and will get me through this. Please, Jesus, give me the courage to press through.

Personal Garden

PSALM 8:5-6

When Keith and I decided to partner with a local Community Supported Agriculture (CSA), we did not know what we were getting into. The idea of jointly sharing in a farmer's crop seemed like a cool way to buy organic vegetables at a discount. The goal was to lower the grocery bill by not purchasing organic vegetables from a grocery store.

After a little trial and error, I finally figured out what to do with all this new, cool food. Instead of grocery shopping and then picking up our CSA share, I let the CSA share lead the grocery shopping. I was already using a weekly meal plan to manage our food budget, but with the CSA, I could simply manage it in reverse.

I got creative with what we received. Instead of making spaghetti for two meals, and then trying to figure out what to do with the cabbage, we passed on the spaghetti and made coleslaw to pair with pulled BBQ chicken. I roasted the beets, added a Dijon mustard sauce, and served them alongside a baked chicken.

The leafy greens were used for salads throughout the week. They also became a part of a weekly frittata. Turnips and other roots were frozen for future use, and zucchini was made into no-carb lasagna. Cucumbers were added to tomatoes and red onions for Keith's favorite summer salad.

The farmers of our CSA sent out a list a few days before shares were scheduled to be picked up. It was like getting a sneak peek under the tree a few days before Christmas morning. By planning ahead, I did not buy unnecessary items from the grocery store. No need to buy spaghetti sauce when tomatoes were in abundance. I made my own roasted marinara sauce, instead. We used some and froze the rest for future use.

Shopping became more efficient. Eggs were always on the grocery list, but now they were used for dinner in a frittata with a side salad. Carrots (including the tops) were used in smoothies so there was no need to buy extra spinach. Strawberries were used for homemade sorbet so no ice cream was added to the list. If we were scheduled to have guests, we added them to angel food cake for a beautiful trifle.

It was a great experience. Keith and the kids really got into it. Our daughter and I scoured the internet looking for cool recipes to use with our upcoming share. Other times, our searches were for techniques for storing food for future use. Who knew watermelon radishes could be fermented?

Even though we paid a fee of roughly $30 each week for the CSA for 7 months, our vegetable supply lasted almost 9 months, and our grocery bill dropped almost 15%. It was a great savings.

When the season came to an end the first year, we really missed our weekly treasure chest. Keith asked one day, "What happened to the vegetables?" When I told him the season was over, he looked at me blankly and said, "What does that mean?" I had to laugh. I knew then we would sign up for farm shares when the season opened again.

Your Turn…Your Perspective: In what ways have you gotten creative to save money? How have you been financially impacted by your community?

Prayer: Lord, I pray for ways to enjoy my new way of managing money. Please help me to embrace frugality and choose a good attitude about my situation. I thank You for the nudge to be a better steward of the resources You have provided.

Day 159
Frozen Organics
PSALM 145:15

I was always looking for ways to decrease our food budget. It was the largest part of our budget after debt reduction and I was constantly aware of how much could be allocated to our debt snowball if it was not spent on food. Organic meats were the largest expense. Keith was a meat-eater and did not enjoy meals where non-meat protein took center stage. I could enjoy a hearty bowl of black bean soup for dinner while he dug through the bowl looking for chunks of chicken or turkey.

A new grocery store opened in town and I found it to be the best source for a large portion of our shopping list. I was able to get nuts and flours for bulk rate prices. Spices were incredibly reasonable, and there was also a large selection of items I could not find in regular grocery stores. One day as I was scanning the aisles, I noticed a marked down section in the freezer.

It turned out the store found a way to recapture lost revenue. Instead of throwing away meats too close to their "sell by" date, they froze them and lowered the price. The meat could then be sold from the freezer at a reduced rate for an additional 4-6 months. Instead of losing money by throwing away the item, they simply made less profit by selling it at a discounted price. It worked for me! It was the same as buying fresh meat in the store and putting it in the freezer at home.

The store may not have been thinking of our family when they switched to this strategy, but I was incredibly thankful just the same. This was a glimpse into the seriousness with which we approached debt reduction. Frozen, organic meat got me excited.

Switching to frozen versus fresh meat resulted in small savings in the beginning, but I kept at it. I even created a motto when deciding whether the sacrifice was worth it: "Every dollar not going to student loans does not go to student loans!" The small savings we made on discounted organic meat purchases amounted to at least a month's worth of student loan interest saved each year.

Inevitably, when we shared this story with our FPU classes, we received strange looks. It was extreme. But for us, extreme was where the savings lived. We were determined to not live like most people. Most people kept their student loans for decades. We were determined to get rid of ours. Most people did not delay purchasing a home or taking a vacation until they were completely debt-free, either.

Keith often stated that everything about our journey was out of the ordinary. We chose to not be normal; we chose to not be defined by debt or status. We were simply intentional in rectifying our financial mistakes and made radical decisions to make it happen.

Buying discounted meat should not have been a big deal, but for some reason, to me it was. There were so many distractions, so many reasons why we should spend our money in other places. Buying discounted meat acted as a lifeline back to our initial mission to be debt-free. It tethered me to our goal and served as a constant reminder to stay focused. All I needed to do was hold on and keep moving.

Your Turn…Your Perspective: What money saving strategies do you have? How have you had to defend them to others?

Prayer: Lord, thank You for the desire to follow Your plan. I pray it constantly remains stronger than the desire to please others. Help me to stay focused, regardless of how long it takes.

Day 160
Returns

NEHEMIAH 9:15

Food was a big part of the healing process for Keith and me as we worked through our medical issues. At the prompting of a naturopath, we switched to an all-organic diet years earlier and worked to keep our food costs as low as possible.

However, each physician chose a different system to detox the body and inevitably our food protocol changed. Our core foods literally changed every 4-6 months. I tried to stay on top of things as best I could. It was a merry-go-round of fruits, vegetables, fish, meats and supplements. It was a lot to manage.

I decided early on it was valuable to shop at grocery stores with a generous return policy, and I kept receipts for months. Every time our food list changed, I went through our freezer and pantry, and returned all the items which no longer fit our newly outlined food regimen. Many times, the refunded amount was well over $100. In most instances, only an in-store credit was available. It worked for me.

No item was off limits. The pound of buckwheat flour which cost $3.49 was just as likely to be returned as a $39.99 jar of protein powder. We needed all the grocery assistance we could get, and I was not going to let pride keep me from saving $3.49. Every return yielded money which went back into the grocery budget.

During one doctor's visit, I discovered I was allergic to rice. I lived a gluten-free lifestyle for 15 years and the main ingredient in gluten-free flour was brown rice. My migraine-style headaches were a result of literally overdosing on brown rice. All the gluten-free foods in our house were returned or donated.

Over and over, I did food exchanges. Occasionally, a receipt would slip through the cracks and I found myself with an item which could not be returned. Those items were then donated to the local food pantry if they were dry goods, or were given away to friends. Our friends thought we were weird for taking back groceries, but I did not care.

Many of them questioned our entire money management strategy, so not having an endorsement for my return process did not matter much to me. Ultimately, it kept us from increasing the food budget. It took a great deal of money to buy everything needed to start a new food protocol and returning items we could not use was a great way to make a dent.

I did struggle, however. I would hear callers on the Dave Ramsey show, and our own FPU class members, talk about feeding a family of four on $150 a week (or a month!), and our budget was four or five times their amount. It was frustrating to know payments to our debt snowball were smaller because we ate organic foods.

It all came down to good health. Time and time again, I asked myself if the money spent on organic food was worth it. But each time I went back to our core principle for healing. If you do not have good health, nothing else really mattered. Returning what we could not use helped keep it plausible for me. It felt good to reuse what I could, when I could, to make it all work in the end.

Your Turn...Your Perspective: What questionable budgetary choices have you had to make on your financial journey? How do you justify your decision?

Prayer: Lord, I pray for the courage to do the things others deem as weird while in this financial season. I pray to not give in to those who criticize my choices. Please help me stay in tune with the Holy Spirit. Help me stay in Your will.

Day 161
No New Meals

Keith was not a cook. When we got married, he told me "you can cook whatever you want, as long as I get full." It was music to my ears since experimenting in the kitchen was something I enjoyed. Three years into paying our debt snowball, however, I realized a great way to tighten up our food budget was to cut back on experimenting in the kitchen.

That meant no one-time use ingredients. No overly expensive ingredients. The tarragon shrimp salad stuffed in fresh tomatoes was no longer a summertime treat. Gone were the fish tacos with fresh mango salsa. The braised chicken with dried apricots, walnuts and pineapple was a thing of the past. It was a hard decision since cooking was something I really enjoyed. Since eating out was a rarity, experimenting in the kitchen became a form of entertainment for me.

I learned a mantra during my time in leadership with Mary Kay Cosmetics which I chose to apply to our meal situation: "I do not have to do this for the rest of my life, but I do need to do it today." By choosing this mindset, I saw the change as an emotionally healthy decision. I chose to not feel deprived by the change but embraced the opportunity to be creative in a new way.

I learned to experiment with recipes using ingredients already in the pantry. Stuffed peppers became a new staple meal, along with Shephard's pie. Our food budget decreased, and the extra money was moved to the debt snowball. We still enjoyed sharing our meals together even though they were the same meals we ate the week before. Ultimately, the lack of variety really was not noticed by anyone but me. And since I knew it was only temporary, I chose not to dwell on it.

"Power" cooking was also a technique I used in the past and began to do so again. One or two days a month I made large quantities of spaghetti sauce, chili, and Shephard's pie to freeze. Experimentation was only a few times a year and the rest of the time I worked from a set meal rotation. Instead of getting excited about debuting a great new chicken dish, I chose to focus on how much money we were able to move to the debt snowball.

Over time, the entire family got involved in rallying me on in the kitchen. We made a game out of how to stretch a meal. One week we ate meatloaf four days in a row! The kids were disappointed to see it was all gone. I was thankful two pounds of ground turkey, two eggs, salsa and oatmeal stretched into four meals for a family with strong appetites. It felt like I was feeding my family with two fish and five loaves of bread. The meatloaf just did not run out. I could see God's hand at work in our budget once again. And I was thankful.

In the beginning, I missed trying out new recipes. In this season, I chose to focus on the day when we would be out of debt. Experimenting in the kitchen would again bring a new level of enjoyment to our lives. The cost of the sacrifice was small compared to the gain of being completely debt-free.

Your Turn...Your Perspective: What lifestyle change are you willing to make in the short term to achieve a goal which seems just beyond your reach? How do you communicate the change to those around you?

Prayer: Lord, thank You for provision. Thank You for helping me to see the sacrifice for what it is – short term. Thank You for perspective.

Vegetables for a Friend

2 CORINTHIANS 8:15

It was CSA time again. It was a huge success for us the first time we used it so we thought we would try it again. Farmers allowed people to pre-pay for shares of crops for the season. Regardless of whether the crops were plentiful or in short supply, the members of the CSA shared alike. We thought it would be a great way to save money on organic vegetables and expose the kids to a new experience at the same time.

The CSA shares consisted of a variety of vegetables. We were able to try new things (who knew beets and kohlrabi would find their way to our table?) and enjoy long-time favorites (cucumber and tomato salad for Keith and collard greens for me). It was a good financial decision and we enjoyed using some of our vegetables and storing others for the winter months. Since I grew up putting vegetables away for the winter, it was not a stretch for me to do it again. I knew eventually I would begin our own organic garden, but for this financial season of our life, a CSA was a great investment.

The only drawback to the CSA was you were required to pick up your share each week at a designated time and place. There was very little flexibility. If you did not pick up your vegetables at the designated time, it was your responsibility to have someone else pick them up or you would forfeit your share for the week. It would then be donated to a food pantry.

Once, a family emergency called us out of town quickly and we ended up being away for 10 days. I did not want to let our share go to waste. I appreciated the CSA donating on our behalf, but I wanted to bless someone we knew if we were able to do so. I prayed and asked the Lord who needed our share the most while we were away.

We knew a friend was having a rough time financially and could benefit from not having to buy vegetables. We decided to donate our share to her. It felt good to bring a little relief to someone else's food budget and our friend was thankful. She sent pictures of the meals she prepared with the vegetables and talked for weeks about the experience every time we saw her. Her excitement was contagious.

The experience showed us the benefit of giving from the heart. Even though we chose to not do monetary giving outside of our tithe while we worked on our debt snowball, this was a great way to give. It was also a reminder to not take for granted what God gave.

We were able to make room in our budget for the CSA. It was simply a decision to do so. So many others did not have the luxury and I did not want to lose sight of what it meant to eat high quality food. Many sections of Kansas City were considered food deserts and did not have affordable, high-quality fresh food. We were blessed to ensure our home was not among them. Neither was our friend's.

Our journey was not always easy. But this small act made it feel more special. The joy of making a difference in someone else's life was incredibly gratifying.

Your Turn...Your Perspective: What non-monetary ways can you be a blessing while on your journey to financial freedom?

Prayer: Lord, please help me to keep my eyes open for opportunities to bless others. Even if my help comes in the form of non-monetary gifts, please help me to continue to be a blessing to Your people.

Day 163
Bonus Time
PSALM 115:14-15

Keith loved his job; he was definitely a "company man." He was diligent, and all his customers loved him. His supervisors always gave him great performance reviews and he received many awards and commendations. They frequently received emails of praise from other leaders in the organization and shared them with him.

He never complained when the work was complicated. He just found a way to make it work and then adjusted the process to make sure the complication did not happen again. He was a team player and worked hard at self-improvement. It was his desire to be the best at his work. He was constantly striving to be better.

Imagine Keith's surprise one year when he received a substantial bonus for his efforts. He was shocked and humbled. And the timing of the award showcased God's hand in our lives. We were in the middle of a season of continuous medical expenses when the bonus was received. All our debt snowball money had been diverted to either medical bills or car repairs for the last several months. We experienced one financial hit after another. It was frustrating, and we fought to simply stay afloat financially.

It felt as if we were in the boxing ring with the financial version of Muhammed Ali or Joe Frazier. Everywhere we turned, more money was punched out of our budget. Our debt was only decreasing by pennies since we were only able to make minimum payments. Still, we kept going. We kept paying cash for our medical expenses and continued to pay what we could on our debt.

The day we received the news of the bonus was a day of celebration for lots of reasons. We were excited to know others recognized Keith's abilities and contributions. But, we also knew the Lord was still at work on our behalf. Because we chose not to complain and grumble about our circumstances, we saw the bonus as a reprieve from the many financial blows we had recently faced.

The first thing we did was tithe. Next, we went out for a nice dinner. And finally, we made a sizable payment to our student loans. The opportunity to make a new dent in our student loan debt felt wonderful. It was a moment of resolve to not give up, but instead to stay the course. We saw the bonus as a reward for our persistence.

As time progressed, more bonuses showed up. Each time one arrived, we thanked the Lord, paid our tithe, and sent the rest to student loans. We were both eager to get out of debt and began to opt out of going to dinner to celebrate the bonus. We opted instead to pay as much as possible on our student loans and not accrue any extra interest.

We knew our future would be filled with as many dinners out as we wanted once we got past our debt. It was good to see it shrinking and we looked forward to the day when it was gone for good. In the meantime, "bonus time" continued to be "pay more on student loan time." Praise the Lord!

Your Turn...Your Perspective: Think of the last time you received a reminder to stay the course. What was it? How long after receiving it did you see it as a gentle reminder from the Lord?

Prayer: Lord, thank You for the reminders of Your faithfulness. They give me hope and provide the light for the next leg of my journey. Please continue to whisper the encouragement I need to complete the task at hand. I trust You, Jesus.

Day 164
Then It's Settled

PSALM 10:14A; PHILIPPIANS 3:14

One day as I was looking through the mail, I noticed an official looking envelope addressed to Lisa Goodman. Goodman was my maiden name, but the address was current. The combination seemed odd. "Lisa Goodman" had not lived at our address in a very long time.

I opened the envelope and found the letterhead of an attorney's office on the east coast. As it turned out, I was grandfathered into a class action lawsuit brought against my former employer. I was a part of the settlement even though my tenure there was short and several years earlier.

The documentation was sent to verify my address so my settlement check could be forwarded. I was shocked. I sat on the sofa rereading the letter over and over again. We were in the midst of a long month financially. We were high on the number of expenses requiring attention, but low on the amount of extra money available to pay debt. We did not complain about it, but it was frustrating nonetheless. The news of the settlement served as a welcomed relief to our very tight financial picture.

Fast forward a few months and the check finally arrived. The timing again was perfect. We were able to pay off our current debt and began to tackle the mountain of student loan debt waiting for us. The randomness of the settlement payout was not lost on us. We knew it was a gift from the Lord and were thankful for it.

Our journey to debt reduction took so many twists and turns – we were definitely on the scenic route. It was incredibly discouraging at times to constantly have other expenses pulling at our money. We could no longer predict when we would be debt-free because of all the detours. The settlement check was like an oasis in the middle of our financial desert. It was an unexpected blessing which gave us just a little reprieve before the heavy financial hitting began again.

As I journaled about the experience, I thanked the Lord for the increase. It was obviously a surprise which He knew we needed. It was a reminder to keep pressing on toward our finish line. We embraced the challenge to live our lives for Christ, including how we managed our money. It also meant making sacrifices along the way.

We deposited the check, paid off the next obligation in our debt snowball, and kept going. There was no pause for celebration, no splurge on a nice dinner, no shopping trip to update our wardrobe, and no weekend getaway. We used it all on our debt repayment.

We took the time to thank God for His provision and quietly went back to work cleaning up our financial mess. It was a great reminder to stay focused on the goal at hand. We would have plenty of time after we were debt-free to enjoy the fruit of our labor.

Your Turn…Your Perspective: When was the last time God gave you a reprieve in the midst of a long run? What was your mindset when the reprieve showed up? What caused you to see God's hand in it?

Prayer: Lord, thank You for a reprieve. Thank You for giving me just a moment of financial rest along my journey. I pray You help me continue to keep my eyes on the end goal and not get sidetracked by the weight of it.

Day 165
No Need to Compare

2 CORINTHIANS 8:3

Christmas and birthdays were always a time of sharing for our blended family. We celebrated birthdays with the kids on the weekend after, and split Christmas vacation with their mother. I was the primary shopper for gifts and put a lot of thought into the gifts we gave the kids. I wanted them to enjoy the giving/receiving aspects of their celebrations, but also felt it was important for them to understand our desire to be debt-free. Since being debt-free was primary, the giving budget was much smaller than I wanted.

In the beginning, it was hard for me to not succumb to the pressure to compete. I wanted the kids to be pleased with our choices in gifts for them. They were kids, and I knew they would have a lot of excitement about unwrapping gifts. It was my desire for them to have as many presents to open as possible, but still stay true to the budget. Throw in the desire for quality gifts and I had quite a dilemma on my hands.

After a few years of feeling frustrated and disappointed at their responses to their gifts, I realized I needed to shift my perspective. The budget was primary, and quality was secondary. Quantity therefore would have to suffer. I could simply not buy all the gifts I wanted to buy and still stay in the budget. It just would not work. It was a difficult decision to make, and I chose to ask myself a hard question: Who was I trying to please?

Ultimately, I knew it was not about pleasing the kids. It was about pleasing the Lord. As long as we carried debt, we were not pleasing Him. The delayed gratification of our family being in a better financial situation in the years to come needed to outweigh the momentary disappointment of the size and quantity of the gifts given to our kids. Most kids quickly forgot their gifts and ours were no different. It was up to me to make peace with the limitations of our budget.

It was not an easy decision for me. It was all in my mind. Keith was very supportive but did not really understand why this was such a big deal. I was not able to explain why it was so important for our kids to have healthy memories of their gift experiences with us. I just knew their childhood memories would include time with us in Kansas and I wanted those memories to be good ones. Celebrations around birthdays and Christmas were at the center of those memories.

I was not sure if the kids would ever fully understand why our giving was the way it was, but I knew it was our responsibility to teach them God's ways of giving. It was my hope they would remember with fondness the full extent of their time with us, and not just the price tag associated with our gifts to them. There was no way of knowing what the future held. I simply must trust the Lord and pray for them to feel our love. In the meantime, I protected my mind. I chose not to allow the enemy to eat away at my self-esteem with the lies of inadequacy.

Your Turn...Your Perspective: Have you ever been disappointed in a gift you received? Has someone else ever been disappointed in a gift you have given to them? How did you work through it?

Prayer: Lord, I pray You help me to stay focused on the things I can control and not focus on the things I cannot control. Thank You for the desire to serve and please You above all others.

Day 166
You Go. We'll Stay

MATTHEW 7:12

Our parenting plan called for Keith and me to have the kids every other President's Day while they were growing up. One year, Valentine's Day fell on the Saturday of our long President's Day weekend. We made the decision years earlier to limit our date nights when the kids were with us. Since they spent roughly 300 days a year with their mother, we chose to focus on them when they were with us.

A few weeks before February 14th, I was in the middle of devotion and felt the Holy Spirit prompting me to open our home for free babysitting for other couples on Valentine's Day. It was a completely random thought for me. It certainly was not one I would have come to on my own. I knew it must be from the Lord.

I shared my idea with Keith and he agreed it must be a divine thought. Neither of us were ones to offer babysitting, even though we would help out a friend or two in a pinch. We agreed it would be a great way to serve our friends and honor the Lord's request. We began to set the plans in motion.

We asked the Lord to show us whom to ask. He revealed five couples to us and three accepted our invitation. They were all shocked at the offer. They asked if we were sure we wanted to take on their multiple kids (of multiple ages) for the evening. We explained God's hand in the invitation and reiterated our desire to help.

There were only a few guidelines for the parents: they could drop off their kids as early as 4P.M. but they needed to pick up their kiddos by 10P.M. No one could spend the night. We would feed all the kids so no need to bring food or snacks. We wanted our friends to enjoy their evening without needing to worry about their kids.

We explained to our kids what we were doing, and they were just as excited as the parents. Their friends got to hang out at our house for a Valentine's Day party!

The big day arrived. Six kids and their parents arrived at our door by 4:05P.M. We made a big circle and prayed for the evening to be enjoyed by all. We waved goodbye to moms and dads, and the fun began. We made French bread pizza for dinner, and the kids got to decorate their own red velvet cupcakes. The boys were downstairs with action movies, and the girls were upstairs with Disney princesses. We had a blast.

By 10P.M., only our two kids remained, and our house was a mess. Each set of parents gratefully offered their thanks as they left, but we were the thankful ones. We did not even think about how much fun our own kids would have. Seeing the joy on their faces was a side benefit of the evening.

I knew with certainty we would not have allowed ourselves to be used by the Lord this way if we were in a different place financially. Even if we spent Valentine's Day just with the kids, we would probably have gone away for the long weekend. If we were debt-free, we would not have seen a staycation with the kids as "enough," and would have looked outside of our home for entertainment.

Since we were focused on spending as little money as possible, we chose to stay home to celebrate. Doing so allowed us to be blessings to three families in a really special way. Wow!

Your Turn…Your Perspective: Name a time when you served someone by stepping outside your comfort zone? What did you learn from it? How did you feel afterwards?

Prayer: Lord, please help me to be obedient to the promptings You give to step outside my comfort zone. Please help me to be open to serving You by serving others. I praise Your holy name.

Day 167
Consequences
1 TIMOTHY 6:18

We tried to support our kids in their extracurricular activities as often as possible. Because they lived four hours away, advanced planning was always necessary. Attending a school or extracurricular event meant extra gas, a possible hotel room, and lots of time on the road. Because of this, we taught the kids to let us know as early as possible in order for us to attend.

On one such occasion, there was a banquet our son wanted to attend. It was sponsored by an organization geared towards providing leadership skills to young men, and it would be the first of its kind for him. He asked us several months in advance if we would take him. Because it was also a fundraising event, the tickets were more than we would have otherwise paid for a banquet. The cost for the three of us was well over $100.

Keith and I discussed it and decided to support the event. We reallocated the money necessary to pay for the tickets, booked a hotel room, and put the event on the calendar. It would be nice to share the experience with our son, and we were looking forward to attending.

About a week before the event, our son made some poor choices at home. They were major poor choices and showcased selfishness, lack of respect, and a general disregard for the property of others. It was a very big deal.

Keith and I struggled with parenting from a distance. We often discussed how to hold our kids accountable for our value system when we were not there on a daily basis, including enforcement of consequences. Some consequences were held and enforced over the summer, but others were not so simple. After having a frank discussion with our son after the incident, there was a decision to be made. The incident was too big to be left until summer. It needed to be dealt with promptly or the impact would be lost.

We decided to remove the banquet. He would not be allowed to attend. We called the event organizer and explained the situation. Because it was a fundraiser, the money was non-refundable. Not only did we have to deal with the disobedience of our son, but the consequences which we thought were best would cost us over $100. Was the money for the tickets more important than teaching the lesson to our son? We stood at the crossroads and prayed for guidance.

We told the organizer to give the tickets to another student and his parents who would not be able to attend otherwise. We then told our son he could not attend. We explained the importance of him following the value system we put in place, and the impact of his disobedience. We told him we loved him. We told him we expected better from him.

In years past, I do not know if I would have been so open to giving up the tickets. I am not sure if I could have seen past the need for consequences to "throw away" $100. I was thankful to have grown to a place where I was no longer defined by the cost associated with a consequence. I was thankful to no longer live with such a mindset of lack.

Your Turn…Your Perspective: Name a time when consequences cost you money. What emotions did you experience because of the lost? How did your actions change after the experience?

Prayer: Lord, I pray to be able to move beyond reacting to money and situations. Thank You for seeing the value in experiencing my own consequences. I pray to stay true to Your path.

Day 168
Money for Monuments

MATTHEW 25:15

Our daughter was privileged to be accepted into her middle school gifted and talented program. It was quite an accomplishment and we were extremely proud of her. She worked hard in all her classes and was especially excited to be among the elite students in her school. One of the highlights of her eighth-grade year in the program was a trip to Washington, DC with all the other gifted and talented students from around the school district.

Information for the trip was sent home to parents in the fall with the trip scheduled for March. Each child was responsible for $750 for transportation and lodging, and another $100 for meals during the trip. Our daughter really wanted to go. She presented us with the information and asked if we would pay for her to attend.

After discussing it, we realized the great opportunity to teach her the value of money through this trip. We told her we would pay half of the cost of the trip, but she needed to be responsible for coming up with the rest. If she wanted to take the trip, she needed to earn the funds to contribute.

The school set up a payment schedule and we used it as the baseline for our family schedule. It was a great exercise in percentages and budgeting since a certain percentage needed to be paid by a specific date. We then helped her brainstorm different ways for her to earn her portion. Her list included a bake sale, babysitting, and a letter to family and friends requesting their support.

We explained the "opportunity cost" of investing in her future by paying for half the trip. We believed in her and were willing to accept staying in debt a few months longer to help her reach this goal. We gave ground rules for our contribution and made sure to explain the consequences of not following them. She was required to maintain her grades and not have any disciplinary issues. This included timely follow-up on all payments.

We talked through all the details several times to make sure she understood. We explained our trust in her to keep her word on the agreement. We also emphasized the importance of maintaining her integrity with us and the school. We were all depending on her to do her part.

It was a great first experience in the consequences of choices and the management of money. Our daughter did not think we were serious about pulling our funding and came very close to not being able to attend the trip. She missed a few assignments and was demoted to 2nd chair in band due to talking in class. When reminded of our agreement, she pleaded for another chance, and we chose to show grace. It was our hope she would learn the value of honoring commitment and being true to her word.

Time would tell if our exercise in integrity, budgeting and planning worked. In the meantime, we continued to look for opportunities to instill Godly principles in our kids.

Your Turn…Your Perspective: How do you challenge the young people in your life to make good choices? Who challenged you during your developmental years? What was the experience that impacted your life the most?

Prayer: Lord, I pray for the courage to always act with integrity. It is so easy to "get by." I want to honor You in all my commitments and represent You well in everything I do. Please let me be quick to discern when I am veering off course. I pray for Your constant reminder to live for You.

Day 169
The Agreement

PROVERBS 20:7

When our daughter asked us if we would pay for her class trip to Washington, DC, we thought it was a great opportunity to teach her how to work for what she wanted. We told her we would pay half, but she needed to raise the other half herself. We helped her set up a payment schedule. We then adjusted our budget to manage our portion.

A few weeks later, our daughter called to tell us her grandmother made a large donation to her trip fund. She turned the money into her teacher and was calling to tell us we did not need to pay our portion for the month. In her mind, her grandmother's donation counted against the total of the trip and not just her portion. Since it was a gift, and she did not actually work for the donation, she felt the need to let us know.

After chuckling at her innocence, we explained our commitment again. Any money collected by her would be applied to her portion of the cost. We would take care of our portion. The payments were already budgeted, and we would honor our commitment.

She sat quietly on the phone and soaked in our comments. She could depend on us to do our part; she just needed to do hers. We did not need her to help fulfill our obligation. She was free to focus only on her portion.

I knew her silence was a trust indicator. Although she did not ask the questions out loud, I knew what she was thinking: Will they really do their part? What if something happens and they can't fulfill their part of the cost?

The next morning during devotion, I pondered the conversation with our daughter from the day before. A sobering thought indicated a teachable moment for me. I knew what my daughter was thinking the day before because I stood in her place on many occasions.

How many times had I done the same thing to the Lord? How many times did He give me a promise only for me to try and help Him fulfill it? It happened more times than I wanted to acknowledge.

Just as we assured our daughter we would come through for her, the Lord assured me He would come through for me. All I needed to do was believe Him. My actions always showed whether I followed through on my belief. Would I continue to worry about the thing He promised to handle? Would I "let go and let God?" Would I fret, wring my hands, and cry out, "Oh, Lord!?" Would I praise Him and rest easily in the confidence of the fulfillment of His promise?

I wish I could say I always got it right, but many times I chose the route our daughter chose, and thought God needed my help. As I finished my devotion, I thanked the Lord for the reminder once again to trust Him to take care of all my needs. I prayed I would not forget it so easily this time.

Your Turn…Your Perspective: When have you tried to "help" the Lord with a request? What was the result? What did you learn?

Prayer: Lord, thank You for the reminder of Your provision. Thank You for chuckling at my foolishness but not holding it against me. Please help me to remember all the promises You have already kept as I wait patiently for the fulfillment of others. I thank You, Jesus. I trust You.

Day 170
State Line

PROVERBS 20:28

Long before our kids were old enough to apply to college, we laid out our expectations of them. These expectations came complete with guidelines for our support for college expenses. The biggest portion of our debt was the interest on Keith's student loans. We were determined they would not experience the financial overload associated with years of repayment.

One of the big guidelines for our support was choosing an in-state school. They were fortunate to have two states to choose from since we lived in Kansas and they lived in Missouri. Both states were packed with high quality schools with every subject imaginable: technology, communications, seminary. Big schools, medium sized schools, and small schools.

For years, we reinforced our commitment to higher education and the importance of choosing a school the entire family could afford. We did not know if they understood just how serious we were about our decision to only support in-state tuition. Our job was to be consistent in communicating our seriousness; their job was to listen to our words of wisdom.

When we discussed with other parents our position on college costs and the importance of the choice of school, we got strange looks. Many of them believed it was the child's choice since they were the ones attending the school. Keith and I recognized the key word which caused our raised eyebrows – child.

The person making the decision in those scenarios was indeed a child. We believed children should not be left alone to make such an important decision, especially when their decision impacted our money. It was not a popular position, but we were prepared to accept criticism for our decision. In the meantime, we did our best to expose our kids to the schools they would have the option of choosing.

Summers were filled with camps and many of those camps were held on college campuses. Christian camps, STEM camps, and art camps were all chosen with the secondary purpose of exposing our kids to colleges within the two states. We also took them to college graduations whenever we could. We were committed to exposing them to as many in-state options as possible.

We also prayed. We prayed for the wisdom to impart God's ways of money to them. We prayed for outside influences to be minimized. We prayed for their grades, their teachers, their extracurricular activities to all lead them down the path of the Lord, and not the way of the world. We prayed for them to exercise good judgement. We prayed for their friends. We prayed, and prayed, and prayed.

With prayer and exposure to multiple options, we believed we were setting our kids up for a successful college career. We were hopeful the Lord would impact their lives mightily during this season and truly believed finishing college debt-free would create an incredible opportunity for them to experience Him in a new way.

Your Turn…Your Perspective: What financial decisions have you made which were questioned by others? What was your response?

Prayer: Lord, help me to resist the urge to go the way of the world. Please give me the courage to follow Your path, even when it is not a popular one. I pray for wisdom in my decision making and wise counsel to help direct my way. Please grant discernment.

Day 171
Future Alma Mater

PSALM 34:10

Our kids were incredibly bright, and we worked hard to encourage them scholastically. One way we did this was by helping them work through future career choices. Our thought was to have career conversations early, plan activities around those conversations, and help them to eliminate the ones which no longer fit.

Our daughter wanted to be a veterinarian so we arranged for her to shadow a local animal doc with his own practice. After a day with Fluffy, Fifi and friends, she realized it was not what she expected. Veterinarian school was off the list at 12 instead of 22.

Our son loved gaming so we arranged for him to go to a camp where he could build his own mobile app. His enthusiasm turned out to be lack luster. He did not completely cross it off the list, but he better understood what it would be like to design games for a living.

We spoke openly with our kids about college and our expectations. They knew we would contribute to their educational fund, but also knew they would be required to contribute as well. We talked about the importance of establishing good study habits and not just doing the minimum. These discussions were held early and often. We learned the value of constantly reinforcing the important messages of life. The Bible was our guide.

We knew our message of being prepared for college would take time to sink in with our kids. The challenge was to keep the message fresh. Little did we know we were about to get a little help.

Dave Ramsey and his daughter Rachel Cruze wrote a book called *Smart Money, Smart Kids*. We were on a road trip shortly after it was released and were listening to the audio version in the car. The kids were watching a movie in the backseat, listening with their headphones. At some point, they stopped the movie and began listening in. They began to listen just in time to hear Rachel talk about the horrors of student loan debt. Praise the Lord!

A message we spoke of for years was now embraced by our kids. I did not care if they got it from Rachel Cruze instead of us; we just wanted them to get it! The chapter opened a great dialogue on how the entire family played a part in them each getting through college successfully. The rest of the trip set the stage for the Jones family college game plan:

-     Work to ensure a higher potential for scholarships. Lots of applications would be submitted.
-     Attend an in-state college or university to keep costs low.
-     No student loans. Period.
-     Access to all their academic records and bank accounts. Our money did not support anything we could not monitor.

Our kids knew they would receive our financial support when these four areas were met. We continued to pray for them to stay focused. It was too big a deal to get this one wrong. Their futures depended on it.

Your Turn…Your Perspective: How did the finances of education impact your life? What would you change if you could do it all over?

Prayer: Lord, I pray for the courage to have hard conversations about money. Please help me to not be fearful. I want to trust You in every area of my life, including my finances.

Day 172
Life Is Not a Game

PROVERBS 28:25

Game night/movie night was how we described family time in our house. Our daughter preferred to watch movies and our son preferred to play games. So, we alternated. During one game night, we were playing the Game of Life and our daughter was really having a rough time. She had four kids, lost her job three times, and could not seem to catch a break.

It created quite a bit of comic relief for the rest of us, but she was not happy. Frustration was the primary emotion as she continued to work her way around the board with her car filled with kids.

When she finally got another job after being terminated the third time, she ended up with a lower paying job. The new job made it hard for her to take care of her family. She pleaded with Keith and me to allow her to try again for a different career. Could she please pick again?

We exchanged looks, and Keith kindly told her she must play out the hand "Life" dealt her. He told her he was sure she would be just fine in the end and would make it through. We all wanted to win, and he was sure she would ultimately be a winner, regardless of whether she came in first place or not.

She was not happy and did not think it was fair. She thought she should be able to pick another career since her current "Life" was so hard.

It was difficult not to laugh. How many times did I ask myself the same questions? How many times did I request a "do over" for the challenging periods of my life? Except my life was not a game. As much as I wished I could have been given another chance, I must play the cards in my hand.

While our daughter was distraught over her current circumstances, we knew it would be over in a few hours. Our hope was for the lesson from the experience to remain for much longer. It was the reason we loved to play the game. It was a great way to expose our kids to the many curve balls real life offered.

Sure enough, our daughter rebounded quite nicely and was able to retire with dignity. She did not win the game but played well and said she learned a lot. She was smiling as the game ended and was able to laugh at her very slow start. We played the game often and knew she would use what she learned the next time.

Keith and I recapped the conversation later in the evening, when it was just the two of us. We both agreed it was a great example of how to persevere. We talked about all the times we wanted a "do over" from the financial mess we created for ourselves, but it was not to be. Instead, we played the hand life dealt us and chose to make the best of our situation. Ultimately, we "played well" and learned a lot.

As it turned out, our daughter was not the only one who would be able to "retire with dignity." We were thankful we would, too.

Your Turn…Your Perspective: What "Game of Life" lessons have you experienced recently? How were you impacted? What did you learn? Who did you share your lessons with?

Prayer: Lord, thank You for my "Game of Life" moment with my finances. Thank You for the lessons I have already learned and have put into practice. Please give me patience and courage for my journey.

Day 173
Costly Coat

ISAIAH 48:17

It was not easy teaching the kids our value system. They were only with us roughly 60 days each year. April, May and June were the hardest months because those were the months farthest away from what we began to teach them each July.

One of the lessons, which was constantly being retaught, was with our son. He struggled to keep up with his belongings. Lunch boxes, water bottles, towels. He lost them all during one summer or another. We paired lots of different consequences with his actions in hopes he would learn how to pay closer attention. It was an exercise in patience like none other.

Each year in preparation for their summer visit, we started conversations in mid-June about what they needed to bring with them on July 1 – swim stuff, hair care items, a jacket for cold buildings, medications. We asked about it all multiple times to make sure they packed it.

One year, even after several promptings, our son came without a jacket. He knew he was supposed to bring one, but forgot it nonetheless. As frustrated as we were with his forgetfulness, he still needed a jacket. So off we went to find a lightweight summer jacket which did not cost a fortune.

The rest of the summer went relatively well. It was a busy five weeks filled with lots of laughter, some intense moments of character building, and fellowship with friends and family. We were winding our time down with the kids, with just a few days left before we took them back to St. Louis.

I picked the kids up from the last day of camp and we were heading home when our son announced he left his jacket at camp. "Seriously?! On the last day of camp, when none of us are going back there, you leave your jacket?" I asked. It was not a good moment. When would he learn this lesson? What did we need to do differently to drive home the point to take care of his belongings?

I chose to say no more, and we drove home in silence. I shared the conversation with Keith later and we decided the consequences for this needed to be steeper than they were in the past. We decided our son needed to reimburse us for the cost of the jacket. If he had remembered to bring his jacket with him at the beginning of the summer, we would never have purchased this one. And now this one was lost.

We paid the kids a commission each week based on how well they performed their "work." Work was defined as their chores around the house, and their attitude while performing them. Saturday was pay day. As we all sat around the table on our last Saturday of the summer, we discussed the jacket. We told our son he needed to reimburse us for the cost of the jacket. We also informed him he would need to pay for anything else he lost in the future. The time had come for him to feel the full weight of the consequences.

He was not happy about it but passed over the payment. It was a lesson best learned before the consequences got any steeper. Only time would tell how well he learned it.

Your Turn…Your Perspective: What has been the costliest consequence you have ever had to pay? What did you learn from the experience?

Prayer: Lord, how many consequences have I paid because I did not learn the lesson sooner? I pray to be more in tune to the lesson You are trying to teach me. Please keep me open to Your voice and Your plan.

Commission Only
PROVERBS 11:18

Keith and I were intentional in using our time with the kids as completely as possible. Sixty days a year was not a lot by most people's standards, but we were determined to make the most of it. One example of how we did this was in the way we approached money management. We learned from Dave Ramsey to place our kids on a commission structure, instead of simply giving an allowance.

We chose to tailor Dave's plan a little, however. We set an available dollar amount and assigned each of them "work" responsibilities. Their commissions were paid in full when all their "work" was completed each week. There was one caveat – their behavior was also included in our expectations. The Jones' Family Cornerstones. If the cornerstones were not followed, their "pay" was decreased.

We started each summer with a "grace week." It was designed to remind the kids of Kansas expectations. We created a list of duties which defined the completion of their work. When all the items on the list were completed for the day, they would be fully compensated. If they did not complete all the items, they would only be partially compensated. We posted the list close by as a reminder. We reminded them of the importance of positive body language and tone of voice. We went through each item as many times as was needed in the first week. We also reiterated the "cost" of them not making the adjustment after grace week.

We spoke often of our desire to pay them their full commission each week. Ultimately, their income was controlled by their decision to do the "work" assigned to them, and to manage their attitudes in the process. These were the same two criteria used by most companies when hiring and retaining quality staff. We saw our system as a small part of the much bigger plan to grow them into productive adulthood.

Saturday was pay day. Keith and I kept a calendar in the kitchen for each of the kids. It listed highs and lows of the week for each of them. We wrote the items as quickly after noticing them as possible. It helped us get the facts accurate and was visible to the kids for them to adjust their behavior or work ethic as needed.

When pay day came, we all sat around the table with the calendars and the commissions. We began and ended in prayer. We talked through each high and low and gave everything a dollar amount. We gave big praise for the wins of the week, but there were often tearful discussions around the challenges.

Prior to pay day, Keith and I consulted on actions to "grace out." Jesus showed us grace every day, and we needed to do the same. If we were out as a family really late, and our son forgot to clean the bathroom, it would be discussed and we would probably "grace it out." Our daughter might have an inappropriate attitude adjustment "graced out," or maybe not. Grace was not to be assumed. It was discussed, and Keith and I made the final decision. And if it was really bad, Keith made the tough call of determining the final cost.

We knew it was a lot of work, but for us, it was worth the effort. If our kids retained even a portion of what we taught, they would be well on their way to self-sustainment. Ultimately, we wanted to give them the best chance possible to create a positive future.

Your Turn…Your Perspective: Who impacted your developmental years? How did their presence affect the life path you eventually chose?

Prayer: Lord, thank You for discipline with my own money. I pray for my attitude. Help me to stay positive as I work my way out of difficult financial seasons.

Day 175
Small Choices

PROVERBS 6:20-22

Birthdays were always a big deal in our house. We put a lot of thought into how they were celebrated, especially for the kids. A big dinner complete with china, crystal, candles and a sparkling cider toast was a part of every birthday celebration, and the person of honor chose the menu. The menu selection was as much a "gift" as the wrapped items and the card.

Another big deal in our house was adherence to the Jones' Family Cornerstones. The very first Cornerstone was to "Follow Directions First Time Asked." It was based on a concept we learned through the Love and Logic Foundation. The idea was to teach your kids the power to make good choices while the consequences were small. When it was time to make bigger, life changing choices, hopefully they would be more prepared.

Since becoming a teenager, our daughter struggled to stay true to the "follow directions" Cornerstone. Keith and I felt like broken records as we held the same conversation with her about paying attention and following through on requests. It did not seem to be sinking in. A few weeks before her birthday, I made the customary request for her birthday menu. Just as we expected, she neglected to provide it.

This was an established tradition in our household. Our daughter knew the routine. It should not have been a stretch for her. It was not uncommon for our son to give us his menu several weeks in advance. He looked forward to the opportunity to choose the menu, but our daughter was simply not cooperating.

Keith and I had a decision to make. Did we ask again for her to give us the information we already requested and go against our Jones' Family Cornerstones, or did we deliver the consequences associated with her disobedience and pray she learned from it? We chose to deliver the consequences.

We obviously still celebrated her birthday, but she removed her opportunity for a full birthday dinner by not providing the menu when it was requested. We decided I would choose her birthday menu based on what groceries were already in the pantry. It was still a nice meal complete with china, crystal, candles and a sparkling cider toast, but there were several of her favorite dishes missing from the table.

When we picked the kids up to start her birthday weekend celebration, we discussed with our daughter the need to stay true to our decision. We reminded her how much we loved her. We also reminded her of the consequences of her choices and she said she understood. We still had a great birthday celebration, but we knew she was disappointed in not choosing her menu.

It was our desire for this birthday to provide lasting memories on the importance of making good choices and in a timely manner, even if they seemed insignificant at the time. We prayed she would remember the disappointment caused by poor choices, and recognize the consequences are magnified when the choices are of greater significance. Only time would tell how well she learned the lesson.

Your Turn...Your Perspective: What seemingly small choices have you made which have had larger than expected consequences? What did you do to prevent similar consequences from happening again?

> *Prayer: Lord, my choices have created significant consequences in the past. I pray for wisdom and discernment as I continue on this journey of Christ-centered financial wellness. Please help me to think through my options before making decisions in hopes of choosing better. Thank You for grace.*

Day 176
For You or For Me?

PROVERBS 28:3

Our kids got along really well as they were growing up. They were two years apart and spent a good bit of their time together. Birthday celebrations were also an area where they supported each other well.

One year, the support backfired. Our daughter missed an opportunity to fully shape her birthday celebration. She was disobedient, and while her birthday celebration was filled with examples of our love, her birthday menu was severely limited.

When it was time for our son to choose his birthday menu a month later, I noticed it was filled with many of our daughter's favorite foods. I was expecting to see a request for salmon, turkey burgers and fries, broccoli, and red velvet cupcakes. Instead the list was meatloaf, mashed potatoes, carrots, apple pie and ice cream.

I thought I knew what was going on and told Keith what I suspected. He agreed we should not say anything. Instead, we decided to let the day play out. If we were right, the opportunity to discuss the situation would present itself when the time was right.

On the day of our son's birthday celebration, we were all excited. We invited guests to join us for the big event and spent the early part of the day wrapping gifts and cooking. Apples were peeled for the pie, meatloaf was prepped, and sparkling cider was chilled. Our guests arrived to find a table overflowing with all the items our son requested to help celebrate his special day. Our home was filled with people and laughter.

We sang happy birthday, and everyone joined in for the toast to the guest of honor. Everything was great, except the birthday boy. He barely ate and did not have dessert at all. When I asked why he was not enjoying apple pie and ice cream, he said he really did not want any. I reminded him that he chose the entire menu, including dessert. It was time for the hard conversation.

It did not take much prodding to discover what Keith and I already suspected. Our son chose all the items our daughter lost the opportunity to choose for her birthday celebration. And now he was disappointed because he missed out on the fullness of his own celebration. We were enjoying his sister's birthday meal, not his.

It was a beautiful gesture, but he missed the mark. In his attempt to please his sister, he missed the opportunity to get what he wanted. What made matters worse was she did not even notice. He hoped for her acknowledgement of his sacrifice, and she did not offer it. It was a reminder to not attempt to impress others to gain their favor.

The Love and Logic Institute taught the importance of allowing children to learn life lessons while the costs were relatively low. Keith and I could have addressed the menu issue long before the big day but would have missed an incredible life lesson in doing so. By allowing the dinner menu to come full circle, our hope was for both of our children to learn the important lesson of not trying to please everyone at the expense of yourself. Time will tell how well they learned.

Your Turn…Your Perspective: When was the last time you forfeited an opportunity by attempting to please someone else? What was the end result?

Prayer: Lord, the only one I want to please is You. Please help me to not give in to the temptation to attempt to please others at the expense of You or myself. I pray for the peace which comes with knowing I am following Your plan for my life. I thank You for the courage to be myself.

Day 177
Sandwich Making Time
PROVERBS 6:6, 8; NEHEMIAH 6:3B

Whenever we spent weekends with our kids in St. Louis, we tried to also include one of our nephews. He was the same age as our son and they got along quite well. We typically stayed in an extended stay hotel which served a hot breakfast and was equipped with a full kitchen. We brought food for lunch and dinner to keep from eating out. The cost of the extended stay hotel was much lower than the cost of feeding a family of four with big appetites for an entire weekend.

Making our meals in the hotel also made it affordable for our nephew join us. If the cost of feeding a family of four was high, imagine adding another male child with a healthy appetite to the equation.

One Saturday we were preparing to go out for the day with our kids and our nephew. We ate a hearty breakfast, but I knew we would be out for several hours. We needed to pack a lunch to keep from spending money for five people to eat out.

I told our daughter it was "sandwich making time." Our nephew showed a puzzled expression and asked me what I meant. I explained we would be out for several hours but would not be eating out. Instead, we would prepare lunch ahead of time to save money. I further explained we were able to stay in the hotel for several days and not spend a great deal of money because we planned ahead for lunch, ate the free breakfast offered by the hotel, and came back to our room for dinner. Our kids told him we did this often.

I knew our nephew thought our way of doing things was odd. Our kids thought the same thing. None of them understood how much money we saved by bringing our own food. Since they were not contributing any of their money, this meant we allowed them no opinion in how we spent ours.

By bringing our own food, we were able to use our limited budgeted on activities and not on meals. We were able to go out and explore the city. Our excursions rarely cost much money, but it was more than would be available if we ate out.

Like most kids, our kids simply wanted to be entertained. They gave no thought to the cost of the weekend. We knew it was our responsibility to be good stewards. We chose to be the adults and manage our resources.

Our hope was one day our children would understand why we structured our trips the way we did. When we finished paying off all our debts, we would be in a better position to spend money eating out. In the meantime, we continued to showcase what it meant to be good stewards of our resources by making sandwiches.

Nehemiah said in Nehemiah 6:3, "I am doing a great work and I cannot come down [off the wall]. Why should the work stop while I leave it and come down to you?" Our "wall" was becoming debt-free. We would not stop our work until it was completed. Creating a future of Christ-centered financial wellness depended on it.

Your Turn...Your Perspective: Consider a time when you had to explain why you made a specific financial decision. Did you feel the need to explain yourself? What did others think of your choice?

Prayer: Lord, I want to stay on my wall. I want to not allow the opinions of others to keep me from the goal I have to honor You with my finances. Please help me not be moved by those around me. I thank You for a clearly defined path to wealth Your way.

PROVERBS 10:22

The day of my 16-year old nephew's accident was a normal August day. I went to work, left a few hours early for a doctor's appointment, and was looking forward to a quiet evening at home with Keith. There was nothing to alarm me when I got a call from my mother during my doctor's appointment. I made a note to call her back when I got in the car. A few minutes later I got a call from a friend of the family. Now I was alarmed. I rarely got calls from Harold and getting this one on the heels of my mother's call caused the hair to stand up on the back of my neck. Something was wrong.

I called Harold first. He told me it was bad, and I needed to come home. I called Keith and we met at home. I tried to get more information, but not much was available. All I knew was a terrible ATV accident took place and Jonathan was severely injured. He was being Heli ported to a trauma unit 50 miles away. It was not good.

We immediately went into action. The first call we made was to our life group asking for prayers. The next calls were to supervisors to explain what we knew, and to inform them we would not be in on Friday. Then flights and a rental car were booked. Next, we packed.

We left Kansas City the next morning, headed to South Carolina. The money for the tickets were transferred from our emergency savings account to our checking account, and a few hundred dollars in cash came from our in-home security box. We made our lunches to limit the amount of money spent in route, and traveled with only carry-on luggage to avoid baggage fees. The money for the rental car was ready and waiting in our checking account when we got to the counter.

Jonathan died on Saturday. We stayed in South Carolina for another week.

At a time when grief and other heart-heavy emotions were high, we were fiscally calm. All our bills were paid. We booked our return tickets knowing the cash was available to pay for them. We did not worry. We were able to be a part of the support network for our family without regard for financial implications.

We were not afraid to look at our bank account; we knew our emergency fund would support our trip. We paused our debt snowball payments and planned to rebuild our emergency fund once we were clear of our current emergency. In the meantime, we were free to focus on what was most important – assisting with the Celebration of Life for Jonathan.

Once we came home and began to pick up the life pieces we dropped ten days prior, I realized what a blessing it was to not have to worry about money during one of the most difficult times of my life. It was also a reminder of the importance of getting out of debt as quickly as possible. Our $1000 emergency fund held, but a fully funded emergency account was still needed to hedge against more expensive emergencies.

Until then, we would continue to be swift with our debt reduction and pray for God's favor over our finances. We were determined to get rid of our debt as quickly as we could.

Your Turn…Your Perspective: What was your biggest financial emergency? How did you get through it?

Prayer: Lord, thank You for diligence and a plan. Thank You for not allowing me to settle into complacency. I pray for the courage to stay focused on becoming debt-free, even during an emergency. Show me Your path and I will follow it. I praise Your holy name.

Day 179
One Way Tickets

PROVERBS 16:33

When Keith and I got the call about Jonathan's accident, we needed to make decisions quickly. The accident was bad, and we needed to get home as fast as we could. It was a Thursday evening and the next flight out was not until Friday morning. We were in a full-on emergency. Fortunately, our emergency fund was there for us; any other money we needed would come from payments to our debt snowball.

I held my breath as I started looking for airline tickets. Everyone knew last minute tickets could be incredibly expensive. It was difficult to balance the emotion of a life-threatening accident with practicality. I did not want a 14-hour drive to South Carolina in a heightened emergency state, but we could not rule out driving as a possibility.

We also did not know how long we would be gone. We knew Jonathan's injuries were severe and the prognosis did not look good. What did all this mean in terms of time? We decided to simply book one-way tickets. We needed to be smart with our money and it seemed like the smart thing to do.

I thanked the Lord as I booked two one-way tickets into Augusta, GA for only $139 each. We then went to our favorite discount warehouse travel site and booked a rental car for the weekend. We would have a better idea of what we needed to do by Sunday evening. For the time being, we focused on simply getting to South Carolina.

After Jonathan passed away and the family began to make final arrangements, it was clear Keith and I needed to stay in South Carolina for another week. We did not panic. Our household expenses were covered because we lived on a budget. We booked our return one-way tickets, and again, they were only $139 each. Because our airline tickets were so reasonable, we were able to book another rental car to get us through the week. At a time when our emotions were high, it was a blessing not to have to deal with expensive travel costs.

As I reflected on the season of loss, I could not help but thank the Lord. I dealt with a very traumatic event with a level head and sound reason. I did not have a financial meltdown through it all.

I did not waiver or respond fearfully at the thought of spending money. I felt very adult in how I handled everything. I wondered if the inexpensive airline tickets were God's gift as a reward for embracing the emergency and resting in the reality of His provision.

Our financial muscles were growing. The new financial discipline we were learning caused us to think differently about each financial situation. We looked for alternatives which were the best use of time and money, and not just at the bottom line. It felt good to be faced with a crisis and come out of it on the other side knowing we used our financial muscles to create the best outcome. We were thankful.

Your Turn…Your Perspective: How well do you manage your finances in a crisis? What keeps you grounded? Who could you call if you needed a sounding board?

Prayer: Lord, help me to learn how to better manage a money crisis. Help me to not be afraid to spend my emergency fund on emergencies. I pray to keep a level head and not make decisions too quickly. Help me to seek guidance if I need it. I want to grow in financial maturity. Show me the way.

Day 180
Refrigerator

MATTHEW 6:21

So much of my Southern upbringing revolved around food. We celebrated with food. We debated with food. We studied with food. We mourned with food. Food was at the very center of our lives. When my nephew died, I told my mother we needed to clean out the refrigerator because food would be coming.

Sure enough, within hours of the announcement, food began to arrive. Chicken (baked, fried, barbequed) came. Vegetables (green beans, tomatoes, collard greens, corn) came. Rice (fried and steamed) came. Potatoes (in salad, baked, mashed) came. Ribs (beef and pork) came. Ham came. Fish came. Pies and cakes came.

People accompanied the food. They offered their condolences and sat with us in an attempt to absorb some of the hurt, some of the pain. None of us could wrap our minds and hearts around our precious 16-year-old "Jay" no longer being among us. Our family and friends came. His classmates came. They all brought food.

They came early and stayed long. It was their way of participating in our grief in a small way. We all sat and reflected, shared laughter and tears, and partook in a meal together. It was the Southern way. They provided all they could give: food and their company.

We ran out of refrigerator space on the second day. It was August in South Carolina and we were in dire need of the cooling power of the box. Turning the food away was certainly taboo. There must be another way.

We began to send food home with friends asking them to return it the next day. We would then set up the buffets all over again. We could not store all the food or eat it fast enough. Caravans of serving containers, filled with food, made their way into the homes and refrigerators of our friends and families.

The next day we heard a delivery truck pull up outside. I went to the door to see a very large refrigerator being unloaded from the truck. A family friend, who owned an appliance store, heard of our dilemma and sent a refrigerator to our aid. I stood watching in humbled amazement as the guys unloaded it and plugged it in.

There was so much Godliness in the refrigerator: It symbolized the grief our family was experiencing through the lens of our community. It symbolized the desire of those around us to assist in whatever way they could. The refrigerator symbolized the joy associated with giving, even when the circumstances were less than ideal.

Our friends did not have to go through the trouble of providing such a generous gift. Instead of thinking of lost revenue, the thought was to provide support. Instead of the bottom line, the thought was of sympathy and kindness. The thought was not of resale, but of the renewal of spirit.

Having an extra refrigerator did not change our circumstances. It did not decrease our grief. It did not lessen the impact of our loss. It did, however, show the love and support of friends and our community. It showed God's grace displayed among His people.

Your Turn…Your Perspective: How have you put yourself aside to help someone else? What has been the most selfless act someone has performed for you? How did each experience impact you?

Prayer: Lord, I thank You for perspective. I am often consumed with my own life and lose sight of the situations of others. I pray to always have compassion for those around me during their time of need. I pray for the ability to set aside the needs of myself for the needs of others. Please help me keep You at the center of my thoughts so I can treat others as You treat me.

Day 181
Atlantis

PROVERBS 19:21

My nephew was obsessed with Atlantis. At first, I thought he was referring to the Greek mythological city until my brother shared the truth with me – Atlantis was a resort in the Bahamas. But it was not just any resort. It was a five-star resort with a multitude of activities.

Jonathan believed he needed to see it, live it, and experience it. At least once a year for at least five years, he asked to go. In his mind, going to Atlantis was equivalent to a weekend trip to the beach. It was a beach after all; he did not see why it was such a big deal. "Daddy, can we go?" was a question he asked continuously.

Year after year, my brother said no. Year after year, he attempted to explain to my nephew just how much a trip of this magnitude would cost for their small, single parent family. Instead, they took smaller trips for long weekends. They went fishing or hunting. They took in the occasional college football game.

My nephew died at the age of 16 without seeing Atlantis. At his celebration of life, my brother spoke of Jonathan's desire to visit the world-famous resort. It was his only regret as a parent. He wanted his son to see it. If Jonathan had lived, the trip would have been his graduation gift.

There was sadness in the air as those in the auditorium absorbed what my brother shared. A once in a lifetime trip for a really cool kid would not be realized. It seemed unfair. On one hand, we could relate because we all wanted to give our kids the best. On the other, we understood what it meant to manage the practicality of life. Both were necessary in creating balance for our kids.

My brother may have wanted my nephew to experience Atlantis, but it was also important for him to learn the importance of being a good steward. Saying no to Atlantis meant saying yes to league basketball in the summers. Saying no to Atlantis meant saying yes to a car for him to drive. Saying no to Atlantis meant saying yes to a cell phone with a large data plan.

It was a bittersweet moment as I listened to my brother speak of the trip which would take place without the guest of honor. Here was a father, whose heart was broken to the core, planning to continue with the celebratory trip of a lifetime without his firstborn son. I felt such joy and admiration. I also felt respect and complete love for my brother who, without knowing it, shared what a great parent he had been to his son.

By saying no to Atlantis, my brother showed my nephew what it was to be well loved. One missed trip could never replace the affection my nephew received every day. What my brother was not able to show in tangible things, he made up for in the other indescribable ways he showed love for his son. No amount of money could replace the gift he gave to my nephew.

My brother's only regret was a trip to Atlantis. What a blessing to have only one regret in such an important relationship.

Your Turn…Your Perspective: Name a time when saying "no" was difficult. Name a time when someone told you "No." How did each experience make you feel? What was the end result?

Prayer: Lord, please help me to foster good relationships. I do not want regret. Help me to make the tough decisions today which will lead to healthy interaction with others long term. Please give me boundaries where they are needed. Help me to love others the way You love me, even when it means not giving in to wants and desires.

Day 182
Life Support

DEUTERONOMY 2:7

Our church used the model of "life groups" to promote a small church feeling within a larger congregation. Our life group was a ragtag group of seven couples. They were a community for Keith and me. We were all so different, but the love and support we felt was incredible. The group consisted of blended families, empty nesters, newlyweds, families with small kids, families with teenagers, and everything in between.

We celebrated birthdays and anniversaries, and shared pot lucks and tail gates. Bible study ranged from in-depth studies on spiritual warfare to seven-minute videos with discussion questions. We were all at difference places on our spiritual journey and supported each other as best we could. We all experienced at least one difficult season during the time we were together as a group. And each time, the group rallied around the couple currently in need.

August 2015 was our turn. We got the call informing us Jonathan was injured in an ATV accident on Thursday, August 13. We were on a plane to South Carolina the next morning. Because we did not know what we were walking into, we purchased one-way tickets and decided to deal with the return flights once we got to South Carolina and knew more about the situation. Because my family lived in rural South Carolina, we also rented a car.

Jonathan died on Saturday, August 15. My brother made the decision to have the Celebration of Life on Saturday, August 22 so all of Jonathan's friends could attend without missing school. Our emergency trip home lasted ten days. Total cost for the entire trip was just under $1000.

We were thankful for our emergency fund. We did not worry about how to pay for the trip. We paid cash for every purchase. Having the cash to pay for the trip meant we did not have to deal with the concerns of monetary expenses during a time when all other emotions were on high alert.

When we returned to Kansas, our life group was waiting for us. Not only did they pray for us and cry with us, they also pitched in and gave us a beautiful monetary gift to help replenish our emergency fund. We were overwhelmed with gratitude and appreciation. It was a beautiful gesture and showcased just how much like family this group was to us. We were hurting, which meant they were hurting too. They knew they could not lessen the pain of our aching hearts, but instead chose to lessen the strain of our financial burden.

Our life group showed their love for us was big enough to make the gift worth the sacrifice. And we were so thankful. They saw the journey of debt reduction we were traveling and made the decision to walk alongside us. We were thankful for an incredible group of friends. We were also thankful they chose to share life (and all its challenges) with us.

Your Turn...Your Perspective: How much room do you have in your budget to assist those in need? How will you pay for your next emergency?

Prayer: Lord, thank You for my own friends and their support. I pray to support them in any way I can and thank You for extending my family to include them. Help me to be there for them when they have a time of need.

Day 183
Grief Therapy

PSALM 34:9

The first week back home after Jonathan died was a hard week. I spent the previous 10 days being "the rock" for my brother who was a single dad. I did not really focus on myself and my own grief. Returning home and re-entering my life and routine proved to be more difficult than I thought it would be. My grieving period was just beginning, and I was not sure how I would get through it.

Jonathan was like my own child. We were 30 years and 19 days apart. In many of my best memories of family, he was at the center. During our first week home, I spent a lot of time remembering those good times. I knew time was at the center of my healing process and I chose to look at every day as another step forward. There was more forward momentum on some days than others, but I continued to attempt to find my way to my new normal without Jonathan.

A few weeks later, Keith was scheduled to travel to Washington DC for a business trip. He knew I was having a hard time with my grief and asked if I would go with him. I would be fine at home for the week and was actually looking forward to some time alone. But Keith was concerned. He had given me a great deal of space to grieve but did not want me to grieve alone. He was insistent and would not let go of the suggestion.

I finally relented and agreed I would go with him if we could find a ticket under $300. Even though I did not want to spend the money, I knew the trip would be helpful in moving past my grief. We lived in the DC Metro area prior to moving to Kansas City. I had not been back in over three years and Keith thought it would do me good to be able to catch up with friends I missed since we moved away. I was off to DC for some grief therapy.

We had known about his upcoming trip for several months and saved a small amount of money each month in case I was able to accompany him. We were able to purchase the airfare for under $300 and the hotel expenses were already covered. We chose a hotel with a kitchenette, along with free breakfast and dinner to lower the cost of meals. I did not want to spend any additional money on eating out and entertainment.

I thought about our journey to debt-freedom and all we accomplished so far. When we first got married, there was so much debt and so many minimum payments. We would not have been able to purchase a ticket without incurring more debt. At a time when I needed the support of friends and a change of scenery, our diligence to continue working towards debt-freedom created a tangible benefit. Even though an expensive family emergency (airfare for two, rental car, extra expenses) was in our recent past, we were still able to make room in our budget for me to make the trip.

We vowed to rebuild our emergency fund and restart our debt reduction efforts the next month, but this small financial detour made a huge impact on us both emotionally. Paying off our debt snowball was still far from complete, but we knew it was a worthwhile sacrifice for me to accompany him. We incurred no new debt, but instead received a lifetime gift of healing.

Your Turn...Your Perspective: What benefits do you see from being steadfast on your debt-reduction journey? How will you manage a slight detour from your plan? How do you know what detour is a want or a need?

Prayer: Lord, I have no way of knowing what the future holds. I pray to be diligent now so I can face whatever comes my way with financial margin on my side.

Earned, Not Given

Moving to Kansas put some separation between me and Jonathan, since I did not get home as often as when I lived in Virginia. It was a huge adjustment for both of us. Even though I knew God called me to move to Kansas, leaving Jonathan left a huge void in my heart.

Our birthday celebrations were a big deal. When I lived in Virginia, I always went home for his birthday celebration. When Keith and I got married and began paying off our debt snowball, we cut our trips to South Carolina to once a year. It was hard for me to miss birthdays, but I reasoned it would only be for a short amount of time. We did make room in the budget for birthday gifts.

My nephew's birthday was a few months after he passed away, and I knew it would be difficult for my brother. My own grief was still fresh. I could only imagine the intensity of his grief. I wanted to support him (and myself) by making a special gift to celebrate Jonathan's birthday.

I designed the gift and priced out what it would cost to create it. Shipping needed to be considered also since my brother lived several states away. I then shared my idea with Keith and explained what I wanted to do. He knew how much I was hurting and wanted to help me get past my grief as best he could.

It was not a great deal more than we would have spent on Jonathan's gift had he been alive. But it was, nevertheless, more. Staying on budget was incredibly important in our house. But so was this gift. As much as I wanted to stay on budget, I wanted (and needed) to spend the extra. Keith agreed without a second thought. I hugged him close and thanked him for the sacrifice.

I told my brother the gift was coming, and anxiously waited for him to call and tell me he received it. I hoped it would provide comfort to him and I wanted him to know we were thinking of him. I also wanted him to know we were praying for him during what we knew would be a difficult time.

When the call came, we all cried. Jonathan would have loved the gift. It was a canvas print with the silhouette of a basketball player making a layup on an outside court at sunset. The words "Earned…Not Given" were etched at the bottom. Even though he was only 16 years old, he already knew his life motto. It was beautiful to capture his maturity on canvas and preserve the memory.

When my brother asked me to make a second canvas to hang in the boy's locker room at Jonathan's high school, I did not hesitate. This time I used my personal money to pay for it. It was a small price to be able to bring hope and encouragement to Jonathan's teammates, and to all the young men who would eventually go through the locker room and see his life motto. I saw it as an investment for his memory to be able to live on in the gym he loved so much. It was the best way I knew to celebrate the first birthday without him.

Your Turn…Your Perspective: How are birthdays celebrated in your family? What traditions do you honor on a regular basis which require financial planning? When was the last time you gave sacrificially? What impact did the experience have on you? On the recipient?

Prayer: Lord, I want to think of others more than I think of myself. I want to provide comfort to those in need. Please help me to keep my eyes open for ways to assist those around me who are hurting from the loss of a loved one or from difficult circumstances. I pray for the margin to give like You do.

Day 185
Play4Jay

A few months after my nephew passed away, we got a notice from our estate planning attorney with reminders to update our will. Because we were a blended family, our wills were more complicated than the average family. In addition to the nuances associated with blended families, my will also contained a clause to provide funds to both my nephews. Since my older nephew was no longer with us, I needed to remove him from the will.

My brother was in the process of setting up a scholarship fund in honor and memory of my nephew. Jonathan was an incredible student-athlete, and the scholarship was designated to provide funds for two seniors to assist with their college education. The student-athletes needed to live in the county where my nephew lived, be accepted into a two or four-year college, and have at least a 3.0 GPA.

So many people were positively impacted by my nephew while he was alive. It was my desire to help his impact be far reaching, even in his death. Since we were several years away from becoming debt-free, there was not a lot I could contribute financially to the cause initially. It was difficult for me to sit on the side-lines while other donations poured in, but I knew my calling was to take care of my own household first.

I decided to do what I could with our available resources. When it came time to make the adjustments to my will, I redirected the funds earmarked for Jonathan to the Play4Jay scholarship fund. It was a way to remember him and build on the legacy of excellence he established in his young life. If something happened to me before we completed paying off our debt snowball, at least the funds would be available.

It seemed like such a small change, but for me it was a really big deal. I wanted to support my nephew's legacy and still honor our commitment to become debt-free before supporting non-profit organizations. It was tough to not give in to the desire to be a part of the initial launch of the scholarship fund.

The first year, only a few students applied for the scholarship. Many told my brother it was too soon to launch the award, but he was committed to honoring Jonathan's memory during the first school year after his death. Nevertheless, a winner was chosen from each of the two school districts represented in the county.

In choosing recipients, all identifying information was removed to make the scoring process as im-partial as possible. Once the winners were chosen, the applicants' names and identifiable information were revealed by the committee. My brother was given the list to make contact and inform the winners of their awards. Imagine his surprise when he discovered the first recipient of the Play4Jay scholarship lived on Jay Street.

Instantly, my brother knew he made the right decision to start the scholarship, and I could not wait to add to the coffers in the years to come.

Your Turn…Your Perspective: What cause do you have which began from a difficult season in your life? How did it assist during your healing process?

Prayer: Lord, I pray for resolve to stay on the financial path laid out for me. There are so many great things I can do with the resources You have given. Please help me to not be sidetracked by the good, but to keep working for what is great. By persevering, I know I will be able to bless others and myself long term.

Day 186
Family Resources

PROVERBS 2:4

I grew up in a blended family. In the book, *The Smart Stepfamily,* author Ron Deal identified 67 different types of blended families. Fortunately for us, our stepfamily was a relatively healthy one. While we experienced our share of quarrels, most of my memories of interactions with my stepbrothers and my biological brother were really good ones. We did not have cable TV, but the VCR entertained us quite often.

My stepbrothers were at our house almost every weekend and most of the summer. There was a calendar which dictated whose turn it was to wash dishes, and our big meals were lunch on Saturday and dinner on Sunday. As we got older, we each made career choices and life decisions according to our skillsets. Most of us moved away and a few moved back closer to home. We all carved out a plan for our lives but did not forget the family unit we enjoyed as kids. Even after my stepdad passed away, we all kept in touch.

At one extended family gathering, Keith and I spent a good bit of time with my stepbrother and his wife. I talked with them a few times a year but had not seen them in quite some time. They only met Keith once or twice before. It was a pleasant surprise to see how much the four of us had in common. We were all able to share in conversation openly, and thoroughly enjoyed our visits, many of them lasted late into the evening.

At one point in the trip, we discussed health. Keith spoke of his diagnosis of heavy metal poisoning and the difficulty it caused. Through a series of questions, we realized my stepbrother was familiar with the process Keith was going through. He explained to us how he assisted others in the past and offered his expertise to us. We were all wide-eyed in wonder at how the Lord orchestrated the moment. Here was a subject matter expert sitting under the carport sharing cake and iced tea. What a blessing.

Throughout the rest of our time in South Carolina and over the next few months, we kept my stepbrother up to date on our progress, and he gave us ideas and recommendations on our next steps. He clarified confusing areas of the case and confirmed information. We asked questions and he provided answers. He did not trivialize our lack of understanding and took the time to walk us through each scenario.

We were able to be vulnerable with him. We put down our guard about just how little we knew about the process. We shared our concerns and he helped put our minds at ease. Information was free-flowing and plentiful. It was a wonderful feeling to be able to trust the source of the information.

It was not lost on me that none of this would have been possible if we had not been transparent at the beginning of our conversation. We could have glossed over Keith's health issues and pretended all was well. It would not have been the first time we chose not to go deep about the full extent of our health issues.

Not sharing would have caused us to miss an incredible blessing. Our openness not only created an opportunity to learn more about how to manage Keith's situation, but paved the way for a deeper, more meaningful relationship with my stepbrother and sister-in-law. That was truly the bigger blessing.

Your Turn…Your Perspective: How have family dynamics impacted your life? How transparent do you choose to be with friends and family? Explain your answer.

Prayer: Lord, please help me not be embarrassed to share my circumstances with others. I pray for wisdom to know when to share and with whom. I thank You for this journey to be better with money.

Day 187
Pray...Don't Worry
LUKE 12:22-23; JOSHUA 1:9

Almost four years into our journey to become debt-free, we entered a season of emergencies. These included major car repairs for my vehicle, Keith's car died completely, legal fees, a death in the family which required next day airfare and rental car fees, expensive medical tests, and out of network doctors in a different city which required multiple trips and hotel stays. All of these occurred within a four-month period.

I struggled to breathe. We paid off a hefty amount of our debt by then, but still owed $60,000. Our $1000 emergency fund was used and reused. All extra money was diverted to cover emergency expenses almost monthly. We only made minimum payments on our debt. It was a fight to mentally stay in the game, knowing no big dents were being made in what we owed. It was as if we were held hostage by emergencies.

I chose to continue to do what I knew to do. I continued to pray. I continued to show up at church, work and volunteer commitments. We continued to live our life, recognizing this was a season which would pass. They always did. We just needed to hold on in the meantime.

I also continued to read. I read the Bible every morning. I also kept a book on CD with me in the car. I called it the "book of the week." One of the books of the week was *Think and Grow Rich for Women*. The original, *Think and Grow Rich,* was written by Napoleon Hill in 1937. The Napoleon Hill Foundation commissioned author Sharon Lechter to publish an updated version for women. It was released in 2014.

I found incredible comfort in the book. In one passage, Ms. Lechter correlated worrying to praying for what you do not want to happen. I listened to the passage again. To worry was equivalent to praying for the opposite of what you wanted. Worrying negated praying. If I was going to worry, what was the point in praying?

It took a conscious effort to make the switch in my brain. I needed to "think" about not worrying until it became natural. I found scriptures to help keep me focused and sustained in Proverbs 3:5-6 and Philippians 4:6-7. I recited them every time a worry thought crept into my mind. I also wrote them on index cards.

It was not easy. Nor was it quick. Worry was a constant companion for many months. My head knew we would get through our current financial season, buy my heart was struggling to keep it together. One day after the emergencies were more behind us than in front of us, I realized it had been weeks since I asked the question, "Lord, how on earth?" It was my "go to" cry of angst when I felt stressed and overwhelmed.

Slowly, the emergencies receded, and we were able to redirect funds to the debt snowball and began to pay more money towards student loans. My pattern of behavior was shifting from fear to faith, one day at a time. I also noticed my attitude adjusted. My anxiety level did not increase as much when an issue arose. And more importantly, anxiety did not stay with me very long. I was thankful for Ms. Lechter's charge to not negate my prayers by worrying. Hope was again my focus.

Your Turn...Your Perspective: What is your response to worry? What situations cause the greatest anxiety in your life?

Prayer: Lord, I pray I can stay focused on You and not on my circumstances. I pray I am mindful of the need to not be afraid. I know You are with me and I am thankful. I choose to not worry. I choose to not be afraid. In Jesus' name.

Day 188
Taillight

PROVERBS 23:7; PHILIPPIANS 4:19

Keith came in one Saturday, after a morning of errands, with a grave look on his face. I was a little alarmed when he sat down and told me he needed to share something. I held my breath with no idea what he would say next.

He told me he was out and about and misjudged the amount of space behind him. He backed into a light post and damaged the taillight on his car. He told me he went to the dealership to get it assessed and they ordered the part and would call when it was ready for installation. He told me he would pay for it out of his personal money.

I sat still, slowly exhaled, and asked if he was okay. I assumed something so much worse than a broken taillight. I was thankful there was no real disaster and I was thankful he was not hurt. I was thankful we were only dealing with a broken taillight. But I was also sad.

We had been on this journey of becoming debt-free for almost five years, and my husband still expected me to have a meltdown over something as small as a taillight. It cost under $100 to repair the car, including parts and labor. He was prepared to pay for it himself. It meant he did not think I would agree for it to come from the car repair line item in our budget.

I acted poorly during so many financial situations in the past. Time after time I was irrational when dealing with any situation which took money away from paying the debt snowball. Time after time I responded to the situation with little faith in our process or our plan. Each hit to the budget was like a boulder crashing in.

I thought by now Keith would have noticed my recent shift in financial maturity. I thought he would have remembered how well I handled the last few medical crises and the previous car repair issue. The taillight incident was a painful reminder of all the growth I still needed to achieve in my newfound financial maturity. Keith believed I had not yet arrived in the land of the financial faithful.

I got up and went to him. I hugged him and told him I was glad he was safe. I told him not to worry about using his own money. We would pay for the taillight with our car repair sinking fund. I thanked Him for trusting me to manage our money, and for loving me through all my financial growing pains. There was no need to call attention to my brand spanking new financial maturity. I obviously was not mature enough yet for the difference to be noticed by anyone but me.

I knew my change in attitude was a permanent one. One day soon, Keith would notice, and it would be cause for a great celebration. In the meantime, there was a lot of opportunity to practice.

Your Turn…Your Perspective: Name a time when your financial immaturity was on full display. Now name a time when your financial maturity prevailed. How did each impact your current financial state?

Prayer: Lord, I pray for my own financial maturity. I pray to make wise choices with my money and grow beyond fiscal temper tantrums. Please help me grow in my faith that You really will supply all my needs, according to Your riches in glory.

Day 189
Great Opportunity?

LUKE 14:28-29; GENESIS 12:4, 21:5

Devotional time was always important to Keith and me. We tried to spend at least 30 minutes each day communicating with the Lord. We often shared insights from our quiet time with each other and it was amazing to see how much we gleaned from the other's devotions.

One day after his quiet time, Keith shared his discovery of a big leadership change coming for him at work. It was interesting to hear this because he was always resistant to moving into leadership. I asked him how he felt about it, and he shared his apprehension. He was not sure he could do it. I reminded him the Lord always provided a plan for those He called into leadership. If the Lord directed him, the plan would emerge.

He shared his new insight with a colleague while on a business trip several weeks later. The conversation led to an introduction to a recruiter for a master's degree program specifically designed for those interested in public leadership. Keith was excited about the leadership options which would open because of this degree.

But was it really God's plan? Did Keith need another master's degree to fulfill God's call to becoming a leader in his workplace? I was not sure, but his energy and enthusiasm about work was higher than it had been in years. Ultimately, if God wanted Keith to receive a second master's degree, He would make a way.

The big problem with the program was the cost. While it offered an incredible opportunity to develop leadership skills, it also came at an incredible cost of $60,000. Student loans were obviously not an option. No debt would be used, so we would have to find funding from a different source.

Keith tried everything. He pursued grants, employer funding, scholarships and everything in between. He was so discouraged and began to question if he truly heard from the Lord. I reminded him of the many times in the Bible when the Lord spoke into the life of someone but did not bring fulfillment right away.

Abraham and Sarah waited 25 years for Isaac's birth after being told by the Lord of the "upcoming" birth of a son. They took matters into their own hands because they did not trust God's timing and the result was chaotic. I shared with Keith he would be doing the same thing if he pushed to make graduate school happen instead of waiting on the Lord.

Finally, after searching for funding with no success for several months, Keith withdrew his application. It was difficult to not be discouraged. Over time, he was able to let go of the disappointment and focus his energy on other areas of development. He found a mentor, enrolled in a leadership development program, and sought out stretch assignments to develop his leadership skill sets. He did not know when the Lord would fulfill the promise, but in the meantime, he was determined to get ready. It was a beautiful lesson in patience and faithfulness.

I was thankful I remained supportive and did not discount what Keith knew God spoke into his life. We were both expectant to see how, and when, God would reveal the path to His plan.

Your Turn…Your Perspective: How do you handle the delays you experience in God's plan for your life? What approach do you take to prepare yourself for the assignments you receive from the Lord?

Prayer: Lord, thank You for glimpses into the future You have laid out for me. I pray for patience to wait for Your timeline to unfold. Please help me to not get ahead of You or detour away from Your plan. I thank You for all You do to get me ready for the assignments you have for me.

Day 190
The Love of Giving

1 TIMOTHY 5:8

I went to college on scholarships. Plural. I earned lots of little scholarships. One of the largest was a multi-year award for residents of South Carolina who lost one or more of their parents. The James F. Byrnes Foundation was a blessing. It worked to not only provide support for a college education but also built a sense of family for the students. It was a vital part of my college years.

It truly would have been much more difficult without their support. In fact, the sense of community continued long after the financial support ended. It was not uncommon to find former recipients still participating in the larger community decades after graduating from college.

Keith was a huge advocate for Veterans who fell through the cracks of "the system." As a Marine, he knew firsthand what it meant to serve. It was painful for him to see Veterans who were not able to navigate post-war life well. He could not assist with their emotional healing but chose to serve as a mentor when possible. He also assisted many by providing money for their transportation needs after they found employment.

Our passion for these organizations made it important for us to support them through giving. An agency whose mission was to support Veterans with transportation needs, and the James F. Byrnes Foundation were both in our monthly budget. We wanted to support them because we loved and believed in their mission.

After taking Financial Peace University, however, we realized we needed to adjust. FPU taught to discontinue all giving outside of tithing until we were completely out of debt. This allowed debt reduction to be intensified and eliminated competing priorities in the budget. Once we were debt-free, extra giving could be added back into the budget.

I admit this was hard for us. We wanted to give back right then. We wanted to show gratitude by supporting our causes. We wanted their missions to continue and wanted to be a part of their growth. The idea of removing these two organizations from our monthly budget left a void for each of us. We were committed to our goal of financial freedom, however; and knew it was a short-term sacrifice for a long-term gain.

We chose to keep our eye on the goal of becoming debt free first. Funding the competing priority of extra giving would have prolonged the amount of time we were in debt. Even though it was not an easy decision, we knew it was the best decision. Slow and steady wins the race, right? If we wanted to win well, we needed to give the plan a chance.

We each called our charity's point of contact and shared why our donations would be suspended. Both were gracious and thanked us for our support and we thanked them for the work their agencies did. We both looked forward to resuming our support in the future. We knew doing so would have the added meaning of financial freedom.

Your Turn...Your Perspective: What parameters define your giving? How do you determine what, when, and how to give? How does your giving support your passion or cause?

Prayer: Lord, I want to have a heart to give. Please help me to be disciplined enough to get out of debt as quickly as possible to give even more in the future. I trust Your plan for my life. I know my current season is meant to strengthen me financially. With Your help, I can do this.

Day 191
Fine Print

PROVERBS 20:10

One day while I was driving to work, I heard a weird noise. It was time for an oil change so I described the noise to our mechanic when I dropped the car off the next day. I called Keith and we agreed, since the cost was low enough, we would have the repair completed along with the oil change. It felt really good to have enough money in the car repair envelope to take care of a small emergency along with routine maintenance.

A few hours later, we learned our mechanic needed to keep my car longer than originally thought. The part needed to be ordered and would not be in until Friday. We were in a little bit of a bind. We needed to drive to St. Louis to pick up the kids for the weekend and our mechanic did not recommend driving 400 miles with the turbo drive in need of repair. Even though our mechanic provided a loaner car, he was not keen on us putting 400 miles on it. Keith was driving his $1500 car during this season of our debt snowball, and we did not trust it on the road for 400 miles. We decided to rent a car.

Typically, we rented our cars from our favorite discount warehouse, but the prices for even a compact car were well outside of the money we allocated for the rental. We only needed the rental car for one day and did not want to spend over $100 to rent a car for such a short period of time.

I checked a few discount travel sites online and found a compact car for around $40 for the day. Perfect! Just what we needed. The terms were for us to pick the car up by 10P.M. on Thursday night and drop it off by 10P.M. on Friday night. I skimmed all the fine print on the discount website and booked the car.

There was only one problem. I did not build in enough time for travel delays. We ran into major traffic delays going to St. Louis and more delays coming back. We were supposed to return the car by 10P.M., but it was after midnight before we made it back to the airport in Kansas City. The fine print, which I skimmed right before booking the car, clearly stated a late charge of $90 would be added if we returned the car after 10P.M.

A late charge! Really? Our discount warehouse never charged a late fee. Our very uncomfortable (for four tall people) compact, supposedly cheap rental car, ended up costing us over $140 for one day! I was so frustrated. The thought of the wasted money (which was pulled from debt reduction) caused my eyes to burn with hot tears. I just hung my head and let them fall. In my attempt to save money, I cost us more.

We were doing all we could to beat our debt into submission, and at every turn, we seemed to be met with crazy resistance. It felt so overwhelming and unfair. I was so ready for it to all be over. Keith did his best to comfort me, but we both knew I would have to work my way through it.

The amount was so small, but the impact was so big. There was more money diverted from the debt snowball. More time in debt. As hard as it was to accept, my error was simply an oversight and a hard lesson was learned from the experience. It was easy and sometimes costly to forget the unexpected. Once again, only time and prayer could heal my hurting heart.

Your Turn…Your Perspective: What financial situation has caused you the most pain? How did you get through it? What changes did you make in your life because of the experience?

Prayer: Lord, thank You for all the trials in my life which You use to grow me. I pray to not get lost on the path to You. Help me to not lose hope, but to constantly seek Your face (full of light) in the dark places.

Day 192
My New Normal

I was blessed with some great mentors and bosses in my life. My first boss out of college was a kind man with a big heart and a smile to match. He would do anything for anyone. Under his leadership, I was able to hone my communication skills and learned to ask for what I needed.

My favorite Mary Kay mentor taught me how to decorate a room, be a gracious hostess, and listen to those around me to anticipate their needs. She taught me to set big goals, be consistent and never shrink away from a challenge. I was to meet it head on, knowing Jesus was with me the entire time. Most importantly, she taught me to not be afraid to showcase my faith.

There were also a few bosses who aided in my development as a leader from a different perspective. Learning how not to treat people was just as valuable as learning how to motivate them. I found myself with one such boss during the middle of our debt snowball.

I was in a new position and was excited about the opportunity. I knew it would stretch me and my abilities. The person who hired me envisioned changes for the department which fit my skillset perfectly. We were both excited to implement them and see how it would all unfold. Unfortunately for me, she was transferred six months after I started. The person who replaced her did not share her vision and had very little desire to continue what we started.

I found myself in a work environment which once held great potential, but now seemed lackluster at best. My expertise was not valued, and I was systematically removed from the inner workings of the department. I no longer knew what was happening around me. My access to information was cut off, outside of a very small circle of colleagues. My pride was wounded, and I became increasingly frustrated.

One day during devotion, I came across Ecclesiastes 11:5-6. Keith and I changed Bible versions monthly to gain fresh insight into God's Word. This particular month, we were reading in "The Message" version. The passage spoke so clearly to me. I realized I was to bloom where I was planted and see the good in what felt like a bad situation. I began to pray for the Lord to show me my purpose for being in my current position.

Over the next few months, I chose to open my eyes and join the Lord at work. I began to serve as a mentor to several women in the office and sought out new projects which exposed me to leadership in new ways. I prayed for my boss and asked the Lord how to be of service. It was a slow process, but eventually I no longer dreaded going to work. I began to embrace my work environment for what it was, not what it could have been. This was my new normal.

I was thankful the seeds of bitterness did not take root. Bitterness was not something which grew in one place. Once it began to grow in one part of your life, it would not be long before other areas fell victim to it. Our journey was too important for me to allow bitterness any room in my life. I vowed to stay in my position and serve Him as long as necessary. I would give my best at all times.

Your Turn…Your Perspective: How do you respond to your professional value being tested? What is your response to having to remain in a challenging environment?

Prayer: Lord, please help me to serve You well, even when I don't feel like it. Help me to not be distracted by the present situation. Keep me focused on the plan You have placed before me.

Will You Share with Me?

SONG OF SOLOMON 8:7

One of the big expenses in our budget, which was constantly under scrutiny, was the cell phone bill. Even with all the competition among the carriers, the expense kept rising. We paid a good bit of attention to it to make sure it stayed in line.

It was important to manage the need for coverage against the cost. We both traveled for work, my family lived in rural South Carolina, the kids lived in St. Louis, and we chose not to incur the expense of a home phone. We needed cell phone coverage to always be available. As a result, we opted to stay with major carriers.

The family plan we started with when we first got married worked fine for us, but not for our cell phone provider. After a few years, it was slowly phased out. The increases in the new plan were small at first but were still more than we wanted to pay. Keith did not want to switch companies, so we needed to find another way to make it work. We decided to cut our data plan.

While most people were clamoring for as much data as they could get, we decided to cut our data to the minimum. We turned off social media apps to keep them from constantly using data for updates. We checked for free Wi-Fi at every place where we spent more than a few moments. We made sure all the data optimization features were enabled. We did everything we could to keep the costs low.

We got good at staying within our lower allotment of data, but occasionally we ended up getting close to our monthly limit. It was then we made the hard decision to shut down data completely until the billing cycle reset. It was not an easy decision, but our goal of becoming debt-free made the discomfort worth it.

There were many painful months when the data ran out before the month. But we did not waiver. Instead of increasing the data, and therefore increasing our cell phone bill, we chose to simply do without. Instead of seeing data as a necessity, we viewed it as a privilege. And when it ran out, the privilege was suspended until the next month.

We never made a big deal of the lack of data. It only happened a few times a year, and rarely impacted our lives for more than a few days. It was a small sacrifice for the money we were able to save. It was a small sacrifice for the overall goal of becoming debt-free. It was a small sacrifice for our future.

We simply saw data limitation for what it was – a small inconvenience in our very convenient life. The reminder helped to keep us grounded and keep our eye on the goal. One day we would be debt-free and data would not stand in our way.

Your Turn…Your Perspective: What are your most expensive creature comforts? Which ones would you be willing to give up to meet your current financial goal?

Prayer: Lord, thank You for creature comforts. Thank You for helping me not take them for granted. I pray You help me remember the value of the sacrifice and to always stay in tune to Your greater plan.

Day 194
Debt Thermometer

HEBREWS 13:5

A few years into paying on our debt snowball, I came up with the grand idea to create a visual aid to keep us motivated. Our remaining debt was still well over $100,000, and the medical bills were coming in constantly. I needed a reminder of our goal. I needed something to help me see our progress.

I decided on a debt payment thermometer. Each time we paid off $1000, we would color in a line. It would help us to visualize our progress. I found examples online and set about creating our thermometer. I taped it to the pantry in our kitchen and felt quite pleased with our new visual. The excitement was short lived.

The first few weeks the thermometer was up, we did not color in any lines. A visit to our new doctor consumed all our extra money and left nothing to pay toward debt. The minimum payments going out to debt were well under $1000 per month which meant no coloring. The next month we were only able to color in one line.

I looked at it several times each day. Sometimes I found myself just standing there staring at it. I willed the thermometer to move. The sooner we were done with debt, the sooner we could move on to the rest of our lives. Come on thermometer! MOVE!!! MOVE, THERMOMETER, MOVE!!!

The next month was more of the same. Expensive medication, rare and costly blood tests all required more of the precious dollars I wanted to send to pay off our student loans. The payoff thermometer was not moving, and I began to feel anxious. I doubted if we would ever get through the huge thermometer on the wall. I became paralyzed with doubt and uncertainty. I was afraid we would always be bound by the debt staring back at me from the thermometer on the wall in our kitchen.

I was in a tailspin over a piece of paper hanging on the side of the pantry. It consumed all my thoughts at this point and I was bound by fear and frustration. What was supposed to be a motivator became an incredible frustration for me. It was so discouraging to look at the thermometer every day, and still see so much debt left to be paid. It was disheartening.

After about three months of non-stop emergencies, I began to pray in earnest. I was not sure why it took so long to turn to the Lord. I was thankful I finally did. I prayed He would change my attitude about our journey. Finally, I realized the thermometer had become my idol. I saw the colors on it as more than just progress. The colors and upward movement began to define me. It was time to remove it.

The lesson of how easy it was to allow an idol to take first place in my life was not lost. I did not want to allow it to happen again. I wanted Christ at the center of my life. To do so meant I would trust His plan and His timing.

Your Turn...Your Perspective: What things in your life consume your thoughts? How can you turn them over to God? What would it feel like to not be in control of them? What would you turn towards when these things are removed?

Prayer: Lord, thank You for Your Word. It truly does soothe my soul. I thank You for the reminder to keep my eyes on You and not on my circumstances. Please continue to reveal to me any areas in danger of becoming idols so they can be purged. You are primary in my life. And I am thankful.

Day 195
Keeping Up with the Other Joneses

PROVERBS 22:4

One of the hardest lessons I learned about living in a blended family was not to compare our household with the household of our kids' mother. Before we got married, Keith and I decided to establish the priorities of our home based on what we believed the Lord wanted for our family. This meant getting out of debt as soon as possible. Since the amount of our debt was so large, we knew it meant being very frugal with the amount budgeted for our time with the kids.

It was relatively straight forward to budget for the expenses associated with getting the kids to and from Kansas City. My struggle was associated more with how we spent our time together. Road trips associated with their visits meant packing a lunch for the four of us instead of stops for fast food or a sit-down meal.

We rarely went to movies, opting instead for games and movies at home. When we did go to movies, it was a matinee with a coupon for popcorn and drinks. We typically picked one summer blockbuster to experience as a family. Everything else was seen on DVD once it was available in the library.

We did not take vacations, except for the occasional trip to South Carolina to visit my family. Instead, we found free activities around our city and took day trips a few hours away for an adventure. We were constantly on the go and our time together was always enjoyable. Staycations were our friend.

We explored Kansas City and the surrounding community. There was always a stack of movies fresh from the library for us to choose from on movie night. I made sure a new game appeared under the Christmas tree to increase our options on game night. But in the back of my mind, I struggled to accept that my efforts were enough. We only occasionally ate out and it was considered a treat for all of us.

It took me years to not feel anxious over our time with the kids. In my mind, I knew we were doing the right thing, but my heart was harder to convince. My desire to create memorable experiences was at odds with the sensibility of getting out of debt. I wanted our kids to enjoy their time with us and needed to reconcile potential activities with our monthly budget. I was struggling to keep up with the other Joneses – our children's opinion.

To be free of the weight of comparison, I needed to choose to not be moved by their opinion, just as I chose to not be moved by the opinions of others. It was not easy.

I knew God's Word clearly outlined our responsibility as parents to set the right example for our kids. I eventually learned to see the experience as an opportunity to teach our kids a different perspective on handling money. The way we lived taught them how to work for what they wanted. It taught them to prioritize wants and needs. It taught them the power of using cash for purchases to prevent overspending.

I also finally realized, even the opinions of our kids could not deter us from following God's plan for managing our finances. It was one of the hardest lessons I learned on our journey to financial freedom.

Your Turn...Your Perspective: In what ways are you moved by the opinions of others? How do you reconcile God's plan for your life with what is popular?

Prayer: Father, thank You for the hard lessons of choosing Your way of financial stewardship. Thank You for my desire to serve You being stronger than the desire to please those around me. I pray always to embrace Your ways of managing money. Help me not be moved by the opinions of others.

Seconds

PROVERBS 10:3A

Organic vegetables were the bane of my existence during our debt snowball. They were expensive but necessary to our overall health and detox as we worked to rid our bodies of heavy metal poisoning. I worked to find ways to get them as cheaply as possible and succeeded in finding a small organic farm around the corner from where we lived.

I was familiar with the basics (tomatoes, zucchini, yellow squash, onions, etc.) but was pleasantly surprised to learn they offered other items like O'Henry sweet potatoes. We fell in love. They were perfect for mashed sweet potatoes which were a big hit with my family and visitors alike.

Since they were only $2 per pound (a real steal for organic), I made sure we kept them in the house. Near the end of the season, the farm did not have quite enough to fill our order and threw in some "seconds" to make up the weight difference. Since they were not first quality, they did not charge us. I was thankful for the discount, but more curious about the "seconds." Was it like shopping for secondhand clothes?

I grew up on a farm and we sold a few of our vegetables, but mostly kept everything we grew for ourselves. We lived on the vegetables we grew in the summer for at least nine months of the year. The less than first quality vegetables were eaten immediately, and the others were canned or frozen. We did not have seconds.

When I asked our neighbors, they explained how they sold the first quality produce, and kept the seconds for themselves. Seconds were what the farmers ate. "Well," I thought, "I used to be a farmer and I will be a farmer again!" Especially if it meant my family could eat organic vegetables at a discount.

There were some larger organic markets around our city, and when I visited, I always asked about seconds. Sweet potatoes, white potatoes, beets, radishes, and other hearty vegetables were all open for negotiation. Peaches, tomatoes, zucchini and cucumbers were more perishable, but I purchased them as seconds whenever possible. The amount we purchased depended on what was available and how long the seconds would last.

Over time, we realized our best purchases were sweet potatoes. We found another organic farmer who sold us O'Henry sweet potato seconds at a fraction of the price of first quality potatoes. We stored them in our basement and loved getting creative – sweet potato chicken hash, mashed sweet potatoes, chicken vegetable soup with cubed sweet potatoes, and more. Keith and the kids loved the meals, and I loved the savings.

Shopping for seconds was a reminder of how fiscally mature we had become since the first budget we created. We no longer ate extravagant meals but stayed with simple food. I did miss experimenting, and I missed creating beautiful food, but I was learning how to make simply into beautiful. It was all about perspective.

I knew the day would come when I could expand my ingredient list. In the meantime, eating simple, cheap food (even if it was organic) went a long way to getting our debt eliminated. There would be plenty of time to do more in the kitchen when our debt was behind us.

Your Turn…Your Perspective: What adjustments have you made to reach your financial goal sooner? What else are you willing to give up now to create the future you desire?

Prayer: Lord, thank You for diligence. Thank You for the desire to get out of debt being stronger than the desire to have an elaborate life. I pray to not lose sight of the beauty of simplicity after I become free.

Day 197
Trustees

PROVERBS 8:20

When Keith and I first completed our wills, we were new students of Dave Ramsey's Financial Peace University. All we knew was we needed a will and we were pretty much clueless beyond this knowledge. Even though we were naïve, we wanted to at least get something in place. The kids were young, and we wanted to make sure everyone was protected financially in case one of us passed away. We did not have any real understanding of the process beyond the basics.

When it came time to choose our trustees, we might as well have said, "eeny, meeny, miny, moe." There were no criteria for choosing trustees. We simply chose people who seemed pretty level headed overall, but we did not have insight into their financial lives. We also did not know what ability they might have to execute our financial wishes. Instead of praying and asking the Lord for guidance, we literally just picked people we knew and liked.

Money was incredibly tight and primarily spent on debt reduction. The initial cost to prepare our wills felt as if we spent a small fortune. When the sinking feeling showed up, indicating we may have made a mistake in our choice of trustees, we simply prayed nothing would happen to both of us at the same time. We knew it was not the best approach, but we honestly did not know who to name as replacement trustees. In our minds, it did not make sense to spend more money changing our trustees when we still did not know if we were making the right decision.

Two years later, when our estate attorney sent a reminder to review our wills, we jumped at the chance. By then, we knew more about managing our personal finances and how to make good choices. We experienced a lot more life and possessed a much better understanding of what it meant to ask someone to serve as the trustee of our wills.

This time, we entered into the process of updating our wills with a clear goal and criteria for executing our wishes. We started with prayer and really listened to what the Lord said to us. Our wills were a reflection of our complicated lives, and we needed someone we could depend on to be firm with the implementation of our wishes. We needed someone who also shared our belief in managing money as outlined in the Bible.

After many days of prayer and discussion, we made our decision. We approached our friends and explained our request. They were quite surprised at our choice because they were much younger. We shared just how much we respected their own approach to marriage and money, and knew they would exercise our wishes with care and respect.

The couple we chose spent a few days praying, and then accepted the role they hoped never to fill. We were thankful and appreciative because we dodged what could have been a very messy situation by not changing our trustees earlier. And, we were especially thankful for the grace God showed us through our friends.

Your Turn…Your Perspective: Name a time when you took too long to make a financial decision. What was the outcome? How would you handle it differently if given another opportunity?

Prayer: Lord, thank You for being patient with me as I learn how to live my financial life as You have instructed me. I pray to keep my heart open to receive Your instructions about every area of my life. I pray for good friends to travel this journey with me.

Day 198
Selling the Past

PROVERBS 30:8B

Almost like clockwork, every few months Keith and I went through our home looking for things to sell. Everything was open to discussion. The longer we were in debt, the less things we found.

Finally, we got around to giving a second and third look at movies and music. Each of us owned an extensive collection. We went through our collections early on and took out the duplicates. Next came the ones we doubted we would ever watch again. By the time we were in year four of paying on our debt snowball, we were looking at items which held some level of significance.

At the same time, our focus was shifting. The longer we worked on becoming debt-free, the deeper our faith became. Music and movies which held significance early on became easier to sell; we no longer saw the value in holding on to them. Or, at least, I did not.

It turned out Keith was having a harder time letting go. He was a DJ for years as a younger man and absolutely loved all types of music. His library was extensive. He had been collecting for years and developed a special attachment to all of it. When we streamlined years ago, it was easier because we only got rid of duplicates. Now we were deciding to cut into what was left. It was much more difficult than either of us thought it would be.

One day, not too long after our decision to cut again, I approached Keith with a thought. I suggested we hold onto the collection for a little longer and find something else to sell. This journey was hard enough without the added loss of a beloved collection.

He hugged me and thanked me for the offer, but it was time to let go of the past. The music was a subtle reminder of all the poor choices he made in his life. And while it was difficult to do, he saw selling the collection as a way of letting go of the past once and for all.

We did come upon a small compromise. Technology made it easy to digitally recreate the portions of the library Keith wanted to keep, but the majority was sold without much reverie.

So much of the journey we were on was reactionary. We reacted to the debt at the beginning of our journey. We reacted to the medical bills and car repairs which pounded us through it all. We reacted to the need to adjust food and medication almost quarterly. It finally felt good to actually think through a scenario and not have to react.

Keith decided to let go of his music collection to pour more financial fuel on our burning desire to be out of debt. It was worth more to him than the space held by a collection from a past life. I was thankful he loved us enough to let it go. And I loved him even more for doing it.

Your Turn…Your Perspective: What have you been holding on to which needs to be purged? Why is it so difficult to let it go?

Prayer: Lord, thank You for my desire to live Your way. I know the sacrifice will be worth it in the end. Please continue to show me glimpses of what it looks like to live for You in every area of my life.

Day 199
Bargain Postage

ISAIAH 23:18: JAMES 1:2-4

I was on a mission to save money wherever I could. Keith and I made all financial decisions together, but I was the gatherer of information. I worked hard to make sure we did not lose any money on any purchase. Most times it worked; sometimes it did not.

We were in a difficult season of debt elimination where our doctors were located in Dallas, TX. Every two to three months, we made the eight-hour drive to Dallas. The trips were physically and financially taxing. Hotel stays, food, medical visits, blood tests and medications were all included in our budget allocation. We chose to stay in a hotel with a kitchen, and packed the car with meals and snacks to limit what we spent eating out.

Another area where we attempted to save was postage. Many of the companies we used to order our supplements from offered free shipping when a specific dollar amount was reached. One provider, however, did not. We both used the supplements from that source and went through roughly three to four bottles a month. At over $80 a bottle, the cost got big really quick.

The shipping and handling costs were an additional $11 per order. I needed to find a way to get the supplements at a cheaper price, but I could not find them anywhere. They were a proprietary blend of minerals and were only sold through licensed medical professionals. If we were to continue with the protocol, we would have to pay the $11 shipping and handling cost each time we ordered. Because of the price of the supplements, and the need to have money available for other medical needs, we were not able to order more than 4 or 5 bottles at a time.

I approached the office manager of the supplier and asked if I could send her prepaid envelopes. She said if we paid the shipping, the "handling" cost would go down to only $6 per order. We looked to save anywhere we could, right? We all then agreed to the arrangement, and I promptly mailed her the prepaid envelopes.

It backfired. I did not ever find out exactly what happened, but the next order (over $300 in supplements) never arrived. It was December and I knew it might take longer because of holiday deliveries, so I built in an extra two weeks before we needed the supplements. By the second week in January, I knew I made a terrible mistake. In an effort to save $5, I cost our family over $300 in lost supplements because they never arrived.

I was sick with frustration, and we still needed the supplements. I told Keith what happened and sat quietly as he processed it all. I loved my husband for many reasons, but the one which came to mind then was his calm and practical demeanor. He was not angry. He did not even match my frustration. He simply kissed my forehead and thanked me for trying to save money anywhere I could.

I could not stop the tears. I wanted so much to be debt-free, and I cost us $300 of our hard-earned income. But I also learned a valuable lesson. Weigh the savings against the "cost" before deciding. Duly noted. It never happened again.

Your Turn…Your Perspective: Name a time when the desire to save money cost you money instead. What was the end result?

Prayer: Lord, even in my frustration, You are with me. I pray for the strength to get through the tough times on this journey. You never told me it would be easy, but I know it will be worth it in the end when I am free from debt.

Birthday Bouquet

ISAIAH 55:2

Keith and I always made sure the kids were given the opportunity to purchase a birthday gift for their mother while they were with us. As they got older, we allowed them more freedom in the choice of gift, as long as the total cost did not exceed the budgeted amount. One year, they decided to redo the floral arrangement in her dining room. Off we went to the local craft store for a bouquet of silk flowers to fill the large vase we purchased.

As we entered the store, I reminded them of the budget, and then hung back to allow them time to wander and make their choices. Soon, our daughter was in full shopping mode with her selections, and our son added in a few stems to keep from being left out of the decision. They were having a blast choosing a variety of exotic stems and were creating a stunning bouquet. There was only one problem – neither of them once looked at a price tag.

I let them finish the bouquet before asking about the cost. The look on their faces was one of confusion and dismay. *"Surely the bouquet is in the budget,"* their expressions said.

Next, we did the only thing to do. We pulled up the calculator app to see exactly how much their masterpiece would cost. They blew through the budgeted amount with just three or four stems and their eyes got wide as the number kept getting higher. Then the sad looks showed up. There was no way their bouquet would make it out of the store. The final cost was literally $110 more than the budget.

I asked them what they would like to do next, and our daughter was the first to speak. I could tell she was disappointed because she thoroughly enjoyed being creative. She told me they needed to choose another gift. I asked our son what he thought we should do and he agreed with his sister. I let them ponder the thought for a few minutes before I spoke again.

I explained that they did not have to choose a different gift. They just needed to choose different stems. I took them to the sale section and pointed to all the stems which were on sale. Many were under $1. They could still build a beautiful bouquet for their mom's dining room table and stay within the allotted budget.

I told them to pick their two favorite regular-priced stems and fill the rest of the bouquet with sale-priced stems. They went to work. I stood back and watched them choose the stems, this time with a calculator. They swapped out stems and worked to get as close to the budget as possible. It took a lot longer to create the second bouquet, but I was in no hurry. I wanted them to take all the time they needed to learn this incredibly valuable lesson.

The second bouquet was beautiful. And came within budget. Two missions accomplished – gift for their mother on budget, and teaching our kids how to shop within our means. Priceless.

Your Turn…Your Perspective: When was the last time you blew your budget? How did it make you feel? What was your response?

Prayer: Lord, thank You for the many opportunities You give me to learn Your ways. I pray to not get caught up in the moment and lose sight of the ultimate goal. Please help me be mindful of my budget and my goals, especially when my emotions are running high.

Day 201
Cell Phone Jail

PROVERBS 11:26

The newest technology and a debt snowball were opposites. Chances were good a person working to reduce debt did not have the latest technology. Our house was no different. Our cell phones were never the latest and greatest. We always got the model year lower than what was currently advertised. It made pricing much more affordable.

I never really understood the cell phone industry. I always felt as if I were "sold something" when we went into a cell phone store. The industry made an enormous amount of money, and Keith and I did not want to part with any more of ours than necessary. So, when I realized within the first few months I made a mistake in buying my latest phone, I chose to suffer through it.

I hated my phone. I complained a little too loudly one day and Keith heard me. His solution was to simply get another phone, but I did not want to pay the contract fees. In my mind, I made the decision and I needed to live with it. Keith's point was reliability. We did not have a home phone and my cell phone was the only way to reach me. If it was unreliable. It needed to go.

It got incredibly frustrating. We argued about it for months. It reached a point where I did not want him to see my frustration because I knew he would either say something or think something which would spark another heated discussion. But the phone just kept getting worse.

One day during my Bible study, the Holy Spirit showed me a different perspective. I did not want to spend the money on the phone because, to me, it was all about preserving payments to the debt snowball. But what about preserving my marriage? Ooh.

What I did not realize was Keith saw me continuing to hold on to the phone as an act of defiance. I was willfully going against his request. As I thought about this, I asked myself if a $200 buyout was worth the priceless damage to our relationship. Did I want to save a dollar more than I wanted to save the open communication of our marriage? I was so focused on the money, I missed the impact on our marriage.

I immediately went to Keith and apologized. I told him of my revelation from the Holy Spirit and asked for his forgiveness and he apologized for holding a grudge. So many of our heated discussions revolved around money, and we forgot our journey of debt reduction was filled with opportunities to learn how to better communicate and understand the other's perspective. He simply wanted me to be safe and did not care about the cost. I completely overlooked and discounted his desire to protect me. It was a powerful lesson for both of us.

We adjusted the budget to include the cell phone payout and then bought me a new phone. The added cost was worth the peace in our household and resulted in a stronger commitment to better communication for both of us. I was thankful we found our way through it without doing major damage to the foundation of our marriage. It was a lesson I would never forget.

Your Turn…Your Perspective: When was the last time you missed a listening opportunity? What was the impact?

Prayer: Lord, I pray for a mind which is open to communication with those around me. I pray to have compassion and show grace to others. Please help me to serve others and be open to their service.

Day 202
How Much Are the Payments?

PSALM 33:10

We were leasing our cell phones. We were slowly making our way through our debt snowball and were also streamlining expenses. The decision to buy me a new phone gave us an opportunity to review our cell phone plan and make sure it was the best fit. We might not be able to get blood out of a turnip, but we wanted to be sure we squeezed every penny out of this next purchase.

We were paying $21 a month for my current phone. As we reviewed the budget and the cell phone bill, I was prompted to do some deeper math. My heart dropped when I finished my calculation. My "it's only $21 a month" phone was actually costing over $500. And while we realized there were other cell phones which were even more expensive, we knew it was time to get out of the cell phone financing business.

This new information about the actual cost of our phones was punctuated by the realization that leasing phones meant a perpetual cell phone payment. It was a fiscal model which did not fit with a life of Christ-centered financial wellness. We were ready to get out.

Before our revelation, we bought into the "go along to get along" mentality of most consumers. We chose to remain uneducated about how we were spending our money in this area. But no more. We decided to no longer blindly give our money over to the multi-billion-dollar industry without doing our homework and better understanding just how our money was spent.

I went online to view my options. I wanted to better understand exactly how to not pay over $500 for a cell phone. Fortunately, we already learned the value of purchasing an older model phone. Instead of getting the latest release, we waited until a new release was announced and then purchased the older one at a discount. It turned out we could do even more.

A few weeks after our discovery of just how much money we were giving away, I found a promotion online which allowed us to purchase the older model phone for only $179. It was the exact same phone which was being offered for $22 a month. Purchasing the phone for $179 outright instead of paying $22 monthly for two years meant we saved over $300.

We also learned to never buy phone accessories from the cell phone store. The profit margin was as much as 500% on some items. Instead, I ordered the protective case and screen cover for my new phone online. Even after these purchases, we did not go over our $200 budget. And because we now owned the phone instead of leasing it, we dropped insurance, saving an additional $60 per phone per year. I felt like we were finally learning how to think through our purchases, and honor God with our money in all areas. What a blessing!

Your Turn…Your Perspective: Name a time when you discovered you could have saved money on a purchase. How did you find out? What emotion did it stir in you? What did you do with your new knowledge?

Prayer: Lord, please open my eyes to hidden costs. Please help me not be complacent in how I spend. Show me where I need to dig in and ask, "Why?" Help me to never again make a purchase without reviewing all my options.

Day 203
Discovery Series
PSALM 145:16

When Keith and I moved to Kansas City, I was pleasantly surprised to find a very active arts community. I enjoyed the variety of cultural opportunities in the DC Metro area and looked forward to getting familiar with what Kansas City offered. In DC, I experienced the Kennedy Center, Constitution Hall, and the Smithsonian museums in addition to the many productions available at area churches, playhouses, and community centers.

Keith and I spent most of our time together enjoying one free event or another. Two of my girlfriends and I were intentional in taking in a new and unusual cultural event every year from June through October to celebrate our birthdays. Ethiopian food, high tea in a mansion, jazz brunch in a museum, free concerts on the National Mall were all in my memory bank from my time in Northern Virginia.

My cultural experiences in Kansas City were severely limited, however, by the tight budget we set up. We were determined to get rid of the mound of debt brought into our marriage which meant no concerts and no symphony. We also did not venture out to many sporting events, and few movies were seen in the theater.

Most of what we did attend was free. I found websites and list-serves which sent updates of the latest free activities around the city. There were museums and exhibits, outdoor movies, and Shakespeare in the park.

We enjoyed the Christmas symphony production at the Kauffman Center on the night of the dress rehearsal. We got our jazz fix by attending free block parties downtown. Free hand bell concerts each year offered more cultural variety.

What I enjoyed most though was the Harriman-Jewell Discovery Series. Founded in 1965, the goal of the series was to expose the arts to the entire Kansas City community without cost being an issue. The artists were typically at the beginning of their professional careers, but it did not diminish the beauty of the performances.

Violinists, cellists, pianists, vocalists and more all delighted the audience for free. It was always an incredible experience. If our budget were not so tight, I would have gladly paid to attend these concerts, and would not have been disappointed. But I did not have to break the budget at all. Even the parking was free.

I was thankful to experience the culture of the city without breaking the budget. The Harriman-Jewell Discovery Series did for me exactly what it intended to do for all. Until we could budget for the arts again, a free concert was the prize for a little patience.

I knew in my heart those free concerts were a gift from the Lord. He recognized my desire to be a part of the culture of our city and honored our commitment to be debt-free before indulging. I did not waste energy lamenting over the concerts we did not get to attend (i.e., Patti LaBelle, Women of Faith, TobyMac and others). Instead, I accepted the gifts of the Discovery Series with grace. I was thankful for the generosity of Richard Harriman and William Jewell College for making them available, and for my Lord and Savior putting us in the city where they existed.

Your Turn…Your Perspective: What creature comforts do you enjoy? How do you manage them within the constraints of your current financial goals?

Prayer: Lord, thank You for the opportunity to have a little fun. I know it's a small thing, but it is important. And I am thankful You provide the creature comforts which make this journey a little easier. Please help me not lose focus. I praise Your name.

Day 204
Envelopes for Christmas

PROVERBS 23:5

One year I received a rather large bonus right before Christmas. We saw it as an incredible blessing and were very thankful. The bonus allowed us to increase payments to our debt snowball for the month. We had been working hard at debt reduction for about three years and cut our expenses repeatedly to send the most amount of money possible to our debts.

One of the areas we recently cut was the amount of money we spent on gifts for our kids and family members. We switched to homemade gifts for the family, and simply tightened the budget for gifts for the kids. It was hard for me to not spend as much on the kids. I wanted them to enjoy the holidays with us and gift giving was a big part of the experience. But I also knew we must be good stewards of our income which meant getting out of debt as quickly as possible.

A few weeks earlier I noticed an advertisement for a musical. I knew we would all enjoy seeing it, and the dates coincided with the time the kids were with us for the holidays. But while I knew it would be fun entertainment for the entire family, I also knew it would not be wise to purchase the tickets. Each time the same advertisement arrived in email, I deleted it. Maybe another time, when we were debt-free.

When I got the bonus, I not only saw it as an opportunity to put more money towards our debt, but I also saw it as an opportunity to splurge a little and make a great holiday memory for our family. I told Keith about the musical and asked if we could take the kids. He thought it was a great idea. We decided to share our gift by taking along our sister and nephew. We all had a blast.

The budget needed to be tweaked to accommodate the added expenses. The hotel we needed while visiting family was already booked with funds in the budget allocated to pay for it. We just needed to add the tickets to the musical. We also decided to take the family out for dinner prior to the musical and needed money for a day trip for a niece's graduation. If we weren't careful, we could easily overspend the holiday.

I did not want the gift of the bonus to be lost by not planning how it would be used. Instead of leaving everything to chance, Keith and I planned out the amount we would spend for each portion of the holiday and set up an envelope system. Each section of the holiday received its own cash envelope. We paid for the hotel stays with cash. We paid for dinner before the musical with cash. We created a separate cash envelope to manage the expenses associated with graduation. It was all planned out.

The holiday was a huge success. Everyone enjoyed the musical and dinner. Our niece's graduation helped us reiterate the importance of college to our kids. Our hotel expenses were paid without fanfare. The absolute best part, however, was having cash leftover. We finished the whirlwind holiday with almost $50 remaining in our envelopes. It was an amazing win as well as a reminder of how far our money could go when we chose to have a plan for it. It was a valuable lesson for our journey of Christ-centered financial wellness.

Your Turn…Your Perspective: How do you handle windfall money? How did you handle your last windfall? What would you change about the experience?

Prayer: Lord, thank You for a plan. Thank You for the desire to be good stewards. I pray to be mindful of this experience in the future and do not lose sight of what it means to manage well the resources You have given.

Day 205
Elf

As with most families, we had a list of must watch movies. During the holidays, our list included *A Miracle On 34th Street, It's a Wonderful Life,* and *Elf.* If we watched them all in one night, it was a special treat. Even though we enjoyed the others, *Elf* was our absolute favorite. Throughout the year, we kept the enthusiasm of Christmas cheer going by using every opportunity possible to recite the lines from the movie. It made for great entertainment and family memories.

We followed our parenting plan for holiday visitation, which meant the kids were with us on Christmas Day every other year. We worked hard to make sure those Christmases were filled with special traditions. We did not put the tree up until we picked up the kids in order for them to be a part of it. Quiche and spiced apples for breakfast was the staple on Christmas morning, and of course, our movie time.

In the months before I received the bonus, I found a special promotion on Groupon for *Elf,* the Broadway musical. It was live in St. Louis during the time we would be there celebrating with family. I wanted to purchase tickets so badly. The Groupon rate was excellent for a family of four, but I knew better than to suggest it to Keith. We kept a strict budget for gifts for the kids and never went over. In addition, I finished shopping months earlier, and there was no more gift money available. Again and again, I saw the promotion come and go. Each time, I watched and prayed for the funds to take our kids; each time, I let the expiration date pass.

So when the bonus came in, I knew it was the answer to a very materialist prayer. I immediately approached Keith with the idea of us making the tickets a part of the kids' Christmas gifts. He agreed with the importance of sharing this event with the kids. We knew they would enjoy seeing the musical version of the movie we all loved so much.

We also chose to purchase two additional tickets for our sister and seven-year-old nephew to experience the musical with us. Neither of them (nor our kids) had been to a Broadway show before. It was beautiful to watch them wide-eyed with excitement. The singing and dancing were spectacular, and the cast managed to capture all the great parts of the movie. They even gave us a few new lines to recite. It was a grand evening.

Including dinner for the six of us, the evening cost about $250. It was a big splurge for us, one which would not have happened without the sizeable bonus. Even after four years, we still owed about $60,000 on our debt snowball. While we knew the $250 could have easily been spent on student loan interest, delaying our debt-free scream by a few weeks was worth the incredible memories we created.

Our kids did not know the final cost of the evening, but they did understand the sacrifice. While it was not expected, it was a wonderful surprise for me and Keith when they thanked us for the evening. We, too, were thankful.

Your Turn…Your Perspective: Think of a time when you splurged on a memorable event. What was the best part of it?

Prayer: Lord, thank You for small reprieves in our journey. Thank You for honoring our work ethic and our desire to live our lives for You. Help us, Lord, to continue to provide a good example for our kids. Please help them to see the value in following You.

Day 206
The Gift

PROVERBS 3:4

We budgeted every year for a Christmas gift for our children's mother. It was our responsibility to ensure she was celebrated as their mother. When the kids were younger, we picked out the gifts for them ourselves, but as they got older, we gave them the responsibility of choosing the gift. They were told how much they could spend and would proceed to come up with the gift. If they needed help, I would recommend ideas.

One year, we asked the kids if they knew what they wanted to give their mother. Our daughter chimed in immediately with her idea. It turned out she and a girlfriend were making cookies and broke her mother's KitchenAid® mixer. They tried to fix it and her mother attempted to find a replacement part, both to no avail. Our daughter asked if we could replace it.

My heart sank. There was no way we were buying a KitchenAid® mixer for Christmas. The price exceeded our budgeted amount by a long shot, and to make matters worse, a KitchenAid® mixer had been on my wish list for years. If I did not have one, we certainly were not buying one for someone else.

I listened as our daughter continued to explain how badly she felt for breaking her mother's mixer. She told us she saved $40 to put towards the cost of the mixer and hoped we would supply the rest. I opened my mouth to say, "Uh, no…try again," when I was immediately silenced by the Holy Spirit. I literally could not speak. Keith kept his eyes straight ahead, refusing to look at me. When I could speak again, I told our daughter we would discuss it and let her know our decision later in the day.

That evening, Keith and I stole a moment of privacy. Before I could speak, he told me he would support whatever decision I made. Great. Now it was all on me. I wanted to remind him he was the head of our household and the decision was his to make, but he already made a decision. His decision was to let me make it! Ugh. As much as I loved my husband, I hated it when he and the Holy Spirit ganged up on me. And it certainly felt like I was fighting a losing battle with this one.

In my heart, I knew what we must do. My mind, however, was not in agreement at all. Talk about sacrifice. I was not sure I was ready to make such a big one. The budget would have to be redone (taking money away from student loans), and I would have to shop for my beloved KitchenAid® mixer only to give it away.

We sat together quietly for a long while. My chest was tight with the emotion of the decision. I could obey the Holy Spirit's call to kindness or hold on to my own selfish desire. The choice was mine to make. My mind spun with the tug of war. I did not want to do it, but I also did not want to be disobedient.

I took a deep breath and told Keith we needed to go shopping for a mixer. He just said, "Okay." We collected our daughter's $40 and we all then headed out and found a great deal on a KitchenAid® mixer at our local warehouse store. When our daughter saw the price, her eyes got wide. I explained our decision to sacrifice to help her show appreciation to her mother. I reminded her it was the thought of the gift (not the price) which mattered most. It was a teachable moment for us both.

Your Turn…Your Perspective: What was the last sacrifice you made? What impact did it have on your spiritual walk?

Prayer: Lord, thank You for obedience being better than sacrifice. I pray for a heart open to giving more than selfish gain.

Day 207
Shared Chicken

PROVERBS 28:27

Over the years, Keith and I began to meet more and more people with environmentally-based illnesses. The category was not even one we knew existed until we were referred to an environmental specialist for our own "mystery" illnesses. There were so many specialists on our list of attempts to find answers, it was good to finally feel as if we were on the right track.

Friends of ours were on a similar journey, but his illness was very different. It took years for them to discover his diagnosis of Lyme's Disease. They too, experienced the need for expensive supplements, obscure blood tests, and trips to other cities in search for answers. One discovery which seemed to make a difference was eating an all-organic diet. Doing so seemed to decrease our friend's symptoms. It got to a point where not eating organic food actually inflamed his condition. His wife knew then, at least for him, keeping organic groceries in the budget was a necessity.

Our friend's diet was very strict. And as a result, organic chicken became a staple. I often made soup with organic chicken breast and vegetables to assist. One morning during devotion, I felt prompted to gift our friends some organic chicken. It was a staple in our house, and I knew how expensive it was to use it every day.

We were in the first pay period of the month. Because of the expenses which were paid in the first few days of each month, we budgeted less grocery money from this pay check. If we were to give our friends organic chicken before the middle of the month, it would create a deficit in our own home. But, I knew from past experiences not to question this sort of prompting by the Holy Spirit. Inevitably a blessing was given or received when I chose to be obedient instead of hoarding our possessions for our own use.

I told Keith what I was prompted to do and headed out to shop for groceries. *How would I make this work, Lord?* was the question in my mind as I walked to the poultry section of our favorite discount warehouse. Organic chicken breasts were my typical purchase and I learned how to stretch them. But how would I stretch them from our house to our friend's house? I prayed silently for guidance. Then it came to me.

Instead of buying all chicken breasts for our house, I bought whole chickens. I hated working with whole chickens. I know hate is a strong word, but it described my feelings at the time. The only way to share organic chicken with our friends, at the beginning of the month and not go over the food budget, was to buy whole chickens. We knew it was not a lot, but we also knew they would appreciate it. We were also thankful to be able to share a blessing.

Our own journey taught us the importance of not discounting the impact of small generosities. We were required to get creative in how we gifted others when we removed all giving outside of tithes from our budget. It was important to remember the intent of the gift. To someone else, raw chicken was far from being gift-worthy. In our world, it was the best gift, simply because it was all we had to offer.

Your Turn…Your Perspective: What was the smallest gift you have ever given? What was the largest? What impact did each have on you and the person(s) receiving it?

Prayer: Lord, thank You for obedience. Thank You for small generosities, those given and those received. Please help me continue to keep my eyes on You and not be concerned with the opinions of others.

Day 208
Headed Upward

PROVERBS 20:10

Cable in Kansas was expensive. Ever since we moved to Kansas from Northern Virginia, I struggled with the amount of our cable bill. Each year I negotiated with the cable company, and many years we changed companies all together. I did not want to pay a fortune for cable. A simple solution in my mind was to cut cable completely, but Keith was not ready to do it.

Our friends did not understand why we complained. Our cable bill was lower than most. They looked at us with expressions of confusion when we explained the increase of 15-20% each year. They were trying to figure out how we "survived" on basic cable, let alone cut what we did have even further.

Since no one paid our bills but us, we chose to no longer discuss the rise of the cost of cable with our friends. Instead, we continued to search for the next promotion and cut our coverage to the bare minimum. We did this for three additional years until the costs were no longer justifiable.

The deciding factor to eliminate cable came when Keith saw a video blog showcasing just how much money could be saved by cutting cable. The speaker walked us through all the reasons why cable would only continue to increase in cost. He also showed all the "cable free" options for streaming our favorite shows, including baseball (go Cardinals!). The time finally came to cut the cord.

We were in unchartered waters, but it was not the first time. We knew we would find our way; it was just a matter of time. We did our research to determine the best way to stream and which apps were the best to view our favorite shows. We hoped it would be a smooth transition.

Unfortunately, the cable company decided to fight back. Several networks blocked the streaming of their shows without a cable account. Sure enough, all our favorite shows were on networks with this arrangement. There were two choices: go back to cable or no longer watch television. We refused to go back. The cost was literally too great.

It was amazing how much scripture and non-fiction could be read without television. We used Amazon Prime to add a little variety to our evenings, and the library was still our best friend for movies. An antenna allowed us to watch the championship games. Debt reduction was worth the sacrifice of not being exposed to mind-numbing entertainment which truly added little value to our lives.

We stood firm and did not go back to cable. Over the next few years, the desire for television lessened even more. Pretty soon we reached a point where our television would not be turned on for weeks at a time.

Charlie "Tremendous" Jones once said, "You will be the same person in five years as you are today except for the people you meet and the books you read." Cutting cable ensured we would be better for ourselves and others in the next five years and beyond.

Your Turn…Your Perspective: What decisions have you made lately which others have called insignificant? What was your response?

Prayer: Lord, I don't want to be controlled by convenience. Please give me discernment to make decisions based on what I need and not what is comfortable or the norm. Help me to always seek You and Your plan as I make the small decisions of life.

Day 209
Farming Grace

MATTHEW 6:3

Keith and I loved our Community Supported Agriculture (CSA) farmers. I grew up on a farm and vowed I would never work in the dirt after I left it, but I could not deny the beauty of a fresh tomato or turnip from the garden. Our first year with the CSA was a success in our minds, and we were eager to sign up again.

Our new dietician loved the idea of the CSA initially so we proceeded to sign our contract committing to pay for 26 weeks of organic vegetable consumption. We picked up the first two weeks and anxiously looked forward to what they would feed us through the summer and fall months.

The problem was the four-day meal rotation our dietician instituted for us. I thought I could make the CSA work with the meal rotation, but it was proving to be difficult. It was nearly impossible to eat the same foods every four days when there was so much variety. I was faced with a major problem and was not sure how to fix it.

Our dietician confirmed my suspicions. We needed to opt out of the CSA. The problem was the signed contract already in place, obligating us to pay our portion for the season. My heart sank. I knew we needed to honor our farmers and fulfill our contract, but we were not prepared to pay for vegetables we could not eat.

We were still about $50,000 in debt, and medical expenses were averaging around $2500 a month. My anxiety level was rising as I thought of our situation. I did not know what to do. A contract was a contract. If our current financial situation did not teach me anything else, it was to pay what we owed, when we owed it.

A few days later, I was thinking of the season of incredible waste we were in during my prayer time. I felt the Lord telling me to reach out to our farmers and explain our situation. We owed it to our debt-reduction money to at least ask. Nothing would change if they said no, but what if they agreed?

I put my pride aside and sent an email to "Mrs. Farmer," and explained our situation. I told her we would honor our contract if necessary, but we also needed to ask for it to be voided. The very next day I received a response graciously releasing us from our contract. She told me they completely understood and hoped we would be able to join the CSA again when our eating plan returned to normal. She wished us well, and even refunded the monies we already paid.

What a blessing! I felt humbled and relieved all at the same time. "Mr. and Mrs. Farmer" did not have to help in any way. They chose to do so because they believed it was the right thing to do. Who would not want to do business with these people? We would certainly be back among their veggie eaters as soon as we were able.

As I thought about the grace extended, I was reminded of how it came to be. I asked for it and put my pride aside. I asked for grace; it was granted. I also knew there was a time in my life when I would have been too prideful to ask. I would have missed an incredible opportunity to see someone's kindness at work. I would also have missed God's grace being extended. Two blessings would have been missed because of foolish pride. I was so thankful I was spiritually mature enough to be humble. Thank You, Jesus.

Your Turn…Your Perspective: When was the last time you asked for grace? When was the last time you extended it?

Prayer: Lord, please help me not be ruled by pride. I pray for the courage to ask for what I need. I thank You for extending grace. Please help me to be gracious to others.

Day 210
I Trust You, Jesus

MATTHEW 6:34; 2 TIMOTHY 1:7

Because of Keith's disability, we received a monthly medical stipend. The terms of the settlement called for his case to be reviewed every two years. During the review, his condition was analyzed, and an updated decision rendered. The review could cause the monthly stipend to either go up, down, or go away completely.

A few months before the scheduled review, I realized something. Even though his condition was still not improving, and our medical expenses increased instead of decreasing, I was carrying a spirit of worry and fear about the decision. I was afraid of potentially getting a lower (or eliminated) monthly stipend. I was afraid of the possibility of having to decrease payments to our debt snowball to absorb the expenses currently covered by the stipend. I finally realized my trust was in our income and not the One who provided it.

I learned years earlier to not allow the spirit of fear to take root in my life. When it took root, fear could literally choke out hope. I did not want my hope to be choked out by fear. Once I became aware it, I began to pray for deliverance.

I knew I needed to be intentional to move past the fear. I did not want it to have a foothold in my life. Ultimately, I knew payments to our debt snowball were not dependent on the settlement. Regardless of whether it stayed or went away, our journey would continue. And God proved Himself faithful many times over with all the blessings we experienced on our journey.

Checks showed up out of the blue. There were unexpected bonuses, monetary gifts from friends, amazing savings on necessary purchases, along with countless others. We experienced a constant stream of blessings.

I was at a crossroads with my attitude. I could continue to allow the fear of a possibility to consume me, or I could focus on the reality of God's provision. I could choose to be afraid of a future I could not control, or I could remind myself of all the obstacles the Lord helped us overcome. I could choose to be paralyzed by the unknown or I could take the Lord's outstretched hand and allow Him to lead me along the path He mapped out for me.

I asked the Lord for forgiveness. I asked Him to forgive my lack of faith and I thanked Him for the constant reminders of His faithfulness and His ability to provide all our needs according to His riches in glory. I recommitted myself to His plan and was thankful my hope rested in Him, not in the abilities of Keith and me to earn a living.

Because we put our hope in God, and not in ourselves, we knew our journey would be victorious. We knew our efforts would not be in vain. God's timing was not our timing, but His promises were, and would always be, true. With or without the income, I chose to trust Jesus.

Your Turn...Your Perspective: What do you worry about? How do you find your way out of it? Take a moment now to reflect on all that God has done for you.

Prayer: Lord, thank You for deliverance. Thank You for showing me when I stray from a path of faith. In my humanness, I sometimes forget exactly how capable You are. I am thankful You choose to remind me, so I can find my way back to a place of faith.

Day 211
Meal Plan Mania

PROVERBS 27:23; PHILIPPIANS 4:19

The food budget was back on the chopping block. It was time to find more cuts in the budget in hopes of squeezing more money out for debt reduction. With both of us working our way through heavy metal poisoning, an all-organic diet was a necessary evil. But, it worked against the idea of minimizing all expenses to increase payment to the debt snowball.

The key was to be intentional about not waiting until the last minute to plan a meal. I needed to survey the freezer and pantry days ahead of time, and not try to do it the night before grocery shopping. No more guessing how many jars of pasta sauce were in the pantry. No more buying a bag of frozen salmon filets only to get home and find out a bag and a half were already in the freezer. So frustrating.

I knew the root of my problem. I grew up living just above poverty level. My dad died when I was four and my mom was a teacher. She always had a part-time job to make ends meet. I was never hungry, and we were never without lights or water, but the struggle to survive hung in the air. Food was the one thing which was always plentiful. The silent mantra was: "If there is food in the house, we are not poor."

I took this mindset into adulthood. Keep the pantry stocked at all times and you will not be poor. But this thinking was counterintuitive to a shrinking food budget. If I was going to thrive, I would have to shift my paradigm about what it meant to be poor.

Was I poor if I did not have twenty cans of tomatoes in the pantry? Was it really necessary to have multiple 3-packs of chicken breasts in the freezer? What did it say of our financial state if I did not have several bags of pasta and jars of pasta sauce on hand? Would I be able (and willing) to shift my thought process to purchase fewer quantities of food to better use our grocery money?

My thoughts of inadequacy about not having large quantities of food in the house were rooted in a spirit of lack. But it was all a lie. For my entire adult life, I lived with the mentality of a food hoarder. It was never intentional, but it was there nonetheless. I finally came to terms with my paradigm and knew it would have to change if we were going to make headway financially.

The reality was I served a God who would supply all my needs according to His riches in glory. Not having an overflowing pantry meant I would have to trust Him to provide what we needed when we needed it. I did not need to hoard food to protect myself from poverty. We were far from poor and lived in the greatest country in the world. We had the freedom to shop with the confidence of knowing more would be available when we needed it.

I did not realize how much my grocery shopping habit was rooted in lack until I made the conscious decision to confront it head-on. Yet again, this journey to financial independence proved to be about so much more than money.

Your Turn…Your Perspective: What bad shopping habits do you have? How is your mindset about money currently being challenged?

Prayer: Lord, thank You for constantly shaking up my old thoughts on money. I thank You for the courage to be different. I pray I stay open to the change You have in store for me as I grow through my journey to financial peace and freedom from debt.

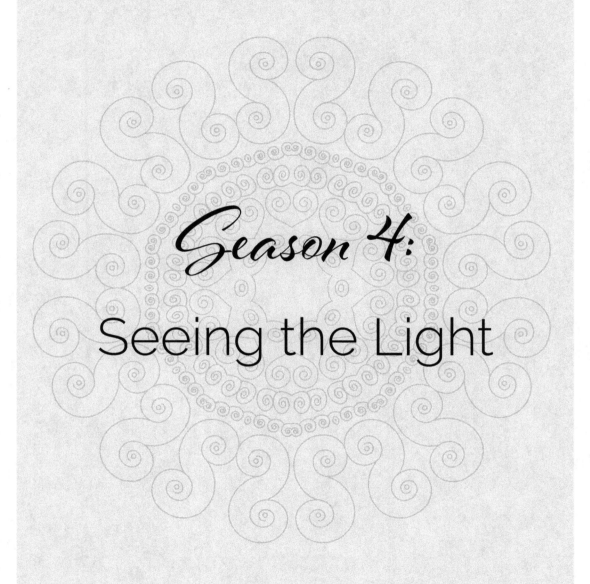

Season 4:

Seeing the Light

Day 212
Weary

PROVERBS 22:29; GALATIANS 6:9; PSALM 55:22

When Keith and I started our journey to financial freedom, I knew it would not be an easy or short process. My thought was we would cut our budget to the bare bones and plough through the debt as soon as possible. I expected setbacks but had no way of knowing just how many we would experience. I felt like a boxer being beat to a pulp in the ring. After several years of constant debt reduction (with many detours called medical expenses and car repairs), I was tired of the journey. I was ready to live the rest of our life. It was hard to stay motivated, but I knew I must stay focused.

Keith and I talked often about our progress. He was not having as much of an issue with how long it was taking to finish our goal. He was sympathetic to my frustrations but did not really understand why I was struggling. He supported me as best he could, but I needed to figure the rest out on my own. We just kept paying our bills and whittling away at our debt.

We made all financial decisions together. We kept personal play money and the family play money in the budget. I became the queen of Groupon, Living Social and any site which might give us free or low-cost options for entertainment.

I prayed a lot. I found scriptures on perseverance which I read and memorized. I wrote them on index cards and carried them in my purse. I pulled them out to review when I was especially anxious about whatever current financial situation was in front of us.

We also taught Financial Peace University at our church. It lifted my spirit immensely to help others with their journey. It was rewarding in ways I could not have ever known. It was incredible to watch others come into a better understanding of how to win with money God's way.

More than anything, I chose to remain hopeful. It was truly a decision. Our journey was a long one and I knew I needed to stay joyful while we worked our way through it. The day to day routine of a very tight budget made it almost impossible to do activities outside of our home, so I chose to get creative.

I chose to focus my energies on the home we would build when paying off our debt snowball was completed. I created a Pinterest board and designed our new home. I researched the building process and picked out finishes, floors and tile. When it came time to build our new home, we would not need extra time to choose design elements.

I realized if I stayed in a place of weariness, I would miss out on God's blessings. I knew we were on the right path, and the harvest the Lord promised was not far away. I was thankful He loved us enough to make us better through the journey. A friend of mine once said, "Everyone wants a testimony, but no one wants the test." Our testimony was going to be incredible. I just needed to stay focused for a little while longer.

Your Turn...Your Perspective: Have you ever felt weary? What scripture refreshes your soul? If you do not have one, I encourage you to take the time to find one.

Prayer: Lord, thank You for Your reassurance. It sustains me. I continue to choose to focus on You. I know Your timing is perfect. I know You will honor my commitment to You and the journey You have set before me. Please help me to keep open to see You at work. Help me to not be so focused on me that I miss the opportunity to join You where You are working.

Let Me Teach You

As Keith and I embraced the principles of Christ-centered financial wellness, and began to implement them in our lives, we could not keep our new discovery to ourselves. It was as if a veil was lifted from our eyes. We were seeing clearly from a financial perspective for the first time in both or our adult lives.

We wanted everyone we knew to experience what we experienced. Not only did we introduce hundreds of people to Financial Peace University, but we also sat with many and taught them how to budget their money. We even took it a step further.

We were both Federal employees who experienced the benefit of working for a large "organization." We also knew most people did not fully understand the benefits of working for the federal government. We knew federal service was a big part of our financial success and wanted others to know what we knew.

We offered to sit and explain the federal hiring process to every person who shared frustration about their job situation, regardless of whether they were unemployed or underemployed. Most people were really confused by the very complicated system and steered clear of it. Those who decided to tackle it saw few results from their efforts. From the weird job titles to the mystery pay scales, we took our time and educated them on the process of successfully navigating the federal hiring system. For most, it was quite a paradigm shift.

Time after time, people were amazed at what they learned. They often said, "I had no idea all of this was available." It was as if their eyes were open to a whole new world which was previously non-existent to them. They were always thankful.

We understood the power of a good income and a financially stable work environment. We wanted to help increase the income of as many people as possible. We knew a few hours of time spent could change their professional life and put them on the track to a career and not just a job. Long term, the time we spent with them could be the difference in hundreds of thousands of dollars of income.

We never took any money. It was a way we chose to serve our community. We saw it as a chance to pour into others the way someone else poured into us. We knew our time could have been spent enjoying leisure activity, but we also recognized the value in helping as many other people as we could.

Helping others also helped to keep us busy while we worked on our own debt snowball. It took the focus off us. For those few hours, we did not think about the mountain of debt we were working hard to clear. For those few hours, we did not think about our own situation. It was a blessing to bring value to someone else's life while we were cleaning up our own.

Your Turn…Your Perspective: What volunteer experience has brought the most joy to your life? How have you been blessed by someone volunteering to assist you?

Prayer: Lord, thank You for reminding me of the value of helping others. Please help me never forget the importance of community. I pray to spread Your love to Your people in whatever way I can.

Day 214
Frivolous

PROVERBS 19:9A

One day I was in our favorite wholesale club with a little extra time on my hands. I wandered each aisle taking in all the displays and then passed a display for our favorite travel mug. We removed all plastic containers from our home the year before, and as a result, I replaced our plastic travel mugs with stainless steel. They were seasonal items, so I purchased two packages (each containing two mugs), one set for me and one set for Keith.

Unfortunately, a few months earlier, I lost one of the mugs when I left it in a rental car. Not only was I annoyed at leaving the mug behind, but it left us with only three mugs for both of us for the week. I really liked having four mugs because we could go two days without needing to wash them. It was not a big deal, just inconvenient. I grabbed a two-pack of mugs and happily finished the shopping.

When I got home and began to unload the groceries, I saw the mugs. Immediately I felt convicted for the purchase. "Do you 'need' these mugs or do you 'want' these mugs?" a still small voice asked. I immediately knew the question came from the Holy Spirit.

"*They're just mugs,*" I thought. "*What's the big deal? They only cost $20.*" No response. I waited a little longer and still no response. I wanted confirmation. I wanted affirmation. I wanted a pass on frugality. Still, no response.

The longer I stood in the kitchen, the more I knew the mugs were to be returned. We did not need five travel mugs. The "big deal" was all about being frivolous. If I could spend $20 on unnecessary travel mugs, what else would I be willing to justify purchasing?

It was such a slippery slope. One small purchase justified could easily lead to a slightly larger purchase justified. If one small inconvenience was allowed, it could easily lead to the next inconvenience being allowed. With every justification, our debt remained with us a little longer. Did I really want to delay it any further?

Our journey to freedom from debt was all about denying self. We denied ourselves larger clothing and entertainment budgets. We denied ourselves the privilege of dining out. We denied ourselves travel money to visit friends and family, and so many other "wants." We questioned every purchase through the lens of "Is this really necessary?" The travel mugs were no different.

I returned the mugs and added the $20 to paying the debt snowball. We continued to wash our travel mugs each night and did just fine. Every year I looked at the mugs in the store and asked myself again, do we "need" these? Each year I passed on the purchase.

We kept our mugs for almost four years before we replaced them. When we finally did, we were debt-free. There was no fanfare when they were purchased, but I knew my decision-making ability was much stronger because of the timing of the purchase. It felt good to "win." It felt good to be a good steward.

Your Turn...Your Perspective: Think of a time when you were called out on a seemingly small infraction. What was the bigger issue? How did you respond? What did the experience teach you about discipline? How can you apply the lesson learned to your current financial goal?

Prayer: Lord, please help me be in tune to the still, small voice of the Holy Spirit. I want to be open to hear from You. I want to be obedient in the small things. I know the small sacrifices over time will yield debt-freedom. I pray I stay focused and follow Your plan.

I Trust You?

ROMANS 13:8

One of the last areas left to bring under Godly submission was the use of our American Express card. We thought because we paid it off every month, we were in control of things. We used it mostly to build up hotel points for the times we needed to stay in St. Louis when visiting our kids and Keith's family. We put everything on the card. All our monthly utilities were automatically charged to the card. Gas, groceries, travel expenses were all charged to the card. Our monthly bill ranged anywhere from $3000 to $6000 each month. We would let the money to pay the bill sit in our checking account to earn a little interest and then sent a lump sum payment to American Express on the day the bill was due.

We thought we were doing the right thing. We thought we were maximizing our cash flow by allowing American Express to fill in the gap. But we were ignoring the warning signs. We spent more because we could "float" money from one pay period to the next by charging an item to the card. I routinely overspent the food budget. The amount spent on entertainment was often more than we budgeted. I would make extravagant meals when friends came over for dinner. And we rationalized it was okay because we always paid the bill in full each month.

One month, the American Express bill was $7000. When I saw the number I almost became ill. I could not believe we spent $7000. What was worse was not fully knowing what we spent it on. Spending so much without knowing it caused me great alarm. I called Keith. We prayed right then and decided we would no longer use the American Express card. I spent the next few days changing over all our automatic payments to come from our checking account. It was also the month we started grocery shopping with cash.

I was terrified for the first few purchases. I was used to buying what I wanted and borrowing from the next paycheck if we needed more. It took real discipline to stay within the amount budgeted for the pay period. We began using our debit card for gas and simply stopped eating out as much. When we did eat out, we knew the amount we could spend ahead of time.

It was amazing to see how much tighter I could get our grocery budget. Within the first two months of switching to cash, I was able to cut almost $100 from our grocery budget. We also cut our family entertainment money in half. I created two menus to use when first time guests came over for dinner. After they visited us twice, we simply served whatever would normally be on the menu. Our guests loved us being comfortable enough to treat them like family.

Discontinuing the use of the American Express card was like a rite of passage for me. It signified being "all in" to the plan God laid out for us. No longer borrowing from the upcoming paycheck, spending only what was available, and cutting back on the "wants" of life was a huge turning point. I wanted the Lord to trust me with more and saw living without a credit card as one of the first steps in finally feeling trustworthy with money.

Your Turn...Your Perspective: What areas of your life have you not turned over to Christ? What's stopping you?

> *Prayer: Lord, thank You for my wake-up call. I trust You, Jesus. As hard as it will be to give up the ways of the world, I know Your way is a better way. I pray to always be aware of Your provision of my needs.*

Day 216
Canisters

We were making changes in our diet and kitchen routine yet again. After four years of searching for answers, we still did not have a system which worked. Our new nutritionist recommended we make more radical changes to our meal preparation and food storage, in addition to the changes to our diet itself. No more plastic storage containers.

We switched all our smaller storage containers to glass the year prior, but I resisted making the change to glass for the storage of larger items like sugar, flour, rice, etc. It was an expense I did not want to make unless it was absolutely necessary. It was now time to make the switch and I was off to find large glass storage containers.

I started at one of my favorite home stores. When we were dating, I took Keith with me to look around. He was always fascinated by the sheer volume of eclectic stuff. It was a fun (and cheap) date because we rarely made a purchase. We did a lot of dreaming on those dates. Neither of us knew how valuable those early dream dates would be later in our lives.

Since we got married and started paying on our debt snowball, there was very little money in the budget for household items. Dreaming was about all we could afford to do. To have the opportunity to actually make a purchase was a special treat and my excitement was high as I pulled into the parking lot.

An hour later, I exited the store with three perfect glass canisters. The sticker shock did not really show up until I got the canisters home. I felt the sting in the store but dismissed it under the guise of necessity. After all, it was our nutritionist who told us to switch to glass canisters. The purchase was for "medicinal purposes."

But the closer I got to home, the more I realized I had gotten carried away. I was so excited to spend money on household items, I forgot the primary mission of the assignment – spend as little money as possible. Coming home with three canisters totaling over $40 really did not count as "as little as possible."

I did not bother taking the canisters in the house. I got back in the car and headed back to the home décor store. As much as I wanted to keep them, I could not justify spending so much on canisters. At least not yet.

The disappointment I felt in having to make the return was not about the canisters. I was disappointed in how fast I allowed myself to be overcome with the thrill of the purchase. I lost sight of the goal so quickly. I was ready to just take the first option I found instead of doing a little window shopping and comparing prices.

Even after all the years digging ourselves out of debt, I still had not learned my lesson. Would I ever get to a point where I felt comfortable making purchases without giving in to the temptation of stuff? I prayed I would. I prayed I learned to be wise and cautious. I prayed to tame the emotion associated with spending.

I often told Keith I did not want to be the reason our family did not prosper. I did not want my lack of self-control to limit what the Lord allowed us to manage. The experience in the home décor store told me there was still work to do. I prayed for wisdom and thanked the Lord I did not get too far off track.

Your Turn…Your Perspective: What area of your financial life needs closer managing? How do you keep your head about you when faced with financial temptation?

Prayer: Lord, please keep me mindful of spending. I pray for discipline when the time comes to loosen the money reigns. Please help me to be a good steward.

Budget Birthdays

PROVERBS 21:1

As we were working our way through our debt, we were careful to not overspend on our kids' birthdays. We were determined we would not be "Disney Parents." A Disney Parent was a "noncustodial parent who indulges his or her child with gifts and good times during visitation and leaves most or all disciplinary responsibilities to the other parent."[6]

We spent roughly 60 days a year with our kids. The every-other-weekend parenting model did not fit a 4 hour one-way. drop-off/pick up schedule. Instead, we worked our visitation around their school holidays, 6 weeks in the summer, and their birthday weekends. We also decided to spend their birthdays in Kansas City where we lived instead of in St. Louis where their mother lived.

Even though it meant a lot of time driving (16 hours on the road instead of 8 hours), it gave the kids two additional Sundays each year to attend church in Kansas. They both enjoyed our church and we wanted to expose them to Jesus in everyday life as much as possible.

We also wanted them to know it was possible (and fun) to have a birthday celebration without breaking the budget. We put a lot of thought into their birthday celebrations, but still used a very modest budget. I would spend hours in the months leading up to their birthdays thinking about activities and gifts they would enjoy. Many times, I chose a list of activities from online specials, and then Keith and I would make the decision together on the top two or three options.

For our daughter's 14th birthday, we gave her the opportunity to choose from three different activities as a part of her celebration: a manicure and pedicure, putt-putt for the family, or a movie. The first two options were online specials, and the movie would have been a matinee with coupons for popcorn & drinks. She also received three small gifts and a birthday dinner. We were able to have a meaningful celebration with a total cost of under $50. She had a blast and we were thrilled.

The process was repeated for our son's birthday. His activity choices were an afternoon with dad at a batting cage, bowling for the family, or a movie matinee. His first two options were also online specials and his budget was the same. We added a birthday dinner and games to round out his celebration.

The kids learned to expect the unexpected for their birthdays. They became accustomed to us taking a different approach to how we spent our time together. We chose not to share too many details about our plans with them to not create disappointment when we needed to adjust.

We worked hard to lay a foundation of budgeted celebration for our kids. Birthdays were to be celebrated but did not have to be budget busters. It was a lesson we prayed they would remember as future events and celebrations come their way. It was our desire to teach them how to enjoy the celebration without regard to how much was spent. Time will tell if it made the impact we wanted. It was all in God's hands.

Your Turn...Your Perspective: How do you celebrate the birthdays of your loved ones? What ways have you been creative in making the celebration memorable without extravagance?

Prayer: Lord, thank You for the lessons in frugality. I pray I am mindful of all the free ways to enjoy my city and my life. Please help me to enjoy the small pleasures of my surroundings as I work my way through to financial wellness. Please help me stay the course. I want to finish well.

Be My Valentine

PROVERBS 3:14

When I was single, the holiday I dreaded most was Valentine's Day. I knew of lots of single women who struggled with Christmas and Thanksgiving, New Year's Eve and their birthdays. But for me, it was Valentine's Day. I did not date much as an adult, and only experienced a few years when there was someone special in my life on February 14.

When I met Keith and we began to settle into a courtship, I looked forward to the experience of sharing Valentine's Day with him. As we worked through the "getting to know you" phase of our relationship, I shared my desire to do something special on V-Day. His birthday was two days earlier, and as a result, he disliked Valentine's Day for a different reason. His birthday was always overlooked in relationships in anticipation of what would come a few days later.

So, it seemed we both were in this love-hate relationship with the day for lovers. We knew we needed to find a common ground for both of us to feel validation in the month of February.

After we got married and decided to not spend money on celebrations, it was a little bit more of a challenge to do anything other than mutter, "Happy Valentine's Day." The first few years, we made cards and created small tokens of affection to present to each other to celebrate.

We slowly settled into our marriage and began our ministry of Christ-centered financial wellness. The medical bills were coming in constantly, and decreasing our debt snowball was not moving very fast or going very far. We were in the fight of our financial lives and worked together to stay on track financially. We did all we could to keep the debt reduction going while also finding the money needed to pay for all the treatments and supplements associated with both of our illnesses.

One year, Valentine's Day was in the middle of a new health challenge. There was a new doctor several states away, and the expenses associated with traveling for medical care were daunting. Hotel costs, meals, gas and toll charges were all added to the budget in addition to the cost of the care itself. It was one expense after another for several months.

I used some of my play money to buy birthday and Valentine's Day cards for Keith. I presented him with the birthday card earlier in the week along with a favorite meal. On Valentine's Day, I laid his card on his place setting at the table before leaving for work.

When I returned home, I realized I did not get a card from him. What came next was a true gift from God. NOTHING! No sadness. No disappointment. No anger. I experienced none of the negative emotions I previously associated with not being "properly" remembered on February 14. I did not question Keith's love for me and I did not question his desire to keep romance in our marriage. What I realized was the importance of perspective. Every year would not be celebratory. Every year would not be filled with fanfare. And, we would be better for it.

Your Turn…Your Perspective: What expectations have challenged you recently? How have they impacted you financially?

Prayer: Lord, thank You for perseverance through the trials. Thank You for perspective. I pray to not get caught by the little things which can take my eye off the end goal if I am not careful.

Money Talk

PROVERBS 16:8

One of the reason's Keith and I were successful in moving through our debt snowball so quickly (even with all the medical bills and car repairs) was transparency. Transparency was often the topic of discussion in our FPU classes, and with our married coaching clients. The transparency of our own purchases was modeled for our clients since we decided early on to not ever spend money without a discussion.

We were transparent with our clients and we were transparent with each other. We chose to discuss every purchase regardless of the amount. We also each received an allowance to use any way we wished, along with a monthly clothing allowance. Keith typically combined his into one lump sum and preferred it in cash. I kept mine separate with some in cash, but reserved the rest for online purchases.

If I went shopping and bought a new dress with my clothing allowance, I shared how much I spent when I got home. If he wanted a new gadget, he bought it and shared the purchasing decision with me. It was still our individual money being spent, but the transparency was important.

There was also a small amount of miscellaneous money in the budget each month which we used to buy gifts, attend the occasional sporting event, or go to a movie or restaurant. The money in the miscellaneous envelope was never spent without a discussion. We both needed to agree on how it was spent. If the cost was larger, we saved for a few pay periods to save enough money to do what we wanted to do.

This was hard for so many of our coaching clients. They saw money as being very black and white. "If it's mine, why do I have to share how I spent it?" was often the question we received. "I don't see the point in discussing every purchase," was another comment. In our minds, it kept communication at the center of the relationship. If a couple could communicate about money, it made it easier to communicate about everything else. Transparency kept secrecy at bay and helped prevent impulsive behaviors from taking over.

We knew some considered our methods extreme. Financial infidelity was a big deal for many couples, and we did not want to fall prey to it. We also did not want our clients to become its victims. Our desire to be debt-free and teach others to do the same was big enough to take what was called extreme and make it normal.

If we could live in transparency with a monthly spending budget of $80 each, we knew we would be fine when our monthly spending budget was $800. If we could teach our clients to live a life of financial transparency, we believed the dangers of overspending and impulsiveness would be limited.

Transparency became second nature to us. We continued to teach it and model it for others to see. We chose to stay in open dialogue about all areas of our budget. It made all the difference in creating harmony in our home.

Your Turn...Your Perspective: What tools do you have in place to help promote financial discipline? How transparent are your conversations with your spouse or accountability partner? In what area do you struggle the most? How can you strengthen this area of your financial life?

Prayer: Lord, I pray for financial transparency. I do not want to hide. I want to be open and honest with myself and others about how I manage the resources You have given me. Please help me to always be mindful of the need for discipline in managing my money.

A New York State of Mind

During our fourth year of debt reduction, we were on a path of non-traditional treatment for our heavy metal poison and found a Naturopath in New York City with a reputation for diagnosing mystery illnesses.

Unfortunately, our new potential Naturopath traveled a great deal, and only saw new patients a few times a year. The good news was the infrequency gave us time to begin saving for the trip. It would be an expensive one. Once an appointment was scheduled, we would have only a two-week window to get plane tickets purchased and reserve a hotel room.

In anticipation of the upcoming appointment, we began saving several hundred dollars a month for the trip. Our estimated cost was about $1000. We prayed the window of opportunity did not open before we saved enough to pay cash. If the appointment was available too soon, we would not be able to go. Because we made the decision to not incur any new debt, using a credit card to pay for the trip was not an option. "Lord, please help us save quickly" became a daily part of our prayer time.

Visiting NYC as a couple was something we placed on our bucket list years prior. We discussed going when we lived in the Washington, DC metro area, but did not have the resources to enjoy the city the way we wanted. Now we were planning a different type of trip.

It was so tempting to make a vacation out of our medical visit. The plane tickets would be purchased regardless of whether we stayed two days or an entire week. But obviously, our hotel costs would triple if we extended our stay. So would our food budget. A $1000 trip might become closer to $2000 or even $3000.

As much as we wanted to sightsee in New York, we decided to stay on course. A quick trip to New York for a doctor's appointment was all we allowed. No Broadway show. No trip to Time Square. We would leave "tourists in New York" on our bucket list a while longer. When the time came to sightsee in the Big Apple, we would do so without a cloud of student loan debt waiting for us when we returned.

Many of our friends questioned our decision. Why not take a small detour? We worked so hard. Did we not deserve a vacation? We would already be there, so what's the harm? For us, the harm was the detour. If we did this detour, what about the next? Spending money on medical (even expensive, non-traditional, insurance-did-not-cover-it medical) was necessary; sightseeing was not. Ultimately, we were the ones paying for the trip, and outside opinions did not add much value.

In the end, we decided to save only enough for the medical version of the trip. We used the rest of the money for student loan repayments. We stood firm on the plan to finish paying off our debt snowball before we enjoyed bucket list items. It did not matter if others did not understand. Ultimately, pleasing God and being obedient to what He requested of us was more important. We knew He would honor our obedience one day. In His time, in His way.

Your Turn…Your Perspective: Think of a time when a sacrifice was necessary to reach a goal. What did you do? How was your decision supported by the ones around you?

Prayer: Lord, please help me stay on course. It is so tempting to do what is easy, but I know following You is what brings true peace. I thank You for loving me enough to require a higher standard. I pray to not lose sight of it.

Day 221
Centering Prayer

One of the things I prayed for when I was single was a husband who loved the Lord. I believed it was possible to find a husband who put God first, and I refused to settle. When Keith and I got married, my prayer was answered. He had a heart for the Lord and wanted to please Him first.

Keith came to me one day and told me he discovered centering prayer. Centering prayer was "a popular method of contemplative prayer or Christian meditation, placing a strong emphasis on interior silence."[7] I knew Keith desired to have a deeper prayer life, and he was committed to becoming a prayer warrior and wanted to grow his prayer life. We were fortunate enough to have a centering prayer retreat location just a few miles away from where we lived. Keith expressed his desire to attend and we both agreed it would be a good use of time.

He signed up for a Saturday session and spent the better part of the day learning the techniques. When he returned home, he shared what he learned and asked if "the house" would reimburse him for the cost. He went on to explain how we would benefit as a family from all he learned.

I stopped him before he went any further. I did not need to hear any other explanations. Keith was standing before me, after spending a day learning how to better worship the Lord through prayer, asking if our household budget could pay for it instead of him using his fun money. He was not asking about a sporting event. He was not at a bar or club. He was in a church learning how to pray.

Keith knew the budget just as I did. He knew what money was available and what monthly expenses needed to be met. Of course, the house would reimburse him.

As we made the adjustment and absorbed the expense of the day from our "fun" money, two thoughts went through my mind. The first was one of wonder at just how the Lord answered my prayer from so many years earlier. I could not have imagined how blessed I would be with the husband He gave me.

The second thought was one of introspection. Did Keith really expect me to say no to his request for the house to reimburse him? This was not a piece of exercise equipment he was requesting. It was the foundation of faith. Prayer was certainly not whimsical or random. What did it mean for him to feel the need to ask me for reimbursement instead of knowing it would be available to him? I knew the answer and it saddened me.

Keith asked because he knew how hardcore I was about the budget. He did not know if I would say yes. He only knew I protected the budget at all cost. It was so easy for me to lose perspective. I put getting out of debt ahead of living more times than I cared to count. I teetered dangerously close to allowing the act of getting out of debt to become the idol I fought so hard to avoid.

I knew I was at a crossroad. When would I trust God to provide everything we needed? When would I trust the progress we made in managing our money well? When would I completely put God first and not be tempted to elevate little "g" gods to first position?

Your Turn…Your Perspective: How is your prayer life? What changes can you make to get closer to the Lord? In what area do you need to trust Him more?

Prayer: Lord, help me, Lord, to resist little "g" gods. I pray to trust You always and not rely on my own abilities. Please help me to strengthen my prayer life.

Day 222
You Can't Beat It

PROVERBS 3:9-10

Keith and I were on a parallel journey when we got married. It was the journey of debt reduction and giving. The first month we were married, we sent out 19 minimum payments in addition to utilities and household expenses. It was a huge amount of our budget, and completely overwhelmed me. After much deliberation, we decided to cut our tithe and give an offering instead. It lasted about a year.

The idea of not tithing really bothered us both. In our minds, every day we did not tithe was a day showcasing lack of faith. What started out as a financial relief slowly became a sinking feeling each time we gave our gift to our local church. It felt as if we were trying to "get over on" God. The day came when the heaviness of disobedience was no longer something we wanted to experience.

The next month, we decreased our debt snowball payment and began to tithe again. We did not see it as slowing down our debt reduction. We just finally understood that the Lord would honor our commitment in His own way and His own time. Our job was to simply honor Him with our tithe.

A few years later, I began to get a check in my spirit about our tithe. I felt we needed to tithe on our gross income which was something I honestly never did before. It would mean decreasing payments to our debt snowball by over $650 each month. I did not know what Keith would think.

I kept praying to see if I got a different answer, and finally realized I was waiting on the Lord to be contrary to His Word. It was never going to happen. He was never going to tell me **not** to tithe. I could trust His Word or trust our own ability to earn income. I could not do both.

When I approached Keith with the idea of tithing on gross, I did not know how he would respond. I did not know if he ever tithed on gross and was not sure if he would agree. It took a lot for me to wrap my mind around the idea, and he could easily be in the same place as me spiritually. I decided to trust the Lord and simply tell Keith what I was thinking.

It was beautiful music to my ears when Keith told me he already knew it was time to tithe on gross. He was praying for me to come around to the idea. Wow. I felt humbled and blessed knowing Keith was praying for my spiritual growth in this way. It was yet another example of why it was important to be led by a man who chose to follow the Lord.

And then the blessings came. Literally two weeks after we started tithing on gross, checks began showing up in our mailbox. Insurance reimbursement checks came. A settlement check was a pleasant surprise. An overpayment for our initial lease agreement from our complex caused our jaws to drop.

We knew it was God's way of showing us what happened when we trusted Him. He would take care of us every step of the way. We learned a valuable lesson during a very difficult time in our lives. "You can't beat God giving." The truth of those words resonated in our hearts as we saw firsthand what they meant.

Your Turn…Your Perspective: Do you trust the Lord through tithing? What has been the result? If not, what's stopping you?

Prayer: Lord, thank You for your generous grace. Thank You for the lessons in faith. Thank You for my desire to grow in relationship with You. I praise You and I thank You for my own journey of debt reduction and giving.

Day 223
Proper Instruction

PROVERBS 1:8-9

The student ministry at our church was wonderful. It was not uncommon to hear disappointment from both middle and high school students anytime their services were not held. In addition to Sunday and Wednesday services, the ministry offered a variety of service opportunities, mission trips and larger local events.

Church camp was always in the budget, and it was not uncommon for us to orchestrate visits to Kansas for our kids to participate in a church event. We wanted to expose them to as many student ministry events as possible. Knowing how much they enjoyed their time at church made it even more important to immerse them in the student body of Christ.

During one visit, our kids came home from church asking about an upcoming church event. Keith and I already knew about the event from the promotional material. We also knew it would not be possible for our kids to attend because of the visitation schedule. We chose not to mention it to them because we knew they could not attend. Our plan backfired because they heard about the event at church.

Our son mentioned it first. He asked if it would be possible for them to attend. Our daughter immediately chimed in and told him they could not go because it was expensive. I already knew the fee was $99 per child. I seized the chance to make this a teachable moment to educate our kids on the importance of budgeting, and to not be afraid of an opportunity because of cost.

I addressed our son first. I reminded him of our custody arrangement and the opportunities available to them in both of their cities. I reminded him of how great it was to have exposure to so many different types of events, and I assured him there would be other events with the student ministry for them to participate in moving forward.

Then I addressed our daughter. I reminded her of the importance of Christian education and our desire to expose them to Christ-centered events. I explained the importance of not throwing an idea away simply because of cost. I also explained the meaning of "opportunity cost" as money not being available for one purchase because it was used for another purchase.

I assured her we would continue to review each event individually. They could attend some, but not others. In any case, it would never be simply because of cost. We were frugal in some areas of our lives to have money available to spend in other areas. It was never a matter of an item or event being "too expensive."

I'm not sure if they got what I said or not. As with every teachable moment, I knew it could be years before we knew if our parenting choice made an impact. Our job was to continue to nurture the seed planted and pray, pray, pray. Their lives were filled with so many choices. I was thankful, at least for the moment, their choices aligned with serving God. I prayed it would become a way of life for them.

Your Turn…Your Perspective: Think back to your childhood. How did your parents discuss difficult money decisions with you? How did they impact your financial growth?

Prayer: Lord, I pray to not be ruled by the fear of cost. Please help me not shy away from an item simply because of cost. I pray to be a good steward, make wise money decisions, and prayerfully consider each person. I want to conquer my fear of money. Please show me the way.

Paradigm Shift

PROVERBS 1:24

Keith and I did not always have the mindset of living completely free of debt. Before we read *The Total Money Makeover* by Dave Ramsey, and subsequently attended his 9-week course Financial Peace University, our focus was on paying down our debt, not necessarily getting rid of it.

During our first year of marriage, we knew our debt to income ratio was too high. But we did not yet understand zero debt as the remedy. We were still "normal" in our thinking. Pay down debt; get more debt. Pay down debt; get more debt. Debt always defined our lives and we honestly did not know any better. We did not know what a life without debt looked like.

An example of our thinking back then was our plan for vehicles. We both brought older vehicles into our marriage. We knew the day would come (sooner instead of later) when we needed to replace them both. After we paid everything except the student loans, we planned the purchase of our next vehicles.

We decided it would be "best" if we got one large car loan instead of two small ones. Doing so would give us some leverage to get a "better" deal. We were actually excited about the plan. Instead of tracking how much debt we paid off in terms of how close we were to being debt-free, we tracked our debt reduction in terms of how quickly we could add more.

I remember the day I realized our paradigm shift. We recently replaced both of our vehicles and paid cash. Both vehicles were purchased with over 100,000 miles and both were over 10 years old. I knew our financial picture would have been dramatically different if we were still functioning under our old way of thinking.

Instead of no car payments, lower property taxes, and no real change in car insurance, we would have a huge car payment, much higher property taxes and much higher car insurance. Our disposable income would have dropped significantly, and we would have been tied to a car payment for another four or five years.

As I thought about all we accomplished in terms of debt reduction, I was embarrassed at how foolish we were. We made so many mistakes financially. I was thankful for the paradigm shift, and the fog of living a life of debt clearing. It was like we received financial glasses which cleared our monetary vision. For the first time in our lives, we were equipped to avoid the same financial mistakes we dove head-first into previously. We were not yet equipped to avoid them all, but were making significant progress.

I just knew how blessed we were to have another chance to do right by the resources the Lord entrusted to us. We were not the same couple we were when we started. Our financial muscles were growing and getting stronger with ever obstacle we overcame.

I looked to our future and saw such hope. We were so far removed from hope when we started our journey. I realized how different our legacy would be because we decided to go against what we knew and walk into what we believed God wanted for us. It was our saving grace.

Your Turn…Your Perspective: How are your thoughts about money and finances different than in years past? What was a turning point for your new views of money?

Prayer: Lord, thank You for paradigm shifts and new ways of thinking. Thank You for the courage to do things differently. I pray for a permanent change in my mindset. I want to master money, Lord, and live a life of Christ-centered financial wellness. Please show me the way.

Day 225
Windfall

PROVERBS 1:26

Several times during our journey to debt reduction, I asked the Lord for a windfall. We did not play the lottery, so I knew it would not come from a string of numbers. Maybe we would win the HGTV Dream Home or get a knock on the door from an investigator telling us of an inheritance from an unknown relative. I did not care how we got the windfall. I just wanted one. All our money issues would be over with a windfall.

I would then allow my mind to wander and make a list of all the things we could do with our new-found wealth. Tithe first, debt-freedom second. What next? Hmmm…pay cash for a house. Take an elaborate trip. Donate anonymously. Set up a legacy for our kids. So many options.

I knew it was healthy to dream about the future, but I was not so sure about this type of dreaming. I spent days planning alternate endings to our financial mess. It was an escape from our dismal reality. It was also my way of coping. But there was no windfall. While the Lord blessed us with financial assistance on our journey, He chose not to remove our debt all at once.

I found myself asking God why He didn't remove all our debt. Were we not worthy? Over time, I realized it was not as much about worth as it was about diligence. If we received a windfall, how would we learn all the financial lessons we now knew (and taught to others)? If we received a windfall, how would we teach our kids the correct financial path? If we received a windfall, would we appreciate the new, debt-free life we were carving out? There was no way to know. Our current situation confirmed we needed to learn firsthand.

The news headlines were filled with stories of people with windfalls making poor decision after poor decision, many ending in bankruptcy or the loss of even more than money. Professional athletes, lottery winners and even friends, time and again felt the dangers of receiving wealth without wisdom. As much as I wanted to get out of debt quickly, I could see countless lessons learned because of our slow, deliberate season.

We finally began to understand how to adjust our budget on the fly without going over. We learned the importance of properly researching major decisions and wise negotiation. We chose Plan B and Plan C because Plan A cost too much. We used all the food in the pantry and the freezer when the food budget took another hit instead of overspending. All because we did not receive a windfall.

We continued to steadily plod our way through our debt, and in the process, strengthened our money management muscles. In doing so, we started making better money decisions. Our poor financial choices became fewer and farther between. Each decision gave the opportunity to grow in our ability to use sound judgement as it related to money. The emotional fallout of emergencies became a thing of the past. Bonuses and random checks in the mail were handled more thoughtfully.

We were slowly becoming wise and financially savvy. The less debt left to pay, the more comfortable we felt with the remaining money in our bank account. The gradual process made the transformation much more valuable. Not receiving a windfall became a gold mine of peace and contentment. What a blessing.

Your Turn…Your Perspective: How have you dealt with your desire to have more? In what ways have you struggled with contentment?

Prayer: Lord, thank You for not always giving me what I want. Thank you for teaching me what it means to work a little harder. Thank You for Your patience as I work my way to contentment.

Day 226
Clear the Mechanism

JOSHUA 1:6

One of my all-time favorite movies was *For Love of the Game* starring Kevin Costner. It was an incredible baseball story about a washed-up pitcher trying to make some major decisions in his life. For me, it was one of the best underdog stories ever made. Like all great movies, it was filled with awesome one-liners and scenes which stood out on their own as true testaments of great acting.

In *For Love of the Game*, pitching was the center of Billy Chapel's life. And as was the case with any really good career athlete, he used a system to get into "the zone." He used a phrase which helped him to block out the noise of the crowd and focus on the signals from the catcher and the eyes of the batter. He would say out loud, "clear the mechanism." All noises and movement would slow to a stop, and for a single moment, it was just Billy and the ball making the decision.

We were several years deep into our journey of debt reduction when Keith and I watched the movie again. It was not on our annual watch list, but every now and then it came up in conversation and we would load the DVD player. It was always a good time.

As we watched it, the familiar phrase took on new meaning for me. I loved hearing Billy Chapel call for time to stop so he could concentrate. But now, I realized I could do the same thing. I too, could clear the mechanism. All I needed to do was stay focused on my own situation and circumstances, and not be moved by what the people around me were doing. I needed to stay the course and execute the plan I knew God outlined for us. I needed to stop trying to figure out God's next move and just rest in His sovereignty.

For me, it was easier said than done. I wanted to trust God completely, but often got impatient with His timing. I wanted to believe He knew what was best, but what I saw around me in the moment caused me to doubt. I wanted to be courageous and not be afraid of the incredible amount of debt still left to repay.

As we watched the movie, I clearly saw the decision I needed to make. For once and for all, I needed to trust God to take care of our financial mess in His way and in His time. We were to continue to live by a budget and not give in to the impulse to spend. I understood the importance of using the courage He gave me to go against the norm. I could not allow myself to be pulled back into the old ways of managing money.

I shared my new insights with Keith, and he agreed with my revelation. Together we knew we could make it through. We would be courageous. We would be resilient. We would prosper. We would change our future by not repeating our past. We would walk in the abundance God called us to experience. We would clear the mechanism.

Your Turn...Your Perspective: How do you "clear the mechanism?" What big assignment has God given you recently?

Prayer: Lord, thank You for glimpses of what my future can hold. Thank You for hope. Please help me not succumb to the fear of my current circumstances. Help me stay focused on You and use the courage You gave me to do the hard stuff.

Day 227
Daddy/Daughter Date
1 PETER 1:15

When our daughter was 14, Keith and I decided it was time for her first daddy/daughter date. It was a very big deal. We talked about it for months prior to picking the kids up for the summer, and were sure to include it in the July budget. She was getting older and we wanted her to understand what it meant to be treated like a lady. Who better to teach this than Daddy?

We knew she watched our interaction as a couple. We also knew it was important for her to understand for herself the importance of having high standards in dating. We decided Keith would take our daughter to a higher-end seafood restaurant. It was one of our favorites, even though we only went once every few years. Since it was a little pricier, we only dined there with a gift certificate.

We did not have a gift certificate for the daddy/daughter date, but still wanted her to experience it. White tablecloths, candlelight and an extensive selection of well-prepared food to go along with one-on-one time with Daddy was worth the cost.

In the days leading up to the dinner, we were all excited. Our daughter seemed nervous, and frankly, so was Keith. He wanted her affection but was determined not to buy it. This date seemed like a great opportunity to make headway in really getting to know the young woman she was becoming.

The night of the dinner, I went to help her get dressed. When I asked if she was nervous, she shyly replied, "Yes." She asked if the restaurant was expensive. I told her it was somewhat expensive, but Daddy and I felt she was worth the money spent on the evening. I reminded her of how much we both loved her and told her to relax and try to enjoy the evening.

We took pictures before they left and savored this "first" for our family. I knew how much it meant to them both and I prayed it was a success. They were gone for three hours! When they came home, our son and I were anxious to hear all about the experience. I knew they both enjoyed themselves the moment they walked through the door. They were grinning from ear to ear.

We all sat in the middle of the floor as both my husband and my daughter recapped the evening. It was a beautiful thing to experience. I knew none of us would ever forget it.

After the kids went to bed, Keith and I were able to unpack the evening by ourselves. He thanked me. He thanked me for suggesting it. He thanked me for being open to spending the money. He thanked me for supporting him in raising "our" kids.

All I could do was hug him. God put us together, and our "together" included two kids. As much as I wanted my own children before I got married, I could not have imagined a better family. I was thankful to be a part of God's plan.

Your Turn…Your Perspective: What precious memories do you have which were worth the cost?

Prayer: Lord, thank You for the value placed on experiences with those we love. While I pray to always be mindful of the cost, I also pray to never lose sight of the importance of family and community. Thank You for giving us the ultimate example in Your Son Jesus Christ.

Day 228
Forgive Me

When Keith and I decided to create a ministry centered on financial stewardship, we knew we would be working with broken people. We did not think about how some of these broken people might be married to each other and blame their spouses for their brokenness. Time and time again, we coached couples where blame was at the center of their marriage and distressful financial situations.

Much of the problem was lack of communication and assumptions made by both. In most instances, one spouse was working extremely hard to manage the money and the other spouse was not involved in the managing portion at all. In every instance, we found couples who were no long dreaming of a future different than their present situation. It was as if they could not see past the current financial hardship.

Some of this blame was years old. In one instance, the scenario creating the rift was over 15 years old. The wife spoke about the incident as if it happened yesterday. The pain in her eyes and her voice was fresh. She never forgave her husband for a bad business decision he made years prior.

When I realized how old the offense was, I knew we were dealing with an issue much more serious than the budget. This wife no longer trusted her husband to lead them financially. His mistake years earlier severed her trust like the branch of a small tree snapped by a Kansas tornado.

I did not think she realized how much damage her lack of trust caused and she did not see her part in their current situation. She did not see how his confidence to make competent financial decisions continued to be eroded by her opinion of him. She did not see how fearful he was to mention anything dealing with money.

As the couple sat at our dining room table one beautiful Sunday afternoon, I could see his eyes pleading with her to release him. I could tell from his expression this was not his first attempt to reach her. But she could not see it. She was still deeply rooted in the memory of what she saw as a financial betrayal.

With both of our husbands looking on, I took both of her hands in mine, looked deep into her eyes and said these simple words: "You have to forgive him. Your future depends on it." As the tears began to flow down all our cheeks, she slowly began to see how her inability to trust her husband was creating pain for them both.

They both asked the other for forgiveness. The heaviness which accompanied them when they arrived several hours earlier began to lift and a spirit of hope filled the space around them. They sat, holding hands, as we began to map out a strategy for them to move forward.

After they left, Keith and I looked at each other and vowed to learn from what we just witnessed. We hoped to have a long and happy marriage, and knew forgiveness was primary if our goal was to be realized. We were thankful to get a glimpse of what happens if trust was not at the core of our home and our union. Our vow was to protect our marriage with forgiveness. By doing so, we knew every area of our marriage would be able to thrive.

Your Turn…Your Perspective: Do you harbor unforgiveness against someone? How has it affected you? How has it impacted your relationship with them and with others?

Prayer: Lord, please help me to not live in the past. Please give me a heart which leans towards forgiveness and not towards distrust and blame. I pray for compassion for those who disappoint me. Help me to manage my expectations and see my loved ones through Your eyes.

Stand Where the Fruit is Falling

DEUTERONOMY 8:15; PSALM 23:4

Priscilla Shirer was one of my favorite authors for a very long time. So many of her messages resonated with me for years after reading them. There were several times in my life when God used one of her books to minister to me during a particularly difficult season. After finishing one of her books a few years into paying our debt snowball, I decided to search for others I may have missed.

Since we were not buying books, I went to our library website. Instead of searching by title, I did a search on the author's name. I was surprised to see a book pop up which did not belong to her. It turned out she wrote the foreword to the book, and not the book itself. It peaked my curiosity. If Priscilla Shirer liked the book enough to write the foreword, it must be a good find. I was not disappointed. *Flash* by Rachel Anne Ridge was a beautiful story of hope and inspiration. It touched my heart and mirrored my own story in many ways.

The book was filled with life nuggets realized by the author through her relationship with a wayward donkey named Flash. I laughed, and I cried. I took notes. I shared passages with Keith. It was a gem of a book which served as a reminder of the Lord's presence on our journey. I could relate to Rachel. While her life was nothing like mine, her desire to serve the Lord seemed as transparent and real as my own. Her failures and flaws showcased the same disappointments I experienced in my own journey. It was clear the Lord was helping me embrace the growth associated with my journey through her words.

About half way through the audiobook, I started a chapter on horse apples. I knew nothing about horses but listened intently anyway because I knew Rachel would tie it all together for me. She was in a place in her life where she felt very aware of what she did not have. I was in the same place. She felt inferior and uncertain of what she had to offer, and I was feeling the same things. She was struggling with envy. So was I. I leaned in to hear more of our story unfold.

Our story was steeped in the need for graciousness during valley experiences. I learned years ago to not discount the valleys in life. A mountaintop was always next. It just took a while to show up sometimes. Rachel's current valley experience was no different. It was another lesson in faith and the need to trust Him completely. As the chapter came to an end, Rachel revealed the nugget: "Stand where the fruit is falling."

"Stand where fruit is falling" means this: "Position yourself where the good stuff is. Find the goodness and get there…the goodness can only come when you're standing in the right place."[8] Wow! I listened to the passage over and over to make sure I did not miss it. I must be in the right place to receive the goodness God made available. The problem was the "right place" rarely felt right.

What was my right place? It was a rented duplex. It was medical bills. It was student loan debt. Those were all my "right places" during this valley experience. I knew I would have other right places during the next season. But for the present, I was to pick up the fruit in those places. It was there. I just needed to acknowledge it and look past the package. The next mountaintop was coming, as soon as I picked up the fruit where I stood.

Your Turn…Your Perspective: Where is your fruit falling? Are you currently in a valley or on a mountaintop?

Prayer: Lord, thank You for the reminder to stand where the fruit is falling. Thank You for the valley experiences and the growth I experience through them. Please help me not allow discouragement to consume me. Fill me with hope.

Express Lane or Scenic Route
HEBREWS 13:5-6 GNB

Anxiety was very real for me during most of the time we worked on our debt snowball. I wanted to be debt-free as soon as possible, sometimes to a fault. It was a struggle to allow myself any relaxation or entertainment because I wanted to be done with debt yesterday. I knew we needed to pace ourselves. We did not want to run out of steam and begin using debt again. But we also recognized the importance of not unplugging completely from life and having no enjoyment.

It was a hard balance for me. Our journey was so long, and detours kept appearing. The medical bills began to show up just a few months after we started to pay off debt, and the combination of the two was really overwhelming. Donating to charitable causes, giving to family and friends, buying "stuff" for ourselves and the kids were all questioned at one point or another.

My motto was: "What money doesn't go to student loans, doesn't go to student loans." It was hard to balance wanting to create cool memories with the kids versus deeper budget cuts to increase payments to the debt snowball. I struggled with the need to pay as much as possible on our debts.

While Keith wanted to be out of debt as much as I did, his approach to debt reduction was not as intense as mine. He did not always agree with completely denying ourselves to keep the debt snowball payments as big as possible. It was the one area on which we did not always agree.

Keith constantly reminded me to "enjoy the journey." My answer back was, "How can I enjoy it when I want to be debt-free yesterday?!" We struggled a lot, even over simple things. I wanted to spend the entire summer in the house with the A/C up around 78 degrees to keep the electric bill low. He wanted to be comfortable with the A/C around 72 degrees and just pay the difference.

It was a constant tug-of-war. I did the only thing I knew to do, and I suspected he was doing the same thing. I took it to Jesus. I prayed constantly for the Lord to help us find common ground. What good would it do to be debt-free if we were at odds on how to get there? I knew neither of us wanted to cross the finish line without both of us sharing in the joy.

It took a while, but we finally got to a place of agreement. We found a way to balance the journey to becoming debt-free with the destination of financial freedom. We listened to each other more and tried to find solutions which made us both feel heard and understood. It was amazing how much stronger our marriage became through this period. It was another reminder of how important it was to be in one accord, regardless of the situation.

Your Turn…Your Perspective: How do you manage your needs versus your wants in terms of finances? Do you have an accountability partner? How has having one (or not having one) impacted your life recently?

Prayer: Lord, please help me embrace every part of this journey to financial wholeness. I want to experience You each step of the way. I thank You for the desire to serve You through my finances. I praise Your name.

Day 231
Little "g"

1 TIMOTHY 6:17; EPHESIANS 4:22-24

I loved to read. It was one of the ways I relaxed and explored the world. When I met Keith, I was pleasantly surprised to find we enjoyed the same types of books. After we married, Keith's taste in books slowly began to change. He discovered Christian, non-fiction authors. He shared his findings and slowly I embraced the genre.

Over time, both of our mindsets changed. Fiction became a thing of the past. We experienced a spiritual transformation as we shifted almost entirely away from books which only provided entertainment. Reading authors who shed light on God's Word was what we craved. As we continued paying our debt snowball, our book choices included authors who showcased God's principles of handling money.

One such book was Andy Stanley's *How To Be Rich: It's Not What You Have, It's What You Do With What You Have.* It impacted our lives significantly and challenged my perspective on Godly wealth. One statement in the book stayed with me for days. Andy stated, "When riches become the basis for your hope – the source of it – you're headed down a slippery slope."[9] I asked myself if this was my motivation for becoming debt-free. Was I putting my hope in being debt-free? Did I think life would be complete once we had margin?

When Keith and I embraced the idea of being completely debt-free, I saw it as an opportunity to finally have enough. But Andy's words challenged my motives and my desires. Why did I really want to be debt-free? What would change in my life when money did not have the names of creditors associated with it? Was debt-freedom all about my personal comfort, or was my motivation spiritual in origin? I honestly did not know.

I pondered the questions for days. I wanted my motives to be Godly, but I knew deep in my heart I was in danger of riches becoming the basis of my hope. I wanted to be debt-free so badly. Was it possible to do so and not allow the feeling of accomplishment to overtake me?

My life was filled with examples of little "g" gods taking the number one spot in my heart. I believed the little "g" god of having a husband and family was the reason I was 43 before I got married. The little "g" god of running a successful business was the reason I was no longer a Sales Director with Mary Kay. I did not want to be stuck in debt because I made a little "g" god out of being debt-free. I often told Keith I did not want my sin to be the reason we were not successful. Here was my chance to prove it.

I finished Andy's book and spent the next few weeks in prayer and meditation on contentment. I knew it would take more than a few weeks for a change to settle in, but it was a start. A pastor once said, "things cease to have control over you when you give them a name." It was equivalent to turning on a spiritual spotlight. The "things" were bathed in light, and darkness was left with no choice but to flee.

Over time, I became aware of a shift in my motives. I did not have such a negative response when money left my hands. I became aware of times the "old man" mentioned in Ephesians 4:22-24 appeared. I kept praying. I knew the change would not take place overnight, but I was committed. My "new self" was emerging.

Your Turn…Your Perspective: What little "g" gods do you have in your life? How do they impact how you manage money?

Prayer: Lord, thank You for loving me enough to call me on my motives. I pray to be renewed daily and to trust You for all I need.

Day 232
Online Envy

PROVERBS 12:5

I was never a big shopper. When Keith and I were dating, he was pleasantly surprised to find out I did not find wandering around the mall a form of entertainment. I shopped for clothes the same way I shopped for groceries – go in, get what was needed, and come out. If something caught my eye while I was looking for something else, I might stop and try it on, or I might not. It was just not a big deal for me.

I did, however, enjoy online shopping. Being tall made it hard to find my size in stores so catalog shopping was my primary shopping experience since college. In the days of free shipping, I ordered two sizes and two colors of everything, tried it all on, kept what worked, and sent the rest back. It was like having my own private fashion show. I did it so often, one store sent me a Christmas gift! Sad but true.

I checked my favorite websites a few times a week and set alerts for items I wanted. My wish list was a collection of wants and would-be needs, waiting for my budget to make room for them.

When Keith and I got serious about getting out of debt, I did not think much of my online shopping. In my mind, it was harmless. I knew I would not be shopping with credit cards, so I did not see the point of changing my behavior, or how I viewed online shopping.

Over time, however, I realized I was pining for what I could not have. Every time I went to an online store, I was reminded of what I could not buy. Many times, the items I wanted sold out before the price got low enough for me to make a purchase. I was torturing myself.

A short time later, I decided to unsubscribe from all the stores. No more alerts, no more discounts. The reality was my clothing budget would be low for several years. Online window shopping did me no good and I was better off not knowing. It took several months to wean myself off my weekly trips online to see what was new, but I persevered. I was determined to release myself from self-imposed torture.

Becoming debt-free was so important to us. But being debt-free and miserable was not going to be fun. Removing online browsing was the best way I knew to grow my contentment with my tired wardrobe and small clothing budget. It would not be forever, but for this season of low spending, it was very necessary.

Gradually, I was not tempted to check the sites. When I needed clothing, I simply took my clothing budget to a local store to find what I needed. On the few occasions when I did shop online (i.e. Black Friday or my birthday), it was a treat. I appreciated the experience much more than I did when I logged on weekly and pined for what I could not have. My entire perspective on shopping changed. There was no need to look if I could not buy.

In the end, I realized my issue was not about the websites and missing out on specials and promotions. It was about being content with what I owned and where I was in my life. Online shopping was simply the symptom of a much bigger contentment issue. Once I realized this, I knew how to attack it. I began to pray for greater contentment. Prayer changed everything, and greater contentment brought peace of mind.

Your Turn…Your Perspective: What things push your contentment boundaries? How do you overcome the temptation?

Prayer: Lord, thank You for the desire to be content in all things. Please help me to be satisfied with what I have instead of constantly wanting what is just beyond my reach.

Too Many Berries

1 CORINTHIANS 4:2

Keith and I went through a heavy medical season where we made a smoothie for breakfast every morning. We used a vegan, gluten free, organic protein powder, along with non-dairy milk, avocado, spinach and mixed berries. It was a great way to get more vegetables in our diet for the day and the avocado made the smoothie creamier without the added sugar of a banana. We used organic, frozen berries and additional aronia berries since research showed them to be beneficial in managing blood sugar levels.

While neither of us were diabetics, we knew the risk and wanted to guard against it. Adding aronia berries to our smoothie made a difference for both of us. They were a great way to keep diabetes from disrupting our lives without the need for any medication. The problem was the berries were not cheap. I did not have a green thumb and there was no room in our home to grow the berries ourselves. We decided to use our grocery budget for life sustaining food, and the aronia berries were a logical choice. It was a sacrifice which made sense to us.

On one trip to the natural grocery store, I noticed there were only four containers of aronia berries in the frozen food section. Instead of asking the manager if they were simply low on inventory, I made the decision to buy all four containers. I typically kept two containers on hand, but four was a bit much. In a moment of weakness, I made a poor financial decision. I became a berry hoarder and did major damage to the weekly food budget. Even though I knew we would eventually use the berries, I negatively impacted our food budget when it was not necessary. There was no need to buy all four containers.

What harm would have been done if the berries were no longer available? Several other stores in the area also carried them. I could have purchased powdered berries online to add to our smoothies. We could have found another natural product to use as a substitute. And frankly, four containers would not have solved the crisis anyway. It simply would have prolonged the inevitable.

The poor choice also impacted meal planning for the rest of the week. My overspending forced me to rethink the rest of the grocery shopping because there was less money to shop for the other items we needed. I still had to make sure there were enough groceries for the week. Three years in to paying off our debt snowball and I made a rookie mistake. I made a purchase without considering the impact it would have on our budget. It was a valuable lesson I wished I had learned better the first time around.

It was a reminder for us to constantly be aware of our end goal. My reactionary way of managing our grocery budget taught me another definition of impulse purchases. Quantity needed to be managed also. Just as buying an item not on the grocery list could upset the balance of things, so could buying too many of an item found on the grocery list. Both upset the financial stability of the monthly budget. Both potentially caused damage long term. I must always think before purchasing…even if it's on the list.

Your Turn…Your Perspective: When was the last time you blew your budget? How long did it take for you to recover? What lessons did you learn? How will you adjust for the future?

Prayer: Lord, I'm still learning. I pray for grace when I make "rookie" mistakes. Thank You for helping me learn from my mistakes and recover from them quickly. Help me to not lose sight of the end goal of financial freedom. Thank you for the gentle reminders to always look to You for counsel.

Day 234
Patience Pays

PHILIPPIANS 4:11-13; GALATIANS 6:9

Our rental home was built to be a rental home. The builders cut corners to save money because, ultimately, they knew they would not be living in it. The cut corners were small things, but they annoyed me. I knew I would have required a higher standard if it were my own home and not a rental.

One big frustration was a leak in the basement. Every time there was a heavy driving rain, the point of entry for the water line leaked. The maintenance guys sealed and resealed it. It still leaked. The reality was it needed professional attention, but professional home repairs were expensive, and our landlord did not want to spend the money. It made me so mad!

I decided to look for another place to live. We were still $68,000 away from becoming debt-free so buying a home was still not an option. I was "forced" by our debt snowball to look for other rental homes. I liked the area we lived in (safe, close to church and work, quiet) and did not want to move too far from where we currently lived.

My search immediately created frustration because rent for a different home with the same basic characteristics would be at least $200 more per month. A move would also require a two-year lease. The pictures of the other potential rental homes indicated we would be moving into a much older home, which also meant other potential maintenance issues. There would be the cost of moving (deposit, first month's rent, and utilities) and the hassle of packing and moving. You guessed it. We did not move.

I was deflated for weeks. I felt powerless to fix our situation. My calculations showed at least two more years in our current home before our $68,000 was paid. I was not looking forward to it. I wanted out, but at what cost? Again, the Holy Spirit reminded me of my ongoing (often losing) battle with contentment. The basement was not the issue. The costs of other rentals in the area were not the issue. The debt was not the issue. Contentment was my issue yet again.

The abandoned search for another rental home was another reminder to be content regardless of the circumstances. The reality was, while the leak was a nuisance, it was not life threatening. The moisture was only there for a short while and no mold or mildew resulted from it. And even though I would have held the builder to a higher quality standard, this was just a temporary location for us. We continued to treat the rental with care (being good stewards), continued to pound away at our debt, and continued to get ready for the day when the Lord would allow us the opportunity to build our own home.

I knew contentment was something I needed to do a better job of mastering before the Lord would allow us out of this season of debt. I often told Keith I did not want my lack of obedience (or poor faith walk) to be the reason our family missed a blessing. Yielding to the Lord in the area of contentment became my prayer. I prayed for deliverance. It was an uphill battle for me and I knew I would not conquer it without the help of the Holy Spirit.

Your Turn...Your Perspective: "The fruit of the Spirit are love, joy, peace, patience, kindness, goodness, faithfulness, gentleness, and self-control" (Gal 5:22-23). Which ones need some focus?

Prayer: Lord, thank You for revealing to me where my spiritual journey needs work. Thank You for helping me see the value in increasing my patience. It is a fruit of the Spirit I need in larger quantities. Show me the way, Father. I want mastery for my life in this area.

Resisting Pride
JEREMIAH 9:23

One year for Christmas, we were struggling to find Angel Tree tags for the kids. Angel Tree gift tags were a part of our celebration every year to provide gifts for underprivileged kids in our community and teach our own kids the value of serving others. We wanted them to understand how fortunate they were to have two Christmases to celebrate when other children barely got one.

In the years when they were with us for Thanksgiving, Angel Trees were easier to find. We shopped with the kids while they were with us for the holiday, then returned the gifts in early December. The years when they were with us for Christmas were a little more complicated. Most agencies wanted the gifts back a few weeks before Christmas. One year, with only a few weeks remaining before Christmas, I struggled to find an agency.

We refused to be deterred, however. Keith and I discussed it and decided to press on. We did not want to change our tradition of the kids giving someone else a gift for Christmas. I went back to the church, explained our dilemma, and got a few more leads to call. I knew we were running out of time.

I finally reached someone who could assist. They were excited we called because they just received a request from a family in need of electricity for the month of December. They were in danger of having their electrical service cut off for non-payment. For only a few hundred dollars, the family would have lights and heat.

I was silent. As much as I wanted to help, this request was significantly outside of the budget we set for Angel Tree gifts. I took a deep breath and explained our budgetary restrictions to the woman at the other end of the line. I was actually embarrassed to tell her we could not assist. My pride welled up quickly. Surely, we could spare a few hundred dollars, right? These people needed us. What would they do if we did not assist? The agency would think we were cheap, or worse. Poor. I did not want them thinking we were poor, did I?

The swirl of questions and accusations raced through my head. I did not know the woman on the other end of the line and what she thought should not matter. But it did. It took incredible resolve to decline the request. We were intentional in not going overboard for Christmas. It was important for payments to the debt snowball to remain significantly intact during the holiday season. We must stick to the plan.

Finally, after what seemed like an eternity, the woman spoke. She said she certainly understood. She asked if we were following Dave Ramsey's plan. I told her we were. She told me she and her husband were also working through their debt snowball and she was disappointed at not being able to assist the family either. We encouraged each other a little, exchanged pleasantries, and the call ended.

I thought of how close I had come to succumbing to pride. It was a fight through the barrage of negative thoughts pressing me to "protect" our reputation. It took significant effort to not believe the lies playing in my head. Christine Caine once said, "We have a choice. We can believe the facts, or we can believe the TRUTH." I was thankful I chose to believe the TRUTH. We were not poor; we were intentional. The day would come when we could assist a family in need. In the meantime, we would stay true to our plan.

Your Turn…Your Perspective: How do you resist giving in to prideful temptation? Name a time when you were not able to resist. What were the consequences?

Prayer: Lord, thank You for the TRUTH. Thank You for the perseverance to finish the race set before me and not be sidetracked by great opportunities assigned to someone else.

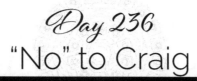
Day 236
"No" to Craig

PROVERBS 6:4

When Keith's beloved truck died three months after my car died, we scrambled to replace it. Our emergency fund was still being rebuilt after purchasing my replacement vehicle, and there was only $1500 available to replace his. We found a 15-year-old SUV with well over 250,000 miles on it, but we knew it would not last long. We decided to set aside a portion of our debt snowball money for the day when we needed to replace it. We prayed we would have time to save enough to purchase a newer vehicle.

A few months later, our car purchase fund was up to a few thousand dollars. We started looking to see what it would buy. We found a car on Craig's List and decided to check it out. I was feeling really gun shy because we made a poor choice with my replacement vehicle and I did not want to do it again.

The car was in a small town about an hour away from where we lived. We would not be able to take it to a dealership to get it inspected because of the remote location. Strike One. No inspection, no purchase was my new car-buying motto. Unless we could find a certified mechanic in a neighboring town, the deal was a bust.

During the test drive, we discovered several electrical issues with the vehicle. Strike Two. Who buys a vehicle whose electrical panel was all lit up like a Christmas tree? Surely, not us! It was also not in the best condition and was too small. Strike Three and Four. In my mind, we were done. Keith, however, seemed to be seriously entertaining the thought of purchasing this car.

I sat for a moment, attempting to gather my thoughts before I spoke. There was no way we were buying this car. His $1500 car was still working, and I had more faith in it than I did in what sat before us. I needed to find a way to remind him of what a poor decision it would be to buy the car.

Slowly, I shared my concerns. He heard me, but I could tell he did not really "hear" what was said. I could not figure out why he was so attached to this vehicle, so I tried again. Still, he did not get it. Finally, I looked him squarely in his eyes and told him there was no way we were buying this car. I did not release his gaze until I saw some hint of understanding.

The ride home was a quiet one. Neither of us had much to say. I prayed he would not be angry for long. A few hours after we got home, Keith came and hugged me. He apologized for being unreasonable and thanked me from walking him back from the ledge. I laughed and reminded him I was the one typically on the ledge about to take the deep plunge.

We were a team and needed to support each other in every way. This situation was no different. I was thankful our relationship was filled with strong communication. It made difficult times easier to get through. We both had a voice in our marriage and respect was a foundational component. Not only did we avert a car disaster, I felt blessed to not also have a marriage disaster. It was a reminder of the importance to always speak in love.

Your Turn…Your Perspective: How many strikes did you reach before realizing you were on the verge of a poor purchase? What did the experience teach you?

Prayer: Lord, please help me avoid financial disasters during this season of my life. I pray for a support network and people who love me enough to tell me the truth. I thank You for the desire to serve You with good money choices.

Picnic in the Park

PROVERBS 3:15

Fall was always my favorite time of year. It could be because my birthday is in October and the temperature was low enough to enjoy outdoors without combusting. I loved how the leaves changed, and the entire landscape prepared to hunker down for winter. It always made me appreciate the gift of life the Lord gave. I also loved picnics. And, of course, I loved them most in the fall.

One year, Keith and I drove to St. Louis for parent/teacher conferences. It was the start of a new school year and we always made a point of being visible to both the kids and their teachers. We wanted to be sure everyone involved in their education knew we were to be included in all decisions concerning the kids. Trial and error taught us this was best done in person.

It was the year both our kids were in middle school. When we set up the conferences, we were told one set of teachers would be available earlier in the day, and the others would be available later in the afternoon. Because we were firmly in the middle of paying off our debt snowball, we chose to pack a lunch instead of eating out. We loaded the cooler with ice and our meal, and headed to our first set of appointments.

When it was time for lunch, we stopped at our favorite gas station for iced tea. I warmed up our meal using the microwaves in the convenience section of the store. I thought we were going to simply eat in the car, but Keith informed me he had a surprise.

I loved surprises and perked up immediately to see what was in store. We drove a short distance and made a few turns. The road opened into a beautiful park. Because it was the middle of a school day, the park was completely deserted. It was all aglow with fall colors and the sun was shining brightly in a clear, blue sky. It was absolutely beautiful. I felt so special.

We took a blanket out of the car, spread out our lunch, and proceeded to enjoy the scenery and the company. We recently started working on goal setting for the next few months of our lives, and it seemed like a perfect time to finish it. It was a wonderful afternoon and we both enjoyed the uninterrupted time together.

As I later thought about our lovely picnic in the park, I realized it was made possible because of our debt snowball. If we were out of debt, we would not have packed a lunch. Instead, we would have found a nearby restaurant and stopped in for a meal. It would have been crowded with employees racing to get back to work and we would have been caught in the frenzy. It certainly would have lacked the serene setting of the park.

So much of my life was spent being frustrated at our circumstances. I wanted to be out of debt so badly. Surrounded by beauty, I was reminded to be patient and enjoy the journey. I knew we would one day be debt-free, and another world of opportunity would open for us.

In the meantime, the Lord chose to sprinkle the blessing of a picnic in the middle of an ordinary fall day. I was thankful Keith was listening when He whispered His plans. I was thankful for a picnic in the park.

Your Turn…Your Perspective: What helps you remain joyful on your journey? How do you stay focused on your current financial goal?

Prayer: Lord, thank You for the little blessings in my life. Thank You for helping me to live in the present and not miss the beauty of my current situation. Please help me to stay focused on our plan and not get ahead of You.

Day 238
Rescue Me!

PROVERBS 5:10

Keith and I took every opportunity to educate as many people as we could about God's ways of managing money. Complete strangers in the line at the grocery store, church members, colleagues at work, people we met at networking functions were all likely candidates. We listened for the telltale signs of people who were living in financial darkness. We were not shy about sharing with those who wanted to know more.

A constant topic was student loans. Most people believed student loans were normal and paying them off early was not possible or necessary. We worked to educate them of the dangers of their attitude.

Most people did not know student loans accrued interest daily, and they never stopped to calculate the amount of money lost in interest each and every day. The idea of keeping more of their hard-earned money in their accounts did not seem plausible to most. We knew otherwise.

Most of our debt, when we began to attack it, was interest accrued on deferred student loans. In every case, the balance was higher than the original loan amount by at least 10% (or a lot more for the oldest ones). Even though signatures were required to receive the original loan, people did not seem to realize interest charges began immediately and continued to accrue during deferment. Since our eyes were opened and we now knew better, we saw it as our personal mission to debunk the myth for everyone else.

As I was having a debunking conversation one day, a young friend of mine stated she was not concerned about her student loans. She already decided the solution to her problem was to marry well. At first, I thought she was kidding. Then I realized she was not. She was serious and I was speechless. It took several moments before I could respond to her perceived solution. She was woefully misled.

I felt sad. I was 43 when I got married and many of my friends never got married. If this young woman thought marriage was the secret to debt reduction, she was in for a rude awakening. Her "prince charming" very likely would also have student loan debt. He could, in fact, be hoping to also "marry well" and have his debt taken care of by his new bride. There was no guarantee. Her idea of marrying someone wealthy enough to take on her six-figure student loan debt was not a realistic debt repayment plan at all.

I told my young friend our story. I shared the difficulty we experienced finding our way as newlyweds with so much debt to manage. I told her of the many money discussions which filled our dating years and spilled over into married life. I shared how I knew I would not have given Keith a chance as a potential mate if my own finances were not so messed up. I tried my best to help her see the best option for a healthy marriage was to get rid of as much debt as possible before the relationship began.

Did she hear me? Honestly, I do not think she did. Her debt was large, and her income was not. She was in survival mode and did not see the lifeline debt reduction offered. With almost $150,000 in student loans, her choices got more limited every time she made a minimum payment. I prayed she would one day see the benefit of fighting through.

Your Turn…Your Perspective: What is your rescue story? What situation did you wish was magically removed? What happened to cause reality to set in?

Prayer: Lord, please help me be bold in Your message. Help me not be afraid to educate Your people on the dangers of debt. Give me courage, Lord, to speak the truth in love.

Wishing for a Windfall
1 CHRONICLES 29:15

I was listening to the Dave Ramsey Show one day and a couple was in the studio to do their debt-free scream. When Dave asked what the hardest part of the journey was, the wife said it was working through the very large dollar amount and the many years (and sacrifices) it took to get there. She stated there were many times she wished a windfall would show up and take the burden away.

I could certainly relate. Our journey was not much different. Our total amount paid was $146,000 by then. When we included the $65,000 in medical bills, and an additional $12,000 in car repairs and replacement vehicles, over $220,000 was spent on life and debt in four years. I could think of many days when I wished a private detective would show up to tell me some unknown relative left me or Keith a large chunk of cash.

The HGTV Dream Home contest winner was my personal favorite windfall fantasy. I even did the research to find out how to get the prize in all cash. I shake my head at myself now, but back then it would have been such an answer to prayer. In every scenario, we cashed in everything and chose the lump sum instead of the monthly stipend. My fantasy was complete with a tithe to our local church.

We would pay off all our debts. Any money left over (and there was plenty left over in my fantasy!) created a three to six-month emergency fund. Then we would begin contributing 15% into our Roth 401k plans, start college funding, and pay cash for a house.

Since no fantasy was complete without a happy ending, we would live happily ever after giving lots of money away in the process. I worked my way through this fantasy more times than I could count. It got to a point I began to limit my entries into the HGTV contests to only one per contest to keep from being consumed by the fantasy.

My saving grace during these fantasy excursions was not stopping. I never stopped working. I never stopped budgeting. I never stopped looking for ways to save money. I never stopped searching for ways to bring more money into our household. I never stopped plugging the holes in our budget to stop the outpouring of unnecessary cash from our checking account. I did not sit and wait for the fantasy to become reality.

What I learned from the experience was I could not handle a windfall. If I could have handled a windfall, the Lord would have given us one. Financial maturity leads to financial security, and I obviously needed to mature a little more before we reached security.

Once I realized what my trips to fantasyland really meant, I stopped going. Spending time imagining a future, which held a limited chance of occurring, was no longer appealing. I focused more of my mental energy on learning to be financially mature, and less on wishing. It was a powerful lesson for me.

Our plan to get us out of debt must be intentional and on purpose. It was based on consistent work and follow through. Only then would the Lord bless our efforts. Every time an unexpected "windfall" showed up in our mailbox, I saw it as our financial maturity increasing. It was a great way to stay motivated.

Your Turn…Your Perspective: Describe one of your trips to "fantasyland." How did you find your way back?

Prayer: Lord, thank You for not giving me everything I want but always providing everything I need. Please help me see when I am unrealistic in my expectations without losing the ability to dream.

Day 240
First Things First

A friend of ours traveled a great deal in his job. He loved his work, but after years on the road as a single person and almost seven years on the road as a married man, he was ready for a change. His sons were at the age where having a man in the house on a consistent basis was important. And, of course, his wife did not want to continue to carry the load at home on her own. He knew it was time to come home for good.

His dilemma was what to do when he came off the road. He was not the typical desk job guy and would not do well in a traditional 9-5 position. He was incredibly talented with his hands but did not want to do manual labor. He was also a skilled musician with amazing operational skills. He struggled to find a way to turn those skills into viable employment in his hometown.

One day he brought his dilemma to our life group for prayer. He loved what he did and was really good at it. His colleagues respected and admired him. He even thought of his work as a ministry and often prayed for and with the musicians and production crew. When anyone was struggling with an issue, they took it to our friend. He was the voice of reason for many people over the years.

We prayed and talked with him about his concerns. He did not want to simply quit his job but was certain it was the right time to leave his current position. An incredible new job opportunity became available for his wife around the same time. It meant she would be able to absorb some of the lost income. They were debt-free which made their budget much smaller and the decision somewhat easier. Ultimately, he needed to decide if he trusted the Lord enough to let go.

A few weeks later, he got some help with his decision after his younger son suffered a traumatic event. While he was not physically harmed, the emotional impact of the experience was deep. Our friend knew immediately what he needed to do. He called his employer and offered his resignation. His employer tried to convince him to stay, but our friend's mind was already made up. His family needed him at home.

It was liberating for our friend to decide to choose family over income. He still did not know what he would do to replace his salary, but his family loved having him at home and he was a great stay-at-home dad.

None of this would have been possible if they were in debt. If our friend and his wife were in debt, their decision would have been made based on income and not just the needs of the family. It was likely he would not have been able to simply walk away.

It served as a reminder to us as we worked on our own journey to debt-freedom. It showcased how important it was to get out of debt quickly. Our friends were able to view their situation through the lens of what was best for their family, and not what was best for their creditors. It was great to watch them manage the situation without fear of not having enough. We prayed for the day when we would be able to do the same.

Your Turn…Your Perspective: When have you had to stay in a position because of money? How would your life be different if you had been free to leave?

Prayer: Lord, I pray for the perseverance to continue this journey to debt-freedom. Please help me stay focused on You and to be mindful of detours designed to steal my time and financial resources. Help me to keep my financial life as simple as possible during this season. I know my time of financial peace is coming.

Day 241
New Beginnings

PROVERBS 8:19

One of my younger friends was moving into her first apartment. She was so excited. She had been working for a few years and was also completing her master's degree. She was still living at home with her parents and was eager to strike out on her own. I encouraged her to stay at home a little longer to get a better handle on her finances, but she was determined to start the next phase of her life.

I could relate to her desire to be independent but was really concerned about the financial choices she made. Her income was on the lower end of the spectrum and her debt was high. Credit cards, personal loans and old debt in collections were all vying for her income. She was hoping her master's degree would open the door to more income, but there was no guarantee. The payments on her student loans would also begin six months after she finished graduate school and add to her already burdensome debt load.

After I shared my concerns with my young friend, I was faced with my own dilemma. Should I continue to share my concerns and risk her shutting me out of her life and decisions long term? Or, should I support her in her journey as best I could? I saw so much of myself in her and wanted to support her as much as I could. In the end, I opted to keep my mouth shut unless she asked for my opinion.

It was difficult to watch her make poor choices. She signed up for more student loans for a certificate program after she finished her master's degree. She rushed into renting a two-bedroom apartment instead of waiting for an efficiency or one bedroom. And, although she received a promotion at work, all her new income was directed at the expenses of her apartment (rent, utilities, etc.). I held my breath, hoping she would ask for my advice.

No request came. I was sad for her but knew she would have to find her own way. Instead I gave her some household items left from my days as a single woman. I gave her artwork and kitchen gadgets, rugs, and décor. I gave no advice. I wanted to keep our relationship as positive as possible and chose to be excited for her new beginnings instead of holding my breath waiting for the other shoe to drop.

My friend talked about getting a part-time job to assist with her new expenses. Her current income was just not enough to make ends meet. I prayed she would see the seriousness of her situation but knew her financial wake-up call was still too far away for her to feel alarmed.

The next five years of her life would be crucial to her future. How she managed them would determine if she retired as a millionaire or ended up living in debt for a good portion of her life. While I prayed she would wake up and embrace the hard work needed to correct her circumstances, ultimately it was her decision to make. In the meantime, I decided to just be her friend and only offer advice when it was requested, and, of course, continue to pray for her.

Your Turn…Your Perspective: How has having debt in your life (or the lives of people you care about) changed your outlook on the future? What changes can you make today which will impact your future in a significant way?

Prayer: Lord, thank You for opening my eyes to see the devastation debt can inflict. I pray I can be gracious to those who have not yet seen how debt can derail their futures. I pray to seek wise counsel from those around me and to think through each financial decision before acting. I pray to not live in financial oblivion.

Day 242
Get Rid of It

MATTHEW 6:33; EPHESIANS 4:22-24

It was time to find more stuff to sell. The longer we were in debt, the less significance stuff held. If we could sell it and apply the proceeds towards a student loan payment, we were closer to becoming debt-free. My grandmother's beloved gooseneck rocker was the only item never considered.

During one such purge, I opened the coat closet. There hung my mink coat. It brought more pain than joy in the almost 15 years I owned it. Regardless of how I tried, I could not shake what a horrible decision it was to buy it. I was actually ashamed to wear it. People for the Ethical Treatment of Animals (PETA) was not my problem. My shame was firmly rooted in my misplaced desire to own it in the first place.

I always felt as if I were living a lie when I wore it. It was like a façade I slipped into every year on really cold days. I could not get past the negative feelings I seemed to put on when I wore it. I knew deep in my heart it was because I purchased the coat hoping to create an image of success. The impact of the purchase was no longer evident in my bank account, but it left a deep wound emotionally.

I was a fashion consultant for almost ten years. I always taught my clients to never wear anything which did not make them feel good. If you needed to pull or tug at an article of clothing to look right, do not wear it. Any time I wore my mink coat, I mentally pulled and tugged, trying to feel good about it. The lesson I taught others was still just outside my reach. I continued to try to make the image fit the real me.

I made progress over the years and worked my way through the need to have status symbols. But the mink coat still reminded me just how deeply rooted the need to belong was in my life. My desire for others to think of me as successful was so great, I literally put owning a coat ahead of both food and shelter.

Strangely, it took me years to put my finger on why I felt unworthy when I wore it. I honestly do not think I really understood the negative emotion associated with owning it until I looked at it hanging in the coat closet during my search for more items to sell. Then and there, I knew it needed to go.

The coat was a connection to a former version of myself. In Ephesians 4:22-24, Paul spoke of putting off the old self which was corrupted by its deceitful desires in order to be made new. By selling the mink, I ceremonially shed the prideful desire associated with its purchase.

I truly was a new version of myself. I no longer needed a status symbol. I was comfortable being who I was, regardless of what others thought; the need to impress others was no longer something I valued. As sad as it was for me to acknowledge all the negative energy associated with the coat purchase, I was thankful to finally let it go.

A week later the coat was gone and $500 was applied to the student loan balance. I doubted if I would ever purchase another one. The opportunity cost of owning a mink coat was much higher than I wanted to pay again. I was finally moving past the need to let a piece of clothing define who I was as a person. I knew I was on the path to a place where any success achieved was honoring God, and not self-seeking.

Your Turn…Your Perspective: What "old self" façades do you need to purge? How have they impacted your life?

Prayer: Lord, please help me to not be defined by stuff. I pray You show me when my actions are not honoring You. Help me to be aware of old desires which may need to be "put off" again.

Day 243
Bank Receipt

HAGGAI 2:8; JOB 6:8

Keith and I often played a little game. We would create a surprise to share and the other person would close their eyes and wait to be led. Sometimes the surprise would be the dental floss left off the grocery list the week before. Or maybe it was a piece of mail we knew the other was waiting expectantly for, and it finally arrived.

The surprises were always small and typically carried little to no financial value, but we loved to give them nonetheless. They always brought smiles and laughter, and we cherished them.

One day, Keith came home from running errands and told me of a new surprise for me. I was giddy with excitement. The last surprise was several weeks prior, and I could not wait to see what this one was. He sat me in a chair in the kitchen, told me to close my eyes, and hold out my hands. I quickly complied and squeezed my eyes tight so he could see I was not peeking.

He gently laid a piece of paper in my hands. I could tell it was a receipt of some sort but was not sure of anything else. There was very little money not attached to debt reduction at the time, so I doubted he made a purchase. I was curious to see.

When I opened my eyes, my suspicions were confirmed. It was a receipt from a bank ATM machine, but I could immediately tell it was not ours. The amount of the withdrawal was $300, and the ending balance was over $23,000! This was certainly not our bank account.

I looked up at him in confusion. The receipt belonged to the person who used the ATM before Keith. The person left the receipt dangling, and Keith removed it to start his own transaction. As he looked at the amounts, a profound thought dawned on him. One day, when we were free from debt, our checking account would look like the receipt. Our financial life would be on solid footing.

I looked at him in amazement. I was so thankful for the glimpse into our future even though we were so far from the account referenced on the receipt. It was much easier to believe we would never get out of debt. It was much easier to think we would always struggle financially. It was much easier to resign ourselves to a life of less than, instead of abundance.

But we did not choose to take the easy route. We chose instead to do the hard part and stick to our plan to become debt-free. We knew deep in our hearts that God would reward our efforts and we would one day be debt-free.

The receipt was a reminder of God's plan for us. It was a reminder of the payoff we would receive from the hard work we already completed as well as the hard work still to come. It created a hopefulness I did not often allow myself to experience. It served as a ticket to the life we would have if we just kept going, putting one financial foot in front of the other.

Your Turn…Your Perspective: What situation or item has God used recently to give you hope? How did you respond?

Prayer: Lord, thank You for hope. Thank You for the small things You use to remind me of Your plan for my life. Please help me never take my eyes off You.

Day 244
Tithe Trust

JOB 28:17

Church was more than just Sunday mornings for Keith and me. We met while serving at our church and it just seemed natural for us to continue serving after we got married. We were new to the city and took great care in finding a church home. We did not want to be church hoppers. Instead, we wanted to settle into a place where we could grow spiritually. We also wanted a place where our kids could grow and be excited about learning God's Word.

We were meticulous in every area associated with choosing a church except one. Not once did we ask about the church's fiscal responsibility. We never thought about praying for God's guidance in terms of the church's financial solvency and how it handled its budget. It honestly never crossed our minds to ask.

It took us a few false starts to find our church home. Finally, after two years of searching, we found the one. As we settled in, we began to hear language which was music to our ears. The church was in the midst of a $2 million building project and was paying cash for it! Keith and I looked at each other with shock and awe as we leaned in to hear more.

The project had been underway for a few years and enough money was raised to begin. The church secured a construction loan, but there were no plans to use it. They asked for continued prayer to raise enough money to complete the project without debt.

Keith and I were giddy with excitement!

We actually found a church whose financial principles matched our own. And we were not even trying. We knew it was a gift from the Lord, and a lesson we should never forget. It was an example of what could happen when people gave freely to the Lord through tithes and offerings. It reminded us of the importance of having financial margin in our lives so that we could give. We were thankful to find a church home where the emphasis was placed on being wise with the resources God gave to each of us. It made us want to embody it all the more by becoming debt-free ourselves.

Choosing a church home was a serious matter, and every area should be reviewed. We learned the importance of looking beyond the surface. If our tithes were going to be counted among the members, our experience taught us the importance of understanding our responsibility to make sure the mindset of church leadership was similar to our own. To do otherwise would set us up to be frustrated.

Even though we stumbled into the importance of aligning ourselves with a church which held our fiscal beliefs, we knew it would forever be a part of our decision-making process. What a gift it turned out to be. So much of what we learned revolved around our own handling of money, and now we knew it applied to our church home also.

Your Turn…Your Perspective: How involved are you in the financial management of your church? How do you respond to the financial decisions made by your church leadership?

Prayer: Lord, thank You for a deeper understanding of Your Word as it applies to my finances. I pray to always be mindful of the charge You have given me to be a good steward of the resources You have blessed me with.

Day 245
Dishwasher Love

PSALM 128:1-2

The original plan was to only live in our little rented duplex for a year while we settled into our new city. Once we knew more about our new hometown, the plan was to buy a home and ditch the rental. We unpacked but did not give away any boxes. After all, we would be packing again soon.

Because we were not supposed to be in our duplex long, I was okay with our cheap dishwasher in the beginning. I believed our time together would be short lived, so I dealt with its poor performance without much frustration. I chose to "grin and bear it." Scrubbing the dishes to remove all food particles was required prior to putting them into the dishwasher. It was small and slow. Each cycle took almost 4 hours, yet the dishes were often not clean when it finished.

The more time we lived in our duplex, the more I hated our dishwasher. I ranted often about how ridiculous it was to use, and was very vocal about my disdain. Keith would gently rub the dishwasher and tell it I did not mean to upset it. He would then tell me I needed to apologize to the dishwasher or it might stop working all together. The silly comments lifted my spirits for the moment, and I would get back to my tasks in the kitchen.

One day I realized my frustration with the dishwasher was a direct result of my level of contentment. I wanted to be debt-free so we could build our dream home. I was not satisfied during our season of renting and I felt "forced" to use cheap appliances. I was choosing to live in the future where I would have nice appliances and not in the present where our living expenses fit our budget. I was so focused on what I did not have, I could not see what I did have.

I was face to face with yet another example of my own discontentment.

It became the subject of my prayer time. I knew we would be renting for quite some time, and frankly did not want to carry such high levels of discontentment for any longer than necessary. My contentment was a constant battle for me and I wanted to be set free from it. I could stay in a place of discontentment or move to where the Lord wanted me. It was my decision.

Once again, I adjusted my perspective. Would I ever learn to be content with what I already had?

I told the dishwasher I was sorry and meant it! I also became intentional in not complaining about our home. It was not easy. The thought of what our home did not have would often creep into my mind. I made a conscious choice to dismiss the thought each time and focus instead on the blessings of our life. Slowly I was able to adjust my thought process and find the good in our current home. I was able to be content in my circumstances. Prayerfully, discontentment would become a condition of the past.

Your Turn...Your Perspective: What areas of your life currently showcase discontentment? How long does it take for you to become aware of your discontentment? What do you do about it?

Prayer: Lord, please help me to stay focused on the journey and not be sidetracked by the destination. Help me to not look to the future, but to enjoy the blessings of today. I pray You continue to call me out when my contentment is out of focus.

Day 246
The Rock

PROVERBS 24:3-4; MATTHEW 16:18; 1 CORINTHIANS 14:40

To bide my time while we plodded through our debt, I did research. I researched ways to trim our food budget. I researched how to save on heating and cooling costs. I researched scripture to keep my spirits high. I researched ways to make the most money on the stuff we sold. I researched just about everything you could imagine.

I spent most of my time, however, researching what our home would look like when we were finally able to build. I designed our home on Pinterest boards. My thought was to do as much legwork as possible while we were getting out of debt so we could hit the ground running when we were ready to build our home.

As I searched thousands of websites over the years of our debt reduction, I kept stumbling back to one piece of property. It was constantly on and off the market. Every time it came on the market, I cheered. Every time it was removed, I was disappointed. It was perfect for us, mainly because it appeared no one else wanted it.

It was a rock. One massive piece of solid earth which would redefine the term excavation. The site prep work would be extensive to literally chisel a foundation out of this huge piece of rock. But I loved it. It was tucked away, slightly obscure, and it was in a great neighborhood which held its value. Our home would be on the lower end of the price point for the neighborhood since we were determined to not build too much house.

One month, when I noticed the lot was on the market again, Keith and I decided to drive by and take another look. Because it was so obscure, we could not actually walk the lot, but we were still able to see it from the street. We drove back and forth as slowly as we could, stopping often for cars to pass us by.

Maybe it was the drudgery of paying off debt for so long with not many extras (car repairs and medical bills were not the extras I wanted). Maybe it was the boredom of living in a bland, rented duplex with ugly carpet. Maybe it was spring fever. I do not know what happened to us that day, but I do know we got a little ahead of ourselves. We began to talk earnestly about throwing caution to the wind and purchasing the lot.

We did not have any savings outside our starter emergency fund of $1000. All our money went to debt reduction. We also did not have money for a down payment, and no collateral for a land loan. We started thinking about "creative" finance opportunities. Every legal idea was explored.

I honestly do not remember who came up for air first. I do know it was a reality check on how important it was to keep our blinders on. It was the same reason I did not go window shopping. We finally decided to not check on the property anymore until we were ready to start our project. If it was meant to be our home site, it would still be there when we were ready to build.

We were thankful we came to our senses before it was too late. We knew it was the Lord's hand on us. We knew He kept us. And, when the time was right, He would release us from this season of the mundane and we could build the home of our desires with blessings in tow. What a great day it would be!

Your Turn…Your Perspective: How do you manage getting too close to your financial point of no return? Whose voice do you hear when you're coming out of it?

Prayer: Lord, thank You for protecting me from myself. I truly appreciate Your guiding hand always being on me. I pray for continued patience as I choose to follow 1 Corinthians 14:40 and always be decent and in order. Please help me stay mindful of You on my journey.

Baseball Friends

We were fortunate two years in a row to have the hometown Major League Baseball team in the World Series. The city was electric. I had never experienced such excitement before and was happy to be a part of the experience. The entire city was on cloud nine and stayed up late into the evenings to watch history in the making.

As imagined, ticket prices soared. A $20 nosebleed seat during the regular season was marked up literally 1000% and higher. Tickets were sold to simply stand in the stadium. It was amazing. Keith and I did not even discuss the possibility of going to a game. We were happy to watch each one at home or with friends. We acknowledged the "once in a lifetime" experience but did not feel the need to move money from paying our debt snowball to be up close and personal.

A day or so after one of the home games, I saw a photo posted by a friend on social media. She and her husband and another couple posed happily for a selfie. I was quite surprised to see them at the game. I knew they still were working on their own debt-reduction strategy. I also knew there was still a good bit left for them to pay. It would be years before they were debt-free.

A thousand questions and thoughts flooded my mind: *How on earth can they spend so much money on a baseball game? What a lack of judgement! I can't believe they are being so irresponsible. Incredible, what were they thinking when they spent money on baseball tickets instead of paying down interest on student loans?* On and on I went, belittling my friends to God and Keith for their "poor choices."

As I came up for air in mid-rant, I felt the conviction of the Holy Spirit. Who was I to judge? Did we not just spend $250 on tickets to a Broadway musical and dinner out? Did I not get a pedicure every month? Surely those funds could have been redirected to the debt snowball. Maybe my friends were gifted the tickets and did not actually have to pay for them at all. And heaven forbid, maybe they chose to save for a special event and decided to divert some of the money to the game.

Wow. I hung my head in shame. Here I was condemning my friends when I knew nothing of how the transaction took place. I was so fueled by my own righteous indignation, I never stopped to think of the primary factor at the center of my judgement. IT WAS NONE OF MY BUSINESS!

Instead of being happy for my friends, I chose to judge. Instead of thinking positively about the situation, I chose to look for the worst financial characteristics and attach them to my friends. I was so embarrassed and I was also humbled. I saw the chastisement for the life lesson it was.

My friends and their choices on an evening out were of no concern to me. I was better served by turning my attention to my own behavior and my own choices. I should choose to show grace instead of judgment and criticism. Lesson learned.

Your Turn…Your Perspective: When was the last time you condemned someone because of their choices? How did it impact you?

Prayer: Lord, please help me to not look at the worst in a person. Please help me to not be judgmental. I pray for compassion for those around me. I pray I continue to keep my eyes focused on my own journey and not be critical of the journey of those around me.

Day 248
Diamonds or Bricks

2 CORINTHIANS 5:9; DEUTERONOMY 30:19

We reached the four-year mark of working on debt-freedom before we found out my phantom medical issues were also heavy metal poisoning. Keith and I were being treated for different forms of the same illness. It was a complicated process and required multiple trips to Dallas, expensive tests, and oxygen therapy for both of us among other things. It was exhausting and took up the bulk of the cash in our checking account. What did not go to the actual visits to doctors went to the medications to manage both illnesses, and to the purchase of organic food which became a lifeline for both of us.

At first, I was discouraged. With the initial trip to Texas, we had officially spent over $50,000 on medical expenses trying to put a name to our mystery illnesses. There was still about $60,000 in debt left to pay. It did not take rocket science to figure out we would have been debt-free if not for the extensive medical bills. We also knew more medical bills were coming.

I was at a crossroad. Did I want to carry diamonds or bricks? Fifty pounds of diamonds weighed the same as fifty pounds of bricks. If I chose to carry bricks, I would focus on the $50,000 already spent on medical bills. If I carried diamonds, I would focus on paying cash for the medical expenses and not incurring any new debt.

If I chose to carry bricks, I would focus on both of us being sick with a rare illness. If I carried diamonds, I would focus on us having the same illness. The solutions would be similar which would lower the medical costs. We were able to use the same oxygen tank and used many of the same medications. The changes to our diet were also the same.

If I chose to carry bricks, I would focus on us spending the first four years of our marriage fighting both financial and medical battles. If I chose to carry diamonds, I would focus on us having a solid game plan. Both our medical and financial issues would soon be over.

I knew it was all about perspective. Did I choose to look at the glass as half empty or half full? Would I be a pessimist or an optimist? Would I trust God's plan or suffer through my own? I needed to make the final decision whether diamonds or bricks, knowing it would impact the rest of my life, Keith and our marriage. It was a foundational decision which would impact our entire future.

I chose diamonds. As I studied God's Word, I saw it specifically talked about God setting before us blessings and curses It was our choice which of the two we accepted. I chose the blessings. I chose to see the blessings in our circumstances. With all Keith and I experienced in the first few years of our marriage, we proved to ourselves we could stand strong against any adversity. God set blessings and curses before us. We chose to acknowledge the blessings and are better for it.

Your Turn...Your Perspective: What diamonds and bricks do you have in your life? Which do you choose to carry and why?

Prayer: Lord, thank You for perspective. Thank You for Your Word which is a constant reminder of Your promises. Thank You for the resolve to stay focused on the blessings and not choose to focus on the curses. I praise Your name for the trials I have experienced. They have made me better and more reliant on You.

Two Million Dollar Delay
PROVERBS 15:6; ROMANS 2:11

When I arrived in Northern Virginia in 2000, one of the first things I did was look for a church home. It took me almost a year to make my final choice. Once I did, I settled in and began to serve and grow. It did not take long to learn about the church's proposed building project and why it was needed. The church held two services on Sundays, but space for other activities was severely limited.

Staff worked out of rented office space in a nearby strip mall. Vacation Bible School was held at an elementary school down the street. A banquet space for retreats and special programs was always a part of any proposed outreach initiative. The church spent a large portion of the budget each year on a variety of rental spaces.

A proposal was made to build a second building on the land the church already owned. It would house the office staff and become the primary space for all activities. It would eliminate the rental payments going out each year. However, getting the proposal passed by county and state legislation proved to be very difficult.

It took an incredible amount of effort to get all parties to agree to the building project. At one point, a contingent from the church testified before the U.S. Supreme Court hoping to receive the approval needed to build. Finally, after almost 15 years of prayer and lobbying, the church received permission.

Because the construction industry was in one of the worst economic periods in the history of building, prices for services and supplies dropped significantly. The cost to build ended up being almost $2 million less than the original estimate from years earlier! It was an incredible example of God's delay not being His denial.

The congregation believed the Lord would allow the building project to take place. They were determined to not stop until approval to build was granted. The result was a beautiful, very functional building with a price tag $2 million lower than expected. What a blessing!

I chose initially to focus on the church's frustration and ultimate celebration as I thought about our own building project. Our roadblocks were not political or the result of changes in zoning regulations. Ours were debt snowball payments, medical bills, car repairs, and life in general.

On the surface, all I saw was more waiting. It was hard not to be frustrated. I witnessed firsthand what the Lord could do with delays. What my head knew was not so easily translated to my heart, however. As much as I believed He would come through for us, I did not know how He would do it.

Instead of choosing self-pity, I finally chose to remember my former church's tenacity and perseverance. It gave me hope for a happy ending to our very long journey through debt reduction. If they could get through it, so could we. If they could continue to trust God, so could I. I chose to wait to see what my God would do with our delays! It would be beautiful to see!

Your Turn…Your Perspective: What request are you waiting for the Lord to fulfill? How are you staying steadfast in the meantime? What reminders has He given you to remind you of His faithfulness?

Prayer: Lord, help me to remain faithful on my own journey to financial wholeness. Please give me reminders of Your greatness when I lose sight of Your power. I pray I do not forget Your desire for me to trust You with every aspect of my life. What You have done for others, You will do for me. I praise Your holy name.

Day 250
Birthday Friends

PROVERBS 17:8

Keith and I befriended a young couple shortly after we arrived in Kansas City. Several years later, the couple got married. It was beautiful to see their relationship come together as a union blessed by God. We enjoyed each other's company on many occasions, and spent hours solving every spiritual problem known to man. We were never short on conversation when we were with these two.

Because of our schedules, it was increasingly difficult to find time to spend with our friends. When "Mrs. Friend" and I texted each other with possible dates for us to get together, it literally took months for us to finally meet face-to-face. On one occasion, we settled on a date in July for them to join us at our table for dinner with our kids. But when it was time for them to reciprocate, we could not settle on a date. After many texts, we eventually chose October 8 – my birthday.

I told Keith I did not want to divulge the significance of the day to our friends. I did not want the evening to be about me. I wanted it to be a reconvening of friends, coming back together to share in good food and conversation. We would have plenty to discuss without my birthday being front and center.

I also nixed a birthday dinner for just the two of us because our medical expenses were rising. We saw no end in sight for the next few months. I did not want to spend money on an extravagant meal when so much money was going out for doctor's visits and supplements.

I forgot about social media, however. We were not only friends in person, we were also social friends on at least one platform. It did the honors of highlighting my upcoming celebration for my friends. So much for not telling them.

My birthday arrived, and Keith was there with a card and kisses. I went to work, and at the appointed time, we rang our friends' doorbell. We settled into a wonderful meal and enjoyed robust conversation. It was a great evening and I actually thought we pulled off not making it about me until it was time for dessert.

Our friends promptly explained a second phase of the evening was ahead of us in celebration of my special day. After ice cream and me opening my card, we all piled into their car to head off to my surprise. A few minutes later, we arrived at the theater where our friends treated us to a movie.

"Mr. Friend" called Keith earlier in the day to make sure we were available after dinner and explained how much they wanted to do something extra for us. It was a beautiful evening and I felt so special. It was great to share my birthday with two very special people and my favorite guy.

Keith and I were very intentional in limiting our entertainment to focus on debt reduction. Having our friends treat us to a movie, in honor of my birthday, felt like God provided a little bit of grace to keep us refreshed on our journey. It was the first movie we had seen in months, and it was awesome!

We were both thankful for the gift.

Your Turn…Your Perspective: How have you blessed someone recently? How has someone blessed you recently? How did each experience make you feel?

Prayer: Lord, I thank You for good friends. I pray for the opportunity to be a good friend to others. I pray to see the gifts You provide in the smallest of circumstances. I praise You for providing everything I need.

Day 251
Steady Plod

One of the things Keith and I learned about our journey to debt-freedom was how different it would be from how most people managed money. Most people saw having debt as a normal (and necessary) way of life. Those who were considered "successful" with money were the ones who learned how to manage their debt and knew how to use it appropriately.

By listening to "The Dave Ramsey Show," and studying the Bible for ourselves, we learned to go against the norm and live a life completely free of debt. We finally got to a place in our lives where we were not defined by our credit score. We learned to embrace the idea of saving for purchases instead of relying on debt.

It did not happen overnight. As much as I wanted to be completely free of debt as quickly as possible, I learned from the journey. I learned to embrace the path we were on and not attempt to rush past all the money lessons the Lord was showing us.

Keith and I learned to plod. To plod meant to take it slow. To plod meant to be deliberate. To plod meant to think first and spend second.

We first learned about steady plodding in a sermon at a church we attended shortly after moving to Kansas City. The sermon was not about money. Instead, it focused on having the faith to persevere through the trials of life. We were certainly persevering. Over time, we began to refer to our journey to freedom from debt as a steady plod. Each time we were able to pay off a debt, we celebrated a victory. Each time we experienced a financial setback, we took a deep breath and started moving forward again.

It was a slow dance of progress…two steps forward, one step back. Mark time for six months. The rhythm was choppy and made no sense. As much as we planned, we could not always anticipate what might happen from day-to-day, let alone from month-to-month. Through it all, we continued to steady plod.

The idea of a steady plod became the foundation of our life and ministry. We chose to embrace the calling the Lord gave us to show as many people as possible how to do it themselves. Each person would ultimately make the decision to continue on the path of the status quo, or make the shift to a life of financial wellness.

Steady plodding was all about taking one moment at a time, and not losing hope. Steady plodding was about believing financial freedom was possible, regardless of how long it took to achieve. Steady plodding was about not giving up when setbacks happened. Steady plodding was about drawing a line in the sand and saying once and for all, "no new debt!" Steady plodding was about getting creative and making tough choices to find a new way to do things instead of settling for debt as the only option.

Steady plodding was a paradigm shift. It was a way of life. It was our new life and we were excited to see how God would bless us because of our choice to steady plod.

Your Turn…Your Perspective: In what ways are you open to a new way of thinking about money? What "line in the sand" have you drawn recently? What area of your finances do you still need to surrender to the Lord? What's holding you back?

Prayer: Lord, I pray for the desire to steady plod. Show me the areas of my financial life where I am still impatient. Please help me surrender them to You. I want to trust the plan You have for my life. I want to learn the lessons while Your plan unfolds. Help me to do both.

Day 252
Flying Blind

JEREMIAH 17:5, 9:11

In Max Lucado's book, *God's Story, Your Story*, he tells the story of a pilot who was literally flying blind. Sixty-five-year-old Jim O'Neill suffered a stroke shortly after taking off in a small Cessna airplane from Glasgow, Scotland heading to Colchester, Essex in 2008. He was able to find his radio and issued a call for help. An air traffic controller heard the request and dispatched a seasoned military pilot to assist him. Because he could not see the instrument panels in his own plane, O'Neill would need to completely rely on the other pilot to get him to safety.

The seasoned pilot helped O'Neill navigate to the nearest airport by instructing him to make a series of small adjustments: "A gentle right turn, please. Left a bit. Right a bit."[10] When it was time to land the plane, O'Neill again needed to rely completely on the seasoned pilot to instruct him in landing the plane. Not only could he not see the instrument panel, he also could not see the runway. After eight attempts, O'Neill was able to successfully land the plane with the guidance of the seasoned pilot.

As I read the book, I realized my life was very similar to this story. I needed to constantly rely on God and the "small adjustments" I was prompted by the Holy Spirit to make. It was my responsibility to be obedient and follow through on what I was prompted to do.

This was especially necessary in relation to our finances. It was not enough to just believe God could provide. I must have faith He would provide, even when His provision was not always what I wanted or when I wanted it. I needed to trust Him and His plan for our lives. I needed to trust He knew better than we did and kept our best interest in mind.

We too were flying blind. We did not know what was in store for us in the years to come. We did not know why we would need the financial muscles we were developing. All we knew was it was necessary. If it was not, the Lord would not have allowed us to experience all we experienced along our journey to financial freedom.

I wanted to be debt-free so we could start building a home. He continued to take me on the "scenic route" in order to grow my character. I wanted to be debt-free so we could vacation as a family. He gave us the opportunity to learn how to grow as a family at home. I wanted to be debt-free so we could take the kids on a mission trip. He showed us ways to volunteer in our own community and show our kids how to be gracious and kind to people right next door.

Our journey to debt-free living truly became a blind faith walk. Even though I had to learn to do so, I chose to have faith. I chose to trust God's plan for my life. I chose to take the journey set before me and walk it with my eyes open. I wanted to see what unfolded every day. I knew His plan was perfect and I knew the result would be incredible. I chose to follow the Lord's plan instead of creating my own.

Your Turn...Your Perspectives: When was the last time you needed a "course correction?" Did you choose to be obedient? What was the outcome?

Prayer: Lord, thank You for loving me enough to have a plan for my life. Thank You for the Holy Spirit who lives inside of me and prompts me to direct my course. I pray You continue to show me corrections and keep me on the path You have laid out. I know I have free will, but what I truly want is to align myself to Your Will. I know in doing so, I will complete this journey and hear from you, "Well done."

Day 253
One for You, One for Me

HEBREWS 13:16

One year, our daughter was a little stuck while shopping for her Angel Tree gift. The name she received came with no details about what the recipient wanted for Christmas. The gift tag said, "clothing accessory." She really did not know what to do with so little information. There was no favorite color, no size associated with the gift, no extra facts to assist her.

I chose the tag on purpose because I wanted to give her the opportunity to really think through the Angel Tree process. While we did not know the recipient, I surmised by the lack of information that her life was more about survival than anything else. It was my hope for my daughter to provide a slice of sunshine for this young lady by giving her something completely unexpected.

Our daughter wandered around the store for about 30 minutes without much success. Outside of staying in the budget, our one stipulation to the kids was the item they chose must be something they would enjoy having themselves. Without size information, articles of clothing would not work. She looked at scarves and other accessories, but nothing caught her eye. Finally, she ended up in the jewelry department. I hung back to allow her to shop at her own pace but was curious about how she would work through her dilemma. She asked my opinion a few times, but I was careful not to offer any information unless it was requested.

She stopped in front of a watch display and started spinning the carousel. Suddenly, she saw it. A large turquoise watch with bling around the face stared back at her. Her eyes got wide. She turned to me and grinned so big it was contagious. I took my cue and joined her. She was so excited. I asked her what she was thinking, and she said she knew it was the perfect gift. Her real dilemma was her desire to have one for herself also, but there was only enough money to purchase one watch. I reminded her of our original goal – a gift for her unknown friend. If she wanted the watch for herself, she would first need to find a different, less expensive gift for the Angel Tree. If there was enough money after the gift was purchased, she could have the watch.

I gave her some space to make her decision. I could see she was really struggling and prayed she would make the right choice. I knew how much she wanted the watch. It took her another 15 minutes to make her decision and I was filled with pride when she chose to buy the watch for the young woman from the Angel Tree. I asked her how she felt, and she said she knew she had made the right decision. I hugged her and told her I thought so too.

What our daughter did not know was the exact same watch was already wrapped and waiting for her under our Christmas tree. It gave me great joy to see the look of surprise and appreciation on her face a few days later when she unwrapped it. Her expression was *my* favorite gift.

Your Turn...Your Perspective: What sacrifices have you made which have come back to you? Who did you share it with and why?

Prayer: Lord, I pray for the courage to go against what is popular and do what I know is the right thing to do. I pray to not give in to the world's way of giving. I thank You for the desire to serve You through giving.

Creative Christmas

PROVERBS 3:32

It was Angel Tree time again. The kids were older and finally began to fully embrace the idea of selecting a gift for someone they did not know. They approached the shopping trip with much more effort than they did when we started the tradition. It was good to see they were finally catching on to the idea of giving to others.

One year we were struggling to find suitable Angel Tree gift tags. Our stipulation for the kids was no gift cards. We wanted them to experience shopping for the person receiving the gift, and not just go to the register and purchase a gift card. In our minds, gift cards took away the joy of choosing something special.

All the Angel Tree tags at our church were gift cards. And while we were able to find another Angel Tree with actual gift recommendations, we would not be able to get the gifts back in time if the kids were to assist with picking them out. I finally called a church member who ran a non-profit. I knew their organization did not have an Angel Tree but thought she might be able to point me in the right direction.

My friend knew a single parent with five kids in need of some assistance. My first thought was our budget could not support buying Christmas gifts for five kids. I shared my concerns with her and she helped me to think outside the box. Instead of taking the kids to shop for individual gifts, shop for a family gift and supplies to make Christmas goodies. What a great idea! I always wanted to make Christmas cookies and here was my chance! I knew our kids would have a blast with the project.

I confirmed the plan with Keith and we were off to the store. Typically, our kids received a set amount of money to buy their gift. Because we were purchasing gifts for the family instead of individuals, we combined the money, took some out for cookie supplies, and spent the rest on games the entire family could enjoy. I stocked up on sprinkles, icing and cookie cutters to go along with our famous red velvet cupcakes.

We had a blast! Christmas music played throughout the house as we cut, frosted, and sprinkled sugar cookies for hours. The red velvet cupcakes were made and placed in a cupcake box. I taught our daughter how to make a decorative bow, and the cookies were placed in decorative cookie tins. Next, we wrapped the games.

Keith and the kids made the special delivery to the family on Christmas Eve. The kids were ecstatic (both the givers and the receivers), and the single parent was humbled and thankful. It was a teary afternoon.

The kids relayed the experience when they returned home, and the joy of their time with our new friends was visible on their faces. They went on and on about the kids, the cookies, and the cupcakes. It was a joy to see them excited about giving and I was so thankful they enjoyed the experience.

I was also thankful I kept an open mind about changing from two Angel Tree gifts to one family. Choosing to be stuck in the routine of the past would have caused our entire family to miss the blessing of this family. Our new form of "Angel Tree" giving was a huge hit. And, we created another beautiful Christmas memory for our young family.

Your Turn…Your Perspective: Describe your favorite Christmas giving experience. How does it compare to your current giving pattern?

Prayer: Lord, I pray to keep an open mind about giving and receiving. This season of my life will require different thoughts on both and I want to be ready. Please help me to think outside of the box with my own giving and to not limit the value of the gift given by attaching expectations.

PROVERBS 22:1

My mother often told me I was my grandmother's granddaughter, and this was certainly true in the case of shoes. My grandmother loved high-heeled shoes, and so did I. I had platform boots and pumps, spiked heels, chunky heels, pink heels, blue heels. I loved to express myself with shoes. A favorite was a pair of black leather pumps with a gold twisted heel. They were fabulous!

My friends knew of my love for shoes, and I often got shoe-related gifts – calendars, ornaments, notepads. You name it, I received it as a gift. Keith even gave me a cake ladle with a shoe handle for Christmas one year.

Unfortunately, I also inherited foot issues from my grandmother. The bones in my feet seemed to have a mind of their own, just like hers. They did not grow straight, but instead took a path all their own. Eventually, pain began to accompany my crooked feet.

After experiencing pain for quite some time, I finally scheduled surgery on my foot. The recovery was incredibly painful and took over a year. My podiatrist told me I needed to give my feet lots of room to heal. I needed square-toed, low heel shoes to allow my newly aligned toes room to be comfortable.

I owned a few pair of shoes which fit the description, but most of my shoe wardrobe was off limits. I purchased a few new pairs to get me through the healing season and looked forward to the day when I could enjoy my shoe wardrobe again. But after about 18 months, I realized this was not the case. I would never be able to wear the majority of the shoes in my closet again.

I was so disappointed, but it was time to donate. I knew others could benefit from them and saw no value in having a closet full of unused clothes and shoes. But this time was different. I did not want to just give them to strangers. These shoes were a part of me and I felt compelled to find a suitable home for them.

A few months later, Keith and I started a new FPU class. A few weeks into the class I realized one of our class members would be a perfect recipient of my shoe wardrobe. Each week she came to class wearing a cool pair of shoes and loved fashion in general. I asked her what size she wore, and sure enough, we were the same size. I explained my situation and asked if she would like my shoe wardrobe. Her eyes got wide, and she immediately said yes.

The next week I gave her almost 30 pairs of shoes. We hugged and laughed, and shared quite the girl moment before loading her car with the boxes. I admit it was hard to see them go, but I knew it was the right thing to do. I even managed to suppress the pang of envy when she walked into class a few weeks later wearing the patent leather platform boots Keith gave me for Christmas our first year together.

Finding another shoe-lover for my wardrobe of shoes was like a rite of passage for me. I could have kept them in hopes of enjoying them again someday, but I felt God leading me to be generous. I was thankful I did not allow greed to keep them from being enjoyed by another shoe queen. Grandma (and Jesus) would be proud.

Your Turn…Your Perspective: Name a time when you gave away something you really valued. Name a time when you did not. How did each experience make you feel?

Prayer: Lord, please help me not to be controlled by greed or selfishness. I pray I am always aware when these two ugly character traits come lurking. Thank You for the desire to give.

Day 256
Murphy

PROVERBS 12:27; JAMES 1:12; GALATIANS 5:22-23

While we were working our way out of debt, Keith and I stayed in an extensive relationship with Murphy. Murphy was short for Murphy's Law: "Anything that can go wrong, will go wrong."

In Financial Peace University, we learned to guard against Murphy by having an emergency fund. If debt reduction was still in process, the emergency fund was to be $1000. The idea was to put a stopgap in place to keep from using credit cards or other debt when an emergency happened. Once debt reduction was completed, the emergency fund increased to 3-6 months of household expenses.

For us, those emergencies never seemed to end. Because our cars were older model vehicles, emergency car repairs happened frequently. There were also the larger routine maintenance costs which needed to be included in the budget. Our $1000 emergency fund always came to the rescue.

Our biggest Murphy experiences were medical bills. After more than four years of debt reduction, we paid off over $180,000 in debt and cash flowed an additional $70,000 in medical bills. We would surely have incurred additional debt if we did not have our emergency fund. In every case, the starter emergency fund was rebuilt after the emergency ended. It required us to pause debt reduction to rebuild it, and it was then available for us to use the next time an emergency surfaced. It was a necessary detour from debt reduction.

The process was incredibly frustrating for me. Keith took it all in stride, but I found it difficult to keep a good attitude. I felt as if our life was on hold until we got past the debt, and in our path, was this huge toll station named "Murphy." Not only did it slow us down, it required a payment to get past.

It felt as if we were being held hostage. In my mind I knew it was a process and we were making great strides. My heart was another matter. I often felt anxious and impatient at the delays. I wrung my hands and uttered, "Oh, Lord," more times than I could count. My telltale sign of anxiety (rubbing my head) also showed up. Most times, I did not even realize how deeply the anxiety was ingrained. None of those were attributes the Lord asked us to embody. They were certainly not in the list of Godly attributes found in the Fruit of the Spirit.

I continued to work to get to a place where Murphy showing up did not affect me so negatively. I knew it was important for us to be debt-free and the delays were simply a part of the journey. Debt-freedom would come at the appointed time.

My job was to continue to persevere and put one foot in front of the other. If I said I trusted the Lord, those two actions were the outward demonstration. We would continue our steady plod, knowing the effort would all pay off in the end. The magnitude of our journey would make the victory so much sweeter when we finished.

Your Turn...Your Perspective: How do you handle setbacks? What type of setback makes the biggest emotional impact on your life?

Prayer: Lord, thank You for hope. Thank You for reminding me perseverance brings the reward. I pray You continue to keep me focused on You and not on our circumstances. I praise Your holy name.

Day 257
Butterfly Effect

PSALM 115:16; PHILIPPIANS 4:6-7; EPHESIANS 3:20-21

I had a beautiful friend who experienced some ugly things in life. There was a period of about six years where it truly was "if it ain't one thing, it's another" for her. She experienced crisis after crisis and hit brick wall after brick wall. She continually fought through it and was determined not to become even more of a statistic than she already was.

I met my friend at one of her lowest points, and my heart went out to her. I wanted to help her in ways I could not because we were not financially able. We were still deeply in debt ourselves and just beginning to get our financial head above water. We did not have the margin in our lives to help anyone else.

I wanted to write a check and just pay away her problems, but could not. I wanted to invite her into our home for a season of respite, so she could get on her feet, but could not. I wanted to buy her groceries and put gas in her car for a month or two, but could not. My heart was broken for her and there was nothing I could do except pray. So, I did.

I prayed for a breakthrough for her. I prayed for protection for her and her children. I prayed for God to reveal Himself in new ways for her to trust Him deeper. I prayed for peace which passed all understanding in her life. We were both experiencing the Butterfly Effect. Butterflies don't become butterflies until they push through their cocoon. Their beauty does not become beautiful until it experiences some pain.

My cocoon of debt was squeezing in on me, reminding me of what I could not do for others because of our lack of margin. My friend was young enough to be my daughter and I realized just how much I wanted to be a blessing to her and others like her who simply wanted a hand-up and not a hand-out. I wanted to be able to provide a shelter of comfort to her in a time of need. But I could not.

My cocoon of debt prevented all I wanted to do. But, it also empowered me. I could not assist my young friend or others like her at the moment, but I could soon. And when I could, I would. My cocoon showed me just how confining it was to live with debt. It made me made mad with the desire to be different. I would be a butterfly. I would be debt-free.

My friend's cocoon of debt was squeezing on her also, forcing her to think about her future. Many questions crossed her mind. Did she want the next six years to be different than the last? What could her life be like if she created financial margin? Did she (could she) trust God to get her through? Was she willing to do the work to make the next choices better than the last ones? Her cocoon of debt previously prevented it. But not for long.

She decided to be a butterfly. She would soar to places she could not imagine. God would make sure of it when she trusted Him with her life and her cocoon. She would conquer her circumstances and share the beautiful testimony He was creating in her. I had no doubt.

Your Turn…Your Perspective: What "cocoon" is currently financially binding you? What are you going to do about it? When you are debt-free, what will you do with your newfound freedom?

Prayer: Lord, thank You for the reminders of why it's important to be debt-free. Thank You for the prompting to not be comfortable until all debt is gone. Thank You for the opportunity to be a hand-up to those in need after I help myself.

Day 258
Jewelry Repair

PSALM 10:4

I have always had sensitive skin. As a result, I did not wear costume jewelry. I only wore 14kt gold, stainless steel, and a small amount of 925 sterling silver. In the past, I bought gold jewelry pretty regularly and managed to create quite the wardrobe of pieces. But buying gold and debt reduction were counterintuitive.

Over the years, my gold jewelry reached a state of disrepair. There were several pairs of gold earrings which were no longer wearable because of the need for maintenance. It finally got to a point where I only had two pairs of earrings I could wear. It was time to spend the money and repair the jewelry.

During lunch one day, I decided to walk out into the local shopping district and get an estimate from the jewelry store located a few blocks from my office. The store was nice, and I spent my time browsing the cases while I waited my turn. Because the shop was in the heart of downtown, I knew the overhead for the location was steep and the jewelry display cabinets matched the rent. All the items displayed were quite pricey.

When the shop owner asked how he could assist, I showed him my earrings. He could indeed repair them. Happy to have my earrings on the mend, I asked the cost. After calculating some numbers, he told me it would cost $200 to repair the earrings. Whoa!

I was not expecting the cost to be quite so much. My facial expression must have given away my surprise because he told me he would be happy to set up an installment program and I could pay him a little at a time for the repair. I thought about it for a moment and finally agreed. I filled out the paperwork and left my precious earrings with the shop owner.

Even as I walked out of the store, I knew I made a mistake. Two hundred dollars to repair two pairs of earrings? It seemed like a ridiculous amount of money. Even more, I would have to tie up my fun money for three months to pay for it. What if I needed the money for something else?

The familiar feeling of being trapped by poor money choices began to creep into my mind. My heart physically hurt, and I could hear the Holy Spirit loudly prompting me to undo this. I made it all the way back to my desk and managed to sit there for thirty minutes before I walked back to the shop.

I asked for my earrings back and explained the need to save for the repairs instead of doing an installment plan. The shop owner was visibly disappointed in the lost sale and we both knew I would not be back. He asked if I were sure I did not want to reconsider. I politely thanked him and said I was. My earrings and I left the shop a few minutes later.

I knew I avoided a really bad money decision. I was thankful I did not succumb to pride yet again. It would have been a costly mistake. A few weeks later I found a different repair shop where I was able to get the repairs done for only $80. Following the prompting of the Holy Spirit proved to be a huge savings, in more ways than one. I was thankful I chose to listen to His still small voice.

Your Turn…Your Perspective: Name a time when you went against the urgent pressing of God. How did it impact you? What did it cost you? What did it teach you?

Prayer: Lord, thank You for the lessons I have learned about the dangers of pride. Thank You for helping me to listen to the prompting of the Holy Spirit. Please help me to stay open to Your voice.

Day 259
Yellow Unicorns

LUKE 12:48B; PROVERBS 29:18; ACTS 3:19

One summer, when they were both in middle school, our kids attended our church's student ministry camp. A few weeks before camp, we found out we would be a part of the Yellow Unicorn team. We were encouraged to bring as many yellow items as possible. We were also told to bring several changes of clothes for each day because of the water-related activities. Since the camp was held on a college campus, we also needed to take bed linens and towels.

I got busy planning what everyone needed, but I did not set a budget. I'm not sure why I did not think a budget was necessary for this trip. I allocated money for when we got to camp, but did not budget for what we needed to purchase in preparation for it. Four years into paying off our debt snowball and I did not think to do a budget. Unbelievable.

What a financial disaster! Five yellow t-shirts for each of us. Yellow notebooks. Yellow bandanas. Yellow yarn for our daughter to make bracelets for all of us. I also bought extra changes of clothes and underwear for the kids (without thinking through the cost of each item). In addition, I bought disposable cameras (no cell phones allowed), sleeping bags, and more snacks than any of us could eat in four days…just in case.

I spent over $500 **preparing** for camp. Swipe…swipe…swipe went the debit card. I was an equal opportunity shopper. Every day for almost a week, I brought bags into the house with additional items for the trip. I shopped without ever considering how much I was spending.

The amount did not become real until I sat down to do the weekly reconciliation of our checking account. My heart sank. Almost all our debt snowball money was gone – spent on yellow. What on earth was I thinking when I spent all our debt snowball funds on yellow? I knew I must find a way to salvage it.

I was able to return many of the items, but the majority was not returnable for one reason or another. I felt like such a failure. Keith was gracious when he found out the final number, but I knew I let us down financially. It was an expensive lesson I would not forget. A budget was not just for everyday expenses, it was also useful when planning for trips, holiday spending or other random events. I knew what to do. I just did not think to do it. I missed a major opportunity to serve my family.

I asked forgiveness from Keith, and the Lord. I knew I was not a good steward with the resources for the month. I often told Keith I did not want my sins to be the reason we did not prosper. Fortunately, both Keith and the Lord forgave me. The "times of refreshing" Peter wrote about in Acts 3:19 could and would be mine.

I learned my expensive lesson. Neither Keith nor my Father in Heaven reminded me of my failure. Both continued to show me grace and gave me the opportunity to redeem myself. It was a blessing to still be trusted after making such a big mistake. I hoped to not disappoint either of them this way again.

Your Turn…Your Perspective: Describe your last "moment of weakness" purchase. Think of the last time you needed to ask for forgiveness. How did you handle both the purchase and the need to ask forgiveness? Have you ever been asked to forgive? Did you?

Prayer: Lord, thank You for forgiveness. I pray I am as forgiving when someone else needs grace. I pray I remember always the importance of asking for and accepting forgiveness. Help me to also think before I spend. I want to learn to be a better steward of what You have given me to manage.

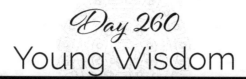

Day 260
Young Wisdom

DEUTERONOMY 11:18A; MARK 4:8

Keith and I gave our kids the opportunity to handle money and make their own financial decisions as often as possible. Since they did not live with us year-round, we only had about 2 months a year to teach them what we learned about money face-to-face. One year at church camp, we got to see if it was working.

We were two of the designated chaperones for the trip but opted to not chaperone our kids' rooms. We were able to see them during meals and assembly, but their group leaders were in charge during all other times.

One morning during breakfast, our daughter asked if I wanted to join her and her roommate. I quickly accepted, seizing the moment to spend some time with her and get her perspective on the sessions the night before. She had other plans however.

Our daughter called me over because she wanted reinforcement. She was in the midst of delivering a lecture to her roommate on why she did not need to buy a fifth t-shirt. Her roommate already purchased one of every item in the camp gift shop and was working her way through the college bookstore searching for other things to buy. The young lady had already spent over $300 and there was still another day of camp to go before returning home.

I chose not to interject myself into the conversation, but instead watched as our daughter worked hard to convince her new friend not to spend all her money on stuff. I was proud of how well she articulated herself. And, I was proud of how passionate she was in attempting to be a voice of reason.

In the end, our daughter's roommate did spend all her money. She did not even leave enough for dinner on our last night so several of her friends chipped in to pay for her meal. She went home with several t-shirts, sweatshirts, mugs, book bags and other miscellaneous items. Our daughter was disappointed. She did not prevent her friend from spending all her money.

I consoled her by helping her focus on what she learned from the week. She tried to educate her friend on the importance of choosing carefully before purchasing. She tried to impart the importance of budgeting. She tried to teach her friend the value of prioritizing. She was the voice of reason.

In the end, her friend made her own buying decisions. I reminded our daughter of another lesson – she knew enough about spending and saving to teach someone else. She was learning how to share and explain finances in a way others could understand. A very special lesson indeed.

Keith and I were laying a solid financial foundation for our kids. We were thankful the Lord allowed us to see how the life lessons we were teaching took root in good soil. Our daughter was only 13 at the time and the future held many crossroads where her understanding of God's principles on managing money would test her. We were determined for good seed and good ground to prevail. Our goal was simply to continue to give her as many opportunities as possible to strengthen her foundation. She was off to a great start.

Your Turn…Your Perspective: Think of a time when you attempted to give someone wise counsel. What happened? What happened the last time someone offered you wise counsel?

Prayer: Lord, I pray for boldness in my finances. Help me to not be silent with what I am learning, but to proclaim the "good news" of life without debt. I want my financial life to reflect You with every money choice I make.

Day 261
Diapers

PSALM 10:3; 2 CORINTHIANS 12:7-10

A friend of mine was having a baby. She and her husband had been trying to get pregnant for quite some time and were just about to go the route of in vitro fertilization when she got pregnant. Everyone was excited for them.

A few months before the baby was due, several of her friends and family members held a baby shower for her. Having attended many baby showers in the past, I knew she would receive a ton of cute little onesies and outfits for her new baby boy. I also knew, from spending a lot of time with my other friends after the births of their babies, just how many of those onesies would never be worn or worn only once or twice before they were too small. So instead of going with cute, I opted for a more practical gift. I bought diapers.

I decided to make my purchase at my favorite big box store. I knew it was the cheapest place to purchase large quantities of diapers because a friend mentioned it just a few weeks earlier. Our budget during this time was really tight. It was July, which meant our grocery bill would almost double because the kids were with us. It also meant camp fees and an increase in the amount of money we put aside for gas to shuttle the kids back and forth each week. And finally, July meant a little extra money needed to be set aside for entertainment. We tried to budget for a matinee for the family or dinner for one evening.

When I got to the store and looked at the selection of diapers, I realized I did not have enough to buy a name brand. I panicked. What was I going to do? There was more than enough to buy the store brand diapers, but not nearly enough to buy the name brand.

My mind swirled with doubt. What would my friend think when she unwrapped the gift and saw the store brand logo? Would her friends think I was cheap? Maybe I could convince Keith to allow me to increase the budget to get the name brand diaper. Maybe I should just go to a different store and buy fewer name brand diapers in order to stay in my budget.

I stood there for a very long time allowing my mind to swing back and forth through the options. I was ashamed to be so paralyzed by pride. Every time I thought I conquered it, there it was again. The big question was if I would allow pride to blow our budget for a box of diapers for a friend.

I finally summoned the courage to load the store brand diapers into the cart and headed to the check-out line. But, I did not go to the baby shower. I could not find the courage to have my store brand diapers opened in front of everyone. Instead, I made an excuse for not coming, and missed the special day because of pride.

In reality, the saddest part was revealed when I finally gave my friend the gift a few weeks later. She thanked me profusely and said those were the diapers she and her husband decided to use. I purchased exactly what she needed and wanted.

Once again, I allowed pride to steal my joy. I prayed it would be the last time. It was painful to know I missed such a special day because of it.

Your Turn…Your Perspective: What is the thorn in your flesh? What has it cost you?

Prayer: Lord, please help me to not be controlled by pride or any other sinful behavior. Your grace is sufficient. Please help me trust it.

Library Love Affair

PSALM 1:1

President Harry S. Truman said, "not all readers are leaders, but all leaders are readers." Even before Keith and I knew of the quote, we were believers who brought large book collections into our marriage. During early budget cuts, we knew our book buying would need to be budgeted. Even buying used books started adding up.

I am not sure when we turned to the library to feed our book cravings. I was simply thankful we did. Our county library system was a godsend. Traditional books, e-books, audiobooks, and books on CD were all available to us. We were also able to access their inter-library loan program. If the county library did not own a title (in whatever format we needed), they searched for it through inter-library loan. Our books sometimes came from other county and university libraries from around the world. It was a blessing.

Our library made it possible to completely remove book buying from our budget. We also removed DVD rentals since their DVD library was extensive. We cut it all out. Everyone in our house was issued a library card and we could each check out up to 30 items (books, DVDs, etc.) at a time. It gave us lots of options to choose from. We did not mind waiting a few months to see new video releases or read the latest book on leadership, finances or spiritual growth. There was always a stack at home to keep us busy.

Over the years, using our public library saved us hundreds of dollars. It was all redirected to debt reduction. If a book was purchased, it came from our individual play fund. No "house" money was used for books or movies. The rare exception was a DVD or book purchased to give as a gift.

Our kids understood the process and looked forward to using their library card to stock up on their favorite books and movies. We all trekked to the closest branch at the beginning of their visit each summer. Star Wars and Star Trek marathons were scheduled for lazy Sunday afternoons. Each could also be found lounging around our duplex with a book of choice. Our son transitioned from readers into chapter books a summer early because of the extensive collection available through our library.

The more we learned about leading God's people on the journey to financial stewardship, the more we wanted to learn. We began to share our library tip with anyone interested in tightening the budget further. Our frugality was often met with snickers. Were we too cheap to spend $1 on a movie rental? Did we not get tired of waiting until Christmas to watch the summer blockbuster?

We just let them laugh. We knew we had stumbled onto a great money saver. Being good stewards meant getting out of debt as soon as possible. Having a love affair with our library proved to be a big part of our action plan. Every book not purchased was interest paid on a student loan. Every DVD not rented got us closer to home ownership. We held on to those hopes and stayed the course. We thanked our Lord for the library every step of the way.

Your Turn...Your Perspective: What is the smallest strategy you use in managing a budget? What was your thought process when you chose to implement it? Have you ever had to defend your strategy? If so, how did if feel?

Prayer: Lord, help me to never allow the criticism of others to deter me from my plan. Thank You for the resolve to become debt-free. I pray to constantly search for ways to cut my budget and get to a life of Christ-centered financial wellness as soon as possible. Please help me stay the course.

Day 263
Turbo Drive

PSALM 1:3

One month, when I took my car in for routine maintenance, the mechanic told us the turbo drive on the car was malfunctioning. It was one of those repairs which required opening the system up before you really knew what the problem was, and how much it would cost. Our mechanic told us the worst-case scenario would be around $1300 and asked if we wanted to proceed with the repair.

Keith and I reviewed the budget and opted to redirect a portion of our debt snowball money to get the car repaired. We saved $125 every month for routine maintenance, but the debt snowball funds served as the first line of defense when we needed more cash to manage emergency expenses. We scheduled the appointment and dropped the car off for servicing.

I was surprised by my response to the car repair. In the past, a car repair of this size would have caused me a lot of anxiety. I would have fretted over the money not being spent on student loan repayment and would have felt frustrated. I would have spent days going over our finances in my mind, recalculating how much we "could" have put towards debt reduction if the car did not need a repair. I would have worked myself into a frenzy because our repayment timeline was altered once again.

But I was now a different woman.

I finally realized car maintenance and repairs were inevitable. And even though we planned for the smaller ones, there would be times when we would need to divert funds to pay for the larger, more complex repairs. The diversion of money from paying off debt to car maintenance was a necessary part of our journey. I could allow negative emotions to rule my thoughts in this area, or I could choose to focus on getting the repair completed and restart payments to the debt snowball the next pay period.

At a time in my life when negative emotions about money were primary, it was nice to have a glimpse of what my emotional thought-life was supposed to look like. I guess I was finally getting the hang of what it meant to not be controlled by my money and my circumstances. I was making progress.

A few hours after we dropped off the car, the mechanic called to let us know the extent of the repair. Imagine my excitement when I learned the repair consisted of replacing a hose and not the entire system. The cost was closer to $150 instead of $1300. Praise the Lord!

What if I allowed worry to overtake me? So much energy would have been spent on nothing. I would have lost sleep and missed the joy around me for no reason at all. My fear would have replaced my faith and I would have missed the beauty of glimpsing what a future without worrying about money looked like.

I was thankful I got it right. God was always in control, and if we chose to keep our eyes on Him, we would not lose sight of the goodness around us, even when faced with difficult situations.

Your Turn…Your Perspective: What is your current emotional state as it relates to money? When unexpected expenses show up, which emotions show up first? Are they positive or negative?

Prayer: Lord, I want a breakthrough in my thinking, even if it's only a small one. I pray to continually choose to stay rooted in Your Will. Help me to completely let go of my money worries. I trust You, Jesus.

Day 264
Mixmaster

I think I started baking when I was around 10 years old. My mother owned a Sunbeam Mixmaster stand mixer and used it to whip up magic each Sunday. I got my baking gene from her.

Saturdays were filled with me baking cookies. I cultivated a few old faithful recipes like pecan crispies, oatmeal raisin, and peanut butter; but was also open to trying new ones like wedding balls and coconut macaroons. Brownies and blondies made the list every now and then, but cookies were my thing. I even spent about 5 years working on the perfect oatmeal raisin recipe (shortening made a chewy cookie, butter made it crispy).

Years later, my brother and I pooled our money and bought our mom a KitchenAid mixer. She passed the Sunbeam Mixmaster on to me. My first stand mixer. I loved it! We made beautiful music (and cookies) together. I did not care that it was old. I figured I would eventually replace it, but never got around to it.

As a newlywed, my baking increased. It was a great bonding opportunity with the kids. We learned how to make gluten-free Angel food cake, experimented with zucchini muffins (a disaster), and mastered red velvet cupcakes complete with homemade cream cheese frosting. My 30 year old Mixmaster held strong and rose to each new adventure.

But I still longed for a KitchenAid mixer. It was the Cadillac of mixers and I had wanted one for years. Ultimately, it was a "want" and not a "need." Plus, the price point was way too high to justify purchasing one. A ton of debt was still left to pay off, and my Mixmaster worked just fine. Window shopping would have to suffice until after we finished paying off debt.

One day, I was in a hurry and attempted to cream frozen butter with my Mixmaster. I forgot to take it out to reach room temperature and needed to get a cake in the oven quickly. In my haste, I bent the beaters. Shoot! I was able to straighten them out enough to get the cake mixed, but I could tell there was significant damage to "Old Faithful."

My first thought was, "Yay! Now I can buy a KitchenAid!" My day of owning one was at hand. I killed my Mixmaster and could now buy my beloved KitchenAid. Keith would definitely understand. My "want" suddenly became a "need."

The sinking feeling set in quickly as if to keep me from moving too fast. Almost immediately, I knew my time for a KitchenAid was still a ways away. The Holy Spirit was telling my heart to be patient. As much as I wanted to race out and buy a new KitchenAid, I knew it was not time.

I did not even make the request known to Keith. I went online, found replacement beaters, and ordered them. The entire purchase (including shipping) was less than $20. I would have to wait a little longer for a KitchenAid. My Mixmaster was back in service within the week, and we continued to enjoy all its culinary creations. Longevity still prevailed, and I got another chance to work on patience and priority spending.

Your Turn…Your Perspective: Give an example of a time when a big "want" derailed your financial goals. What did you do about it? What did the experience teach you?

Prayer: Lord, please help me manage wants and needs. I know only what I do for Christ will last. I pray to not get sidetracked by my many "wants." Please help me keep purchases in perspective. Help me always be open to the prompting of the Holy Spirit.

I-70 Bound

ECCLESIASTES 3:1

The main interstate between Kansas City (where we lived) and St. Louis (where our kids lived) was I-70. It was a straight 4-hour trip from our house to their mother's house. Because we made the trip as often as we did, we had the routine down to a science. We knew which exits were best for coffee, which exits were best for iced tea, and (of course) which exits had the cleanest bathrooms. All four of us knew the routine well. Each time we made the trip, we all settled in for the ride.

On one such trip back to St. Louis to take the kids home, the low battery light came on. We were only about an hour into the trip and in an area which was not well populated. Since we traveled as much as we did, car maintenance was something we took seriously. We traveled too much to not take care of our vehicles.

The situation surprised us both because we had not seen the light before, but we did not want to take any chances. We mapped out the closest auto parts store in the next populated area and made the small detour. Sure enough, we needed a new battery. We checked the car maintenance fund to see how much money was available. Because we saved for car repairs monthly, there was more than enough to purchase what we needed.

Everyone piled out of the car while Keith went in and decided which battery to purchase. The service guy took him through all the choices for our make and model of vehicle. He asked questions about warranties and dependability as he considered our options. After a few moments, he made his decision and paid for the battery. He chose not to buy the cheapest one, but instead purchased one with a decent lifespan. The store clerk assisted with the install in the parking lot, and our detour took less than an hour.

As we all piled back into the car to settle in for the rest of the journey, Keith and I looked at each other with grins on our faces. It was a car battery, not bad luck. It was $149 which would be taken from the car repair envelope. It was not the end of the world. It was also just a slight delay which only meant we would get home later. More importantly, we were not stranded on the side of the road.

The incident was not drama filled. It was not a credit card purchase. It was not really even a big decision. It was a blip on the screen of life which we would scarcely remember months later. It felt so good to make a necessary decision which did not send us into a financial and emotional tailspin. We did not use money allocated to pay bills to get the car repaired. We used car money to get the car repaired. It was a decision made completely free of negative emotion.

I knew I would never forget what it felt like to be able to take care of our family financially. It could have been a very different story if we were not financially prepared for such an event. It also felt good to know our kids were able to see how to handle an emergency car situation with a level head and cash. I was thankful we chose to be prepared by continuing to add to our car maintenance fund on a monthly basis. What a blessing it turned out to be on one of many trips on I-70.

Your Turn…Your Perspective: Do you have a car repair envelope? How do you respond to a situation which requires more time and money than you have available?

Prayer: Lord, thank You for the diligence to stay prepared. I pray for financial margin in my life. I pray to keep a level head when faced with emergency situations. Thank You for provision.

Day 266
He Who Angers You

PROVERBS 11:6; JAMES 1:19

I got a call one day from my mother informing me of her upcoming knee surgery. I looked at the calendar and my heart sunk. I was scheduled for a week of training and would not be able to go home for the procedure. Since the training was a special leadership development program, competition to get in was tough and no absences were allowed. I knew I would not be able to participate and still be with my mother for her surgery.

The program was large enough to need two groups for attendees. Training for each group was scheduled several weeks apart. The only way for me to stay in the program, and go home for my mother's surgery, was to change groups. It was a long shot, but I asked anyway. Imagine my surprise when they agreed to try.

Unfortunately, moving me was a logistical nightmare. I needed to be placed in a new coaching group and my new coach must agree to take an additional person. Class size and group activities would be adjusted in both groups – all to accommodate my request. The program manager told me he required a few days to be sure all the changes could be accommodated.

I immediately began looking at airline tickets. The surgery was a few weeks away, and I was not sure if tickets would be super cheap or through-the-roof expensive. I held my breath and prayed for a reasonable rate. I was amazed to find a ticket for under $200!

I knew it would not be available for long. I really wanted to buy it, but my group change request was not yet confirmed. If I bought the ticket, and the logistics did not work, we would be out almost $200. If I did not buy the ticket, I ran the risk of the ticket price increasing. I struggled and checked my email constantly. I was tempted to send a request for an update on the status of the move but did not want the program manager to know my level of impatience. I waited, and waited, and waited. The ticket price did not change.

Friday came and went with no email, and I was anxious all weekend. I told myself not to work myself into a frenzy. Finally, Monday afternoon as I was preparing to leave for the evening, I received an email confirming my transfer between groups. It was time to buy a ticket, but now it was over $350!

I was heartbroken and angry. If the email had come sooner, we would have saved well over $150. I brooded for days. Finally, on day four of being angry, Keith looked at me and said, "He who angers you controls you." Then he left me with my thoughts. I knew he was right and began to pray. Slowly the Lord helped me shift my perspective from entitlement to gratitude.

In my moment of wanting to get the cheapest possible flight, I forgot the blessing of the transfer. I was now able to be a part of the leadership development program *and* go home for my mother's surgery. I received the blessing of both, and I sat there angry because I did not also get a cheap ticket.

Conviction is a humbling feeling. It can motivate you to be better or bitter. I spent almost a week bordering on bitter (certainly angry). Keith called me on it, which sent me to my knees. I'm thankful the Lord chose to show grace. I chose to be better.

Your Turn…Your Perspective: When was the last time you lost perspective? How do you avoid bitterness when circumstances do not go as you anticipated?

Prayer: Lord, thank You for the reminder of perspective. I pray to not lose sight of the good found in every circumstance. When I do, please draw me near and guide me back to You.

Day 267
Misplaced Faith

PROVERBS 13:18

The more we talked about our financial journey, the more people began to associate Keith and me with getting out of debt. We often found ourselves standing with individuals looking for assistance with their financial picture. We were happy to help.

After one such request, we found ourselves sitting with a young woman whose budget needed some tweaking. After a few suggestions, she was amazed to "find" several hundred extra dollars available in her family's monthly budget. Seeing how much of a difference a few changes made gave her the courage to ask for additional help.

The woman and her husband purchased a new vehicle using a car loan. Her husband did not want the loan, but she insisted. There was more than enough money in their savings to purchase the car outright, but she did not want to use any of it. She did not feel comfortable removing money to purchase the car.

She was struggling from misplaced faith. After she finished sharing the story and asked what I felt they should do, I took a deep breath. I knew my next words would significantly impact her and I did not want to get them wrong. It was not the time to jump right in and offer my opinion. I knew I needed to be slow to speak and wait for the Holy Spirit to guide me.

I started by asking more questions. How much did they have in savings? What did they spend on the car? How much were the payments? Did they have a budget when they made their purchase? She answered all my questions and began to see where I was headed with them. The more questions I asked, the more clarity she received. When I stopped asking questions, she simply stared at me. I asked her what she was thinking.

Through our conversation, she realized they spent more on the car because they got a loan. They would have purchased a less expensive vehicle if cash were used. She realized the property taxes and car insurance on the new vehicle were 15-20% higher. The new car would cost more than she imagined.

The lesson I was hoping she learned took a little more prodding to come to the surface. After a few more questions, another light bulb came on in her eyes. She slowly realized her misplaced faith. By holding on to the money in savings, and choosing instead to get a car loan, she put her faith in her family's ability to earn instead of trusting the Lord to supply all their needs.

She did not want to use the money from savings because of her fear they would need it for something bigger. While the Lord calls us to save and be prepared for mishaps in life, He also calls us to owe no man anything. It was one thing to have the realization of sin, but was something totally different to remove it.

When I saw the woman in church the next Sunday, she was grinning from ear to ear. It was contagious so I was already laughing when she shared the good news. They took money from savings and paid off the car! Her excitement was a beautiful sight and I was thankful to have been a part of it.

Your Turn…Your Perspective: Describe a time when you experienced misplaced faith. How did you overcome it?

Prayer: Lord, I want to trust You. I do not want to be afraid to pay cash for large purchases. I want to walk in faith and not by sight. I want to be bold with my finances.

Day 268
Out of Order

Our debt-free journey was a few years old when we ran into some friends. They were Financial Peace University graduates and were members of the first class we taught. The last time we talked with them, they were trying to decide if it was time to buy a home. We encouraged them to rent for a while longer since they were still paying off a large amount of debt and did not yet have an emergency fund.

As we were catching up on life, they shared they were in the process of purchasing a home. It was an uncomfortable moment of silence for my friend. She thought she disappointed us by making the purchase. It hurt my heart to see her discomfort. The way she handled the conversation showed she knew, in her heart, it was not a wise decision. It was sad to see her place more emphasis on what we thought of their decision than on the decision itself.

We were disappointed, but not in the way they expected. We were not disappointed in their decision to purchase a home while still in debt and without an emergency fund. We were disappointed because they were willing to expose their family to so much risk. We knew THEY knew how financially danger-ous it was to purchase a home out of order. Yet, they felt the risk was acceptable.

We all knew the Bible stated to "count the costs" before beginning any project. And this scripture specifically referred to a building project. Dave Ramsey taught in Financial Peace University that a "cost" many people did not appropriately consider was risk. We knew firsthand how unwise it was to not con-sider it. We hoped our friends would know it also.

Our friends shared our strong desire to own a home. And we all knew how much risk came with the decision to purchase before being completely debt-free with a fully funded emergency fund. It was not a risk we were willing to take. We counted the costs and chose to err on the side of caution even though it would delay our own building project by several years.

We already experienced financial detours which would have been difficult to navigate if we spent any more on housing. We chose to continue to take the path of low risk and wait a little longer before purchasing a home. And, since our housing expenses were well below the 25% suggested in FPU, a large portion of our budget was available for debt repayment.

As for our friends, we wished them well and said a silent prayer. We hoped they would not experience the full weight of the risk they chose. It would not change us or how we felt about them, but I knew their lives would forever be affected by their decision. The encounter was a reminder to us to stay on the path God laid out in His Word. Our time of home ownership would be a blessing because we chose to wait. It gave us a great goal to work towards.

Your Turn...Your Perspective: When was the last time you had to make a tough decision to stay on your plan? Have you ever decided you knew what was not in your best interest? What was the result?

> *Prayer: Lord, please help me stay in order, even though it is not easy or popular. Help me to be mindful of the "cost" of risk. I pray to not allow my desires for more to get ahead of what I can afford.*

Day 269
Financial Infidelity

PROVERBS 6:15

Over the years, Keith and I coached a lot of couples. Some were in healthy marriages and were just looking to gain a better understanding of how to manage their money. Others, however, were in a really bad financial state. Of the ones not doing well with money, almost all of them experienced some level of financial infidelity. "Financial infidelity is any money decision – a big one, a small one, one you can afford, or one you can't – that's made without the knowledge or consent of your partner."[11]

When I first saw the title of Bethany and Scott Palmer's book, *First Comes Love, Then Comes Money,* I was intrigued. As I began to read it, I was convicted. I did not think I was unfaithful to Keith. Bethany and Scott revealed otherwise. What seemed "harmless" in my mind could become a major concern if left unchecked.

Keith and I believed ours was a healthy money relationship. However, we realized through our reading we both committed financial infidelity in our marriage more than once. My financial infidelity almost always revolved around the grocery budget. It was not uncommon at this point in our marriage for me to overspend the grocery budget and justify it as needing to feed my family.

His was related to car repair/car maintenance. Our cars needed to be maintained, right? What was wrong with going ahead and getting the repair, even though we did not discuss it and there was no room in the budget? In his mind, he was taking care of his family and keeping us all safe.

After reading about financial infidelity, we realized we were in dangerous territory. Small infidelity often led to bigger infidelity. It was a slippery slope of trust. It did not matter the dollar amount. The issue was purely emotional. We took the voice of our spouse away when we chose to not include them in the decision.

The more we read, the more we could see our own relationship revealed. We also saw glimpses of our friends and coaching clients. Constant communication was so important, and we began discussing every money decision. It diffused so many unnecessary arguments and "intense moments of fellowship." After making the switch to communicating about all financial decisions, our conversations about money became so much more positive. We chose to discuss every purchase.

Once we were on the right track, we assisted those clients experiencing the same issues in their marriages. We made a habit of sharing the Palmer's book with all our married clients. We often spoke of how emasculating it was to a husband to find out his wife was hiding purchases. We explained to husbands how fearful their wives were when they hid the family's financial well-being from them.

Marriage is a partnership and money is a huge part of it. We chose to keep the lines of communication open in our own marriage and worked to help our clients do the same. Our goal was to help as many people avoid financial infidelity as possible.

Your Turn…Your Perspective: Have you witnessed the effects of financial infidelity in your own relationship or others'? What was the impact?

Prayer: Lord, I continue to pray for transparency with my money. Please help me to not hide, from myself or anyone else. I thank You for grace and compassion in my finances, even as You desire for me to be a better steward of the resources You have given.

Nix the Tailspin

We had been in the thick of debt reduction for almost 5 years when I noticed the shift. Years three and four were tough. An incredible amount of medical expenses, crazy car issues and a lot of life emergencies hammered us with one financial hit after the other. It was literally months of paying no more than minimum payments on our debt. We were worn out – spiritually and financially.

Some days I felt as if I were in a trance, simply going through the motions of life. It was all we could do to get to the end of another week. It was all we could do to just keep going.

One day, I told Keith I was going for a walk. I had not ventured out much over the last few years because we were very careful with the amount of gas we spent and did not do many unnecessary trips. Add to the mix a general state of not feeling well, and staying home made more sense than exploration. But on this day, I wanted a change of scenery. I needed a change of scenery.

I found a trail near our house, and just began to walk and talk with God. The beauty of nature was always calming to me, and I was thankful for the time to step away from our financial situation and be in awe of the wonder of God.

As I walked, I began to think about the last few weeks and months. We had been back and forth to Dallas, TX from Kansas City for medical care, and it was not easy or cheap. The trips were filled with hotel stays, expensive out of network doctor's visits and medical labs, wear and tear on the vehicle, gas, and tolls. We spent a lot of money attempting to find answers to our medical mysteries. It was exhausting.

What the Lord showed me during my time with Him on the trail was profound. He reminded me of the medical meltdown I experienced three years earlier when we were faced with a $600 medical bill. Even though the money to pay for the visit was available in our checking account, I was frustrated at the need to use it for medical care. I wanted it to go to the debt snowball and could not emotionally handle it when faced with the realization of the funds needing to be redirected.

The Lord showed me just how far I had come in the last few years. I could now approach each financial situation with greater clarity and peace of mind than in the past. I could also logically review the facts and join Keith in the decision-making process without going into a tailspin emotionally. The delay in reaching the end of our debt snowball no longer frustrated me quite as much as it did in the beginning. God showed me the strengthening in my financial wellness muscle and the deepening of my faith in Him.

During my time with Him on the trail, He showed me the good which came from the experience. I could not deny the growth and maturity I had gained. And while the light at the end of the tunnel was still not visible, I knew I was now equipped to get through the journey. I was both thankful and hopeful. We would get through it. I no longer doubted it.

Your Turn…Your Perspective: What experience have you had which caused you to grow spiritually? What was the turning point when you knew you'd make it through?

Prayer: Lord, thank You for glimpses of hope. Thank You for reminding me just how capable You are of getting me through whatever circumstance I am experiencing. Thank You for peace.

Day 271
Buy and Not Build

ISAIAH 5:8

Shortly after Keith and I got married we were driving around our new city with the kids looking at houses. We were deeply in debt with a very sketchy plan for getting rid of it. Debt was still a way of life for us and we did not yet know we could actually live without it. We stumbled into a new housing community late on a Saturday afternoon.

Because it was later in the day, we were the only guests visiting the model home. The agent was happy to chat with us, and over pretzels, he shared why building a home was a better way to enter home ownership. I was star struck. In my mind, it made so much sense. We would have the opportunity to build exactly what we wanted. Keith was not so convinced, but went along mainly because he could not convince me otherwise.

We were going to build a house! We were going to build a house as soon as we cleared some debt. We were going to build a house as soon as we could find some financing. We were going to build a house as soon as we could afford a mortgage payment.

The reality was it would be a while before we could build a house. But I was okay. While we continued to make our way out of debt, I occupied my mind by designing our home. I spent hours digging around the internet looking for the perfect kitchen layout, the perfect free-standing soaking tub for the master bath, the perfect sectional for our media room. I found the perfect quartz countertop, the perfect bamboo flooring, the perfect toilets, the perfect kitchen sink. I found it all and neatly organized my photos on Pinterest. I accumulated so many "likes," you would have thought I was an interior designer.

I made design plans for almost four years. It was not supposed to take so much time, but it did. The medical bills and car repairs may have delayed our debt-reduction plan, but they did not slow down my research. I knew the day was coming when we would be able to choose a lot, a builder, and get started on our dream home.

I do not remember when the thought first hit me. In addition to planning every square inch of our dream home, I also spent my time learning everything I could about God and money. I found blogs and books to read, speakers to follow, and "The Dave Ramsey Show" to listen to on a daily basis. At some point along the way, I realized it actually did cost more to build than it did to buy.

Building meant paying full retail instead of getting a discount. Building meant the added expense of personalizing the space even before we moved in. Building meant all the additional items would not be included in the mortgage, like window treatments and landscaping. Building meant more money.

I slowly realized our first home together as a family would probably not be one we built. If we were going to continue on our journey of Christ-centered financial wellness, it would be more practical to buy. Building may or may not come down the line. It was a thought I needed to embrace if I were to achieve contentment in this area. It was time to be a big girl and allow practicality to reign. I knew I could do it.

Your Turn…Your Perspective: What areas of contentment do you struggle with most? How has a lack of contentment in an area derailed your financial plans in the past?

Prayer: Lord, thank You for growing pains. Even though You sometimes choose to bless me with extravagance, I know practicality is best. I pray for contentment in all areas of my life.

Day 272
The Speed of Cash

PROVERBS 30:24-25

We were in Dallas for yet another visit to our doctor. It was not an easy day for either of us. It was a day filled with pokes and prods, oxygen and tests. We were both exhausted as we sat in our hotel room eating a drab meal of carrots and chicken breasts. The conversation was about the details of the day and where we would go from there, both in terms of our finances and our health. It all seemed so overwhelming. We were both so ready to be done with our debt and our health issues, but neither seemed ready to leave us.

While I remember what we were eating at the time, I do not remember what part of the conversation led to Keith's next question. With a look of trepidation in his eyes he asked, "What do you think about us saving to pay cash for a house?"

I let the question hang in the air for a lot longer than I should have. My mind was racing. I obviously did not hear him correctly. What I *thought* I heard was my husband asking if I would continue to live in a rental duplex for at least another five years. This was instead of getting a mortgage and purchasing a home the moment we were out of debt, with an emergency fund and down payment in place. I *thought* I heard my husband ask me to put off our future for an even longer time to pay cash for our home.

I was slow to speak because I did not trust my voice. I felt betrayed and frustrated. The first few years of our marriage were not anything like I expected because of the massive amount of debt we carried with us like a family heirloom. It was a daunting task to get so much of it paid off, and we sacrificed so much in the process already. And now my husband was asking me to sacrifice even more by delaying a home purchase.

The conversation was not fun for either of us. It was not filled with dreams of color swatches and window treatments. It did not have anything to do landscape designs or whether we would buy a gas grill or a charcoal one. It was not about our desire to have a home filled with laughter and friends. It was all about the call to completely surrender to God's plan for our lives.

We were not only choosing to follow God's plans for our finances, but we were also teaching others to do the same. Where was our faith? Did we trust God to provide for us completely? Would He not make a way for us if we chose to honor Him this way?

We both sat there in a dazed state. And as much as I did not want to surrender to God and submit to my husband, I knew I was called to do both. We both chose this path. We both chose to trust His provision. He did not fail us in the past, and we knew He would not fail us in the future. This was simply a new opportunity to trust Him and His provision.

We decided to buy a home at the speed of cash. We would continue our steady plod and be in awe at how God chose to honor our commitment to Him, and His plan for our lives. I did not doubt He would do amazing things which could only be attributed to Him. I looked forward to seeing how He did it.

Your Turn…Your Perspective: When was the last time you chose to trust God for something big in your life? What was the end result? How did it impact your ability to trust Him for more?

Prayer: Lord, please give me the courage to make the hard financial choices. I pray to be patient and trust Your plan for our lives. Thank You for loving me enough to protect me from myself when I ignore what You know is best for me. I trust You, Jesus.

Day 273
The Last to Go

PROVERBS 6:3; ROMANS 14:13

Through our years of teaching Financial Peace University and providing coaching services to our own clients, Keith and I met people at all stages of financial well-being. Some were committed to becoming (and staying) debt-free, but many were not. We were able to spot the difference almost immediately because we spent time on both sides of the conversation ourselves. We were not completely committed to the plan in the beginning. We tried a modified approach to getting out of debt and it did not work. We finally began to make headway on our debt when we decided to not incur any new debt. It was a huge paradigm shift and the beginning of the real journey to become financially well.

Slowly, we closed all our credit card accounts and committed to not using them for future purchases. We paid cash for what we needed and reviewed carefully what we wanted. The last card to go was the American Express card. It took us years to let go of it because we "thought" it was necessary.

We still planned to build a home and needed a construction loan. The loan officers we spoke to all said the same thing. It would be almost impossible (and a lot more expensive) to secure a construction loan without a credit score. Traditional mortgages were candidates for the manual underwriting process, but not construction loans. We could forgo building a home and use a manually underwritten loan to buy, but we really wanted to build.

We decided to keep the American Express account open and used it for hotel stays to keep our score active. We justified our decision because of our "special circumstance." A construction loan was important, and we were building. It was okay, right? We knew the world's way of managing money would allow it, but what would Jesus say?

I never felt authentic when we used the card. Instead, I felt like a fraud. Our own selfish desires caused us to hold on to the opportunity for debt. Did we need to build? No. We wanted to build. Why should we not build? Did we not deserve to build? Was there not a way to build without a credit score? I asked myself these questions over and over in my mind. I wanted to be true to the process because I believed it worked. But did I really believe it worked when we still kept a credit card account open? Back and forth I volleyed the questions in my mind.

The entire time, we continued to teach FPU and help as many others as possible find their way out of debt. We chose to be transparent about our own dilemma. We did not want to justify our actions but chose full disclosure to give hope to others. The Bible calls us to not allow our own actions to cause another to stumble. Choosing full disclosure was a way to help others see our own struggle – it was the only way to be authentic.

When we decided to pay cash for our house, the need for a credit score disappeared. It also meant the need for a construction loan disappeared. We would no longer have to compromise on our desire to completely live without credit. It felt good to be in a place of authenticity.

Your Turn…Your Perspective: Name a time when you did not feel financially authentic. What was the end result? How did it impact you spiritually?

Prayer: Lord, thank You for the desire to be authentic. I pray to always be aware of the slippery slope leading away from it. Please help me stay alert for how my walk impacts those around me. Guide me on this journey.

Day 274
Soldier Dollars

We were in Dallas, TX for a doctor's appointment. It was a day of pokes and prods for both of us and we were weary. The allergy testing room was filled with others just like us. We were all looking for solutions to environmental health issues of one kind or another.

The kindred spirit which existed among the patients was tender. Everyone there meant it when they said, "I know how you feel," because they did. They all spent hard earned money to venture to Dallas, seeking treatment from one of the best in the business. The costs associated with each visit reflected our doctor's status in the industry which made paying for care daunting for most of us. Many resorted to debt to pay for their care.

We were careful not to judge. Just because we were in the process of being delivered from debt did not mean others were ready to do the same. We were fortunate to be able to continue working while we sought solutions to our heavy metal poisoning, but many others were not able to do so.

I was chatting with the guy sitting next to me. I honestly do not remember what we were discussing or how it related to our care. But he made a statement I will never forget. He said, "Dollars are like soldiers. If you're going to send them off to war, it had better be worth it."

It struck me. Hard. The financial resources in our possession were not to be trivialized. They were hard-earned and did damage wherever you sent them. In the grocery store, they slayed aisles of processed food just as easily as they slayed organic meats and vegetables. They fought with the same vengeance for medical bills as they did for movie night for a family of four. They were not partial to any opportunity. Wherever you sent them, they waged war.

So why did I so often want to send them off to fight trivial, meaningless battles? Every time I made a random purchase without thought of what other opportunities would not then be available, I sent my precious soldier dollars off to fight a futile battle.

At the same time, whenever Keith and I tightened our budget even more, we sent our soldier dollars off to fight for our financial freedom. When we chose to cut cable TV from our budget, stopped eating out without a gift card, and chose to not give gifts to each other, we were in effect allowing our money to wage war on our debt.

With our medical expenses rising, and our debt still needing the full weight of our soldier dollars to get us through, being reminded of their power made an incredible impact on me. For the first time, I was able to have a visual of what our concentrated efforts looked like. Our money was working hard for us. We needed to ensure it did not work in vain.

Your Turn…Your Perspective: When has your money worked for you the hardest? When was the last time you made a random purchase which felt like a waste of money? How did both instances make you feel?

Prayer: Lord, thank You for perspective. I pray for the discipline and tenacity to stick to my financial plan. Please help me stay focused on my goals and cross the finish line. Show me how to be more strategic with my money.

Day 275
The Itch

1 CORINTHIANS 14:33

We were well into our fourth year of paying off our debt snowball when Keith got car fever. We had spent over $10,000 on car repairs and replacement vehicles by then, and he was driving the 1994 Toyota 4Runner we purchased a few months prior. It was not expected to survive our debt snowball. In the meantime, we were saving a few hundred dollars a month for the day when it died and needed to be replaced.

One day, Keith came home with excitement in his eyes. A used car dealership opened down the street from where we lived. and he stopped in to take a look around. After finding out a little about the company, he told the salesman he was in the market for an older model Toyota Tundra. Toyota trucks held their value well, and even one over 10 years old would cost well over $10,000.

After listening for a few moments, I asked the million-dollar, elephant-in-the-room question. "How are we going to pay for it?" We were both quiet. We just sat there for a few long moments as we both processed what was happening.

I knew he was ready for a better vehicle. I knew he missed driving a truck. I knew the sacrifice we were making to become debt-free. I also knew Keith was aware of these things, too. I was typically the one who needed to be reeled in from a poor money decision. It was tough to watch him struggle with this one.

But the truth was, we made the commitment to pay cash for all purchases. It was the line we drew in the sand years earlier. We were determined to not create any new debt. It was the only way to get out once and for all. We made the commitment together and would stand united in the tough times until we completed our goal.

I said nothing else. He had to be the one to come to a final decision. I prayed for discernment for Keith because I knew he sacrificed comfort so I could drive a slightly better vehicle. We made frequent trips to St. Louis (four hours one way) to spend time with our kids, and decided my vehicle was the best for road trips.

My heart ached for him to make the right decision. I did not want a financial setback because of a truck. But I also knew Keith was feeling the weight of our long journey to financial freedom. I needed to support him the only way I knew how. I needed to pray.

I prayed for two weeks. Finally, the day came when he told me he canceled the search for the truck. He apologized for losing sight of our vision. I reminded him of all the times I lost sight, and how he talked me off the money spending ledge. I was just doing the same. Our future was important to both of us. We were a team and we had to support each other.

On our wedding day, we stated we would be there for each other through the highs and the lows. The journey to financial freedom continued to be filled with both. We were determined to make the best of the lows on our way to the highs.

Your Turn…Your Perspective: When was the last time you were on the edge of the money spending ledge? What happened? Who do you have in your life who serves as an accountability partner?

Prayer: Lord, I need resolve. I pray for perseverance through my financial journey. Please help me to seek wise counsel before making big financial decisions. I pray for discipline and determination. I will get through this, Jesus. With Your help.

Day 276
Entitlement to Gratitude

2 CORINTHIANS 9:7; GALATIANS 6:7-8

A few years ago, I was listening to a Christian radio program ("Life, Money, Hope with Chris Brown") which focused on what the Bible said about money. During a show one day, a caller asked Chris when the reaping was going to start. She told him she felt she was sowing well, but not seeing the benefits. In her mind, she was not getting what she deserved compared to what she was giving.

The caller was referring to the law of sowing and reaping. "Do not be deceived. God cannot be mocked. A man reaps what he sows. Whoever sows to please their flesh, from the flesh will reap destruction; whoever sows to please the Spirit, from the Spirit will reap eternal life" (Galatians 6:7-8). She was basically saying "I have given to the Lord. I have done my part. When do I get mine?" I knew exactly what she meant because I asked myself the same questions on many occasions. "Okay, Lord. I have done what you asked me to do. Where is my reward?"

Chris confirmed what I already knew. Most of us, at one time or another, shared the caller's feelings. He talked about our view of our current situation being seen through a "foggy" lens. There was an idea in our mind of what our lives "should" look like. The lens of our life, being out of focus, caused us to not believe we deserved our current situation. When we looked through a foggy lens, we believed we should have more or be better off than our current situation allowed. Chris called this feeling "entitlement." Wow. I thought only kids felt entitled! I accused an entire generation of kids of being entitled and completely missed my own feelings of righteous indignation.

Chris then invited the caller to shift her perspective from entitlement to gratitude. Immediately, I could see myself through the eyes of this foggy lens (specifically relating to our financial picture). Instead of thinking I was entitled to us being out of debt immediately, the goal was to be grateful we were able to attack our debt so fiercely. I was to be grateful we were making such great progress. Instead of feeling frustrated because we were still renting, I was to be grateful for a place to live. Our rent was much less than 25% of our income. The rent did not increase the entire four years we lived there. Our home was clean, safe, and filled with love and the presence of the Lord. Instead of being frustrated because my boss did not see my worth. I was to be grateful for my job, along with the income and flexibility it provided. It was amazing what a simple shift in perspective brought.

When I chose to be grateful, there was so much more peace. When I chose to feel entitled, and thought I was not getting everything I deserved, my overall attitude suffered. Listening to the show helped me realize gratitude was a choice. Every day I got to choose to be grateful. The more I chose gratitude, the more thankful I became. The less I chose to feel entitled, the more joy I experienced in my life.

Your Turn...Your Perspective: What areas of your life cause you to feel entitled? How do you shift your perspective?

Prayer: Lord, thank You for perspective. Thank You for the benefit of other people being transparent so I can learn from their struggles. I pray You show me when I am not being grateful. Help me to see it in myself quickly and switch my perspective. Help me to show grace when I see it in others. I thank You for the trials of my life. I know Your "perfect" work is being completed in me because of it.

Promotion Potential

PHILIPPIANS 4:19; GENESIS 39:2-3

Keith got a promotion. Praise the Lord! He was one of six people who performed the same job for the entire country but was the lowest paid member of the team. He never complained. He loved his job and was very good at it. His solution to being underpaid was to continue to work hard and do the best job possible. His dedication and professionalism did not go unnoticed. He often received commendations and awards, but never a promotion. He just continued to trust and believe the Lord would provide.

When God did provide, it was above and beyond all we imagined. In addition to getting a promotion, Keith also received a Quality Service Award. This was an additional pay increase added on top of the promotion. The result was a $12,000 increase in annual income! He was both excited and humbled. It was more money than he ever made in his life. He chose not to complain about his status and the Lord blessed his humility because of it.

Even though Keith received his bachelor's degree in Business years earlier, he resisted finding a position which matched his education and potential. He was a mailman for over 10 years and was happy walking the streets of St. Louis, handing out envelopes to his neighbors. When he lost his job, and found it difficult to find another, he began to look outside of St. Louis. His degree was instrumental in him landing an internship in Washington, DC. Suddenly, he was in a position where education was valued. He was among professionals with master's degrees and doctorates. For the first time in his life, he was being compensated for his mind, and not his ability to haul mail or follow the commands of military leaders. He slowly began to embrace the opportunities education could create.

It was wonderful to watch God's provision at work in our finances. From the time we began paying on our debt snowball when we married, to the three-and-a-half-year mark, our income increased by over $60,000. There was just over $68,000 left to pay before we would be debt-free. To God be the glory! There was more debt behind us than in front of us. Keith's new income would continue to help us manage the balance between expensive medical bills and debt reduction.

Our level of determination reached an all-time high. The pay raise spurred us on to find even more money in our anorexic budget. We adjusted our tithe to accommodate the new income and moved all remaining money to the debt snowball. We did not go out to celebrate Keith's new promotion, but instead watched a movie at home as planned. At a time when we could have been discouraged because of the length of time remaining to pay off debt, we chose to stay focused and dug into it even deeper.

We were rewarded for our efforts with the gift of a promotion. It helped us stay hopeful and remain mindful of the importance of not detouring away from our goal to be debt-free. We could see God's hand at work in our lives once again. It was yet another reminder of God's timing not being our own.

Your Turn...Your Perspective: What are your plans for the next pay increase you receive? Have you ever worked in a position where you were underpaid or undervalued? If so, how did you handle it?

Prayer: Lord, please help me stay focused on the finish line. I thank You for the ways You have blessed this journey and encouraged me to keep going. I pray to not lose hope or the desire to serve You by being financially free. I praise Your name.

Day 278
Not Worth It

PROVERBS 1:5

Keith needed a new cell phone, so we put money in the budget to buy him one. I happened to be in our favorite discount warehouse one day and noticed a sign announcing our carrier was having a promotion. In addition to the new phone, we would also get a $25 gift card to the warehouse. Since it was the primary place we shopped for groceries, I was quite excited. I called Keith and asked him to meet me at the store.

When we started asking questions about the promotion, the cell phone representative could not give us straight answers. He could not explain the difference in the prices. He could not tell us why one phone looked as if it would be purchased out right and another looked like a lease. He said, "I'm not sure," on several occasions and kept calling his boss for answers. While I was okay with someone checking with their manager to get answers, we were not okay with those answers when they came back. They still could not adequately answer our questions. The promotion seemed confusing and we were not sure if it was the right plan for Keith and our budget.

The sales person assured us it was a great deal. He showed us all the perks of the phone and demonstrated all the new, cool features. He crooned about why this was the best deal possible and continued to attempt to woo us. I felt like we were being "sold." It was not a feeling I enjoyed, and I knew from experience to walk away when it showed up. Keith and I looked at each other; immediately knowing we were thinking the same thing.

In the end, we decided to not get his phone from our discount warehouse. The $25 gift card was a lure, but it was not enough for us to sign up for a cell phone plan we did not understand. If we were learning anything on our journey to managing money better, it was to never buy anything we did not understand.

As we walked away from the counter, it felt good to know we made a wise decision. We considered the opportunity cost of our money. It was not just about the gift card, but about how the purchase of the phone impacted our budget. For the first time in a long time, we felt like informed consumers. With knowledge there was power, and after our experience with the salesman, we felt powerful. We knew our due diligence saved us money in the long run, even if we did not get to save $25 on groceries.

It took us several weeks to decide on a new phone for Keith. We did more research, asked more questions, and were ready when a different promotion became available. There was no confusion and we knew exactly what we purchased. It felt great.

It is often said that "managed money works harder." We saw this principle in action through the purchase of Keith's cell phone. We looked forward to seeing it many more times in the future.

Your Turn...Your Perspective: What's your natural response to a sale or promotion which is ending soon? How do you process the true cost of such a transaction? Think of a time when you did not handle it well. What would you do differently?

Prayer: Lord, I pray for the day when I am in control of my money. Please show me how to make informed decisions. I pray for guidance on becoming a better steward of the resources You have entrusted to me. Show me how to win with money, Lord.

Day 279
Trust the Tithe
LUKE 6:38; MATTHEW 8:26

For several weeks, I felt prompted to change from tithing on our net income to tithing on our gross income. When I ran the numbers, I realized it would mean an additional $650 to tithing, and away from our extra debt payment. My first reaction was alarm. I did not want to remove $650 from our extra debt payment. I did not want to delay getting out of debt, but how could I say no to tithing? Since it was not a decision I could make alone, I knew I needed to talk with Keith. I had no idea what he would say.

When I shared my prompting with Keith, he told me it was something he wanted to do for quite some time. He was praying I would come to the same decision. While I was thankful Keith was praying for me, his statement created mixed emotions. On one hand, how great was it to have a husband who prayed for me, a husband who knew me? It was an answer to a prayer I prayed for many years before being married. "Please, Lord, send me a Godly husband. One who will pray for me."

On the other hand, Keith knew I would not be excited about the change to tithing on gross. He knew I would struggle decreasing our extra debt payment. He knew it long before I did. What did his knowledge say about my faith? Did I not trust the Lord's provision? What was I afraid of? How materialistic could I be? I was embarrassed and ashamed.

Keith hugged me and reminded me we cannot give more than God gives. My desire to be an obedient and cheerful giver must be stronger than my desire to be debt-free. If I got it reversed, it meant getting out of debt would become my god (note the little "g"). It would defeat the entire purpose of being debt-free. We wanted to get out of debt to better serve the kingdom with our income. I did not want to get it out of order. Serving the Lord must be first and primary in my life. To do otherwise meant allowing false gods to come first. As much as I wanted to be out of debt, I did not want to be enslaved to the idea of freedom from debt. I wanted to be sure my motives for increasing our tithe were pure.

As I prayed about the new knowledge of my spiritual state of being, I began to come to terms with the reality of our situation. Even though I wanted desperately to be out of debt, I wanted to love and serve the Lord more. I did not want to give more because I was expecting to get something in return. I wanted to give more because I wanted to give, and because I chose to be obedient. I wanted the opportunity to give to be a blessing instead of feeling as if it were a chore. To do so, I must trust the Lord and trust the faithfulness of the tithe.

It was important for me to understand why tithing on gross was strengthening my faith muscles. We would have to depend more on Him than on our income for our freedom from debt. And ultimately, dependence on Him is exactly where I wanted (and needed) to be.

Your Turn...Your Perspective: Describe your giving pattern. Have you ever struggled with how much to give? What did you do?

Prayer: Lord, thank You for the desire to serve You through giving more. Thank You for helping me to trust You to be the One who provides for my needs. I pray to not get things out of order. I pray I am constantly aware of how You come first and everything else, including debt reduction, comes after You. Thank You.

I'll Raise You

HEBREWS 2:7

The weeks before I shared with Keith the prompting to begin tithing on gross income were tough ones. I wrestled with it for much longer than I wanted to admit. I tried to justify it.

We were being good stewards, weren't we? We were not frivolous in our spending and our budget was incredibly tight. Not only was it tight, but we adjusted it every few months to squeeze even more money out of it. Surely this was sufficient to show what good stewards we were. Did we really need to increase our tithe?

Without realizing it, I moved becoming debt-free to first place in my life. It was ahead of God. Not good. If I avoided tithing on gross, I would be idolizing debt-freedom. This would not be the first time I put something ahead of God. My track record boasted a column full of losses every time I did. There was no way I wanted to sabotage our efforts to lead a life free of debt because of a choice to not trust God.

I knew what we needed to do. I knew we must make the switch and begin to tithe on our gross income. Keith was already ready to do so. I was the one holding up our blessing. It was time to take the leap of faith and trust God with a full tithe. It did not matter if we "lost" $650 each month if we were faithful to the Lord. He always provided for us and would continue to do so.

The crossroad was clear. God and Keith wanted us to tithe on gross. Would I join in submission or would I continue to justify why tithing on our net income was sufficient? The question was the introduction to a bigger question: Would I trust God to provide all our needs?

I was finally ready to lay our debt reduction on the altar and walk the full path of obedience. We adjusted our tithe and debt snowball allocation and continued the journey before us without ever looking back.

And just as boldly, God showed up. He chose to honor our commitment and sacrifice by sending more resources our way! Within one month of our decision to tithe on gross, Keith received three raises! One. Two. Three. Boom! What a blessing!

As we shared our story with others, we made sure to point out the raises were a gift. God did not **have** to increase our income in response to our decision to tithe on gross. He **chose** to do so. And I believed it happened in part because we did not expect it. We knew tithing was a basic act of obedience for those who professed to know Jesus as their Lord and Savior. We were the ones with the requirement, not Him. It was yet another reminder of our role in all of this. God was the owner; we were the managers. We were just thankful to be entrusted with His belongings and His blessings. It was our job to manage them well.

Your Turn…Your Perspective: Have you ever made a commitment to something, hoping to be rewarded for your efforts? What was the outcome? Have you ever had higher expectations of someone because you helped them in some way? How did your level of expectation impact the relationship?

Prayer: Lord, thank You for the reminder that You own it all. Thank You for the opportunity to manage Your resources. I pray for wisdom and discernment as I continue this journey. Help me not lose sight of the few things You request of me. I praise You and I thank You.

Day 281
No Envy for Me

LUKE 3:14; PSALM 37:7; 1 CORINTHIANS 2:9

A colleague of mine got a great new job. It suited her perfectly and there was no doubt in my mind she would do well in the position. It was also the type of position which would shape her career and put her on the fast track within our organization. The long-term career implications were very positive.

While I was happy for her when I heard about her new position, I felt a twinge of envy. I was struggling to find my place within our organization and did not fit in. I could not see where my current position would lead me long-term. I sought out mentors to help me brainstorm how to redirect my career, but still had not found my way.

When I felt the envy creeping in, I found myself with two choices: I could feed it or kill it. Feeding it was the easiest choice, but not the best. Feeding it meant feeling sorry for myself. It meant asking God why He did not bless me the way He blessed my colleague. It meant using words we taught our kids not to use. "It's not fair!" Feeding the envy meant not sending a congratulatory email and it meant succumbing to office gossip which suggested my colleague was not qualified.

Even though it was easier to feed it, I did not want to do it. I knew deep in my heart I must resist the desire to feed the envy if I were to grow in my walk with the Lord. How could I ask Him to bless us in the future when I was unwilling to accept His current plan for my life?

Killing the envy, on the other hand, was speaking the truth out loud. It was a reminder for me to trust God for what I needed. Killing the envy meant immediately sending an email congratulating my colleague, and letting her know how excited I was for her and her new opportunity. Killing the envy meant looking up scriptures to support God's promises and speaking the words, "I trust You, Jesus," over and over until the envy subsided. Killing the envy meant continuing to do my current job well which meant not complaining when things did not go my way and prime assignments were yet again given to someone else. Killing the envy also meant continuing to look for a position which better fit my skillset.

This was not the first time I felt a delay in the answer to a prayer. I experienced it many times when I was a Sales Director with Mary Kay Cosmetics. I experienced it many times when I wanted to be married but lacked Godly suitors. I knew in my heart God's delay did not mean denial. It was my choice to either continue to trust Him or believe the lie of being better on my own without His support. I chose to trust Him. I chose to find comfort in the three answers I knew to be true. Yes. No. Not now.

I continued to look for a new position. And I continued to ask the Lord to show me His direction for my career. I was thankful I did not allow myself to get sidetracked by envy. Envy was one of many tools the enemy used to derail us from God's plan. I chose not to be moved. I chose God's plan.

Your Turn...Your Perspective: Think of a time when you were sidetracked by envy. What did you do? What other traps of the enemy have you fallen into? How do you pull yourself out? What safeguards do you have in place to prevent you from being sidetracked again?

Prayer: Lord, thank You for showing me when I am entering the danger zone of sin. Your Word says in every temptation You provide a way out (1 Corinthians 10:13). I pray You help me to keep my focus on You. I thank You for helping me to embrace Your plan for my life, even when I don't understand it.

Day 282
Not Yet

PROVERBS 8:18

I was talking to a friend one day and she asked how our debt snowball was going. She and her husband were also working through debt reduction, and it was not uncommon to share stories and encourage each other a few times a year. We had not spoken in a while and I was excited to catch up.

As we worked our way through the conversation, my friend took a sudden turn and asked why on earth we were still renting. She reminded me their mortgage was a fraction of what they paid in rent because they purchased an older home. She told me we could easily get into a home with a smaller mortgage and redirect the money saved to our debt snowball. She spent about 15 minutes attempting to convince me what a great idea it was to stop renting and buy a home as soon as possible.

I just listened and let her talk the entire time. I could have interrupted to defend our position. I could have justified why we chose to continue renting and focused on our debt elimination plan. I could have matched her words with my own, highlighting all the statistics mentioned in the FPU class we both experienced.

I did not speak until she completed her checklist of great reasons for home ownership. My heart was a little sad because my friend and her husband completed FPU the year before and knew the plan. They knew why the class taught not to purchase a house before getting out of debt. They also knew comparing mortgages to rent was like comparing apples to oranges. The comparison did not include risk.

We would be in a much better financial place to buy a home after we were out of debt with a fully funded emergency fund. We all heard the same information in the class. They were already homeowners before the class, which meant the information did not apply to them. But it did apply to us.

I thanked my friend for her advice. I told her we were going to follow the plan. We were too close to the finish line to give up. I told her we would continue to trust the Lord to provide for us, knowing our home purchase would bring great joy when the time was right. We did not want to get our financial life out of order after working so hard to get it in order. She was not convinced, but it was not my place to change her mind.

For 15 years I chose to live an abstinent lifestyle. Keith and I maintained an abstinent relationship for three years before we got married. In my mind, buying a home this close to our debt-free finish line was the same as choosing to have sex outside of marriage. It simply was not worth it. In both instances, the commitment was to the Lord. He laid out a game plan in His Word. We chose to follow it.

The Bible is very clear on debt. We were the ones who chose to be out of order. When Keith and I started on our journey to debt-freedom, we made a conscious choice to no longer be out of order. We made the conscious choice to be patient and trust God's plan for our lives. We would continue to press in, get rid of our debt and build an emergency fund before purchasing a home. How others felt about our decision ultimately did not matter. He was the only One we needed to please.

Your Turn...Your Perspective: How have you had to justify your financial choices to friends and family? How comfortable are you with you plan? Can you resist others adjusting your plan?

Prayer: Lord, thank You for resolve. Thank You for the perseverance to stay the course on my journey. Please help me be gracious with those who do not agree with my plan. Help me to be a light to others currently in financial darkness.

Day 283
Faith Zone

PROVERBS 20:24

Keith and I knew we wanted to take Dave Ramsey's financial coaching training program very soon after we took Financial Peace University. Because of the expenses associated with the program, we decided to until we were debt-free. In the meantime, I busied myself by researching financial coaching and learning all the nuances of starting a coaching business. I spent four years as the Director of the Women's Business Center of Northern Virginia and knew we needed to create a Unique Selling Proposition (USP) to give us an edge.

Our family ministry was financial stewardship. We were committed to helping as many people get out of debt as possible. FPU was a great tool, but we saw almost immediately how many of our students needed more time and attention. Becoming a Master Financial Coach was a natural next step.

We discussed creating multiple streams of income to make the business profitable. We envisioned a career of motivational speaking in our future, in addition to coaching. We also needed a product to sell.

I began to pray and talk out loud about a product. What could we sell? What sort of inspiration could we put in the hands of our potential clients as a way for them to remember us, and want to work with us? How could we separate ourselves from other financial coaches? The days and weeks passed. No ideas came to mind.

One night I was in the shower thinking about our future product. Suddenly, I saw it. The picture in my mind was of this devotional. I said, "Lord, are you serious? A devotional? I'm not a writer. I don't know how to write a devotional."

I shared what I knew was a divine assignment with Keith, and immediately the fear set in. *Would anyone buy it? What would the critics say? Would I be able to put my life out front for all to review? Did I know enough about the Bible to write a devotional? Surely someone else could do this. Lord, why me?* The questions overwhelmed me. I was terrified. I was entering unknown territory and had no idea how to proceed. I was certainly outside of my comfort zone.

It took months for me to embrace the call I knew I was given by the Holy Spirit. God knew I could not do it with my own strength. I had to depend on Him. Writing this devotional was no different than depending on Him to lead us through our journey to be debt-free. He already proved Himself as faithful in so many areas of my life. Surely, He would be faithful in this, too.

Over time, I found my way. Keith and I made the necessary adjustments to our household and our budget to make sure we honored the Lord with a quality product. I prayed for insight and guidance. I prayed to be obedient and not allow pride and fear to overtake me. I prayed to reach someone with the finished product.

The rest would be up to Him. I truly felt safe in His hands and could not wait to see how He used us and this devotional. There was no doubt in my mind; He would get the glory from this project. He would use this to further His kingdom. I was excited to see how it all worked out.

Your Turn…Your Perspective: When have you been paralyzed by fear? How did you overcome it? What part did your faith play in you getting through it? How has your prayer life been different since the experience? Do you trust Him more?

Prayer: Lord, I want to trust You with the big stuff in my life. I want to be used by You to reach others. Help me to not be afraid to trust the plan You have for my life. Show me Your way.

Day 284
Press In...Press On

PROVERBS 2:7; EXODUS 4:10-13; JUDGES 7:6-8; HEBREWS 13:5-6

It was never my desire to write a devotional. I did not go looking for an opportunity to put my financial life on paper for others to dissect. I used devotionals for years and was a big fan of them. I reused them and bought new ones. I considered them all a vital part of my daily time with the Lord. I even looked for one centered on finances and could not find one. But I never thought to write it myself.

When the Lord gave me the assignment to write this devotional, it completely overwhelmed me. And, I was rarely ever overwhelmed. I knew nothing about writing in general, let alone writing a devotional. I certainly did not think I knew enough about the Bible to instruct someone else. I was completely out of my league.

Then I remembered reading of Moses and his fear of leadership and public speaking. I also remembered Gideon and his army of 300 men going up against over 100,000 Midianites. I remembered the Lord telling me (and you) He would never leave nor forsake us. These thoughts left me with a decision. Either write the devotional and leave the rest up to Him, or allow fear to rule my life and rob me of the joy of obedience.

Obstacles came at me left and right. Work became incredibly stressful and came home with me in my mind on a regular basis. Our new dietician put us on a four-day meal rotation where we could not eat the same food more than once every four days. It took me over a month to finalize the meal plan, and the prep literally quadrupled my time in the kitchen. I thought I would finish writing in a year, but instead, it took over three.

It was incredibly difficult, but I pressed in and pressed on. I refused to quit. I lay before the Lord often, asking if this was really His plan. Did I have it in me to finish? Why did the finish line keep moving? When would it be over? Are we there yet?

The process was so much like our journey to debt-freedom. We hit many obstacles there, too. Mounting medical expenses (almost $70,000 at the 4-year mark) required us to redirect money from our debt snowball causing a much longer debt-reduction plan. Constant car repairs and two replacement vehicles in less than three months. Emergencies, emergencies, emergencies seemed to rule our checking account.

Through it all, we somehow pressed in and pressed on. I learned to seek comfort from the Holy Spirit when I felt overwhelmed. I learned what it was to trust His plan even when I did not understand it. The hardest part was being patient with the process. I wanted to finish the book now! I wanted to be out of debt now!

Neither happened right away, and I needed to learn to be okay with where I was on the journey. I was often amazed when I looked back at how much debt we repaid in a six-month period. I was in awe when the Lord gave me the words to over 20 devotionals in one weekend. He continued to show Himself faithful.

So much of my spiritual growth came from this season of life. Low points often led to keen awareness of the Holy Spirit and His presence in our trials. It was not easy, but we saw it as necessary. The growth we experienced was so evident and we refused to allow negative energy to negate the spiritual progress. We continued to press in and press on, knowing it would all be worth it in the end.

Your Turn...Your Perspective: How have you had to "press in and press on?" In what ways have you been bound by the fear of failure?

Prayer: Lord, thank You for the ability to press into You and to press on toward the completion of my goals. Please help me stay focused on You. Show me Your way.

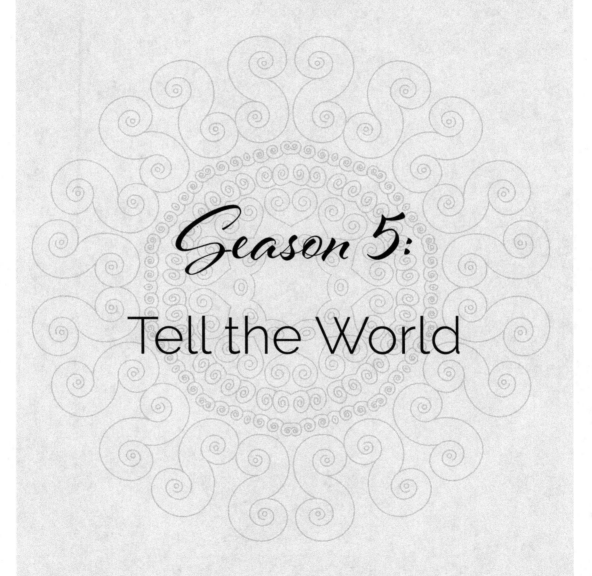

Season 5:

Tell the World

Day 285
Good Money After Bad

PROVERBS 30:14

When the Lord gave me the assignment to write this devotional, I knew there was a lot to learn. First, I needed to learn how to write a devotional. I needed to learn about self-publishing. I needed to learn about marketing. It was all so overwhelming. I also severely underestimated how much time it would take. My initial estimate from inception to a completed project was one year. Boy, did I have a lot to learn.

Because I did not know what I did not know, I signed a contract with an independent publisher way too early. They were Christian-based and seemed to know what we would need to make our project a success. The regret was almost immediate.

We signed the paperwork and sent them a huge chunk of money to help us get started publishing our first book. The honeymoon phase ended very quickly. While our salesperson was very accessible and full of information, our execution team was just the opposite. Since we did not have a finished manuscript, they did not have much time for us. Our questions were often met with delayed responses or no responses at all.

The warning signs were there from the beginning, but I convinced Keith it would all work out. As soon as we finished the manuscript, we would have the full weight of the agency behind us. Weeks turned into months. They kept asking when we would have a manuscript to release. The added pressure was not helping me write any faster, and the anxiety was taking its toll.

How long did it really take to write a daily devotional? Did I have what it took to finish? Was this book ever going to be published? What if we made a mistake in signing a contract so early? Oh Lord! What did I talk us into doing?!

Each question grew teeth and cut into my confidence. Did we made a mistake signing a contract before we finished our manuscript? What seemed like a proactive plan at the time began to look more like an extreme lesson in poor financial decisions.

About six months after we signed the contract, I met another publisher at a women's event. Sure enough, she confirmed my worst fear. We spent too much money on a package which would not serve us well at all.

It had been a long time since I felt such loss and shame. I felt as if I let our family down in a huge way. Our funds were limited, and I wasted our resources by being hasty. I yet again asked Keith for his forgiveness for not being a good steward. He held me close and reminded me of all we learned. Our money bought us an education on the process. It was not wasted.

I was thankful for a forgiving husband who followed Christ. I was thankful he trusted me to continue what I felt I failed to achieve. We prayed and asked God to continue to lead us through and make our way clear. We hoped we learned all the costly lessons necessary to finish the assignment.

Your Turn…Your Perspective: When has a financial decision proven to be a mistake? What did you do when you discovered your error? Who else did it impact?

Prayer: Lord, thank You for Your forgiveness when I completely miss the mark in my own financial journey. I pray for the courage to manage the resources You have entrusted to me with wisdom and skill. Please help me always be mindful of Your plan, not just mine.

Day 286
On a Budget

PSALM 35:10

It was time to build a website. We knew when the Lord told us to write this book we would need a website. And while I was technically capable of doing it, it was not something I wanted to tackle. We did not want it to look like it was built by someone who did not build sites often.

We were clueless where to begin. Even though I was in the business world when we lived in Northern Virginia, my contacts were old. I honestly did not even know what we needed or how to compare pricing. We did not have a name for the company, no mission or vision statement, no tag line. Nothing.

We also did not have much money. We obviously knew we would pay cash for whatever we chose to purchase, but our primary focus was getting out of debt. My mantra during this time of our marriage was "if it doesn't go to student loans, it doesn't go to student loans." Every purchase was viewed through this lens of how it impacted extra payments to student loans.

A friend recommended a friend who did "great work." We met with them both over coffee and laid out our very unclear vision for our little company. We did not have answers to most of their questions and the entire experience seemed disconcerting. Even though they were nice enough, it seemed like we were getting in over our heads. I felt a huge responsibility to spend our money well and did not want to make a mistake by choosing the wrong company to assist us in getting our website and brand created.

A few weeks later the proposal arrived. My heart dropped. The estimate for everything was $8000. How could this be? How on earth did we get to this number? Did they forget we were a small company simply trying to market a devotional? Was this website to be built in gold?

Keith and I sat with the proposal for quite some time. Was I feeling fear or resolve? Was this a test of our faith or a test of our decision-making process? Were we really supposed to spend $8000 on a website while we were working our way out of debt? We prayed. We prayed for days. Finally, we made our decision. The company might create incredible websites, but it would not create ours.

We could not justify spending so much money on a website. It was just too much for what we needed. We politely declined the proposal and kept looking. It took several months and three additional proposals before we found the incredible work of our graphic designer. We paid a fraction of the original fee and were thrilled with the finished product.

Our persistence and determination to protect the resources God entrusted us with paid off beautifully. We knew we learned a valuable lesson about what it meant to be good stewards. It was a lesson which would serve us well as we made other business decisions in the future.

Your Turn…Your Perspective: What recent financial decisions have you made with "disposable" income? When was the last time you viewed a purchase as unacceptable because of cost, even if you had the money to pay for it? What emotion did you experience?

Prayer: Lord, please help me be mindful of what I need versus what I want. I want to always be mindful to not view my income as disposable. Please help me use my newfound skills with every financial decision.

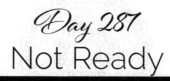

Day 287
Not Ready

LUKE 14:33

Over time, people began to look at Keith and me as ambassadors for debt elimination. When we ran into people we knew, they would say things like, "Hey! Aren't you guys the 'get out of debt' people?" We simply laughed and owned our calling. A lot of the people we talked to were not yet ready to get out of debt. They believed they were managing their debt well and were above being ruled by debt. Many felt it would take too much effort to live a debt-free life.

One such couple went to our church. They were not debt-free, but felt they were managing their financial situation. They were blessed with a good income and were not in a state of crisis. They talked about wanting to tighten down their financial management process, but were not yet committed to making it happen. We tried not to be judgmental, but instead showed compassion and offered to help in any way we could.

One day, they asked if we would review their budget with them. We told them we would be happy to assist and set the date. When they arrived, they did not have all their budget numbers, but requested we simply work with what was available. They knew we could not provide an accurate assessment but did not see it as an issue. We knew the real issue was they were not ready to see the truth.

It was a sad realization, and unfortunately, not uncommon. Living with the lie of "I have my debt under control" was a dangerous place. We saw it often and even lived it ourselves. All it took was one small hiccup and the house of cards called debt would come crashing down. They did not understand the danger of not working harder to get out of debt.

With this couple, we did what we always did. We worked with the numbers they gave us. We used hypothetical examples to fill in the places where true financial data was missing. We walked them through how to set their budget based on how much money came into their household each pay period. We made suggestions about places to cut back to make room for a debt snowball payment in their budget. We recommended selling some things to get a jump start on their process.

They sat silently and nodded softly at our recommendations and suggestions. We encouraged them to put some structure around what we presented to them with regular coaching sessions. They said they would consider it. We ended in prayer and walked them to the door. When they left, Keith and I looked at each other with an all-knowing expression. We knew they were not going to act.

It was disappointing to know the truth, and not be able to convince others of it. For us, debt reduction created the same sense of urgency as sharing the Gospel with the unsaved. There was too much at stake to not accept the truth as soon as possible. But just as we could not convince every person to live for Christ, we could not convince every person to get rid of their debt. We chose to do the only thing we could; we continued to pray. We prayed they would not have a crisis too big to handle before making the right decision. We prayed they embraced the truth as soon as possible.

Your Turn…Your Perspective: What prompting from the Holy Spirit are you avoiding? What are you afraid of?

Prayer: Lord, please help me to always be financially proactive. I do not want to be complacent. I want to grow in my knowledge and understanding of what Your word says about money. Teach me Your ways.

Tighten Up
MATTHEW 6:19

We were getting close. Almost five years into our plan, medical bills were still flowing into our mailbox like lava. But, we were down to the last $32,000 in debt. Two student loans were the only remaining loans. I did the math and realized we could be debt-free in six to twelve months, depending on how much we needed to put aside for medical expenses. The light at the end of the tunnel was getting brighter.

We started looking at our budget with new eyes. What else could we cut out? What could we trim to a bare minimum? The amount spent on medical each month was getting larger, not smaller. We needed to look elsewhere if we were going to trim the budget and add payments to the debt snowball.

We decided to cut our play money to $100 a month. We used it for the occasional dinner away from home or any gifting needs for the month. We also combined it with the money set aside for the kids if there was a special activity we wanted to share with them. It paid for the few books or movies we purchased as well as any conferences or events. Most months, we saved a good portion of it to use at a later point in time.

We did not think twice about cutting the play money allotment. We were used to staying home for date night. Making our play money smaller would not really impact us. We were wrong.

Almost immediately after cutting the play money, opportunities to do stuff began to appear. Tickets to a fun outing with friends would have cost $60. We passed. A "once in a lifetime" concert was in our city. We did not even discuss it. Tickets to a baseball game. Nope. We passed on them all.

It was amazing to see so many opportunities to spend money show up in such a short period of time. We saw them as the distractions they were and chose not to be moved by them. We were too close to give in to small pleasures.

We knew more magnets would attempt to draw our money away from us and keep us in debt, but we were determined to stay the course. Scriptures supporting our goal became our primary focus. We chose to keep our heads down and not look around at what others were doing. We would be debt-free. Sooner, not later.

The time would soon come when we could enjoy the fruit of our labor without debt hanging around charging us interest. But it was not there yet. We resolved to keep going. Our finish line was in view and our blinders were firmly in place. "Stay focused," we told ourselves.

We often told our FPU classes, "you do not need to do this for the rest of your life, but you do need to do it today." We simply chose to hang in there a little while longer.

Your Turn…Your Perspective: What was the last "finish line" you were determined to reach? How did you encourage yourself as you got to the end? What distractions did you have to persevere through?

Prayer: Lord, help me resist the distractions of lifestyle. I pray for the strength to stay focused on my journey and your plan for my life. I know freedom from debt is a part of Your plan. Thank You for the small wins to keep me.

The Commission Pinch

PROVERBS 13:11B

Most of our clients received regular salaries, but there were a few who worked on commission. Inevitably they believed budgeting was impossible for them since their income varied from month to month. We welcomed the challenge of helping them understand how essential budgeting was to their households.

An example was a friend and her husband's household income. He received a salary plus commissions, and she worked part-time. They sent her income straight to savings and applied his salary to their basic expenses. But his salary was often not quite enough to cover everything which meant they needed his commissions to make up the difference. Not having the basic expenses covered by the salary made her nervous. We called it the commission pinch. It also caused her to not want to tithe in an effort to "save money."

When they requested a coaching session, we were happy to help. A review of their household expenses showed more than enough income to take care of their household expenses, including tithing. The solution was simply a shift in perspective. All they needed to do was reverse how they managed their existing income.

Instead of sending the income from her part-time job straight to savings, we added it to her husband's base salary. When those two incomes were combined, the family was able to meet all their monthly expenses, including tithing. Any extra monthly expenses would come from his commission check, and all remaining income would go to savings. The savings amount varied, based on the final amount of commission received.

They were amazed. In just a few hours they made the shift from feeling poor with a large income to having enough money to tithe, cover all expenses, and comfortably add to savings each month. We were excited to be a part of their transformation. It felt good to help them add a few simple tweaks to their budgeting process.

What we did not know was the affect this change would have on the wife. In the past, she did not feel her income added value. Even though it went to savings, it was not tangible. By rearranging their income allocation, she felt like a full contributor to the family financially. Her husband did not even know she felt this way. It was beautiful to watch them realize how much it meant for her to contribute directly to the budget.

Keith and I never knew how we would be impacted by the people we assisted during our coaching sessions. We never knew what lessons we might learn which could be directly applied to our own life and marriage. As we sat with this couple, we learned the importance of never underestimating the value of working as a team.

The lesson caused us to cherish our own communication style even more. I also realized what a gift this lesson would have been for me during my commission-only days. If I knew the lessons we taught our clients when I was commissioned, I may have been able to save my business. I chose not to dwell on what could not be changed. I trusted the plan the Lord laid out for me instead.

Your Turn...Your Perspective: What is your current financial struggle? If you're married, in what ways do you need to adjust how you manage your finances for both of you to feel included? If you're single, who do you have as an accountability partner to assist with reviewing your budget with fresh eyes? Why did you choose this person?

Prayer: Lord, I pray for wise counsel. I pray to keep an open mind and seek out help when I feel stuck. Please help me not be ruled by pride. I thank You for this journey to be a better steward of all the financial resources You have entrusted to me.

Day 290
Extra Money

As Keith and I coached more clients, we began to see patterns emerge. We learned to recognize the looks of hopelessness. We also knew we would inevitably have the discussion of what to do with the "extra money" they "found" in their budgets, after fully embracing the concept.

As they learned how to define every dollar of income, they soon discovered "extra money" in their budgets. The first reaction for many was "Woohoo! Let's go play!" It was our job to slow them down and remind them of the end goal. The use for the "extra money" was the same, regardless of the amount. It was to be applied to whatever stage of financial growth they were currently working to complete.

If they were just starting out, the extra money was applied to help build the starter emergency fund. If their starter fund was in place, the extra money went to the debt snowball. If they were debt-free, the extra money was applied to the fully-funded emergency fund. Next was retirement, college funding for the kids, or paying off the mortgage. There was always a purpose for the extra money, just like every other dollar in the budget.

It was not always intuitive. Many of them felt a sense of relief at having extra money in their budgets, but it often burned a hole in their pocket. They wanted to add more items to the budget to absorb it. They wanted to travel and buy more stuff. They saw the "extra money" as newfound freedom to spend.

We knew it would take time to shift the mindset from spending to making a dent in the current financial step. The key was to balance the desire to do more with their extra money along with the need to be fiscally responsible. It was our job to help them walk though how to do this strategically.

We helped them to think about the future and paying cash for the next vehicle purchase. We reminded them of the goal to send the kids to college without debt, and the need to save for the new HVAC system. Our job was to be the voice of reason in their lives until they could hear their own financial voices.

We learned to call on the emotion they experienced when they first began budgeting. It was not about them reliving fear or anxiety again, but a reminder of the importance to not repeat bad habits. Once we helped them see the importance of shoring up their financial picture with their extra money, they were better able to balance new spending with a plan.

We gave them hope. We showed them the power of their income and helped them embrace sound financial decision making. We encouraged them to dream about the future. Many would become millionaires and philanthropists, simply because they learned what to do with the "extra money" found through budgeting.

What I loved most was how so many of our clients discovered their financial options for the first time. They no longer felt controlled by their circumstances, but instead, felt in control. They could create a plan which worked, regardless of how much extra money was available. It was truly a blessing to watch them take control of their financial lives and lay a foundation of good money decisions.

Your Turn…Your Perspective: How do you maintain discipline when "extra money" is available? What long term financial goals are you currently tracking?

Prayer: Lord, I want to be a good steward. I want to think before I spend. Please help me to stay aware and sensitive to the needs of Your people. I pray for the tools to help me manage my income in a way which honors You.

Day 291
Earned or Paid

PROVERBS 1:27-28; PROVERBS 14:12

In addition to teaching Financial Peace University and following its principles, Keith and I also regularly listened to "The Dave Ramsey Show." A caller's question frequently asked was also one we often addressed in our classes and coaching sessions. "Do you really want me to use my savings to pay off my debt?"

At least once a session we got this question, and oftentimes many more during the 9-week class. Each time, the answer was the same. Interest earned was a blessing, interest paid was a penalty. In addition, interest earned was almost always lower than interest paid, meaning the money would not earn as much as it would save when applied towards eliminating debt.

Very rarely did our class members and coaching clients embrace this concept immediately. The idea of using savings to pay down debt was counterintuitive for most. They saw this as the removal of their safety net. They wanted to hold on to savings at all cost, even if it meant more money in interest paid on debt.

Keith and I worked to reach each person on a spiritual level. We attempted to show them the other side of their unwillingness to let go of debt. By holding on to savings and allowing interest on debt to grow, they were choosing to not trust in the Lord. They were trusting in their own abilities instead.

The world's way was to carry debt and use "other people's money" to get what you wanted. But the Lord's way was different. Romans 13:8 stated to "owe no man anything." Following the Lord's way was to remove debt as quickly as possible. By choosing to hold onto money when they owed others, they were choosing the self-centered view of the world. To take a Christ-centered approach to life meant removing all debt as quickly as possible and living only on what one could afford to purchase with cash.

Not everyone was ready to submit all they owned to the Lord. I remembered how hard it was for me to bring all I owned under submission. Not everyone was ready to trust Him to provide during the debt-reduction phase of their lives. Not everyone wanted to take the leap of faith and be fully committed to put themselves all into His plan. I struggled myself when His plan did not reveal itself fast enough, and certainly understood.

Ultimately, we knew it was each class member's and client's choice whether to follow God's financial direction, just as it was ours. We continued to pray with them, and encouraged them. We worked hard to not be judgmental; it was not too long ago when we were of the same mindset. We wanted the scales to be removed from their eyes, just as they were removed from our own. We wanted them to see God's way as the right way and the best way.

Many never saw the full beauty of a debt-free life because they refused to relinquish their current small gain for a much larger gain in the future. All we could do was hope they would eventually take the leap of faith. Doing so would open their eyes to what we were able to see. God's provision was better and more abundant than anything we could have done on our own.

Your Turn…Your Perspective: Name a time when you struggled to trust the Lord. What happened?

Prayer: Lord, please help me trust Your plan for my life and my finances. It is so much easier to follow the world and the expectations of the past. I want to embrace new expectations. Help me manage my money differently so I can be free of fear. I want to have financial peace.

Day 292
I Held Strong

PSALM 26:4

I was talking with a girlfriend one day when she mentioned she was car shopping. Her current vehicle was literally at the end of its useful life. She had bandaged and spit-taped it for as long as she could. As much as she hated the thought, it was time to buy another car.

Financially, I knew she could not afford another car. She was making ends meet, but adding a monthly expense the size of a car payment would not be a good fiscal decision.

I held my breath as she talked about taking enough money from a mutual fund to use as a down payment for a car. I did not want to see my friend go into debt. I knew she could not afford it, and I did not think she knew just how much of a bad idea it was.

I slowly released my breath and quietly asked if she ever considered paying cash for a car instead of getting a loan. The phone line was quiet for a moment and I held my breath again. I did not want to offend her, but I also did not want her to incur any debt. While we had been friends for years, and discussed many things, we rarely discussed money. I did not know how she would respond to my question.

She said she never really thought about paying cash for a car. When she said she would consider it, I saw my opportunity. I gave her several scenarios of how she could pay cash for a car and countered her reasoning for a car loan. I reminded her of interest working for her in her mutual fund, but how it would work against her if she got a loan. I also reminded her how much easier it would be to overspend with a car loan instead of having a set amount to spend outright when paying cash. I literally begged her to not get a car loan.

Several months passed. Every time we spoke, I waited to hear if she decided what to do. As more repairs were needed on her current car, it was clear she was running out of time. Soon she would be forced to do something. If a decision was not made soon, she would either be stranded on the side of the road or feel rushed to replace her car right away. Neither was a good option.

I shared my thoughts again on paying cash, encouraged her to be proactive and think it through completely. After we got off the phone, I prayed and asked God to give her the courage to do the right financial thing.

A week or so later, my friend sent pictures of her new ride. Her message said: "Thank you, Lisa, for giving me the advice of not getting a car payment. Had several sales people try to talk me into it. I HELD STRONG!"

It was music to my ears, and a clear answer to prayer. Thank You, Jesus! One more debt averted.

Your Turn…Your Perspective: Name a time when someone you knew was about to make a bad financial decision. What did you do? What would you do differently if you knew then what you know now? What did you learn from the experience?

Prayer: Lord, I pray for the courage to speak truthfully to those around me about managing their money Your way. Please help me to always put Your truth ahead of my comfort.

Day 293
Out of Control

1 PETER 1:7

I always did what I thought was a budget. As a new college graduate with my first apartment, I wrote out my expenses each month and dutifully listed out all my bills. The problem was the money left over. I never thought about actually giving myself an amount to spend each month and then sticking to it. I estimated what I would spend for groceries but gave no thought if I went over. It was merely a suggestion.

I never thought to budget an amount for clothing, eating out, or saving. I simply listed out all the things I knew I needed to pay, and then spent the rest. In the months when the expenses were higher, I remember experiencing anxiety. Those were the months I used a credit card more often and felt guilty later. I knew I was living beyond my means but did not know how to fix it.

Inevitably, I would put myself on a monetary diet and forbid spending any extra money. This lasted for a few months while I got the credit card balances down, and sure enough, I would binge. I would spend way too much on random, impulsive purchases and then spend days feeling remorse at losing control. Sometimes I returned items to the store, other times I did not.

I lived this way most of my adult life. Spend too much, feel remorse, tighten up my spending, fall off the wagon, and do it all again. It was a vicious cycle; one I did not know how to stop.

When my income was commission-only, it shifted a little. Since I did not get paid if I did not work, I fell into a habit of racing to work ahead of the payments. I would pay for a purchase with a credit card and then book appointments quickly to earn enough money to make the payment when the bill came in. The negative emotions I experienced because of the purchase always remained.

It was a different vicious cycle, but the result was the same. I never felt settled, financially. I never felt in control. Each new purchase caused me to question whether I would make it to the end of the month. I would deny myself, then rationalize I "deserved" to spend money on a nice meal or a new dress. The cycle would continue.

When Keith and I finally began to understand and embrace the concepts of Christ-centered financial wellness, I came face-to-face with my struggles with money. I realized I never really budgeted. Instead, I began to understand how to adjust the budget to fit the expenses of the month. I learned to view each month as a separate entity. I learned to say "no" to myself, but also show grace.

I realized my life would have been incredibly different if I learned these skills earlier in life. But I also knew God's plan for my life would use my experiences for His purposes. Instead of feeling remorse at all the mistakes I made in the past, I learned to use them to help others avoid making them in their own lives. I was thankful to be able to help others conquer their finances the way I learned to conquer my own.

Your Turn…Your Perspective: Describe some financial "out of control" experiences? How did they impact how you manage your finances today?

Prayer: Lord, thank You for my own personal financial wilderness. Please help me never to forget the low seasons and to always work to reach the high ones. I thank You for giving me a plan.

Day 294
Cash Flow

PROVERBS 20:21; ISAIAH 55:8

When we first decided to not build our home until after we were completely out of debt, I did not know it would take over five years before we could begin to save for the down payment. I was so ready to move on with the rest of our lives and stop renting.

As we moved along our journey of debt elimination and got closer to Christ-centered financial wellness, I began to see the value of our situation. This was put into context even more when our medical expenses reached almost $80,000. We were able to cash flow all of it because our housing expenses were so low.

By not buying a house before we became debt-free, we were able to keep our housing costs down to only 12.5% of our net income. Dave Ramsey encouraged everyone to keep housing expenses below 25% of their net income. We were well below the threshold.

What I once saw as an incredible inconvenience turned into a blessing and a savings. We spent much more than 12.5% a year on medical, and I do not know if we would have been able to do so if we used the full 25% on housing expenses. If we had given in to the desire to own a home before becoming debt-free, our journey to healing would have been delayed as we saved even longer to pay for our extensive medical care.

As much as we wanted to own a home, renting proved to be a valuable part of our debt elimination strategy.

Once again, the Lord gave us what we needed even though it was not what we wanted. By following His plan and not our own, we avoided the added frustration associated with a tighter budget. We would never know how many medical decisions would have been postponed because of lack of funding. We would never know how much time would have been lost in our healing process because we could not afford to pay for them. But God knew.

God knew our income needed to be redirected to medical expenses. God knew our budget could not bear the weight of maintaining a home and paying for treatments and medications. Because we chose to be obedient, we were able to receive the blessing of good medical care in a timely manner. It was a blessing we did not even know we needed. It was an opportunity to learn the valuable lesson of trusting Him.

Isaiah 55:8 states "'…for My thoughts are not your thoughts, neither are your ways My ways,' declares the LORD." My thoughts would have caused our financial situation to be much more constrained. My ways would have put us into a home we could not afford. My thoughts would have depleted all margin from our budget. My ways would have increased the amount of time we were in debt. My thoughts would have changed how we approached our medical treatment, and my ways would have caused me to miss the blessing of patience.

My life prior to starting this journey to know God's ways of managing money was filled with instances when I did not trust His thoughts or His way. Fortunately, I was finally learning the value of following and trusting Him.

Your Turn…Your Perspective: When has a delay in your life become a blessing from God? How did you realize it? How did it impact you?

Prayer: Lord, thank You for Your thoughts. Thank You for Your ways. I pray for peace in the process. I pray to trust You wholly regardless of what is happening around me. I trust You, Jesus.

Day 295
Vacation Envy
PSALM 49:16; PROVERBS 4:27

In our fifth year of debt reduction, I was really beginning to feel the pinch. We whittled our budget down as low as it could go. We were still experiencing a crazy amount of medical expenses, along with the requisite car repairs.

Summer and our time with the kids were upon us, but it would be another year without a vacation. I set up several day trips and different activities around the city for us to enjoy as a way to compensate. We were still very much in the midst of debt reduction and chose not to allocate money for a trip. We could not justify spending money on a vacation when so much debt was still left unpaid.

The kids were teenagers and I really wanted the opportunity to create vacation memories with them. They were obviously getting closer to leaving the nest, and it would not be long before our time with them changed. We had yet to experience a vacation as a family, and based on our current plan, it would be at least another year before we would be able to take one.

A few days after pondering this thought, I reached out to a friend to ask a question. My call went to voicemail and I got a text from her about an hour later. She and her family were on vacation. A stab of envy pierced me deep in my heart. I knew my friend was not debt-free and said they were working with Dave Ramsey's plan, but they chose to budget for a vacation anyway. I began to question our own decision to not budget for a vacation and thought we might be too extreme in our thought process.

Ultimately, I knew Keith would not agree to a vacation. And frankly, it was too late to put anything in place for the few weeks we had left with the kids. Camp was already paid for, and the kids not attending for any reason other than health or an emergency was foolish and a waste of hard earned money.

A few days later, I reached out to a different friend to discuss a different issue only to find out she and her family were also on vacation. "Did anybody stay home anymore? Were we the only ones not taking a vacation?" The envy was heavy and hung on me like a wet blanket. It had been a long time since I felt sorry for myself, but the feeling was closing in. I recognized it for what it was and begin to pray.

I prayed for resolve to stay on the path Keith and I set for ourselves, our family, and our future. We could not live the lives of other people; we must continue to stay on the course God laid out for us. It was a hard lesson to focus on and it took great effort to wrap my mind around it. I knew Keith and I made the right decision by not making room in the budget for a vacation.

None of us were lacking happy memories from our time together. Vacation memories would come in due time. We must stay the course and not get sidetracked by the decisions of others. It was not an easy lesson for me, but I knew I would be better for it in the end. Our summer was still a success, with lots of "remember when" moments. Vacation or no, we were a family. Nothing else really mattered.

Your Turn…Your Perspective: How have your plans been derailed by the plans of others? What did you learn from the experience?

Prayer: Lord, thank You for the reminder to stay focused on You and not to get sidetracked by the plans of others. I pray for contentment in every area of my life. Please help me to be mindful of how great Your plans are for me.

Day 296
The Thought Counts More

PROVERBS 3:13

One year for Christmas, I was sitting in the middle of the living room floor wrapping gifts with our daughter. It was reminiscent of when a friend and I used to have "wrapping parties" where we would make dinner, bring in all the gifts we needed to wrap, and worked until we got it all done. It was a great bonding time.

Although I moved away from South Carolina almost two decades earlier, I fondly remembered the laughter and celebration of our parties. Now, during the years when the kids were with us for Christmas, our daughter and I got to have our own wrapping party. We played Christmas music and I showed her how to make beautiful bows out of different types of ribbon. We both enjoyed it.

On this occasion while we were wrapping, she asked why we removed the price tag from gifts. I loved teachable moments. I prayed for them because 60 days a year did not guarantee they would always show up on their own. I prayed for any opportunity to share the wisdom of the Lord with our kids. For this teachable moment, I told her it was more about the thought than the cost.

She scrunched her face the way she did when she did not understand something, and I knew more explanation was needed. I asked if she liked a good sale. She smiled enthusiastically and told me she did. I asked her if finding a cashmere sweater on clearance for $5 was a good deal. She laughed and told me of course! I asked if she would consider giving the sweater to a friend for Christmas. She knew exactly which friend would like it.

I asked her if she would tell the friend the sweater cost only $5. She paused. "Well, I'm not sure," she said. "I don't want her to think I'm cheap." I then explained how knowing the cost of a gift could sometimes take away from the time and effort put into choosing it. I reminded her it was still a cashmere sweater and asked if it was any less valuable because it only cost $5. She agreed it was not.

Next, I asked if she ever spent $5 on supplies to make a gift for a friend. She said she had. I asked how much time it took to make the gift. She said a few hours. I asked if her friend liked the gift and she said she did. Then I asked if the $5 cashmere sweater held more value than the $5 handmade gift. It took her a long time to answer. I wanted her to come to the conclusion on her own, so I sat quietly and let her ponder.

After several minutes she finally told me she did not know which gift held the higher value. I told her neither gift held a higher value because both gifts came from the heart. It was all about the thought. When someone took time to consider the gift and the receiver before choosing, the dollar amount did not matter. It was why homemade gifts were so valuable to some while others lit up at the sight of an item purchased on sale.

She said she understood, but I was not sure she did. I knew the lesson was not complete until she was given the opportunity to experience it more fully. I prayed she would not fall into the trap of believing only gifts with large price tags were worthy of giving. I prayed she would see gift giving as a gift in and of itself.

Your Turn…Your Perspective: What was the most sincere gift you have ever given? What gift did you give purely to impress? How did each experience impact you?

Prayer: Lord, please help me resist the temptation to impress others and only give from the heart. I pray to not get caught up in cost, but to be mindful of the thought of each gift, given and received. I thank You for loving me enough to teach me Your ways.

Day 297
Work Value

COLOSSIANS 3:23

One of our friends was blessed with an amazing job. He was quite talented, and his employer recognized it. Years earlier, he quit his job when he and his wife relocated to Kansas City. It was hard for him and his employer because he loved his job and he was a valuable asset to the team. But the move to Kansas City was important to their family life, and ultimately, he knew resigning was the right thing to do.

Fast forward a few years, and our friend got a call from his former employer asking if he would please come back. His employer could not find a suitable replacement. Our friend brought the issue to our life group for prayer. Part of him was apprehensive, and part of him was as giddy as a kid on the first day of school. What should he do? He missed working for his former boss, but was it right for his family? Was work-life balance possible?

The other side of the story was our friend's new work life. He found it difficult to find work he enjoyed when he moved to his new city. He even questioned his value to his family and to the community. It was a difficult time for him; he was struggling to find his way. His wife was supportive, and ultimately just wanted him to settle into their new life. He wanted to settle in also but could not seem to find a position suitable to his skill set. He missed the feeling of accomplishment he felt in his former position.

What should he do? We all prayed with him and asked the Lord to help him reconcile the need to support his family financially with the desire to have a career and not just a job.

He decided to present his must haves to his former boss. It would be a moot point if they could not agree to the terms of him returning to the team. The position was the same, but our friend needed some things to be different for him to consider the request. He would need his travel to originate in Kansas City and not the home office. He needed more structure around his salary. For him to consider going back, he needed to have a fixed salary with benefits.

Our friend presented his needs to his former employer and told him he would be happy to come back, but under the new terms. If his former employer wanted him back, these criteria were necessary. If the terms were not accepted, it was simply not meant to be.

His employer did want him back and agreed to the terms. Both men were excited to be working together again, and our friend was thankful to be back in a work environment he loved with a job he did well. He spoke of how profound it was to be viewed as valuable. He also thanked the Lord and his earthly father for helping him develop a strong work ethic. He felt humbled to now be able to contribute to his family in a meaningful way. A new chapter, with the same title, was about to begin.

It was interesting watching our friend go through the experience. It was a reminder of how important it was to, not only know your worth, but also your values. He was thankful the Lord helped him find purpose.

Your Turn…Your Perspective: When have you made a decision which centered on your value system? What was the end result?

Prayer: Lord, please help me to be mindful of the values You have placed in me. I want to know my worth is in You and not in the position I hold. I pray for guidance in career choices. Help me to be bold enough to stand up for what I need.

Day 298
Food for a Friend

MARK 12:33

During our fifth FPU class, tragedy struck. One of our former class members passed away suddenly, leaving a wife and two kids. They completed the program a few months earlier and went to work implementing the new information even before the class ended. They took the proverbial "bull by the horns."

They followed the plan and were looking forward to reaping the benefits of their hard work when his time on earth ended. Fortunately, he knew Jesus as his Lord and Savior and was in a much better place, but the rest of us were still left to miss his presence.

When I heard about the loss, I immediately called his wife and shared our condolences. There were few words, but I wanted her to know we were thinking of her and praying for her. I thought of my nephew and the loss our family experienced just a year earlier. I remembered all too well how important it was to be surrounded by friends and family, even when solitude was the natural choice.

The next day, I showed up at their home with boxes of food. Breakfast, lunch and dinner, complete with condiments and dessert. All food was fully prepared so only a microwave would be needed. Then we sat. I let her share what she wanted to share and tried to keep my own grief at a minimum. I hoped and prayed it would be enough to help ease a little of the stress of incoming family members and funeral arrangements.

I thought of all the people who appeared on our doorsteps just a year earlier with food. For the first time, I thought of their preparations to assist us, and how those preparations must have impacted their household budget. I depleted our "fun" money and some of our grocery money to assist our friend. How much did our friends and neighbors spend to assist us? What groceries did their families go without to provide for ours?

In the past, so much of wanting to be free of debt related to impending joy. The joy of a vacation paid in cash, leaving only pleasant memories and not the dread of next month's credit card statements. The joy of watching a child graduate from high school knowing student loans were not waiting. The joy of giving to our charities of choice and seeing the fruit of our labor blossom in the hands of a hardworking non-profit staff.

Those were all worthy examples of the joy of living a debt-free life. They were not the ones which flooded my mind as I left my friend's home the day after her husband died, however. All I could think about that day was how thankful I was to have the resources to relieve just a little of the strain by providing a meal. I was thankful they chose to purchase the correct amount of term life insurance while they could. I thought of what peace of mind my friend experienced, knowing money would not be her first concern.

I was thankful our friends made the decision to get their finances in order before it was too late. I was thankful we did the same thing and were able to share in the provision of the Lord. I was thankful there was financial margin in our life. I was thankful for the comfort of a meal shared with a grieving family.

Your Turn…Your Perspective: Think of a time when you wanted to share in someone else's grief. What did you do? How did it impact you financially? What would you do differently if given the opportunity? Do you have adequate life insurance?

Prayer: Lord, I pray for guidance as I get my financial house in order. Help me to be proactive and not procrastinate. I also pray to not focus so much on myself, but to be mindful of the needs of others. Help me to always have a giving spirit.

Day 299
The Gift of Time

One of the benefits of being a long-time federal employee was the amount of vacation time earned. I cashed in all my time when I left my federal job in 2000. As a result, I started from zero when I came back. Keith did not cash in his time when he left federal service so he picked up where he left off when he came back.

He earned two full days of vacation time every month, and rarely took time off. We were only allowed to carry a month's worth of vacation from one year to the next which meant he always maxed out the amount of time he could rollover to the next calendar year.

Instead of just losing the extra time, he donated it. There was always a need to support a colleague whose vacation and sick time were already depleted because of health issues.

One year, the recipient was in the office of a friend. Keith gave the gift of a full pay period of vacation time. His friend shared updates about the recipient and her healing progression. It was as if we were able to have a window into her sick room to share in her experience from a distance.

The woman was single with not much family. Her vacation and sick time ran out months earlier. The agency's approval of her request to receive donated vacation time relieved stress on lots of levels. She was able to continue to be paid a salary which meant she also received healthcare benefits. Without it, her employment would be terminated either through disability or retirement.

It was hard to work on getting well when her focus was on money. Her dilemma served as yet another reminder of how important it was to get our financial house in order. We knew all too well the overwhelming cost of medical care and we empathized with her situation. We were fortunate to both be able to work through our illnesses and not have the added financial stress our new friend experienced.

The financial and emotional weight of her situation was heartbreaking. And while we were able to give the gift of time, we knew it would eventually come to an end. What would she do then? Would others step up and donate enough to keep her going? I did not know why her situation resonated with me so much. I had never met her. I just knew her circumstances showcased another "why" in the growing list of reasons for us to be debt-free.

No one knew when a life-threatening illness will strike. No one knew when a job or benefits would be affected. No one knew when outside assistance would be needed. This woman needed all of those, and we were fortunate because we did not. It was two sides of the same coin. I was thankful we were on the more positive side, but I could not negate the pain associated with what she experienced.

The woman eventually passed away. And while I never met her, I would never forget the lessons I learned because of her: Lessons of financial and physical wellness. Lessons of the ability to share whatever was available to share. Lessons of community. So many lessons learned from the gift of time.

Your Turn…Your Perspective: When was the last time you gave the gift of time? What did it look like? How did you benefit from being the giver?

Prayer: Lord, I pray to never discount the value of work and benefits. Please help me to not take my resources for granted. I am grateful for all You have given. Please help me be mindful of those less fortunate. I pray for health and financial freedom.

Day 300
Locality Pay

PSALM 24:1

Keith and I both worked for the Federal government. Even though we worked for different agencies, it was considered one large employer. Federal employees from all agencies received access to the same healthcare and retirement benefits, along with a very structured pension plan and pay scale.

In order to keep employee pay as competitive and equitable as possible, the Federal government used a locality pay system. It meant the person working in a very expensive city received slightly more for the same work as a person living in small town America. The goal was to ensure everyone was paid according to the standard of living in their area.

The locality pay for Kansas City was included in the largest group which comprised most of the United States. These were the cities whose cost of living was relatively average.

When we were in year four of paying our debt snowball, we found out all Kansas City Federal government employees would receive a pay raise. A study was done determining the cost of living in Kansas City to be slightly higher than the rest of the United States. To compensate for the increase, an adjustment in the locality pay was needed. Since Keith and I were both Federal employees, it meant our household would receive two pay raises. The net result was an additional $1200 a year for our household.

We saw the extra money as the blessing it was. A few months earlier we decided to increase our tithe from tithing on net income to tithing on our gross income. Incredible blessings of abundance began to show up. We were amazed at the money we saved on purchases, the items people gifted us, random checks which appeared in the mail, and now a net increase to our household.

We saw God's hand at work in our lives and in our finances. We saw Him honoring our commitment to live for Him. We were choosing to manage well the resources and income He gave us. We saw Him giving us more to work with because we were finally beginning to be good stewards. It was humbling to watch it all unfold.

These new blessings made us even more determined to become debt-free. It fueled our desire to live a life of Christ-centered financial wellness, even more than before. There were so many ways we wanted to help grow the Kingdom, but we must get past the hurdle of debt before we could do any of it.

We continued our steady plod to freedom from debt, fueled by more income and one belief – what we were doing was bringing honor to God. We chose to continue to be diligent in all areas of our life to grow as close to Him as possible. The fruit of our labor was visible for all to see.

Your Turn…Your Perspective: When have you received a financial blessing because of sacrifice? How did it impact your life?

Prayer: Lord, thank You for increase. I pray to look for it in every-day experiences. Please help me stay focused on the journey and the lessons, and to look less at the obstacles. Please help me stay in a place of humility and grace.

Day 301
Thanks, Uncle

Keith's employer, like many Federal agencies, offered their employees a student loan repayment plan. Every year, tenured employees were able to apply to have a portion of their student loans reduced. There was an elaborate formula to determine what amount each person was eligible to receive, and the amount of the award varied every year depending on several factors.

We applied annually and received reduced repayment allocations ranging from $800 to over $3000. Since the student loans were at the back end of the debt snowball, it was the only reduction they received in the first few years. We never took the repayment reductions for granted. We saw the student loan reduction in repayment fund as the gift it was, and thanked the Lord for it each time it was received.

Because our debt was so big and consisted mostly of large student loans, the repayments were a huge help in getting the balances lower while we worked on the smaller debts. I breathed a sigh of relief each year when the repayment was approved, and the amount was revealed. I saw the repayment as God's way of helping us to get a handle around our debt.

I often saw payment on our debt snowball as being equivalent to using a tea cup to dip water out of the ocean. At least the student loan repayments were bucket sized. The experience was a constant reminder of the need to stay focused and steadily plod our way through. Our debt overwhelmed me at times and it was a nice reprieve to get a boost from the repayment.

While we chose to pursue repayment each year, we opted not to take part in the student loan forgiveness program. The idea of staying in debt for ten years to get the remaining debt forgiven was not a viable option for us. It was a plan Keith considered before we got married, but after finding Dave Ramsey and reading *The Total Money Makeover*, we knew getting out of debt as soon as possible was a much better route for us.

As it turned out, we ended up completing repayment of our entire debt snowball (while paying out over $110,000 in medical and emergencies) in a little over five years. We saved thousands of dollars in interest by pressing in and getting rid of the debt instead of waiting for it to be forgiven.

Many of Keith's coworkers scratched their heads at why we did not participate in the forgiveness program. They did not understand our desire to be rid of debt as soon as possible. They understood participating in the repayment plan, and many joined us in having portions of their debt paid each year. But they did not agree with our decision to pay off all our debt sooner instead of waiting out the 10-year period to receive forgiveness.

It did not matter to us if others understood our reasons. Loan forgiveness came at a much higher price than we were willing to pay. Getting five years of our life back was worth so much more than minimum payments. We knew our decision was the right one for us.

Your Turn…Your Perspective: When was the last time you made a financial decision which was the opposite of what was popular? What was your response to criticism?

Prayer: Lord, thank You for being resolute. Thank You for not being moved by those around me. Thank You for a plan and progress, even if it feels slow at times. Help me to always show compassion to those whose views are different from mine.

Day 302
As Needed

PROVERBS 25:13

One of my friends was a nurse on a cancer ward in a local hospital. It was hard work and emotionally draining, but she was incredibly good at her job and her patients loved her. One of the things they loved most was her empathy, but her empathy was a double-edged sword. Even though it allowed her to connect with her patients on a real and personal level, it was hard for her to leave her emotions at work.

Inevitably, she took thoughts of her patients home with her, and had a hard time letting go of the ones who passed away. It was hard to watch her struggle with the work she loved doing, but which also brought so much pain.

Mt friend and her husband were debt-free. They chose a life of Christ-centered financial wellness as the foundation of their union and paid off their debt within a year of getting married. Since they were debt-free, their household expenses were much lower. As a result, she and her husband were in a position to decide what impacted their lives significantly.

My friend quit her job as a full-time oncology nurse and transitioned to a cancer day clinic where she worked on an as needed basis. No longer was she required to work the graveyard shift, instead she was able to set her own hours and more closely align her schedule to her husband's. She also no longer saw her clients at their worst which was typically the case on the cancer ward at the hospital. Instead, she saw them in various stages of recovery and was able to build relationships with them while they were healthier.

She thrived. It was great to watch her smile again. She was no longer weighed down with the sorrow of losing patients who meant so much to her. She was well rested because she no longer worked odd hours and could enjoy her husband and their marriage.

As I watched my friend talk about her new job one day, I thought of the significance of this opportunity. The couple decided to become debt-free early in their marriage. As a result, they could make choices which would not have been available to them if they continued to simply make the payments on their student loans. Their freedom and flexibility were two blessings others were not often afforded due to choices made in the past.

I saw their circumstance as a reminder of our own journey, and the importance to keep going. We were determined to not get sidetracked by the size of our debt. I saw it as motivation to keep pressing into God for the strength to finish our goal, even though almost four years had passed since we started. Our friends motivated me to continue to live for Christ and embrace His ways of managing money.

It was a wonderful blessing to watch this couple make choices. Their choices were made from a place of strength and fiscal maturity instead of having to settle for what was available because they needed the income to pay debt. It was a place Keith and I were working hard to reach. Our friends had no idea just how much we were inspired by their choices to live a life of Christ-centered financial wellness.

Your Turn…Your Perspective: Who has been a financial role model for you? What has been the biggest lesson you have learned from them? Who can you begin to mentor?

Prayer: Lord, thank You for role models, even those who do not know I am watching. I pray my life can be an example to others and showcase how to truly live for You. Help me make all my financial decisions through the lens of Your plan for my life.

Day 303
Good, Better, Best

ROMANS 12:16

Keith and I were quick to share our secret to growing a healthy, blended family. We saw a family therapist. He performed our pre-marital counseling and our marriage ceremony. He was just as much a part of our family as the four of us.

We did not plan to see him so much, but we almost immediately saw changes in our own behavior and the behavior of the kids after we spent time on his couch. So, we made seeing "Mr. Alex" a part of every summer visit. Keith and I saw him before we picked up the kids to map out our strategy for the summer. We discussed our areas of concern and the things we were looking forward to experiencing.

We later went back as a family within the first few days of the kids getting to Kansas. Alex always shared a bonding exercise with us. He instinctively knew what we needed to get our visit with the kids off to a great start.

One year, the bonding exercise was all about what was good, what was better, and what was best. For fifty minutes, we drilled on the subject to make sure we all understood. There would be many times when we would each have to sacrifice what was "good" or even "better" for us individually to achieve what was "best" for the family.

We did not know how much we would need the lesson just a few weeks later.

Our daughter would be a freshman the coming fall, which required an adjustment to our summer schedule to accommodate the need for freshman orientation. We lost a week of time with them because of it. We also needed to adjust the camp schedules and other activities to get her back to St. Louis for orientation, but she wanted more. She wanted to attend registration.

In the past, the kids' mother registered them. But this year, our daughter wanted to experience the freedom of registering herself as a freshman. The problem was registration was on a Wednesday and literally lasted about 15 minutes. We would have to take off a full day of work to drive four hours for her to experience 15 minutes. We would then get back in the car and drive another four hours home. The kids would also miss a day of camp which was already paid for. It was not feasible.

As we sat as a family and discussed it, emotions were running high for all of us. We wanted her to fully embrace all aspects of high school and wanted her to experience this first high school registration. We also needed to be true to our budget and time constraints. It may have been a good decision for her, but it was not the best decision for the family.

I have no doubt our conversation would have ended on much harsher terms if we did not go through the exercise with Alex. It was a reminder yet again to keep the cost of family counseling in our budget. The cost of the co-pay was nothing compared to the impact those fifty minutes each week made on our family.

Your Turn…Your Perspective: What outside counsel do you have to assist you with tough decisions? How had having outside counsel helped recently?

Prayer: Lord, I pray for wise counsel in my life. I pray to never forget the importance of having perspective.

Day 304
Behind Enemy Lines

PROVERBS 19:17; JOHN 10:10A; MATTHEW 28:19-20

Keith and I began our journey of financial freedom with Crown Financial Ministries. While we were dating, we took a ten-week class offered by Crown which helped us understand the foundational principles behind being debt-free. We learned how our income could be better used to further the work of the Kingdom if we did not have debt. This lesson was reinforced when we began to follow the principles of godly money management taught by Dave Ramsey.

The thought of assisting in growing God's kingdom gave us even more incentive to get out of debt. Prior to Crown and Dave Ramsey, I never really gave much thought to actively participating in growing the Kingdom. I paid my tithes and thought I was done. The rest was up to the church leadership to figure out. All of this began to change as we dug deeper into God's Word and began to realign our thought process to what we learned.

Suddenly, I wanted to be a part of the call to care for those less fortunate. I wanted to be more active in making a difference in whatever way I could. It was no longer about simply serving on Sunday mornings, but was about being a part of the bigger picture of influencing others for Christ.

Because we were not debt-free, we missed out on opportunities to assist others financially. I did not want to delay helping any longer than necessary. I did not want to miss the opportunity to pay the electric bill for a couple who lost their income or sponsor an entire family for Christmas. These were some of the things we dreamed of being able to do when we were debt-free. They were thoughts which never crossed my mind before our debt-free journey began. I wanted to contribute to the fight against Satan in a bigger way.

I also began to look at mission work differently. Prior to starting our journey to freedom from debt, I never desired to take a mission trip. After seeing what an impact we were able to have on our kids and their attitudes about giving, serving, and living for Christ, my thought process began to change. I wanted our kids to experience a mission trip to a third world country. I knew these trips would help our kids see past the "first world" mentality prevalent among a lot of young people.

Our incentive to become debt-free was no longer just about our family being able to take a vacation. We felt a calling to do more to grow God's kingdom and knew we must get out of debt to do so. We chose to keep going and not be deterred by the constant detours. Our new-found purpose of using our debt-freedom to grow the kingdom became just as much motivation as the earthly uses for our money.

We chose to be on purpose and focused. We were behind enemy lines, fighting the fight to reclaim the resources which were blessings from the Lord. We wanted to use those resources to serve Him and assist others the way Jesus requested. It was exciting and gave us the push to keep going. Every day we chose to stay in the fight was a day we won.

Your Turn...Your Perspective: What passion do you have which is currently unfulfilled? Do you have a plan to get it finished? How does your financial situation affect your passion and your ability to fulfill it?

Prayer: Lord, thank You for the sense of urgency I feel to get out of debt. I want to make a difference even in a small way in the fight to positively impact Your people.

Day 305
Financial Margin

PROVERBS 10:15

Financial margin was a term I never heard before we began the journey to find out what God had to say about money. It was never in my thoughts. After learning what it was, I knew financial margin was what I lacked in my life. I often described myself as never having "quite enough money." I could pay my bills, but never felt my savings was big enough. I thought it was normal to have debt. Everyone has debt, right?

I never thought about debt decreasing financial margin. It never occurred to me to think of increasing savings by limiting spending. It never occurred to me to be intentional in determining the level of financial margin I needed in my life and in my bank account.

Businesses used profit margins to determine the health of their company all the time. But I never thought of me having financial margin. I never thought of my finances in terms of them being healthy (or not). The more I looked at money through the lens of the Bible, the more I began to see just how much I needed to rethink how I viewed my financial health.

It was not uncommon for lenders to ask about debt-to-income ratios when structuring a loan. It never occurred to me to view it as a statement of my financial margin. A high debt-to-income ratio meant low financial margin. When people spoke of lowering their ratio, what they were really saying was they were increasing their financial margin.

Financial margin became my focus. It was equivalent to a person choosing to make a complete change to eat healthier instead of just going on a diet. Diets often failed because they were viewed by most as temporary measures. The previous ways of managing food would return over time. I began to view financial margin the same way. Keith and I began to focus on creating financial margin and setting up a financial system which could be sustained.

Our financial margin included a change in mindset. Debt was no longer an option. Once we made the shift, it was easier to embrace God's ways of managing money. We no longer tried to rationalize our "wants" to make them "needs." It was amazing how purchases no longer seemed as important when they stood between us and financial margin. It did not mean we did not make purchases. It did not mean we did not have a desire for things. What it did mean was a different perspective.

Over time, we began to see margin develop. Suddenly, our net worth was positive! Suddenly, our retirement accounts were bigger than our outstanding debt. The light at the end of the tunnel was slowly coming into focus. Each month the light became brighter. Amazingly, too, money emergencies no longer created anxiety. For the first time for each of us, we had hope.

Your Turn...Your Perspective: What level of financial margin do you have? How has having financial margin (or not having it) shaped your life?

Prayer: Lord, thank You for the desire to have financial margin. Thank You for Your Word clearly defining a strategy to have it. I pray to always be mindful of the value it brings to my life.

Day 306
Emotion of Choice

PROVERBS 28:13 AMP; JOHN 15:2

One of the most profound lessons the Lord taught me on our journey of Christ-centered financial wellness was how to trust Him with our circumstances. So much of my financial life, prior to embracing His ways of managing money, revolved around financial crisis.

Financial fires seemed to be everywhere, and I never knew why. I was constantly worried about money. Where could I find more? How could I stretch what I had to make it go farther? Why did "Susie" or "Joe" seem to be better off financially? So much negative emotion around the subject of money.

Things were no different when I got married. When I was single, I desperately prayed for a husband who could rescue me from my financial woes. I found it ironic when the Lord sent me a man whose financial life was just as messed up as mine. Fortunately, Keith was motivated to find a new plan for our finances. I was thankful he was motivated since I almost resigned myself to a life of debt. I honestly did not think there was any other way.

Even though I embraced the idea of being debt-free, it was hard to let go of old habits. It seemed my old anxiety continued to show up time and again to remind me of my money failures. My poor money mindset continued to sabotage the call to debt-freedom.

Despite it all, I chose to remain faithful. Once I saw the plan laid out in Dave Ramsey's book, *The Total Money Makeover,* I realized freedom from debt was actually possible. And while ours was a very large amount of debt to tackle, for the first time in my life, I knew I could get out of debt and stay out of debt.

My problem was I still needed to grow in fiscal maturity. John 15:2 says: "He cuts off every branch in me that bears no fruit, while every branch that does bear fruit he prunes so that it will be even more fruitful." So much pruning…so much pain. Would it be worth it? I needed to trust Jesus and choose to believe the answer was yes.

Slowly (ever so slowly), I was able to find my way through my fear of not having enough. Keith could not help me, only Jesus could. With every financial crisis, my resolve was strengthened. The, "Oh Lord, what are we going to do?" questions became fewer and farther between. I knew what we would do. I knew we would dig in, trust God, and find the money we needed through budget cuts and our emergency fund.

Five years into our journey to debt-freedom, we received a tax bill for $2056. A creditor reported a negotiated debt cancellation as income to the IRS. Our income for the year was recalculated, and it generated a tax bill. We were $24,000 away from being debt-free when the bill arrived.

In the past, the sight of a letter from the IRS would have caused my palms to sweat and my heart to race. This time, I calmly opened the letter, reviewed the information, and discussed it with Keith. We redirected the majority of our debt-reduction money to the IRS envelope and paid the bill. No fanfare. No drama. No anxiety. So different from the past and so thankful for the opportunity to see growth.

Your Turn…Your Perspective: What money situation causes you anxiety? How do you get through it?

Prayer: Lord, thank You for the pruning. Thank You for making me stronger. Thank You for growing my trust in You.

Day 307
I'm Tracking

MATTHEW 6:22

Keith and I got really good at doing a monthly budget. What was a tedious process in the beginning became more streamlined as we settled into our new normal. There were lots of opportunities to learn the nuances of budgeting. From lost income to bonuses and pay raises, our income went up and down.

We learned how to make the adjustments quickly and efficiently. We understood the importance of getting our budget done before the next month began. We discussed the changes and planned how to spend every penny. When changes were necessary, we reviewed the budget and figured out how to cover the expense without incurring any new debt.

After a year or so of consistently tracking our income, it became engrained into who we were. I honestly could not imagine what our financial life would be like without a monthly budget. We successfully created a habit with money.

The discipline of tracking a budget month in and month out began to spill over into other areas of my life. I did not plan for it to spill over, but it did. We found a spreadsheet which helped us to track our time. We cut cable and decreased the amount of time we spent watching television. The movies we borrowed from the library were returned unwatched; we just couldn't get to them. We realized we wanted to spend our time doing things to better ourselves, not watching others live out their dreams.

I also began to pay more attention to my weight. I started weighing myself every morning and became more aware of which foods worked for my body and which did not. I signed up for Weight Watchers again and found new ways to manage meal planning and prep.

I also began to put exercise in the schedule. It was only ten minutes each day, but it was more than I consistently did in the past. I could tell a difference in how I felt when I committed to my ten-minute workout. Gym memberships and paid classes were not an option, so I found videos on YouTube instead.

The idea of tracking what added value to my life was sinking in. I wanted the discipline I was seeing financially to move over into other areas of my life. Just as was the case with our initial budget, these changes were not easy. I fell off the Weight Watchers wagon time and again. The ten-minute workout routine was restarted and restarted. I would go for weeks without creating a new weekly time plan.

Still, I kept working at it. I knew the discipline would eventually be hardwired if I kept trying. The only way to fail was to quit altogether, and I did not want to quit. I did not want to fail. I knew I would be better when I was able to consistently track these areas of my life, just like I was better because we tracked our finances.

I prayed for God to give me the desire to work out. I prayed for God to remove the taste of sugar so I would not crave sweets. I prayed for God to stretch out my time and help me to be a good steward of the time He gave. Progress was slow going, but I trusted Him anyway. I would continue to track my way to success, one area of my life at a time.

Your Turn…Your Perspective: What areas of your life would be better if you tracked them? What's holding you back? What one thing can you implement this week to get you started?

Prayer: Lord, thank You for the discipline to track what adds value to every area of life. Please help me to seek You for the strength and courage I need to bring all my life under submission to You.

Day 308
Straight Ahead

PROVERBS 13:5, 4:27; JOHN 17:16

Keith and I listened to the Dave Ramsey show almost every day. Not only did it help us to hear how to handle potential scenarios we might encounter in our financial coaching business, but the debt-free screams also kept us motivated. We cried with the screamers. We laughed with them. They gave us hope. They gave us encouragement. They were just as much a part of our journey as Dave Ramsey himself.

One of the things Dave always asked the debt-free screamers was if there were cheerleaders or naysayers in their life. Most had both. We could certainly relate. We experienced our share of both also.

As hard as it was to admit, the naysayers in our lives caused us quite a bit of sadness. It was hard to see their sneers when we described why we chose not to participate in an event or make a random purchase. They scoffed at our ideas of being debt-free and living a cash life. They also made offhand comments when we discussed our plans or next steps.

There were even a few who lashed out in anger when we chose to not support their cause or event. The words "shame on you" were yelled at us. We were called selfish for choosing to get out of debt instead of giving to whatever charitable need was front and center.

Through it all, we kept our poise, and remained quiet when our initial explanations were challenged. We did not attempt to defend the names we were called. We just took it. We looked straight ahead at our goal and did not allow the negative energy of others to keep us from reaching it. We knew the charge we were given by the Lord, and we knew His plan for our lives could not be executed as long as we lived by the ways of the world.

It was hard, but we knew it was necessary to stay the course. It strengthened our resolve and helped us become even more determined than ever to get out of debt. We vowed to not be moved by the ideas of others.

As time progressed, the naysayers affected us less and less. It was as if we possessed a shield which got stronger with each debt we paid off. We learned who we could share our plans with, and who we needed to keep quiet around. We continued to be gracious when an offhand comment came our way, and simply smiled and said nothing.

The experience taught us what it meant to be in the world, but not of it. It taught us to not give up, but instead, to press in. It was a part of our testimony, and one day others would benefit from what our experiences taught us. It motivated us to keep going and we were thankful for the lesson.

Your Turn...Your Perspective: Name a time when the opinions of others caused you sadness. How did you handle it? How did the experience change your life?

Prayer: Lord, thank You for the difficult reminders of being different. Thank You for showing me how to show grace to those who do not believe what I believe. Please help me always be kind and generous.

Day 309
Spilled Milk

One of the things most people do not know about negotiating settlements with creditors is the income it creates. When a settlement is reached, and the amount paid is less than the amount owed, the difference generates income in the eyes of the IRS. The creditor is required to create a 1099-MISC tax form showing the income.

The problem is most of them do not generate the form in a timely manner. Nor do they send it to you. Instead, they send it directly to the IRS. They, in turn, audit your tax return, and seeing the increased income, send you a bill.

The first time we received one of these bills, the settlement occurred a full two years prior. We were finally making some headway with our debt. By reducing our debt, we created a good-sized chunk of money to send as an extra debt payment each month. But the medical bills were huge, and it was the year of thousands of dollars in car repairs.

When the IRS envelope came in the mail in the past, it filled me with anxiety. I knew an envelope from the IRS was never a good thing. The question in my mind was always: *How much will it cost us, and can we afford it?* These notices in the past resulted in lengthy, intimidating phone calls to set up a payment arrangement. The IRS was worse (and more powerful) than student loan companies. We learned early on to put them at the head of the line and attempt to get rid of them as quickly as possible.

This time, however, there was no cringing. Caution, maybe, but no cringing. We opened the envelope, reviewed the notice, and realized what happened. We then adjusted payments to the debt snowball and made plans to send the IRS their $800 payment during the next pay cycle. Without any fanfare, it was over. No wringing of hands. No intimidating phone call. No "Oh, Lord, how are we going to get through this?" cries.

It took a few days for it all to sink in for me, and Keith was the one who pointed it out. We were having dinner and he told me he was proud of me. I looked up, surprised but thankful for the acknowledgement. But I did not know what it meant. He reminded me of the experience and how it affected me in the past.

I sat and thought about it for a moment. I finally learned to not cry over spilled milk. The payment was necessary, and we were going to pay what we owed. There was no need lamenting over what else we could have done with the money. It was a beautiful lesson to learn. Fortunately, I learned the lesson early.

A few years later, a $2000 tax bill showed up because of a 1099-MISC from a former creditor. Because I already learned the lesson, this one did not phase me either. It took a little more time to pay (two pay periods instead of one), but we paid it. We then reset the debt snowball payments and kept going. It was a wonderful feeling to no longer fear an envelope.

Your Turn…Your Perspective: When was the last time you were financially paralyzed by fear? How did you grow through the experience?

Prayer: Lord, thank You for progress on my own journey. Thank You for the lessons I have learned. I know I am better and stronger because of all I have experienced. I pray to remain mindful of it all and not allow myself to drift into complacency.

Day 310
No Drama

PSALM 41:3; JEREMIAH 17:7-8

About five years into our journey to debt-freedom, we experienced yet another season of almost no debt reduction due to emergencies. Medical bills, car repairs, an unexpected tax bill from the IRS all showed up within weeks of each other.

With each new additional expense, Keith and I sat at the kitchen table with our budget and redirected our spending for the month. A trip to celebrate with a friend for her 50th birthday was canceled. We even delayed paying for summer camp for the kids in case those funds needed to be used as a stopgap. We talked through due dates and financial timelines. We made the necessary adjustments to the budget.

Once we crafted a plan, we quietly went about the rest of our evening. Another financial disaster diverted.

The unexpected tax bill was the last to arrive. During my quiet time the next morning, I reflected on this series of financial hits. I realized this set was slightly different than all the others. In the past, I felt physical pain when an emergency arose. I experienced sweaty palms and rubbed my head a lot. The phrase, "Oh, Lord!" was my verbal indicator of stress, and I said it a lot. I worried.

This time, however, there was no utterance of, "Oh, Lord!" I did not rub my head, and my palms were not sweaty. There was no tremble in my voice to indicate my nervousness in our ability to get through the current situation. I simply sat with Keith, discussed the issues, created a game plan, and made the adjustments in the budget. We thanked the Lord for the resources to get through another round of financial hits.

Emergencies ceased to be emotional. They were simply a car repair, or a medical bill, or an unexpected something. They no longer sent me into a tailspin and I no longer felt derailed by a financial event. I simply and logically sought a solution with Keith through prayer and we implemented it. It was done.

The days of having money drama, along with the current crisis, seemed to be passing. I felt more secure in our ability to get through them. I knew we were not out of the woods yet, but I could begin to see the forest clear a little. There were glimpses of light in front of us which sparked a hope I never experienced previously. We still needed to finish paying off our debt and build a fully-funded emergency fund, but I felt confident God would get us through those too.

As I sat with this new thought in the early morning, I sensed God's presence with me. I knew He was telling me I had learned a valuable lesson through this latest emergency. I finally learned to trust His plan. Even though our own plan was altered by the extra drain on our budget, and our debt reduction was delayed yet again, I felt Him reminding me to trust Him.

We would be okay. The lesson of trusting God through all circumstances was being hardwired.

Your Turn…Your Perspective: What areas of your life do you need to turn over to God? Why are you still holding on? How do you move forward to complete surrender?

Prayer: Lord, thank You for a very long learning curve. Thank You for Your patience. Thank You for the reminder to trust You always. Please help me always be mindful of the decision to let You lead me in all areas of my life.

Day 311
Questions from a Child

PSALM 49:17

Keith and I worked hard to be transparent with our kids about our financial life. We wanted them to learn God's ways of handling money and hoped to keep them from making the financial mistakes we made. We used material from both Dave Ramsey and The Love and Logic Institute. The combination worked well.

Because they were only with us 60 days a year, we chose to be very intentional in our communication. We talked freely about how we funded summer camp, why we ate the majority of our meals at home, the importance of taking good care of possessions, and our debt snowball. We discussed it all.

We also paid a commission instead of giving them an allowance. The idea was to teach the concept of money being tied to work. You got paid when you worked in the real world, and the training ground for the real world was our home. We wanted them to understand they were not entitled to anything but must work for what they wanted.

Their commission was required to be broken into three parts: spending, saving, and giving. We explained the concept of tithing and made sure they understood the difference between giving and tithing. They were required to tithe on the income they earned.

Each summer we would go back to the beginning and review it all. We followed up with shorter discussions when they were with us during the school year. Repetition was the only way to hardwire the skill, and we wanted to be sure it was hardwired during their time with us.

One summer, as we were having the discussion of tithing, our son asked how much we tithed. We tithed online which meant they did not see us physically write a check each week. Until this time, we shared a lot of the outgoing side of our budget, but not so much about the income side. We knew we needed to answer the question and be transparent in this area also.

It was not easy for me to share. As much as I wanted to teach our kids God's ways of handling finances, I did not want to show them our checkbook. I grew up not knowing anything about my mother's finances and a big part of me felt it was not a child's place to have such intimate knowledge. But in my heart, I knew we needed to be completely transparent.

Not knowing my mother's income, and how she managed her money, did not help me manage my own money any better as an adult. If anything, the lack of knowing contributed to the poor financial skills which were my foundation. My preconceived ideas about money were steeped in fear of money and the belief of wealth being unattainable. They were rooted in a spirit of lack and shaped my entire life.

I would either positively or negatively impact our kids' financial health by sharing our income. Either way, I would contribute. We told them how much we tithed and helped them calculate our income. We used it as a teachable moment and prayed God would multiply the knowledge. Time would tell how well we did.

Your Turn…Your Perspective: What difficult money conversations have you needed to have lately? How did God use them to grow you? What did you ultimately learn from the experience?

Prayer: Lord, please help me to not be fearful about money. I don't want to live in secret. I pray I have a heart of transparency as it relates to money and other areas of my life. Please allow light to shine into the dark places of my life.

Free Your Mind

PSALM 66:10

Our lives changed tremendously after we broke the spirit of lack. We both spent our entire lives chained to it. It shaped every financial decision and the choices we thought were necessary. It literally defined who we were, impacted what we thought we could ultimately achieve, and was the cause of most of the financial baggage we carried.

Keith grew up on welfare and I grew up a part of the working poor. We both grew up in single parent homes. The financial despair associated with the mentality of our homes greatly influenced how we got into the mess we were in. We did not know any better. The spirit of lack was like a film over our eyes which hindered the fullness of God's grace in our financial minds from the very beginning.

For us, the debt-reduction process was as much about clearing our mindset as it was about clearing our debt. We needed to go through the challenges we experienced in order for God to cleanse us of the negativity entwined with our souls. We needed to be purged of all the mental waste associated with money in the same way silver and gold were freed from their impurities before their full value was exposed.

Once we realized the root of our financial issues as a spirit weighing on us like a boat anchor, we were in a better place to deal with it. We prayed for God's assistance, expressed our desire to trust Him with our financial lives, and set about walking in faith. And, as is the case with any big prayer request, when you ask God to help you with something, He gives you opportunities to practice.

As we continued to whittle away at our debt, there were many practice sessions to make sure the spirit of lack was indeed broken. We did not see them as practice sessions at the time, however. We just knew we experienced more than our fair share of financial roadblocks during our journey, and we handled each one slightly better than the last. We grew in our faith and grew in our understanding of God's principles of money.

It was amazing to see the difference this mindset made on our financial lives. Situations which derailed us (primarily me) in the past became small annoyances at best. We were no longer sent into a tailspin such as when a repair on a vehicle was needed. Setbacks were no longer viewed in desperation, but were carefully discussed and prayed upon. Decisions were made and executed.

We became less hasty in our decision-making process and had fewer instances of impulse purchases. The emotions associated with purchases lessened over time, which in turn, created more joy and fulfillment in our current circumstances. We became more content, and I was even able to enjoy the journey a little more.

We learned to not feel anxious when Plan A did not work. We spent more time researching every option before settling on our final choice, and no longer associated a delay with missing out on something. We experienced margin in our lives and did not feel pressure when last minute budget changes surfaced. We let go of the guilt associated with saying "no" to our kids, our friends, and our family. We had truly become free.

Your Turn…Your Perspective: What experiences has God used to refine you recently? What did you learn from the process? How will it change how you respond to challenges in the future?

Prayer: Lord, thank You for the refiner's fire. Thank You for loving me enough to remove all my impurities. Please keep me humble and open to continued refinement.

Day 313
Birthday Books

PSALM 33:11

Even before Keith and I were on the journey of Christ-centered financial wellness, we made the decision to not buy each other gifts for holidays and birthdays. The decision came as a suggestion from Keith shortly after our honeymoon. Earlier, we decided to use our wedding and honeymoon as gifts to each other for the year of 2012. After the honeymoon, when we were faced with the true magnitude of our financial situation, Keith suggested we continue the practice of not purchasing gifts for each other.

It was not as if a fairy godmother or magic genie was available to pop in and provide money for gifts. Funds would have to come from our budget, and it was already bursting at the seams with debt payments. It was actually a relief to know we did not have to find room in our budget for one more thing. No gifts just seemed like the best choice.

Neither of us realized how long it would be without gifts. Five years of birthdays. Five years of anniversaries. Five Christmases. Five Valentine's Days. Five Mother's Days. Five Father's Days. All without gifts.

My girl genes were a little disappointed every now and then. Keith did not really care about receiving gifts, but after a while, I was a little disappointed at not having something to open from my husband. But each time the feeling surfaced, I reminded myself of our mission. Did I really want to delay our goal of freedom from debt for a little something? Were wrapping paper and gift bags more important than being debt-free? I knew the answer. It was a short-term sacrifice for a long-term gain. We would have many more years with gifts than without, if we could just stay the course.

In year four, there was a wrapped gift at my place setting for my birthday. I cocked my head at Keith and asked with a smile, "What's this?" I could not keep the surprise and excitement out of my voice. I really wanted to open something for my birthday and my husband knew it. I quickly unwrapped the gift.

When I saw what was inside, I immediately began to cry. It was a library book on audio. A book of stories about great women in the Bible. I cried even more when I looked up and saw the expression on Keith's face. He told me he knew how much I wanted to open something on my birthday. He wanted to honor my desire but stay true to our decision to keep as much money allocated to paying the debt snowball as possible. He asked God for guidance and He led him to the book.

It was hands down one of the best gifts I ever received. I loved the commitment we made to each other, and our journey. I loved how creative Keith was in giving me my heart's desire. I was thankful God gave me a compassionate husband who also exhibited great discipline. I was thankful we chose to honor God by staying true to our commitment to becoming debt-free and live a life of Christ-centered financial wellness.

Your Turn…Your Perspective: What is the best birthday present you have ever received? Who gave it to you? What gift have you given to someone else which impacted their lives significantly?

Prayer: Lord, my heart's desire is to serve You even when I want what I want. I pray for the discipline to stay the course and trust that You will honor my commitment. I thank You for perseverance.

Santa's Helpers

DEUTERONOMY 15:4

Our friends were across the entire financial spectrum. Some were deeply in debt and others were completely debt-free, including the mortgage. Most were somewhere in between. Everyone was in a different financial season, and it was always interesting to hear their stories. One friend shared a particularly heartwarming story.

Our friends lived a life with no debt. They became debt-free years earlier and spent a good bit of time helping out in their community. Through a series of conversations, they learned of a family in need. Months passed without employment for either the husband or the wife and they were struggling to make ends meet. Their two little ones were young enough to not fully understand the impact of their financial situation, but old enough to be excited about Santa arriving in a few days.

As our friends found out more information about the couple, it became clear no Christmas would be celebrated. No tree, no gifts, no decorations, no special meal. The family was in a tough financial place and there was no extra money available for a celebration. The amount of money coming in would not allow for the essentials to be met, let alone anything else.

Our friends decided to assist. They arranged for the family to be out of their home for the afternoon, and then jumped into action. Gifts were purchased for the entire family. Something small for the parents and several gifts to open for each of the kids. They purchased a Christmas tree. They purchased decorations for the tree and the entire house. They also purchased groceries for the family, including food for a holiday meal.

Not only did they buy a tree and decorations, but they put them up. The tree was trimmed with all new ornaments and lights, stockings were hung, and holiday décor pieces were placed in just the right locations. Even candles were put in holders and garland hung where appropriate. The works!

Our friends were so excited. Time was running out before the family was scheduled to return and they raced to finish. When the family came home, they were elated. The kids screamed, "Santa was here! Santa was here!" They jumped for joy at all the gifts under the tree. Mom and dad were in tears. They did not know who to thank, but were thankful nonetheless.

When our friends told the story, they were still filled with emotion even though the event took place years earlier. For them, the story was twofold. It was not just about being able to share with a family in need.

For our friends, it was also about what could happen when you lived a debt-free life. With no money going to payments to anyone (no mortgage, no credit cards, no student loans, etc.), it was amazing what a family's income could do. Our friends knew the blessing they shared with the family would never have happened if they were not debt-free.

Dave Ramsey always talked about a person's income being their largest wealth building tool. Our friends learned another great use for their largest wealth building tool. Giving. What a great lesson to learn.

Your Turn…Your Perspective: Describe a time when you were the giver or the receiver in an over-the-top giving experience. How did it impact your life?

Prayer: Lord, I want to be generous. I want to be debt-free and allow my income to be used to help others. Please help me keep a heart of generosity, even as I work on my current financial goal. I thank You for the reminder of how much joy comes from helping others.

Day 315
Three Years to Freedom

There was a sweet little couple in one of our FPU classes who really touched our hearts. They were debt-free in the past and made the mistake of co-signing a loan for a family member. It started a spiral of poor choices which ended in them getting a mortgage on the house they owned free and clear. Years later, they were rid of all debt except the mortgage, but found they did not quite have enough money to make ends meet. They heard about FPU during the announcements at church and joined our class.

As was the case with many of our FPU class members, we sat down with them during the first week and helped them work through their initial budget. They were overwhelmed by the numbers. They did not know how they would be able to keep their house. What made matters worse was they were only three years away from paying it off. But if they did not get their finances in order, they would be forced to sell. They were desperate for a solution and we were committed to walking with them to find one.

We helped them get a zero-based budget completed. This meant every dollar of income coming into their account each month was assigned a designated purpose. They discovered income they did not know was there previously because it was never used with purpose. Our new friends were so excited to find out they really did have enough money to make ends meet each month.

What the couple did not have was any extra money. They were nervous about not having an emergency fund and there was no money left in their budget to save. The first step was to simply put away $1000. For our new friends, this seemed like a daunting task. We recommended selling something. They were not sure what they could sell but were committed to finding something to get them closer to their starter emergency fund.

The next week, our new friends came back to class grinning from ear to ear. We were excited to hear why they were so excited. They told us they took to heart the idea of selling stuff around the house to get the starter emergency fund completed. They sold their gun collection! Not only did they have their $1000, but also a few dollars were left over to celebrate their anniversary with a nice dinner. We were so proud of them.

Less than two months later, our friends were faced with several emergencies. Two deaths, and a parent with a sudden illness, required multiple trips out of town. Hotel stays, gas and food for the journeys were needed. But our friends were ready. Each time they were able to make the trip and be with family. And each time, they found a way to replenish the emergency fund.

The couple was so thankful for what they learned. Once they understood the power of a zero-based budget, they were armed to manage any crisis as they encountered it. Gone was the anxiety of potentially losing their home; hope in their future was the replacement. They came to us thinking they could not even make ends meet but they left with a better plan for their money. They gained so much peace of mind. It was beautiful to watch.

Your Turn…Your Perspective: How far are you from reaching your next financial goal? How can you speed up the process? What are you willing to give up now for a more fiscally secure future later?

Prayer: Lord, help me see the financial forest instead of just the trees called my immediate circumstances. I pray to not get so bogged down in my current situation that I miss the lesson. Please help me be mindful of the need for wise counsel when I cannot figure out my next steps. Thank You for the courage to keep going.

Day 316
Dreaming

PSALM 25:13; HABAKKUK 2:2

Keith and I enjoyed listening to books on CD when we were on road trips. St. Louis was an eight hour round trip and we almost always finished a book during the journey. When we started going to Dallas for medical visits, we were able to get two books on CD (a sixteen hour round trip) completed most times. It was during one of these Dallas trips when our conversation turned to dreams of our future.

We were listening to a book on personal financial development and realized we no longer dreamed about our future. Our journey to financial freedom was over 4 ½ years long. We paid off almost $150,000. We also cash flowed over $65,000 in medical expenses and spent another $18,000 or so on car repairs and replacement vehicles. The combined total of cash leaving our checking account for debt payments and/or life events since we got married was well over $230,000. There was still more than $40,000 left to pay on debt, and medical expenses were still coming in. We were emotionally and financially exhausted. It was hard to dream when your mind was as overloaded as ours.

As we talked through the book, we could not remember when we stopped dreaming. We used to dream of building a home together, having vacations with the kids, giving more to charities, and generally having a more relaxed view of our financial picture. Somewhere along the way, we stopped discussing any of it. The reality of being in the financial trenches for 4 ½ years straight took its toll on our ability to think of the future.

We experienced so many setbacks. We were in fight or flight mode for so long, we forgot to protect our dreams. As we listened to the authors talk about the importance of couples being with one accord in relation to their financial dreams, we realized we dropped the ball. We needed to make an adjustment. We needed to have something to look forward to when the time came to celebrate being out of debt.

We talked about what our dreams looked like and discussed the desire to not lose sight of our goals again. We finally decided to have a dream session each month. We already came together each month for our budget committee meeting and realized we now needed to come together to dream. We shared all of what we wanted for our future, even things which seemed incredibly unrealistic. We needed to be intentional about looking at the future if we wanted it to look anything like what we envisioned. Habakkuk 2:2 states: "…write the vision and make it plain." It was true with business goals, and it was true with debt-reduction goals. We needed to make it true with the goals associated with our future too.

We asked questions and sought answers about our future. Where would we go on the first vacation we took after becoming debt-free? How would we incorporate external giving back into our budget? How old would the kids be when we took our first family mission trip? How would we refocus the energy we had concentrated on debt reduction? What was next in terms of ministry opportunity? All of these and more became a part of our Dream Dates.

It was beautiful to be able to dream again and have our hope renewed. We were careful to not allow the reality of our situation keep us from thinking about the future. It needed to be protected…and then ushered in.

Your Turn…Your Perspective: What dreams have you put on hold? What can you do to begin to put them in action again?

Prayer: Lord, thank You for the ability to dream. I pray You help me to not get bogged down in my reality so much I forget to think of the future. Help me to stay mindful of my dreams.

Day 317
Scam

PSALM 5:6

Keith called me at work one day and said he received a call from the IRS. The caller gave his badge number and proceeded to tell Keith he owed $8932 in back taxes. He had 24 hours to set up a payment plan or there would be a warrant issued for his arrest. The caller proceeded to transfer Keith to the section supervisor for verification of banking information.

I started to laugh, and Keith followed suit. We were being scammed! Several thoughts crossed my mind. The first was how familiar we were with the IRS and how they operated. We knew they would never contact us by phone. They preferred certified mail. In the first few years of our marriage, we owed the IRS every year. We were never able to pay in full and set up a payment arrangement each time. The request for payment always came through certified mail.

We also knew we did not owe any money to the IRS. Our last tax bill was over $3000 and was paid by April 15. Even though it took us a few years to get a handle on our finances, we finally figured out how to manage our taxes. No longer did we experience the penalties, interest and fees associated with not paying our taxes on time. There was no unpaid debt lurking in the background.

If the scam call were a few years earlier, our response would have been quite different. A few years earlier, we did owe the IRS. A few years earlier we did have random old debt lurking around. A few years earlier we would have surely panicked at the call. The panic may have caused us to believe the call and pay the scammers.

It was a sobering reminder of just how much progress was made on our financial journey. We worked hard to clean up our financial mess and managed to come within striking distance of getting it all paid off. The reality of what we accomplished helped us think rationally, and not be fooled by the maliciousness of scammers.

We were confident our financial footprint was clean and knew enough to protect ourselves from fraud by having ID theft protection and paying our bills on time. We also limited the possibility of being hacked by closing accounts and not using debt.

We used cash for purchases and checked our online accounts often. The same week as the IRS scam, we stopped several other fraud attempts by simply being aware and monitoring our financial footprint. We did not panic. We simply followed the same plan we used with our financial coaching clients. We called the bank, identified the fraudulent charge, and waited for the item to be removed.

We knew what to do to protect ourselves.

The IRS scam call was a beautiful reminder of the financial peace we possessed. Even though we were not yet out of debt, we knew how to manage our money and take care of our financial obligations. It felt like a test and we passed with flying colors. What a blessing to feel competent with the resources the Lord entrusted to us! What a blessing to finally be wise with our finances.

Your Turn…Your Perspective: How fraud-proof is your financial picture? Do you have identity theft protection? If not, please get some today!

Prayer: Lord, I pray for financial wisdom. Help me to be keenly aware of those who seek to take advantage of me financially. I pray for discernment as I make financial decisions. Please show me what areas of my financial life still need more growth.

Day 318
Holidays with Friends

PSALM 21:3

Keith and I both loved to entertain, so much so, we made it one of the standard objectives of our family: DO LIFE AROUND THE TABLE.

We especially loved to entertain when the kids were with us. We tried to have families with kids their age join us for a meal at least once or twice during each extended visit. It was not uncommon to invite friends to join us for their birthday celebrations, or just because they happened to be in town visiting. We all enjoyed sharing our table.

Over the years, I realized the one time of the year we were not intentional about having friends over was Christmas. When the kids were with us for Christmas, we tended to hunker down and stay to ourselves. The years they were with us for New Year's Day were filled with memories of people visiting, but not Christmas.

As I thought of this one year in November, I realized it was because most people (our family included) celebrated their own holiday traditions for Christmas. I really wanted to find a way to incorporate our friends into our family traditions. They were an essential part of our lives and the lives of our kids. There must be a way for them to share and enjoy Christmas with us.

I was excited when I found the solution. We could just celebrate Christmas with our friends before we all began to celebrate with our families. I shared my excitement with Keith and asked if he was okay with us having a Christmas celebration with non-family members in the week leading up to Christmas. With his support, I began to reach out to friends to create the guest list.

When we picked the kids up for the beginning of the holiday, we shared our plans of our planned celebration. They were just as excited as we were. We all set about preparing our home for guests. They cleaned and rearranged furniture, and I planned and prepped our menu. On the day of the event, you could feel the energy grow in our little duplex. We were ready for our guests to arrive.

It was a beautiful evening. We laughed. We ate. We ate more. The kids played games, watched movies, and made themselves tired with activity. The adults lingered around the table and shared philosophical conversations, rich with the experiences of the others. It was a magical evening. It was referenced often when our conversation with the kids turned to "remember the time when…"

I learned a valuable lesson from the evening. I learned the importance of recognizing those who are not blood relatives, but who still impact your life the way family does. I learned the value of creating tradition around what is important, and not just what is expected. I learned to make room for others to impact the lives of our kids. An expanded grocery budget was certainly worth the memories created.

I was thankful to have a village to raise our children.

Your Turn…Your Perspective: Name five friends who have richly blessed your life. Call them and tell them.

Prayer: Lord, thank You for my own friends. I pray for their financial journeys. I pray we can support each other as we live in the community we have created. Help them embrace Your ways, just as I have.

Day 319
800 Club

EZEKIEL 28:5; ROMANS 12:2

We were at the tail end of paying off our debt snowball when it reached its peak. My credit score plummeted to the low 600s at its lowest point, and eight years later, after time and diligence in repaying all my debt, it peaked at 820. Never was my credit score so high. In my former life, I would have celebrated. But in this new life, where I lived without debt, the number no longer held any real meaning.

Nevertheless, the lack of meaning did not keep me from feeling pride at my accomplishment. I silently thanked the Lord for helping me get a handle on my debt and become a part of an elite group of people whose credit scores were over 800. I did not want to find pleasure in the accomplishment, but I did.

All my accounts were closed except for an American Express card. Keith and I kept the card open longer than we thought we would. We used it to book hotel rooms, but it finally dawned on us to put a buffer in our checking account for the sole purpose of managing our hotel reservations. Most hotels put a hold on debit cards, and with a buffer in our account to absorb the hold, we no longer needed the American Express card. Shortly after my credit score peaked at 820, we closed the account.

With no credit accounts open and active, my credit score began to drop. Like a rock. The month after we closed the American Express account, it dropped 50 points. Just like my credit score, my heart sank. My brain knew my score would go down. And since we no longer wanted any debt, it would eventually go to zero. But I did not expect the disappointment I felt watching the new number.

I worked my entire life to achieve a credit score of over 800 and found it ironic to achieve it only as a part of letting go of it completely. A score of zero was counterintuitive. I was always told to build up my credit, not get rid of it. I opened my first credit card account in college, and except for being debt-free for a year or so after selling my house, I always carried debt and a credit score.

To be in a place where I should be excited about my score dropping to zero was an odd experience. I questioned whether I really wanted to let it go. I knew I should let it go, but for the briefest of moments, I wanted to hold on to it. It was like a badge of honor and I wanted to show it off.

Fortunately, the moment passed after a few days. I did not mention what I felt to Keith. I just quietly prayed my way through it and allowed the moment of pride to pass. Keeping a credit score meant keeping debt and there was no way we were going to keep debt. My score would soon be zero and I would have a new accomplishment to celebrate. It would mean more to have a zero score than it could ever mean to have a score over 800.

A score of zero would mean true Christ-centered financial wellness. It meant depending on Christ for every need, and never again depending on a bank. I now looked forward to my score going down to zero. I looked forward to celebrating the biggest accomplishment of my financial life.

Your Turn…Your Perspective: In what ways have you followed the world's view of managing personal finances? In what ways have you gone against the world's view?

Prayer: Lord, thank You for the truth, the truth of Your provision. I pray to continue to not be conformed to this world. Thank You for leading me to financial freedom.

Day 320
Prepared

HAGGAI 2:7B

I was looking at a social media feed one day and saw a strange post. I reread it several times to make sure I understood it. A friend's husband unexpectedly passed away. He was 42 years old. He was not ill. His heart simply just stopped working.

I was in shock. I could not begin to imagine what our friend was going through. They thought they would have years to spend together but now would not. I prayed for her to hold on to the peace of Jesus Christ.

We met when they attended our Financial Peace University class a few months prior. I immediately called her to offer our condolences. When she picked up the phone, the first thing she said was "thank you." Because Keith and I put such an emphasis on being prepared when they took our class, they owned an adequate amount of life insurance. It was a humbling moment. At least financially, she would be okay.

I took her food the next day and sat with her a while. She once again thanked me for our guidance and shared what a relief it was to not have to think of money right then. She walked me through their discussions after our class when they made the decision to increase their life insurance coverage. Because of their due diligence, and at a time when her life was literally turned upside down, there was a financial anchor. There was a slice of peace in the midst of the storm.

They also paid off all their debt a few months after the class ended. The sigh of relief on her face when she shared this was palpable. It was one less thing she needed to manage during a time when doing anything other than breathing was difficult.

As I shared the conversation with Keith later, we were both somber. It was a difficult time for our friend, but it was an eye-opening moment for us also. How many couples went through our class? How many did we sit with for financial coaching? How many actually did the hard part and executed an estate plan? We knew our friends did not think they would need to use their estate plan so soon after creating it. It was only a few months since they finished our class.

The tragedy was a reminder of how little we know of the future. We certainly could not predict it. The most we could do was prepare for it as best we can. The best we could do was educate as many people as possible on the importance of being prepared.

Our family ministry of Christ-centered financial wellness was born out of our own adversity. Because we chose to not keep what we learned and experienced to ourselves, we created an opportunity to impact the lives of hundreds of families. We were thankful to make even a small difference for this family and others. We were thankful to see a win, even during a time of loss.

Your Turn…Your Perspective: Do you have ten times your annual income in term life insurance? If not, please increase your coverage immediately. It is the best way to say, "I love you," to your family.

Prayer: Lord, thank You for being with me, even during the difficult seasons of life. I pray to not lose sight of You. Help me to embrace the life of Christ-centered financial wellness and not procrastinate. Please keep me in Your perfect peace.

Day 321
Blessed to Tow

JEREMIAH 9:24

I flew back to help my mom recover from knee surgery. It was a full week and I wanted simply to get back home. My flight was scheduled for 5:30A.M. which meant I was up well before the sun. Just as I was boarding my flight out of Columbia, SC bound for Washington Dulles, I found out my connection from Dulles to Kansas City was cancelled. It was too late to go to the information desk in Columbia so off to Dulles I went.

When I arrived at Dulles, I found few options. I could either spend the day flying all over the country to get home five hours after my original arrival time; or I could sit tight in the airport for the same amount of time and take the next flight to Kansas City. As frustrating as it was, I opted to just wait. I settled in with my breakfast and lunch vouchers, and busied myself with my laptop.

Keith picked me up at the Kansas City airport seven hours later. I was exhausted. I just wanted to go home and have a quiet evening. As we were getting on the interstate, we noticed a pick-up truck on the side of the road. It did not look good. The front tire was at a weird angle, and the position of the vehicle made it dangerous to attempt to change it. We pulled ahead and stopped. Keith got out to see if he could lend a hand, and it was worse than we thought. In addition to a tire blowout, the transmission had also died. There was nothing we could do to help. Or was there?

I reminded Keith of our AAA service. But it was tied to the individual, not the vehicle. As long as we were with them, the couple from Nebraska could have their truck towed anywhere within 50 miles. Keith shared our offer with the couple and they gladly accepted. The tow truck arrived, and between our vehicle and the cab of the tow truck, we got ourselves and the family of five to a local repair shop.

They thanked us over and over. We told them over and over how it was not a big deal. We were thankful to be in the position to assist. We knew it would be an expensive repair. The least we could do was offer a free tow.

The entire experience made a huge impact on me for so many reasons. First, it was a reminder to stay focused on getting out of debt so we could be ready when emergencies showed up. Second, it was a reminder of the importance of putting aside money to properly maintain our vehicles on a regular basis. Third, it was a reminder of the magnitude generosity plays in the lives of those who need it. And finally, it was a reminder of how God sometimes has other plans.

Had I made my original flight, we would not have been available to assist our new Nebraska friends. Had I allowed the delay to annoy me, I would not have possessed a generous attitude when we passed them on the highway. We might not have even stopped. And, I almost certainly would not have been cheerful which may have caused me to not have remembered the terms of the AAA membership. God was able to use us because our lives were interrupted. While I did not always embrace interruptions, I was certainly thankful for this one.

Your Turn…Your Perspective: How has your life been altered by a recent interruption? What was your attitude before, during and after? How did it impact you financially?

Prayer: Lord, please help me get to a place of generosity and patience. I pray for you to use my journey to make me more compassionate to the needs of others. Please remind me of this if I begin to slip back to the ways of the old me.

Day 322
I Want

PROVERBS 28:6; PHILIPPIANS 3:12-14

People were always in awe of the amount of discipline Keith and I exercised with our finances. We accepted their praise with humility because we understood the value in sharing our story. It was our hope to do more than simply garner praise from people, however.

We wanted to inspire others to have the same discipline in their own finances. We wanted them to see the value in how we lived our lives and make similar adjustments in their own. Our process was really simple in nature. It was just hard for most people because it went against the strong "I want" desire most of us lived by.

One of the ways we were able to make such big headway with our debt was because we did not often give in to the "I want" desire. It was not easy, but we knew we needed to stay the course if we were going to reduce our debt to zero. If we gave in to the "I want" mentality, we knew with certainty we would fail at becoming debt-free.

It was a defeat we were determined not to experience. God gave us a glimpse of what our future could be when we embraced the idea of debt-freedom. We did not want to disappoint Him anymore than we wanted to disappoint ourselves.

My "I want" list included buying a home, traveling, and investing for the future. Keith's "I want" list included exercise equipment, giving to family, and college planning. There were smaller "I want" lists for both of us which included book buying and entertainment along with sporting events and newer vehicles. It varied through the years, but the core "I want" items never really changed. It was always a conscious choice to stay focused on the goal of debt reduction.

We needed to talk each other off the ledge of "I want" many times. It was painful at times to watch Keith admire a truck when he drove a much smaller car which was really too small for his 6'4" frame. We both knew a truck for him was in our future, but not until the debt was done.

I constantly struggled to manage my contentment issues around owning a home. I wanted to decorate, buy furniture, and create a prayer room for each of us. We wanted to entertain and buy a grill and patio furniture. But not until the debt was done.

It would have been easy to just give in to "I want," especially when we got to the end and only a few student loans were left to pay. Our debt-reduction zeal garnered us very high credit scores, making both a car loan and a mortgage easily attainable. A few signatures here and there, and we could have everything on our "I want" list.

We knew the discipline of the delay would be worth the effort in the end. Philippians 3:14 says, "I press on toward the goal to win the prize for which God has called me heavenward in Christ Jesus." Our prize was coming. We just needed to hold on and not give in to "I want."

Your Turn…Your Perspective: What "I want" do you have in your life? How well do you manage them?

Prayer: Lord, thank You for guiding me on this journey. Thank You for giving me the courage to not give in to the "I want" list of my life. I pray to keep You and the race You have set before me as the ultimate prize.

Day 323
Tip

PSALM 15:5

It was Thanksgiving and our turn to share the holiday with our kids. Since we alternated major holidays according to the custody arrangement with their mother, we were only able to spend Thanksgiving with them every other year.

We planned to enjoy Thanksgiving with Keith's family, and decided to stay in St. Louis for the entire holiday. It did not make sense to pick the kids up on Tuesday night, drive four hours back to Kansas, and then drive four hours back to St. Louis on Thursday. We used our loyalty points to get a discounted rate on the hotel and settled into our weekend retreat.

Dinner was not until much later in the day so we busied ourselves in our room after breakfast on Thanksgiving Day. When the cleaning lady appeared at our door, we requested towels and told her she did not need to do a full cleaning. She insisted on at least cleaning the bathroom for us.

As she went about her tasks, we asked her to share a little about herself. She shared our daughter's first name and stated how much she was looking forward to spending time with her family later in the day.

We always made sure to leave our hotel cleaning people a tip and a note of thanks at the end of our stay. The kids would write the note because it was our way of teaching them to be generous and kind to those who served for a living. I felt prompted to give this cleaning lady her tip upfront instead of waiting until we checked out days later. Since they shared the same name, we told our daughter to quickly write the note and present it with the tip to her namesake.

With a not-always-shy voice, our daughter managed to thank the cleaning lady for serving us and offered the note with the $20 bill. The look on the older woman's face was one of shock and humility. The tears which welled in her eyes caught all of us off guard. She shared how she spent the last of her money on gas earlier in the day and did not have money to buy the supplies she needed to make her portion of Thanksgiving dinner. She prayed on the way to work for God to show her favor and provision.

We were surprised by her honesty and transparency, and humbled to have been used as a part of His plan. We were simply trying to use the moment to teach our children about generosity. We had no idea how extensive the lesson would be.

Our daughter was especially moved by this older woman with her same name. She could tell the woman worked hard and earned little. She was made painfully aware of how a seemingly small amount of money could impact the life of another. She hugged her namesake and wished her a Happy Thanksgiving. She also thanked her for taking care of us. Keith and I followed our daughter's lead and hugged the woman also. The tears in my own eyes would not stay put. The moment was incredibly tender. The true meaning of Thanksgiving was on display in our room and I was thankful to experience it.

Your Turn…Your Perspective: What seemingly small gesture have you made recently which impacted someone else? How has someone else's generosity blessed you?

Prayer: Lord, I pray for those who serve. They are so often invisible to us. I pray to see them with new eyes and acknowledge them with kindness and generosity. Please help me to show grace to those who serve me.

Day 324
Two A.M. Encounters

PSALM 40:4; JOHN 4:23

My first 2A.M. encounter with God was in July of 2000. All was quiet, and distractions were low. It was the night (or morning) I was told by the Holy Spirit to set the goal to become a Sales Director with Mary Kay Cosmetics in record time. People questioned it, but I knew what I heard and set about the task to get it done.

I learned a lot from those early encounters. Namely, to not question what I was told by the Lord. As the financial hole I dug for myself got deeper, there were more and more 2A.M. mornings. Money was a constant worry for me during the decade of running my own business. I was never sure if I would have enough, how it would show up, or when it would show up. I prayed…a lot. I begged God to supply my needs even though He had proven Himself faithful to me time and time again.

Still, I chose to question His ability to provide. I struggled constantly to stay in a place of faith. It took hard work to keep my mind focused on Him and not on my circumstances. There was a constant battle to not live in financial fear. And because He knew I was not yet sure, the 2A.M. encounters kept coming. They came constantly until I began to believe.

My 2A.M. encounters with Him were the reassurance I needed to make it through. He gave me scriptures to comfort me, business ideas to implement, and confirmation of my direction. He rarely chastised me, unless I was intentionally disobedient, and His presence was always prevalent. I never doubted Him being with me.

My encounters shaped my faith and grew me spiritually. I was eager to soak up His words and encouragement. I knew they were a huge part of me sustaining my business for 10 years. I finally stopped fighting the early morning wake-up call and began to embrace my time with the Lord.

As I learned more about managing money and trusting His plan for it, my 2A.M. encounters lessened. At the height of my financial desperation, I experienced two or three a week. I experienced just one or two a year after Keith and I began to implement the strategy taught in Financial Peace University. It was not because I was married. It was all because I finally had a sound financial biblical foundation to stand on.

Over time, I became less anxious about purchases and spending. Fear was replaced with resolve. The decision to evaluate our budget to find cuts became a monthly occurrence, and we sacrificed and dug in to stay on task. We also learned how to approach financial challenges with critical thought instead of being reactionary. We grew closer to God and each other through it all.

As we neared the financial finish line, my 2A.M. encounters began to shift in focus. My call to join the Lord became more about how to serve Him, and less about how to pay our bills. I still knew instinctively to get up if I awoke between 2A.M. and 3A.M. but was no longer so sure of the reason. Prayer and journaling became my assignment from the Lord instead of a desperate cry for financial guidance.

Your Turn…Your Perspective: Describe an encounter you have had with God. What made it memorable? How did it change you?

Prayer: Lord, thank You for loving me through the difficult times. I pray to never lose sight of how much You will do for me. Please help me be mindful of the beauty of time spent in Your presence.

Day 325
Gift Card Giving

MATTHEW 6:4

For Christmas one year, we received several gift cards to a chain restaurant. It was not one we tended to frequent, but our kids loved it. We decided to wait until they were with us and then use our gift cards to have a rare family dining out experience.

The four of us settled in and stared at our menu. With over $100 in gift cards, we were each able to get pretty much what we wanted. It was one of the few times we allowed the kids free reign in ordering. It was fun to watch them go back and forth over what to order. "We get to order appetizers AND dessert?!" They were wild with excitement.

Our server was a wonderful woman named Judy. Judy was not new to serving. She obviously knew the secret to happy customers because she was engaging, helpful and added great value to our dining experience. We fell in love with her from the very beginning. We learned a lot about Judy as we enjoyed our meal. With over 20 years of service at the same restaurant, she absolutely loved her job. Even the kids loved her.

As our evening came to an end, we were all full and satisfied. Judy delivered our check to the table and told us what a pleasure it was to serve us. When I looked at the check, I realized we were not even close to using all the money available on our gift cards. But, there also was not enough left for a second visit for the four of us. We could keep the gift cards and add money to them for another visit or…

I leaned over and shared the receipt with Keith. I reminded him about the gift cards and just how much was left over. I quietly explained what I wanted to do and asked his thoughts. He thought it was a wonderful idea. We put all the gift cards in the card holder and placed it on the table. When Judy returned, we told her to keep whatever was left. She was used to the gesture but did not yet realize the size of her tip.

She came back a few moments later with shock and tears in her eyes. I slid over so she could sit with us in the booth. We told her we were very thankful for her kindness and wanted to repay the gesture. She kept saying thank you over and over. It made my heart full to watch the depth of her gratitude.

The kids did not quite understand what was going on. After Judy left, we explained the tip and how we thought it was a great opportunity to showcase how much we appreciated her service. They thought it was cool and told us we were cool, too. Nothing like getting approval from your kids!

As we left the restaurant and began the drive home, I thought about Judy. I thought about the gift cards. I thought about my level of giving in the past and how much more I seemed to want to give lately. I knew it was primarily because I chose to embrace God's ways of managing money. I was never a minimal tipper, but I rarely went above and beyond the way we did with Judy.

Part of my hesitancy in being more open-handed was not feeling financially secure enough to go above and beyond. The other part was simply not knowing how to be generous. I was thankful once again for the journey Keith and I chose to take. I was constantly amazed at the growth we experienced because we chose to honor God with our finances.

Your Turn…Your Perspective: What's your best giving story as a giver? As a receiver?

Prayer: Lord, I pray I can see the beauty of my financial journey. I pray to be open to giving to others and not just think of myself. Please strengthen my giving muscle so I can be more like You.

Day 326
I'm Debt Free!

DEUTERONOMY 6:6-7

Keith and I worked hard to teach our kids what we learned about managing money God's way. We worked to teach them debt was not viewed favorably in the Bible. We made the decision to become debt-free and never use debt again. Since we were serious about being debt-free, it meant they needed to be serious about it too.

We were in Wal-Mart one day, and our daughter remembered she needed razors. We had purchased some for her a few months earlier, but she took them with her when she returned to her mother's house. This meant there were no razors for her personal use in Kansas.

She asked if she could have more, and I explained we already purchased what she needed and would not be buying any more. I told her she could use her own money to purchase them if she needed them. She thought about it for a moment and said she understood.

Since our daughter had not brought any money with her, she asked if the "house" could loan her the money until we returned home. I asked her if she knew what it meant to borrow money. She said she realized she would be in debt and promised to repay it as soon as we returned home. With those conditions, we all (including the "house") agreed she could pay back the cost of the razors when we returned home.

Keith and I decided not to remind her. We wanted to see how long it would take her to get rid of the debt. We did not charge her interest, but explained what interest was. She knew, in a different debt situation, the amount borrowed would accrue interest every day it was not repaid.

Within an hour of us returning home, she came into the kitchen with the exact amount she had borrowed and proudly handed it over. I hugged her and told her I was proud of how responsible she was. I also asked her if she learned anything. She told me she learned to always have money with her in case she wanted to purchase something.

At dinner later in the evening, our daughter cleared her throat and stated she needed to make an announcement. We all turned to look at her as she said, "Three, two, one...I'm debt-free!" We all cheered loudly. It felt amazing watching her grin from ear to ear at her accomplishment.

People did not understand why we made such a big deal of explaining debt to our kids. They also did not understand why we went to the trouble of creating scenarios where they had to deal with real life money issues.

All we knew was we wanted our kids to grow up to be responsible adults, and it was better for them to learn money lessons while the consequences were small. Having our daughter do her debt-free scream was a priceless example of the fruit of our labor.

Your Turn...Your Perspective: How do you teach financial concepts to the children in your life? How do you determine when to let them "fail?"

Prayer: Lord, I pray for the opportunity to impact those around me with my journey. I know I cannot have a testimony without first experiencing a test. I pray to continue to persevere and not stop until I complete this hurdle. I thank You for the opportunity to make a difference in my life and in the lives of others.

Day 327
Beauty from Ashes

PSALM 112:3; ISAIAH 61:3

A friend experienced the unfortunate loss of a child. It created a sadness most people will never understand, and it cannot be described. And even though I recently lost my 16-year old nephew, I could not imagine what it felt like to lose a son. I was talking with my friend a few months after the funeral and we began to discuss how to begin to put life back together. A payout from the insurance policy arrived a few days prior, and my friend was struggling with what to do with it.

I knew I must share what I knew in terms of being responsible with the money, but the last thing I wanted was to sound like a financial coach. I prayed for compassion. Compassion in my voice. Compassion in my choice of words. Compassion in my silence. Compassion in the questions asked. I prayed for wisdom and for the Lord to guide the conversation.

Hesitantly, I asked the amount of the policy payout. I held my breath, praying the entire time for my friend to hear my desire to assist and not view my question as snooping. After the answer to the initial question was answered, I slowly asked the other questions on my mind.

Over the next few minutes, the information I needed to assist was shared by my friend. Through years of listening to "The Dave Ramsey Show," and working with our own clients, I knew how to respond. I slowly walked my friend along the path leading to financial freedom and offered to assist in mapping it out. I knew the importance of not getting too excited. I was trained in how to read personality types and recognized the need to speak slowly and softly. It did not matter how long it took. I vowed to talk with my friend as long as needed to insure all her questions and concerns were addressed.

My friend struggled with the idea of using the money to get out of debt. I tried to explain the importance of viewing the insurance payout as the beauty from the ashes. Isaiah 61:3 spoke of embracing the goodness received after a bad situation. It could obviously never replace my friend's son, and there was never a question of what my friend would have preferred. We both knew life was much more valuable than an insurance payout. I also knew the value of being a good steward, especially from our own financial journey emphasizing the importance of being debt-free. Ultimately, I knew my friend would have to make the final decision with what to do with the money. All I could do was pray for discernment.

I decided not to ask again about how my friend chose to use the insurance payout. I spoke as a friend, not as a financial coach. With a coaching client, we would have set up next steps at the end of the call in addition to setting up a timeline to completion. My friend was not a client, however, and I offered my assistance as a friend, not a coach. I did not have a right to impose my normal coaching "homework." All I could do was pray for the best financial outcome.

We never spoke of the insurance payment again, leaving things as if the conversation never happened. I continued to pray and support my friend in every way I could, and trusted the Lord to do the rest.

Your Turn…Your Perspective: Describe the last time you were on the giving or receiving end of a difficult conversation. How did the result impact you?

Prayer: Lord, I know You are with me. I thank You for the good and the bad. I pray for the peace to make it through the bad and thank You for the joy of the good. Please help me be sensitive to the needs of those around me. Help me to always be compassionate.

Day 328
Weird

LUKE 12:42

Keith and I worked hard to make sure our kids understood why our life was different. The concept of delayed gratification was foreign to them. Volunteering to serve those less fortunate was also not something they experienced often. We wanted them to know what it was like to not just think about themselves. As a result, we did not alter our serving when they were with us. Instead, we took them with us. We also created extra opportunities for them to volunteer to grow their serving muscles.

During the summer and Christmas holiday visits, there was at least one day of volunteering every few weeks. One year we took down the Christmas decorations at a homeless shelter. Another Saturday during the summer, we were all at the church cleaning playground equipment and painting curbs. When we volunteered to host tables at the church's marriage seminars, the kids were assigned to help with childcare.

We took every opportunity we could to let our kids see volunteering in action. They were never excited about going, but were always excited they went. The people we encountered blessed our lives tremendously and the blessing extended to our kids. Sometimes they met new friends, and they always learned something new.

We also wanted them to know about giving. Every week after we paid them their "commission," we discussed how much they would give in church. Since their service was in a different part of the church, the "how was church for you?" question always included their giving experience.

We talked with them about the difference in giving and tithing. We did not shy away from the question of how much we tithed; it was important for us to model what it meant to give generously and be transparent. They also saw us donate clothes and shoes to service organizations. We included them in the decision to donate clothing as they outgrew it.

In the beginning, we knew they thought we were weird. Their perception of us did not matter, however. We knew our ways lined up with what the Lord wanted us to do, and it was our job to pass those thoughts and ideas on to our kids. Our goal was for our thought process on giving and volunteering to eventually become a natural way of thinking for them also. We chose to be intentional in how we approached giving and volunteering. We did not give in to the pressures to raise our kids the way other people wanted.

We knew it could be years before we saw any fruit from our efforts. We continued to steadily plod our way into examples of giving and serving, knowing the more exposure we gave them, the better chance they had of embracing our way of living. We were excited to share in their growth in the meantime.

Your Turn...Your Perspective: Think of a time when your ways of serving and giving made an impact on someone's life. What was the experience? How did it make you feel to influence someone?

Prayer: Lord, I pray to always have a heart to serve. It is not the most natural thing for me to do, but I want to be a good steward in this area also. Show me where I can make a difference even as I continue to grow my financial wellness muscle.

Day 329
Linchpin

A friend of mine worked for the same Fortune 500 Company for more than 20 years. She was good at her job and enjoyed the variety her projects allowed. Over about a 5-year period, however, changes in leadership began to impact her work environment.

The caliber of her projects decreased. She was asked to frequently travel to more obscure locations, and she was no longer challenged by the assignments offered. But even though she was not as thrilled with the new changes, she continued to work hard and produce a quality product.

Then the day came when her new assignment was the worst possible fit for her and her skillset. Not only would the project require frequent travel to the far northeast part of the country during the winter months, but it was neither a career-shaping assignment nor did it adequately utilize her abilities.

My friend needed to decide. Should she take the assignment and endure the poor terms which came along with it, or should she approach her management team and request a different assignment which better fit her expertise? She prayed about it and enlisted others to pray with her for quite some time before choosing to turn down the position. She honestly felt her superiors would fire her for not accepting the assignment but was willing to accept the consequences of her decision.

Sure enough, a few months after turning down the initial assignment, she was put in a situation where she would either need to resign or accept a different assignment which fit her skillset even less. After much prayer, she chose to resign.

Resigning was not an easy decision for her, but she knew it was the right thing to do. It was the right thing for her career and the right thing for her peace of mind. She made the decision based not only on what she needed financially, but on what she needed for career fulfillment and quality of life. And although she had been out of the job-search market for over 20 years with no idea what to expect, she knew it was what was also necessary for her overall Christ-centered financial wellness.

Author Seth Godin said in his book *Linchpin:* "Perhaps your challenge isn't finding a better project or a better boss. Perhaps you need to get in touch with what it means to feel passionate. People with passion look for ways to make things happen."[12]

My friend had passion and decided to "look for ways to make things happen." And because she was on a journey of Christ-centered financial wellness, she was able to do so. She chose to not be limited by her work environment. She chose to embrace the unknown and trust the Lord to provide for her needs. And He did.

Your Turn…Your Perspective: Who has been an example of faith for you recently? What inspiration did you receive from them? How have you applied it to your own life?

Prayer: Lord, thank You for the examples of faith we are able to see in others. I pray to be inspired by their boldness and courage. I want to take action also. I want to be bold and courageous in You.

Day 330
Freedom Cry

PSALM 119:14

Keith and I chose to be very transparent about our debt. We shared our financial numbers with our Financial Peace University classes and our coaching clients. We shared our budgets with anyone who asked for extra assistance. We talked with our kids openly about our debt and where we were on the journey to get rid of it. We did not hide any of it from anyone. It was our desire to inspire others by our own experiences as much as possible.

There was a sense of urgency to help everyone interested in making a change. Even though they might not know yet how important it was to be debt-free, we knew. And because we knew, we wanted them to "get it" as quickly as they could. Our solution was to give them access to as much of our financial life as possible to help them see the importance of getting to a debt-free status as soon as possible.

We helped many people be hopeful and stay inspired, and we used "The Dave Ramsey Show" to keep us hopeful and inspired. We listened to the show every day and often started our daily recap with, "Did you listen to Dave today?" In most instances, the question referred to someone who was on the show to do a "debt-free scream."

These people shared incredible stories about their journey to becoming debt-free. They talked about their debt, how much they paid off, and how long it took to do so. They also shared how they found out about the principles of Financial Peace, what they learned along the way, and how the process impacted their lives. It would not be uncommon for them to have family in the audience for support. Crazy props, signs and t-shirts were often a part of the moment.

They traveled from all over the country (and the world), sometimes scheduling their time on the air with Dave months in advance. They all went to Nashville or called into the show so they could "count it down" and yell "we're debt-free!" The audience always erupted with applause, and in some instances, the tears freely flowed.

My tears often flowed as well. Tears of joy. Tears of sadness. Tears of amazement at what they overcame to finally be able to yell those important three words. Their story was our story. Their frustration was our frustration. Their hope was our hope. If they could do it, we could too. We would do it. It was just a little longer before it would be our turn.

Keith and I listened intently every day to people sharing their stories. We knew we would never meet them, but also knew our lives would never be the same because of the testimony they chose to share. The debt-free screams gave us hope to continue to remain steadfast in our own journey. They helped us look forward to the day when we would go to Nashville to do our own debt-free scream.

Your Turn...Your Perspective: How do you stay motivated when working on a goal? What role have you recently played in motivating others?

Prayer: Lord, thank You for the testimonies which keep me going. Please keep me humble but transparent with anyone who can benefit from my story. It may not be easy, but I want to honor You by helping anyone I can. Give me courage, Lord, to be the difference for someone else.

Ticket, Please!
PSALM 37:21; GENESIS 12:2

When Keith and I decided to move forward with the creation of LisaYJones Ministries, we knew we needed to get some business education. I was gun-shy about relying too much on the business skills I cultivated in the past. Those businesses were built on debt and I knew the days of using debt were gone.

Dave Ramsey had a platform around doing business debt-free, and during the last year of our debt snowball, he came to Kansas City to impart wisdom to our business community. We were still paying off debt but made the decision to use our fun money to purchase tickets to the all-day event.

We were both excited to attend and looked forward to how God would use us and the experience. A few weeks before the event, however, we found out Keith would not be able to attend. A last-minute business trip would take him out of town. We discussed what to do with his ticket and I suggested we gift it to someone.

This was a huge step for me. Keith was always the more generous one. I tended to hold back, and think more, before giving. I wanted to give, but I took the idea of "put your own mask on first" a little too seriously sometimes. Giving was just not my first thought.

So, for me to be the one to suggest donating the ticket, instead of attempting to recoup the cost, was a huge step towards increasing my level of generosity. I felt God's blessing on our decision and set about finding someone to gift. It was harder than I thought. I identified a few front runners, but they all politely declined for one reason or another.

What was supposed to be a quick, "Do you want a ticket?" was taking a lot more time and energy than I anticipated. "Why is this so hard, Lord?" I did not understand. Before I knew it, the event was the next day and I had yet to find a home for the ticket.

Finally, I quieted myself and asked God to show me who should have the ticket. Without much time passing, He gave me a name. We were friends on social media, had exchanged pleasantries a few times, but I did not really know her. I just knew God told me to give her the ticket. I messaged her and made my offer. And frankly, I gave up. I was expecting another, "no thank you."

I got just the opposite. She was literally on her knees in prayer when my message came through. My frustrating attempt at generosity turned out to be her answer to prayer. She quickly said, "YES!" and thanked me profusely. The event was the catalyst she needed to get her business turned in the direction God wanted.

What was supposed to be a simple act of generosity turned out to be much more. God showed me the importance of bringing EVERYTHING before Him before taking action. But, in the end, He still used my misguided attempt at generosity to bring all honor and glory to Himself. I was thankful to be the vessel He chose.

Your Turn…Your Perspective: Name a time when you gave with impure motives. What was your reasoning? What was the end result? Looking back, what would you do differently?

Prayer: Lord, thank You for my increased desire to be generous. I pray it is a muscle which continues to grow. Please help me to always stop and listen and seek Your guidance in all decisions, even the seemingly small ones. I pray You bless me to be a blessing.

Day 332
Poor People Have Poor Ways

MATTHEW 25:18

I was having coffee with a friend one day when the conversation turned to money management. She knew Keith and I followed Dave Ramsey and taught Financial Peace University. We talked about how difficult it could be to stay focused on the financial goals set for the family. It all came down to mindset. We both agreed a person must want more for their future to embrace the discipline of financial stewardship today.

My friend shared a saying her grandmother used to always utter, "Poor people have poor ways." She said she did not understand the saying for the longest time, and the full meaning did not come into focus for her until after she was an adult. Even though I understood immediately what my friend's grandmother meant, I would not have understood it before Keith and I began to be intentional about managing our money.

Being poor was not as much about not having money, as much as it was about choosing the behavior and attitudes associated with poverty. Being poor was all about having a minimalist mindset.

I pondered her comment for many days after our time together. "Poor people have poor ways." It was a reminder of how important it was to make wise choices and to think positively. The consequences of those choices were far reaching and affected a person's life for more time than most people realized.

I thought of coaching clients we met with a few days earlier. They believed because they made a great living, a budget was not necessary. Purchases were made without thought of the long-term consequences. Credit was used carelessly even though they made more than enough money to pay cash for their purchases. They chose the most expensive version of most items instead of looking for the best overall value. We discussed many times the importance of not making impulse purchases and monetary decisions, but their consumption of things indicated our conversation missed its mark.

It was disheartening to see the behavior continue month after month, and I began to think our business relationship needed to be severed. I did not believe they were committed to the changes we originally agreed upon. It became clear that despite their significant income, they were poor people with poor ways.

Richard Francis Burton said: "Broke is a temporary condition, poor is a state of mind." Our clients made plenty of money but were incredibly poor. Their poor state of mind would continue to stifle their wealth opportunities, and ultimately, limit the legacy they passed on to their children and grandchildren.

Keith and I both spent the first part of our adult lives as poor people with poor ways. But, we made the decision to put the past behind us and create a legacy of abundance for our family. We did not have a lot of material possessions but certainly were not poor. Our state of mind became of one of wealth and abundance. We knew the legacy we passed on to our kids would be one of great faith. It would take a great deal of effort and time, but was worth all of it. We were no longer poor people, and we did not have poor ways. We were thankful for the transformation and what it meant to our family.

Your Turn…Your Perspective: What "poor ways" do you have in relation to money? What changes in your mindset are on the horizon?

Prayer: Lord, thank You for the desire to serve You with my finances and financial decisions. Please help me to get rid of my poor ways. I want to live in abundance and think in abundance. Show me what changes are needed to make it happen.

Day 333
Overflow

PSALM 106:5

Some friends were working on their debt snowball during the same time we were working on ours. We were a little farther ahead of them in terms of time, with farther to go in terms of amount. They were inspired by our tenacity and it helped to spur them to get out of debt.

They made some radical changes in their lives to tighten down their budget and their lifestyle. It was humbling for them to sell toys they loved and enjoyed, take work assignments which put a strain on their family, and make other sacrifices; all in the name of short-term sacrifice for long term gain.

About two years into their journey, "Mrs. Friend" called to share some good news. She worked for a rather large company and recently completed her annual performance review with her boss. Everyone was incredibly impressed with "Mrs. Friend's" work during the last 12 months. As a result of her hard work and dedication to her clients and the company, she was going to receive a bonus.

"Mrs. Friend" was obviously excited about the recognition and knew she and her husband would use any cash received to cut into their remaining debt. She was not expecting to hear what came next. Her bonus was to be in the form of company stock options. Lots of it. The current value was over $30,000.

"Mrs. Friend" was beside herself. She clearly saw the hand of God at work in her career, her life, and her finances. She and her husband continued to do the hard part of digging themselves out of their financial situation, and at times, were not sure they would ever get out of debt. The promise of this bonus gave them hope and shed a strong light at the end of a very long tunnel.

Our friends were beginning to understand the discipline needed to live a life of Christ-centered financial wellness, and could see God honoring their commitment to living His way by providing for their needs in a very tangible way.

God honors hard work and the commitment to getting out of debt. The two ideas went hand in hand. Do the hard things, make the hard choice, and God will show up and give you a push. It may not always be a $30,000 push, but it is a push nonetheless.

With a push, God allows you to live in overflow where your debt-reduction efforts seem to be magnified. He allows you to experience a small reprieve in the journey as if in preparation for the next big obstacle.

We were excited our friends were able to experience God's overflow. We prayed it would be what they needed to see the benefit of in staying the course until they finished.

Your Turn…Your Perspective: What overflow blessing have you experienced lately? How did your experience impact your view of your current financial goals?

Prayer: Lord, please help me recognize the overflow in my own life. I thank You for the financial reprieves which show up when I least expect them. I pray to always be mindful to give You all honor and glory for any gift You choose to give. I thank You for being with me on my journey of Christ-centered financial wellness.

Day 334
Open Sesame

PSALM 40:17

Before we discovered Christ-centered financial wellness, I was always intimidated by the mail. Envelopes representing any type of financial institution made me nervous. I was constantly afraid I overspent or was overdrawn. The never-ending fear of forgetting to pay a bill gripped me. I did not want to know about any of it. I allowed the envelopes to pile up month after month, choosing instead to stick my head in the sand.

Keith's financial life mirrored much of my own and he cultivated his own blend of avoidance tactics. Together, we made quite the financial pair.

When we got married and made the commitment to face our finances head on, we slowly began to let go of the unhealthy financial habits and began to make better choices. One of those choices was the simple act of opening each piece of mail which came to our home. It was an exercise in perseverance and discipline and it was not easy. I often approached the mail with so much fear, my palms sweat and my hands shook. But we were determined to no longer be ruled by fear.

The mail was not kind in the beginning. There were several IRS statements demanding more income taxes. There was old debt which finally caught up with the address changes. Student loans came out of deferment. There were new creditors collecting on old debts. You name it, we had it. It was overwhelming, embarrassing, and humiliating to be tracked down with such vengeance because of poor financial choices.

Over time the fear began to be replaced with curiosity. *Who has found us today?* we asked ourselves. "Oh look! It's a duplicate! No new creditors. Yay!" Slowly our attitudes about the mail changed as we made headway on cleaning up our financial mess.

Then we noticed the mail itself began to change. Instead of the non-descript envelopes bringing bad news, we started to find good news in the envelopes. A plain white envelope revealed a check from a previous employer. An envelope resembling a medical bill was actually an overpayment being refunded. Another weird-looking envelope revealed paperwork for a class action lawsuit, and several months later, the check showed up in yet another blank-looking envelope.

It was amazing. In the five years we worked on debt reduction, we easily received close to $1000 in random overpayments and refunds. It completely changed how we approached "junk mail." We got excited when we saw a random envelope because we knew possibilities were inside. Our piqued curiosity often rewarded us with the gift of a push toward the finish line.

There was no way to know how much money we would have missed out on if we continued to live in fear of the mail. The lesson of not living in fear firmly took root, and we were thankful to have learned it. It forever changed our mindset about financial wellness and helped us to trust God's plan for our lives, even when we did not understand it.

Your Turn...Your Perspective: What fear has controlled your life? How did you overcome it? What did it teach you?

Prayer: Lord, I pray for the courage to face financial fear. Please help me approach each random financial experience as an opportunity to grow closer to You. Please strengthen my resolve to get through this. Help me, Holy Spirit.

Day 335
Community of Peace

PSALM 45:12

One of the ways Keith and I stayed accountable to our goal to become debt-free was by teaching Dave Ramsey's Financial Peace University. We were fortunate to have a home church which saw the value in offering the class. As the demand for more information on managing finances became evident, we jumped at the opportunity to facilitate.

We loved our class members. They were like our children, financially speaking. We were invested in their future and wanted to make sure they got the tools they needed to succeed with money. And just like children, each class was different. Some classes were small, which created the opportunity for more intimate conversation. Other classes were larger, which offered more robust discussion and diverse examples to explore. Some were oozing with debt; others were completely debt-free.

One class was packed with couples and singles of all ages and backgrounds. We all got along fabulously, and each lesson was punctuated with laughter and mutual admiration. It was a struggle each week to get them to leave because the discussions were so lively.

We were happy to celebrate with the attendees on graduation night. They were excited to be on their own, but several admitted being a little nervous. We held their hands for nine weeks, and now it was time for the financial training wheels to come off. Could they sustain what they learned once they went back to their lives? Were the tools and skillset they learned hardwired enough to not go back to the way they used to manage money? They were not sure.

After class was over, one couple approached us and asked if we could get together every now and then to discuss how things were going. They wanted to simply come together just to talk.

We thought it was a grand idea and made the decision to open it up to all our past graduates. The FPU Support Group was born. The group gathered every quarter to discuss the good, bad, and the ugly associated with Christ-centered financial wellness. There was always laughter, and many times tears. There were big wins to celebrate, and support when needed for epic failures.

We gathered in homes and brought food and questions. We each were the teacher and the student, taking away as much as we brought. We did life together.

It was amazing how much value these new friends brought to our lives as we continued to work our own way out of debt and then encouraged many of them to do the same. They became a pivotal part of our story. We knew they were our cheerleaders, and we were theirs.

Living a life contrary to the world was not an easy task. Our little community offered support to others choosing to go against the grain and live their financial lives God's way. What a blessing it was – to us and to them.

Your Turn…Your Perspective: What support network do you have in place? Who are your accountability partners? How have they stretched you recently? If you do not have one, what's stopping you?

Prayer: Lord, I thank You for community. I pray for the wisdom to constantly seek wise counsel. Thank You for the reminder that I am not alone.

New Consultant

PSALM 41:1; ACTS 9:18

When I started my business with Mary Kay Cosmetics, I did not wear make-up. Burgundy lipstick and loose powder were all I owned, and I wore it every day. I had never seen an eyeliner, and did not know what skin care was, let alone how to customize it to the skin type of others. I would need quite the education if I was going to be successful as an independent beauty consultant.

Consultant meant knowledge. Consultant meant experience. Consultant meant having the ability to assess a situation and provide viable options. On the day I became an independent beauty consultant, I possessed none of those abilities and my friends and family knew it. So, it was no surprise when they did not flock to become my clients. Even though I represented an award-winning company, I still needed to prove myself as a consultant.

When Keith and I began to grow from the financial principles we learned from Dave Ramsey and Crown Financial Ministries, we shared what we learned with our friends and family. There was only one problem. We were without credibility.

Our friends and family knew we were in the middle of a financial mess. They knew we did not know any more than they did about how to manage money. In their minds, they were doing a better job than we were. Our message was falling on deaf ears.

We were the ones who allowed debt to take over our lives. They were managing their debt just fine. We were the ones who were "broke." There was plenty of money to pay their bills. We were the ones who were overwhelmed by our circumstances, not them. They did not trust the depth of our biblical financial knowledge. Our friends and family were not impressed.

It was a long, hard battle to educate them on the financial truths we chose to live by. And honestly, most of them never embraced it. It was disappointing and disheartening to find a way out of the darkness of debt, but not have more of those closest to you choose to follow you.

We created and executed a successful plan for ourselves but were not successful in helping many of our friends and family to make change in their own lives. We could allow their decisions to impact our relationships, or we could quietly go about our own process of debt reduction and just make ourselves available if they ever changed their minds.

Over time, a few of them came around. Every now and then, we received a phone call or a text with a question relating to a financial matter. Instead of pouncing on the person with all our tools and education, we simply answered their questions and let them know we were here to answer other questions if they needed us.

We did not flaunt our knowledge in their faces at gatherings. We also did not allow their choices to influence our own. It was a fine line to walk. We chose to love our family and friends where they were, and not alienate them because our views were so dramatically different. We would always be there if they needed us.

Your Turn…Your Perspective: Name a time when your friends or family did not embrace your passion. How did you respond? How did it impact your relationship?

Prayer: Lord, thank You for removing the scales from my eyes. I pray to be an example for others to follow to remove their scales. Please help me to not be judgmental.

Day 337
Come Celebrate with Us

PROVERBS 19:4

When Keith asked if I wanted to renew our vows for our 5th anniversary, I jumped into motion. Our journey was not what I ever envisioned when we got married. We had been through more than our fair share of frustration in the first five years of marriage.

We started with $191,000 in debt, along with a crazy amount of medical bills. It took its toll on us, but we were on our way out and thankful. We were down to the last $40,000 in debt while cash flowing over $100,000 in medical expenses. During the same time, we launched a financial coaching business and were helping couples just like ourselves find their way to financial freedom. We taught six FPU classes by then, and our graduates were facing their financial messes head on.

Rarely did a week go by without someone at church stopping us for advice on one financial topic or another. We became known as the "debt elimination" couple and loved helping anyone and everyone.

We also managed to create a relatively healthy blended family. It was not easy, but we were determined not to give up. While we still experienced the occasional parenting challenge with our kids, our challenges were more related to parenting teenagers and not because we were a blended family. We were thankful and ready to celebrate our milestone anniversary.

We decided to keep the celebration small. We were so close to becoming debt-free and did not want to lose momentum by planning and paying for a huge celebration. So instead of sending out invitations to a host of friends and family, we opted instead to invite only our life group. They had been with us every step of our journey and knew intimately the ups and downs we experienced.

As we prepared for the small ceremony in the prayer room at our church, I knew it would not be fiscally responsible to pay for a reception. Instead, we decided to share a meal with our friends at our favorite restaurant. We did not dine at the restaurant often (only when we were given a gift card) and thought our vow renewal would be the perfect time to visit again.

We told our friends of our plans to have dinner after the ceremony and asked if they would join us. We explained we could not pay for their meals but would love to celebrate with them. They all graciously accepted.

I knew in the past my pride would have prevented me from being so transparent about our finances. I knew I would have put my desire to please others ahead of our goal of being debt-free. As I looked around the table and reveled in the laughter of our friends, I was thankful I had matured enough to know good friends come without a price tag. I was thankful for the lesson in transparency.

Your Turn...Your Perspective: Describe a time when pride affected a financial goal. What was the lesson?

Prayer: Lord, thank You for the lessons You continue to teach me. I thank You for the growth and maturity I have experienced on this financial journey and look forward for more in the future. Please help me to never lose sight of the gift of financial stewardship.

Day 338

Rhythm

ACTS 4:32; ZECHARIAH 13:9

We were making it. It was the start of year five of our debt reduction and there was a dim light ahead which signaled we were in view of the end of this season of our life and our marriage. We were down to the last $30,000 in debt. Medical expenses were still incredibly high, but no new debt was created to manage them.

The drama associated with the early days of trying to get everyone a little money, and still survive as a family, had given way to the turmoil associated with massive debt payoffs. But now, even the turmoil was fading. We were making progress on the debt and were learning quite a bit about ourselves and money in the process. We were also beginning to teach others what we knew through our coaching business. All we needed to do now was simply keep our nose to the ground and get over this last chunk of debt.

I was writing in my journal during my quiet time one morning when I realized how calm it was in our financial world. We were not finished by any means, but the emotional ups and downs associated with money decisions in the past seemed to be fewer and farther between. We were responding well to the challenges which came against us and were beginning to embody making traction in our financial lives.

And while we were not without emotional scars from the constant battle waged between us and the creditors who wanted our money, I felt like we were in a place of healing. We had found a rhythm.

German philosopher Friedrich Nietzsche said: "that which does not kill us, makes us stronger." Keith and I were witnesses to just how true this was. I could not see any way out of our financial mess when we started this journey four years earlier. We did not know how to budget, did not understand how our interest was calculated, did not communicate with each other and reacted to every financial scenario which came our way.

Now, we budgeted every dollar which came into our home, communicated openly about all purchases, dreamed of the future together, and planned our way out of any emergency. We were different people. We were proactive about our money and no longer reactive. We weighed each monetary decision against the whole of our financial life and evaluated its impact. We were not afraid to say no to ourselves, our kids, or other people.

It was a place neither of us had ever been before, and I was beginning to understand why our journey needed to be so grueling. We were in the refiner's fire and were cleansing ourselves of all the old money habits which kept us bound. The new people who were emerging understood God's place in our finances and were not afraid to acknowledge Him as owner of it all. It was no longer simply about the material things we could purchase, but was more about how we could use our resources to further His Kingdom. It was beautiful.

Taking the moment to reflect on where we were gave me hope for where we were going. A life free of debt would be ours and it would be the beginning of a season which was still yet unchartered. I could not wait to see what God had in store for us. There was no doubt in my mind it would be amazing.

Your Turn…Your Perspective: Where do you see God's hand at work in your financial life? Do you trust Him?

Prayer: Lord, thank You for hope. Please help me to fight for it, regardless of the financial mess around me. I pray for insight and wisdom to stay on the path You have mapped out for me. I trust You, Jesus.

What Doesn't Go to Student Loans

PROVERBS 21:17

Getting to a place of Christ-centered financial wellness and breaking the spirit of lack were not easy for us. It took us years to even identify them as something we needed to achieve. It took another few years for us to put the time in to achieve them. The journey was well worth it, and the end result was huge. We were no longer ruled by our emotions. We no longer believed there were no options when it came to purchases. We were finally in a place where we viewed each purchase on its own characteristics.

Along the way, we made a lot of mistakes. We justified purchases which should never have been made. We convinced ourselves we needed more, over and over again. We gave in to the desire to be like "the Joneses." We spent much more than was necessary and created buyer's remorse.

Looking back, I realized our journey was as much about the change of habits as it was about getting out of debt. I truly believed, part of what took us so long to get out of debt, was learning the lessons we needed to stay out of debt. If we got out of debt, but continued the same habits, we would end up right back where we started.

It took us five years to get out of debt. But there was no doubt in my mind. We were done with debt.

During the last few years of debt reduction, a theme emerged. As Keith and I talked through our purchases, and the expenses associated with our household, we began to look at each item through the lens of the phrase: What doesn't go to student loans, doesn't go to student loans.

We were ready. We wanted to be done with debt. We wanted our income back. We wanted a future which was filled with hope and possibility, not payments and limitations. So, we now began to approach each purchase knowing it would impact the timeline for becoming debt-free.

If we purchased movie tickets, $50 in interest would accrue on student loans. If we took a vacation, hundreds of dollars in interest would accrue on student loans over time. If we increased our spending for Christmas gifts, more money would be diverted from paying the debt snowball. Dinner out for the family meant more days in debt.

Each expenditure was discussed this way over and over in the last years of our debt snowball. "What doesn't go to student loans, doesn't go to student loans" became the mantra we cited when any decision about purchases was made. We resolved to be done with debt, and rethinking how we viewed our income was a huge part of how we made it across the finish line.

It was not easy. But it was very worth it. The joy we felt when we made the last student loan payment was indescribable. Our resolve paid off and we were debt-free. No longer would we have to pay interest. We were finally in a place where we could actually earn it.

Your Turn…Your Perspective: What area of your life needs increased discipline? How has God challenged you to change it?

> *Prayer: Lord, thank You for resolve. Please help me make the hard choices to delay pleasures. Thank You for teaching me the discipline needed to stay out of debt once and for all.*

Day 340

Resist the Free

ISAIAH 55:1

I was having coffee with a girlfriend one day and we discussed just how busy we both were. It was a very active few weeks in the Jones' household, and from the sound of it, my friend and her husband were also experiencing a good bit of busyness.

We talked about how nice it would be to sit quietly at home during the upcoming weekend and just watch a movie and be still. Just the suggestion of nothingness sounded delightful. But even as I discussed doing nothing with my friend, there was a place of uneasiness niggling in the back of my brain.

I pondered the thought for a moment before confessing to my friend. As much as I wanted a respite at home, there was a free concert in the city on Saturday night and I truly wanted to go. It had been several months since I was able to enjoy some culture, and a night at the symphony sounded divine, especially since it was free.

I shared my desire with my friend. I was not expecting her to give me advice. I was simply expressing my dilemma out loud. I knew the right thing was to stay at home, but it would be months before another free symphony opportunity presented itself, and I did not want to miss it.

My friend looked at me with incredible sincerity and said, "You know, it might be good to resist the free."

Wow! What a statement. It made so much sense. As much as I wanted to attend the free concert, it truly was not in my best interest. My friend voiced the simplest, but most profound, thought I had heard in a long time. Do the right thing. Stay home and rest. Free is not always free when you weigh the opportunity cost. The opportunity of the evening out would cost me rest and rejuvenation. Was it worth it?

As I pondered the conversation later in the day, I realized I already learned to "resist the free" in my finances. It should not have been a stretch to do the same thing with my time. I mastered not giving in to the temptation of "buy one, get one at ½ off" when I only needed one of an item. I mastered not purchasing an item when it was not in the budget, even if it was on sale. I mastered going without a "want" to have the money necessary to take care of a need.

Resisting the free was a major strategy Keith and I used to get out of debt. Resisting the free became a habit we carried with us into the new season of financial wellness and freedom from debt. Resisting the free became a way of life with our finances. It was time for it to become a way of life with my time.

My friend reminded me, the habit we worked so hard to form in our financial life, added incredible value in other areas of our lives as well. She helped me to see just how much "free" could cost if it was viewed without context. I was thankful she loved me enough to challenge me. I was thankful I was humble enough to be challenged.

Your Turn…Your Perspective: Describe the last time you resisted the free. What about the last time you did not? How did each impact you?

Prayer: Lord, thank You for good friends and the reminder to guard against the free. Thank You for priorities and perspective. Please help me always be mindful of what is good, better and best, especially as it relates to time and money.

Day 341

Like Family

MARK 4:24

Over the years, Keith and I decreased the amount of time we spent in St. Louis with the kids, and began to spend more and more time in Kansas. Even though it meant we drove at least 16 hours roundtrip on I-70 to bring the kids home with us, there were two important factors to our decision.

Coming back to Kansas for the weekend meant the kids were at home with us. They were assigned chores and other household responsibilities. It gave us an opportunity to teach them our value system a few more times through the year. Coming back to Kansas also meant we all attended our church together and the kids enjoyed being a part of our church's student ministry. Even if we did not have the opportunity to teach them our work ethic, we were thankful to be able to expose them to God in a way they enjoyed.

The second reason we chose to come back to Kansas, even on short weekends, was cost. As we got deeper into paying off our debt snowball, we realized the importance of keeping our travel expenses to a bare minimum. Returning to Kansas meant no hotel costs. No hotel costs meant more money to the student loans and other debts. More money to the debt snowball meant debt-freedom would arrive sooner instead of later. Hotel stays became reserved for the trips when we needed to be in the area to manage affairs with the kids.

On one such visit to St. Louis, we got a late morning start. As a result, we were still in the room when housekeeping came by to freshen up our surroundings. She was very personable and engaging. In just a few moments we learned her name and knew her goal of going back to school to earn her degree. She was the same age as one of our nieces and seemed to have the same desire to be better.

Cleaning hotel rooms was hard work and I knew she faced a tough task ahead. It was hard to break the cycle of work to get back to school once you left. I knew many people who took a semester off never to return. I prayed she would succeed in her desire to finish her education. I prayed she would not give up on her dream when it got tough but would stick it out until she finished her goal.

Our trip was relatively uneventful and the majority of the money we allocated remained unspent. Normally the money would have been moved to paying the debt snowball, but I asked Keith if we could increase the size of our tip for this young woman. Something about her drive and determination made me want to help her. He agreed, and I gave her a significant amount over our normal tip.

In addition to the tip, I gave her my card. I hoped she would stay in touch. I wanted to invest in her the way Keith and I invested in our nieces and nephews. I did not know if she would accept the offer, but I wanted to extend it. I benefited tremendously from older women taking me under their wing when I was younger. If I could do the same for her, maybe it would make a difference. Time would tell. In the meantime, I added her to my prayer list. God would do the rest.

Your Turn…Your Perspective: What was the biggest "hand up" you ever received? Ever gave?

Prayer: Lord, thank You for the reminder to help in whatever way I can. Thank You for the reminder to give more than encouragement whenever possible. I pray I do not ever forget my own humble beginnings.

Day 342

Kid Love

DEUTERONOMY 11:19; EPHESIANS 6:4

One of the first things Keith and I did when we started dating was take "The 5 Love Languages" survey. Author Gary Chapman wrote a book by the same name and created the inventory as a tool to help couples learn how to love each other better and more deeply. Instead of showing love in the manner a person wanted to receive love, couples were instructed to show love the way the receiver wanted to receive love.

All was well when the giver and receiver shared the same language, but it got a little interesting when their languages were different. It was equivalent to me speaking Spanish to Keith and him responding in French. If we were not careful, miscommunication was likely and good intentions would be met with frustration. It became a valuable tool for us in our marriage.

As the kids got older, their personalities became more and more distinct. One day I realized we were in danger of miscommunicating with them if we did not stop and dig a little deeper. Were we loving them the way they wanted to be loved? I knew we might not always see eye-to-eye with them (especially during the teenage years), but I still wanted to be sure we loved them the way they needed.

I looked online and found the teen version of the 5 Love Languages survey. The free survey was modified to consider the special emotional needs of teens. We pulled out our laptops and asked both kids to take the survey. The results were quite revealing.

Aside from our daughter's desire to limit touch, we did a pretty good job. Both kids scored high in the need for time. We already knew our son enjoyed playing board games and our daughter enjoyed watching movies as a family. We established "game night, movie night" years earlier to accommodate them both. And it did not hurt to have free, in-home entertainment since, early on, there was rarely money in the budget for us to be entertained outside of the house.

What was created as a way to stay engaged with them, and not spend a lot of money, became the anchor of our time together as a family. We were trying to create memories around inexpensive activities and inadvertently supplied what they needed from us to know that we loved them.

It felt good to know we got it right. So much of how we raised our kids created questions for us because it seemed parenting God's way was not very popular by the world's standard. It was hard enough to keep them engaged when so much of how we lived was contrary to everything else they knew. At least in this one area, we not only managed to please God by honoring our budget, but we also managed to please our kids. We were incredibly thankful to have the confirmation.

Your Turn…Your Perspective: What was your favorite childhood memory where no money was spent? What about your favorite adult experiences where no money was spent? What are your love languages?

Prayer: Lord, thank You for the times when I get money management right. I pray for the courage to follow Your ways and not the ways of the world.

Day 343
Over Tipped

PROVERBS 22:9

During a trip to visit my family in South Carolina one year, we stopped in Nashville to have dinner with friends. They brought their kids to join us since our kids were with us. The five kids got along really well which made for a wonderful reunion.

We chose a nice Italian restaurant and settled in at a long table near the back. We were quite an animated group with two conversations often mingling into one, and the food and company were both enjoyable.

While we did not know which restaurant we would visit when we budgeted for the trip, Keith and I knew we wanted to enjoy a nice meal with our friends. As a result, we budgeted quite a bit for the evening. Even with multiple appetizers, desserts for all of us, and coffee for me, we still came well under our budgeted amount.

We also knew we would be at our table for a while. Seeing our friends only happened once a year at most. It was important to take the time to catch up on their lives and share a little of our own journey from the last year. Because we knew our server would expect us to leave soon after our meal was over, we budgeted a generous tip. We did not want our server to miss out on tips from other patrons simply because we wanted to linger.

A 20% tip was our starting point, and we often tipped at a higher rate. Prior to choosing a life of Christ-centered financial wellness, I saw 20% as the maximum amount and adjusted my tip down if I did not feel the service was valuable enough. But after we started living our lives based on Christ-centered financial wellness, I became a lot more comfortable giving generously. I was often surprised at how good it felt to give more.

I did not pay much attention to the bottom part of the bill. I checked to make sure we were charged for all the items we ordered, and also not charged for items we did not order. I did not know how much the tax was in Tennessee and did not concern myself with attempting to figure it out. By not checking the bottom of the receipt closely, however, I did not see the extra 18% gratuity already included. I forgot our party was over eight people, which would prompt the restaurant to add gratuity. Unknowingly, I added a 30% gratuity on top of the total.

I did not realize my error until I saw the server's eyes register shock when I told him no change was needed. My first reaction was frustration. I had given too big a tip. Fortunately, the reaction only lasted a split second before I realized just how much money was left in our envelope. Even with the enlarged gratuity, we were still well under budget for the trip.

I reasoned the shock I saw in the server's eyes was there because the tip was out of the ordinary for him also. He was young enough to probably not be a server because he wanted to be, but because he had fewer job opportunities available. His expression told me we positively impacted some goal in his life. I was glad I did not allow the oversight of the added gratuity to dampen the generosity we were obviously supposed to give. It was a great lesson to not only give with an open hand, but to also give with an open heart.

Your Turn…Your Perspective: Name a generosity story when you were the giver and when you were the receiver. What did you learn from each experience?

Prayer: Lord, thank You for the lessons on generosity I have experienced. I pray I stay open to giving and not become calloused towards those in need. I pray to follow Your lead and give like You do.

Floral Giveaway

JAMES 2:1

Keith and I loved our local auto repair shop. They were a great team of people and cared for our cars in a way neither of us ever experienced previously.

The owner did a good bit of networking and worked to be the source of information for all their clients. At some point years ago, he created a relationship with another small business nearby. This business was a florist. On the surface it seemed odd for a car repair shop and a florist to have a business relationship.

Each Monday, the florist delivered a fresh vase of flowers to the auto repair shop. The attached card identified where the flowers came from with the hope of sending new business to the florist. Every Friday, the guys at the auto repair shop gave away the flowers.

They did not have a formula to decide who received the flowers. A lot of times they were given to a woman who just received some really bad news about her vehicle. Or maybe they were given to the new mom who came in looking a little frazzled. Sometimes they were given to the guy, who had been down and out for a while, to give to his wife when he went home. They instinctively knew who needed them.

The flowers were always a bright spot for me when I dropped off my car, and I admit to being the recipient of the vase many times. I enjoyed those Fridays immensely since I did not receive flowers often. I no longer bought them for myself, and Keith bought them for me only occasionally. It was always a treat to be the recipient of the flowers from the auto repair shop.

One week, when Keith and I stopped to pick up our car after some routine maintenance, there were two vases of flowers. Apparently, no one was given the flowers from the week before and both vases of flowers were still there this particular Friday afternoon. Our technician insisted I take both vases. I protested, but he would not take no for an answer. It was late Friday and both vases needed a home.

We stopped by the car wash on the way home, and as we drove up to pay, Keith told me I needed to bless the woman at the window with one of the vases. I thought it was a great idea and was ready to share my gift with her when our transaction was completed. As we pulled up to the window, we realized there was not just one woman in the booth. There were two.

The first commented on the flowers and said how pretty they were. It was the perfect opportunity to pass them on. She was shocked and filled with emotion when I told her the vase was hers. I also saw a look of disappointment on the face of the second woman. I caught her eye and proceeded to hand her the second vase of flowers. She was visibly shaken by the gesture and thanked us profusely.

Both women were impacted greatly by the gesture, and it felt good to be able to bless them with the beauty of the flowers. I was often blessed to receive, and it felt good to be on the giving end. Yet again, blessed to be a blessing.

Your Turn…Your Perspective: How have you blessed someone recently? How did it impact you to give?

Prayer: Lord, I pray for the opportunity to bring joy to others. I pray I never lose sight of how important it is to see others and acknowledge them even in a small way.

Day 345
Free

2 TIMOTHY 2:6

A very dear friend was an attorney for over 25 years. He was very good at what he did and carved out quite a specialty as a political advisor. He worked for several state administrations and possessed a resume filled with accomplishments.

The problem with working in the political realm was the constant change of administration. Every few years, my friend would be off to a different assignment. He seemed to take it all in stride and always landed on his feet. Each new position brought a new set of challenges which he tackled head on.

Over dinner one evening, he mentioned being a little troubled with his latest change. He was still in between positions and was struggling with his next move. The practical side of him wanted to take the next new challenge and continue to add accomplishments to his resume. His heart was pushing him in an entirely different direction, however. His head wanted him to continue the life he built several states away. His heart wanted him to return to his home state and begin a real estate law firm.

There were many obstacles to consider if he decided to move home. First and foremost, he was not licensed in his home state and would need to take the Bar exam. He also was not well known in his home state. His contacts were limited, and he would be starting over without a professional support network. He did not know how long it would take to start a new specialty law firm in a new state.

I listened intently as he talked about his dilemma. Moving home had been in his heart for years, and it seemed to be pressing him even more during this latest transition. I asked questions to help him put a few more pieces to the puzzle in place. I finally asked the one question which changed everything. I asked my friend if he was in debt. His eyes got bright as he proudly informed me of his debt-free status.

What my friend neglected to consider was his freedom. Since he did not have debt, his household expenses were minimal. He only needed a few thousand dollars a month to take care of his basic needs. I explained how this opened a world of possibilities for him. He could literally take any job he wanted in his home state. With his basic expenses met, he would be free to focus all his energy on building his practice.

The power of being debt-free was weighing in and asserting itself. If he still carried student loan debt from law school, his options would have been severely limited. If he chose to have credit card debt or car loans, he would have needed a much higher minimum salary requirement. If he chose a lavish lifestyle, he would not be able to start a second career in a new state from scratch. His choice to live below his means was giving him the flexibility to follow a dream.

I was excited to watch my friend's dream begin to take root. There was no doubt his new career would be just as successful as the first. The foundation was firmly set – without debt.

Your Turn...Your Perspective: What decision in your life has been most affected by debt? If the decision were made today, how would it be different?

Prayer: Lord, thank You for helping me stretch towards debt-freedom. Thank You for giving me the burning desire to be free once and for all. I pray to persevere until I reach the financial goal You have placed before me.

Season 6:

Living Free

Day 346
Freedom

2 CORINTHIANS 9:8

The day we became debt-free was the Saturday before Easter, April 15, 2017. Keith and I loved the Easter celebration and were always spiritually filled from it. It was no different in 2017. The Good Friday service was beautiful, and we enjoyed serving together. Saturday was to be a quiet day. We would attend Easter service later in the evening and serve there also. Our church encouraged regular attenders to join in on Saturday to make room for visitors on Sunday.

I settled myself in my favorite chair early Saturday afternoon. It was payday week and it was time to electronically "touch" our money. We used a system which allowed us to divide out our income into various categories to execute our budget. It was a lifeline during the many years of debt reduction and medical bills.

Before the start of each month, Keith and I spent every penny of our expected income by allocating our money to a specific purpose: food, gas, medical expenses, money for the kids' visits, insurance payments, car insurance, etc. Every expense was budgeted in advance. When we got paid, I simply assigned the money coming in to its predetermined location. Any deviation was discussed before making an adjustment.

The software tool showed all deposits and withdrawals from all accounts and I electronically reconciled our accounts through the tool. Keith and I then both used the mobile app to monitor our money.

When I first saw the five-figure sum of money showing as a deposit, I frowned. *What's this?* was the question I asked myself. Since the budget tool only gives basic transaction information, I switched to our online checking account registry to make sure an error had not occurred. I immediately recognized the name of the depositor.

My heart raced. Could it be? I looked at the number again, then went back to the online tool to review the balance on our student loan accounts. The balance due on the student loans was indeed lower than the amount of the deposit.

"Honey!" I called to Keith. "Please come here for a moment." When he showed up a few moments later, I looked at him, grinned and said, **"WE'RE ABOUT TO BE DEBT-FREE!"**

We looked at the numbers again, in awe at God's grace. On the Saturday before Easter, when we were in the midst of serving and celebrating the glory of the resurrection of Jesus Christ, our finances were also resurrected. We were debt-free. A click of two buttons on two different websites wiped out the last of our student loans. We performed those two clicks after we paid our tithes on the increase we just received.

The increase was the principal and interest due to us from an error which occurred years earlier. It had literally taken 5 years to fix it. But God's delay was never God's denial. We received it just in time to use it to become debt-free. Praise the Lord for perseverance. Praise the Lord for not giving up. Praise the Lord for favor!

Your Turn...Your Perspective: Name something which has been eluding you for a long time. How have you persevered? What has it taught you?

Prayer: Lord, I thank You for helping me to not give up. Your delay truly is not Your denial. I trust Your ultimate plan for my life and pray to stay focused on You, regardless of what my situation looks like.

Day 347
The Second Time

PSALM 51:6; ROMANS 8:37; 1 PETER 2:9

I kept pinching myself. We were debt-free! It was an amazing feeling. It took five long years but we finally crossed the finish line. We put in the work, stayed the course, and could finally shout to the world, "WE'RE DEBT-FREE!"

Being debt-free was not without its own challenges. The spiritual warfare began almost immediately. My mind whispered: *You've been here before. What makes you think you can stay debt-free? How is this time any different than the last? You'll be back in debt before you know it.*

The doubt was real, and I knew I needed to address it. I failed miserably in the past with money and my track record was horrible. Keith was not much better, and we admittedly made a ridiculous mess of our finances. So why should we believe we could stay debt-free this time? The fear the question created was creeping into the back of my mind. I saw it for what it was and went to work attacking it the only way I knew how.

I prayed. A lot. And often.

I asked God for clarity and peace. This was supposed to be a celebration, not a time of doubt and uncertainty. We did the hard part and were reaping the reward. I did not want to lose all the momentum we built by doubting our ability to maintain it.

My journal became my friend. I reminded myself through its pages of all we already accomplished. I looked at the blessings and miracles God already provided. I played the good video in my mind to replace the negative clips the enemy was attempting to use to derail my joy.

I went back to scripture and surrounded myself with the promises of God. We were more than conquerors through Him who loved us. He led us out of the darkness of debt into the marvelous light of financial wellness.

Slowly over the next few weeks, I settled into our new status. I gradually realized the difference between this debt-free journey and the last. When I became debt-free before, it was not a journey at all. I was transported from a place of debt into a place of no debt. No mental change occurred, and there was no adjustment in mindset.

This time would be different because I was different. All the trials we experienced would serve as a "hot stove" reminder any time our financial wellness mindset was challenged. We did the work and successfully formed the habit of living below our means. We were then rewarded by our means increasing.

Debt-free did not mean we would not be faced with obstacles in the future. But it did mean we were armed with the resolve and the determination to protect our new way of life. I was thankful to be up for the challenge.

Your Turn…Your Perspective: How do you protect your mind from negative thoughts? What new money behaviors need to be hardwired in your life? What's your plan to make the shift permanent?

Prayer: Lord, thank You for the tools to fight the battle being waged in my mind. Thank You for the reminder of Your sovereignty and Your ability to conquer all. I pray for the courage to continue to walk on this new path You have laid out before me.

Day 348
In the Middle

PSALM 119:127; 1 CORINTHIANS 2:9

Baby Step 2…check! We were debt-free and moving onto the third of Dave Ramsey's 7 Baby Steps.[13]
1. $1000 Beginner Emergency Fund
2.   Use the debt snowball payment allocation to pay off all your debt, except the house
3.   A fully funded emergency fund of 3 to 6 months of expenses
4.   Invest 15% of your household income into retirement
5.   Start saving for the kids' college education
6.   Pay off your home early
7.   Build wealth and give generously

We were now ready to build our emergency fund for 3-6 months of expenses. I was also ready to start saving for a house, and therefore, wanted a three-month emergency fund. Keith was not interested in ever being in a financial crunch again. He wanted a six-month fund. We were at an impasse.

We talked through it for a few weeks before settling on four months. Four months gave us a nice sized emergency fund to use while we switched gears to saving for the house. We then agreed to move the emergency fund to six months after we moved into our new home.

As I thought about the discussion, and our very different perspectives on what the ideal savings number should be, I realized just how far we had come. Five years earlier, feelings would have been hurt after the discussion. Five years earlier, we would have struggled to explain our position. Five years earlier, we would each have felt compelled to convince the other to come over to our side.

We experienced so much growth in five years: We beat debt and started a new debt-free era of life. We learned how to budget. We learned self-control and how to say "no" to ourselves and others. We became better decision makers. We became more patient and faithful.

We did not realize how much we needed the lessons we learned in the five years of debt reduction. Our individual relationships with Jesus strengthened through the trials we experienced, and our marriage was stronger than ever because we learned to trust each other. What we came to realize was we would not have changed a thing about our journey.

The conversation and ultimate decision on the size of our emergency fund was a reminder of all the side benefits we received by following Christ. 1 Corinthians 2:9 (GNT) states: "What no one ever saw or heard, what no one ever thought could happen, is the very thing God prepared for those who love him."

Who knew what making the decision to become debt-free, and stay debt-free, would do for every other aspect of our lives. We were so thankful to be able to see a glimpse of what God ordained. We could not wait to see what He had in store for us next!

Your Turn…Your Perspective: How have you seen God's hand at work in your life through trials? What have you learned from the experience?

Prayer: Thank You, Lord, for Your plan. Thank You for guiding me on a journey bigger than we could ever have imagined. I pray to keep my eyes open and watch You work!

Day 349
Audacious Faith

PSALM 24:3-4

As Keith and I shared our journey with others and talked about spending over $300,000 cash on life and debt in 5 years, we inevitably we got the question: "How did you do it?" We gladly shared.

The answers were always the same – Jesus and lots of prayer. We spent lots of time on our knees. The answer also included "lots of sacrifice." We went without vacations, dinners out, new movie releases, baseball games, and much more. We kept our budget tight and our eyes open for new opportunities to sell as much as we could. But the biggest thing we did was believe it could be done. We kept believing, regardless of the circumstances. We kept believing even when the debt payoff was slow. We just kept believing. We had audacious faith.

Steven Furtick, author of *Sun Stand Still: What Happens When You Dare to Ask God for The Impossible*, said: "Audacious faith starts when you choose to step out in a strength not your own."[14] I certainly did not have financial strength when we started. I was literally weak in the knees when we put all our debt together and began to devise a plan to pay it all off. My head spun as we totaled up all the debt payments and attempted to align them with our paychecks. My heart even hurt with fear whenever a strange envelope showed up in the mailbox, announcing itself as yet another creditor demanding to be paid.

Still, through it all, I believed God would get us through. His Word was clear. We were to be debt-free. And if we trusted Him, we would be. So we dug in and fought to make headway in our debt reduction. Payments to the debt snowball slowly picked up speed, and even when we experienced setbacks, we knew we would one day be debt-free.

It was a long journey. I spent lots of time asking God for guidance and understanding. There was also lots of time to grow my audacious faith. It got bigger each time we paid off another loan and it became stronger with every pay raise and bonus. The random checks which showed up in our mailbox were fuel to the audacious faith fire. We knew we could do it. We knew we WOULD do it.

The fear began to subside, and the angst went away. Emergencies held less power over me. We ceased having to stop everything to figure out how to pay the unexpected expense, and decisions were made with a lot less fanfare. We stopped, analyzed the situation, moved the money around, and paid the bill.

It was amazing to feel peace instead of panic, and refreshing to not have a financial meltdown when the budget needed to be adjusted. It was simply a blessing to see God's work as we continued to activate and reactivate our audacious faith.

Your Turn…Your Perspective: When was the last time you exercised audacious faith? What stumbling blocks did you experience? How did you get through it?

Prayer: Lord, thank You for guiding me through tough financial experiences. Thank You for showing Yourself to me. I know Your Word will guide me. I pray to have audacious faith.

Money Personalities

PSALM 34:12

Five years was a long time to be in debt. And of course, we did not know it would take so long when we started our journey of Christ-centered financial wellness. We just knew we wanted to be debt-free and our lives needed to radically change to make it happen.

Once we got the basics of budgeting down, we began to work on the other parts of our money lives. This included as much research as we could get our hands on. The library became our best friend. Books, books, books. We read them, we listened to them on audio, and we began our journey to better understand how we ended up in the financial mess we were in.

One such book made a major impact on us. It was *The 5 Money Personalities* by Scott and Bethany Palmer. We stumbled across them a few months earlier when we discovered their book. *First Comes Love, Then Comes Money.* We saw their business and ministry as a great help to us and began to dig into this new book.

What we learned was incredible and eye-opening. The book shed light on the premise that each of us identified with two different money personalities which dictated how we responded to money. The Palmers told us a money personality was a way to "think about and deal with money in a [way which is] unique [and] highly personal."[15]

Boy, did we each have a unique and personal way to think about money! Talking about money with Keith was like speaking a foreign language sometimes. He could not relate to what I was saying or why, and I was just as oblivious to him speaking about his money needs and wants. Once we realized we each aligned to two very different money personalities, we began to experience a new way of communicating about money. It was beautiful.

I used to be so frustrated when we talked about money. And because of our huge amount of debt, medical bills, and car issues, we talked about money…a lot! After we learned how to frame our conversations in terms of our money personalities, conversations about money became calm, did not last as long, or happen as often.

There was less tension in our marriage and we actually began to dream about life after debt. Our language shifted towards each other, and we began to realize just how much commonality we experienced when it came to money. We learned how to balance our money personalities and found great comfort in seeing just how supportive the other was when we discussed the topic. We were on the same money team, even though there were four very different money personalities with us.

People asked us how we were able to get through $300,000 of life and debt in five years, and we were quick to share what we learned. While it was not easy in the beginning, we found our way through it. Understanding how we each viewed money was a huge part of our process, and our success. We then set about telling everyone we could. Our mess became a message.

Your Turn…Your Perspective: If you're married, how is your communication with your spouse about money? What do you need to improve? If you're single, do you have a money accountability partner? Why or why not?

Prayer: Lord, thank You for tools and resources to help me understand I am not alone. I pray to stay open to all the lessons You want to teach me about money.

Redeeming the Time

PSALM 49:18; GENESIS 12:2

It was still hard to believe we were debt-free. The journey seemed to take forever. The beginning was tough, the middle was long, and the end seemed to take forever to arrive. It was not easy to work on our goal of Christ-centered financial wellness and freedom from debt when there were so many obstacles. The adage of taking "two steps forward and one step back" seemed to be our banner throughout the entire journey.

Medical bills consumed entire debt-reduction allocations, and sometimes caused us to pull from sinking funds. It was frustrating and disheartening to spend so much money on medical tests only to have healthcare providers improperly diagnose our issues. The reality of car repairs going from minor to major, with added miles, increased our frustration. It was one thing after another, year after year.

Through it all, we chose to stay focused. Even in the months when there was nothing extra to add to the minimum payments, we chose to keep a good attitude. It truly was a choice. We believed God would use us and our story to bless others. Surely, He would redeem the time we spent in the valley of debt. We trusted Him and His Word.

Time and again, we were able to see glimpses of His plan for our lives. Just when we were close to giving up, a reprieve would come. A random check in the mail. A friend stopping by with a gluten free pizza and an offer of conversation. Help with meals, the gift of clothing, and gift cards to use for the occasional dinner out. All were viewed as gifts from the Lord. We saw the gestures as His way of showing us His faithfulness to our commitment to live for Him. He was redeeming our time.

Each reprieve felt like a safety net, meant to keep us from falling into despair. We thanked Him profusely and did not discount the value of the gift or the giver (both earthly and heavenly). We verbalized our thanks and passed on the kindness as often as we could. We also chose to be the giver to others when we could, and continued to make the hard choices to say "no" to those things which did not fit His plan for us.

We endured the strange looks from church members and colleagues, friends and family who did not understand the financial decisions we made. Even our kids did not always understand why our lives were so different than the families around us. We would not be moved. We would not allow anything or anyone to keep us from standing firm on the call to become and stay debt-free.

We knew God would honor our sacrifice and hard work one day. We knew He would use us as examples to others who struggled with the idea of whether achieving debt-freedom was actually possible. So we chose to be transparent. We chose to stand in a glass house for all to see how we lived. We chose to keep our heads low and not look around us at what others were doing. We trusted Him, and we trusted His plan. We knew the day of celebration would be grand, and we could hardly wait.

Your Turn…Your Perspective: How has God redeemed time you have spent in a desert or valley experience? What did He teach you? How have you used the experience to impact the lives of others?

Prayer: Lord, thank You for your faithfulness. Thank You for helping me stay focused on You and not on my circumstances. Thank You for instilling in me the desire to serve You and others while on this journey. You have blessed me to be a blessing.

Day 352
Rent Freeze

1 CHRONICLES 29:12; DEUTERONOMY 29:5

I was strategic when choosing our duplex. Keith and I were not yet engaged, but I thought we were headed towards marriage. I chose a location which gave each of us a decent commute. I also chose a property which would be large enough for Keith and the kids to move into if we did get married. But it needed to be affordable enough for me to manage on my own if we did not get married.

Once we discovered Dave Ramsey's plan and realized our housing expenses should be no more than 25% of our take-home pay, we knew I chose well for us as a couple. However, as a single person my rent would have been way too high. With our combined income, the rent payment was 21% of what we brought home each month. It would have been almost half of my income alone. Disaster avoided!

It was sobering to realize what a financially dangerous situation I set up. I was thankful I did not have a major financial emergency before we got married and joined our finances.

At the time there were 19 different payments leaving our checking account because of poor financial decisions made in the past. Coming in under the recommended limit for housing made it feel as if we made at least one good financial decision. It was encouraging to know we were on the right track. We saw it as an example of better times ahead of us, and they certainly were.

We were not expecting what happened over the next five years. OUR RENT NEVER INCREASED! During the same time, our income almost doubled. As we finished paying off our debt snowball, our housing expense was only 14% of our take-home pay. What started out as a decision made without much understanding, turned into a huge financial opportunity. Because our rent never increased, we were able to focus on other areas of our financial lives with the income which would have gone to cover housing expenses.

The income from every raise and promotion was applied to the debt snowball and/or medical expenses instead of being allocated to housing expenses. It was an incredible blessing which we did not take lightly. As much as I wanted to purchase a home and get out of our rental duplex, it served us well during the debt-filled season of our life.

We knew our journey of debt reduction and healing would have been much longer if we spent more money on housing expenses. There were many months where medical bills consumed all available income, and money for the debt snowball was unavailable. If our rent were higher, those medical procedures would have been postponed, and our healing process likely would have been longer.

Just as the children of Israel wore the same shoes during their 40 years in the desert, we received a reprieve from increased rent during our desert season of debt. God proved His faithfulness to our family once again.

Your Turn…Your Perspective: Name a time when God provided for you in a big way. What did you learn from the experience?

Prayer: Lord, thank You for sustaining me through every situation. I know You are guiding me, even when I do not see it. I pray to never forget all the ways You provide for me.

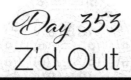

Day 353
Z'd Out

PSALM 66:11-12

Even though Keith and I were barely treading water financially when we first got married, we made the decision to hire a financial coach. Neither of us were blessed with a good financial upbringing and both made a crazy number of mistakes financially. A debt of $191,000 was a lot to overcome when you knew what you were doing. It was next to impossible to do when you were clueless about how to attack it. Add almost $110,000 in medical bills to the equation and even the bravest of souls might back down.

One of the first things our financial coach did was teach us how to use a money management tool. Instead of simply looking at our online checking account to determine the health of our finances, our coach taught us how to allocate each dollar of income ahead of time. We learned how to plan for all expenses and save for those purchases which did not occur monthly. The tool became an essential part of our debt-reduction strategy, and we used it every month to plan our way out of debt.

Another tip we received from our coach was to never actually delete an envelope from our budget. We could create as many electronic envelopes as we needed to manage our budget, and we did. At any given time, there were over 75 active envelopes. Some of them were only used once or twice a year (i.e. travel to family and holiday spending), while others were used each month (i.e. rent, food, tithing). When we no longer needed an envelope, our coach taught us to add a "Z" at the front of the name to force it to the bottom of the list. If we ever needed to run a report on the transactions assigned to inactive envelopes, we would be able to do so.

Once Keith and I became debt-free, there were several envelopes which needed to be "z'd out." Our debt-reduction envelope was a staple in our budget from the very beginning. If it was a good month, several thousand dollars would flow through it. Other months, those filled with car repairs and medical expenses, it received little or no money at all. The last two student loan envelopes also needed to retire.

I cannot describe the joy I felt to retire those envelopes. It was the end of an era. It was the end of being saddled with debt and living in fear. It was the end of being owned by a bank or student loan company. No longer would our income be demanded by someone else. No longer would we have to view our budget through the eyes of what was left after debts were paid.

It was such a small thing – the removal of a few electronic envelopes. But the impact was huge. WE WERE DEBT-FREE! And our budget proved it. No more debt payments could be found. No more money was lost to interest paid. We made it out of the hole of consumer debt and were thankful.

We knew God honored our commitment to living a life of Christ-centered financial wellness by allowing us to get to the other side of debt. He also knew we learned our lesson and would never view debt as an option again. We were grateful to have earned His trust in us.

Your Turn…Your Perspective: What financial milestone have you reached recently? What lesson came with it? Who have you shared your milestone and lesson with? Why did you choose this person?

Prayer: Lord, I thank You for hope. I pray for a steadfast spirit to keep going until I reach my next financial goal. Keep me focused on You always and help me to not lose sight of the plan You have for my life.

Day 354
Emotional Growth

ECCLESIASTES 9:11; JOSHUA 5:6

We had been debt-free a few weeks, and I was still reveling in the reality of our accomplishments. We were so thankful the Lord allowed us to reach this particular finish line. It was hard fought and worth every ounce of the blood, sweat and tears we shed throughout the five-year journey.

Strangely, I was still afraid we did not actually learn enough to make certain our new status was permanent. I was afraid **I** did not learn enough. I was debt-free once before. The euphoria was short lived, however. Because my habits did not change, four years after I paid off all my debt, I was right back in debt again.

I remember feeling ashamed and embarrassed at being back in debt. I remember questioning my abilities to manage money. I remember wondering if I would ever understand what it meant to build wealth. It was a low point in my life and I did not want to experience it again. I did not want to repeat the disappointment. I did not want to be like the children of Israel and spend a lifetime wandering through the desert of debt. I wanted to be free from the mental chains of debt once and for all.

I kept asking myself these questions: *Was what I learned during our journey of becoming debt-free enough to keep me away from debt in the future? Did I finally learn not to just become debt-free, but STAY debt-free? Had I finally found the mental process I needed to think through money situations and make the right decisions?*

I sat with the questions for weeks after we made the last payment to our student loans. I wanted desperately to be sure we learned what we needed to know. I kept waiting for the Lord to give me a sense of peace, for Him to say, "You can do this, My Child." But, it never happened.

During my quiet time one morning, about a month after we became debt-free, it finally dawned on me. The Lord was not going to actually TELL me we would make it. He needed me to have faith in our abilities TO make it.

We became debt-free because we trusted in Him. We became debt-free because we were in tune to His Word and His ways. We became debt-free because we learned His principles of managing money and building wealth. We became debt-free because we chose to live our lives by His plan. I experienced none of those things the first time I became debt-free.

What we learned to make it through to debt-freedom was exactly what we needed to achieve our goal of Christ-centered financial wellness. We did learn what we needed to live a life free of debt. I learned how not to repeat the mistakes of the past. Freedom from debt was ours once and for all. It was a beautiful feeling.

Your Turn…Your Perspective: Are you debt-free? If so, how did it feel to get there, and are you doing what is needed to stay there? If you are not debt-free, how do you think it will feel to be debt-free? What can you do today to make sure you never use debt again?

Prayer: Lord, thank You for providing the lessons I need to successfully complete the journey to Christ-centered financial wellness. Thank You for the confidence to know I can do this. Help me always remember and never go back.

Day 355
House Anxiety

PSALM 119:72; JAMES 1:8; EPHESIANS 3:20-21

After we got over the initial shock of being out of debt, house fever began to set in again. Keith and had already decided to save and pay cash for a house about a year prior to getting out of debt. But it was different when we could actually save for our purchase instead of just talking about it.

We still needed to save our fully-funded emergency fund. We chose to save four months of expenses before we purchased our home, and then move it up to six months afterwards. There were still a lot of medical bills, and 2017 was shaping up to be the most expensive year of medical-related expenses since we got married.

I soon questioned whether we should save to pay cash or just get a mortgage. The question kept creeping into my mind: *Are we sure we want to wait?* I admit to slowly giving in. The market was strong and not hinting of slowing down. Would we be able to find a nice home in our price range? Surely it would be okay to get a small mortgage, right? The questions were pelting my mind like a Kansas hail storm. My resolve weakened, and I was not sure how to hold on.

James 1:8 said, "A double-minded man [is] unstable in all his ways." Either I believed debt was not an option for us at all and we should save to pay cash, or I believed a little debt (like a mortgage) was okay. Five years of fighting to get out of debt left a bad taste in my mouth, so why was I wavering now? Was I allowing the seeds of doubt to convince me waiting and saving was too much to do? Why was I in such a hurry to forget all we learned, after fighting so hard for the opportunity to make new choices and change our future?

It hit me one day like a ton of bricks. I never actually thought we would save enough to purchase a home. Our journey was so long, I was not sure we could do it again. I was not sure **I** could do it again. The medical bills were still consuming so much of our available cash, and there was no end in sight. I fell victim to the same lie I tried to keep my clients from believing. I believed it was too much to complete.

Once the lie was revealed, I reminded myself of all Keith and I accomplished in five years. Our income was higher than ever before, and we were debt-free. Even with the medical bills, we could still save a substantial amount of money each month. When it was time to buy, we would have the benefit of cash on our side.

Trust the plan. I believed it was God's plan, so why not trust it? There were so many examples of how He did exceedingly, abundantly more than we could ask or think in the past. It was time to believe with finality that He could do it again.

I learned a huge lesson. I would never stop needing to fight the urge to follow the status quo. Even with all we accomplished, the draw of the world was (and always would be) strong. I knew just how important it was to stand strong on our position of no debt, and never allow it to be an option. Only then would I truly walk in Christ-centered financial wellness.

Your Turn…Your Perspective: What financial wavering have you done recently? What was your final decision? How did the experience strengthen your faith?

Prayer: Lord, I pray for resolve. Thank You for the examples I have of what walking in financial obedience looks like. Please help me keep my eyes focused on You and the goals You have laid out for me. Please help me grow in my faithfulness and trust You always.

Day 356
Forgot

The first month after paying off the last of our student loans started like any other. The budget was set the week before the month began. It was not very different from the months before with the exception of the huge chunk of cash which was now allocated for savings instead of student loans. Our financial lives seemed relatively void of stress.

This new season was one neither of us were used to living in. I had once been debt-free years earlier when I sold my home and made enough profit to pay off all my debt, but my mindset did not change then. Within a few years I was in debt again, and Keith was never debt-free as an adult.

This time was different. This time I knew what to do with my money, both the amount which came regularly and the extra which still showed up from time to time. We were armed with the benefit of financial wisdom and had the battle scars to prove it. We looked forward to building both wealth and a legacy.

The next stop on our journey was to amass 3-6 months of expenses. We opened a money market account to hold our shiny, new, fully-funded emergency fund and got to work contributing to it. It felt amazing.

Fast forward a few weeks. I was driving home from work on a Friday afternoon, ready to settle in for the weekend. Friday night was date night in our household, and both Keith and I were looking forward to a quiet evening with dinner and a movie borrowed from the library.

As I sifted through all the mental notes in my mind, I felt one which seemed to be stuck in the back. The weekend promised to be quiet and I was looking forward to not doing much. But the thought was trying to get my attention. There was something I needed to do but I could not quite put my finger on it. What was it?

When I was able to pull the thought forward in my mind enough to understand it, the shock was unimaginable. It was payday and I totally forgot! The entire day passed, and not once did it dawn on me that it was payday. There was actually money I needed to touch and organize in our online budget software.

I do not ever remember a time when I forgot it was payday. I spent years praying payday would show up early to beat some check or other debit from getting to the bank before my income did. I recall moving money from savings to checking to build a bridge between what was needed and what would arrive with payday. Never before did I forget it was coming, but this time I did. I forgot.

When I shared the thought with Keith later in the evening, we both just sat in wonder. The stress of money was not present in our lives. There was margin, but no angst. No one demanded our money except our landlord who was paid automatically with the rent consuming only 11% of our net income.

We were in control of our financial lives for the first time as a married couple, and loved what it felt like. While we may have forgotten payday, we prayed to never forget the hard work it took to become debt-free.

Your Turn…Your Perspective: Describe the emotion you experience with payday. What would you change?

Prayer: Lord, this is not easy for me right now, but I pray one day it becomes second nature. Please help me learn the discipline necessary to win with money. I pray for margin and no financial stress.

EZEKIEL 33:13A

I was driving to work one day and heard the morning show hosts talking on the radio. The hit Disney movie *Frozen* was to become a Broadway musical. The pre-Broadway run of the show would be in Denver. Our daughter absolutely loved all things Disney and was especially in love with the *Frozen* movie. I thought it would be an amazing gift to give her a trip to Denver for her 16ᵗʰ birthday.

We took the kids to see the *Elf* musical a few years prior and we all enjoyed ourselves. I hoped we could make the trip to Denver fit the budget. I checked the calendar, the ticket prices, hotels in the area, and got all the information I needed before I called Keith. I did not want him to say no. I made sure I compiled everything I needed to convince him this was a good purchase.

I called and made my case. We were debt-free, the cost of the tickets was less than I expected, and the hotel room could be paid with points. The logistics were interesting, but it would not be the first time we spent the majority of a holiday weekend on the highway with the kids. We were all pros at settling in and making the most of a journey.

When he said yes, you would have thought it was *my* 16ᵗʰ birthday! I was so excited. None of us had ever been to Denver, and I loved the idea of exposing the kids (and myself) to new places in addition to having a cultural experience. I booked the hotel and purchased the tickets. I even bought a copy of the *Frozen* DVD so our daughter could have something to unwrap when we celebrated her birthday. We planned to go to Denver for Labor Day which was just a few weeks later. It would be an amazing time for all. Except it was not.

After the presentation of her birthday gift was made and she returned to St. Louis, our daughter's choices over the next few weeks were not good ones. Her actions were well outside of the lines of acceptable behavior. We were faced with the big decision: Should we go to Denver or not?

We always told our kids we would not reward disobedience or disrespect. Our daughter's choices were a clear act of disobedience and disrespect. The trip to Denver was a gift on the surface, but ultimately, it was still a reward. We were within our right as her parents to remove it, and we did not take the decision lightly. Keith and I prayed about it and then knew what we needed to do.

We chose to cancel the trip. My heart hurt for so many reasons. It would have been the first trip we took with the kids since becoming debt-free. It would have been a beautiful culmination to her 16ᵗʰ birthday. It would have been great to visit the beautiful city of Denver. The trip would have been memorable for all of us which made the decision to cancel it even harder.

In the end, we sent the tickets to friends who lived in the area, and they enjoyed the musical in our place. We did not ask for payment; the cost was worth the lesson learned. Though we all experienced the disappointment of the canceled trip, the life lesson from the experience was one we hoped none of us would soon forget.

Your Turn…Your Perspective: When has a poor choice cost you more than you were willing to pay? How did you respond to the loss? What did you learn about yourself?

Prayer: Lord, please give me the courage to make the tough choices in my own journey of Christ-centered financial wellness. I pray to not count lightly the cost of poor choices.

Seeds of Faith

PSALM 30:7; MATTHEW 17:20; 1 CORINTHIANS 12:9

People often asked us how we were able to stay so focused for so long. It took five years and $300,000 to get through our debt snowball. It was a daunting task which weighed heavily on us, but we were determined to get through it. God's Word was clear on debt being foolish. We wanted to honor Him in our finances and be true to the ministry He gave us.

We dug into the faith we were given, and held on to it for dear life. We believed we would be delivered from our debt if we remained faithful through the process. It was not always easy, and we experienced many times when one or the other needed to be strong for both of us. We chose to stay transparent with each other and give support when our resolve waivered.

We knew we would never be able to get through our massive debt on our own strength. We knew we must lean on God and depend on Him to clear it all. We prayed often and kept our eyes open to watch Him work. We worked hard to keep good attitudes and not allow the weight of our circumstances to overtake us. When we failed, we quickly asked for forgiveness and tried again.

We talked about our feelings often and encouraged each other as best we could. We celebrated the small victories but did not lose sight of the next goal. We worked hard to keep our eyes on our own journey to not be distracted by the journey of others.

It was not easy, but we chose to believe God would deliver us if we stayed faithful to the process. We chose to believe we would one day experience life without debt and have a future different from our past. Each decision was weighed through the lens of our goal, and we pondered each one carefully before a decision was made.

When we came across someone who seemed hopeless in terms of their finances, we used our own faith as a way to help them find their way. We poured hope onto their financial wounds like salve and reminded them that God's promises applied to them also.

We sprinkled faith wherever we went in hopes others would scoop it up and claim it for themselves. We rejoiced when we were able to increase the faith of others and tried hard not to be disappointed when we could not.

Ultimately, we knew each person would have to choose to believe their circumstances could be different, and then put in the effort to make it happen. In the meantime, we chose to remain hopeful for those we met on their journey in the same way we were hopeful for our ourselves on our own journey. God was faithful, and we knew He would see them through, just as He saw us through. Our faith became the sustaining power we needed to reach our goal, and we hoped others would lean on their faith to get to their own finish line.

Your Turn…Your Perspective: How would you describe your level of faith? How has it changed during your current financial season?

Prayer: Lord, I pray to add value to others whenever possible. Please help me to embrace the community around me and give where I can. Show me how to serve Your people.

Day 359
The Future

PROVERBS 14:24

About a month after Keith and I made the last student loan payment and became debt-free, we received a dinner invitation. We were familiar with the couple but knew very little about them. We served together at church and gave each other the cursory church hug as a part of the greeting, but never spent more than a few minutes in their presence. Keith and I both looked forward to getting to know them better.

At promptly the requested hour, we arrived at their home with dessert in hand. The evening was off to a great start. The food was wonderful, and they were gracious hosts. We brought no expectations for the evening and settled in to see how the Lord would use the time we were given. What a blessing it turned out to be.

The couple was about 10-15 years ahead of us in terms of the ages of their kids and success with their career paths. Everything about their life seemed to mirror what we hoped for our future. It was as if we were being given an opportunity to see what our lives would be like if we continued on our current path.

As we shared the stories of meeting our spouses, stories of the challenges and joys of raising our kids, stories of living for Christ, and even stories of how we managed our finances, Keith and I were overjoyed at how much we were able to glean from this amazing couple. Their lives were not perfect, but they chose to keep God in their midst and sought Him first.

Our friends were experiencing the fullness of what it meant to sow good seed and reap its harvest. We were fortunate enough to enjoy the transparency of a relationship years in the making on our first night with our new friends.

Keith and I often talked about finding a couple or two to surround ourselves with on the next leg of our journey. We were the mentors for so many people as we assisted them in navigating debt reduction, but who would mentor us on what our lives would be like after debt? Who would we go to with our tough questions about financial matters?

It was not about how much money a couple made, but more about the strength of their Christ-centered financial wellness. We understood and embraced motivational speaker Jim Rohn's philosophy: "You are the average of the five people you spend the most time with."

As we entered into the new phase of Christ-centered financial wellness, we knew we needed to add some new friends to our community. We did not expect to find them so quickly, or so randomly. Five hours after we arrived, we left our new friends' home feeling blessed in so many ways. It was a wonderful evening, filled with answers to prayers along with laughter and good food. We knew we were on the right path and hoped to spend many more evenings with this exemplary couple.

Our community expanded to include these two new friends who were maybe even our new mentors. We were thankful God chose to bless us with them and looked forward to many more shared blessings in the future.

Your Turn…Your Perspective: Who are the five people you spend the most time with? How do they impact your life? How do you impact theirs? Who do you need to add to your circle?

Prayer: Lord, thank You for recognizing every need I have. Thank You for providing mentors every stage of my own journey of Christ-centered financial wellness. Please help me continue to add value to all my relationships. I praise Your name for sustaining me.

Day 360
Stunned

JOB 28:18; ISAIAH 55:8-9

We were a few months into our new life of being debt-free when I told Keith we needed to see a financial advisor. As financial coaches, we understood the importance of budgeting and goal setting, but also referred those more advanced clients to financial advisors for the execution of long-term investment strategies. Since we were debt-free and beginning to look at long-term investing for ourselves, it was time to choose an advisor.

We settled in to chat with "Mr. Advisor" and instantly liked him. He was warm, engaging and void of the arrogance sometimes found in the field of financial advisors. He was a family man and appreciated our desire to set up our future with generational wealth in mind. He asked us to share our story and how we came to be in his office late on a Wednesday afternoon in mid-December. Shouldn't we be Christmas shopping?

As we shared our story, he shook his head in amazement. It seemed, while many of his clients were debt-free, none of them took quite our route to get there. He applauded our efforts and our determination. He told us our financial future would be bright if we continued with the tenacity with which we started.

He then asked about our house and we explained our plan to save and pay cash for a home in the next three to four years. The look of excitement on his face turned to one I can only describe as alarm. Watching him made me uncomfortable. Why would our financial advisor be alarmed at us wanting to stay out of debt completely? After a few moments of reviewing his notes and gathering his thoughts, he shared what was on his mind.

We were old. At almost 50, Keith and I were entering the biggest wealth building years of our life. And while it was great for us to be debt-free, the price we paid to get there was not investing for retirement. We chose to divert funds we would have used for retirement to increase the amount of money we sent to debt reduction. The result was a modest retirement account instead of a robust retirement account.

Our new financial advisor shared the importance of timing. Housing costs would only continue to rise which would make it even more difficult to save for what we wanted in a home. In the meantime, our six-figure house savings account was just sitting in a money market account, earning next to nothing.

We were stunned. We thought our plan to save and pay cash for our home was the right decision. It certainly would keep our debt-free status intact. But "Mr. Advisor" made it clear. It was not the smartest move. Get a mortgage and then do what we did best. Pay it off quickly.

Keith and I left with few words spoken between us. Our entire world was literally turned upside down. We prayed and asked God for guidance. It became clear this was the direction He wanted us to take. We learned years ago to trust Him, even when we did not understand Him. This time was no different.

Your Turn…Your Perspective: Name a time when you thought you were on the right financial path, only to discover you were not. What did you do? How did it impact where you are financially today?

Prayer: Lord, I trust You with every aspect of my life. I do not always understand Your ways, but I am learning to lean on the faith You have given. I pray to hear Your voice and to make wise financial choices. I pray for wise counsel to guide me.

Day 361
Zero Is Good

JOB 28:19

About a week after our financial advisor told us to get a mortgage, we started the process to do so. Keith was highly attached to our credit union and their mortgage rates were competitive. As a result, I knew we would use our existing credit union to finance our home.

Both Keith and I were still a little gun shy about getting a mortgage. We spent years wrapping our minds around paying cash for our home, and here we were, considering debt again. Even if a mortgage was considered "acceptable" in the short term, it was still debt to us. It felt weird to think about interest rates and payments.

When we chose our mortgage broker, we expressed the importance of only requesting a mortgage which would equate to under 25% of our net income. Most mortgage loan applications qualified buyers for much more than the amount we recommended. It was the one mistake we saw with many of our financial coaching clients. They bought too much house because their loan agent did not take into account how much it would actually cost to live. We would not be purchasing at the top of our eligibility.

The call from our loan agent a few days after we filled out the online application came as a surprise to both of us. It turned out, Keith's credit score was zero and mine was dropping like a rock. She was calling to see if it was a mistake.

It was not a mistake. We were debt-free. There was no loan information available to calculate a credit score. My score would continue to drop until it also reached zero. Our accounts were not frozen; there was no computer error.

Once we explained the report (or lack of report in Keith's case), our agent said she would get back with us in a day or two. And she did. She called two days later to tell us we were approved for the amount requested. We were all set to begin a search for our new home!

I asked her what happened after she found out we did not have credit. She said she simply presented our case to the mortgage board. Our loan would be manually underwritten since we did not have credit scores. We were debt-free with a great combined income which was quite stable. There was no reason not to give us a loan. Being debt-free was a benefit since it showed the mortgage board we were fiscally responsible. Wow!Days later, I still reveled at our good fortune during my quiet time with the Lord. I asked again why we were instructed to get a mortgage instead of saving to pay cash for our home. The Lord showed me the awe of getting a mortgage without a credit score. By choosing to get a mortgage, and being approved without a credit score, we proved it could be done. We created a testimony for others to follow and a barrier was broken. Most importantly, He was exalted in the process. We were so thankful to once again be used to fulfill His glory.

Your Turn...Your Perspective: What money myths have you uncovered? How have they impacted your mindset about your financial journey?

> *Prayer: Lord, the world says I cannot live without debt. I thank You for reminders that, not only can I live without debt, but I can also thrive without debt. I pray for the resolve to become and stay debt-free.*

Day 362
Time to Build

It was hard to believe we were actually house hunting. Seven years after we moved to Kansas City, six years after we got married, five years after we thought we would be ready, it was time to search for our new home. To say Keith and I were excited was the understatement of the century.

The one area we dreamed about during our time of eliminating debt was home ownership. We took pictures. We tried on furniture. We discussed layouts and bedroom sizes. We kept the fuel in our goal to become debt-free by dreaming of one day owning a home.

What started out as a new build project with a mortgage, which probably would have made us house poor, turned into a ready-to-move-in purchase. The ready-to-move-in purchase was made smaller in scale when we decided to pay cash. After our financial advisor shed light on the importance of getting retirement kicked into high gear, we were again considering a ready-to-move-in home with an affordable mortgage option. We were more than ready to find a home to purchase and kick our rented duplex to the curb. Except we could not find what we wanted.

The neighborhoods we liked were almost all filled with two-story homes. We wanted what was equivalent to a ranch with a finished basement. Most of the homes which were ranch models with finished basements were four bedrooms. We wanted five. And those were just the big items which we could not settle on.

The list of small things we wanted, like a double wall oven and a screened in deck on a walkout lot, were unavailable in our price point. Or, the price point took us to a neighborhood farther out than we wanted to go. It was all quite frustrating. After years of wanting to purchase a home, we did not want to spend years looking for one. It seemed our desire for home ownership was going to take more time than we hoped.

One day our realtor called with a suggestion. "Have you thought about building?" Of course, we thought about building! It was all I dreamed about for years. But the farther we got into our debt elimination plan, the more I realized how expensive building could be. "Why not just look at some neighborhoods and see what's out there?" she said.

So, I looked. And I found the most amazing lot, in the most amazing sub-division. It all seemed too good to be true. Keith loved it, too. We squeezed each other's hand tightly as we talked about the possibilities. It was literally everything we could have hoped for. We began to pray. And the Lord answered.

In a series of 2A.M. encounters over three nights, the Lord told me our home was to be built in this neighborhood. He said it would be a five-bedroom ranch with a finished basement. Our price point would hold. *But how Lord?* I finally trusted what I could not see, and we started negotiating for the lot. And we purchased it – for $50,000 under asking price! Once again, God did what we could not do and provided more than we could have imagined. Amazing! It was time to build.

Your Turn…Your Perspective: Name a time when God showed up in a big way for you. How did it make you feel? How has the experience sustained you during more difficult times in your life?

Prayer: Lord, I trust You. I do not always understand how or why, but You have proven Yourself to me time and again. I pray to never doubt just how capable You are of providing my needs and sometimes, even my wants.

Day 363
Can't Have It All

JOB 28:16

Everyone said building a home was more expensive than buying one. It was true for most. The reason most people overspent on building was because they chose to spend more on certain elements of the home than they budgeted. In the world of constructing a new home, it was called going over your allowances.

An allowance was an agreed upon amount given to the buyer to spend on certain items. Typically, there were allowances for appliances, lighting, flooring and tile, sod and site work, etc. Some allowances were estimated by the builder (i.e. site work) and some were negotiated based on the level of "bling" the buyers wanted. If the builder's estimates were low, buyers could easily find themselves well over budget.

Keith and I were determined not to go over budget. We worked too hard to become debt-free and create margin in our lives to overspend on our home. We saw it as a blessing from the Lord to be able to build, and we did not want to disappoint Him or ourselves by overspending. We vowed to do things differently.

Instead of opting for allowances in our contract, we chose a very different approach. We picked out every single element for our home BEFORE we signed the contract. We wanted to know exactly how much our home would cost prior to committing to anything. The builder, his realtor, and our realtor all looked at us with raised eyebrows. Seriously? You want to choose everything ahead of time? Can I get that in writing?

We were dead serious. Four weeks later, all elements of our home were chosen, and the estimates were delivered to the builder. It was time for him to tell us how much our home would cost to build. We were $60,000 over budget! The good news was we had not committed to anything. The bad news was we would not get all we wanted in our new home.

I was incredibly disappointed for about five minutes. Then I realized how much money we saved by finding out we were over budget ahead of time, avoiding financial disaster. Instead of lamenting over not having hardwood floors throughout the entire main level, I chose to be thankful for wisdom. It saved us a ton.

Our builder, Keith, and I went to work adjusting our wish list to create a home we could all agree on. Our builder wanted a home which represented his esthetic. Keith and I wanted a home which met our needs and included the important wants.

I got to keep the double wall oven and cooktop, but without the upgrades. Keith got to keep the insulated garage. We did not get tiled shower for the kid's bathroom and the laundry room was not even close to what we wanted. Our entire lighting selection was redone, and the trim choices were scaled back significantly.

Still, it was an incredible exercise in perspective. It was an experience we would never forget and reminded us that, even though we could not have it all, we were blessed beyond measure. We were thankful we chose to deny ourselves a little of what we wanted in the moment to set up a masterful future. We owed it all to God teaching us years earlier how to let go of what was not important.

Your Turn…Your Perspective: Name a time when your emotions were high during a monetary transaction. What happened?

Prayer: Lord, thank You for perspective. I pray to not lose sight of what is ultimately important as I balance my wants against my needs. I pray for Your guidance to stay objective when spending emotionally.

Day 364
Prayer Room

MATTHEW 27:57; JAMES 4:3

One of the few things we loved about our rented duplex was the layout. In Kansas, it was called a Reverse 1½ story. The main level held the master bedroom, laundry room, and all common living areas. The basement was finished, complete with extra bedrooms. Ours was a three-bedroom unit which meant our kids lived downstairs. It was perfect for our family.

When we were thinking through the home we wanted to purchase, we decided to keep the same layout. It worked well for us and we were not planning on moving again any time soon which meant the single-story layout would continue to be beneficial for tender knees as we got older.

The difference for us, however, was the number of bedrooms. We needed more room. We both were privileged to be able to work from home. When we both worked from home on the same day, it was like musical chairs trying to manage the need for tabletop space in our dining room, and privacy for conference calls. We figured out early on that our new home would have two offices.

What we did not anticipate, however, was the need for solitude. We each took our relationship with Jesus Christ seriously and relished the alone time we created with Him every day. Neither of us liked starting our day without Him, and it was many times a challenge to carve out some quiet time when the other person was nearby.

We literally scheduled time to make sure we both got the time we needed with Jesus. I tended to wake up first during the week with Keith getting first dibs on the weekend. If the schedule needed to vary for any reason, we just worked it out.

When the movie *The War Room* came out in 2015, we both desired to increase our time with Jesus. Journaling for a few minutes in the morning, with a short prayer and scripture, no longer seemed to be enough. The movie showcased just how important it was to have a dedicated space set aside to commune with the Lord. As we began to look for our new home, we realized it would not have two offices. It would have two prayer rooms.

Our relationship with the Lord had deepened tremendously during our time of debt reduction. From 2A.M. encounters and the divine plan for us to reside in Kansas City to the many nights of praying for financial and medical relief, we knew our alone time with God was incredibly important.

By making the hard choice to not purchase our home before we were debt-free, we were in a strong financial position to be able to afford a five-bedroom home and convert two of them into prayer rooms. It seemed like the ultimate opportunity to dedicate our home (and our prayer time) to the Lord.

We were thankful and excited to see how God would use our prayer rooms to grow our faith and strengthen our marriage. We looked forward to many days on our knees.

Your Turn…Your Perspective: Where do you spend time with the Lord? What can you do to make your time more impactful?

Prayer: Lord, You said in James 4: 2-3 that we have not because we ask not. I am asking for favor to complete the journey set before me. Help me to always keep You in the midst.

Day 365
Fertile Ground

When Keith moved to Kansas City in June of 2011, he was not excited. The plan was to move to St. Louis to be in the same city as the kids. But as hard as he tried to find a new position or a transfer to St. Louis, there were no employment opportunities available. The closest he could get was Kansas City.

He knew no one in Kansas. I was searching for a position to join him, but one had not yet materialized. He was completely alone.

One morning, as he was getting dressed for work, he was lamenting to the Lord about his situation. He was alone in a foreign city. He was 4 hours away from his kids and 14 hours away from his soon to be wife. It was hard to be motivated about his surroundings when he felt so isolated.

During this time, he felt a prompting from the Holy Spirit. He knew exactly what Keith was experiencing. As a way to comfort him during this dark season of transition, He uttered these words to him:

"I put you in Kansas so that your pending marriage can be planted in fertile ground."

It was those words which sustained him until I joined him several months later. It was those words which sustained us both when we wished we could be near the kids on a regular basis and not have to wait a month or more to see them again. It was those words which sustained us as we battled the financial war our debt waged on us. God put us in Kansas for a reason.

When we made the decision to build our home, neither of us knew what to expect. Early in the process, we chose to be actively engaged. We wanted to attend inspections and meet the sub-contractors. We wanted them to know how special this home was to us in hopes that they would build it with pride and care. As I was thinking of this during my prayer time one morning, the Lord prompted me to go and pray over our land. When I mentioned it to Keith, he agreed we could never pray too much.

When we arrived at the build site, there was a huge mound of dirt at the front of the lot. The digging of the foundation was complete, and the earth was open to receive our prayers and the blessed oil we brought to anoint it. We sat in the car and prayed before getting out to walk our property and pray over it. It was during this time that Keith reminded me of the promise God made to him seven years earlier.

The dirt which would become our home was the fertile ground referred to by God. The journey to get to it was long and arduous, but we finally made it. Our family home was the culmination and the beginning of a promise God gave, and we were humbled to be in a position to receive it.

Matthew 13:8 says, "Still other seeds fell on fertile soil, and they produced a crop that was thirty, sixty, and even a hundred times as much as had been planted." This was our mandate from the Lord and we were excited to begin fulfilling it. We did not yet know how our harvest would unfold, but we trusted God's plan for our life and looked forward to all which was to come.

Your Turn…Your Perspective: What promise has God given you that you are waiting to unfold? What are you doing to prepare?

Prayer: Lord, thank You for your promises. Thank You for something to hold on to when all else seems to be failing. I trust You, Jesus. I cannot wait to see how this season of my life unfolds.

Day 366
Heat from the Light

PSALM 37:9A

As we were going through our debt snowball, we had a small community of close friends, most of whom we met through our church. When we became debt-free, we set about letting our friends know. Many of them were debt-free themselves, but there were just as many who were working through their own journey's debt reduction.

When we shared our news with one such couple, they wildly applauded us and then begged for the details. What was the last debt? How do you feel? What are you going to do first? Wow! Congratulations! The questions and comments kept coming, and honestly it felt great to share. The journey was long, and we were often discouraged. It was great to bask in the completion of such a huge goal with our friends.

As the evening came to an end and "Mr. Friend" walked us to the door, he shared again how excited he was for us. He listened to the Dave Ramsey Show almost as much as we did, and he heard the incredible stories of debt-freedom from people across the country and around the world. He said it was especially meaningful to hear this from someone he actually knew. He said it made it real.

He and his wife were on their debt-reduction journey for almost as long and experienced their own share of ups and downs. They continued to work on their goal even after falling off their commitment a few times. They were determined to finish so they, too, could be debt-free.

"Mr. Friend" shared how, because of our newly found freedom, he could not only see the light at the end of the tunnel, but he could also feel the heat from the light. It was as if their breakthrough was just around the corner. With all the setbacks they experienced, it would have been easy to give up and slip back into the old way of managing money. But the heat from the light was the reminder not to give up.

The heat from the light. The metaphor was packed with many meanings for all of us. As we made our way through the debt snowball, it got a little brighter with each debt paid off. Every time we refused to make a poor money decision, we walked a little straighter toward the light. One foot in front of the other. One payment after another. Toward the light.

It was a powerful reminder for Keith and me to continue to share our story, just as we did when we were going through the debt-reduction process. Others would still be able to benefit from our journey and our experiences. As much as we were thankful to be free of debt, we could not lose sight of the lessons learned. Those lessons would be the ones others used to keep their hope alive.

The heat from the light was hot for our friends, and we were thankful to have provided a little fuel to their fire of financial freedom. There was no doubt they would come face-to-face with the light in the near future and knew we would be there to celebrate them just as they celebrated us.

Your Turn…Your Perspective: How comfortable are you in sharing your financial picture with your friends? How have you been blessed by the financial journey of others?

Prayer: Lord, I pray for the courage and the strength to not give up. I pray for the heat to feel hot on my face and burn bright before me as the reminder to keep going to meet my financial goal. I thank You for the encouragement and the reminder that You will be with me every step of the way.

Bibliography

1. https://studentaid.ed.gov/sa/types/work-study (Day 3)

2. *The Automatic Millionaire.* David Bach. 2004. Page 35 (Day 31)

3. http://www.jackhayford.org/teaching/articles/a-time-of-altars/ (Day 39)

4. https://www.pickthebrain.com/blog/raise-kids-become-great-adults/ (Day 88)

5. Flexible Spending Account. https://www.healthcare.gov/have-job-based-coverage/flexible-spending-accounts/ (Day 94, 142)

6. http://www.fathers.com/s5-your-situation/c18-divorced-dad/dont-be-a-disney-dad-guest-blog (Day 217)

7. http://contemplativemonk.com/meditation-centering-prayer/ (Day 221)

8. *Flash.* Rachel Anne Ridge. 2015. Page 146 (Day 229)

9. *How To Be Rich: It's Not What You Have, It's What You Do With What You Have.* Andy Stanley. 2013. Page 49 (Day 231)

10. *God's Story, Your Story.* Max Lucado. 2011. Pages 67-70 (Day 252)

11. *First Comes Love, Then Comes Money.* Bethany and Scott Palmer. 2009. Page 1 (Day 269)

12. *Linchpin – Are You Indispensable.* Seth Godin. 2010. Page 92 (Day 329)

13. https://www.daveramsey.com/baby-steps (Day 86 and Day 348)

14. Audacious Faith – *Sun Stand Still: What Happens When You Dare To Ask God For The Impossible.* Steven Furtick. 2010. Page 32 (Day 349)

15. *The 5 Money Personalities.* Bethany and Scott Palmer. 2013. Page (Day 350)

Day	Scripture	Verse
1	James 3:16	For where you have envy and selfish ambition, there you find disorder and every evil practice.
2	Deuteronomy 8:16	He gave you manna to eat in the wilderness, something your ancestors had never known, to humble and test you so that in the end it might go well with you.
3	Proverbs 6:9-11	How long will you lie there, you sluggard? When will you get up from your sleep? A little sleep, a little slumber, a little folding of the hands to rest and poverty will come on you like a thief and scarcity like an armed man.
4	James 1:17	Every good and perfect gift is from above, coming down from the Father of the heavenly lights, who does not change like shifting shadows.
5	Proverbs 11:24-25	One person gives freely, yet gains even more; another withholds unduly, but comes to poverty. A generous person will prosper; whoever refreshes others will be refreshed.
6	James 2:15-16	Suppose a brother or a sister is without clothes and daily food. If one of you says to them, "Go in peace; keep warm and well fed," but does nothing about their physical needs, what good is it?
7	Proverbs 12:20	Those who plan evil are full of lies, but those who plan peace are happy.
8	Proverbs 15:25	The LORD tears down the house of the proud, but he sets the widow's boundary stones in place.
8	John 14:2	My Father's house has many rooms; if that were not so, would I have told you that I am going there to prepare a place for you?
9	Proverbs 12:24	Diligent hands will rule, but laziness ends in forced labor.
10	Psalm 119:24 GNT	Your instructions give me pleasure; they are my advisers.
11	Romans 7:8	But sin, seizing the opportunity afforded by the commandment, produced in me every kind of coveting. For apart from the law, sin was dead.
12	Job 34:19 ERV	He does not respect leaders more than other people. And he does not respect the rich more than the poor. God made everyone.
12	John 10:10	The thief comes only to steal and kill and destroy; I have come that they may have life and have it to the full.
13	Psalm 32:8	I will instruct you and teach you in the way you should go; I will counsel you with my loving eye on you.
13	1 Kings 19:11-12	The Lord said, "Go out and stand on the mountain in the presence of the Lord, for the Lord is about to pass by." Then a great and powerful wind tore the mountains apart and shattered the rocks before the Lord, but the Lord was not in the wind. After the wind there was an earthquake, but the Lord was not in the earthquake. After the earthquake came a fire, but the Lord was not in the fire. And after the fire came a gentle whisper.

Day	Scripture	Verse
14	Psalm 33:18 ICB	But the Lord looks after those who fear him. He watches over those who put their hope in his love.
14	Matthew 14:29-30	"Come," he said. Then Peter got down out of the boat, walked on the water and came toward Jesus. But when he saw the wind, he was afraid and, beginning to sink, cried out, "Lord, save me!"
15	Proverbs 12:19	Truthful lips endure forever, but a lying tongue lasts only a moment.
16	Psalm 145:18	The Lord is near to all who call on him, to all who call on him in truth.
16	1 Chronicles 4:10	Jabez cried out to the God of Israel, "Oh, that you would bless me and enlarge my territory! Let your hand be with me, and keep me from harm so that I will be free from pain." And God granted his request.
16	Isaiah 55:11	So is my word that goes out from my mouth: It will not return to me empty, but will accomplish what I desire and achieve the purpose for which I sent it.
17	Matthew 25:16	The man who had received five bags of gold went at once and put his money to work and gained five bags more.
18	Psalm 41:2 ERV	The Lord will protect them and save their lives. He will bless them in this land. He will not let their enemies harm them.
19	Proverbs 15:19 GNB	If you are lazy, you will meet difficulty everywhere, but if you are honest, you will have no trouble.
20	Hebrews 2:8	You have put all things in subjection under his feet. For in that He put all in subjection under him, He left nothing that is not put under him. But now we do not yet see all things put under him.
21	Proverbs 13:7	One person pretends to be rich, yet has nothing; another pretends to be poor, yet has great wealth.
22	Luke 12:27-28 ERV	"Think about how the wildflowers grow. They don't work or make clothes for themselves. But I tell you that even Solomon, the great and rich king, was not dressed as beautifully as one of these flowers. If God makes what grows in the field so beautiful, what do you think he will do for you? That's just grass—one day it's alive, and the next day someone throws it into a fire. But God cares enough to make it beautiful. Surely he will do much more for you. Your faith is so small!"
23	Genesis 22:14	So Abraham called that place The Lord Will Provide. And to this day it is said, "On the mountain of the Lord it will be provided."
24	Matthew 6:20	But store up for yourselves treasures in heaven, where moths and vermin do not destroy, and where thieves do not break in and steal.
25	Ezekiel 28:4 CEB	By your wisdom and discernment, you made yourself rich, and you filled your storehouses with silver and gold.
26	Proverbs 3:3	Let love and faithfulness never leave you; bind them around your neck, write them on the tablet of your heart.

Day	Scripture	Verse
26	Proverbs 18:24	One who has unreliable friends soon comes to ruin, but there is a friend who sticks closer than a brother.
27	Psalm 73:24 NLT	You guide me with your counsel, leading me to a glorious destiny.
27	2 Corinthians 4:8-10	We are hard pressed on every side, but not crushed; perplexed, but not in despair; persecuted, but not abandoned; struck down, but not destroyed. We always carry around in our body the death of Jesus, so that the life of Jesus may also be revealed in our body.
28	Luke 12:25-26	Who of you by worrying can add a single hour to your life? Since you cannot do this very little thing, why do you worry about the rest?
28	Proverbs 13:12 NLT	Hope deferred makes the heart sick, but a dream fulfilled is a tree of life.
29	Matthew 6:1	Be careful not to practice your righteousness in front of others to be seen by them. If you do, you will have no reward from your Father in heaven.
30	Hebrews 2:6 GNB	Instead, as it is said somewhere in the Scriptures: "What are human beings, O God, that you should think of them; mere human beings, that you should care for them?"
30	1 Thessalonians 5:17	Pray continually.
31	Proverbs 12:11	Those who work their land will have abundant food, but those who chase fantasies have no sense.
32	Proverbs 14:23	All hard work brings a profit, but mere talk leads only to poverty.
33	Proverbs 11:15 ICB	Whoever guarantees to pay what somebody else owes will suffer. It is safer to avoid such promises.
34	Luke 12:15	Then he said to them, "Watch out! Be on your guard against all kinds of greed; life does not consist in an abundance of possessions."
35	Deuteronomy 15:5	If only you fully obey the Lord your God and are careful to follow all these commands I am giving you today.
36	Proverbs 13:10	Where there is strife, there is pride, but wisdom is found in those who take advice.
37	Psalm 34:13	Keep your tongue from evil and your lips from telling lies.
37	Luke 8:17	For there is nothing hidden that will not be disclosed, and nothing concealed that will not be known or brought out into the open.
38	Psalm 37:11	But the meek will inherit the land and enjoy peace and prosperity.
38	Isaiah 61:3	And provide for those who grieve in Zion—to bestow on them a crown of beauty instead of ashes, the oil of joy instead of mourning, and a garment of praise instead of a spirit of despair. They will be called oaks of righteousness, a planting of the Lord for the display of his splendor.

Day	Scripture	Verse
39	Proverbs 12:9	Better to be a nobody and yet have a servant than pretend to be somebody and have no food.
40	Proverbs 11:14 AMP	Where there is no [wise, intelligent] guidance, the people fall [and go off course like a ship without a helm], But in the abundance of [wise and godly] counselors there is victory.
40	Matthew 25:18	But the man who had received one bag went off, dug a hole in the ground and hid his master's money.
41	Luke 12:31 NLT	Seek the Kingdom of God above all else, and he will give you everything you need.
41	Jeremiah 29:11	"For I know the plans I have for you," declares the Lord, "plans to prosper you and not to harm you, plans to give you hope and a future."
42	Proverbs 1:32-33	"Gullible people kill themselves because of their turning away. Fools destroy themselves because of their indifference. But whoever listens to me will live without worry and will be free from the dread of disaster."
43	Colossians 3:22 ERV	Servants, obey your masters in everything. Obey all the time, even when they can't see you. Don't just pretend to work hard so that they will treat you well. No, you must serve your masters honestly because you respect the Lord.
43	2 Corinthians 12:6-8	Even if I should choose to boast, I would not be a fool, because I would be speaking the truth. But I refrain, so no one will think more of me than is warranted by what I do or say, or because of these surpassingly great revelations. Therefore, in order to keep me from becoming conceited, I was given a thorn in my flesh, a messenger of Satan, to torment me. Three times I pleaded with the Lord to take it away from me.
44	Job 1:9-10	"Does Job fear God for nothing?" Satan replied. "Have you not put a hedge around him and his household and everything he has? You have blessed the work of his hands, so that his flocks and herds are spread throughout the land."
45	Psalm 128:5	May the LORD bless you from Zion; may you see the prosperity of Jerusalem all the days of your life.
45	Isaiah 43:18-19 (Berean Study Bible)	Do not call to mind the former things; pay no attention to things of old. Behold, I am about to do something new; even now it is coming. Do you not see it? Indeed, I will make a way in the wilderness and streams in the desert.
46	1 Chronicles 29:17a ERV	My God, I know that you test people, and that you are happy when people do what is right.
46	Matthew 11:30	For my yoke is easy and my burden is light.
47	Job 30:25	Have I not wept for those in trouble? Has not my soul grieved for the poor?

Day	Scripture	Verse
48	Psalm 37:16 AMP	Better is the little of the righteous [who seek the will of God] Than the abundance (riches) of many wicked (godless).
49	Proverbs 1:10	My son, if sinful men entice you, do not give in to them.
50	Proverbs 11:28	Those who trust in their riches will fall, but the righteous will thrive like a green leaf.
51	Proverbs 19:22	What a person desires is unfailing love; better to be poor than a liar.
52	Proverbs 27:9	Perfume and incense bring joy to the heart, and the pleasantness of a friend springs from their heartfelt advice.
52	Psalm 107:9	For he satisfies the thirsty and fills the hungry with good things.
53	Deuteronomy 10:14	To the Lord your God belong the heavens, even the highest heavens, the earth and everything in it.
54	Proverbs 29:14	If a king judges the poor with fairness, his throne will be established forever.
55	Psalm 15:1-2 GNB	LORD, who may enter your Temple? Who may worship on Zion, your sacred hill? Those who obey God in everything and always do what is right, whose words are true and sincere.
56	Psalm 39:6 ERV	Our life is like an image in a mirror. We rush through life collecting things, but we don't know who will get them after we die.
57	Proverbs 28:19	Those who work their land will have abundant food, but those who chase fantasies will have their fill of poverty.
57	Revelation 3:8	I know your deeds. See, I have placed before you an open door that no one can shut. I know that you have little strength, yet you have kept my word and have not denied my name.
58	Psalm 25:12	Who, then, are those who fear the Lord? He will instruct them in the ways they should choose.
59	Isaiah 45:3	I will give you hidden treasures, riches stored in secret places, so that you may know that I am the Lord, the God of Israel, who summons you by name.
59	Exodus 14:21	Then Moses stretched out his hand over the sea, and all that night the Lord drove the sea back with a strong east wind and turned it into dry land.
60	Deuteronomy 7:13 NLT	He will love you and bless you, and he will give you many children. He will give fertility to your land and your animals. When you arrive in the land he swore to give your ancestors, you will have large harvests of grain, new wine, and olive oil, and great herds of cattle, sheep, and goats.
61	Proverbs 13:8	The rich can pay a ransom for their lives, but the poor won't even get threatened.
61	Matthew 5:14	You are the light of the world. A town built on a hill cannot be hidden.

Day	Scripture	Verse
62	Proverbs 19:14	Houses and wealth are inherited from parents, but a prudent wife is from the Lord.
63	2 Thessalonians 3:8-9 TLB	We never accepted food from anyone without buying it; we worked hard day and night for the money we needed to live on, in order that we would not be a burden to any of you.
64	Luke 12:24	Consider the ravens: They do not sow or reap, they have no storeroom or barn; yet God feeds them. And how much more valuable you are than birds!
65	Proverbs 23:6	Do not eat the food of a begrudging host, do not crave his delicacies.
66	Haggai 2:4 GNT	But now don't be discouraged, any of you. Do the work, for I am with you.
67	1 Chronicles 29:16 ERV	Lord our God, we gathered all these things to build your Temple. We build it to honor your name.
67	Mark 10:8	And the two will become one flesh. So they are no longer two, but one flesh.
68	Proverbs 3:10	Then your barns will be filled to overflowing, and your vats will brim over with new wine.
69	Psalm 35:27 CEB	But let those who want things to be set right for me shout for joy and celebrate! Let them constantly say, "The LORD is great— God wants his servant to be at peace."
70	Proverbs 19:20	Listen to advice and accept discipline, and at the end you will be counted among the wise.
71	Haggai 1:14a GNB	The LORD inspired everyone to work on the Temple.
72	Proverbs 21:5	The plans of the diligent lead to profit as surely as haste leads to poverty.
73	Proverbs 28:12a AMP	When the righteous triumph, there is great glory and celebration.
74	Proverbs 17:18 NLT	It's poor judgment to guarantee another person's debtor put up security for a friend.
74	Titus 2:7	In everything set them an example by doing what is good. In your teaching show integrity, seriousness.
75	Titus 1:7 ERV	An elder has the job of taking care of God's work. So people should not be able to say that he lives in a wrong way. He must not be someone who is proud and selfish or who gets angry quickly. He must not drink too much, and he must not be someone who likes to fight. He must not be a man who will do almost anything for money.
75	2 Timothy 2:15 ERV	Do your best to be the kind of person God will accept, and give yourself to him. Be a worker who has no reason to be ashamed of his work, one who applies the true teaching in the right way.

Day	Scripture	Verse
76	1 Timothy 6:6-8	But godliness with contentment is great gain. For we brought nothing into the world, and we can take nothing out of it. But if we have food and clothing, we will be content with that.
76	Philippians 4:19	And my God will meet all your needs according to the riches of his glory in Christ Jesus.
77	Psalm 112:1	Praise the Lord. Blessed are those who fear the Lord, who find great delight in his commands.
77	Deuteronomy 1:2-3	It takes eleven days to go from Horeb to Kadesh Barnea by the Mount Seir road. In the fortieth year, on the first day of the eleventh month, Moses proclaimed to the Israelites all that the Lord had commanded him concerning them.
78	Proverbs 16:6	Through love and faithfulness sin is atoned for; through the fear of the Lord evil is avoided.
78	Ephesians 5:21	Submit to one another out of reverence for Christ.
79	Psalm 30:6 AMP	As for me, in my prosperity I said, "I shall never be moved."
80	1 Corinthians 14:40	But everything should be done in a fitting and orderly way.
81	2 Corinthians 8:12 NLT	Whatever you give is acceptable if you give it eagerly. And give according to what you have, not what you don't have.
82	Psalm 119:36 GNB	Give me the desire to obey your laws rather than to get rich.
83	Proverbs 1:25 NLT	You ignored my advice and rejected the correction I offered.
84	Luke 12:29 TLB	And don't worry about food—what to eat and drink; don't worry at all that God will provide it for you.
84	Jeremiah 33:6 NLT	Nevertheless, the time will come when I will heal Jerusalem's wounds and give it prosperity and true peace.
85	Nehemiah 9:21	For forty years you sustained them in the wilderness; they lacked nothing, their clothes did not wear out nor did their feet become swollen.
85	John 10:10	The thief comes only to steal and kill and destroy; I have come that they may have life, and have it to the full.
86	Proverbs 12:15	The way of fools seems right to them, but the wise listen to advice.
86	John 10:10b NKJV	I have come that they may have life, and that they may have it more abundantly.
87	Proverbs 8:11	For wisdom is more precious than rubies, and nothing you desire can compare with her.
88	Proverbs 13:22a NKJV	A good man leaves an inheritance to his children's children, But the wealth of the sinner is stored up for the righteous.

Day	Scripture	Verse
89	Proverbs 21:20 ESV	Precious treasure and oil are in a wise man's dwelling, but a foolish man devours it.
90	Acts 20:35	In everything I did, I showed you that by this kind of hard work we must help the weak, remembering the words the Lord Jesus himself said: 'It is more blessed to give than to receive.'"
90	Luke 12:30 TLB	All mankind scratches for its daily bread, but your heavenly Father knows your needs.
91	1 Kings 17:16	For the jar of flour was not used up and the jug of oil did not run dry, in keeping with the word of the Lord spoken by Elijah.
92	Proverbs 11:1	The Lord detests dishonest scales, but accurate weights find favor with him.
93	Psalm 16:7	I will praise the Lord, who counsels me; even at night my heart instructs me.
94	Proverbs 3:28	Do not say to your neighbor, "Come back tomorrow and I'll give it to you" when you already have it with you.
95	Proverbs 30:25 ERV	Ants are small and weak, but they save their food all summer.
96	Proverbs 15:22	Plans fail for lack of counsel, but with many advisers they succeed.
97	Psalm 136:25	He gives food to every creature. His love endures forever.
98	Psalm 33:19 ICB	He saves them from death. He spares their lives in times of hunger.
98	2 Timothy 1:7	For the Spirit God gave us does not make us timid, but gives us power, love and self-discipline.
99	1 John 4:16	And so we know and rely on the love God has for us. God is love. Whoever lives in love lives in God, and God in them.
99	Isaiah 55:8	"For my thoughts are not your thoughts, neither are your ways my ways," declares the Lord.
99	Ephesians 3:20	Now to him who is able to do immeasurably more than all we ask or imagine, according to his power that is at work within us
100	Proverbs 3:27	Do not withhold good from those to whom it is due, when it is in your power to act.
100	Deuteronomy 29:5	Yet the Lord says, "During the forty years that I led you through the wilderness, your clothes did not wear out, nor did the sandals on your feet."
101	Acts 20:35b	Remembering the words the Lord Jesus himself said: "It is more blessed to give than to receive."
102	Luke 9:24-25 HCSB	For whoever wants to save his life will lose it, but whoever loses his life because of Me will save it. What is a man benefited if he gains the whole world, yet loses or forfeits himself?

Day	Scripture	Verse
103	1 Chronicles 29:11 CEB	To you, Lord, belong greatness and power, honor, splendor, and majesty, because everything in heaven and on earth belongs to you. Yours, Lord, is the kingship, and you are honored as head of all.
103	2 Timothy 1:7 AMP	For God did not give us a spirit of timidity or cowardice or fear, but [He has given us a spirit] of power and of love and of sound judgment and personal discipline [abilities that result in a calm, well-balanced mind and self-control].
104	1 Corinthians 12:8 GNB	The Spirit gives one person a message full of wisdom, while to another person the same Spirit gives a message full of knowledge.
105	Romans 11:36 CEV	Everything comes from the Lord. All things were made because of him and will return to him. Praise the Lord forever! Amen.
106	Proverbs 6:5	Free yourself, like a gazelle from the hand of the hunter, like a bird from the snare of the fowler.
107	Matthew 25:14	Again, it will be like a man going on a journey, who called his servants and entrusted his wealth to them.
108	Proverbs 11:16	A kindhearted woman gains honor, but ruthless men gain only wealth.
109	Proverbs 28:20 GNB	Honest people will lead a full, happy life. But if you are in a hurry to get rich, you are going to be punished
109	Proverbs 15:17 GNB	Better to eat vegetables with people you love than to eat the finest eat where there is hate.
110	Ecclesiastes 5:14	Or wealth lost through some misfortune, so that when they have children there is nothing left for them to inherit.
111	Proverbs 1:29	"For you closed your eyes to the facts and did not choose to reverence and trust the Lord.
112	Deuteronomy 15:6	For the Lord your God will bless you as he has promised, and you will lend to many nations but will borrow from none. You will rule over many nations but none will rule over you.
112	Hebrews 12:11	No discipline seems pleasant at the time, but painful. Later on, however, it produces a harvest of righteousness and peace for those who have been trained by it.
113	Proverbs 28:21	To show partiality is not good— yet a person will do wrong for a piece of bread.
114	Proverbs 10:5	He who gathers crops in summer is a prudent son, but he who sleeps during harvest is a disgraceful son.
115	Proverbs 16:3	Commit to the Lord whatever you do, and he will establish your plans.
116	Hebrews 11:4 NLT	It was by faith that Abel brought a more acceptable offering to God than Cain did. Abel's offering gave evidence that he was a righteous man, and God showed his approval of his gifts. Although Abel is long dead, he still speaks to us by his example of faith.

Day	Scripture	Verse
117	Psalm 3:8	From the Lord comes deliverance. May your blessing be on your people.
118	Proverbs 13:20	Walk with the wise and become wise, for a companion of fools suffers harm.
119	Mark 5:25-26	And a woman was there who had been subject to bleeding for twelve years. She had suffered a great deal under the care of many doctors and had spent all she had, yet instead of getting better she grew worse.
120	Proverbs 24:5	The wise prevail through great power, and those who have knowledge muster their strength.
121	Proverbs 22:7	The rich rule over the poor, and the borrower is slave to the lender.
122	Ecclesiastes 4:9	Two are better than one, because they have a good return for their labor:
123	2 Corinthians 9:12	This service that you perform is not only supplying the needs of the Lord's people but is also overflowing in many expressions of thanks to God.
124	Proverbs 20:18 GNB	Get good advice and you will succeed; don't go charging into battle without a plan.
124	Hebrews 12:11	No discipline seems pleasant at the time, but painful. Later on, however, it produces a harvest of righteousness and peace for those who have been trained by it.
125	Proverbs 17:26	If imposing a fine on the innocent is not good, surely to flog honest officials is not right.
126	James 2:14	What good is it, my brothers and sisters, if someone claims to have faith but has no deeds? Can such faith save them?
127	Romans 8:28	And we know that in all things God works for the good of those who love him, who have been called according to his purpose.
127	Matthew 7:14 NKJV	Because narrow is the gate and difficult is the way which leads to life, and there are few who find it.
127	Romans 8:28	And we know that in all things God works for the good of those who love him, who have been called according to his purpose.
128	Philippians 2:3 NLT	Don't be selfish; don't try to impress others. Be humble, thinking of others as better than yourselves.
129	Proverbs 4:24	Keep your mouth free of perversity; keep corrupt talk far from your lips.
129	Ephesians 5:33	However, each one of you also must love his wife as he loves himself, and the wife must respect her husband.
130	Proverbs 14:5	An honest witness does not deceive, but a false witness pours out lies.
131	Psalm 73:25 CEB	Do I have anyone else in heaven? There's nothing on earth I desire except you.
132	Proverbs 22:6	Start children off on the way they should go, and even when they are old they will not turn from it.

Day	Scripture	Verse
133	Proverbs 1:30-31	Since they would not accept my advice and spurned my rebuke, they will eat the fruit of their ways and be filled with the fruit of their schemes.
134	Proverbs 30:9 ERV	If I have too much, I might deny that I need you, Lord. But if I am too poor, I might steal and bring shame to the name of my God.
134	1 Corinthians 10:13	No temptation has overtaken you except what is common to mankind. And God is faithful; he will not let you be tempted beyond what you can bear. But when you are tempted, he will also provide a way out so that you can endure it.
135	Proverbs 30:15a ERV	Greedy people know only two things: "Give me," and "Give me."
136	Proverbs 10:2	Ill-gotten treasures have no lasting value, but righteousness delivers from death.
137	Proverbs 18:11	The rich think of their wealth as a strong defense; they imagine it to be a high wall of safety.
137	2 Corinthians 12:7	or because of these surpassingly great revelations. Therefore, in order to keep me from becoming conceited, I was given a thorn in my flesh, a messenger of Satan, to torment me.
138	Proverbs 16:11	Honest scales and balances belong to the Lord; all the weights in the bag are of his making.
139	Proverbs 16:16	How much better to get wisdom than gold, to get insight rather than silver!
140	Proverbs 11:4	Riches won't matter on the day of wrath, but right living will rescue from death.
141	Proverbs 13:23	An unplowed field produces food for the poor, but injustice sweeps it away.
141	1 Corinthians 15:10	But whatever I am now, it is all because God poured out his special favor on me and not without results. For I have worked harder than any of the other apostles; yet it was not I but God who was working through me by his grace.
142	Romans 13:7	Give to everyone what you owe them: If you owe taxes, pay taxes; if revenue, then revenue; if respect, then respect; if honor, then honor.
142	Romans 8:28	And we know that in all things God works for the good of those who love him, who have been called according to his purpose.
143	Proverbs 20:13	Do not love sleep or you will grow poor; stay awake and you will have food to spare.
143	Philippians 4:19	And my God will meet all your needs according to the riches of his glory in Christ Jesus.
144	Proverbs 16:26	The appetite of laborers works for them; their hunger drives them on.
145	Proverbs 4:25	Let your eyes look straight ahead; fix your gaze directly before you.

Day	Scripture	Verse
145	James 1:2-4	Consider it pure joy, my brothers and sisters, whenever you face trials of many kinds, because you know that the testing of your faith produces perseverance. Let perseverance finish its work so that you may be mature and complete, not lacking anything.
146	Ephesians 4:25	Therefore each of you must put off falsehood and speak truthfully to your neighbor, for we are all members of one body.
147	Proverbs 23:23	Buy the truth and do not sell it wisdom, instruction and insight as well.
147	Luke 8:17	For there is nothing hidden that will not be disclosed, and nothing concealed that will not be known or brought out into the open.
147	Mark 12:17	Then Jesus said to them, "Give back to Caesar what is Caesar's and to God what is God's." And they were amazed at him.
148	Lamentations 4:1a GNT	Our glittering gold has grown dull.
149	Proverbs 20:15	Gold there is, and rubies in abundance, but lips that speak knowledge are a rare jewel.
150	Proverbs 29:3a	A man who loves wisdom brings joy to his father.
151	Proverbs 10:4	Lazy hands make for poverty, but diligent hands bring wealth.
152	Proverbs 29:7 ICB	Good people are concerned that the poor are treated fairly. But the wicked don't care.
152	1 Peter 5:7	Cast all your anxiety on him because he cares for you.
153	Proverbs 21:8	The way of the guilty is devious, but the conduct of the innocent is upright.
154	Proverbs 13:21	Trouble pursues the sinner, but the righteous are rewarded with good things.
154	Genesis 12:2	"I will make you into a great nation, and I will bless you; I will make your name great, and you will be a blessing.
155	Philippians 3:7 ERV	At one time all these things were important to me. But because of Christ, I decided that they are worth nothing.
155	John 17:16	They are not of the world, even as I am not of it.
156	Proverbs 6:2	You might get trapped by what you say; you might be caught by your own words.
156	Eccl 4:12	Though one may be overpowered, two can defend themselves. A cord of three strands is not quickly broken.
156	John 10:10b	I have come that they may have life, and that they may have it more abundantly.
157	Proverbs 21:6	A fortune made by a lying tongue is a fleeting vapor and a deadly snare

Day	Scripture	Verse
158	Psalm 8:5-6	You have made them a little lower than the angels and crowned them with glory and honor. You made them rulers over the works of your hands; you put everything under their feet:
159	Psalm 145:15	The eyes of all look to you, and you give them their food at the proper time.
160	Nehemiah 9:15	In their hunger you gave them bread from heaven and in their thirst you brought them water from the rock; you told them to go in and take possession of the land you had sworn with uplifted hand to give them.
161	Matthew 6:25	"Therefore I tell you, do not worry about your life, what you will eat or drink; or about your body, what you will wear. Is not life more than food, and the body more than clothes?
161	Matthew 14:20	They all ate and were satisfied, and the disciples picked up twelve basketfuls of broken pieces that were left over.
162	2 Corinthians 8:15	As it is written: "The one who gathered much did not have too much, and the one who gathered little did not have too little."
163	Psalm 115:14-15	May the Lord cause you to flourish, both you and your children. May you be blessed by the Lord, the Maker of heaven and earth.
164	Psalm 10:14a	But you, God, see the trouble of the afflicted; you consider their grief and take it in hand.
164	Philippians 3:14	I press on toward the goal to win the prize for which God has called me heavenward in Christ Jesus.
165	2 Corinthians 8:3 NLT	For I can testify that they gave not only what they could afford, but far more. And they did it of their own free will.
166	Matthew 7:12	So, in everything, do to others what you would have them do to you, for this sums up the Law and the Prophets.
167	1 Timothy 6:18	Command them to do good, to be rich in good deeds, and to be generous and willing to share.
168	Matthew 25:15	To one he gave five bags of gold, to another two bags, and to another one bag, each according to his ability. Then he went on his journey.
169	Proverbs 20:7	The righteous lead blameless lives; blessed are their children after them
170	Proverbs 20:28	Love and faithfulness keep a king safe; through love his throne is made secure.
171	Psalm 34:10 GNB	Even lions go hungry for lack of food, but those who obey the LORD lack nothing good.
172	Proverbs 28:25	The greedy stir up conflict, but those who trust in the Lord will prosper.
173	Isaiah 48:17	This is what the Lord says — your Redeemer, the Holy One of Israel: "I am the Lord your God, who teaches you what is best for you, who directs you in the way you should go.

Day	Scripture	Verse
174	Proverbs 11:18	Evil people get rich for the moment, but the reward of the godly will last.
175	Proverbs 6:20-22	My son, keep your father's command and do not forsake your mother's teaching. Bind them always on your heart; fasten them around your neck. When you walk, they will guide you; when you sleep, they will watch over you; when you awake, they will speak to you.
176	Proverbs 28:3	A poor person who oppresses others who are poor is like a driving rain that destroys the crops and leaves no food.
177	Proverbs 6:6, 8 GNB	Lazy people should learn a lesson from the way ants live. But they store up their food during the summer, getting ready for winter.
177	Nehemiah 6:3	So I sent messengers to them with this reply: "I am carrying on a great project and cannot go down. Why should the work stop while I leave it and go down to you?"
178	Proverbs 10:22	The blessing of the Lord makes a person rich, and he adds no sorrow with it.
179	Proverbs 16:33	The lot is cast into the lap, But its every decision is from the Lord.
180	Matthew 6:21	For where your treasure is, there your heart will be also.
181	Proverbs 19:21	Many are the plans in a person's heart, but it is the Lord's purpose that prevails.
182	Deuteronomy 2:7	The Lord your God has blessed you in all the work of your hands. He has watched over your journey through this vast wilderness. These forty years the Lord your God has been with you, and you have not lacked anything.
183	Psalm 34:9 GNB	Honour the LORD, all his people; those who obey him have all they need.
184	Proverbs 16:19	It is better not to be proud and to be with those who suffer than to share stolen property with proud people.
185	Proverbs 3:16	Long life is in her right hand; in her left hand are riches and honor.
186	Proverbs 2:4	And if you look for it as for silver and search for it as for hidden treasure
187	Luke 12:22-23	Then Jesus said to his disciples: "Therefore I tell you, do not worry about your life, what you will eat; or about your body, what you will wear. For life is more than food, and the body more than clothes.
187	Joshua 1:9	Have I not commanded you? Be strong and courageous. Do not be afraid; do not be discouraged, for the Lord your God will be with you wherever you go."
188	Proverbs 23:7	For he is the kind of person who is always thinking about the cost. "Eat and drink," he says to you, but his heart is not with you.
188	Philippians 4:19	And my God will meet all your needs according to the riches of his glory in Christ Jesus.

Day	Scripture	Verse
189	Luke 14:28-29	Suppose one of you wants to build a tower. Won't you first sit down and estimate the cost to see if you have enough money to complete it? For if you lay the foundation and are not able to finish it, everyone who sees it will ridicule you.
189	Genesis 12:4	So Abram went, as the Lord had told him; and Lot went with him. Abram was seventy-five years old when he set out from Harran.
189	Genesis 21:5	Abraham was a hundred years old when his son Isaac was born to him.
190	1 Timothy 5:8 NKJV	But if anyone does not provide for his own, and especially for those of his household, he has denied the faith and is worse than an unbeliever.
191	Proverbs 20:10	Differing weights and differing measures the Lord detests them both.
192	Ecclesiastes 11:5-6 MSG	Just as you'll never understand the mystery of life forming in a pregnant woman. So you'll never understand the mystery at work in all that God does. Go to work in the morning and stick to it until evening without watching the clock. You never know from moment to moment how your work will turn out in the end.
192	Lamentations 3:22-23 CEB	Certainly the faithful love of the Lord hasn't ended; certainly God's compassion isn't through! They are renewed every morning. Great is your faithfulness.
193	Song of Solomon 8:7 AMP	Many waters cannot quench love, nor can rivers drown it. If a man would offer all the riches of his house for love, it would be utterly scorned and despised."
195	Proverbs 22:4 GNT	Obey the Lord, be humble, and you will get riches, honor, and a long life.
196	Proverbs 10:3a	The Lord will not let the godly go hungry.
197	Proverbs 8:20	I walk in the way of righteousness, along the paths of justice.
198	Proverbs 30:8b	Give me neither poverty nor riches, but give me only my daily bread.
199	Isaiah 23:18 GNT	The money she earns by commerce will be dedicated to the Lord. She will not store it away, but those who worship the Lord will use her money to buy the food and the clothing they need.
199	James 1:2-4	Consider it pure joy, my brothers and sisters, whenever you face trials of many kinds, because you know that the testing of your faith produces perseverance. Let perseverance finish its work so that you may be mature and complete, not lacking anything.
200	Isaiah 55:2	Why spend money on what is not bread, and your labor on what does not satisfy? Listen, listen to me, and eat what is good, and you will delight in the richest of fare.
201	Proverbs 11:26 TLB	People curse the man who holds his grain for higher prices, but they bless the man who sells it to them in their time of need.

Day	Scripture	Verse
202	Psalm 33:10	The LORD foils the plans of the nations; he thwarts the purposes of the peoples.
203	Psalm 145:16	You open your hand and satisfy the desires of every living thing.
204	Proverbs 23:5	Cast but a glance at riches, and they are gone, for they will surely sprout wings and fly off to the sky like an eagle.
205	Proverbs 28:22	A miser in a hurry to get rich doesn't know that he'll end up broke.
206	Proverbs 3:4	Then you will win favor and a good name in the sight of God and man.
207	Proverbs 28:27	Those who give to the poor will lack nothing, but those who close their eyes to them receive many curses.
208	Proverbs 20:10	Differing weights and differing measures—the Lord detests them both.
209	Matthew 6:3	But when you give to the needy, do not let your left hand know what your right hand is doing.
210	Matthew 6:34	Therefore do not worry about tomorrow, for tomorrow will worry about itself. Each day has enough trouble of its own.
210	2 Timothy 1:7 AMP	For God did not give us a spirit of timidity or cowardice or fear, but [He has given us a spirit] of power and of love and of sound judgment and personal discipline [abilities that result in a calm, well-balanced mind and self-control].
211	Proverbs 27:23 GNB	Look after your sheep and cattle as carefully as you can, because wealth is not permanent.
211	Philippians 4:19	And my God will meet all your needs according to the riches of his glory in Christ Jesus.
212	Proverbs 22:29 GNT	Show me someone who does a good job, and I will show you someone who is better than most and worthy of the company of kings.
212	Galatians 6:9	Let us not become weary in doing good, for at the proper time we will reap a harvest if we do not give up.
212	Psalm 55:22 NKJV	Cast your burden on the Lord, And He shall sustain you; He shall never permit the righteous to be moved.
213	Ecclesiastes 9:10a ICB	Whatever work you do, do your best.
214	Proverbs 19:9a	A false witness will not go unpunished.
215	Romans 13:8	Let no debt remain outstanding, except the continuing debt to love one another, for whoever loves others has fulfilled the law.
216	Proverbs 18:9	Someone who does careless work is as bad as someone who destroys things.
217	Proverbs 21:1	In the Lord's hand the king's heart is a stream of water that he channels toward all who please him.
218	Proverbs 3:14	For she is more profitable than silver and yields better returns than gold.
219	Proverbs 16:8	Better a little with righteousness than much gain with injustice.

Day	Scripture	Verse
220	Psalm 1:2 HCSB	Instead, his delight is in the Lord's instruction, and he meditates on it day and night.
220	Isaiah 35:8	And a highway will be there; it will be called the Way of Holiness; it will be for those who walk on that Way.
221	Proverbs 15:16	Better a little with the fear of the Lord than great wealth with turmoil.
222	Proverbs 3:9	Honor the Lord with your wealth, with the first fruits of all your crops.
223	Proverbs 1:8-9	Listen, my son, to your father's instruction and do not forsake your mother's teaching. They are a garland to grace your head and a chain to adorn your neck.
224	Proverbs 1:24	I tried to help, but you refused to listen. I offered my hand, but you turned away from me.
225	Proverbs 1:26	I in turn will laugh when disaster strikes you; I will mock when calamity overtakes you.
226	Joshua 1:6	Be strong and courageous, because you will lead these people to inherit the land I swore to their ancestors to give them.
227	1 Peter 1:15	But just as he who called you is holy, so be holy in all you do.
228	Proverbs 10:20	The tongue of the righteous is choice silver, but the heart of the wicked is of little value.
229	Deuteronomy 8:15	He led you through the vast and dreadful wilderness, that thirsty and waterless land, with its venomous snakes and scorpions. He brought you water out of hard rock.
229	Psalm 23:4	Even though I walk through the darkest valley, I will fear no evil, for you are with me; your rod and your staff, they comfort me.
230	Hebrews 13:5-6 GNB	Keep your lives free from the love of money, and be satisfied with what you have. For God has said, "I will never leave you; I will never abandon you." Let us be bold, then, and say: "The Lord is my helper, I will not be afraid. What can anyone do to me?"
231	1 Timothy 6:17	Command those who are rich in this present world not to be arrogant nor to put their hope in wealth, which is so uncertain, but to put their hope in God, who richly provides us with everything for our enjoyment.
231	Ephesians 4:22-24	You were taught, with regard to your former way of life, to put off your old self, which is being corrupted by its deceitful desires; to be made new in the attitude of your minds; and to put on the new self, created to be like God in true righteousness and holiness.
232	Proverbs 12:5	The thoughts of the right-living tend toward justice, but the guidance of the wicked is trickery and treachery.
233	1 Corinthians 4:2	Now it is required that those who have been given a trust must prove faithful.

Day	Scripture	Verse
234	Philippians 4:11-13	I am not saying this because I am in need, for I have learned to be content whatever the circumstances. I know what it is to be in need, and I know what it is to have plenty. I have learned the secret of being content in any and every situation, whether well fed or hungry, whether living in plenty or in want. I can do all this through him who gives me strength.
234	Galatians 6:9	Let us not become weary in doing good, for at the proper time we will reap a harvest if we do not give up.
235	Jeremiah 9:23	Let not the wise boast of their wisdom or the strong boast of their strength or the rich boast of their riches.
236	Proverbs 6:4	Allow no sleep to your eyes, no slumber to your eyelids.
237	Proverbs 3:15	She is more precious than rubies; nothing you desire can compare with her.
238	Proverbs 5:10	Yes, strangers will take all your wealth, and what you have worked for will belong to someone else.
239	1 Chronicles 29:15	We are foreigners and strangers in your sight, as were all our ancestors. Our days on earth are like a shadow, without hope.
240	Proverbs 8:10	Choose my instruction instead of silver, knowledge rather than choice gold.
241	Proverbs 8:19	My fruit is better than gold, even fine gold; my crops are better than choice silver.
242	Matthew 6:33	But seek first his kingdom and his righteousness, and all these things will be given to you as well.
242	Ephesians 4:22-24	You were taught, with regard to your former way of life, to put off your old self, which is being corrupted by its deceitful desires; to be made new in the attitude of your minds; and to put on the new self, created to be like God in true righteousness and holiness.
243	Haggai 2:8 GNB	All the silver and gold of the world is mine.
243	Job 6:8	Oh, that I might have my request, that God would grant what I hope for.
244	Job 28:17 GNB	It is worth more than gold, than a gold vase or finest glass.
245	Psalm 128:1-2	Blessed are all who fear the Lord, who walk in obedience to him. You will eat the fruit of your labor; blessings and prosperity will be yours.
246	Proverbs 24:3-4	By wisdom a house is built, and through understanding it is established through knowledge its rooms are filled with rare and beautiful treasures.
246	Matthew 16:18	And I tell you that you are Peter, and on this rock I will build my church, and the gates of Hades will not overcome it.
246	1 Corinthians 14:40 KJV	Let all things be done decently and in order.
247	Proverbs 1:31	They will eat the fruit of their lifestyle. They will be stuffed with their own schemes.

Day	Scripture	Verse
247	Matthew 7:3	"Why do you look at the speck of sawdust in your brother's eye and pay no attention to the plank in your own eye?
248	2 Corinthians 5:9	So we make it our goal to please him, whether we are at home in the body or away from it.
248	Deuteronomy 30:19	This day I call the heavens and the earth as witnesses against you that I have set before you life and death, blessings and curses. Now choose life, so that you and your children may live.
249	Proverbs 15:6	The house of the righteous contains great treasure, but the income of the wicked brings ruin.
249	Romans 2:11	For there is no respect of persons with God.
250	Proverbs 17:8	Receiving a gift is like getting a rare gemstone; any way you look at it, you see beauty refracted.
251	Proverbs 14:2	Whoever fears the Lord walks uprightly, but those who despise him are devious in their ways.
251	Romans 15:4	For everything that was written in the past was written to teach us, so that through the endurance taught in the Scriptures and the encouragement they provide we might have hope.
252	Jeremiah 17:5	This is what the Lord says: "Cursed is the one who trusts in man, who draws strength from mere flesh and whose heart turns away from the Lord.
252	Jeremiah 29:11	"For I know the plans I have for you," declares the Lord, "plans to prosper you and not to harm you, plans to give you hope and a future."
253	Hebrews 13:16	And do not forget to do good and to share with others, for with such sacrifices God is pleased.
254	Proverbs 3:32	The Lord hates those who do wrong. But he is a friend to those who are honest.
255	Proverbs 22:1	A good name is more desirable than great riches; to be esteemed is better than silver or gold.
256	Proverbs 12:27 AMP	The lazy man does not catch and roast his prey, But the precious possession of a [wise] man is diligence [because he recognizes opportunities and seizes them].
256	James 1:12	Blessed is the one who perseveres under trial because, having stood the test, that person will receive the crown of life that the Lord has promised to those who love him.
256	Galatians 5:22-23	But the fruit of the Spirit is love, joy, peace, forbearance, kindness, goodness, faithfulness, gentleness and self-control. Against such things there is no law.
257	Psalm 115:16	The highest heavens belong to the Lord, but the earth he has given to mankind.

Day	Scripture	Verse
257	Philippians 4:6-7	Do not be anxious about anything, but in every situation, by prayer and petition, with thanksgiving, present your requests to God. And the peace of God, which transcends all understanding, will guard your hearts and your minds in Christ Jesus.
257	Ephesians 3:20-21	Now to him who is able to do immeasurably more than all we ask or imagine, according to his power that is at work within us, to him be glory in the church and in Christ Jesus throughout all generations, for ever and ever! Amen.
258	Psalm 10:4	In his pride the wicked man does not seek him; in all his thoughts there is no room for God.
259	Luke 12:48b	From everyone who has been given much, much will be demanded; and from the one who has been entrusted with much, much more will be asked.
259	Proverbs 29:18 CEB	When there's no vision, the people get out of control, but whoever obeys instruction is happy.
259	Acts 3:19	Repent, then, and turn to God, so that your sins may be wiped out, that times of refreshing may come from the Lord
260	Deuteronomy 11:18	Take these words of mine to heart and keep them in mind. Write them down, tie them around your wrist, and wear them as headbands as a reminder.
260	Mark 4:8	Still other seed fell on good soil. It came up, grew and produced a crop, some multiplying thirty, some sixty, some a hundred times.
261	Psalm 10:3 ICB	They brag about the things they want. They bless the greedy but hate the Lord.
261	2 Corinthians 12:9	But he said to me, "My grace is sufficient for you, for my power is made perfect in weakness."
262	Psalm 1:1 HCSB	How happy is the man who does not follow the advice of the wicked or take the path of sinners or join a group of mockers!
263	Psalm 1:3 HCSB	He is like a tree planted beside streams of water that bears its fruit in season and whose leaf does not wither. Whatever he does prospers.
264	Psalm 37:7 GNT	Be patient and wait for the Lord to act; don't be worried about those who prosper or those who succeed in their evil plans.
264	1 Corinthians 15:58	Therefore, my dear brothers and sisters, stand firm. Let nothing move you. Always give yourselves fully to the work of the Lord, because you know that your labor in the Lord is not in vain.
265	Ecclesiastes 3:1	There is a time for everything, and a season for every activity under the heavens:
266	Proverbs 11:6	Good character is the best insurance; crooks get trapped in their sinful lust.

Day	Scripture	Verse
266	James 1:19	My dear brothers and sisters, take note of this: Everyone should be quick to listen, slow to speak and slow to become angry
267	Proverbs 13:18	Whoever disregards discipline comes to poverty and shame, but whoever heeds correction is honored.
268	Proverbs 24:27	Put your outdoor work in order and get your fields ready; after that, build your house.
268	Luke 14:28	Suppose one of you wants to build a tower. Won't you first sit down and estimate the cost to see if you have enough money to complete it?
269	Proverbs 6:15	Therefore disaster will overtake him in an instant he will suddenly be destroyed without remedy.
270	Proverbs 23:4	Do not wear yourself out to get rich; do not trust your own cleverness.
270	2 Corinthians 4:8-9	We are hard pressed on every side, but not crushed; perplexed, but not in despair; persecuted, but not abandoned; struck down, but not destroyed.
271	Isaiah 5:8	Woe to you who add house to house and join field to field till no space is left and you live alone in the land.
272	Proverbs 30:24-25	Four things on earth are small, yet they are extremely wise: Ants are creatures of little strength, yet they store up their food in the summer.
273	Proverbs 6:3	So do this, my son, to free yourself, since you have fallen into your neighbor's hands: Go to the point of exhaustion and give your neighbor no rest!
273	Romans 14:13	Therefore let us stop passing judgment on one another. Instead, make up your mind not to put any stumbling block or obstacle in the way of a brother or sister.
274	Isaiah 52:13 GNT	The Lord says, "My servant will succeed in his task; he will be highly honored."
275	1 Corinthians 14:33	For God is not a God of disorder but of peace as in all the congregations of the Lord's people.
276	2 Corinthians 9:7	Each of you should give what you have decided in your heart to give, not reluctantly or under compulsion, for God loves a cheerful giver.
276	Galatians 6:7-8	Do not be deceived: God cannot be mocked. A man reaps what he sows. Whoever sows to please their flesh, from the flesh will reap destruction; whoever sows to please the Spirit, from the Spirit will reap eternal life.
277	Philippians 4:19	And my God will meet all your needs according to the riches of his glory in Christ Jesus.
277	Genesis 39:2-3	The Lord was with Joseph so that he prospered, and he lived in the house of his Egyptian master. When his master saw that the Lord was with him and that the Lord gave him success in everything he did.
278	Proverbs 1:5	let the wise listen and add to their learning, and let the discerning get guidance.

Day	Scripture	Verse
279	Luke 6:38	Give, and it will be given to you. A good measure, pressed down, shaken together and running over, will be poured into your lap. For with the measure you use, it will be measured to you.
279	Matthew 8:26	He replied, "You of little faith, why are you so afraid?" Then he got up and rebuked the winds and the waves, and it was completely calm.
280	Hebrews 2:7	You made them a little lower than the angels; you crowned them with glory and honor.
281	Luke 3:14	Then some soldiers asked him, "And what should we do?" He replied, "Don't extort money and don't accuse people falsely be content with your pay."
281	Psalm 37:7	Be still before the Lord and wait patiently for him; do not fret when people succeed in their ways, when they carry out their wicked schemes.
281	1 Corinthians 2:9	However, as it is written: "What no eye has seen, what no ear has heard, and what no human mind has conceived" the things God has prepared for those who love him.
282	Proverbs 8:18	Riches and honor are with me, as well as enduring wealth and righteousness.
283	Proverbs 20:24	What the wicked dread will overtake them; what the righteous desire will be granted.
284	Proverbs 2:7	He holds success in store for the upright, he is a shield to those whose walk is blameless.
284	Exodus 4:12	Now go; I will help you speak and will teach you what to say.
284	Judges 7:7 NASB	The Lord said to Gideon, "I will deliver you with the 300 men who lapped and will give the Midianites into your hands; so let all the other people go, each man to his home."
284	Hebrews 13:5-6	Keep your life free from love of money, and be content with what you have, for he has said, "I will never leave you nor forsake you." So we can confidently say, "The Lord is my helper; I will not fear; what can man do to me?"
285	Proverbs 30:14 ERV	There are people whose teeth are like swords and their jaws like knives. They take everything they can from the poor.
286	Psalm 35:10 GNB	With all my heart I will say to the LORD, "There is no one like you. You protect the weak from the strong, the poor from the oppressor."
287	Luke 14:33	In the same way, those of you who do not give up everything you have cannot be my disciples.
288	Matthew 6:19	Do not store up for yourselves treasures on earth, where moths and vermin destroy, and where thieves break in and steal.
289	Proverbs 13:11b	Whoever gathers money little by little makes it grow.

Day	Scripture	Verse
290	Proverbs 13:4	Lazy people want much but get little, but those who work hard will prosper.
291	Proverbs 1:27-28	When panic strikes you like a violent storm, when calamity strikes you like a wind storm, when trouble and anguish come to you. "They will call to me at that time, but I will not answer. They will look for me, but they will not find me.
291	Proverbs 14:12	There is a way that appears to be right, but in the end it leads to death.
292	Psalm 26:4	I do not sit with the deceitful, nor do I associate with hypocrites.
293	1 Peter 1:7 CEB	This is necessary so that your faith may be found genuine. (Your faith is more valuable than gold, which will be destroyed even though it is itself tested by fire.) Your genuine faith will result in praise, glory, and honor for you when Jesus Christ is revealed.
294	Proverbs 20:21	An inheritance claimed too soon will not be blessed at the end.
294	Isaiah 55:8	"For my thoughts are not your thoughts, neither are your ways my ways," declares the Lord.
295	Psalm 49:16	Do not be overawed when others grow rich, when the splendor of their houses increases.
295	Proverbs 4:27	Do not turn to the right or the left; keep your foot from evil.
296	Proverbs 3:13	Blessed are those who find wisdom, those who gain understanding.
297	Colossians 3:23	Whatever you do, work at it with all your heart, as working for the Lord, not for human masters.
298	Mark 12:33	To love him with all your heart, with all your understanding and with all your strength, and to love your neighbor as yourself is more important than all burnt offerings and sacrifices.
299	Proverbs 21:13	Whoever shuts their ears to the cry of the poor will also cry out and not be answered.
300	Psalm 24:1	The earth is the Lord's, and everything in it, the world, and all who live in it.
301	Proverbs 27:18 NLT	As workers who tend a fig tree are allowed to eat the fruit, so workers who protect their employer's interests will be rewarded.
301	Psalm 16:8 KJV	I have set the LORD always before me: because he is at my right hand, I shall not be moved.
302	Proverbs 25:13	Like a snow-cooled drink at harvest time is a trustworthy messenger to the one who sends him; he refreshes the spirit of his master.
303	Romans 12:16 ICB	Live together in peace with each other. Do not be proud, but make friends with those who seem unimportant. Do not think how smart you are.
304	Proverbs 19:17	Whoever is kind to the poor lends to the Lord, and he will reward them for what they have done.

Day	Scripture	Verse
304	John 10:10	The thief comes only to steal and kill and destroy; I have come that they may have life, and have it to the full.
304	Matthew 28:19-20	Therefore go and make disciples of all nations, baptizing them in the name of the Father and of the Son and of the Holy Spirit, and teaching them to obey everything I have commanded you. And surely I am with you always, to the very end of the age.
305	Proverbs 10:15 ICB	Having lots of money protects the rich. But having no money destroys the poor.
306	Proverbs 28:13 AMP	He who conceals his transgressions will not prosper, but whoever confesses and turns away from his sins will find compassion and mercy.
306	John 15:2	He cuts off every branch in me that bears no fruit, while every branch that does bear fruit he prunes so that it will be even more fruitful.
307	Matthew 6:22	The eye is the lamp of the body. If your eyes are healthy, your whole body will be full of light.
308	Proverbs 13:5 ICB	Good people hate what is false. But wicked people do shameful and disgraceful things.
308	Proverbs 4:27	Do not turn to the right or the left; keep your foot from evil.
308	John 17:16	They are not of the world, even as I am not of it.
309	Psalm 34:6	This poor man called, and the Lord heard him; he saved him out of all his troubles.
310	Psalm 41:3 TLB	He nurses them when they are sick and soothes their pains and worries.
310	Jeremiah 17:7-8	"But blessed is the one who trusts in the Lord, whose confidence is in him. They will be like a tree planted by the water that sends out its roots by the stream.
311	Psalm 49:17 ICB	He won't take anything to the grave. His wealth won't die with him.
312	Psalm 66:10 GNT	You have put us to the test, God; as silver is purified by fire, so you have tested us.
313	Psalm 33:11	But the plans of the LORD stand firm forever, the purposes of his heart through all generations.
314	Deuteronomy 15:4	However, there need be no poor people among you, for in the land the Lord your God is giving you to possess as your inheritance, he will richly bless you.
315	Proverbs 8:21	I give riches to those who love me, and I fill their houses with treasures.
316	Psalm 25:13	They will spend their days in prosperity, and their descendants will inherit the land.
316	Habakkuk 2:2 KJV	And the Lord answered me, and said, Write the vision, and make it plain upon tables, that he may run that readeth it.

Day	Scripture	Verse
317	Psalm 5:6	You destroy those who tell lies. The bloodthirsty and deceitful you, Lord, detest.
318	Psalm 21:3 MSG	Your strength, GOD, is the king's strength. Helped, he's hollering Hosannas. You gave him exactly what he wanted; you didn't hold back.
319	Ezekiel 28:5 CEB	Through your shrewd trading you multiplied your riches. But then you became proud of your riches.
319	Romans 12:2	Do not conform to the pattern of this world, but be transformed by the renewing of your mind. Then you will be able to test and approve what God's will is—his good, pleasing and perfect will.
320	Haggai 2:7b CEB	I will fill this house with glory, says the Lord of heavenly forces.
321	Jeremiah 9:24 CEB	No, those who boast should boast in this: that they understand and know me. I am the Lord who acts with kindness, justice, and righteousness in the world, and I delight in these things, declares the Lord.
322	Proverbs 28:6	Better the poor whose walk is blameless than the rich whose ways are perverse.
322	Philippians 3:14	I press on toward the goal to win the prize for which God has called me heavenward in Christ Jesus.
323	Psalm 15:5 AMP	He does not put out his money at interest [to a fellow Israelite], And does not take a bribe against the innocent. He who does these things will never be shaken.
324	Psalm 40:4	Blessed is the one who trusts in the LORD, who does not look to the proud, to those who turn aside to false gods.
324	John 4:23 GNB	But the time is coming and is already here, when by the power of God's Spirit people will worship the Father as he really is, offering him the true worship that he wants.
325	Matthew 6:4	So that your giving may be in secret. Then your Father, who sees what is done in secret, will reward you.
326	Deuteronomy 6:6-7	These commandments that I give you today are to be on your hearts. Impress them on your children. Talk about them when you sit at home and when you walk along the road, when you lie down and when you get up.
327	Psalm 112:3	Wealth and riches are in their houses, and their righteousness endures forever.
327	Isaiah 61:3	And provide for those who grieve in Zion—to bestow on them a crown of beauty instead of ashes, the oil of joy instead of mourning, and a garment of praise instead of a spirit of despair. They will be called oaks of righteousness, a planting of the Lord for the display of his splendor.

Day	Scripture	Verse
328	Luke 12:42 NKJV	And the Lord said, "Who then is that faithful and wise steward, whom his master will make ruler over his household, to give them their portion of food in due season?
329	Colossians 3:24	Since you know that you will receive an inheritance from the Lord as a reward. It is the Lord Christ you are serving.
330	Psalm 119:14 AMP	I have rejoiced in the way of Your testimonies, As much as in all riches.
331	Psalm 37:21	The wicked borrow and do not repay, but the righteous give generously.
331	Genesis 12:2	I will make you into a great nation, and I will bless you; I will make your name great, and you will be a blessing.
332	Matthew 25:18	But the man who had received one bag went off, dug a hole in the ground and hid his master's money.
333	Psalm 106:5	That I may enjoy the prosperity of your chosen ones, that I may share in the joy of your nation and join your inheritance in giving praise.
334	Psalm 40:17	But as for me, I am poor and needy; may the Lord think of me. You are my help and my deliverer; you are my God, do not delay.
335	Psalm 45:12 GW	The people of Tyre, the richest people, want to win your favor with a gift.
336	Psalm 41:1	Blessed are those who have regard for the weak; the LORD delivers them in times of trouble.
336	Acts 9:18	Immediately, something like scales fell from Saul's eyes, and he could see again. He got up and was baptized.
337	Proverbs 19:4 ICB	Wealthy people are always finding more friends. but the poor lose their friends.
338	Acts 4:32 GNB	The group of believers was one in mind and heart. None of them said that any of their belongings were their own, but they all shared with one another everything they had.
339	Proverbs 21:17 GW	Whoever loves pleasure will become poor. Whoever loves wine and expensive food will not become rich.
340	Isaiah 55:1 ERV	All you people who are thirsty, come! Here is water for you to drink. Don't worry if you have no money. Come, eat and drink until you are full! You don't need money. The milk and wine are free.
341	Mark 4:24 ICB	Think carefully about the things you hear. The way you give to others is the way God will give to you. But God will give you more than you give.
342	Deuteronomy 11:19 GW	Teach [God's Word] to your children, and talk about them when you're at home or away, when you lie down or get up.
342	Ephesians 6:4 ERV	Fathers, don't make your children angry, but raise them with the kind of teaching and training you learn from the Lord.

Day	Scripture	Verse
343	Proverbs 22:9	The generous will themselves be blessed, for they share their food with the poor.
344	James 2:1 ERV	My dear brothers and sisters, you are believers in our glorious Lord Jesus Christ. So don't treat some people better than others.
345	2 Timothy 2:6 ICB	The farmer who works hard should be the first person to get some of the food that he grew.
346	2 Corinthians 9:8	And God is able to bless you abundantly, so that in all things at all times, having all that you need, you will abound in every good work.
347	Psalm 51:6 GNB	Sincerity and truth are what you require; fill my mind with your wisdom.
347	Romans 8:37	No, in all these things we are more than conquerors through him who loved us.
347	1 Peter 2:9	But you are a chosen people, a royal priesthood, a holy nation, God's special possession, that you may declare the praises of him who called you out of darkness into his wonderful light.
348	Psalm 119:127	Because I love your commands more than gold, more than pure gold.
348	1 Corinthians 2:9 GNT	However, as the scripture says, "What no one ever saw or heard, what no one ever thought could happen, is the very thing God prepared for those who love him."
349	Psalm 24:3-4	Who may ascend the mountain of the Lord? Who may stand in his holy place? The one who has clean hands and a pure heart, who does not trust in an idol or swear by a false god.
350	Psalm 34:12 ERV	Do you want to enjoy life? Do you want to have many happy days?
351	Psalm 49:18	Though while they live they count themselves blessed and people praise you when you prosper.
351	Genesis 12:2	I will make you into a great nation, and I will bless you; I will make your name great, and you will be a blessing.
352	1 Chronicles 29:12	Wealth and honor come from you; you are the ruler of all things. In your hands are strength and power to exalt and give strength to all.
352	Deuteronomy 29:5	Yet the LORD says, "During the forty years that I led you through the wilderness, your clothes did not wear out, nor did the sandals on your feet.
353	Psalm 66:11-12	You brought us into prison and laid burdens on our backs. You let people ride over our heads; we went through fire and water, but you brought us to a place of abundance.
354	Ecclesiastes 9:11	I have seen something else under the sun: The race is not to the swift or the battle to the strong, nor does food come to the wise or wealth to the brilliant or favor to the learned; but time and chance happen to them all.

Day	Scripture	Verse
354	Joshua 5:6	The Israelites had moved about in the wilderness forty years until all the men who were of military age when they left Egypt had died, since they had not obeyed the Lord. For the Lord had sworn to them that they would not see the land he had solemnly promised their ancestors to give us, a land flowing with milk and honey.
355	Psalm 119:72	The law from your mouth is more precious to me than thousands of pieces of silver and gold.
355	James 1:8	Such a person is double-minded and unstable in all they do.
355	Ephesians 3:20-21	Now to him who is able to do immeasurably more than all we ask or imagine, according to his power that is at work within us, to him be glory in the church and in Christ Jesus throughout all generations, for ever and ever! Amen.
356	Genesis 26:12 ICB	Isaac planted crops in that land and the same year reaped a hundredfold, because the Lord blessed him.
357	Ezekiel 33:13a GNT	I may promise life to someone good, but if he starts thinking that his past goodness is enough and begins to sin, I will not remember any of the good he did.
358	Psalm 30:7	Lord, when you favored me, you made my royal mountain stand firm; but when you hid your face, I was dismayed.
358	Matthew 17:20	He replied, "Because you have so little faith. Truly I tell you, if you have faith as small as a mustard seed, you can say to this mountain, 'Move from here to there,' and it will move. Nothing will be impossible for you."
358	1 Corinthians 12:9	To another faith by the same Spirit, to another gifts of healing by that one Spirit.
359	Proverbs 14:24	The wealth of the wise is their crown, but the folly of fools yields folly.
360	Job 28:18 GNB	The value of wisdom is more than coral or crystal or rubies.
360	Isaiah 55:8-9	"For my thoughts are not your thoughts, neither are your ways my ways," declares the Lord. "As the heavens are higher than the earth, so are my ways higher than your ways and my thoughts than your thoughts.
361	Job 28:19 GNB	The finest topaz and the purest gold cannot compare with the value of wisdom.
362	Job 28:15 GNB	[Wisdom] cannot be bought with silver or gold.
363	Job 28:16 GNB	The finest gold and jewels cannot equal [wisdom's] value.
364	Matthew 27:57	As evening approached, there came a rich man from Arimathea, named Joseph, who had himself become a disciple of Jesus.
364	James 4:3	You do not have because you do not ask God. When you ask, you do not receive, because you ask with wrong motives, that you may spend what you get on your pleasures.

Day	Scripture	Verse
365	Psalm 122:6-7 GNB	Pray for the peace of Jerusalem: "May those who love you prosper. May there be peace inside your walls and safety in your palaces."
365	Matthew 13:8 NLT	Still other seeds fell on fertile soil, and they produced a crop that was thirty, sixty, and even a hundred times as much as had been planted!
365	1 Peter 1:3-4	Praise be to the God and Father of our Lord Jesus Christ! In his great mercy he has given us new birth into a living hope through the resurrection of Jesus Christ from the dead, and into an inheritance that can never perish, spoil or fade. This inheritance is kept in heaven for you.
366	Psalm 37:9a GNT	Those who trust in the Lord will possess the land.

About the Author

Lisa Y. Jones (yes, the "Y" is important...there are a lot of Lisa Joneses!) and her husband Keith paid off over $300,000 in five years. Over $110,000 of it was medical bills. The journey was long and discouraging at times, but they pressed through and were determined not to give up on their desire to live a life without consumer debt.

Today, Lisa and her husband Keith own a financial services firm which focuses on debt elimination (specifically student loans and medical debt) and financial goal setting. They share financial wisdom with those ready to take the next step, both virtually and face to face.

Lisa has the ability to connect with people on a very personal level, inspiring them to have hope and encouraging them to bring about the change they are wanting in their lives. She helps them to create a manageable game plan for their life, business and money while removing the confusion most have in dealing with their finances.

Lisa has a bachelor's degree from Clemson University in Computer Engineering and a Master's degree from Webster University in Information Management. She and her husband are also certified financial coaches through Ramsey Solutions.

More importantly, she is a child of God, enjoying the fullness of being an Heir to the Ultimate Throne.

CPSIA information can be obtained
at www.ICGtesting.com
Printed in the USA
BVHW010842080419
544914BV00018B/1193/P